BYZANTINE COMMENTARIES ON ANCIENT GREEK TEXTS, 12TH–15TH CENTURIES

This is the first volume to explore the commentaries on ancient texts produced and circulating in Byzantium. It adopts a broad chronological perspective (from the twelfth to the fifteenth centuries) and examines different types of commentaries on ancient poetry and prose within the context of the study and teaching of grammar, rhetoric, philosophy and science. By discussing the exegetical literature of the Byzantines as embedded in the sociocultural context of the Komnenian and Palaiologan periods, the book analyses the frameworks and networks of knowledge transfer, patronage and identity building that motivated the Byzantine engagement with the ancient intellectual and literary tradition.

BAUKJE VAN DEN BERG is Associate Professor of Byzantine Studies at Central European University, Vienna.

DIVNA MANOLOVA is Visiting Postdoctoral Fellow at the Max Planck Institute for the History of Science in Berlin.

PRZEMYSŁAW MARCINIAK is Professor of Byzantine Literature at the University of Silesia in Katowice.

BYZANTINE COMMENTARIES ON ANCIENT GREEK TEXTS, 12TH–15TH CENTURIES

EDITED BY

BAUKJE VAN DEN BERG
Central European University

DIVNA MANOLOVA
Max Planck Institute for the History of Science

PRZEMYSŁAW MARCINIAK
University of Silesia in Katowice

Shaftesbury Road, Cambridge CB2 8EA, United Kingdom

One Liberty Plaza, 20th Floor, New York, NY 10006, USA

477 Williamstown Road, Port Melbourne, VIC 3207, Australia

314–321, 3rd Floor, Plot 3, Splendor Forum, Jasola District Centre, New Delhi – 110025, India

103 Penang Road, #05-06/07, Visioncrest Commercial, Singapore 238467

Cambridge University Press is part of Cambridge University Press & Assessment, a department of the University of Cambridge.

We share the University's mission to contribute to society through the pursuit of education, learning and research at the highest international levels of excellence.

www.cambridge.org
Information on this title: www.cambridge.org/9781009088053

DOI: 10.1017/9781009085762

© Cambridge University Press & Assessment 2022

This publication is in copyright. Subject to statutory exception and to the provisions of relevant collective licensing agreements, no reproduction of any part may take place without the written permission of Cambridge University Press & Assessment.

First published 2022
First paperback edition 2023

A catalogue record for this publication is available from the British Library

ISBN 978-1-316-51465-8 Hardback
ISBN 978-1-009-08805-3 Paperback

Cambridge University Press & Assessment has no responsibility for the persistence or accuracy of URLs for external or third-party internet websites referred to in this publication and does not guarantee that any content on such websites is, or will remain, accurate or appropriate.

Contents

List of Contributors		*page* vii
	Introduction: Byzantine Commentaries on Ancient Greek Texts *Baukje van den Berg and Divna Manolova*	1
1	The Politics and Practices of Commentary in Komnenian Byzantium *Panagiotis A. Agapitos*	41
2	Forging Identities between Heaven and Earth: Commentaries on Aristotle and Authorial Practices in Eleventh- and Twelfth-Century Byzantium *Michele Trizio*	61
3	Cultural Appropriation and the Performance of Exegesis in John Tzetzes' Scholia on Aristophanes *Aglae Pizzone*	100
4	Uncovering the Literary Sources of John Tzetzes' *Theogony* *Maria Tomadaki*	130
5	Odysseus the Schedographer *Valeria F. Lovato*	148
6	Eustathios of Thessalonike on Comedy and Ridicule in Homeric Poetry *Baukje van den Berg*	169
7	Geography at School: Eustathios of Thessalonike's *Parekbolai* on Dionysius Periegetes *Inmaculada Pérez Martín*	195
8	Painting and Polyphony: The *Christos Paschon* as Commentary *Margaret Mullett*	214

9 Parodying Antiquity for Pleasure and Learning: The *Idyll* by
   Maximos Planoudes   240
   Krystina Kubina

10 Teaching Poetry in the Early Palaiologan School:
   Manuel Holobolos' and John Pediasimos' Commentaries on
   Theocritus' *Syrinx*   273
   Paula Caballero Sánchez

11 Late Byzantine Scholia on the Greek Classics: What Did They
   Comment On? Manuel Moschopoulos on Sophocles' *Electra*   304
   Andrea M. Cuomo

12 Theodora Raoulaina's Autograph Codex Vat. gr. 1899 and
   Aelius Aristides   339
   Fevronia Nousia

13 The Reception of Eustathios of Thessalonike's *Parekbolai* in
   Arsenios Apostolis' and Erasmus' Paroemiographic Collections   360
   Lorenzo M. Ciolfi

Index   379

Contributors

PANAGIOTIS A. AGAPITOS is Emeritus Professor of Byzantine Literature at the University of Cyprus. His research focuses on textual and literary criticism, with an emphasis on Byzantine rhetoric and its performance, poetics, erotic fiction and the representation of death in Byzantine literature. Over the past thirty years, he has published some eighty scholarly papers, three single-authored studies, the first critical edition of the thirteenth-century verse romance *Livistros and Rodamne* (Athens 2006), the edited volume *Medieval Narratives between History and Fiction: From the Centre to the Periphery of Europe, 1100–1400* (with L. B. Mortensen; Copenhagen 2012) and, most recently, an English translation of *Livistros and Rodamne* for *Translated Texts for Byzantinists* (Liverpool 2021). He is currently working on a narrative history of Byzantine literature (AD 1050–1500).

BAUKJE VAN DEN BERG is Associate Professor of Byzantine Studies at Central European University, Vienna. Her research focuses on Byzantine scholarship, Byzantine education and the role of ancient literature in Byzantine culture. Her recent publications include the monograph *Homer the Rhetorician: Eustathios of Thessalonike on the Composition of the Iliad* (Oxford 2022) and the co-edited volume *Emotions and Narrative in Ancient Literature and Beyond: Studies in Honour of Irene de Jong* (with M. de Bakker and J. Klooster; Leiden–Boston 2022). She is currently preparing a volume with translations of and commentary on various works on ancient poetry by John Tzetzes.

PAULA CABALLERO SÁNCHEZ is Lecturer of Ancient Greek at the University of Málaga, Spain. Her dissertation was published as a monograph by Nueva Roma (Spanish National Research Council, 2018) with the title *El Comentario de Juan Pediásimo a los Cuerpos celestes de Cleomedes: estudio, edición crítica y traducción*. Her research covers the reception and transmission of scientific and literary Greek texts during the Byzantine Palaiologan Renaissance (1261–1453) and the European Renaissance, primarily in a scholastic context, as well as Greek codicology and palaeography. She has collaborated with several Spanish research projects with the aim of delving deeper into the scientific and literary contribution of Byzantine scholars.

LORENZO M. CIOLFI completed his undergraduate studies in philology and Greek palaeography at Sapienza University of Rome and is currently a PhD candidate at L'École des hautes études en sciences sociales (EHESS), Centre d'études en sciences sociales du religieux, Paris. His dissertation project concentrates on the figure and role of John III Vatatzes in the Byzantine and post-Byzantine eras, with particular focus on the emergence of his cult within the framework of Byzantine imperial sainthood. In parallel, he is working on Greek paroemiographic collections in the fifteenth and sixteenth centuries, and their relationship with the developments of Western proverb anthologies.

ANDREA M. CUOMO is Professor of Greek at Ghent University. From 2012 to 2021, he worked at the Austrian Academy of Sciences in Vienna, where he led the *Greek Scholia and Medieval Greek* project funded by the Austrian Science Fund (FWF-P 30775-G25). In 2020, he was awarded an ERC Consolidator Grant for the project *The Meaning of Language: A Digital Grammar of the Greek Taught at Schools in Late Constantinople* (No. 101001328 MELA). He has published on the history of the Greek language, late Byzantine historians and linguistics.

KRYSTINA KUBINA is a research associate at the Austrian Academy of Sciences, specializing in late Byzantine poetry. She has published a monograph on the fourteenth-century poet Manuel Philes (*Die enkomiastische Dichtung des Manuel Philes: Form und Funktion des literarischen Lobes in der frühen Palaiologenzeit*, Berlin 2020), as well as the co-edited volume *Epistolary Poetry in Byzantium and Beyond: An Anthology with Critical Essays* (with A. Riehle; New York 2021).

VALERIA F. LOVATO is a Swiss National Science Foundation postdoctoral fellow at the University of Geneva with a project on middle Byzantine conceptions of *asteiotes*. Her research also encompasses the reception of the Homeric epics in Byzantium and in Renaissance Europe, a topic on which she has published extensively. Her current book projects include an edited volume on Isaac Komnenos Porphyrogennetos and a monograph investigating the interplay between classicizing learning and self-fashioning in the works of John Tzetzes and Eustathios of Thessalonike.

DIVNA MANOLOVA is Visiting Postdoctoral Fellow at the Max Planck Institute for the History of Science and an Affiliate Member of the Centre for Medieval Literature (University of York and University of Southern Denmark). She works on theories of space and dimensionality in Byzantine cosmological and astronomical texts and diagrams. She obtained her PhD in Medieval Studies at Central European University (2014) and was a Marie Skłodowska-Curie/POLONEZ 1 fellow at the University of Silesia in Katowice (2016–18).

PRZEMYSŁAW MARCINIAK is Professor of Byzantine Literature at the University of Silesia in Katowice, Poland. He has held fellowships in Princeton, Berlin, Paris, Uppsala and Dumbarton Oaks and has published on Byzantine performativity, humour and satire. His recent publications include the edited volume *Satire in the Middle Byzantine Period: The Golden Age of Laughter?* (with I. Nilsson; Leiden–Boston 2021). He currently works on the Byzantine perception of animals.

MARGARET MULLETT is Professor Emerita of Byzantine Studies at Queen's University Belfast and Director of Byzantine Studies Emerita at Dumbarton Oaks. She has recently published *The Church of the Holy Apostles: A Lost Monument, A Forgotten Project, and the Presentness of the Past* (with R. Ousterhout; Washington, DC 2020) and *Storytelling in Byzantium: Narratological Approaches to Byzantine Texts and Images* (with I. Nilsson and C. Messis; Uppsala 2018). She is currently working on tents, emotions and hybridity, as well as the *Christos Paschon*. After leaving Dumbarton Oaks, she was Visiting Professor of Byzantine Social History at Vienna and then Visiting Professor of Byzantine Greek at Uppsala. She is now Honorary Professor at the University of Edinburgh.

FEVRONIA NOUSIA is Assistant Professor of Byzantine Philology at the University of Patras. Her research focuses on Greek palaeography, Byzantine literature, education, hagiography, the reception and dissemination of Greek texts in the West and critical editions of Byzantine texts.

INMACULADA PÉREZ MARTÍN holds a PhD in Classical Philology from the Complutense University of Madrid and since 1997 has been a Scientific Researcher at the Spanish National Research Council (Instituto de Lenguas y Culturas del Mediterráneo y del Oriente Próximo [ILC-CCHS], Consejo Superior de Investigaciones Científicas [CSIC]). She is an expert in Greek palaeography, Byzantine culture and transmission of classical texts in Byzantium, and has published several studies on Byzantine scholars and Spanish Hellenists, as well as critical editions of Byzantine texts such as Michael Attaleiates' *History*. She is currently the Director of the Instituto de Lenguas y Culturas del CSIC in Madrid and is preparing the critical edition of Eustathios' *Parekbolai on Dionysius Periegetes*.

AGLAE PIZZONE is a Byzantinist with a background in Classics. She is currently Associate Professor in Medieval Literature at the Danish Institute for Advanced Study, hosted by the University of Southern Denmark. Her research focuses on cultural history and the history of ideas. At present, she is interested in autography and self-commentaries in the Greek Middle Ages, as well as in the Byzantine commentaries on Hermogenes and their early modern reception. She has recently discovered new autograph notes by John Tzetzes in the Voss. Gr. Q1.

MARIA TOMADAKI works as a scientific collaborator at the Göttingen Academy of Sciences and Humanities. Her main research interests are Byzantine poetry, textual criticism, Greek palaeography and the reception of the ancient poets in Byzantium. Her PhD thesis includes the critical edition of 236 iambic poems by John Geometres (forthcoming in Brepols' Corpus Christianorum Series Graeca).

MICHELE TRIZIO is Associate Professor of Ancient and Medieval Philosophy at the University of Bari. He has received PhDs in Medieval Philosophy (Bari 2006) and in Classical Philology (Bari 2010), and has published on Byzantine philosophical texts and Greek–Latin interaction in the Middle Ages. His *Il Neoplatonismo di Eustrazio di Nicea* (Bari 2016) is the first monograph devoted to this Byzantine commentator.

INTRODUCTION

Byzantine Commentaries on Ancient Greek Texts

Baukje van den Berg and Divna Manolova

'Medieval thought leaves some of its richest records in glosses and commentaries on authoritative texts. Whether we want to know how medieval thinkers viewed their treasured inheritance of ancient philosophy and literature, or how they imbued their students with a love for the liberal arts, or how they studied sacred Scripture, our best access is often through their expositions of the texts that they read, taught, and copied.' With these words, Rita Copeland describes the value of medieval scholarship on ancient texts.[1] Even though Copeland writes about the Medieval West, her words hold equally true for the wealth of Byzantine scholarship on ancient authorities that has come down to us: Byzantine commentaries teach us much about the role of ancient literature in the cultural system of different Byzantine periods, about the meaning of these ancient texts for Byzantine readers, and about the wisdom and inspiration Byzantine authors found there for their own scholarly and literary production.

The present volume therefore considers Byzantine commentaries as firmly grounded in their intellectual and sociocultural contexts.[2] Recent studies have emphasized that commentaries – whether ancient, medieval or modern – are universally determined by their specific historical and cultural circumstances: the aims and assumptions of commentators and

---

We would like to thank Panagiotis Agapitos and Przemysław Marciniak for their helpful comments on an earlier version of this introduction. The volume is partly based on the conference 'Preserving, Commenting, Adapting: Commentaries on Ancient Texts in Twelfth-Century Byzantium' (University of Silesia in Katowice, Centre of Studies on Byzantine Literature and Reception, 20–22 October 2017), which was organized in the framework of the project UMO-2013/10/E/HS2/00170, funded by the National Science Centre (Poland), and the project UMO-2015/19/P/HS2/02739, also supported by the National Science Centre (Poland). The latter project has also received funding from the European Union's Horizon 2020 research and innovation programme under the Marie Skłodowska-Curie grant agreement No 665778. We thank Lauren Stokeld for proofreading the volume.

[1] Copeland (2012: 171).
[2] For introductions to Byzantine classical scholarship, see Wilson (1996 [1983]), Pontani (2015), Dickey (2017).

their readerships differ from culture to culture. The choice of what to comment on depends on what commentators perceive as the needs of their target audience.[3] In other words, the questions the commentary addresses depend on the commentator's cultural and historical assumptions and the expectations of the interpretive community, as every commentary is first and foremost an interpretation, a specific reading of a text.[4] By catering to the particular needs of their target audience, commentaries aim to bridge the gap that separates ancient texts and new readerships, be they ancient, medieval or modern.[5]

Even if this may sound obvious to some extent, it is not how Byzantine commentaries have generally been studied. Instead, the Byzantines have mostly been regarded as the conduit through which much of ancient literature has survived into the modern period, and their scholarship has been mined for what it preserves of fragments and readings of ancient texts not otherwise transmitted. Why these ancient texts were preserved, how they were used and what they meant to their Byzantine readership are questions that have only recently begun to be asked.[6] Byzantine commentators resemble their ancient predecessors in that they tend to project their own didactic interests onto the text under discussion and to shape the source author in their own image: for instance, they turned Homer into a teacher of grammar and rhetoric much like themselves.[7] In a similar vein, late antique and Byzantine philosophers interpreted and reinterpreted Aristotle and Plato according to their own philosophical and ideological agenda.[8] An investigation of the ways in which commentators read and interpreted their source texts can therefore tell us much about their didactic, intellectual and cultural endeavours.

Byzantine commentaries commonly concern authoritative texts that were read in the classroom. A twelfth-century father by the name of Christopher Zonaras articulates the significance of studying these ancient texts in a hortatory discourse to his son Demetrios on the importance of education. Demetrios has just finished his grammar studies and is about to continue with rhetoric and prose composition, the next stage in the educational curriculum, in which ancient texts continued to play a central

---

[3] See e.g. Baltussen (2007: 181), Sluiter (2013: 194), Woods (2013: 332), Kraus and Stray (2016: 7).
[4] Kraus (2002: 4, 9, 13).
[5] On commentaries as bridging the gap between text and readership, see e.g. Sluiter (2000: 188), Kraus (2002: 7), Kraus and Stray (2016: 11).
[6] Kaldellis (2009) explores the ideological reasons behind this neglect of the study of Byzantine classical scholarship as a cultural phenomenon in its own right. See also Smith (1996).
[7] On ancient commentators, see Sluiter (1999: 173–4, 176–9) and (2013: 193–6); for Eustathios, see Cullhed (2016: 11*–13*), van den Berg (2022).
[8] For a good starting point, see Golitsis (2012).

role.⁹ Zonaras explains that one should converse with these authors of the past to train both one's mind and one's tongue, that is, to learn how to think deep thoughts and express them with rhetorical elegance. He presents it as a moral obligation not to waste one's intellectual talents and be a 'useless' person but embark on a journey of lifelong learning so as to make both oneself and one's parents happy.¹⁰ The discourse ends on a threatening note: should you fail to heed your father's words, so Zonaras warns Demetrios, 'you will give me grief and a life that is pitiable and more difficult than death; you will disgrace me and clothe me in shame – may this not happen to me, Lord Christ!'¹¹ Much was at stake, it seems, in getting a good education in ancient literature and acquiring the knowledge and eloquence necessary to prove oneself an educated and sophisticated person.

Zonaras' emphatic exhortations tie in with the general idea that knowledge of the ancient authorities studied in the classroom constituted the cultural capital or *paideia* that defined elite identity.¹² The social role of *paideia* became particularly pronounced under the Komnenian and Palaiologan emperors, during the centuries on which this volume focuses. A familiarity with the literature of the past and a perfect command of Atticizing Greek was imperative for anyone contending for high-ranking positions in the imperial or ecclesiastical bureaucracies. Ambition and competition governed the intellectual climate of these periods, and went hand in hand with a desire for display: social and cultural credentials were worth only as much as the public recognition they earned.¹³ Many texts, moreover, testify to polemics among teachers and intellectuals, often with the interpretation of school texts as their battlefield.¹⁴ By rereading and reinterpreting authoritative ancient texts, commentators constantly defined and redefined the cultural capital in terms that were meaningful to their own times. Their works demonstrate, for instance, that, in order to know one's Homer, it was not enough to read just the *Iliad* and *Odyssey*;

---

⁹ The literature on Byzantine education is extensive. For useful starting points, see Browning (1997), Markopoulos (2006) and (2014). For the twelfth century, see also Nesseris (2014); for the Palaiologan era, see e.g. Constantinides (1982), Mergiali (1996), Nousia (2016). For the teaching of the mathematical sciences in Byzantium, see Pérez Martín and Manolova (2020).
¹⁰ See esp. Zonaras, *Hortatory Discourse to His Son* 1–6, 217–30, 278–91 ed. Tsolakis.
¹¹ Zonaras' *Hortatory Discourse to His Son* 307–10: Ἐμοὶ δὲ δώσεις ὀδύνην καὶ ζωὴν οἰκτρὰν καὶ θανάτου χαλεπωτέραν καὶ ἔσῃ μοι ὄνειδος καὶ αἰσχύνην ἐνδύσεις με, ὃ μὴ γένοιτό μοι, Χριστὲ βασιλεῦ!
¹² Commentaries underscore the special status of a canonical or authoritative text and at the same time let commentators share in the prestige of their source text: see e.g. Most (1999: ix and xi), Sluiter (1999: 173–7) and (2013: 192–3, 195), Kraus and Stray (2016: 2).
¹³ On competition, ambition and display, especially in the context of the so-called *theatra*, see e.g. Magdalino (1993: 335–56), Marciniak (2007), Gaul (2011, esp. 23–5), (2018) and (2020).
¹⁴ On polemics and competition concerning the interpretation of ancient texts, see e.g. Garzya (1973), Agapitos (2017), Bourbouhakis (2017: 213). See also Agapitos in this volume.

rather, one also had to be familiar with the grammatical and hermeneutic traditions attached to the Homeric epics.[15] The commentaries discussed throughout the present volume thus open up a perspective on what it meant to be educated, eloquent and erudite in Byzantium from the eleventh to fifteenth centuries.

Commentaries with an explicit patron-dedicatee offer concrete starting points for interpreting the educational, social and cultural importance of knowledge of the ancient tradition. More often than not, however, student-readers and their investment in their teachers' exegesis are present only implicitly in the very acts of producing and preserving the commentaries.[16] A line of investigation that naturally follows from the research presented in this volume, therefore, involves shifting the focus from the Byzantine authors and their exegetical output – not just the commentaries themselves but also the practices and strategies of reading and commenting on ancient texts – to the notoriously difficult question as to how Byzantine scholarship was read, experienced and reused by its contemporary readers. This question includes issues beyond the didactic setting and the framework of patronage relations, such as the pleasure gained from reading ancient texts and the emotional response triggered by learning something new. Delving deeper into contemporary as well as later reception of the commentaries is one of the avenues for future research that this volume hopes to open.

In this book, we define commentary both in a narrow and a broad sense. In the narrowest sense, commentaries – whether marginal scholia or self-standing works – are concerned with explaining an ancient text and the knowledge related to it, often in a didactic context. Defined more broadly, commentaries include treatises on ancient literature and paraphrases of ancient authorities, which likewise demonstrate how these texts were read and taught. In the broadest sense, commentaries can be any literary texts that creatively engage with ancient texts and, thus, shed light on Byzantine attitudes towards their ancient heritage, on practices and strategies of reading ancient literature, and on the importance attached to *paideia*. Together, these different kinds of commentaries and exegetical practices produce a fuller picture of the cultural role of ancient texts in the Komnenian and Palaiologan periods. This volume concentrates on ancient poetry, oratory

---

[15] On ancient commentaries redefining cultural capital, see Sluiter (2013: 195–6, 202–3). Cf. Sluiter (2000: 188): 'writing a commentary is also the reproduction and digestion of what is considered valuable intellectual and cultural material'.

[16] Significant progress in the identification and study of personal notebooks and schoolbooks associated with well-known Palaiologan scholars such as Maximos Planoudes and Nikephoros Gregoras has recently been made by palaeographers working on late Byzantine manuscripts. See for instance Bianconi (2017) and Pérez Martín (2017).

and philosophy, thus largely leaving aside biblical and patristic texts, which were equally central to Byzantine intellectual culture and received many commentaries, not infrequently by the same scholars who commented on secular ancient texts.[17] Many commentaries, moreover, remain hidden in unedited manuscripts or outdated editions. Only with satisfactory editions and detailed studies of individual commentaries in their relevant contexts will we reach a deeper understanding of Byzantine cultural history and the role of ancient texts herein, as relevant to Byzantinists and Classicists alike.[18] The present volume is a step in this direction.

Grammar and Rhetoric, Poetry and Prose

With the strong focus on poetry in Byzantine grammar teaching, it is no surprise that many commentaries concern the ancient poets. The twelfth century saw an intensified interest in Homer, which has been connected with the military ideology of the ruling aristocracy: the *Iliad* and *Odyssey* (especially the former) provided rhetors with appropriate language and imagery for praising their rulers as modern-day heroes.[19] The 'first Byzantine commentary on the *Iliad*' was likely produced by a member of this ruling elite, the *sebastokrator* Isaac Komnenos Porphyrogennetos, son of Emperor Alexios I Komnenos and younger brother of Anna Komnene, who herself wrote a Homerizing biography of her father with the title *Alexiad*.[20] The twelfth century also saw the (re-)emergence of self-standing commentaries, works that existed independent of the texts they commented on rather than in their margins.[21] The monumental works on the *Iliad* and *Odyssey* by Eustathios of Thessalonike (ca. 1115–95) are undoubtedly the best known.[22] The grammarian John Tzetzes (ca. 1110–70/80)

---

[17] However, see the contributions by Agapitos and Mullett in this volume. On the Bible in Byzantium, see e.g. Magdalino and Nelson (2010), Krueger and Nelson (2016), Rapp and Külzer (2019).

[18] Cf. Smith (1996: 405): 'for the classicist it is necessary to have a perception of how the Byzantine scholars through whose hands the classical texts passed to us dealt with the texts, what they thought about them, and how they interpreted them. For the Byzantinist these commentaries ought to be basic source material.'

[19] See e.g. Basilikopoulou-Ioannidou (1971: 124–6 and 131–4), Magdalino (1993: 431) with Cullhed (2014a: 74*–9*), Kaldellis (2007: 242–3).

[20] On Isaac's work on the *Iliad*, see Pontani (2007). On Homeric scholarship in the Byzantine era (with a focus on the *Odyssey*), see Pontani (2005: 136–99).

[21] Kaldellis (2009: 29–30).

[22] The *Commentary on the Iliad* (or *Parekbolai on the Iliad*) is available in the edition by van der Valk (1971–87). Most of the *Commentary on the Odyssey* is still to be consulted in the edition by Stallbaum (1825–6). For a new edition and translation of the first two books, see Cullhed (2016); for Books 3–4, see the digital edition by E. Cullhed and S. Douglas Olson at https://brill.com/view/db/eooc, which will eventually offer a new edition with English translation of

appears to have planned his *Exegesis of the Iliad* as a similarly ambitious work of Homeric scholarship, intended to be the first ever commentary to discuss every aspect of the *Iliad*, so Tzetzes claims in his long prefatory essay.[23] He, however, never managed to complete his project: only the introduction and the commentary on *Iliad* 1 survive.

Even if Homer continued to be read, his poetry did not dominate the scholarship of the Palaiologan era to the same extent. The most prominent scholars of the thirteenth and fourteenth centuries lavished their erudite attention on many ancient authors, notably the Athenian playwrights.[24] Maximos Planoudes (1255–1304/5), Manuel Moschopoulos (ca. 1265– after 1316), Thomas Magistros (ca. 1280–after 1347) and Demetrios Triklinios (fl. 1305–20) produced recensions of and scholia on comedies of Aristophanes as well as the most-read tragedies of Aeschylus, Sophocles and Euripides.[25] Their scholia were often the product of intellectual collaborations and engaged with the work of contemporaries as well as predecessors, which resulted in a fluid textual tradition that is often difficult to disentangle.[26] The Palaiologan scholia are predominantly (if not exclusively) grammatical, concentrating on lexical, morphological and syntactical aspects of the ancient texts.[27]

---

the entire *Commentary on the Odyssey*. On Eustathios' Homeric commentaries, see the contributions by van den Berg and Lovato in this volume, with further bibliography. For an overview of Eustathios' life and work, see Cesaretti and Ronchey (2014: 7*–30*) with further references.

[23] Tzetzes, *Exegesis of the Iliad* 7.2–10 ed. Papathomopoulos. On Tzetzes, see Wendel (1948).

[24] For more general discussions of the reception of the playwrights in Byzantium, see e.g. Marciniak (2004), Baldwin (2009) for Euripides, Easterling (2003) and Magnelli (2017) for Sophocles, Simelidis (2018) for Aeschylus, Tomadaki and van Opstall (2019) for the tragedians, van den Berg (2021) for Aristophanes.

[25] On the respective intellectuals, see *PLP* 23308 (Planoudes), 19373 (Moschopoulos), 16045 (Magistros), 29317 (Triklinios). For an overview of their classical scholarship, see Pontani (2015: 398–434) with further references. On the (Byzantine) scholia on the tragedians and Aristophanes, see Dickey (2007), 28–31 for Aristophanes, 31–4 for Euripides, 34–5 for Sophocles, 35–8 for Aeschylus, with further references to the vast bibliography on the Palaiologan recensions and scholia. For the scholia on Euripides, see also Mastronarde (2017). For Magistros, his commentaries and his circle, see also Gaul (2007) and (2011: 230–66, 387–401). For Moschopoulos and Aristophanes, see also Keaney (1972). On Moschopoulos' scholia to Sophocles' *Electra*, see Cuomo in this volume. For Triklinios, see below.

[26] On intellectual circles and collaborative scholarship in the Palaiologan era, see e.g. Cavallo (2004), Bianconi (2005) for Thessalonike and (2010: esp. 504–12), Gaul (2007) and (2011: 267–71) with a focus on Magistros. On the fluid textual tradition and what this implies for the modern editor, see Cuomo in this volume. See also Smith (1996) on the importance of editions for our understanding of Byzantine scholia and scholarship.

[27] On the grammatical thrust of Palaiologan scholia, see e.g. Webb (1994) and (1997) with a focus on Moschopoulos, Smith (1996: 400), Easterling (2003) for the study of Sophocles specifically, Gaul (2011: 230–1) for Magistros' commentaries in the context of grammar teaching, Cuomo in this volume. See also Gaul (2008) on grammar and lexicography.

A similar grammatical focus emerges from various collections of schedography and epimerisms that were produced in the same period, with different ancient texts as their points of departure. Such grammatical exercises work outwards from a word or phrase in the text in question and relate it to the wider context of ancient Greek language. Often this word is the starting point for discussing more or less related terms, commonly illustrated with citations from other ancient authors.[28] Examples include Manuel Moschopoulos' *Schedographia*, which was based on various pagan and Christian texts and remained influential beyond the end of the Byzantine Empire and into the Early Modern period;[29] the epimerisms by George Lakapenos (fl. ca. 1297–1311) on, among other texts, the letters of Libanios, a much-admired model author throughout the entire Byzantine period;[30] and the epimerisms to Philostratus' *Eikones* by Maximos Planoudes.[31] Schedography had gained traction from the eleventh century onwards and continued to be part of grammar teaching throughout the twelfth century,[32] when some teachers developed the form in ways that gained the disapproval of more conservative intellectuals such as Anna Komnene, John Tzetzes and Eustathios of Thessalonike.[33] Yet the Homeric works of the latter contain material that has close affinities with epimerisms and schedography that are of the more traditional rather than the more modern type, we may presume.[34]

An exception to the predominantly grammatical concerns in the Palaiologan commentaries on the Athenian playwrights is the work of Demetrios Triklinios, whose scholia demonstrate a strong interest in textual criticism and metre.[35] His recensions of the tragedians and Aristophanes significantly improved the texts and remained in circulation

---

[28] On such exercises for teaching vocabulary, see e.g. Webb (1994: 88–9). The most recent study of schedography in the Palaiologan era is Nousia (2016: 52–92); see also Gaul (2008). For epimerisms and schedography in Byzantium, see also Lindstam (1919), Robins (1993: 125–48), Agapitos (2013) and (2015a), Silvano (2015).
[29] For Moschopoulos' *On Schede*, see Webb (1994: 88–9), Nousia (2016: 75–89). For its reception in the Early Modern period, see Nousia (2017).
[30] *PLP* 14379. On Lakapenos and his epimerisms, see e.g. Constantinides (1982: 83–7, 101–3), Wilson (1996 [1983]: 243), Mergiali (1996: 34–8, 52–3). See also Lindstam (1910) and (1924).
[31] On Planoudes' epimerisms, see e.g. Lindstam (1919: 61–87).
[32] See Agapitos (2014), who focuses on the twelfth century. On the popularity of schedography in the eleventh century, see Bernard (2014: 259–66, 270–1).
[33] For Anna, see Agapitos (2013); for Tzetzes, Agapitos (2017), van den Berg (2020) and Lovato in this volume; for Eustathios, Agapitos (2015b). For schedographic innovations by Theodore Prodromos, see Vassis (1994), Agapitos (2015c).
[34] On schedography in Eustathios' Homeric commentaries, see Lovato in this volume.
[35] Gaul (2008: 163), Pontani (2015: 424).

up to and even beyond the first printed editions.³⁶ In this way, Triklinios' work differs not only from that of the other Palaiologan scholars, but also from that of Tzetzes two centuries earlier, whose commentaries on Aristophanes show little interest in textual issues and focus on grammar, meaning and context instead.³⁷ Tzetzes' Aristophanic commentaries, moreover, display the same strong authorial presence as the rest of his work and repeatedly open up a perspective on his exegetical practice as well as the competition involved in interpreting school texts in twelfth-century Constantinople.³⁸ Eustathios' Homeric commentaries testify to a greater interest in textual issues, yet not in Triklinios' systematic way.³⁹ Producing new recensions of ancient texts was not a priority for twelfth-century scholars.

Triklinios' work on Pindar's odes likewise is strongly text-critical and metrical in character, whereas the scholia of his Palaiologan predecessors and contemporaries again have a strong grammatical thrust.⁴⁰ A focus on language and style emerges also from the preface to a lost or never completed commentary on Pindar by Eustathios, who discusses, among other things, the stylistic obscurity and lexical inventiveness of the poet, in addition to the moral value of his maxims and the wealth of historical and mythological material woven into his odes.⁴¹ Triklinios' metrical work has a predecessor in a verse treatise on Pindaric metres by Isaac Tzetzes, which heavily relies on the *Encheiridion* by Hephaestion of Alexandria (second

---

³⁶ On Triklinios and his circle, see Bianconi (2005: 91–182). On Triklinios' editions of the tragedians and Aristophanes, see Smith (1975), Wilson (1996 [1983]: 251–3), Pontani (2015: 424–5) with further references. For recent editions of Triklinios' scholia, see Faveri (2002) for Euripides and Tessier (2005) for Sophocles.

³⁷ Tzetzes' commentaries on the *Frogs*, *Birds*, *Plutus* and *Clouds* are available in the editions by Koster (1962), Massa Positano (1960) and Holwerda (1960) respectively.

³⁸ On Tzetzes' authorial presence, see e.g. Budelmann (2002: 148–53), Pizzone (2017), (2018) and in this volume. For traces of Eustathios' work on Aristophanes, see Koster and Holwerda (1954) and (1955).

³⁹ Browning (1975: 24) and Cullhed (2016: 13*) list textual criticism among Eustathios' diverse interests.

⁴⁰ For Palaiologan scholarship on Pindar, see e.g. Irigoin (1952), 182–5 for Magistros, 247–69 for Planoudes, 270–86 for Moschopoulos, 331–64 for Triklinios. For Magistros' commentary on Pindar, see also Gaul (2007: 284–96). For the metrical study of Pindar in the Palaiologan era, see Günther (1998; for Triklinios, 167–85); for Triklinios' metrical scholia, see also Budelmann (1999: 199–201). Competition may partially answer the questions posed by Smith (1996: 404) about the motivations of teacher-scholars for composing their own commentaries on Pindar (and other authors) even if a commentary was already available. Magistros' polemical remarks criticizing ancient predecessors and Palaiologan colleagues point in this direction. On Magistros' polemics, see e.g. Smith (1996: 401), Gaul (2007: 278–83); on Magistros' defence of his views vis-à-vis rivals, see also Gaul (2011: 232–3, 299–310).

⁴¹ For Eustathios' preface on Pindar, see Kambylis (1991a) and (1991b), Negri (2000), Haubold (2021).

century AD).⁴² Even if such minute study of Pindar's intricate metres may go beyond classroom utility, there is ample evidence that students learned versification and were required to compose verses of their own, which suggests a practical and productive dimension to at least some metrical scholarship.⁴³ A verse treatise on the nine most important ancient metres by Isaac's brother John, for instance, is didactic rather than scholarly in nature and seems to be designed for teaching practice.⁴⁴

In addition to grammatical explanations, many commentaries include longer or shorter paraphrases of the texts under discussion, which likely reflects a much-used pedagogical strategy to promote students' understanding of the text.⁴⁵ In addition to paraphrastic material in scholia and commentaries, free-standing paraphrases of ancient texts existed, particularly of philosophical texts, most notably the works of Aristotle.⁴⁶ Homer's poetry likewise was the subject of various paraphrases: Moschopoulos, for instance, paraphrased the first two books of the *Iliad*, while Manuel Gabalas/Matthew of Ephesus (ca. 1271/2–1355/60) composed a partial prose paraphrase of Odysseus' wanderings.⁴⁷ John Tzetzes paraphrased the *Iliad* and *Odyssey* in political verse and allegorical terms for the edification and entertainment of the foreign-born Empress Irene and, later, the aristocrat Constantine Kotertzes.⁴⁸ The intensified interest in Homer – and ancient mythology more generally – in the eleventh and twelfth centuries went hand in hand with a renewed interest in the allegorical interpretation that had been an important part of earlier Homeric exegesis.

---

⁴² Isaac's treatise is available in the edition by Drachmann (1975). On the treatise and its debt to Hephaestion, see Budelmann (1999: 197–9).

⁴³ On versification in the classroom, see e.g. Bernard (2014: 216–22). In his hortatory address to his son Demetrios, Christopher Zonaras (twelfth century) urges his son to persevere in his studies and keep on practising composition in verse as well as prose (see e.g. 394.91–9, 398.221–3 ed. Tsolakis).

⁴⁴ On John Tzetzes' *On Metres*, see van den Berg (2020).

⁴⁵ Smith (1996: 400), following Turyn (1957: 66–8), calls paraphrasing a dominant feature of Planoudes' work on Euripides. Pontani (2015: 417) refers to Moschopoulos' commentary on Hesiod's *Works and Days* as largely paraphrastic. Eustathios' commentaries and Tzetzes' scholia on Aristophanes also contain paraphrastic material.

⁴⁶ On philosophical paraphrases, see below and Trizio in this volume.

⁴⁷ Moschopoulos' paraphrase is edited by Grandolini (1980–1) and (1982). On the paraphrase of Gabalas (*PLP* 3309), see Browning (1992); on Gabalas' work on Homer, see also Pontani (2005: 271–3). Another example is the so-called Psellian paraphrase of the *Iliad*, on which see Vassis (1991: esp. 16–32). For the Homeric paraphrase by a certain Hermoniakos (dated to the fourteenth century), see Jeffreys (1975), Nilsson (2004: 23–6). Gregory of Cyprus (ca. 1241–90, *PLP* 4590) paraphrased some fables by Aesop: see Kotzabassi (1993).

⁴⁸ *Allegories of the Iliad*: ed. Boissonade (1851); trans. Goldwyn and Kokkini (2015); *Allegories of the Odyssey*: ed. Hunger (1955) and (1956); trans. Goldwyn and Kokkini (2019). On Tzetzes as a commissioned writer, see Grünbart (2005), Rhoby (2010).

Michael Psellos (ca. 1018–78) wrote various allegorical essays on ancient mythology.[49] His interpretation of *Iliad* 4.1–4 inspired a similar essay on the same lines by a certain John Diakonos Galenos, an otherwise obscure figure who is now usually dated to the twelfth century.[50] Tzetzes' *Exegesis of the Iliad* also features allegorical interpretations as well as programmatic statements on myth and allegory.[51] Eustathios articulates his own approach in the prefaces to his Homeric commentaries: his allegorical interpretations are not primarily apologetic but make allegory an aesthetic and didactic practice that allows the poet-rhetor to add an extra layer of meaning to his mythical inventions.[52] Without being employed to systematically Christianize ancient poetry, allegory had the potential to support the moralizing reading that was widespread in Byzantium.[53] The ancient poets were sources of wise maxims and proverbial expressions, which were collected in gnomological collections and woven into many new texts as part of Byzantine literary aesthetics.[54]

Tzetzes' allegorical paraphrases of Homer are among various didactic texts in verse designed for the classroom or as 'edutainment' for aristocratic audiences.[55] Psellos was the first to use political verse for pedagogical purposes in his didactic poems for members of the imperial family.[56] His example was followed by other teachers such as Niketas of Herakleia (ca. 1050–after 1117), who wrote didactic poems on various

---

[49] Psellos' allegorical essays are edited by Duffy (1992; essays 42–7) and studied by Cesaretti (1991: 29–123). On Psellos' biography, see Papaioannou (2013: 4–13).

[50] Galenos also wrote an allegorical commentary on Hesiod's *Theogony*. On Galenos and his allegorical interpretation, see Roilos (2014). See also Cullhed (2016: 30*).

[51] On Tzetzes' allegorical method, see Hunger (1954), Cesaretti (1991: 128–221), Goldwyn (2017).

[52] On Eustathios, see Cesaretti (1991: 207–74), Cullhed (2016: 25*–33*), van den Berg (2017) and (2022: 44–54, 152–81). Another example of allegorical interpretation survives from Southern Italy, not of Homer but of Heliodorus' *Aethiopica*, by Philip-Philagatus of Cerami. See esp. Bianchi (2006: 1–67) for an edition with introduction; see also Hunter (2005).

[53] Moralizing reading is widespread but little studied. For some observations on Eustathios' moralizing reading of Homer, see Lindberg (1985: 134–6). Sophocles was often praised as wise poet: see e.g. Nikephoros Basilakes (ca. 1115–after 1182), *Progymnasmata* 25 ed. Pignani; Easterling (2003: 323). The tragedian looms large in Eustathios' Homeric commentaries and frequently features in a moral-didactic context: Makrinos (2013: 145, 150, 157–60). For moral reflections in book epigrams on the ancient tragedians, see Tomadaki and van Opstall (2019).

[54] On gnomological collections, see e.g. Odorico (1986), Searby (2007). On maxims, see also Messis and Papaioannou (2021). Eustathios discusses many maxims and proverbs in his Homeric commentaries: see Andersen (2014) and Cullhed (2016: 23*–4*). Arsenios Apostolis (1468/9–1535) later used Eustathios' commentaries for his own collection of Homeric proverbs: see Ciolfi in this volume. On proverbs in Eustathios' literary practice, see e.g. Tosi (2017).

[55] The term 'edutainment' is used by Cullhed (2016: 11*). On Tzetzes as didactic poet, see van den Berg (2020), with further references.

[56] On Psellos' didactic poetry, see e.g. Hörandner (2012: 57–62) and (2019), Bernard (2014: 229–51) and (2019: esp. 225–6).

grammatical subjects, some of them in hymnographic metres.⁵⁷ In addition to the *Allegories*, Tzetzes composed didactic verses on ancient poetry, comedy and tragedy,⁵⁸ a synopsis of Porphyry's *Isagoge* and a commentary on various rhetorical handbooks by Hermogenes.⁵⁹ Tzetzes' *Carmina Iliaca*, a hexameter summary of the history of the Trojan War with scholia by the author himself, belong – at least partly – to the same didactic category.⁶⁰ He also composed a *Theogony* in political verse for the *sebastokratorissa* Irene, largely (but not solely) indebted to Hesiod's poem, presenting the genealogies of the ancient gods and heroes without taking recourse to allegorical interpretation.⁶¹ The *Synopsis Chronike* of Constantine Manasses (ca. 1130–87) – also commissioned by Irene – similarly presents mythological and historical lore in literary form.⁶² Familiarity with ancient history and mythology was expected of every educated person in Byzantium, and many scholia and commentaries aim to expand students' knowledge of the mythical, legendary and historical past. Prose treatises such as that of John Pediasimos (ca. 1240–1310/14) on the labours of Heracles served the same purpose.⁶³

Exegetical material on other ancient poets survives, displaying a similar focus on language, style and ancient lore, even if the exact use of these texts and the accompanying exegetical material in the classroom (and beyond) remains to be studied. Among these ancient poets are various Hellenistic poets: Tzetzes commented on Lycophron, whose *Alexandra* offers a wealth of mythological material as well as recherché vocabulary.⁶⁴ Palaiologan scholars worked on Theocritus, whose *Syrinx* received scholia

---

⁵⁷ For the didactic poetry of Niketas of Herakleia, see e.g. Schneider (1999), Antonopoulou (2003), Hörandner (2012: 64–6) and (2019: 467), Bernard (2014: 230, 237–8, 240) and (2019: 226, 228).
⁵⁸ Edited by Koster (1975). See van den Berg (2021) and Roilos (2021). Tzetzes also wrote prose prolegomena to comedy (in the same volume by Koster).
⁵⁹ Nikos Zagklas is preparing an edition of the synopsis of the *Isagoge*, Elisabetta Barili and Aglae Pizzone of the work on Hermogenes (until then available in the outdated editions by Walz [1832–6] vol. 3 and Cramer [1837]). On the latter, see also Pizzone (2020).
⁶⁰ Edition by Leone (1995); Italian translation (with commentary) in Leone (2005). On the *Carmina Iliaca* as an erudite literary piece, see Braccini (2009–10); on the poem as vehicle for teaching Homer, see Cardin (2018); on grammar lessons in Tzetzes' scholia to the poem, see van den Berg (forthcoming). See also Conca (2018) and Mondini (2022).
⁶¹ On the *Theogony*, see Tomadaki in this volume, with further references. On the *sebastokratorissa* Irene, see e.g. M. J. Jeffreys and E. M. Jeffreys (1994), E. M. Jeffreys (2012).
⁶² Ed. Lampsidis (1996). On the literariness of the text, see e.g. Reinsch (2002) and Nilsson (2006).
⁶³ *PLP* 22235. For a recent edition, with French translation and elaborate introduction, see Levrie (2018).
⁶⁴ Tzetzes' commentary on Lycophron remains unstudied: for some observations, see Hornblower (2015: 104–7), Pontani (2015: 380–2). The edition by Scheer (1908) is outdated; see Coward (2022). On the reception of Lycophron in Byzantine literature, see De Stefani and Magnelli (2009).

by Manuel Holobolos (ca. 1243–1310/14) and John Pediasimos.⁶⁵ Even if Theocritus did not write in the much-admired Attic dialect, students were expected to be familiar with other dialects too, as registers of literary language rather than historical phenomena.⁶⁶ Planoudes studied Aratus' *Phaenomena* out of an interest in astronomy.⁶⁷ Andronikos Kallistos (d. 1476/84) worked on Apollonius of Rhodes.⁶⁸ Hesiod's *Works and Days* was studied by Tzetzes, Planoudes and Moschopoulos, while Pediasimos produced scholia on Hesiod's *Shield*.⁶⁹ Tzetzes and Eustathios seem to have worked on Oppian's *Halieutica*, even if only scanty evidence survives.⁷⁰ The latter also produced a commentary on another didactic poet from the Imperial period, the geographer Dionysius Periegetes, whose *Description of the Known World* continued to be read in Byzantium.⁷¹

An innovation in the grammar teaching of the Palaiologan period was a stronger engagement with prose texts. Planoudes integrated prose texts into the curriculum with what has been called the 'Scholastic Anthology' or the 'Anthology of the Four'.⁷² The Anthology contains excerpts from Philostratus' *Eikones*, Aelian's *Natural History*, Marcus Aurelius' *Meditations*, and the Planoudean collection of the *Greek Anthology*; all texts are accompanied by (schedographic) scholia that point to their use in the classroom.⁷³ Together with, for instance, scholia on Philostratus' *Eikones* by Moschopoulos, the Anthology gives insight into the didactic

---

⁶⁵ See Caballero Sánchez in this volume, with further references. Holobolos: *PLP* 21047. Theocritus was also popular in the Komnenian period, as his reception in the learned novels illustrates: see Burton (2003) and (2006).

⁶⁶ See e.g. Webb (1994: 93) and (1997: 16). Treatises such as Gregory Pardos' *On Dialects* (twelfth century) may therefore have served a prescriptive as well as descriptive purpose: see van den Berg (2021).

⁶⁷ See e.g. Constantinides (1982: 72), Pontani (2015: 410).

⁶⁸ *PLP* 10484; Pontani (2015: 449), with further references.

⁶⁹ Tzetzes: ed. Gaisford; Planoudes: see Constantinides (1982: 79); Moschopoulos: ed. Grandolini (1991), see Pontani (2015: 417); Pediasimos: ed. Gaisford, see Pontani (2015: 407). On Hesiod in the twelfth century, see Cardin and Pontani (2017).

⁷⁰ For Tzetzes, see Colonna (1963), Napolitano (1973); for Eustathios, see Dyck (1982), with critical response in Cariou (2016).

⁷¹ The commentary is available in the (outdated) edition by Müller (1861). On the commentary and its context, see Angelov (2022) and Pérez Martín in this volume.

⁷² See Canart (2010: 453–4) and (2011), Webb (1994: 87) and (1997: 5–6), Pontani (2015: 418). On the Anthology and the innovation of introducing prose into the curriculum, see also Gaul (2008: 168, 172–4). For the ancient (and Byzantine) novels in an educational and schedographic context in the Komnenian period, see Nilsson and Zagklas (2017).

⁷³ For the scholia to the *Greek Anthology*, see Luppino (1959–60); for Aelian, see Marcheselli Loukas (1971–2).

methods and linguistic expectations involved in grammar teaching in the school of Planoudes and Moschopoulos and beyond.[74] Other prose authors enjoyed similar popularity, notably Aelius Aristides, whose works received marginal comments by probably the only Byzantine female scholar known to have written (and copied) scholia: the noblewoman Theodora Raoulaina (ca. 1240–1300).[75]

We find another form of commentary on ancient prose authors (and orators in particular) in various literary critical essays by Theodore Metochites (1270–1332).[76] Comparing Aristides to Demosthenes, Metochites concludes that, even if the latter is indeed eloquence personified, the former – working in an autocracy rather than a democracy – is the more useful of the two from a Byzantine perspective; Metochites thus departs from the traditional pre-eminence awarded to Demosthenes and ties Aristides' relevance to the type of eloquence required in an imperial political system.[77] Other essays – included in the miscellaneous *Sententious Notes* rather than transmitted among Metochites' orations – discuss the style and eloquence of prose authors such as Aristotle, Josephus, Philo, Synesios, Dio Chrysostom, Xenophon and Plutarch.[78] A characteristic of Metochites' approach is his combined focus on matters of style and morals.[79] His dispute with the scholar and court official Nikephoros Choumnos (ca. 1250/5–1327) about the best literary style illustrates again that much was at stake in the study and criticism of ancient texts in the competitive world of Palaiologan Constantinople.[80] Scholarship has often pointed to political reasons lying behind the dispute, reading the rivalry between the two men as a rivalry for the position of 'prime minister' under Emperor Andronikos II Palaiologos. Alexander Riehle, however, has

---

[74] On Moschopoulos' scholia on the *Eikones*, see Webb (1994) and (1997).
[75] *PLP* 10943. Nousia (in this volume) provides an edition of the scholia as well as ample bibliography on Theodora and Aristides in the Palaiologan era.
[76] *PLP* 17982.
[77] On Metochites' essay, see e.g. Gigante (1969), Conley (2005: 669–70, 689–90), Pernot (2006), Bourbouhakis (2017: 125–6). The most recent edition is Polemis and Kaltsogianni (2019). For similar comparative essays by Michael Psellos, see Dyck (1986), Bourbouhakis (2017: 118–20).
[78] See *Sententious Notes* 3, 15–20, 71 ed. and trans. Hult (2002). On the *Sententious Notes* in general, see e.g. Featherstone (2011). For Plutarch and Metochites, see also Xenophontos (2018) and (2019). On the reception of Plutarch in Byzantium, see the relevant contributions in Xenophontos and Oikonomopoulou (2019).
[79] See esp. his *Moral Treatise or Concerning Education*, ed. Polemis and Kaltsogianni (2019: 347–429), trans. Xenophontos (2020). Cf. Zonaras' exhortations at the address of his son Demetrios mentioned above.
[80] *PLP* 30961.

recently revisited the dispute and argues that it is built not on political rivalry but on irreconcilable views about literature and its social implications.[81]

Another group of ancient texts that received continuous exegesis and commentary throughout the Byzantine period consists of various grammatical and rhetorical handbooks that remained central to Byzantine education. Moschopoulos, for instance, turned the influential *Art of Grammar* attributed to Dionysius Thrax (second century BC) into a schoolbook in question-and-answer form (*Erotemata*), which continued to be used into the Early Modern period.[82] Tzetzes produced a verse synopsis of various texts of the Hermogenean corpus that was at the core of rhetorical education.[83] His contemporary Gregory Pardos wrote a commentary on Pseudo-Hermogenes' *On the Method of Skilfulness*, and Planoudes did the same for all four Hermogenean treatises.[84] John Chortasmenos (ca. 1370–1431) composed a commentary on the equally popular textbook of *progymnasmata* by Aphthonios,[85] which had long prompted teachers and intellectuals to compose their own model *progymnasmata*, often using subjects from ancient mythology and history as well as biblical stories, from Libanios in the fourth and John Geometres in the tenth century to Nikephoros Basilakes in the twelfth and George of Cyprus in the thirteenth century.[86] Other teacher-rhetors such as George Pachymeres (1242–ca. 1310),[87] Constantine Akropolites (d. before 1324),[88] Nikephoros Kallistos Xanthopoulos (d. ca. 1328)[89] and

---

[81] On their dispute, see e.g. Ševčenko (1962), Gigante (1981: 167–98) and, most recently, Riehle (2014: 13–40). See also Conley (2005: 688–9), with references to literary critical essays by Choumnos. On competition and *theatra*: see above.

[82] On the *Erotemata*, see most recently Rollo (2019) with further references. On Dionysius Thrax in Byzantium, see Robins (1993: 41–86), Ronconi (2012: 72–80).

[83] See n. 59 above.

[84] The commentaries are available in Walz (1832–6), vols. 7.2 (Gregory) and 5 (Planoudes), respectively. On Gregory's commentary, see Kaldellis (2009: 16–17). On Hermogenes in Byzantium, see e.g. Kustas (1970), Lindberg (1977), Papaioannou (2017: 105).

[85] On the importance of Aphthonios in Byzantium, see e.g. Kustas (1970), Papaioannou (2017: 105). For an overview of Byzantine commentaries on Aphthonios' *progymnasmata*, see Hunger (1978, vol. 1: 78–9). See also Kustas (1973: 5–26), Hock (2012).

[86] Libanios: ed. Foerster (1915), trans. Gibson (2008); Geometres: Littlewood (1972); Basilakes: Pignani (1983), trans. Beneker and Gibson (2016); Gregory of Cyprus: Kotzabassi (1993). On *progymnasmata* in general, see Webb (2001); for *progymnasmata* in the Latin Middle Ages, see Kraus (2013).

[87] *PLP* 22186. Ed. Walz (1832–6, vol. 1: 551–96). See also Constantinides (2003: 48).

[88] *PLP* 520. For the manuscripts and editions of Akropolites' *progymnasmata*, see Constantinides (2003: 49).

[89] *PLP* 20826. For the *progymnasmata*, see Glettner (1933); see also Constantinides (2003: 49).

Nikephoros Gregoras (ca. 1292–1361)⁹⁰ likewise produced their own *progymnasmata* as part of their teaching practice.

Many Byzantine texts testify to the linguistic competence, rhetorical skills and wide knowledge in which the educational system trained their authors: they are written in Atticizing Greek and feature an abundance of allusions to and citations from ancient texts (pagan as well as biblical and patristic); they include ancient proverbs and gnomic sayings as vehicles of style as well as moral value; and they imitate, continue or revive ancient genres and the styles of various ancient authors. Many literary works can therefore themselves be read as commentaries on ancient literature, revealing the manifold ways in which the Byzantines dealt with their ancient heritage. Some conspicuous examples include Theodore Prodromos' *Katomyomachia* ('Battle of Cat and Mice'), which draws on ancient tragedy and partly parodies Aeschylus' *Persians*;⁹¹ the *Sale of Poetical and Political Lives* by the same author, conceived as a sequel to Lucian's *Philosophies for Sale*, in which Prodromos puts prominent school authors up for auction;⁹² the anonymous *Christos Paschon*, which tells the story of the Passion with numerous lines from Euripides' tragedies;⁹³ and Planoudes' *Idyll*, a humorous parody drawing on the satirical tradition in the style of Lucian as well as the bucolic tradition in the style of Theocritus.⁹⁴ Such texts support the idea that 'practical usefulness, and symbolic value as a marker of culture or even of mere social polish, can comfortably coexist with deep imaginative and "philosophical" appeal'.⁹⁵ In fact, reading ancient poets and prose authors from a grammatical and rhetorical perspective went hand in hand with a creative and active engagement with the texts of the past in the literary culture of Komnenian and Palaiologan Byzantium.

Philosophy and Science

Scholars have usually studied the philosophical commentary and paraphrase as the literary forms preferred by the Byzantines for the education and practice of philosophy, alongside the philosophical essay

---

⁹⁰ *PLP* 4443. On the *progymnasmata*, see Leone (1970–1).
⁹¹ On the *Katomyomachia*, see Warcaba (2017), Marciniak and Warcaba (2018), Lauxtermann (forthcoming).
⁹² See Marciniak (2013), Cullhed (2014b: 50–8), Nilsson (2016: 193–4).
⁹³ See Mullett in this volume, with further references.
⁹⁴ See Kubina in this volume, with further references. ⁹⁵ Easterling (2003: 331).

and dialogue.⁹⁶ Thus, the reader will find that the didactic setting in which the philosophical commentary functioned in Byzantium tends to be a given in discussions of Byzantine material and is rarely a subject of analysis on its own. As Michele Trizio demonstrates in his contribution to this volume, however, it is no longer useful, productive or, indeed, acceptable to perpetuate the generalizations employed in scholarship so far. Such generalizations include not only presupposing a didactic setting for each and every philosophical commentary, but also assigning a place within the curriculum to thematically grouped commentaries (e.g. stating that commentaries to the logical works of Aristotle belong to the early stages of the curriculum) without acknowledging varying degrees of complexity displayed within each group. For Trizio, 'the real task would be to locate the production of a given commentary on a classical philosophical work within the Byzantine *cursus studiorum*'.⁹⁷ Thus, one way of approaching research into the philosophical commentary in Byzantium is to study contemporary education in philosophy, the related and resulting textual production and the authors whose teaching activity in this field of knowledge is attested. To start with, we may wish to focus on those who occupied the imperially sponsored position of 'consul of the philosophers' (ὕπατος τῶν φιλοσόφων), starting with Michael Psellos, John Italos (d. after 1082) and Theodore of Smyrna (d. after 1112) in the eleventh and twelfth centuries and continuing with John Pothos Pediasimos (d. 1310/14) in the Palaiologan period.⁹⁸ Focusing on the office of the *hypatos* has the potential to be methodologically valuable as it encourages us to question the nature and extent of institutionalization of advanced learning in Byzantium – one possible and, indeed, likely framework within which the didactically targeted philosophical commentary was composed and circulated.

Examples of the exegetical activity of the *hypatoi* do survive. Psellos, for instance, paraphrased Aristotle's *De interpretatione*,⁹⁹ while his disciple Italos commented on Aristotle's *Topics*,¹⁰⁰ and left scholia to *On the Celestial Hierarchy* by Pseudo-Dionysius the Areopagite.¹⁰¹ John Pediasimos, however, is the only Palaiologan *hypatos* whose writings

---

[96] On Theodore Metochites and the philosophical essay in late Byzantium, see Bydén (2002). On philosophical dialogues in Byzantium, see Mariev (2011), Manolova (2017), Karamanolis (2017). On the philosophical commentary in Byzantium, a good starting point is provided by Trizio (2017), Ierodiakonou (2002) and (2012), Barber and Jenkins (2009).
[97] See Trizio in this volume, p. 62.   [98] Constantinides (1982: 113–32).
[99] See Ierodiakonou (2002) and Trizio in this volume.   [100] See Kotzabassi (1999).
[101] See Trizio in this volume.

survive. Among them we find scholia on Aristotle's *Prior* and *Posterior Analytics* and on *De interpretatione*.[102] Focusing on the activity of the *hypatoi* can also be misleading to a considerable degree if one takes into consideration two aspects highlighted by Constantinides in as early as 1982. First, we know of many commentators of philosophical works who did not hold this office or held a higher-ranking position while possibly performing the duties of a *hypatos* at the same time.[103] In the case of the latter, the title of *hypatos* would not be worth mentioning, as it was inferior to their current office. Second, while the historical record preserves the names of certain *hypatoi*, such as, for instance, the thirteenth-century Theodore Eirenikos and Demetrios Karykes, little is known of their teaching activity in Nicaea, and its remit might have been much more limited than the title of *hypatos* might indicate.[104]

The activity of *hypatoi ton philosophon* is a predominantly Constantinopolitan phenomenon and, thus, it draws our attention away from the philosophical education and related exegetical production in other Byzantine cities (chiefly, in Thessalonike). At the same time, focusing on the imperially appointed and sponsored *hypatoi* helps us raise a question discussed in this volume by Michele Trizio and Maria Tomadaki, namely in what ways commentaries and the exegetical strategies they employ are a result and a reflection of a patron's (in addition to the author's) social and literary self-representation.[105] As we discuss the impact of networks of patronage on philosophical exegesis in Byzantium, we will briefly examine several large-scale exegetical enterprises that primarily commented on Aristotle's philosophical corpus, none of which was directed by an imperially appointed *hypatos ton philosophon*.

The exegetical literature related to the patronage of princess Anna Komnene (d. ca. 1153) is probably the best known and better studied. In his contribution, Panagiotis Agapitos discusses the use of Aristotelian material by Theodore Prodromos in his novel *Rhodanthe and Dosikles*, dedicated to Anna's husband Nikephoros Bryennios (d. 1138),[106] while Michele Trizio's analysis centres on the two most prolific Aristotelian

---

[102] See Trizio (2017). On Pediasimos' commentary on Theocritus' *Syrinx*, see Caballero Sánchez in this volume. On Pediasimos' scholia to Cleomedes' *The Heavens*, see Caballero Sánchez (2018).
[103] Constantinides (1982: 116) suggests that the latter might have been the case of George Akropolites (1217–82).
[104] Constantinides (1982: 114–16).
[105] On the cultural and political context of the production of Aristotelian commentaries in twelfth-century Byzantium, see also Frankopan (2009).
[106] Prodromos also composed a commentary on *Posterior Analytics* 2.

commentators of the twelfth century, both of them associated with Anna's patronage, namely Eustratios of Nicaea (d. after 1120) and Michael of Ephesus (fl. first half of the twelfth century).[107] Eustratios, the metropolitan of Nicaea, commented on Aristotle's *Posterior Analytics* 2 and on *Nicomachean Ethics* 1 and 6. Michael, of whose life almost nothing is known, was much more prolific. His extant Aristotelian commentaries include those on *Sophistical Refutations*; on Aristotle's zoological works, such as *Generation of Animals, Parts of Animals, Movement of Animals, Progression of Animals*; on *Metaphysics* 7–14; on *Nicomachean Ethics* 5, 9 and 10; scholia on *Politics*; commentaries on *Parva naturalia* and on Pseudo-Aristotle's *De coloribus*. Both authors were the first to produce extended self-standing philosophical commentaries in Greek on the *Nicomachean Ethics, Parva naturalia* and Aristotle's 'zoological treatises' since the Hellenistic era.[108]

Not surprisingly, the two major publications on the philosophical commentary in Byzantium produced roughly during the past decade focus on Eustratios' and/or Michael's contributions. These are Brill's *Medieval Greek Commentaries on the Nicomachean Ethics* edited by Charles Barber and David Jenkins (2009) and Springer's *The Parva naturalia in Greek, Arabic and Latin Aristotelianism: Supplementing the Science of the Soul*, edited by Börje Bydén and Filip Radovic (2018). Both volumes, which focus on a discrete part of the Aristotelian corpus, present a collaborative approach towards an in-depth analysis of the commentary tradition and strive to revise the traditional narrative that sees Byzantium as a passive repository of ancient Greek wisdom (of both science and philosophy). These publications recognize the long-lasting (beyond the late medieval period and up to the sixteenth century) and wide-reaching (across Europe) influence of Eustratios' and Michael's commentaries and treat them as authors and texts that engaged with Aristotle's philosophy seriously and on their own terms. The more recent of the two, *The Parva naturalia in Greek, Arabic and Latin Aristotelianism*, moreover, adopts a comparative approach and discusses Michael of Ephesus' commentaries on an equal

---

[107] On the practice of commenting on Aristotle in Byzantium, see most recently Trizio (2017), Erismann (2017).

[108] On the commentaries on the *Nicomachean Ethics*, see Barber and Jenkins (2009); on the commentaries on *Parva naturalia*, see Arabatzis (2012), Bydén and Radovic (2018), Bydén (2018). A recent translation into English of Michael's commentary on *Nicomachean Ethics* 10 has been published in Bloomsbury's *Ancient Commentators on Aristotle* series; see Wilberding, Trompeter and Rigolio (2019). On Eustratios' commentary on the *Nicomachean Ethics*, see most recently Trizio (2021).

footing with its counterparts in Latin and Arabic (works by Avicenna, Albert the Great and so forth). It exemplifies a new stage in the research on philosophical thought in Byzantium – one that posits it as interconnected and in dialogue with other intellectual cultures that were comparably engaged with the Aristotelian tradition. In this sense, its methodology is similar to that of the ERC-funded project Reassessing Ninth Century Philosophy: A Synchronic Approach to the Logical Traditions (9 SALT; 2016–20 at the University of Vienna), which studied synchronically the Latin, Greek, Syriac and Arabic philosophical traditions of logic in the ninth century.[109]

Eustratios' and Michael's combined exegetical output, and Michael's in particular, however, should not be interpreted simply, or even predominantly, as individual scholarly achievements.[110] They represent in equal measure (to say the least) their patroness's ambition to fill in the gaps in the commentary literature on Aristotle available in the twelfth century, which in turn might be connected to Anna Komnene's personal strategies of self-representation, as shown by Trizio in this volume. The pursuit of comprehensiveness by means of providing an exegetical reading of the entire Aristotelian corpus is exemplified by two other similar scholarly projects dating to the early fourteenth century and authored by George Pachymeres (1242–ca. 1310) and Theodore Metochites (1270–1332).

In terms of institutional educational framework and questions of patronage, the cases of Pachymeres and Metochites present us with a constellation of factors different from what we have seen so far with the philosophical teaching of *hypatoi*, such as Psellos and Italos, and in the case of Anna Komnene's role in Eustratios of Nicaea's and Michael of Ephesus' exegetical work. Like the *hypatoi ton philosophon*, Pachymeres was actively involved in education while he was teaching at the Patriarchal school in Constantinople.[111] His scholarly output is firmly embedded in the educational environment of early fourteenth-century Constantinople and resulted from Pachymeres' teaching a curriculum that started with logic and physics and finished with theoretical mathematics and theology. He composed the *Philosophia*, an extensive compendium and paraphrase of Aristotelian philosophy in twelve books.[112] Pachymeres also commented on Plato (e.g. on the dialogue *Parmenides*)[113] and wrote a textbook on the

---

[109] On the 9 SALT project, see Erismann (2018). [110] See Kaldellis (2009: 37).
[111] Golitsis (2008).
[112] Golitsis argues that *Philosophia* was composed ca. 1307: see Golitsis (2009).
[113] Gadra, Honea, Stinger and Umholtz (1989).

four sciences of the *quadrivium*. Producing a full critical edition of Pachymeres' *Philosophia* has been the objective of an editorial project within the Corpus Philosophorum Medii Aevi – Commentaria in Aristotelem Byzantina series under the auspices of the Academy of Athens. At present, the Academy has published critical editions of Book 3 *Commentary on Aristotle's* De Caelo,[114] Book 5 *Commentary on Aristotle's* Meteorologica,[115] Book 6 *Commentary on Aristotle's* Parts of Animals,[116] Book 10 *Commentary on the* Metaphysics,[117] and Book 11 *Commentary on the* Nicomachean Ethics.[118] Pachymeres also wrote running commentaries (as opposed to paraphrases) to some of Aristotle's works, such as parts of the *Organon*, the *Physics*, *Metaphysics* and *Nicomachean Ethics*.[119] Thus, Pachymeres' case presents us with the rare opportunity, first, to compare his exegetical strategies in the *Philosophia* (an extended paraphrase) and in his running (lemmatic) commentaries and, second, to analyse his commentaries both within their didactic setting and as expressions of self-teaching and of his personal philosophical explorations. Much progress was made in this regard both by the editors of the *Philosophia* and by scholars such as Pantelis Golitsis. Nevertheless, any current interpretation remains partial and contingent on the publication of Pachymeres' commentaries in their entirety.

A current assessment of the final significant Aristotelian enterprise we will mention in this brief survey shows that its study remains in an even more preliminary phase. Even though it is well known that the *megas logothetes* of emperor Andronikos II Theodore Metochites (d. 1332) produced paraphrases on all of Aristotle's writings on natural philosophy (including *Physics*, *On the Heavens*, *On Generation and Corruption*, *Meteorologica*, *On the Soul* and *Parva naturalia*, as well as Aristotle's zoological works), very few of them are critically edited.[120] According to Bydén, Metochites' paraphrases of Aristotle's writings on natural philosophy were most likely first circulated ca. 1312–13; a possible alternative is a

---

[114] Telelis (2016). [115] Telelis (2012). [116] Pappa (2008). [117] Pappa (2002).
[118] Oikonomakos (2005).
[119] See Golitsis (2012). The commentary on Aristotle's *Physics* is the only one edited so far. It has been published under the name of Michael Psellos, but Golitsis has argued convincingly that it should be attributed to Pachymeres instead. For the edition, see Benakis (2008). For Golitsis' arguments in favour of Pachymeres' authorship of the commentary, see Golitsis (2007). A new critical edition and English translation of Pachymeres' commentary on Aristotle's *Nicomachean Ethics* is currently being prepared by Sophia Xenophontos for the *Commentaria in Aristotelem Graeca et Byzantina* series. On the commentary, see most recently Xenophontos (2021).
[120] For a list of modern printed editions, see the introduction to Bydén and Radovic (2018: 16, n. 52). See ibid., 24, n. 69 for a list of sixteenth-century printed editions of the Latin translation of Metochites' paraphrases.

date ca. 1320–1.[121] There is little we could say about their significance for the history of the philosophical commentary at present, except to use them as an illustration of several core ideas discussed in our survey so far.

First, we have been signposting the relationship, albeit insufficiently articulated in existing scholarship, between the philosophical commentary, the processes of teaching and learning philosophy (especially Aristotelian philosophy) and the institutional and patronage frameworks which may or may not motivate and circumscribe the production of exegetical literature. The case of Metochites yet again differs from those we have seen before. A high-ranking politician and among the wealthiest people in early Palaiologan Byzantium, Metochites was not involved in teaching (except perhaps in his personal exchanges with his disciple and intellectual heir Nikephoros Gregoras) and often played the role of a patron rather than of a protégé. At the same time, he is famously and by his own account an ambitious and very keen student who spared no effort to find himself a teacher of mathematics, astronomy and harmonics. Finally, he had at his disposal one of the best Constantinopolitan libraries – that of the monastery of Christ the Saviour in Chora. With all this in mind, the rationale behind and purpose of Metochites' Aristotelian paraphrases seem less clear. Issues of self-fashioning and of imperial patronage probably play a role in this case as well, but we may also wish to consider the extent to which the practice of paraphrasing relates to self-teaching and learning.[122]

Second, the Metochitean paraphrases, written in the early fourteenth century, demonstrate nicely the profoundly genealogical nature of the practice of writing philosophical (and other) commentaries. While Michael of Ephesus emulated the late antique commentators of Aristotle, Metochites borrowed from Michael and, about a century later, George Scholarios' own Aristotelian commentaries in fact abridged Metochites' paraphrases.[123] Scholars have usually interpreted this 'concatenated' character of the philosophical production of the Byzantines as an indication not only of its embeddedness in the tradition of Greek thought but also as a sign of its dependency, derivativeness and lack of originality. To borrow the expression from Trizio's contribution, however, 'commentaries do not merely attempt to clarify the ancient philosophical texts, but also address contemporary questions of meaning'.[124] Moreover, they hold precious

---

[121] Bydén (2018: 201).
[122] On the murky boundaries between teaching and self-teaching of the sciences in Byzantium, see Pérez Martín and Manolova (2020).
[123] See, for instance, Demetracopoulos (2018), Bydén (2018).   [124] Trizio in this volume, p. 88.

subversive potential, as a commentary of a work does not necessarily have to be supportive of the work's thesis and outlook.[125] Fashioning oneself as another link in the chain of commentators perhaps brought additional cultural capital we cannot fully recognize yet. Furthermore, the extent to which Byzantine commentators oscillated closer to or further away from the exegesis they inherited may be dependent on the requirements of Byzantine education. Finally, we should note that, even though the majority of the extant self-standing Byzantine philosophical commentaries focus on Aristotle's corpus, other authors' texts were also furnished with an exegesis, albeit more rarely, for instance, Plato's dialogues and Synesios' *On Dreams*.[126] One way in which research on commentaries in Byzantium will expand in the future is by studying philosophical exegesis beyond the Aristotelian corpus.

When it comes to science in Byzantium, we define it widely, thus including more than the four mathematical sciences of the *quadrivium*, such as the epistemic fields of geography, medicine and botany.[127] However, science is not among the core areas of focus in this collection, and only the chapter by Inmaculada Pérez Martín addresses an exegetical text composed in connection to a 'scientific' field (geography). Nevertheless, it is worth formulating several general points on the subject, to give further context to the commentaries discussed throughout the volume. Education in natural philosophy, the mathematical sciences and medicine formed part of the same framework of teaching and learning whose institutionalization and ties to patronage were discussed earlier in relation to poetry, rhetoric and philosophy. Similarly, Byzantine science has been accused of being unoriginal and irrelevant in comparison with ancient Greek mathematics. Again, just as in the case of philosophy, scholars have only recently started to reassess the conscious choice of the Byzantines to model their intellectual production on the ancient and Hellenistic traditions they inherited.[128]

In the opening sentence of his 1967 survey of Byzantine science, Vogel stated: 'When the course of Byzantine history is surveyed as a whole, it will be seen that long periods of partial or complete neglect of the sciences

---

[125] Worth considering in this respect is the *Refutation of Proklos'* Elements of Theology, commonly ascribed to the twelfth-century Byzantine theologian Nicholas of Methone. On the scholarly dispute concerning the authorship of the work, see most recently Gioffreda and Trizio (2021).

[126] Two fourteenth-century commentaries to Synesios' *On Dreams* have been preserved. One is anonymous and one was composed by Nikephoros Gregoras. For Gregoras' commentary, see the edition by Pietrosanti (1999) and also Bydén (2014). For the anonymous commentary, see Monticini (2018).

[127] Good starting points are Bouras-Vallianatos (2015) and (2018) on medicine and Touwaide (2020).

[128] Acerbi (2020: 106–7).

alternated with periods of intensive activity.'[129] This is the impression created by the fluctuation between periods of abundant source material and periods almost completely devoid of scientific works amongst the texts preserved in Byzantine manuscripts. Vogel also saw the importance of the Byzantine contribution to the history of science in the role it played for the preservation of Hellenic science (a master narrative current scholarship strives to revise) and sketched its development in three phases, each defined by the dynamics of initial spectacular achievement and subsequent gradual decline (a historiographical model that also requires revision, albeit beyond the scope of the present volume and of this introduction).

Forty-odd years later, Vogel's chapter can now be complemented and revised thanks to the publication of *A Companion to Byzantine Science* within Brill's Companions to the Byzantine World series.[130] In his overview of the mathematical sciences with the exception of astronomy included in the *Companion*, Fabio Acerbi rejects the usefulness of the categories of 'originality', 'relevance' and '(dis)continuity' when studying Byzantine mathematics and qualifies the latter as 'sectional, framing and embedded':

> Byzantine mathematics is *sectional* because it mainly comprises works that do not display a tight deductive structure; as a consequence, they can easily be, or actually are, partitioned in independent sections, or can easily be assembled to generate sectional texts ... Byzantine mathematics is *framing* (and not simply second-order) because it relates, to Greek mathematics and to itself, in the same way as, in a manuscript, a frame-commentary *cum* interlinear glosses relates to the main text: primers elaborate *before*, scholia *above*, compendia *after* ... Byzantine mathematics is finally deeply *embedded* – as a prestigious further step along the social ladder – in the highest socio-political milieux and in a rhetorical tradition that induces subtle modifications in the stylistic codes inherited from Greek antiquity.[131]

If we accept that Byzantine mathematics is framing, in the same way that a frame-commentary is, how do commentaries to mathematical works function in this general picture? Self-standing scientific commentaries in Byzantium are rare.[132] However, at the same time, the generic instrumentarium

---

[129] Vogel (1967: 264).
[130] Lazaris (2020). The companion's bibliography is an excellent and up-to-date starting point for readers interested in Byzantine science.
[131] Acerbi (2020: 155).
[132] See Pérez Martín in this volume and Pérez Martín and Manolova (2020: 93). A special case is the sphere of cosmological knowledge, where, in addition to Byzantine exegesis related to Aristotelian, Platonic, Ptolemaic and Stoic models, we should also add biblical exegesis and, more precisely, hexaemerical commentaries, such as, for instance, the commentaries on *Genesis* by John Chrysostomos and Severianos of Gabala. On this, see Caudano (2020: 217). For biblical

employed for the purposes of scientific exegesis greatly surpasses the limits of the late antique commentary model, and it includes *quadrivia*, monographs, primers, compendia, letters, scholia and collections of scholia, notebooks, introductions, syntheses and synopses, collections of tables, *Rechenbücher*, recensions and so forth.[133] In addition, the nature of the mathematical material (especially in the spheres of astronomy and astrology) and its applied use required continuous adaptation, for example of astronomical tables and the data they contain, or of the methods of calculation and combination. One of the most common adaptations of an astronomical table, for instance, relates to its reconfiguration for a new set of geographical coordinates. Finally, we should signal the importance of translations from Arabic, Persian, Latin and Hebrew – enterprises also motivated by the appreciation of accurate data or improved methods of calculation. The translation of non-Hellenic knowledge as a special case of adaptation and exegesis is a specific feature of the scientific teaching and learning in Byzantium that did not play a role in the study of, for instance, Homer or Aristotle, and is thus worth mentioning here.[134]

To conclude, we ought to state the obvious, namely that more research is needed on Byzantine science and on the role commentaries play in scientific education. However, we may also add that the contemporary approach towards the study of Byzantine mathematics, as outlined by Acerbi above, has the potential to help revise, update and advance scholarly methodologies applied to the study of other aspects of Byzantine intellectual culture and its educational context. Byzantine science is rarely taken into consideration by the general Byzantinist, who is traditionally focused on philology, literature and history. At the same time, the scholars in Byzantium who wrote on Ptolemy, Diophantos, Nicomachus and Euclid are more often than not the same as those who commented on Homer and Aristotle. If the Byzantine authors themselves worked across disciplinary divides, perhaps it is wise to follow their example when studying them.

In its engagement with the Byzantine commentary, this volume operates on two distinct levels. On the first level, it aims at introducing the reader to Byzantine commentaries: it provides an overview of the material available to those interested in Byzantium and outlines the opportunities, as well as the challenges, that the nature of the sources inevitably imposes

---

commentaries preserving traces of an Antiochene (non-spherical) cosmological model in the eleventh and twelfth century, see Caudano (2008).
[133] Acerbi (2020: 110). See also Acerbi (2014) and (2016).
[134] To start with, see Caudano (2020: 213); then, see Tihon (1987) and (1990).

on scholarship in the field. The volume also serves as a guide to current trends in the study of the Byzantine commentary and, furthermore, indicates various directions for future research.

On the second level, however, the editors and contributors collaborating on this collection purposefully go one step further than simply offering the reader a piece of solid scholarship. We wish to redeem the Byzantine commentary. We read, discuss and analyse it on its own terms, and we enquire into the specifically *Byzantine* aims behind the acts of preserving, commenting and adapting. In the research presented on the following pages, the contributors approach the process of commenting on ancient texts as a deliberate and culturally significant choice made by the commentators. Their analyses reveal that the practice of composing commentaries on ancient texts in Byzantium was more than a scholarly endeavour, often in service of an educational need. Commenting was also a creative and targeted enterprise of identity building. The cultural and intellectual identity of the Byzantine commentators is, indeed, profoundly genealogical. The chapters in this volume demonstrate that this genealogical character should not be taken as a sign of derivativeness. On the contrary, the genealogical embeddedness of Byzantine commentary practice should rather be interpreted as evidence for the fact that Byzantine authors were aware of their intellectual predecessors, acknowledged what they conceived as the immediate past of the knowledge corpus available, and worked within existing traditions, while at the same time never losing sight of the contemporary relevance of their source texts and the commentaries they were writing.

A Note on Style

Following a common practice in Byzantine Studies, we have adopted a mixed system of transliteration. Late antique and Byzantine names are generally transliterated, following the *Oxford Dictionary of Byzantium*. Ancient names appear in their common Latinized or Anglicized form, following the *Oxford Classical Dictionary*. Titles of ancient and Byzantine texts are given in English or, where this is conventional, in Latin. References to Eustathios' *Commentary* (or: *Parekbolai*) *on the Iliad* and *Commentary on the Odyssey* include page and line numbers of the *editio princeps* by Niccolò Maiorano (Rome, 1542–9), which are included in the edition by van der Valk of the *Commentary on the Iliad* and those by Stallbaum (1825–6) and Cullhed (2016) of the *Commentary on the Odyssey*. They also give the volume, page and line numbers of the modern editions, which are followed in the TLG.

REFERENCES

Acerbi, F. (2014) 'Types, Function, and Organization of the Collections of Scholia to the Greek Mathematical Treatises', *Trends in Classics* 6: 115–69.
  (2016) 'Byzantine Recensions of Greek Mathematical and Astronomical Texts: A Survey', *Estudios bizantinos* 4: 133–213.
  (2020) 'Logistic, Arithmetic, Harmonic Theory, Geometry, Metrology, Optics and Mechanics', in *A Companion to Byzantine Science*, ed. S. Lazaris, 105–59. Brill's Companions to the Byzantine World 6. Leiden–Boston.
Agapitos, P. A. (2013) 'Anna Komnene and the Politics of Schedographic Training and Colloquial Discourse', *Nea Rhome* 10: 89–107.
  (2014) 'Grammar, Genre and Patronage in the Twelfth Century: A Scientific Paradigm and Its Implications', *JÖByz* 64: 1–22.
  (2015a) 'Learning to Read and Write a *Schedos*: The Verse Dictionary of Par. Gr. 400', in *Pour une poétique de Byzance: hommage à Vassilis Katsaros*, ed. S. Efthymiadis, C. Messis, P. Odorico and I. D. Polemis, 11–24. Dossiers Byzantins 16. Paris.
  (2015b) 'Literary *Haute Cuisine* and Its Dangers: Eustathios of Thessalonike on Schedography and Everyday Language', *DOP* 69: 225–41.
  (2015c) 'New Genres in the Twelfth Century: The *Schedourgia* of Theodore Prodromos', *MEG* 15: 1–41.
  (2017) 'John Tzetzes and the Blemish Examiners: A Byzantine Teacher on Schedography, Everyday Language and Writerly Disposition', *MEG* 17: 1–57.
Andersen, L. (2014) 'Unfolding Compressed Knowledge: Wisdom Expressions in the Homeric Commentaries by Eustathios of Thessalonike', unpublished PhD thesis, University of Southern Denmark.
Angelov, D. (2022) 'Repurposing Ancient Knowledge: Eustathios of Thessaloniki and His Geographical Anthology', in *Imagined Geographies in the Mediterranean, Middle East, and Beyond*, ed. D. Kastritsis, A. Stavrakopoulou and A. Stewart. Washington, DC.
Antonopoulou, T. (2003) 'The Orthographical Kanons of Nicetas of Heraclea', *JÖByz*: 171–85.
Arabatzis, G. (2012) 'Michael of Ephesus and the Philosophy of Living Things (*In De partibus animalium* 22.25–23.9)', in *The Many Faces of Byzantine Philosophy*, ed. K. Ierodiakonou and B. Bydén, 51–78. Papers and Monographs from the Norwegian Institute at Athens Series 4.1. Athens.
Baldwin, B. (2009) 'Euripides in Byzantium', in *The Play of Texts and Fragments: Essays in Honour of Martin Cropp*, ed. J. R. C. Cousland and J. R. Hume, 433–43. Leiden–Boston.
Baltussen, H. (2007) 'From Polemic to Exegesis: The Ancient Philosophical Commentary', *Poetics Today* 28: 247–81.
Barber, C. and D. Jenkins (eds.) (2009) *Medieval Greek Commentaries on the Nicomachean Ethics*. Leiden–Boston.

Basilikopoulou-Ioannidou, A. (1971) Ἡ ἀναγέννησις τῶν γραμμάτων κατὰ τὸν ΙΒ' αἰῶνα εἰς τὸ Βυζάντιον καὶ ὁ "Ομηρος. Athens.
Benakis, L. G. (ed.) (2008) *Michael Psellos, Kommentar zur Physik des Aristoteles*. Corpus Philosophorum Medii Aevi – Commentaria in Aristotelem Byzantina 5. Athens.
Beneker, J. and C. A. Gibson (2016) *The Rhetorical Exercises of Nikephoros Basilakes: Progymnasmata from Twelfth-Century Byzantium*. Cambridge, MA.
Bernard, F. (2014) *Writing and Reading Byzantine Secular Poetry, 1025–1081*. Oxford Studies in Byzantium. Oxford.
  (2019) 'The Eleventh Century: Michael Psellos and Contemporaries', in *A Companion to Byzantine Poetry*, ed. W. Hörandner, A. Rhoby and N. Zagklas, 212–36. Brill's Companions to the Byzantine World 4. Leiden–Boston.
van den Berg, B. (2017) 'Eustathios on Homer's Narrative Art: The Homeric Gods and the Plot of the *Iliad*', in *Reading Eustathios of Thessalonike*, ed. F. Pontani, V. Katsaros and V. Sarris, 129–48. Trends in Classics Supplementary Volume 46. Berlin–Boston.
  (2020) 'John Tzetzes as Didactic Poet and Learned Grammarian', *DOP* 74: 285–302.
  (2021) 'Playwright, Atticist, Satirist: The Reception of Aristophanes in Twelfth-Century Byzantium', in *Satire in the Middle Byzantine Period: The Golden Age of Laughter?*, ed. P. Marciniak and I. Nilsson, 227–53. Explorations in Medieval Culture 12. Leiden–Boston.
  (2022) *Homer the Rhetorician: Eustathios of Thessalonike on the Composition of the Iliad*. Oxford Studies in Byzantium. Oxford.
  (forthcoming) 'Teaching Grammar with Poetry: Grammar Lessons in John Tzetzes' Scholia on the *Carmina Iliaca*', in *Byzantine Poetry in the 'Long' Twelfth Century (1081–1204)*, ed. B. van den Berg and N. Zagklas.
Bianchi, N. (2006) *Il codice del romanzo: tradizione manoscritta e ricezione dei romanzi greci*. Bari.
Bianconi, D. (2005) *Tessalonica nell'età dei Paleologi: le pratiche intellettuali nel riflesso della cultura scritta*. Paris.
  (2010) 'Erudizione e didattica nella tarda Bisanzio', in *Libri di scuola e pratiche didattiche dall'antichità al Rinascimento. Atti del Convegno Internazionale di Studi, Cassino, 7–10 maggio 2008*, vol. 2, ed. L. Del Corso and O. Pecere, 475–512. Cassino.
  (2017) 'La lettura dei testi antichi tra didactica ed erudizione: qualche esempio d'età paleologa', in *Toward a Historical Sociolinguistic Poetics of Medieval Greek*, ed. A. M. Cuomo and E. Trapp, 57–83. Βυζάντιος: Studies in Byzantine History and Civilization 12. Turnhout.
Boissonade, J. F. (ed.) (1851) *Tzetzae allegoriae Iliadis*. Paris.
Bouras-Vallianatos, P., with contributions by S. Xenophontos (2015) 'Galen's Reception in Byzantium: Symeon Seth and His Refutation of Galenic Theories on Human Physiology', *GRBS* 55: 431–69.

(2018) 'Reading Galen in Byzantium', in *Greek Medical Literature and Its Readers: From Hippocrates to Islam and Byzantium*, ed. P. Bouras-Vallianatos and S. Xenophontos, 180–229. Abingdon–New York.
Bourbouhakis, E. C. (2017) 'Byzantine Literary Criticism and the Classical Heritage', in *The Cambridge Intellectual History of Byzantium*, ed. A. Kaldellis and N. Siniossoglou, 113–40. Cambridge.
Braccini, T. (2009–10) 'Erudita invenzione: riflessioni sulla *Piccola grande Iliade* di Giovanni Tzetze', *Incontri triestini di filologia classica* 9: 153–73.
Browning, R. (1975) 'Homer in Byzantium', *Viator* 6: 15–33.
  (1992) 'A Fourteenth-Century Prose Version of the *Odyssey*', *DOP* 46. *Homo Byzantinus: Papers in Honor of Alexander Kazhdan*, 27–36.
  (1997) 'Teachers', in *The Byzantines*, ed. G. Cavallo, 95–116. Chicago.
Budelmann, F. (1999) 'Metrical Scholia on Pindar', *BICS* 43: 195–201.
  (2002) 'Classical Commentary in Byzantium: John Tzetzes on Ancient Greek Literature', in *The Classical Commentary: Histories, Practices, Theory*, ed. R. K. Gibson and C. S. Kraus, 141–69. Mnemosyne Supplements 232. Leiden–Boston–Cologne.
Burton, J. B. (2003) 'A Reemergence of Theocritean Poetry in the Byzantine Novel', *CPh* 98: 251–73.
  (2006) 'The Pastoral in Byzantium', in *Brill's Companion to Greek and Latin Pastoral*, ed. M. Fantuzzi and T. Papanghelis, 549–79. Leiden–Boston.
Bydén, B. (2002) 'The Nature and Purpose of the *Semeioseis gnomikai*: The Antithesis of Philosophy and Rhetoric', in *Theodore Metochites on Ancient Authors and Philosophy: Semeioseis gnomikai 1–26 & 71*, ed. and trans. K. Hult, 245–88. Gothenburg.
  (2014) 'Nikephoros Gregoras' Commentary on Synesius, *De insomniis*', in *On Prophecy, Dreams and Human Imagination: Synesius, De insomniis*, ed. H.-G. Nesselrath and D. Russell, 161–86. SAPERE 24. Tübingen.
  (2018) 'The Byzantine *Fortuna* of Alexander of Aphrodisias' Commentary on Aristotle's *De sensu et sensibilibus*', *JÖByz* 68: 93–109.
Bydén, B. and F. Radovic (eds.) (2018) *The Parva naturalia in Greek, Arabic and Latin Aristotelianism. Supplementing the Science of the Soul.* Studies in the History of Philosophy of Mind 17. Cham.
Caballero Sánchez, P. (2018) *El Comentario de Juan Pediásimo a los 'Cuerpos celestes' de Cleomedes: estudio, edición crítica y traducción*. Madrid.
Canart, P. (2010) 'Pour un répertoire des anthologies scolaires commentées de la période des Paléologues', in *The Legacy of Bernard the Montfaucon: Three Hundred Years of Studies on Greek Handwriting. Proceedings of the Seventh International Colloquium of Greek Palaeography (Madrid–Salamanca, 15–20 September 2008)*, ed. A. Bravo García and I. Pérez Martín, 449–62. Turnhout.
  (2011) 'Les anthologies scolaires commentées de la période des Paléologues: à l'école de Maxime Planude et de Manuel Moschopoulos', in *Encyclopedic Trends in Byzantium? Proceedings of the International Conference Held in Leuven, 6–8 May 2009*, ed. P. van Deun and C. Macé, 297–331. Leuven.

Cardin, M. (2018) 'Teaching Homer through (Annotated) Poetry: John Tzetzes' *Carmina Iliaca*', in *Brill's Companion to Prequels, Sequels, and Retellings of Classical Epic*, ed. R. Simms, 90–114. Leiden–Boston.
Cardin, M. and F. Pontani (2017) 'Hesiod's Fragments in Byzantium', in *Poetry in Fragments: Studies on the Hesiodic Corpus and Its Afterlife*, ed. C. Tsagalis, 245–87. Berlin.
Cariou, M. (2016) 'Eustathe de Thessalonique lecteur des Halieutiques', *RPh* 90: 73–88.
Caudano, A.-L. (2008) 'Un univers sphérique ou voûté? Survivance de la cosmologie antiochienne à Byzance (XIe et XIIe s.)', *Byzantion* 78: 66–86.
  (2020) 'Astronomy and Astrology', in *A Companion to Byzantine Science*, ed. S. Lazaris, 202–30. Brill's Companions to the Byzantine World 6. Leiden–Boston.
Cavallo, G. (2004) 'Sodalizi eruditi e pratiche di scrittura a Bisanzio', in *Bilan et perspectives des études médiévales (1993–1998). Euroconférence (Barcelone, 8–12 juin 1999); Actes du IIe Congrès Européen d'Études Médiévales*, ed. J. Hamesse, 645–65. Turnhout.
Cesaretti, P. (1991) *Allegoristi di Omero a Bisanzio: ricerche ermeneutiche (XI–XII secolo)*. Milan.
Cesaretti, P. and S. Ronchey (eds.) (2014) *Eustathii Thessalonicensis exegesis in canonem iambicum pentecostalem*. Supplementa Byzantina 10. Berlin–Boston.
Colonna, A. (1963) 'Il commento di Giovanni Tzetzes agli Halieutica di Oppiano', in *Lanx satura N. Terzaghi oblata: miscellanea philologica*, 101–4. Genoa.
Conca, F. (2018) 'L'esegesi di Tzetzes ai *Carmina Iliaca*, fra tradizione e innovazione', *ΚΟΙΝΩΝΙΑ* 42: 75–99.
Conley, T. M. (2005) 'Byzantine Criticism and the Uses of Literature', in *The Cambridge History of Literary Criticism*, vol. 2: *The Middle Ages*, ed. A. Minnis and I. Johnson, 669–92. Cambridge.
Constantinides, C. N. (1982) *Higher Education in Byzantium in the Thirteenth and Early Fourteenth Centuries (1204–ca. 1310)*. Nicosia.
  (2003) 'Teachers and Students of Rhetoric in the Late Byzantine Period', in *Rhetoric in Byzantium. Papers from the Thirty-Fifth Spring Symposium of Byzantine Studies, Exeter College, University of Oxford, March 2001*, ed. E. M. Jeffreys, 39–53. Aldershot.
Copeland, R. (2012) 'Gloss and Commentary', in *The Oxford Handbook of Medieval Latin Literature*, ed. R. J. Hexter and D. Townsend, 171–91. Oxford.
Coward, T. (2022) 'Towards a New Edition of Tzetzes' *Commentary on Lycophron*', in *Τζετζικαὶ ἔρευναι*, ed. E. E. Prodi, 359–401. Bologna.
Cramer, J. A. (1837) *Anecdota Graeca e codd. manuscriptis bibliothecarum Oxoniensium*, vol. 4. Oxford.
Cullhed, E. (ed. and trans.) (2014a) 'Eustathios of Thessalonike, *Parekbolai* on Homer's *Odyssey* 1–2: Proekdosis', PhD thesis, Uppsala University.

(2014b) 'The Blind Bard and "I": Homeric Biography and Authorial Personas in the Twelfth Century', *BMGS* 38: 49–67.
(ed. and trans.) (2016) *Eustathios of Thessalonike, Commentary on the Odyssey*, vol. 1: *On Rhapsodies A–B*. Acta Universitatis Upsaliensis. Studia Byzantina Upsaliensia 17. Uppsala.
Demetracopoulos, J. A. (2018) 'George Scholarios' Abridgment of the *Parva naturalia*: Its Place in His *Œuvre* and in the History of Byzantine Aristotelianism', in *The Parva naturalia in Greek, Arabic and Latin Aristotelianism. Supplementing the Science of the Soul*, ed. B. Bydén and F. Radovic, 233–315. Studies in the History of Philosophy of Mind 17. Cham.
De Stefani, C. and E. Magnelli (2009) 'Lycophron in Byzantine Poetry (and Prose)', in *Lycophron, éclats d'obscurité. Actes du colloque international de Lyon et Saint-Étienne, 18–20 janvier 2007*, ed. C. Cusset and E. Prioux, 593–620. Saint-Étienne.
Dickey, E. (2007) *Ancient Greek Scholarship: A Guide to Finding, Reading, and Understanding Scholia, Commentaries, Lexica, and Grammatical Treatises, from Their Beginnings to the Byzantine Period*. Oxford–New York.
(2017) 'Classical Scholarship: The Byzantine Contribution', in *The Cambridge Intellectual History of Byzantium*, ed. A. Kaldellis and N. Siniossoglou, 63–78. Cambridge.
Drachmann, A. B. (ed.) (1975) *Isaac Tzetzae De Metris Pindaricis commentarius*. Copenhagen.
Duffy, J. M. (ed.) (1992) *Michaelis Pselli Philosophica minora*, vol. 2: *Opuscula logica, physica, allegorica, alia*. Stuttgart–Leipzig.
Dyck, A. R. (1982) 'Did Eustathius Compose a Commentary on Oppian's *Halieutica*?' *CPh* 77: 153–4.
(ed. and trans.) (1986) *Michael Psellus, the Essays on Euripides and George of Pisidia and on Heliodorus and Achilles Tatius*. Byzantina Vindobonensia 16. Vienna.
Easterling, P. (2003) 'Sophocles and the Byzantine Student', in *Porphyrogenita: Essays on the History and Literature of Byzantium and the Latin East in Honour of Julian Chrysostomides*, ed. C. Dendrinos, J. Harris, E. Harvalia-Crook and J. Herrin, 319–34. Aldershot–Burlington, VT.
Erismann, C. (2017) 'Logic in Byzantium', in *The Cambridge Intellectual History of Byzantium*, ed. A. Kaldellis and N. Siniossoglou, 362–80. Cambridge.
(2018) 'Writing the History of Aristotelian Logic during the Long Ninth Century', *Medieval Worlds* 8: 162–9.
Faveri, L. D. (ed.) (2002) *Die metrischen Trikliniusscholien zur byzantinischen Trias des Euripides*. Stuttgart.
Featherstone, M. J. (2011) 'Theodore Metochites' *Semeioseis gnomikai*: Personal Encyclopedism', in *Encyclopedic Trends in Byzantium? Proceedings of the International Conference held in Leuven, 6–8 May 2009*, ed. P. van Deun and C. Macé, 333–44. Leuven.
Foerster, R. (1915) *Libanii opera*, vol. 8. Leipzig.

Frankopan, P. (2009) 'The Literary, Cultural and Political Context for the Twelfth-Century Commentary on the *Nicomachean Ethics*', in *Medieval Greek Commentaries on the Nicomachean Ethics*, ed. C. Barber and D. Jenkins, 45–62. Leiden–Boston.

Gadra, T. A., S. M. Honea, P. M. Stinger and G. Umholtz (eds. and trans.) (1989) Γεωργίου τοῦ Παχυμέρους Ὑπόμνημα εἰς τόν Παρμενίδην Πλάτωνος [Ἀνωνύμου Συνέχεια τοῦ Ὑπομνήματος Πρόκλου]. *George Pachymeres, Commentary on Plato's Parmenides [Anonymous Sequel to Proclus' Commentary]*. Corpus Philosophorum Medii Aevi – Philosophi Byzantini 4. Athens.

Gaisford, T. (ed.) (1823) *Poetae Minores Graeci*, vol. 2. Leipzig.

Garzya, A. (1973) 'Literarische und rhetorische Polemiken der Komnenenzeit', *Byzantinoslavica* 34: 1–14.

Gaul, N. (2007) 'The Twitching Shroud: Collective Construction of *Paideia* in the Circle of Thomas Magistros', *Segno e Testo* 5: 263–340.

(2008) 'Moschopulos, Lopadiotes, Phrankopulos (?), Magistros, Staphidakes: Prosopographisches und Methodologisches zur Lexikographie des frühen 14. Jahrhunderts', *Lexicologica Byzantina: Beiträge zum Kolloquium zur byzantinischen Lexikographie (Bonn, 13.–15. Juli 2007)*, vol. 4, ed. E. Trapp and S. Schönauer, 163–96. Göttingen.

(2011) *Thomas Magistros und die spätbyzantinische Sophistik: Studien zum Humanismus urbaner Eliten in der frühen Palaiologenzeit*. Wiesbaden.

(2018) 'Performative Reading in the Late Byzantine Theatron', in *Reading in the Byzantine Empire and Beyond*, ed. T. Shawcross and I. Toth, 215–33. Cambridge.

(2020) 'The Letter in the Theatron: Epistolary Voice, Character, and Soul (and Their Audience)', in *A Companion to Byzantine Epistolography*, ed. A. Riehle, 353–73. Brill's Companions to the Byzantine World 7. Leiden–Boston.

Gibson, C. A. (2008) *Libanius's Progymnasmata: Model Exercises in Greek Prose Composition and Rhetoric*. Atlanta, GA.

Gigante, M. (1969) *Teodoro Metochites: saggio critico su Demostene e Aristide*. Varese–Milan.

(1981) *Scritti sulla civiltà letteraria bizantina*. Naples.

Gioffreda, A. and M. Trizio (2021) 'Nicholas of Methone, Procopius of Gaza and Proclus of Lycia', in *Reading Proclus and the Book of Causes*, vol. 2: *Translations and Acculturations*, ed. D. Calma, 94–135. Leiden–Boston.

Glettner, J. (1933) 'Die Progymnasmata des Nikephoros Kallistos Xanthopulos: Erstausgabe', *ByzZ* 33: 1–12.

Goldwyn, A. J. (2017) 'Theory and Method in John Tzetzes' *Allegories of the* Iliad and *Allegories of the* Odyssey', *Scandinavian Journal of Byzantine and Modern Greek Studies* 3: 141–71.

Goldwyn, A. J. and D. Kokkini (trans.) (2015) *John Tzetzes, Allegories of the Iliad*. Dumbarton Oaks Medieval Library 37. Cambridge, MA.

(trans.) (2019) *John Tzetzes, Allegories of the Odyssey*. Dumbarton Oaks Medieval Library 56. Cambridge, MA.

Golitsis, P. (2007) 'Un commentaire perpétuel de Georges Pachymère à la *Physique* d'Aristote, faussement attribué à Michel Psellos', *ByzZ* 100: 637–76.
  (2008) 'Georges Pachymère comme didascale: essai pour une reconstitution de sa carrière et de son enseignement philosophique', *JÖByz* 58: 53–68.
  (2009) 'La date de composition de la *Philosophia* de Georges Pachymère et quelques precisions sur la vie de l'auteur', *REB* 67: 209–15.
  (2012) 'A Byzantine Philosopher's Devoutness toward God: George Pachymeres' Poetic Epilogue to His Commentary on Aristotle's *Physics*', in *The Many Faces of Byzantine Philosophy*, ed. K. Ierodiakonou and B. Bydén, 109–27. Papers and Monographs from the Norwegian Institute at Athens Series 4.1. Athens.
Grandolini, S. (1980–1) 'La parafrasi al secondo libro dell'*Iliade* di Manuel Moschopoulos', *AFLPer* 4: 5–22.
  (1982) 'La parafrasi al primo libro dell'*Iliade* di Manuel Moschopoulos', in *Studi in onore di Aristide Colonna*, 131–49. Perugia.
  (1991) *Manuelis Moschopuli Commentarium in Hesiodi Opera et Dies*. Rome.
Grünbart, M. (2005) 'Byzantinisches Gelehrtenelend – oder: Wie meistert man seinen Alltag?', in *Zwischen Polis, Provinz und Peripherie: Beiträge zur byzantinischen Geschichte und Kultur*, ed. L. M. Hoffmann and A. Monchizadeh, 413–26. Wiesbaden.
Günther, H.-C. (1998) *Ein neuer metrischer Traktat und das Studium der pindarischen Metrik in der Philologie der Paläologenzeit*. Mnemosyne Supplements 180. Leiden–Boston.
Haubold, J. (2021) 'Impressive and Obscure: Three Christian Sources in Eustathius' *Proem to a Commentary on Pindar*', *GRBS* 61: 344–67.
Hock, R. F. (2012) *The Chreia and Ancient Rhetoric: Commentaries on Aphthonius's Progymnasmata*. Atlanta, GA.
Holwerda, D. (ed.) (1960) *Johannis Tzetzae Commentarii in Aristophanem, fasciculus II continens Commentarium in Nubes*. Groningen.
Hörandner, W. (2012) 'The Byzantine Didactic Poem – A Neglected Literary Genre? A Survey with Special Reference to the Eleventh Century', in *Poetry and Its Contexts in Eleventh-Century Byzantium*, ed. F. Bernard and K. Demoen, 55–67. Farnham.
  (2019) 'Teaching with Verse in Byzantium', in *A Companion to Byzantine Poetry*, ed. W. Hörandner, A. Rhoby and N. Zagklas, 459–86. Brill's Companions to the Byzantine World 4. Leiden–Boston.
Hornblower, S. (2015) *Lykophron, Alexandra: Greek Text, Translation, Commentary, and Introduction*. Oxford.
Hult, K. (ed. and trans.) (2002) *Theodore Metochites on Ancient Authors and Philosophy: Semeioseis gnomikai 1–26 & 71*. Gothenburg.
Hunger, H. (1954) 'Allegorische Mythendeutung in der Antike und bei Johannes Tzetzes', *Jahrbuch der Österreichischen Byzantinischen Gesellschaft* 3: 35–54.
  (1955) 'Johannes Tzetzes, Allegorien zur *Odyssee*, Buch 13–24, kommentierte Textausgabe', *ByzZ* 48: 4–48.

(1956) 'Johannes Tzetzes, Allegorien zur *Odyssee*, Buch 1–12, kommentierte Textausgabe', *ByzZ* 49: 249–310.
(1978) *Die hochsprachliche profane Literatur der Byzantiner*, 2 vols. Handbuch der Altertumswissenschaft XII.5.1–2. Munich.
Hunter, R. L. (2005) '"Philip the Philosopher" on the *Aithiopika* of Heliodorus', in *Metaphor and the Ancient Novel*, ed. S. Harrison, M. Paschalis and S. Frangoulidis, 123–38. Ancient Narrative Supplements 4. Groningen.
Ierodiakonou, K. (2002) 'Psellos' Paraphrase on Aristotle's *De interpretatione*', in *Byzantine Philosophy and Its Ancient Sources*, ed. K. Ierodiakonou, 157–81. Oxford.
(2012) 'The Byzantine Commentator's Task: Transmitting, Transforming or Transcending Aristotle's Text', in *Knotenpunkt Byzanz: Wissensformen und kulturelle Wechselbeziehungen*, ed. A. Speer and P. Steinkrüger, 199–209. Berlin–Boston.
Irigoin, J. (1952) *Histoire du texte de Pindare*. Paris.
Jeffreys, E. M. (1975) 'Constantine Hermoniakos and Byzantine Education', *Dodone* 4: 81–109.
(2012) 'The *sebastokratorissa* Irene as Patron', in *Female Founders in Byzantium and Beyond*, ed. L. Theis, M. Mullett and M. Grünbart, with G. Fingarova and M. Savage, 177–94. Wiener Jahrbuch für Kunstgeschichte 60/61. Vienna.
Jeffreys, M. J. and E. M. Jeffreys (1994) 'Who Was Eirene the *sevastokratorissa*?', *ByzZ* 64: 40–68.
Kaldellis, A. (2007) *Hellenism in Byzantium: The Transformations of Greek Identity and the Reception of the Classical Tradition*. Cambridge.
(2009) 'Classical Scholarship in Twelfth-Century Byzantium', in *Medieval Greek Commentaries on the Nicomachean Ethics*, ed. C. Barber and D. Jenkins, 1–43. Leiden–Boston.
Kambylis, A. (ed.) (1991a) *Eustathios von Thessalonike, Prooimion zum Pindarkommentar: Einleitung, kritischer Text, Indices*. Veroffentlichung der Joachim Jungius-Gesellschaft der Wissenschaften 65. Göttingen.
(1991b) *Eustathios über Pindars Epinikiendichtung: Ein Kapitel der klassischen Philologie in Byzanz*. Göttingen.
Karamanolis, G. (2017) 'Form and Content in the Dialogues of Gennadios Scholarios', in *Dialogues and Debates from Late Antiquity to Late Byzantium*, ed. A. Cameron and N. Gaul, 237–51. Abingdon–New York.
Keaney, J. J. (1972) 'Moschopoulos and Aristophanes', *Mnemosyne* 25: 123–8.
Koster, W. J. W. (ed.) (1962) *Johannis Tzetzae Commentarii in Aristophanem, fasciculus III continens Commentarium in Ranas et in Aves, argumentum Equitum*. Groningen.
(ed.) (1975) *Prolegomena de comoedia; Scholia in Acharnenses, Equites, Nubes, fasc. I.I.a: Prolegomena de comoedia*. Groningen.
Koster, W. J. W. and D. Holwerda (1954) 'De Eustathio, Tzetza, Moschopulo, Planude Aristophanis commentatoribus I', *Mnemosyne* 7: 136–56.

(1955) 'De Eustathio, Tzetza, Moschopulo, Planude Aristophanis commentatoribus II', *Mnemosyne* 8: 196–206.
Kotzabassi, S. (1993) 'Die Progymnasmata des Gregor von Zypern: Fabeln, Erzählung und Ethopoiie', *Hellenika* 43: 45–63.
(1999) *Byzantinische Kommentatoren der aristotelischen Topik: Johannes Italos und Leon Magentinos*. Εταιρεία Βυζαντινών Ερευνών 17. Thessalonike.
Kraus, C. S. (2002) 'Introduction: Reading Commentaries/Commentaries as Reading', in *The Classical Commentary: Histories, Practices, Theory*, ed. R. Gibson and C. S. Kraus, 1–27. Mnemosyne Supplements 232. Leiden–Boston–Cologne.
Kraus, C. S. and C. A. Stray (2016) 'Form and Content', in *Classical Commentaries: Explorations in a Scholarly Genre*, ed. C. S. Kraus and C. A. Stray, 1–18. Oxford.
Kraus, M. (2013) 'Progymnasmata and Progymnasmatic Exercises in the Medieval Classroom', in *The Classics in the Medieval and Renaissance Classroom: The Role of Ancient Texts in the Arts Curriculum as Revealed by Surviving Manuscripts and Early Printed Books*, ed. J. F. Ruys, J. O. Ward and M. Heyworth, 175–97. Turnhout.
Krueger, D. and R. Nelson (eds.) (2016) *The New Testament in Byzantium*. Dumbarton Oaks Byzantine Symposia and Colloquia. Washington, DC.
Kustas, G. L. (1970) 'The Function and Evolution of Byzantine Rhetoric', *Viator* 1: 55–73.
(1973) *Studies in Byzantine Rhetoric*. Thessalonike.
Lampsidis, O. (ed.) (1996) *Constantini Manassis Breviarium Chronicum*. Athens.
Lauxtermann, M. D. (forthcoming) 'Of Cats and Mice: The *Katomyomachia* as Drama, Parody, School Text, and Animal Tale', in *Byzantine Poetry in the 'Long' Twelfth Century (1081–1204)*, ed. B. van den Berg and N. Zagklas.
Lazaris, S. (ed.) (2020) *A Companion to Byzantine Science*. Brill's Companions to the Byzantine World 6. Leiden–Boston.
Leone, P. L. M. (1970–1) 'Nicephori Gregorae opuscula nunc primum edita', *Annali della Facoltà di lettere e filosofia* 3–4: 729–82.
(1995) *Ioannis Tzetzae Carmina Iliaca*. Catania.
(2005) *Giovanni Tzetzes, La leggenda troiana (Carmina Iliaca)*. Lecce.
Levrie, K. (2018) *Jean Pédiasimos, Essai sur les douze travaux d'Héraclès: édition critique, traduction et introduction*. Leuven–Paris–Bristol.
Lindberg, G. (1977) *Studies in Hermogenes and Eustathios: The Theory of Ideas and Its Application in the Commentaries of Eustathios on the Epics of Homer*. Lund.
(1985) 'Eustathius on Homer: Some of His Approaches to the Text, Exemplified from His Comments on the First Book of the Iliad', *Eranos* 83: 125–40.
Lindstam, S. (ed.) (1910) *Georgi Lacapeni epistulae x priores cum epimerismis edita*. Uppsala.
(1919) 'Senbyzantinska epimerismsamlingar och ordböcker', *Eranos* 19: 57–92.

(ed.) (1924) *Georgii Lacapeni et Andronici Zaridae epistulae XXXII cum epimerismis Lacapeni*. Gothenburg.
Littlewood, A. R. (1972) *The Progymnasmata of Ioannes Geometres*. Amsterdam.
Luppino, A. (1959–60) 'Scholia graeca inedita in Anthologiae epigrammata selecta', *AAP* 9: 25–62.
Magdalino, P. (1993) *The Empire of Manuel I Komnenos, 1143–1180*. Cambridge.
Magdalino, P. and R. Nelson (eds.) (2010) *The Old Testament in Byzantium*. Dumbarton Oaks Byzantine Symposia and Colloquia. Washington, DC.
Magnelli, E. (2017) 'Introduction: Ancient (and Byzantine) Perspectives on Sophocles' Life and Poetry', in *Brill's Companion to the Reception of Sophocles*, ed. R. Lauriola and K. N. Demetriou, 1–24. Brill's Companions to Classical Reception 10. Leiden–Boston.
Makrinos, A. (2013) 'Tragedy in Byzantium: The Reception of Sophocles in Eustathios' Homeric Commentaries', in *Dialogues with the Past 1: Classical Reception, Theory and Practice*, ed. A. Bakogianni, 139–61. Bulletin of the Institute of Classical Studies Supplements 126.1. London.
Manolova, D. (2017) 'Nikephoros Gregoras's *Philomathes* and *Phlorentios*', in *Dialogues and Debates from Late Antiquity to Late Byzantium*, ed. A. Cameron and N. Gaul, 203–19. Abingdon–New York.
  (2020) 'Epistolography and Philosophy', in *A Companion to Byzantine Epistolography*, ed. A. Riehle, 255–78. Brill's Companions to the Byzantine World 7. Leiden–Boston.
Marcheselli Loukas, L. (1971–2) 'Note schedografiche inedite del Marc. gr. Z 487=883', *RSBN* 8–9: 241–60.
Marciniak, P. (2004) *Greek Drama in Byzantine Times*. Katowice.
  (2007) 'Byzantine *Theatron* – A Place of Performance?', in *Theatron: Rhetorische Kultur in Spätantike und Mittelalter / Rhetorical Culture in Late Antiquity and the Middle Ages*, ed. M. Grünbart, 277–85. Millennium-Studien 13. Berlin–New York.
  (2013) 'Theodore Prodromos' *Bion Prasis*: A Reappraisal', *GRBS* 53: 219–39.
  (2017) 'A Pious Mouse and a Deadly Cat: The *Schede tou Myos*, Attributed to Theodore Prodromos', *BMGS* 57: 507–27.
Marciniak, P. and K. Warcaba (2018) 'Theodore Prodromos' *Katomyomachia* as a Byzantine Version of Mock-Epic', in *Middle and Late Byzantine Poetry: Texts and Contexts*, ed. A. Rhoby and N. Zagklas, 97–110. Turnhout.
Mariev, S. (2011) 'Παιδεία und ἀστειότης im Dialog *Phlorentios* des Nikephoros Gregoras', *FMS* 45.1: 245–58.
Markopoulos, A. (2006) 'De la structure de l'école byzantine: le maître, les livres et le processus éducatif', in *Lire et écrire à Byzance*, ed. B. Mondrain, 85–96. Centre de recherche d'Histoire et Civilisation de Byzance: Monographies 19. Paris.
  (2014) 'Teachers and Textbooks in Byzantium Ninth to Eleventh Centuries', in *Networks of Learning: Perspectives on Scholars in Byzantine East and Latin West, c. 1000–1200*, ed. S. Steckel, N. Gaul and M. Grünbart, 3–15. Zurich–Berlin.

Massa Positano, L. (ed.) (1960) *Johannis Tzetzae Commentarii in Aristophanem, fasciculus I continens Prolegomena et Commentarium in Plutum.* Groningen.
Mastronarde, D. J. (2017) *Preliminary Studies on the Scholia to Euripides.* Berkeley.
Mergiali, S. (1996) *L'enseignement et les lettrés pendant l'époque des Paléologues (1261–1453).* Athens.
Messis, C. and S. Papaioannou (2021) 'Memory: Selection, Citation, Commonplace', in *The Oxford Handbook of Byzantine Literature*, ed. S. Papaioannou, 132–61. Oxford–New York.
Mondini, U. (2022) 'John of All Trades: The Μικρομεγάλη Ἰλιάς and Tzetzes' "Didactic" Programme', in *Τζετζικαὶ ἔρευναι*, ed. E. E. Prodi, 237–59. Bologna.
Monticini, F. (2018) 'The Inner Source of Dreams: Synesius of Cyrene's Reception in the Palaiologan Era', in *Dreams, Memory, and Imagination in Byzantium*, ed. B. Neil and E. Anagnostou-Laoutides, 82–95. Byzantina Australiensia 24. Boston.
Most, G. W. (1999) 'Preface', in *Commentaries = Kommentare*, ed. G. W. Most, vii–xv. Aporemata: Kritische Studien zur Philologiegeschichte 4. Göttingen.
Napolitano, F. (1973) 'Esegesi bizantina degli *Halieutica* di Oppiano', *RAAN* 48: 237–54.
Negri, M. (2000) *Eustazio di Tessalonica, introduzione al commentario a Pindaro.* Antichità classica e cristiana 32. Brescia.
Nesseris, I. (2014) 'Ἡ παιδεία στην Κωνσταντινούπολη κατά τον 12° αἰώνα', unpublished PhD thesis, University of Ioannina.
Nilsson, I. (2004) 'From Homer to Hermoniakos: Some Considerations of Troy Matter in Byzantine Literature', *Troianalexandrina* 4: 9–34.
  (2006) 'Discovering Literariness in the Past: Literature vs. History in the *Synopsis Chronike* of Konstantinos Manasses', in *L'écriture de la mémoire: la littérarité de l' historiographie*, ed. P. Odorico, P. A. Agapitos and M. Hinterberger, 15–31. Dossiers Byzantins 6. Paris.
  (2016) 'Poets and Teachers in the Underworld: From the Lucianic katabasis to the *Timarion*', *SO* 90: 180–204.
Nilsson, I. and N. Zagklas (2017) '"Hurry up, reap every flower of the *logoi*!" The Use of Greek Novels in Byzantium', *GRBS* 57: 1120–48.
Nousia, F. (2016) *Byzantine Textbooks of the Palaeologan Period.* Studi e Testi 505. Vatican City.
  (2017) 'The Transmission and Reception of Manuel Moschopoulos' *Schedography* in the West', in *Teachers, Students, and Schools of Greek in the Renaissance*, ed. F. Ciccolella and L. Silvano, 1–25. Leiden.
Odorico, P. (1986) *Il prato e l'ape: il sapere sentenzioso del Monaco Giovanni.* Vienna.
Oikonomakos, K. (ed.) (2005) *Γεώργιος Παχυμέρης, Φιλοσοφία, Βιβλίον ενδέκατον: Ηθικά, ήτοι τα Νικομάχεια.* Corpus Philosophorum Medii Aevi – Commentaria in Aristotelem Byzantina 3. Athens.
Papaioannou, S. (2013) *Michael Psellos: Rhetoric and Authorship in Byzantium.* Cambridge.

(2017) 'Rhetoric and Rhetorical Theory', in *The Cambridge Intellectual History of Byzantium*, ed. A. Kaldellis and N. Siniossoglou, 101–12. Cambridge.
Papathomopoulos, M. (ed.) (2007) Ἐξήγησις Ἰωάννου Γραμματικοῦ τοῦ Τζέτζου εἰς τὴν Ὁμήρου Ἰλιάδα. Athens.
Pappa, E. (ed.) (2002) *Georgios Pachymeres, Philosophia, Buch 10: Kommentar zu Metaphysik des Aristoteles*. Corpus Philosophorum Medii Aevi – Commentaria in Aristotelem Byzantina 2. Athens.
  (ed.) (2008) *Georgios Pachymeres, Philosophia, Buch 6: Kommentar zu De partibus animalium des Aristoteles*. Corpus Philosophorum Medii Aevi – Commentaria in Aristotelem Byzantina 4.1. Athens.
Pérez Martín, I. (2017) 'Aristides' *Panathenaikos* as a Byzantine Schoolbook: Nikephoros Gregoras' Notes on Ms. Escorial Φ.1.18', in *Toward a Historical Sociolinguistic Poetics of Medieval Greek*, ed. A. M. Cuomo and E. Trapp, 85–107. Byzantios: Studies in Byzantine History and Civilization 12. Turnhout.
Pérez Martín, I. and D. Manolova (2020) 'Science Teaching and Learning Methods in Byzantium', in *A Companion to Byzantine Science*, ed. S. Lazaris, 53–104. Brill's Companions to the Byzantine World 6. Leiden–Boston.
Pernot, L. (2006) 'Mimesis, rhétorique et politique dans l'essai de Théodore Métochite sur Démosthène et Aelius Aristide', in *Spirito e forme nella letteratura bizantina*, ed. A. Garzya, 107–20. Quaderni dell'Accademia Pontaniana 47. Naples.
Pietrosanti, P. (ed.) (1999) *Nicephori Gregorae explicatio in librum Synesii De insomniis: scholia cum glossis*. Pinakes 4. Bari.
Pignani, A. (ed. and trans.) (1983) *Niceforo Basilace, Progimnasmi e monodie: testo critico, introduzione, tradizione*. Naples.
Pizzone, A. (2017) 'The *Historiai* of John Tzetzes: A Byzantine "Book of Memory"?', *BMGS* 41.2: 182–207.
  (2018) 'The Autobiographical Subject in Tzetzes' *Chiliades*: An Analysis of Its Components', in *Storytelling in Byzantium: Narratological Approaches to Byzantine Texts and Images*, ed. C. Messis, M. Mullett and I. Nilsson, 287–304. Uppsala.
  (2020) 'Self-authorization and Strategies of Autography in John Tzetzes: The *Logismoi* Rediscovered', *GRBS* 60: 652–90.
Polemis, I. and E. Kaltsogianni (eds.) (2019) *Theodori Metochitae Orationes*. Bibliotheca scriptorum Graecorum et Romanorum Teubneriana. Berlin–Boston.
Pontani, F. (2005) *Sguardi su Ulisse: la tradizione esegetica greca all'Odissea*. Sussidi eruditi 63. Rome.
  (2007) 'The First Byzantine Commentator on the *Iliad*: Isaac Porphyrogenitus and His Scholia', *ByzZ* 99: 551–96.
  (2015) 'Scholarship in the Byzantine Empire (529–1453)', in *Brill's Companion to Ancient Greek Scholarship*, vol. 1: *History; Disciplinary Profiles*, ed. F. Montanari, S. Matthaios and A. Rengakos, 297–455. Leiden–Boston.
Rapp, C. and A. Külzer (eds.) (2019) *The Bible in Byzantium: Appropriation, Adaptation, Interpretation*. Journal of Ancient Judaism Supplements 25.6. Göttingen.

Reinsch, D. R. (2002) '*Historia ancilla litterarum*? Zum literarischen Geschmack in der Komnenenzeit: Das Beispiel der *Synopsis Chronike* des Konstantinos Manasses', in *Pour une 'nouvelle' histoire de la littérature byzantine. Actes du colloque international philologique, Nicosie, 25–28 mai 2000*, ed. P. Odorico and P. A. Agapitos, 81–94. Dossiers Byzantins 1. Paris.

Rhoby, A. (2010) 'Ioannes Tzetzes als Auftragsdichter', *Graeco-Latina Brunensia* 15: 155–70.

Riehle, A. (2014) 'Funktionen der byzantinischen Epistolographie: Studien zu den Briefen und Briefsammlungen des Nikephoros Chumnos (ca. 1260–1327)', unpublished PhD thesis, Ludwig Maximilian University of Munich.

Robins, R. H. (1993) *The Byzantine Grammarians: Their Place in History*. Berlin.

Roilos, P. (2014) '"Unshapely Bodies and Beautifying Embellishments": The Ancient Epics in Byzantium, Allegorical Hermeneutics, and the Case of Ioannes Diakonos Galenos', *JÖByz* 64: 231–46.

  (2021) 'Satirical Modulations in 12th-Century Greek Literature', in *Satire in the Middle Byzantine Period: The Golden Age of Laughter?*, ed. P. Marciniak and I. Nilsson, 254–78. Explorations in Medieval Culture 12. Leiden–Boston.

Rollo, A. (2019) 'Gli Erotemata di Manuele Moscopulo e i suoi precedenti', *AION(filol)* 41: 235–52.

Ronconi, F. (2012) 'Quelle grammaire à Byzance? La circulation des textes grammaticaux et son reflet dans les manuscrits', in *La produzione scritta tecnica e scientifica nel medioevo: libro e documento tra scuole e professioni*, ed. G. De Gregorio and M. Galante, 63–110. Spoleto.

Scheer, E. (ed.) (1908) *Lycophronis Alexandra*, vol. 2. Berlin.

Schneider, J. (1999) 'La poésie didactique à Byzance: Nicétas d'Héraclée', *Bulletin de l'Association Guillaume Budé* 58: 388–423.

Searby, D. M. (ed. and trans.) (2007) *The Corpus Parisinum: A Critical Edition of the Greek Text with Commentary and English Translation*. Lewiston, NY.

Ševčenko, I. (1962) *Études sur la polémique entre Théodore Métochite et Nicéphore Choumnos*. Brussels.

Silvano, L. (2015) 'Schedografia bizantina in Terra d'Otranto: appunti su testi e contesti didattici', in *Circolazione di testi e scambi culturali in Terra d'Otranto tra tardoantico e Medioevo*, ed. A. Capone, with F. Giannachi and S. J. Voicu, 212–67. Vatican City.

Simelidis, C. (2018) 'Aeschylus in Byzantium', in *Brill's Companion to the Reception of Aeschylus*, ed. R. F. Kennedy, 179–202. Brill's Companions to Classical Reception 11. Leiden–Boston.

Sluiter, I. (1999) 'Commentaries and the Didactic Tradition', in *Commentaries = Kommentare*, ed. G. W. Most, 173–205. Aporemata: Kritische Studien zur Philologiegeschichte 4. Göttingen.

  (2000) 'The Dialectics of Genre: Some Aspects of Secondary Literature and Genre in Antiquity', in *Matrices of Genre: Authors, Canons, and Society*, ed. M. Depew and D. Obbink, 183–203. Cambridge.

(2013) 'The Violent Scholiast: Power Issues in Ancient Commentaries', in *Writing Science: Medical and Mathematical Authorship in Ancient Greece*, ed. M. Asper, 191–213. Berlin.
Smith, O. L. (1975) *Studies in the Scholia on Aeschylus 1: The Recensions of Demetrius Triclinius*. Leiden.
  (1996) 'Medieval and Renaissance Commentaries in Greek on Classical Greek Texts', *C&M* 47: 391–405.
Stallbaum, J. G. (ed.) (1825–6) *Eustathii archiepiscopi Thessalonicensis commentarii ad Homeri Odysseam ad fidem exempli Romani editi*, 2 vols. Leipzig.
Telelis, I. (ed.) (2012) *Georgios Pachymeres, Philosophia, Book 5: Commentary in Aristotle's Meteorologica*. Corpus Philosophorum Medii Aevi – Commentaria in Aristotelem Byzantina 6. Athens.
  (ed.) (2016) *Georgios Pachymeres, Philosophia, Book 3: In Aristotelis De Caelo Commentary*. Corpus Philosophorum Medii Aevi – Commentaria in Aristotelem Byzantina 7. Athens.
Tessier, A. (ed.) (2005) *Demetrio Triclinio, scolii metrici alla tetrade sofoclea*. Alessandria.
Tihon, A. (1987) 'Les tables astronomiques persanes à Constantinople dans la première moitié du XIVe siècle', *Byzantion* 57: 471–87.
  (1990) 'Tables islamiques à Byzance', *Byzantion* 60: 401–25.
Tomadaki, M. and E. M. van Opstall (2019) 'The Tragedians from a Byzantine Perspective: Book Epigrams on Aeschylus, Sophocles and Euripides', *MEG* 19: 193–220.
Tosi, R. (2017) 'Proverbs in Eustathios: Some Examples', in *Reading Eustathios of Thessalonike*, ed. F. Pontani, V. Katsaros and V. Sarris, 229–41. Trends in Classics Supplementary Volume 46. Berlin–Boston.
Touwaide, A. (2020) 'Botany', in *A Companion to Byzantine Science*, ed. S. Lazaris, 302–53. Brill's Companions to the Byzantine World 6. Leiden–Boston.
Trizio, M. (2017) 'Reading and Commenting on Aristotle', in *The Cambridge Intellectual History of Byzantium*, ed. A. Kaldellis and N. Siniossoglou, 397–411. Cambridge.
  (2021) 'Eustratius of Nicaea and the *Nicomachean Ethics* in Twelfth-Century Constantinople: Literary Criticism, Patronage and the Construction of the Byzantine Commentary Tradition', in *The Reception of Greek Ethics in Late Antiquity and Byzantium*, ed. S. Xenophontos and A. Marmodoro, 193–211. Cambridge–New York.
Tsolakis, E. T. (ed.) (1981) 'Χριστοφόρου Ζωναρᾶ, 1. Λόγος παραινετικὸς εἰς τὸν υἱὸν αὐτοῦ Δημήτριον, 2. Ἐπιστολὲς', *Epistemonike Epeterida tes Philosophikes Scholes* 21: 391–400.
Turyn, A. (1957) *The Byzantine Manuscript Tradition of the Tragedies of Euripides*. Urbana, IL.
van der Valk, M. (ed.) (1971–87) *Eustathii archiepiscopi Thessalonicensis commentarii ad Homeri Iliadem pertinentes ad fidem codicis Laurentiani editi*, 4 vols. Leiden.
Vassis, I. (1991) *Die handschriftliche Überlieferung der sogenannten Psellos-Paraphrase der Ilias*. Hamburg.

(1994) 'Graeca sunt, non leguntur: Zu den schedographischen Spielereien des Theodoros Prodromos', *ByzZ* 86/87: 1–19.
Vogel, K. (1967) 'Byzantine Science', in *Cambridge Medieval History*, vol. 4.2, ed. J. M. Hussey, 264–305. Cambridge.
Walz, C. (ed.) (1832–6) *Rhetores Graeci*, 9 vols. Stuttgart.
Warcaba, K. (2017) *Bizantyński epos dla średnio zaawansowanych: Katomyomachia Teodora Prodromosa jako tekst trzeciego stopnia (Byzantine Epic Poetry for Intermediate Students: The Katomyomachia by Theodore Prodromos as an Example of Genette's 'Literature in the Third Degree')*. Katowice.
Webb, R. (1994) 'A Slavish Art? Language and Grammar in Late Byzantine Education and Society', *Dialogos* 1: 81–103.
 (1997) 'Greek Grammatical Glosses and Scholia: The Form and Function of a Late Byzantine Commentary', in *Medieval and Renaissance Scholarship*, ed. N. Mann and B. Munk Olsen, 1–18. Leiden.
 (2001) 'The *Progymnasmata* as Practice', in *Education in Greek and Roman Antiquity*, ed. Y. L. Too, 289–316. Leiden–Boston.
Wendel, C. (1948) 'Tzetzes Johannes', in *Realencyclopädie der classischen Altertumswissenschaft* VII A 2, 1959–2011. Stuttgart.
Wilberding, J., J. Trompeter and A. Rigolio (trans.) (2019) *Michael of Ephesus, On Aristotle's Nicomachean Ethics 10; Themistius, On Virtue*. Ancient commentators on Aristotle. London.
Wilson, N. G. (1996 [1983]) *Scholars of Byzantium*, revised edition. London–Cambridge, MA.
Woods, M. C. (2013) 'What Are the Real Differences between Medieval and Renaissance Commentaries?', in *The Classics in the Medieval and Renaissance Classroom: The Role of Ancient Texts in the Arts Curriculum as Revealed by Surviving Manuscripts and Early Printed Books*, ed. J. F. Ruys, J. O. Ward and M. Heyworth, 329–41. Turnhout.
Xenophontos, S. (2018) 'The Byzantine Plutarch: Self-Identity and Model in Theodore Metochites' Essay 71 of the *Semeioseis gnomikai*', in *The Afterlife of Plutarch*, ed. P. Mack and J. North, 23–39. Bulletin of the Institute of Classical Studies Supplement 137. London.
 (2019) 'Plutarch and Theodore Metochites', in *Brill's Companion to the Reception of Plutarch*, ed. S. Xenophontos and K. Oikonomopoulou, 310–23. Brill's Companions to Classical Reception 20. Leiden–Boston.
 (2020) (trans.) *Theodore Metochites, On Morals or Concerning Education*. Cambridge, MA.
 (2021) 'George Pachymeres' Commentary on Aristotle's *Nicomachean Ethics*: A New Witness to Philosophical Instruction and Moral Didacticism in Late Byzantium', in *The Reception of Greek Ethics in Late Antiquity and Byzantium*, ed. S. Xenophontos and A. Marmodoro, 226–48. Cambridge–New York.
Xenophontos, S. and K. Oikonomopoulou (eds.) (2019) *Brill's Companion to the Reception of Plutarch*. Brill's Companions to Classical Reception 20. Leiden–Boston.

CHAPTER I

The Politics and Practices of Commentary in Komnenian Byzantium

Panagiotis A. Agapitos

When scholars talk about commentaries of ancient texts in Byzantium, they are usually referring to a variety of works that explain texts from pagan antiquity, where 'pagan' implies that they traditionally belong to Classical Studies.[1] Indeed, in at least one instance in antiquity, the plural οἱ ἀρχαῖοι ('the ancients') does indicate the old Athenian prose writers.[2] However, if the adjective ἀρχαῖος is understood as 'very old' or 'chronologically very far removed', rather than 'antique/ancient' in an archaeological sense, a substantial amount of commentary written in the Komnenian era could be included, because excluding such material would leave the large painting of twelfth-century literature with substantial patches of grey scattered among some brightly coloured sections.[3] Thus, in this chapter I shall briefly attempt to fill in these grey patches and draw a fuller picture in which some of the works discussed in other chapters of the present volume will find their place. Obviously, I will not be able to refer to all texts that might fit under the notional category of commentary but, by making a few indicative choices, it will be possible to present more broadly the politics and practices of commentary in Komnenian Byzantium.[4]

I shall begin my discussion with school education, because it is in this context where commentary is most often to be found. Numerous manuscripts

---

[1] See, for example, Dickey (2007); for a more nuanced approach, see, however, Dickey (2017), Bourbouhakis (2017).
[2] Demetrius, *On Style* 67.4 ed. Chiron.
[3] For a recent example of the exclusionary approach, see Pontani (2015: 366–94) in his presentation of classical scholarship in the Komnenian era; though rich in good remarks and useful as a guide, the overview restricts itself to the study of pagan authors, giving a rather imbalanced picture of Komnenian commentary production as a whole and, therefore, of twelfth-century culture in its historical context.
[4] For reasons of brevity no references will be made to general bibliography on Komnenian history or the lives and works of individual authors. For the historical framework one might profitably read Magdalino (1993), Angold (1996), Magdalino (2008). The handbooks of Hunger (1978), Beck (1959) and (1971) are still useful reference works for literature, along with the relevant entries in the *Oxford Dictionary of Byzantium*.

of the late eleventh to the thirteenth centuries preserve scholia on Hellenic authors, mostly poets, but also prose writers. Among the poets, the respective triads of the three tragedians and of Aristophanes loom large. This immense and complex material, though exhaustively studied by classical scholarship, has not been examined more carefully from the point of view of what it might tell us about Komnenian literary culture. One example might suffice to show what I mean. Codex B of Aeschylus is a manuscript consisting of Florence, Biblioteca Medicea Laurenziana, Plut. 31.3 and one part of Florence, Biblioteca Medicea Laurenziana, Plut. 86.3 (fols. 210r–231v), written by Manuel Spheneas in 1287.[5] Into this manuscript, the scribe inserts, among the older scholia, a scholion on verses 155–6 of the *Persians*. It is the point where the chorus, having seen the old Queen enter the stage, address her in catalectic trochaic tetrameters, while the scholion reads as follows:[6]

ὦ βαθυζώνων ἄνασσα Περσίδων ὑπερτάτη,
μῆτερ ἡ Ξέρξου γεραιά, χαῖρε, Δαρείου γύναι.

ση(μείωσαι) ὡς λέγουσί τινες ὡς ἐκ τούτων τῶν πολιτικῶν στίχων ἐπεκράτησεν ἡ συνήθεια τοῦ διὰ πολιτικῶν στίχων ποιεῖν τὰ βασιλέων προσφωνήματα.

Oh, highest queen of the deep-girded Persian women,
you old mother of Xerxes, hail, wife of Darius.

Note: As some people say, it is because of these city verses that the custom has prevailed to compose the addresses to emperors in city verse.

This reading results from the coincidence that, once the two Aeschylean verses are declaimed with medieval pronunciation, they sound like accentuating fifteen-syllable *politikoi stichoi* ('city verses').[7] The remarkable point here is that the scholion (probably from the twelfth century) comments on a practice readily found at the Komnenian court such as the *prosphonemata* ('laudatory addresses') of Theodore Prodromos written for the circus factions of the city show.[8] It should be noted that this scholion is the only mention we have of this practice beyond the surviving texts themselves. Thus, this snippet of commentary opens up for us a window onto what I would call Komnenian literary modernity, a phenomenon

---

[5] See Turyn (1972, vol. 1: 55–7) on the codicological history of the manuscript's two parts.
[6] Edited and commented on by Jeffreys and Smith (1991).
[7] The term *politikos stichos* is conventionally rendered as 'political verse' in English, but this is misleading since the term has nothing to do with politics but with the *polis*, i.e. Constantinople. I therefore prefer 'city verse' as a more appropriate translation.
[8] For some of these performative poems of Prodromos, see Hörandner (1974: 201–9, 214–17, 253–9, 261–2), nos. IV, V, XI, XII.

strongly related to linguistic and generic experimentation.⁹ 'Modernity' and 'experimentation' have been semantically loaded terms since the Enlightenment and have exercised a particular force in defining cultural production in the visual arts, music and literature from the late nineteenth century to the 1950s. For the purposes of this chapter I shall use, on the one hand, 'modernity' to describe a specific stance of authors towards their own education and the notion of authority inculcated in school. This stance presupposes an implicit or even explicit distancing from authoritative *mimesis* and the accentuation of a writer's own creativity.¹⁰ On the other hand, 'experimentation' will be used to characterize various authorial practices employing all kinds of tools in crafting works that appear 'novel', that is, as textual products defying categorization according to accepted school norms.¹¹ It should be made clear that Byzantine 'novelty' (καινότης) is not to be identified with Romantic 'originality', a concept unknown to most pre-modern cultures.¹²

But let us return to the twelfth-century interest in the use of city verse, which is reflected in another commentary. The manuscript Milan, Biblioteca Ambrosiana, gr. F 101 supra (thirteenth century) transmits the text of the *Iliad* with a facing prose paraphrase and a commentary after each book. On fols. 11v–13v there survives a fragment of a unique metrical paraphrase of *Iliad* 3.71–186 (the opening of the famous *teichoskopia* scene between Helen and the elders of Troy), composed in city verses.¹³ What immediately catches our ear is the pronounced similarity of this paraphrase to the versification style of John Tzetzes, such as his use of new compound words and the rhetoricity developed around the verse's bipartite rhythmical structure.¹⁴ The use of *politikos stichos* in Komnenian

---

⁹ For some observations, see Nilsson (2014) on the novels, Pizzone (2017b: 340–9) on Eustathios and Agapitos (2003: 12–15) on generic experimentation in funerary discourse.
¹⁰ For representative examples of this use of experimentation, see Agapitos (1998b) and (2000), Papaioannou (2013) and (2017), Nilsson (2021: 1–13).
¹¹ On this point, see, indicatively, Agapitos (2003), (2015b), (2015c), Roilos (2005), Pizzone (2017b).
¹² For a discussion of 'originality' in Byzantium, see Littlewood (1995), which includes a broad spectrum of methodologically and conceptually very different contributions. See also Agapitos (2002: 190–214) for a comparison of Byzantine to Japanese literature concerning the very notions of novelty, imitation and aesthetic experience.
¹³ Edited by Vassis (1991b).
¹⁴ See, for example, the novel compound words 3.121 λευκάγκαλος ('having a white embrace'), 3.127 Τρωοϊππότης ('Trojan knight') or 3.152 γλυκοφωνολαλέω ('addressing someone with a sweet voice'). As examples of novel versification, see 3.125 ἐν οἴκῳ ταύτην εὔρηκε· μέγαν δ' ἱστὸν ἱστούργει or 3.155 ἡσύχως προσηγόρευον, ἀλλήλους προσελάλουν. For a comparable passage from Tzetzes, see the long epilogue to his own compact version of the *Theogony* (along with a genealogy of the heroes in the Trojan War) composed in city verses; for a preliminary edition and translation, see Agapitos (2017a: 36–48).

schools is known theoretically, but it remains under-studied, while the sociocultural reasons for its use are still a debated issue.[15]

An important figure, who made use of city verse combined with 'everyday language', is Theodore Prodromos.[16] In two of his surviving *schede* (σχέδη) – exercises for practising grammar and spelling – he uses a mixture of a learned and a vernacular idiom, which could have been seen as idiosyncratic, were it not for the survival of a dictionary composed in the second half of the twelfth century by an anonymous teacher, preserved in the manuscript Paris, Bibliothèque nationale de France, gr. 400 (AD 1343/4).[17] The dictionary was specifically written to support the teaching of schedography;[18] it is composed in *politikos stichos* and includes a high number of lemmata with explanations in the vernacular, or vernacular lemmata explained in the learned idiom. A number of these lemmata coincide with the everyday language Prodromos used in his *schede* and also in his vernacular poems, known as the *Ptochoprodromika*.[19] Thus, the exegesis of schedography became a commentary on the use of ancient authors and the vernacular idiom within Komnenian modernism, given that, before the twelfth century, everyday language did not appear in the school curriculum nor was it used for purposes of literary experimentation. In my opinion, it is from within this innovative school context that Prodromos composed his vernacular poems. Particularly intriguing are two diptych compositions addressed to emperors John II (ca. 1139) and Manuel I (ca. 1150–5), namely, *Carm. Hist.* XXIV + *Ptochopr.* I[20] and *Carm. Hist.* LXXI + *Carm. Maiuri.*[21] Here the poet uses the learned idiom in the first poem of the diptych and then a vernacular idiom in the second poem, while he manifestly raises the level of humorous discourse in the diptych's second part. Prodromos, of course, wrote various commentaries among many other treatises offered to some of his patrons, such as the *sebastokratorissa* Irene. He also systematically created an image of himself as the poet/teacher who is in need of constant financial support.[22] The image of the 'begging' scholar is a recurrent theme in Komnenian culture, found behind various and

---

[15] For a different, somewhat restrictive, approach from the one presented here, see Jeffreys (2009).
[16] Agapitos (2015b) with the relevant bibliography. [17] On this dictionary, see Agapitos (2015a).
[18] On schedography as a very particular type of grammatical drill of Byzantine invention, see Agapitos (2014), Nousia (2016: 49–92).
[19] Critical edition with German translation by Eideneier (1991).
[20] Hörandner (1974: 330–3), Eideneier (1991: 99–107).
[21] Hörandner (1974: 516–19), Maiuri (1914–19: 398–400).
[22] See Zagklas (2014: 66–72), Agapitos (2015b: 2–3).

sometimes quite diverging strategies of social networking. One aspect of these sociocultural politics is the polemics of school commentary and the competitiveness prevalent among teachers of different social ranks that it expresses.[23]

One of the most prolific battlegrounds of commentary was the Homeric *Iliad*, a major school text since antiquity. As mentioned above, from the eleventh century, the *Iliad* was accompanied by prose paraphrases.[24] Parallel to the surviving ancient scholia, as found, for example, in the margins of the famous tenth-century Venice, Biblioteca Nazionale Marciana, gr. 454 (codex A of the *Iliad*), many manuscripts with scholia survive from the eleventh century onwards, like the Oxford, Bodleian Library, Auctarium T.2.7 or the Florence, Biblioteca Medicea Laurenziana, Conventi Soppressi 139. However, a change takes place in the twelfth century, as a number of new texts show. One such text is the gigantic commentary of the *Iliad* John Tzetzes undertook to write in around 1135–8, though he never went beyond the first book.[25] This early work of Tzetzes, in conjunction with his hexametrical *Carmina Iliaca* (a kind of school synopsis of the whole story of the Trojan War),[26] shows him aspiring to carve out a major niche in the capital's competitive school environment. Already, the *Iliad* commentary displays two characteristic literary and philological devices of Tzetzes: (a) the polemical prologue, where critique, sometimes quite acerbic, is exercised against his real or imagined opponents, and (b) mostly autobiographic scholia that accompany the main body of the commentary. Thus, the previously anonymous scholia are presented now as a fully developed exegetical work, where the author figures largely in and around the text as editor and commentator of himself.[27] That academic teachers will launch polemics against each other is, too, well known from reading scholarly historiography. However, the carrying out of such verbal combat in the twelfth century was part of a very specific sociopolitical framework that allowed teachers to rise socially and potentially acquire important political status. For example, take the critique of Tzetzes in the preface to the *Iliad* commentary and in a separate

---

[23] Beyond the pioneering study of Garzya (1973), see Agapitos (2017a: 5–7) with full bibliography. On the competitive environment of twelfth-century Constantinople and rivalries concerning the interpretation of school texts, see also the contributions by Pizzone, Tomadaki and Lovato in this volume.

[24] See Vassis (1991a: 16–28). [25] Critical edition by Papathomopoulos (2007).

[26] Critical edition by Leone (1995).

[27] See Pizzone (2020). On Tzetzes' self-representation as exegete and grammarian, see also van den Berg (2020).

marginal scholion against a student of his, who was writing down what Tzetzes presented in class and was thinking of selling the notes as his scholia, thus forcing Tzetzes to publish his own commentary.[28] This anxious polemical stance of the 'middle-class' teacher can be compared to the detached approach of another prologue, the *Preface to Homer*, composed by no less a high-standing aristocrat and learned man than the *sebastokrator* Isaac Komnenos, third son of emperor Alexios I (1081–1118) and brother of John II (1118–43), where no critique is exercised against any predecessor.[29] Around 1160, another high-standing teacher, Eustathios of Thessalonike, began working on a commentary of the *Iliad*. Eustathios also, even if discreetly, criticized his predecessors and Tzetzes in particular, as is shown clearly in a telling passage from the preface to the *Parekbolai on the Iliad* about the structure of his commentary in comparison to that of Tzetzes.[30] It is, therefore, important to keep in mind that commentaries need to be read within their sociocultural and sometimes even political contexts, as Tzetzes' scholia on Aristophanes and Lycophron amply demonstrate.[31] Not all commentators reached the level of authorial experimentation of Tzetzes, who created the ultimate commentary to his own letter collection – the vast *Histories* in city verse, which he accompanied again with prose auto-exegetic scholia.[32]

One particular type of commentary that I would like to touch upon here is biblical exegesis.[33] By the late eleventh century, a number of grand-scale commentaries of the Psalms and of the New Testament were produced – mostly in the form of *catenae*, collected from material of the early Byzantine period. Two of the most prominent and widely used authors were Theophylact of Ohrid and Niketas of Herakleia. These *catenae* commentaries rarely offer actual interpretations by their compilers. However, around the middle of the twelfth century a new genre emerged, which combined rhetorical homiletics, interpretive exegesis and commentary. The authors of these texts – for example, Leon Balianites, John

---

[28] Tzetzes, *Preface to the Exegesis on the Iliad* 8.1–13 and scholion ad 8.3; Papathomopoulos (2007: 8 and 423).
[29] The text has been edited by Kindstrand (1979); on this neglected Komnenian prince, see Linardou (2016).
[30] Eustathios, *Commentary on the Iliad* 2.42–6 = 1.3.28–33 ed. van der Valk; more broadly for Eustathios' critique of Tzetzes, see Holwerda (1960b), Cullhed (2014: 21*–4*).
[31] For Aristophanes, see Massa Positano (1960), Holwerda (1960a), Koster (1962), Pizzone in this volume; for Lycophron, see Scheer (1958). For a sociocultural reading of these commentaries, see Agapitos (2017a: 27–35); for a political reading, see Agapitos (forthcoming).
[32] The text edited by Leone (2007); on the *Histories*, see Pizzone (2017a).
[33] On the *Christos Paschon* as a commentary on the gospel narrative, see Mullett in this volume.

Kastamonites and Constantine Stilbes – use the term *didaskalia* ('teaching') to characterize their works.[34] We find them transmitted side by side with other oratorical texts in collections like the Madrid, Real Biblioteca de San Lorenzo de El Escorial, Y-II-10 (late twelfth–early thirteenth century) or the Oxford, Bodleian Library, Baroccianus 131 (ca. 1250–70). The *didaskalia* can either be an exegetical analysis of a specific Psalm verse based on the commentary of Niketas of Herakleia, or it can pick up a broader theme of a Psalm or passage from the New Testament using the *catenae* of Theophylact, but reshaping the material in a completely different and quite innovative way.[35] Most interestingly, a number of these *didaskaliai* were delivered at the occasion when the speaker had just been given a particular teaching post (e.g. *didaskalos* of the Gospels), delivering his oration in front of the patriarch and a select audience of colleagues and advanced pupils.[36] Thus, we can see how the commentary of a text becomes, within a specific school context, the starting point for literary experimentation.

Let me very briefly present two examples of this Komnenian literary modernity, which are very different in their subject but quite similar in their approach to integrating commentary into an overflowing narrative. The first example is Eustathios' second oration in praise of patriarch Michael III *ho tou Anchialou* (1170–8), delivered on the Saturday of Lazarus, probably in March 1173.[37] Eustathios organizes his praise of the patriarch around various themes, such as education and teaching, philosophy and theology, rhetoric and schedography, harmony between emperor and patriarch. All of this is placed within a commentary-like narrative, taking as its point of departure the description of the high priest's garments as prescribed by God to Moses on Mount Sinai (Exodus 28). In a highly individualist anagogical exegesis of this crucial Exodus passage, Eustathios creates a symbolical image of the patriarch that has been created out of the material of biblical commentary with the support of rhetoric and its complex devices. The labyrinthine narrative, structured by massive digressions, interlacing imagery and the continuous

---

[34] Many of these texts are still unedited; for basic information, see Katsaros (1988: 213–42) on Kastamonites and Loukaki (2000) on Balianites. A critical edition of Balianites' *didaskaliai* is under preparation by Giannouli (2011).

[35] I owe this information to my colleague Antonia Giannouli, who gave a talk on this very subject in Nicosia in June 2013; I am grateful to her for giving me a copy of her unpublished talk and allowing me to present her findings.

[36] See Loukaki (2005).

[37] On the date of delivery, see Loukaki (2007). The text is now edited by Wirth (2000: 100–40); for some aspects of interpretation, see Pizzone (2017b).

presence of the 'Roman' emperor as counterpart to the 'biblical' patriarch, makes the text of this oration one of the most complex of Eustathios' set pieces which he, as *maistor ton rhetoron* ('senior teacher of rhetoricians'), composed in Constantinople before his appointment to the see of Thessalonike in ca. 1175.[38]

The second example comes from Prodromos' novel *Rhodanthe and Dosikles* (hereafter: *R&D*), written around 1135, some forty years before Eustathios' oration.[39] Prodromos dedicated his novel to caesar Nikephoros Bryennios (d. 1138), husband of princess Anna Komnene.[40] Among many works of a didactic character, Prodromos compiled a commentary on Book 2 of Aristotle's *Posterior Analytics*.[41] In Book 3 of *R&D*, Prodromos depicts a drunken young sailor who falls asleep and, while dreaming, performs gestures that imply he is drinking in his dream. Dosikles, the hero of the novel and narrator in this scene, explains what the cause and effect of dreams are, presenting a succinct Aristotelian analysis.[42] In the same book, Dosikles, in an absolutely critical situation, mistakenly believes that his beloved Rodanthe was dreaming, and goes on to expound how dreams are deceiving creations of the mind, again within an Aristotelian framework.[43] Here, the commentary has taken over the novelistic dialogue, creating a narrative exegesis with a subversive and humorous tone. There is, of course, a difference between Prodromos and Eustathios. The former uses his Aristotelian commentary in this fictional work in a playful mode, while the latter employs the biblical commentary in a serious and clearly political discourse.[44] In my opinion, this element of seriousness marks a change within Komnenian literary modernism, a point to which I shall return.

The two dreams in Prodromos' novel and their Aristotelian background bring us to the teaching of philosophy and the philosophical commentary in the twelfth century.[45] Besides Prodromos' commentary, there survives a

---

[38] On Eustathios' narrative techniques in another of his speeches, see Agapitos (1998b).
[39] Critical edition by Marcovich (1992) but with numerous problems, on which see Agapitos (1993); Italian translation by Conca (1994: 63–303), English translation by Jeffreys (2012: 19–156).
[40] See Agapitos (2000).   [41] Edited by Cacouros (1992).
[42] *R&D* 3.1–42; Marcovich (1992: 36–8), Jeffreys (2012: 51–2). On the use of Aristotle by Prodromos in *R&D*, see MacAlister (1990: 208–12). On the connection between the novels and the interpretation of Aristotle, see also Trizio in this volume.
[43] *R&D* 3.294–318; Marcovich (1992: 47), Jeffreys (2012: 59). On dreams and fictionality in *R&D*, see Agapitos (2012: 279–81).
[44] Prodromos did use Aristotelian material seriously, for example, in the laudatory oration he addressed to Patriarch John IX Agapetos (1111–34), but there the Aristotelian references serve to support the project of the patriarch to have manuscripts copied for the benefit of teachers and pupils; see Manaphes (1974: 239–40).
[45] See the survey by Trizio (2017) and his chapter in the present volume.

commentary on *Posterior Analytics* 2 by Eustratios of Nicaea and a series of commentaries on a substantial part of the Aristotelian corpus by Michael of Ephesus. It has been suggested that the latter scholar, together with a few others, belonged to a circle around Anna Komnene, as George Tornikes seems to suggest in his funeral oration for the purple-born princess.[46] Michele Trizio has cautioned us that 'circle' might be too strong a term to use considering the available evidence.[47] But that some kind of interaction in Aristotelian matters existed between these scholars and Anna Komnene cannot be doubted. In fact, it is Prodromos in his novel who furnishes us with an indirect reference to the study of philosophy and the production of commentaries around Anna. At the very end of *Rhodanthe and Dosikles*, the father of the hero's friend praises, in a funny way, his old nurse, who was solving philosophical problems following the precepts of natural philosophy, but suffered a loss of her eyesight because, according to the speaker, she was reading too many treatises on philosophy of nature.[48] This grotesque story (probably declaimed at the literary salon of Irene Doukaina or of her daughter Anna in the presence of the latter's husband), finds its serious counterpart in what Tornikes had to say about Michael of Ephesus, who complained that he had lost his eyesight because of labouring ceaselessly on his Aristotelian commentaries upon Anna's command.[49] But what these two stories tell us is that commentary, philosophy and literature went hand in hand in the Komnenian era, even if the potential dangers for such pursuits were not negligible, as the trial of Eustratios of Nicaea in 1116/17 demonstrates. It is exactly this interest in innovative philosophical thinking that, following the trial of John Italos early in the reign of Alexios, became a centrepiece of critique raised by learned men trained in philosophy but ultimately serving theology. One such example, where the philosophical commentary becomes the target of theological critique, is the treatise by Nicholas of Methone against Proklos' *Elements of Theology*,[50] written around 1160. Nicholas is probably responding to the growing interest in Proklos that had started a hundred years earlier with Psellos and culminated in the four treatises of the *sebastokrator* Isaac

---

[46] George Tornikes, *Funeral Oration for Anna Komnene* 283.4–9 ed. Darrouzès.
[47] See the exhaustive discussion in Trizio (2016: 22–72).
[48] *R&D* 9.423–30; Marcovich (1992: 161), Jeffreys (2012: 154).
[49] George Tornikes, *Funeral Oration for Anna Komnene* 283.9–12 ed. Darrouzès; on this scene, see Agapitos (2006: 145–7).
[50] Critical edition by Angelou (1984).

Komnenos,[51] this being, in my opinion, yet another expression of modernism in the first half of the twelfth century. In fact, we find an open attack against this kind of philosophy. It was formulated by the newly appointed 'consul of philosophers' (*hypatos ton philosophon*) who, in his inaugural lecture of 1167 addressed to emperor Manuel, clearly expressed the official stance against experimentation in the field of philosophy. This is another aspect of the change in Komnenian modernism to which I referred above. We should note that the said professor of philosophy was no other than the later patriarch Michael III and patron of Eustathios.[52]

It would be plausible to suggest that, during the *longue durée* of the Komnenian era, intellectual experimentation reaches a climax in the 1150s. From the 1160s onwards, textual production focuses much more strongly on theological and legal writing (note, for example, the grand commentaries on the church canons by Alexios Aristenos, John Zonaras and Theodore Balsamon),[53] while the number of writers who are clerics rises noticeably. The Komnenian political elite – by which I understand both state and church officials – was, from the time of Alexios onwards, manifestly concerned with controlling in various ways the innovations that seemed to pose a threat to political, social and intellectual stability.[54] A type of text that resurfaced in this context is the collection of material that aimed to defend orthodoxy from heresy by attacking the latter through the authority of patristic texts and the decisions of the ecumenical councils. The first of these collections is Euthymios Zigabenos' *Armour of Dogma* (Δογματική Πανοπλία), offered to emperor Alexios in ca. 1110.[55] In the original presentation copy, which has been preserved (Vatican City, Biblioteca Apostolica Vaticana, gr. 666), we can see how the text and its various paratextual material is visually laid out on the pages, accompanied by some splendid illustrations, in order to present the emperor as a

---

[51] Three treatises on providence, edited by Isaac (1978: 153–223) and (1979: 99–169), and a treatise on the substance of evil, edited by Rizzo (1971).

[52] Michael's oration was edited and discussed by Browning (1977); recently Polemis (2011) has proposed a date for the delivery of the speech shortly after 1151.

[53] See Troianos (2017: 289–96) with references to editions and further bibliography.

[54] See Agapitos (1998a) for the debate concerning the Feast of the Three Hierarchs and the trial of John Italos. One further case of some importance is the trial of Leo of Chalcedon concerning the worship of God through icons; as Lamberz (2003) has proven, the codex London, British Library, Harley 5665, which is the oldest textual witness to the Acts of the Seventh Ecumenical Council, was copied in 1093/4 to provide the material for the synod of 1094/5, where Leo was finally acquitted.

[55] Edited in Migne (1865).

champion of orthodoxy.⁵⁶ The *Armour of Dogma* is a vast antiheretical collection culled from older florilegia and various patristic texts, organized around general subjects and followed by refutations of various heresies.

As time passed by and new issues of dissent arose, partly stemming from imperial policy, another such collection was produced between 1172 and 1174 by the *sebastos* and city prefect Andronikos Kamateros, a learned man and sometime patron of John Tzetzes. The *Sacred Armoury* ('Ιερὰ Ὁπλοθήκη), dedicated to emperor Manuel, focuses specifically on the theological debates between Constantinople and the Latins and the Armenians respectively.⁵⁷ In contrast to Zigabenos' collection, Kamateros' *Sacred Armoury* displays a very sophisticated and highly rhetorical structure. The main text is framed by a series of paratextual material: a laudatory poem (ἐπίγραμμα τῆς βίβλου) by George Skylitzes – protégé of Kamateros; a summary description (κεφαλαιώδης προτίτλωσις) of the book's contents by the author; general preface (προοίμιον) and a final epilogue (ἐπίλογος) addressed to the emperor. Furthermore, in its first part, the text purports to offer the minutes of a theological debate (διάλεξις) between the emperor and the papal legates on the procession of the Holy Spirit, accompanied by a florilegium of patristic texts on the same topic. The author guides the readers through the excerpted passages by means of a commentary addressed to them and titled 'examination' (ἐπιστασία). Moreover, the florilegium is separately framed by an address (προδιαλαλία) of the author to those who support the Latin position and, at its end, by a second address (προσφώνημα) to the emperor, followed by a set of arguments (συλλογισμοί) on the procession of the Holy Spirit excerpted from the oration on this subject written some sixty years earlier by no other than Eustratios of Nicaea. Kamateros' *Sacred Armoury*, whose structure is, in my opinion, inspired by the *Histories* of Tzetzes,⁵⁸ represents a telling example of late Komnenian modernism in its intellectually restrictive but artistically expansive version, thus making manifest the political role played by commentary in the twelfth century. How a changed political and sociocultural context could influence this perspective can be seen in Niketas Choniates' *Dogmatic*

---

⁵⁶ The manuscript is readily available at https://digi.vatlib.it/view/MSS_Vat.gr.666 (accessed 31 August 2018).
⁵⁷ Bucossi (2014) has presented a critical edition of the work's first part, i.e. the debates with Latins.
⁵⁸ For example, the substantial paratextual material framing the bulk of a compartmentalized text, the 'main' text broken up into different and quasi-independent units of unequal length, the didactic character of the information provided, strong presence of an authorial voice and generic hybridity and mixture.

Armour (Πανοπλία Δογματική),[59] a substantial heresiological florilegium explicitly referring back to Zigabenos' collection.[60] The ex-politician and historian composed his work at the bitter time of his Nicaean exile (1206–17), as he clearly states in his preface.[61] The addressee of the *Dogmatic Armour* is an unnamed friend, while the compilation lacks any commentary by the author or any paratextual material placing its 'message' in a political or ecclesiastical context.

The heresiological florilegium, used in part as a political weapon, leads us to another group of florilegia-like texts which belong to the broad category of admonitory literature. Such texts collect gnomic statements from various sources and put them into use within a narrative frame that treats various topics under an overarching theme. One such text is the *Dialexis* ('dialogue') by Philip Monotropos, composed in 1097. Written with a monastic audience in mind, the *Dialexis* (often referred to as *Dioptra*, 'mirror') presents a dialogue between the body and the soul in four books, composed in city verse.[62] It is a huge textual mosaic with clearly marked prose extracts from other sources and often collages of excerpts, accompanied by a rudimentary exegesis. This specific type of admonitory commentary finds a clearly political expression in three works, concentrated in different ways around the person of emperor Alexios. The first of these works is the poem *Alexiad-Komneniad Muses* (Μοῦσαι Ἀλεξιάδες Κομνηνιάδες), supposedly addressed by Alexios on his deathbed to his son John (15 August 1118);[63] the second is the *Spaneas*, an admonitory poem in 'vernacular' city verses, spoken by an aristocratic father to his son and written in the first half of the twelfth century;[64] the third is the prose *Life of Cyril Phileotes* by Nicholas Kataskepenos (ca. 1140–50).[65] All three texts display the type of florilegium-like gnomologic structure that we find in Monotropos' *Dialexis*. In the *Muses*, an emperor-father advises his emperor-to-be son; in the *Spaneas*, an aristocratic father advises his son by using an eleventh-century florilegium of political conduct (the so-called *Excerpta Parisina*); and in two quite

---

[59] For a study of the work's manuscript transmission, along with an edition of the prefatory material, see van Dieten (1970).
[60] Van Dieten (1970: 58.25).   [61] Van Dieten (1970: 57.16–19).
[62] Partial edition by Lavriotes (1920); for an analysis of the work, see Afentoulidou (2007).
[63] Edited by Maas (1913); for an analysis of the poem, see Mullett (2012).
[64] For an edition of the oldest version (Vatican City, Biblioteca Apostolica Vaticana, Palatinus gr. 367), see Lambros (1917–20); for the identification of the poem's direct gnomologic sources, see Danezis (1987: 27–90).
[65] Critical edition and French translation by Sargologos (1964); for an analysis of the work, see Mullett (2004).

impressive scenes of the *Life of Cyril*, the saint advises emperor Alexios, who visits the former in his hermitage in 1095 and 1105, about how to conduct himself and what to do against the incursions of the Seljuq Turks.[66] Thus, the ancient – Hellenic and Christian – gnomologic material is used as a narrative commentary of admonition with clear political aims and literary ambitions, though coming from different directions: an imperial background (support for and legitimation of John's rule against the claims of his sister Anna), a distinct aristocratic background trying to safeguard its own space of power within Komnenian rule and, finally, the powerful monastic circles also attempting to safeguard their substantial intellectual and economic wealth against imperial encroachment.

By way of conclusion, I would like to return to the school context where I began and offer a few remarks about another type of commentary that appears with full force in the Komnenian era and maintains its momentum well into the fourteenth century. This is the commentary to a larger or smaller group of canons, a hymnographic genre of the eighth century that became a major form of poetic and musical composition in liturgy in the second half of the ninth century. Gregory Pardos, a prominent school teacher who wrote treatises on Greek syntax and dialects and later became metropolitan of Corinth, composed in the 1130s a basic linguistic commentary on twenty-three canons by or attributed to John of Damascus and Kosmas of Jerusalem. Sometime thereafter, Theodore Prodromos also wrote a commentary on the same twenty-three canons, but with theological and literary comments, criticizing his predecessor for his basic and restricted approach. At the same time, John Zonaras (the well-known historian and canonist) wrote a commentary on the Resurrection Canons of John of Damascus.[67] Finally, Eustathios wrote his vast and immensely learned commentary (ἐξήγησις) on the Iambic Pentecostal Canon, attributed to John of Damascus but ascribed by Eustathios to an otherwise unknown John Arklas.[68] Eustathios composed his commentary in Thessalonike between ca. 1187 and 1195, at the end of his long life. In his last work, the learned former professor of rhetoric and commentator of the Homeric poems (*Parekbolai*) combined textual criticism, philological analysis, literary interpretation and allegorical exegesis. Just as with Tzetzes and his *Iliad* commentary, Eustathios discreetly criticizes Gregory Pardos

---

[66] *Life of Cyril Phileotes* 47 and 51; Sargologos (1964: 225–35 and 243–4); on the three works within the broader context of Komnenian literary production, see Agapitos (2017b: 99–101).
[67] On these three commentators, see Giannouli (2007: 17–19).
[68] For a critical edition and a substantial introduction, see Cesaretti and Ronchey (2014). On Eustathios as scholar and writer, see the essays in Pontani, Katsaros and Sarris (2017).

on a few points.[69] However, in contrast to the *Parekbolai*, Eustathios allows himself a greater freedom of interpretation of the actual text in the *Exegesis*, offering us, if I am not mistaken, the first fully focused literary commentary of a Byzantine text by a Byzantine scholar. In a very special way, Eustathios' *Exegesis* of the Iambic Pentecostal Canon represents the synthesis of ancient and medieval Greek philology in Byzantium. What is quite noteworthy, moreover, is that, towards the end of the thirteenth century, a wealthy person in Constantinople, possibly connected to a school situated within a monastery, had a parchment book of 274 folia copied out, with two scribes working together.[70] The codex Alexandria, Patriarchal Library 62 is one of the two main witnesses for the text of Eustathios' *Exegesis*. It is worthwhile to take a look at the contents of this finely executed volume. The book includes the canon commentaries of Zonaras, Pardos and Prodromos. Furthermore, it includes towards its end a series of homiletic and rhetorical set pieces and, surprisingly to us, substantial parts of Tzetzes' *Allegories of the Iliad*, various minor lexical and grammatical works and the largest fragment of Tzetzes' lost chronographical work. Thus, the complete commentary tradition of the twelfth century is reflected in this manuscript, showing us how a teacher in early Palaiologan Constantinople viewed all of this material as one entity and not separated in different thematic (pagan vs. Christian) or generic categories (commentary vs. homily or oration, narrative explanation vs. paraphrasis). Furthermore, the manuscript preserves texts that cover the whole spectrum of Komnenian literary modernity and experimentation from its intellectually innovative phase to its politically restrictive development.

If we are, therefore, to understand the processes of commenting on 'ancient' texts in Komnenian Byzantium as the politics and practices of commentary in its broadest sense (a sense that is imperative for a new history of Byzantine literature), we must look at this thorny yet stimulating subject of research through a Byzantine point of view. It is only then that we shall be able to grasp sociocultural, ideological and aesthetic functions of Byzantine textual production as a dynamic phenomenon belonging to a wider medieval world and not just as an important appendix to Classical Studies.

---

[69] Cesaretti and Ronchey (2014: 172*–84*).
[70] For a full codicological description and reconstruction of the manuscript's history, see Cesaretti and Ronchey (2014: 201*–9*); for the presence of Eustathios' *Exegesis* at the Monastery of St John the Forerunner at Petra in Constantinople, see Ronchey (2017).

REFERENCES

Afentoulidou, E. (2007) 'Die Dioptra des Philippos Monotropos und ihr Kontext: Ein Beitrag zur Rezeptionsgeschichte', *Byzantion* 77: 9–31.

Agapitos, P. A. (1993) Review of Marcovich (1992), *Hellenika* 43: 229–36.

(1998a) 'Teachers, Pupils and Imperial Power in Eleventh-Century Byzantium', in *Pedagogy and Power: Rhetorics of Classical Learning*, ed. Y. L. Too and N. Livingstone, 170–91. Ideas in Context 50. Cambridge.

(1998b) 'Mischung der Gattungen und Überschreitung der Gesetze: Die Grabrede des Eustathios von Thessalonike auf Nikolaos Hagiotheodorites', *JÖByz* 48: 119–46.

(2000) 'Poets and Painters: Theodoros Prodromos' Dedicatory Verses of His Novel to an Anonymous Caesar', *JÖByz* 50: 173–85.

(2002) "Ἡ θέση τῆς αἰσθητικῆς ἀποτίμησης σὲ μιὰ "νέα" ἱστορία τῆς βυζαντινῆς λογοτεχνίας', in *Pour une 'nouvelle' histoire de la littérature byzantine: problèmes, méthodes, approches, propositions. Actes du colloque international philologique (Nicosie, mai 2000)*, ed. P. Odorico and P. A. Agapitos, 185–232. Dossiers Byzantins 1. Paris.

(2003) 'Ancient Models and Novel Mixtures: The Concept of Genre in Byzantine Funerary Literature from Patriarch Photios to Eustathios of Thessalonike', in *Modern Greek Literature: Critical Essays*, ed. G. Nagy and A. Stavrakopoulou, 5–23. New York–London.

(2006) 'Writing, Reading and Reciting (in) Byzantine Erotic Fiction', in *Lire et écrire à Byzance*, ed. B. Mondrain, 125–76. Centre de recherche d'Histoire et Civilisation de Byzance: Monographies 19. Paris.

(2012) 'In Rhomaian, Frankish and Persian Lands: Fiction and Fictionality in Byzantium and Beyond', in *Medieval Narratives between History and Fiction: From the Center to the Periphery of Europe (c. 1100–1400)*, ed. P. A. Agapitos and L. B. Mortensen, 235–367. Copenhagen.

(2014) 'Grammar, Genre and Patronage in the Twelfth Century: Redefining a Scientific Paradigm in the History of Byzantine Literature', *JÖByz* 64: 1–22.

(2015a) 'Learning to Read and Write a *Schedos*: The Verse Dictionary of Par. Gr. 400', in *Pour une poétique de Byzance: hommage à Vassilis Katsaros*, ed. S. Efthymiadis, C. Messis, P. Odorico and I. D. Polemis, 11–24. Dossiers Byzantins 16. Paris.

(2015b) 'New Genres in the Twelfth Century: The *Schedourgia* of Theodore Prodromos', *MEG* 15: 1–41.

(2015c) 'Literary *Haute Cuisine* and Its Dangers: Eustathios of Thessalonike on Schedography and Everyday Language', *DOP* 69: 225–41.

(2017a) 'John Tzetzes and the Blemish Examiners: A Byzantine Teacher on Schedography, Everyday Language and Writerly Disposition', *MEG* 17: 1–57.

(2017b) 'Dangerous Literary Liaisons: Byzantium and Neohellenism', *Byzantina* 35: 33–196.

(forthcoming) '"Middle-class" Ideology of Education and Language, and the "Bookish" Identity of John Tzetzes', in *Ideologies and Identities in the Medieval Byzantine World*, ed. I. Stouraitis. Edinburgh.

Angelou, A. D. (ed.) (1984) *Nicholas of Methone, Refutation of Proclus' Elements of Theology: A Critical Edition with an Introduction on Nicholas' Life and Works.* Corpus Philosophorum Medii Aevi: Philosophi Byzantini 1. Athens–Leiden.

Angold, M. (1996) *The Byzantine Empire 1025–1204: A Political History*, second edition. London.

Beck, H.-G. (1959) *Kirche und theologische Literatur im byzantinischen Reich.* Handbuch der Altertumswissenschaft XII.2.1. Munich.

(1971) *Geschichte der byzantinischen Volksliteratur.* Handbuch der Altertumswissenschaft XII.2.3. Munich.

van den Berg, B. (2020) 'John Tzetzes as Didactic Poet and Learned Grammarian', *DOP* 74: 285–302.

Bourbouhakis, E. C. (2017) 'Byzantine Literary Criticism and the Classical Heritage', in Kaldellis and Siniossoglou, 113–28.

Browning, R. (ed.) (1977) 'A New Source on Byzantine-Hungarian Relations in the Twelfth Century: The Inaugural Lecture of Michael ὁ τοῦ Ἀγχιάλου as ὕπατος τῶν φιλοσόφων', in *Studies on Byzantine History, Literature and Education*, 173–214. London (originally published in 1961).

Bucossi, A. (ed.) (2014) *Andronici Camateri Sacrum Armamentarium, Pars Prima.* Corpus Christianorum, Series Graeca 75. Turnhout.

Cacouros, M. (1992) 'Le commentaire de Théodore Prodrome au second livre des analytiques postérieurs d'Aristote: le texte (editio princeps et tradition manuscrite) suivi de l'étude logique du commentaire de Prodrome', PhD thesis, Paris-Sorbonne University.

Cesaretti, P. and S. Ronchey (eds.) (2014) *Eustathii Thessalonicensis exegesis in canonem iambicum pentecostalem.* Supplementa Byzantina 10. Berlin–Boston.

Chiron, P. (ed.) (1993) *Démetrios, Du style.* Paris.

Conca, F. (1994) *Il romanzo bizantino del XII secolo: Teodoro Prodromo, Niceta Eugeniano, Eustazio Macrembolita, Constantino Manasse.* Turin.

Cullhed, E. (ed. and trans.) (2014) 'Eustathios of Thessalonike, *Parekbolai* on Homer's *Odyssey* 1–2: Proekdosis', PhD thesis, Uppsala University.

Danezis, G. (1987) *Spaneas: Vorlage, Quellen, Versionen.* Miscellanea Byzantina Monacensia 31. Munich.

Darrouzès, J. (ed.) (1970) *Georges et Dèmètrios Tornikès, lettres et discours: introduction, texte, analyses, traduction et notes.* Paris.

Dickey, E. (2007) *Ancient Greek Scholarship: A Guide to Finding, Reading, and Understanding Scholia, Commentaries, Lexica, and Grammatical Treatises from Their Beginnings to the Byzantine Period.* Oxford–New York.

(2017) 'Classical Scholarship: The Byzantine Contribution', in Kaldellis and Siniossoglou, 63–78.

van Dieten, J. L. (1970) *Zur Überlieferung und Veröffentlichung der Panoplia Dogmatike des Niketas Choniates.* Zetemeta Byzantina 3. Amsterdam.

Eideneier, H. (1991) *Ptochoprodromos: Einführung, kritische Ausgabe, deutsche Übersetzung, Glossar*. Neograeca Medii Aevi 5. Cologne.
Garzya, A. (1973) 'Literarische und rhetorische Polemiken der Komnenenzeit', *ByzSlav* 34: 1–14.
Giannouli, A. (2007) *Die beiden byzantinischen Kommentare zum Großen Kanon des Andreas von Kreta: Eine quellenkritische und literarhistorische Studie*. Wiener Byzantinistische Studien 26. Vienna.
  (2011) 'Leon Balianites, Exegetische Didaskalien: Zur Interpunktion im Codex Escorialensis Y-II-10', in *From Manuscripts to Books: Proceedings of the International Workshop on Textual Criticism and Editorial Practice for Byzantine Texts (Vienna, 10–11 December 2009)*, ed. A. Giannouli and E. Schiffer, 79–84. Vienna.
Holwerda, D. (ed.) (1960a) *Johannis Tzetzae Commentarii in Aristophanem, fasciculus II continens Commentarium in Nubes*. Groningen.
  (1960b) 'De Tzetza in Eustathii reprehensiones incurrenti', *Mnemosyne* 13: 323–6.
Hörandner, W. (1974) *Theodoros Prodromos, Historische Gedichte*. Wiener Byzantinistische Studien 11. Vienna.
Hunger, H. (1978) *Die hochsprachliche profane Literatur der Byzantiner*, 2 vols. Handbuch der Altertumswissenschaft XII.5.1–2. Munich.
Isaac, D. (1978) *Proclus: Trois études sur la providence*, Tome 1: *Dix questions concernant la providence, 1re étude*. Paris.
  (1979) *Proclus: Trois études*, Tome 2: *Providence – Fatalité – Liberté, 2e étude*. Paris.
Jeffreys, E. M. (2009) 'Why Produce Verse in Twelfth-Century Constantinople?', in *'Doux remède ...': poésie et poétique à Byzance. Actes du IVe colloque international philologique EPMHNEIA, Paris, 23–25 février 2006*, ed. P. Odorico, P. A. Agapitos and M. Hinterberger, 219–28. Dossier Byzantins 9. Paris.
  (2012) *Four Byzantine Novels: Theodore Prodromos, Rhodanthe and Dosikles; Eumathios Makrembolites, Hysmine and Hysminias; Constantine Manasses, Aristandros and Kallithea; Niketas Eugenianos, Drosilla and Charikles*. Translated Texts for Byzantinists 1. Liverpool.
Jeffreys, M. J. and O. L. Smith (1991) 'Political Verse for Queen Atossa', *C&M* 42: 301–4.
Kaldellis, A. and N. Siniossoglou (eds.) (2017) *The Cambridge Intellectual History of Byzantium*. Cambridge.
Katsaros, V. (1988) *Ἰωάννης Κασταμονίτης: Συμβολὴ στὴ μελέτη τοῦ βίου, τοῦ ἔργου καὶ τῆς ἐποχῆς του*. Βυζαντινὰ Κείμενα καὶ Μελέται 22. Thessalonike.
Kindstrand, J. F. (ed.) (1979) *Praefatio in Homerum*. Uppsala.
Koster, W. J. W. (ed.) (1962) *Johannis Tzetzae Commentarii in Aristophanem, fasciculus III continens Commentarium in Ranas et in Aves, argumentum Equitum*. Groningen.
Lamberz, E. (2003) 'Vermißt und gefunden: Zwei Texte des Sophronios von Alexandria zur Bilderverehrung, die Akten des VII. Ökumenischen Konzils

und eine Patriarchatsurkunde des 11. Jh. in einem griechischen Codex aus dem Besitz des Nikolaus von Kues (Harleianus 5665)', *Römische Historische Mitteilungen* 45: 159–80.

Lambros, S. P. (ed.) (1917–20) "Ὁ Σπανέας τοῦ Βατικανοῦ Παλατίνου κώδικος 367', *Νέος Ἑλληνομνήμων* 14: 353–80.

Leone, P. L. M. (ed.) (1995) *Ioannis Tzetzae Carmina Iliaca*. Catania.

(ed.) (2007) *Ioannis Tzetzae Historiae*, second edition. Galatina.

Lavriotes, S. (1920) Ἡ Διόπτρα: "Ἔμμετρον ψυχοθεραπευτικόν', *Ὁ Ἄθως* 1: 1–264.

Linardou, K. (2016) 'Imperial Impersonations: Disguised Portraits of a Komnenian Prince and His Father', in *John II Komnenos, Emperor of Byzantium: In the Shadow of Father and Son*, ed. A. Bucossi and A. Rodriguez Suarez, 155–82. London–New York.

Littlewood, A. R. (ed.) (1995) *Originality in Byzantine Literature, Art and Music: A Collection of Essays*. Oxbow Monographs 50. Oxford.

Loukaki, M. (2000) 'Les didascalies de Léon Balianitès: note sur le contenu et la date', *REByz* 59: 245–52.

(2005) 'Le samedi du Lazare et les éloges annuels du patriarche de Constantinople', in *Κλητόριον εἰς μνήμην Νίκου Οἰκονομίδη*, ed. F. Evangelatou-Notara and T. Maniati-Kokkini, 327–45. Athens.

(2007) 'Questions de dates à propos de trois discours d'Eustathe de Thessalonique', in *Byzantinische Sprachkunst: Studien zur byzantinischen Literatur gewidmet Wolfram Hörandner zum 65. Geburtstag*, ed. M. Hinterberger and E. Schiffer, 210–17. Byzantinisches Archiv 20. Berlin–New York.

Maas, P. (ed.) (1913) 'Die Musen des Kaisers Alexios', *ByzZ* 22: 348–69.

MacAlister, S. (1990) 'Aristotle on the Dream: A Twelfth-Century Romantic Revival', *Byzantion* 60: 195–212.

Magdalino, P. (1993) *The Empire of Manuel I Komnenos, 1143–1180*. Cambridge.

(2008) 'The Empire of the Komnenoi, 1118–1204', in *The Cambridge History of the Byzantine Empire, c. 500–1492*, ed. J. Shepard. Cambridge.

Maiuri, A. (1914–19) 'Una nova poesia di Teodoro Prodromo in greco volgare', *ByzZ* 23: 397–407.

Manaphes, K. A. (1974), 'Θεοδώρου τοῦ Προδρόμου λόγος εἰς τὸν Πατριάρχην Κωνσταντινουπόλεως Ἰωάννην Θ' τὸν Ἀγαπητόν', *Ἐπετηρὶς Ἑταιρείας Βυζαντινῶν Σπουδῶν* 41: 223–42.

Marcovich, M. (1992) *Theodori Prodromi De Rhodanthis et Dosiclis amoribus libri IX*. Stuttgart–Leipzig.

Massa Positano, L. (ed.) (1960) *Johannis Tzetzae Commentarii in Aristophanem, fasciculus I continens Prolegomena et Commentarium in Plutum*. Groningen.

Migne, J.-P. (1865) *Panoplia dogmatica ad Alexium Comnenum*. Patrologiae Cursus Completus, Series Graeca 130. Paris.

Mullett, M. (2004) 'Literary Biography and Historical Genre in the *Life* of Cyril Phileotes by Nicholas Kataskepenos', in *La vie des saints à Byzance: genre littéraire ou biographie historique? Actes du IIe colloque international philologique HERMENEIA (Paris, juin 2002)*, ed. P. Odorico and P. A. Agapitos, 387–409. Dossiers Byzantins 4. Paris.

(2012) 'Whose Muses? Two Advice Poems Attributed to Alexios I Komnenos', in *La face cachée de la littérature byzantine: le texte en tant que message immédiat. Actes du colloque international (Paris, juin 2008)*, ed. P. Odorico, 195–220. Dossiers Byzantins 11. Paris.

Nilsson, I. (2014) *Raconter Byzance: la littérature au XIIe siècle*. Paris.

(2021) *Writer and Occasion in Twelfth-Century Byzantium: The Authorial Voice of Constantine Manasses*. Cambridge.

Nousia, F. (2016) *Byzantine Textbooks of the Palaeologan Period*. Studi e Testi 505. Vatican City.

Papaioannou, S. (2013) *Michael Psellos: Rhetoric and Authorship in Byzantium*. Cambridge.

(2017) 'Rhetoric and Rhetorical Theory', in Kaldellis and Siniossoglou, 101–12.

Papathomopoulos, M. (ed.) (2007) Ἐξήγησις Ἰωάννου γραμματικοῦ τοῦ Τζέτζου εἰς τὴν Ὁμήρου Ἰλιάδα. Athens.

Pizzone, A. (2017a) 'The *Historiai* of John Tzetzes: A Byzantine "Book of Memory"?', *BMGS* 41.2: 182–207.

(2017b) 'History Has No End: Originality and Human Progress in Eustathios' Second Oration for Michael III *o tou Anchialou*', in Pontani, Katsaros and Sarris, 331–55.

(2020) 'Self-authorization and Strategies of Autography in John Tzetzes: The *Logismoi* Rediscovered', *GRBS* 60: 652–90.

Polemis, I. D. (2011) 'Notes on the Inaugural Orations of the Patriarch Michael of Anchialos', *ByzSlav* 59: 162–72.

Pontani, F. (2015) 'Scholarship in the Byzantine Empire (529–1453)', in *Brill's Companion to Ancient Greek Scholarship*, vol. 1: *History; Disciplinary Profiles*, ed. F. Montanari, S. Matthaios and A. Rengakos, 297–455. Leiden–Boston.

Pontani, F., V. Katsaros and V. Sarris (eds.) (2017) *Reading Eustathios of Thessalonike*. Trends in Classics Supplementary Volumes 46. Berlin–Boston.

Rizzo, J. J. (ed.) (1971) *Isaak Sebastokrator's* Περὶ τῆς τῶν κακῶν ὑποστάσεως. Meisenheim am Glan.

Roilos, P. (2005) *Amphoteroglossia: A Poetics of the Twelfth-Century Medieval Greek Novel*. Washington, DC.

Ronchey, S. (2017) 'Eustathios at Prodromos Petra? Some Remarks on the Manuscript Tradition of the *Exegesis in Canonem Iambicum Pentecostalem*', in Pontani, Katsaros and Sarris, 181–97.

Sargologos, E. (ed.) (1964) *La vie de Saint Cyrille le Philéote moine byzantin (†1110): introduction, texte critique, traduction et notes*. Subsidia Hagiographica Graeca 39. Brussels.

Scheer, E. (ed.) (1958) *Lycophronis Alexandra*, vol. 2: *Scholia continens*. Berlin (reprint of the 1908 edition).

Trizio, M. (2016) *Il neoplatonismo di Eustrazio di Nicea*. Biblioteca filosofica di Quaestio 23. Bari.

(2017) 'Reading and Commenting on Aristotle', in Kaldellis and Siniossoglou, 397–412.
Troianos, S. (2017) *Die Quellen des byzantinischen Rechts*, trans. D. Simon and S. Neye. Berlin–Boston (revised translation of the Greek third edition of 2011).
Turyn, A. (1972) *Dated Greek Manuscripts of the Thirteenth and Fourteenth Centuries in the Libraries of Italy*, 2 vols. Urbana, IL.
van der Valk, M. (ed.) (1971–87) *Eustathii archiepiscopi Thessalonicensis Commentarii ad Homeri Iliadem pertinentes ad fidem codicis Laurentiani editi*, 4 vols. Leiden.
Vassis, I. (1991a) *Die handschriftliche Überlieferung der sogenannten Psellos-Paraphrase der Ilias*. Meletemata 2. Hamburg.
(1991b) 'Iliadis paraphrasis metrica: Eine unbekannte byzantinische Paraphrase der Ilias (Γ 71–186)', *JÖByz* 41: 207–36.
Wirth, P. (2000) *Eustathii Thessalonicensis opera minora*. Corpus Fontium Historiae Byzantinae 32. Berlin.
Zagklas, N. (2014) 'Theodore Prodromos, The Neglected Poems and Epigrams: Edition, Translation and Commentary', unpublished PhD thesis, University of Vienna.

CHAPTER 2

Forging Identities between Heaven and Earth
Commentaries on Aristotle and Authorial Practices in Eleventh- and Twelfth-Century Byzantium

Michele Trizio

When investigating Byzantine commentaries on classical texts, one cannot help but notice that developments have been rather slow in comparison with the ways our colleagues from the departments of Classical and Medieval Studies have approached the ancient and medieval commentary traditions.[1] The particular case of philosophical commentaries written in Byzantium during the eleventh and twelfth centuries is no exception. We know from classical scholars that Aristotelian philosophical commentaries in Late Antiquity were framed within the philosophical curriculum of study in the Neoplatonic schools in Athens, Alexandria and elsewhere. Here commentaries on Aristotle were meant to open the way to the reading of Plato in what can be regarded as a path towards spiritual perfection.[2] Philosophical commentaries were regarded as a key pedagogical tool in medieval universities and *studia* as well. In this case, commenting on Aristotle was intended both to introduce students to Aristotelian philosophy and at the same time prepare them for further theological reading.[3] With regard to eleventh- and twelfth-century Byzantium, however, we know much less. Certainly, education in Byzantium played a role in forming the bureaucratic elite, but a comprehensive study addressing issues such as the institutional framework for the production and circulation of philosophical commentaries in this

---

I would like to express my gratitude to Panagiotis Agapitos, Baukje van den Berg, Divna Manolova and Przemysław Marciniak for their useful comments on a draft of the present chapter. I also would like to thank the anonymous reviewers for their many insightful comments and suggestions. All transcriptions and translations, unless otherwise stated, are mine.
[1] See e.g. Kraus (2002).
[2] See, among others, Festugiere (1969), Goulet-Cazé (1982), I. Hadot (1987a), (1987b), (1991), (1992), Westerink (1990), Hoffmann (1998) and (2009), Baltussen (2007), Golitsis (2008: 8–15), Tuominen (2009: 1–40).
[3] The literature on this topic is vast. See especially the introductory Del Punta (1998), Ebbesen (2002), Weijers (2002) and more recently Bianchi (2013). On Medieval Arabic philosophy: D'Ancona (2001).

period is still lacking.[4] The same holds true for our knowledge of the different authorial practices and interpretive strategies employed by the Byzantine commentators of philosophical texts.[5]

This chapter aims to partially fill this gap by reconstructing the cultural, social and material aspects of the production of eleventh- and twelfth-century Byzantine philosophical commentaries.[6] I argue that, while interpreting the ancient philosophical texts, the Byzantine commentators also advanced their conception of authorship, thus presenting their identity as a commentator to the readers. I will first discuss the present state of our knowledge of philosophical commentaries written in the period under discussion. Next, I will investigate the strong connection in Byzantine texts between the written and spoken word and the importance of orality. Then I will present some lesser-known texts written by commentators in this period, and I will study the textual approaches of commentators such as Eustratios of Nicaea and Michael of Ephesus, in order to point out the survival of various late antique hermeneutics in their commentaries. Finally, I will discuss the self-representation of the Byzantine commentators of this period and provide an example of how visible patronage was from the social point of view and how it reinforced the patron's and patroness's social prestige.

The Cultural and Material Aspects of Eleventh- and Twelfth-Century Philosophical Commentaries

A Problem of Sources

The first problem that I would like to address concerns the institutional framework for the production and circulation of philosophical commentaries in this period. To state that philosophical commentaries were written for teaching purposes and circulated mostly in the Constantinopolitan schools of the time is certainly reasonable. However, in my view, the real task would be to locate the production of a given commentary on a classical philosophical work within the Byzantine *cursus studiorum*. We

---

[4] This is not to say that we lack *in toto* information on the Byzantine schools and their curricula. See, among others, the classic studies by Fuchs (1926), Browning (1962a), (1963), (1981), Speck (1974), Lemerle (1971) and (1977), Markopoulos (2006), (2013a), (2013b), Nesseris (2014). For the later period, Constantinides (1982), Mergiali (1996).

[5] By contrast, there are good studies addressing those very same issues in Homeric scholarship from Michael Psellos to John Tzetzes and in Byzantine novels. See e.g. Cesaretti (1991), Budelmann (2002), Roilos (2005), Pizzone (2017).

[6] The framework for my analysis comes from the remarks found in Cavallo (2002). See also Goulet (2007). On twelfth-century classical scholarship in Byzantium, see Kaldellis (2009).

do actually have information on Byzantine schools and their curricula.[7] Nonetheless, the difficulty in dealing with the Byzantine commentary tradition of philosophical works lies in the lack of information on the exact place that a given text occupies in the curriculum of studies. In this respect, I would like to emphasize the need to avoid generalizations and trivialities of all sorts. For example, it may be true that logical commentaries were located in the lower part of the curriculum; however, a closer look at the production of these particular texts in the period under investigation makes it clear that even commentaries on Aristotelian logical works display different levels of complexity and, accordingly, were probably addressed to students at different stages.[8] In other words, a commentary on an Aristotelian logical or physical work (two disciplines traditionally regarded as propaedeutic to more advanced readings) was not necessarily produced and read at an earlier stage of the curriculum. In this regard, I maintain that the first challenge one encounters when reconstructing the Byzantine commentaries on philosophical works is not having information as accurate as in the commentaries written by the late antique Neoplatonic commentators of Aristotle's works.[9]

A second difficulty is in distinguishing and identifying the different addressees of a commentary from, for instance, its stylistic features. Too often, modern scholars categorize the levels of complexity of commentaries according to the modern perception of these levels. For me, however, the focus should be on determining Byzantine standards for assessing the complexity of a text. Admittedly, we are not as yet able to answer this question.

Die Bücherverluste

In addition to the lack of precise information on the philosophical curriculum in this period, one should add a further difficulty, that is, the lack of the materiality, so to say, of the available sources: *die Bücherverluste*. Our colleagues working, for example, on the circles of late Byzantine scholars of the Palaiologan period are in the fortunate position of having access to the manuscripts authored by these scholars together with their pupils.[10] The stratigraphy of these manuscripts offers a tremendous amount of information that is useful in

---

[7] Cf. *supra* n. 4.   [8] On this issue, see the interesting observations in Pizzone (2016).
[9] Cf. *supra* n. 1. See also P. Hadot (1990), Sorabji (2005: 37–55).
[10] On Pachymeres: Golitsis (2010). On Nikephoros Gregoras, see the introductory Ševčenko (1964) and (1975), Pérez Martín (1997), Förstel (2011), Bianconi (2005) and (2017). On Chortasmenos: Hunger (1957), Cacouros (1997), Gamillscheg (2006). On intellectual circles as reflected in manuscript culture, see Bianconi (2004) and (2008), Orsini (2005), Cavallo (2010a), Menchelli (2010), Gaul (2011).

reconstructing the way master and pupils collaborated in preserving, adapting and reshaping a classical text. However, scholars working on eleventh- and twelfth-century philosophical commentaries face a rather disappointing scenario. Of Michael Psellos, John Italos, Eustratios of Nicaea, Michael of Ephesus, etc., we have not one autograph manuscript. We do not know their book hands, nor can we establish their *modus operandi* on a safe codicological and palaeographical basis. The majority of the manuscripts preserving the works of the philosophers and commentators of this period can be dated between the second half of the thirteenth century and the sixteenth century.[11]

There are notable exceptions to this trend. For example, Vatican City, Biblioteca Apostolica Vaticana, gr. 269 preserves a collection of late antique and Byzantine commentaries on Aristotle. The different hands in this manuscript have been dated to the end of the thirteenth century,[12] but the codex was likely produced at an earlier date, possibly at the end of the twelfth century.[13] Interestingly, in this manuscript, the *mise-en-page* differs from that present in manuscripts from the Palaiologan period. Whereas in the latter the text of the commentaries is transmitted as paratext surrounding Aristotle's text, in the former the text flows continuously through the page and Aristotle's text is included in quotation marks within the commentary. This manuscript was probably produced for private scholarly purposes by scribes who worked in a great hurry with little concern for its outward appearance.

As stated earlier, this manuscript, together with the two twelfth-century fragments of Eustratios' commentary on *Nicomachean Ethics* 1 recently discovered in the bindings of two seventeenth-century manuscripts preserved in the National Széchényi Library (Budapest),[14] suggest that the earlier stage in the transmission of these texts was characterized by a different layout from that utilized in many of the later manuscripts of the *Corpus Aristotelicum*. It appears that the transition between the two layouts may have caused some textual loss, as some of the later manuscripts preserving twelfth-century philosophical commentaries offer an abridged version of the original texts.[15] Since these later manuscripts were often used for the editions in the *Commentaria in Aristotelem Graeca* series, some of the modern editions of these commentaries display a deficient text.[16]

---

[11] See Mondrain (2000).
[12] For a description of the content and the traditional dating of the manuscript, see Mercati and de' Cavalieri (1923: 353–6).
[13] Lutz Koch and Daniele Bianconi, private conversation.   [14] Németh (2014).
[15] Németh (2014) updating Mercati (1915).
[16] Eleni Pappa has informed me that something similar is evident in the text tradition of Michael of Ephesus' commentary on Aristotle's natural works.

There are two other important exceptions to the trend mentioned above. The first is Vatican City, Biblioteca Apostolica Vaticana, gr. 2199, preserving Michael of Ephesus' commentaries on *Parva naturalia* and *Movement of Animals*. Here, the same scribe, a professional whose handwriting dates to the second half of the twelfth century, copied the text and left wide margins for the insertion of marginal notes. However, these have been filled only on fols. 2v–11 by a later Palaiologan hand, who summarized Aristotle's text. The manuscript is competently produced in all respects. More importantly, it is the first known testimony of Michael's commentaries after their composition.[17]

The second is the fascinating Florence, Biblioteca Medicea Laurenziana, Plut 5.13, a manuscript of the *Corpus Dionysiacum* that transmits (fols. 8r–9r, 10rv) three long scholia on *On the Celestial Hierarchy* composed by John Italos, Psellos' controversial pupil and consul of the philosophers in the 1070s.[18] This manuscript has been competently produced and is exceptional in all respects. It preserves the only known witness of Italos' exegesis on Dionysius the Areopagite and, more significantly, the handwriting in this part of the manuscript dates to the very same period of the composition of the scholia, possibly between 1070 and 1080. This is suggested by the close similarities the scribe's handwriting bears with that of several official documents issued in the late eleventh century.[19] Interestingly, after copying Italos' three scholia, the copyist left all remaining margins empty. While it is not possible to ascertain the exact reasons for this, it would be tempting (though highly speculative) to assume that the copyist interrupted his copying of the text following the trial against Italos between 1076–7 and 1082, when Italos' authority was challenged.[20]

Among the reasons for the loss of several of the twelfth-century philosophical manuscripts, scholars often cite the physical destruction of books following the Latin conquest of Constantinople in 1204. Yet, the impact of this event on the production and preservation of manuscripts has not been clearly quantified, and in recent studies alternative explanations have been advanced, which take into account the way philosophical texts of this period circulated. In fact, besides material circumstances, cultural and social factors may also have played a role, such as the way in which Byzantine scholars of this period edited and published their works or the existence of strong competitors, i.e. other books on the same subject which could make a text

---

[17] On this manuscript, see Lilla (1985: 147–9), Németh (2014: 59).
[18] On these scholia, see Rigo (2006). [19] On these handwritings, see Cavallo (2000).
[20] On the trial against Italos, see Gouillard (1985).

obsolete or less appealing.²¹ For example, Michael Psellos' work is dispersed through a myriad of manuscripts, most of which date from the late thirteenth to fifteenth century, something which may suggest that the author did not prepare an edition of his texts. In the case of Psellos, in spite of its fragile transmission, the survival of his works is due to the favourable impact of these texts on the later generation of Byzantine literati.²²

Other Byzantine scholars were less fortunate. Unlike Psellos' writings, the works of his pupil John Italos have been transmitted as a corpus. However, the presence in this corpus of notes and essays by Italos' students signifies that perhaps Italos, too, did not arrange his writings into an edition and that this task was eventually accomplished by one of his pupils. Finally, I mention the case of Theodore of Smyrna's *Epitome* of natural philosophy. Theodore held the chair of consul of the philosophers after Italos, but his *Epitome* had almost no impact on later generations of Byzantine scholars. In fact, the text has been transmitted in fragmentary form in a single manuscript, Vienna, Österreichische Nationalbibliothek, theol. gr. 134 (fols. 238r–262v), a theological miscellany copied around 1300 in the monastery of Stoudion in Constantinople.²³ A possible explanation for this might be that Theodore's *Epitome* lost out badly in competition with other works on the same subject, such as Nikephoros Blemmydes' later *Compendium on Physics*, which survives in an impressive number of manuscripts. In fact, it is conceivable that Theodore's work might never have survived at all: the presence of his *Epitome* in a purely theological miscellany is entirely accidental and probably depends on the fact that Theodore had a reputation as a theologian due to having penned a few anti-Latin writings, perhaps on the occasion of Peter Grossolanus of Milan's visit to Constantinople in 1112.

In spite of these limitations, the literary witnesses from this period still provide several interesting hints for reconstructing the ways Byzantine scholars commented on classical philosophical texts. Among these witnesses, I would like to present a few case studies concerning the role of orality and its connection with written culture. In the next section, I will demonstrate that Byzantine commentators and teachers of this period follow their antique predecessors in conceiving of orality as complementary to the written word. Accordingly, several Byzantine philosophical texts of this period derive from

---

²¹ See Ronconi (2011).
²² See Anastasi (1976), N. G. Wilson (2008), Papaioannou (2012a), Pérez Martín (2013).
²³ On which see Hunger, Kresten and Hannick (1984: 126–32).

oral teachings, either reporting what the teacher said during a class or invoking oral explanations as supplements to the written text.

The Power of Orality

Let me start with one of Michael Psellos' lesser-known texts. At the very end of his yet unedited paraphrase of Aristotle's *De interpretatione*, Psellos writes:

> οὕτω μὲν οὖν ἐγὼ ἐν τῷ λογίῳ τούτῳ θεάτρῳ τοῦ Ἀριστοτέλους πρόσωπον ἐμαυτῷ περιθέμενος, τὸν ἐκείνου περὶ τῶν ἀποφαντικῶν λόγων ἐξωρχησάμην ὑπομνηματισμόν, εὐστόχως μὲν παντάπασιν οὐκ ἂν εἴποιμι, ἐπηβολώτατον δὲ καὶ γενναιότατον· (Michael Psellos, *Paraphrase of Aristotle's* De interpretatione, Florence, Biblioteca Medicea Laurenziana, Plut. 10.26, fol. 176r)

> Thus, while actually impersonating Aristotle before this erudite circle (*theatron*), I performed the commentary on his work on categorical propositions. I may not have always succeeded [in this task], but I certainly tried with the greatest dexterity and excellence.[24]

I find this text very interesting for the following reasons. While endorsing the traditional understanding of a paraphrase as a text in which the paraphrast speaks in the first person, as if he were Aristotle himself,[25] Psellos makes extensive use of performance-related language. The paraphrast presents himself as an actor who wears Aristotle's mask and acts before the *theatron* of his erudite spectators. Actually, the form ἐξωρχησάμην, from ἐξορχέομαι, implies a performance utilizing the medium of dance (see Liddell-Scott, s.v.).[26] Indeed, in Late Antiquity and Byzantium the word *theatron* usually refers to the learned audience of orations and poems. However, in light of Przemysław Marciniak's more inclusive understanding of the term at hand, it is reasonable to believe that by *theatron* Psellos refers to students and maybe even fellows attending his class on Aristotle's *De interpretatione*.[27]

Moreover, the reference to orality in Psellos' text is consistent with similar allusions in the philosophical commentaries, paraphrases and scholia written in the period under investigation. For example in the following text attributed to John Italos:

---

[24] On this text, see Ierodiakonou (2002: 165, n. 31).   [25] See Ierodiakonou (2012).
[26] On Psellos' usage of performance-related language, see Protogirou (2014).
[27] Cf. Marciniak (2007: 278–9).

> οἶσθα γὰρ ὡς τῶν πλεοναχῶς ἐστιν ἡ ἀρετὴ λεγομένων· καὶ τοῦτό μοι καὶ πρὸς σὲ πάλαι εἴρηται διὰ ζώσης φωνῆς καὶ νῦν αὖθις εἰρήσεται τοσοῦτον, ὅσῳ μὲν βελτίω γενέσθαι ἐκ τῶν περὶ ταύτης ῥηθησομένων ἡμῖν λόγων, πρὸς ὅπερ ἀεὶ σπεύδεις καὶ οὗ διηνεκῶς ἐφιέμενος εἶ. (John Italos, *Problems and Solutions* 63, 87.1–9 ed. Joannou)

> In fact, you have learned that the notion of 'virtue' is one of these notions that are expressed in many different ways. And I have already told you this with the living voice and I will repeat it again since that for which you always strive and which you continuously desire, becomes clearer by what I am going to say on this matter.

In this text, the master suggests that part of his teaching is better received 'through the living voice', *viva voce*, or 'through direct oral communication' (διὰ ζώσης φωνῆς). The passage at hand reflects an earlier antique and late antique practice. In fact, in a well-known text, the physician and philosopher Galen writes:

> καὶ διὰ τοῦτό μοι δοκοῦσι καλῶς οἱ πολλοὶ λέγειν ἀρίστην εἶναι διδασκαλίαν <u>τὴν παρὰ τῆς ζώσης φωνῆς</u> γιγνομένην, ἐκ βιβλίου δὲ μήτε κυβερνήτην τινὰ δύνασθαι γενέσθαι μήτ' ἄλλης τέχνης ἐργάτην· ὑπομνήματα γάρ ἐστι ταῦτα τῶν προμεμαθηκότων καὶ προεγνωκότων, οὐ διδασκαλία τελεία τῶν ἀγνοούντων. (Galen, *On the Properties of Foodstuffs* 480.5–9 ed. Helmreich)

> This is why I think that the majority are correct who say that the best instruction is <u>through the living voice,</u> and that it is impossible for anyone to become either a helmsman or an expert in any other craft from a book. These are reminders for those who have previously studied and understood, not complete instruction for the ignorant. (after Powell trans.)

And elsewhere:

> Ἀληθὴς μὲν ἀμέλει καὶ ὁ λεγόμενος ὑπὸ τῶν πλείστων τεχνιτῶν ἐστι λόγος, ὡς οὐκ ἴσον οὐδ' ὅμοιον εἴη <u>παρὰ ζώσης φωνῆς</u> μαθεῖν ἢ ἐκ συγγράμματος ἀναλέξασθαι. (Galen, *Compound Remedies according to Places* 864.1–6 ed. Kühn)

> There may well be truth in the saying current among most craftsmen, that reading out of a book is not the same thing as, or even comparable to, learning <u>from the living voice or through direct oral communication.</u> (trans. Mournet)

Galen exemplifies a widespread belief in antiquity that oral teaching is preferable and more effective than written texts, which are evidently seen as lifeless.[28] Eusebius of Caesarea echoes this very same idea when he writes that the head of the Alexandrian school in sacred learning, Pantaenus, 'commented on the treasures of the divine truths both through direct oral communication (ζώσῃ φωνῇ) and in written words'.[29] In my view, by accepting this earlier belief, Italos achieves two goals: first, to point out that teaching is only complete when the text is complemented by the living voice; second, to connect his own teaching and identity as a teacher with a distinguished and earlier tradition of ancient commentators and scholars who pledged themselves to sharing knowledge orally as well as through the written word.[30] Accordingly, in one of his logical works, Italos refers to his sources and emphasizes that he has indeed read books on the subject, but he has also heard things directly from his master's voice.

> Εἴρηται τοίνυν περὶ τούτων ἡμῖν ἐν ἄλλοις, ὅσα ἐκ τῶν ἀρχαίων βιβλίων ἐξελεξάμεθα καὶ τοῦ μεγάλου ἡμῶν διδασκάλου ἠκηκόαμεν. (John Italos, *Problems and Solutions* 6, 8.4–6 ed. Joannou)
>
> Therefore, we have discussed these matters elsewhere, things that we read in ancient books and things which we heard from our great teacher.

In this case, referring to orality also serves to remind the readers of the author's belonging to a prestigious philosophical lineage embodied by the famous Michael Psellos, who was actually Italos' master.

References to interpretations of a text provided orally by teachers occur frequently in the Byzantine sources of this period.[31] For instance, while commenting on *Rhetoric* 1401a31, Stephanos Skylitzes admits that the passage at hand is an obscure one and adds that 'it created many difficulties for our teachers and earlier commentators' (τοῦτο πολλὰ πράγματα παρέσχε τοῖς διδασκάλοις ἡμῶν καὶ ἐξηγηταῖς).[32] In the same vein, a twelfth-century hand has written several marginal notes on the text of Aristotle's *Metaphysics* attributed to his teacher in the well-known manuscript Paris, Bibliothèque nationale de France, gr. 1853.[33] These notes are

---

[28] See, among others, Richard (1950), Alexander (1990), Mournet (2005: 141–9), Cavallo (2010b), Botha (2012: 21–38).
[29] *Ecclesiastical History* 5.10.4 ed. Bardy.
[30] On Galen's reception in Byzantium, see Temkin (1973: 51–94), Nutton (2007), Bouras-Vallianatos (2015) and (2018).
[31] On exegesis and performance, see also Pizzone in this volume.
[32] *On Aristotle's* Rhetoric 304.29–31 ed. Rabe.
[33] The author of the scholia refers at least five times to his teacher: at fol. 258v marg. sup.: οὕτως ὁ διδάσκαλος. At fol. 269r right marg.: τοῦ διδασκάλου. At fol. 272v left marg.: οὕτω γὰρ ὁ ἡμέτερος καθηγητὴς ἐξηγήσατο. At fol. 287r right marg.: ὡς ὁ διδάσκαλος εἶπε. At fol. 295v left marg.: οὕτως ὁ διδάσκαλος. See Golitsis (2014: 43–50).

no more than a basic explanation of the text, but they are important in that they exemplify a common procedure of integrating written exegetical notes with comments expounded in the classroom.

Teachers are not the only source of orally transmitted explanations of a classical philosophical text. Often, twelfth-century Byzantine scholars refer to comments by fellow scholars working on the same text. For example, Michael of Ephesus' commentary on Aristotle's *Parva naturalia* includes at least four such references.[34] Just as in the case of comments produced by a teacher, notes by fellow scholars in Byzantine sources also reveal the urgency of connecting with an earlier noble exegetical tradition and at the same time of emphasizing the importance and role of the Byzantine commentators with regard to this same tradition. For example, in his commentary on *Posterior Analytics* 2, Eustratios of Nicaea writes that he does not consider himself a professional commentator and that he wrote this commentary 'at the request of friends' (διὰ τὴν τῶν ἑταίρων ἀξίωσιν). In so doing, Eustratios uses a widespread literary *topos* in ancient texts, that is to say, to account, out of modesty, for the composition of a written text by referring to a request from friends, pupils or fellow scholars. The very words which Eustratios uses are taken once again directly from a well-respected authority like Galen (*Compound Remedies according to Places* 887.17 ed. Kühn). In this case, imitating the Galenic text works as a sociolect, signifying to readers that, while endorsing the modesty *topos*, the author wishes to present himself as the heir of a distinguished earlier philosophical tradition and, at the same time, that he intends to be identified as the pivotal figure in the circle of the *hetairoi*.

These case studies make it clear that the commentators and philosophers of this period were anxious to determine their identity within a complex interaction between the power of orality, the prestige of written culture (here seen as an instrument for attaining prestige in the eyes of fellow scholars or pupils) and the readers' or listeners' expectations and social status.[35] This latter point is of particular interest insofar as, just like the scholars of the earlier and later periods, eleventh- and twelfth-century authors display a distinctive awareness of the need to modulate their exegesis according to extratextual criteria such as the social status of the reader or readers of the text.[36] John Italos provides a good example of this

---

[34] Michael of Ephesus, *On Aristotle's* Parva naturalia 85.4–8, 130.34, 131.4–8, 148.9–10 ed. Wendland.
[35] On the interaction between teachers and pupils in the eleventh and twelfth centuries, see Agapitos (1998), Grünbart (2014).
[36] See Agapitos (2017) on John Tzetzes.

tendency when he rejects an interpretation of *Odyssey* 19.562–7 found in the ancient scholia to Homer as 'lower-class' or 'colloquial' (δημῶδες) and unsuitable for a text commissioned by Andronikos Doukas, the son of emperor Constantine X.[37]

So far, I have highlighted some of the strategies of self-legitimation present in the philosophical commentaries of this period. In the next section, I will discuss the ways in which Byzantine commentators of this period approached the classical material, that is to say, the commentators' methodology.

Identities in Context

The Philosophy Professor and the Pious Compiler

The first two characters I would like to introduce are John Italos and Theodore of Smyrna. Theodore took over Italos' position as consul of the philosophers around the end of the eleventh century, possibly a few years after Italos' condemnation in 1082. He composed the *Epitome of Nature and Natural Principles according to the Ancients*, a summary of ancient philosophical views on physics which draws heavily from late antique commentators and from the ancient Greek astronomer Cleomedes. When introducing this compilation, Theodore follows a rather traditional approach and promises to report, for the benefit of the readers, 'in short form' (διὰ βραχέων) that which has been discussed at length in many ancient books.[38] However, he also adds that:

> ἐπεὶ δὲ ταῦτα περί τε τῆς ὕλης καὶ τοῦ εἴδους καὶ τῆς στερήσεως ἐδηλώσαμεν, κἀκεῖνα ἐπισυνάψαι τῷ λόγῳ κεκρίναμεν οὐκ ἐκ τῆς ἔξωθεν ὄντα παιδείας, ἀλλ' ἐκ τῆς ἡμετέρας καὶ ἱερᾶς. (Theodore of Smyrna, *Epitome of Nature and Natural Principles according to the Ancients* 3.25–4.2 ed. Benakis)
>
> For this reason, we have discussed these things regarding matter, form and privation, and we have decided to include them in our work not from the point of view of the pagan doctrines, but from that of our sacred ones.

Theodore remarks that, when discussing the material in his *Epitome*, he will only include those ancient views which are compatible with the Holy Scriptures. Accordingly, he warns the reader that he will read ancient

---

[37] On this text, see Trizio (2013).
[38] Theodore of Smyrna, *Epitome of Nature and Natural Principles according to the Ancients* 1.7–11 ed. Benakis.

physics from the point of view of Revelation and not from that of Hellenic *paideia*. Following these premises, Theodore wrote a basic compendium for unacquainted readers who were not prepared to deal with a more complex discussion of the material. Furthermore, since Theodore's focus is on presenting ancient physical theories through the prism of orthodoxy, he must have thought that, by teaching some rudimentary physics, he could do away with accuracy. In fact, he never mentions any of the ancient sources on which the *Epitome* depends, as if these were not relevant to the pedagogical purpose of the text.

In my view, this text must be seen against the backdrop of the philosophical commentaries and textbooks composed in this period. Even though Theodore's introductory remarks on the appropriate methodology for epitomizing ancient source material are quite traditional, I believe that, when seen in the broader cultural context of this period, his statements are all but accidental. Actually, I argue that this text must be read as a reply to Theodore's predecessor as consul of philosophers, John Italos. In one of his philosophical works, Italos elaborates on the proper methodology for teaching philosophy:

> Δεῖ οὖν τὴν τοιαύτην σημασίαν διελθεῖν εἰς ὅσα τοῖς "Ελλησιν ἔδοξεν· οὗτοι γὰρ τῆς τοιαύτης ἐπιστήμης καθηγηταί· διὸ κατὰ δόξαν ἐκείνοις τὰς ἀπορίας λυτέον, εἰ καὶ πολλάκις τοῖς εὐσεβέσι δόγμασιν ἐναντιοῦται τὰ ἐκείνοις δοκοῦντα (Italos, *Problems and Solutions* 7, 9.9–10 ed. Joannou)

> It is therefore necessary to go through the Greek views on this subject. In fact, they are the masters of this discipline. Therefore, I shall solve the apories according to their opinions, even though often their teaching contradicts our pious dogmas.

Italos' text seems to be the actual target of Theodore's preliminary statement on the appropriate methodology for discussing ancient philosophical views on physics. If this is correct, then Theodore forges his identity as a scholar and as the author of the *Epitome* by establishing a sharp contrast between himself and his predecessor. On the one hand stands Theodore, the pious and unoriginal compiler; on the other stands John Italos, a controversial figure who made it his task to teach ancient philosophy according to the inner principles of the discipline. In this case, the marker for determining the commentators' identity is a methodological one.[39]

---

[39] However, it must be said that elsewhere Italos adopts a more prudent approach. See the texts collected in Trizio (2013: 94–5).

Simplikios Wannabe: Eustratios of Nicaea's Methodology

One of the greatest novelties in the philosophical texts produced under the Komnenoi is surely the appearance of long philosophical commentaries following the model of the late antique ones composed by Simplikios and Philoponos. With the exception of Psellos' paraphrase of Aristotle's *De interpretatione* mentioned above, eleventh-century scholars mostly composed shorter treatises, either abridgements of classical philosophical works or exegetical notes on difficult passages from Aristotle or Gregory of Nazianzos. The reasons for this shift are unclear, but it is plausible that the production of longer commentaries after the late antique model stems from the impulse of private patronage. In our case, the impulse came from an imperial woman, the princess and historian Anna Komnene.[40]

Eustratios of Nicaea authored commentaries on Aristotle's *Posterior Analytics* 2 and on *Nicomachean Ethics* 1 and 6. In what follows, I evaluate Eustratios' methodology against the background of the earlier, late antique commentary tradition. I compare Eustratios' text with his late antique model according to a set of markers: (1) reconstructing the meaning of the lemma in the form of a syllogism; (2) comparing and discussing the meaning of the lemma according to the *variae lectiones* found in the manuscripts available to the commentator; (3) the *lexis/theoria* approach (two levels in the commentary: literal and general explanation of the text); (4) digressions; (5) harmonizing Plato and Aristotle.[41]

(1) *Syllogistical explanation of the text.* Eustratios often rephrases the lemma in the form of a syllogism in order to make the text more understandable.[42]

(2) *Discussing* variae lectiones *found in other manuscripts.* Eustratios occasionally refers to the *lectiones* found in other manuscripts, especially when the text is obscure.[43]

---

[40] See Browning (1962b). On eleventh- and twelfth-century imperial women and philosophical culture, see Garland (2017).
[41] On the importance of these markers for late antique commentators, see the testimonia collected in Sorabji (2005: 37–55).
[42] See e.g. Eustratios, *In Eth. Nic. 1* 43.2–3 ed. Heylbut; *In Eth. Nic. 1* 121.5–7; *In Eth. Nic. 6* 306.23–6 ed. Heylbut; 332.35ff.; 387.16ff. Compare these texts with Simpl., *In Caelo* 99.24ff. ed. Heiberg; 128.1ff.; 446.29ff.; *In Phys.* 171.17ff. ed. Diels; 229.17ff.; 274.9ff.; 276.22ff.; 416.12ff.; 1253.3ff.; Philoponos, *In Phys.* 209.23ff. ed. Vitelli; *In De an.* 232.24ff. ed. Hayduck; 349.10ff.
[43] See e.g. Eustratios, *In An. Post. 2* 84.24 ed. Hayduck; 158.32, 174.28; *In Eth. Nic. 6* 304.5; 339.14–15; 373.9–10. Compare these texts with Alexander of Aphrodisias, *In Metaph.* 75.26ff. ed. Hayduck; 104.20ff.; 145.21ff.; *In An. pr.* 210.30ff. ed. Wallies; *In Sens.* 101.4ff. ed. Wendland; Ammonius, *In De int.* 50.8 ed. Busse; Asclepius, *In Metaph.*, 300.32 ed. Hayduck; Simpl., *In Cael.*

(3) *The* lexis/theoria *organization of the commentary*. Eustratios imitates a late antique way of commenting on Aristotle's texts based on the division of the commentary into a general explanation of the lemma and a more detailed scrutiny of it.[44]

(4) *Digressions and corollaries*. In line with a common practice in late antique commentaries, digressions and corollaries appear, though to a limited extent, in Eustratios' commentaries.[45] Two cases are worth mentioning here. First, in his commentary on *Nicomachean Ethics 6* (272.3–277.17), Eustratios devotes several pages of the printed text to the refutation of Islam. Taking his cue from Aristotle's three types of lives – the life of philosophical contemplation, the political life and the life of those who only pursue pleasures – Eustratios identifies Muslims as followers of the lowest and most grievous way of life in the Aristotelian classification. Accordingly, he adapts the allegation of lustfulness traditionally made against Muslims to the framework of Aristotle's *Nicomachean Ethics* and classifies the Muslims as hedonists.[46] A second, shorter digression is found in the commentary on *Nicomachean Ethics* 1. In *Nicomachean Ethics* 1.5.10, 1096b22–3 Aristotle speaks of those who seek honours in life and, accordingly, pursue political happiness. Eustratios here introduces the case of Socrates, who was an honourable man in that he accepted an unfair sentence even though he could have escaped. However, suddenly Eustratios makes a short digression, introducing elements alien to Aristotle's text:

152.31; 291.25; 597.21; 686.1; 698.11; *In Cat.* 34.28–30 ed. Kalbfleisch; *In Phys.*, 77.6–7; 168.19–21; 368.15–16; 377.25; 399.33; 414.18–20; 441.30–31; 522.24–5; 665.26–7; 691.2–4; 728.10; 753.28–9; 769.16–18; 845.4; 876.22; 912.23–4; 918.11–13; 936.21; 1017.19; 1054.27–8; 1093.6; 1214.34; 1245.2–3; 1317.6; Ps. Simpl. (*re vera* Priscianus Lydus), *In De an.* 320.28–9 ed. Hayduck; Philoponos, *In An. pr.* 20.4 ed. Wallies; 57.24–5; 255.29–30; *In An. post.*, 107.18; 233.10–11; 252.26–7; 264.23–4; 400.20; 408.29; *In Mete.* 10.25 ed. Hayduck; *In Gen. corr.* 76.2–3 ed. Vitelli; *In De an.* 315.24.

[44] On the genesis of this model, see Golitsis (2008: 55–8). For examples, see Eustratios, *In An. post. 2* 171.15–16; *In Eth. Nic. 6* 289.1; *In Eth. Nic. 6* 284.30; *In Eth. Nic. 6* 326.25–7; *In Eth. Nic. 6* 339.13–14; *In Eth. Nic. 6* 384.31. Compare these texts with Prokl., *In Alc. I* 207.19–208.1 ed. Westerink; *In Tim. I* 186.7 ed. Diehl; Ammonius, *In De int.* 265.12 ed. Busse; *In Cat.* 8.13–15 ed. Busse; Simpl. *In Cat.* 22.15 ff.; 68.32–3; 80.13–15; 159.9; 165.31 ff.; 308.22–3; 211.5; 228.1–3; 286.4; 381.31–3; 387.17ff.; *In Cael* 698.10; *In Phys.* 129.16; Philoponos, *In Phys.* 176.26 ed. Vitelli.

[45] See Golitsis (2008: 83–195). [46] On this text, see Trizio (2012).

ἐῶ γὰρ νῦν εἰς μέσον ἄγειν τοὺς καθ' ἡμᾶς, τῆς προσκαίρου ταύτης ζωῆς τὸν θεάρεστον προτιμήσαντας θάνατον μετὰ τυραννικῆς ἀδόξου καταδίκης καὶ τοὺς ἐν ἀναχωρήσει καὶ μονίᾳ θεῷ μόνῳ σχόντας δήλην τὴν αὐτῶν τελειότητα· περὶ γὰρ τῶν καθ' ἡμᾶς οὐδ' Ἀριστοτέλης ἔννοιαν ἔσχηκε. (Eustratios, *Commentary on Aristotle's* Nicomachean Ethics 1 35.33–7 ed. Heylbut)

I will avoid introducing the case of those Christians who preferred leaving their earthly existence in a way that pleased God, namely by dying by the hand of a tyrant inflicting on them an unfair sentence, and the case of those who seek their perfection in a solitary isolation whereby they contemplate God alone. In fact, of these Christians Aristotle had no knowledge.

The text elaborates on the traditional early Christian characterization of martyrs and monks as true philosophers.[47] Accordingly, Eustratios assumes that Aristotle's *Nicomachean Ethics* only describes a model of political and civil happiness, exemplified by Socrates, while the philosophical and contemplative happiness, which Aristotle in books 1 and 10 of this work regards as the highest form of happiness attainable by human beings, only applies to Christian martyrs and monks. While doing so, Eustratios echoes the late antique debate over Socrates as a forerunner of Christ.[48] Within this debate, our commentator stands with Theodoret of Cyrrhus' *Cure for the Greek Maladies* (12.26–8 ed. Canivet), where Theodoret tendentiously interprets Plato's *Republic* 475d, *Theaetetus* 176a–b and *Phaedo* 83a–b to argue that the true Platonic assimilation with God and escape from this life do not apply to Socrates, but can only be achieved within a Christian context by martyrs and monks.[49] Eustratios applies the same interpretive model to Aristotle's distinction between intellectual and political happiness, between the blessed life of the philosophers and that, of secondary importance, of the politicians. In opposition to Aristotle, Eustratios maintains that the former belongs to Christian martyrs alone, while the latter applies to the Greek philosophers of the past.

(5) *Harmony between Plato and Aristotle.* Simplikios' prologue to his commentary on Aristotle's *Categories* (7.23–32 ed. Kalbfleisch) lists

---

[47] See the classical studies by Dölger (1940), Leclercq (1952), Penco (1960), Malingray (1961), Podskalsky (1977: 13–48) and more recently Trizio (2007: 250–2).
[48] On this topic, see Döring (1979), Giannantoni (1986), Droge and Tabor (1992), E. Wilson (2007: 141–69), Edwards (2007).
[49] On this text, see Siniossoglou (2008: 112–46), Papadogiannakis (2013: 78–80), Urbano (2013: 279–86).

the qualities of the ideal commentator. According to Simplikios, (i) the ideal commentator must show a vast and deep knowledge of Aristotle's work; (ii) he must be impartial, neither presenting certain statements of Aristotle's as unsatisfactory, nor defending them as though he were one of Aristotle's disciples; and (iii) with respect to Plato and Aristotle's allegedly different views, he must go beyond the letter (*lexis*) towards the real meaning (*nous*) of these philosophers' views in order to uncover their harmony.[50]

As shown above, Eustratios exemplifies several of these qualities. He accepts Simplikios' methodology as a commentator in all aspects but one: the harmony between Plato and Aristotle. For Simplikios, these hermeneutics serve to show the fundamental unity of philosophical truths within the sixth-century Neoplatonic system. Eustratios, however, was not interested in the agenda of the late antique Neoplatonic school. He was a fervent admirer of the Neoplatonist Proklos, a philosopher who was less inclined to defend the harmony between Plato and Aristotle. Everywhere in his commentaries, Eustratios gives long explanations of the Aristotelian text consisting of excerpts from the work of Proklos.[51] This is particularly evident in Eustratios' defence of Plato's ideal good against Aristotle's critique in *Nicomachean Ethics* 1.4.1096a11–1097a13, which is entirely taken from proposition 8 of Proklos' *Elements of Theology*.[52] Not only does our commentator disagree with Aristotle, but he actually goes further than this in accusing Aristotle of being unfair to Plato and in charging the philosopher with deliberate sophistry.[53] Here the shadow of the middle-Platonist Atticus (the second-century AD philosopher who regarded Aristotelianism as a heresy deviating from authentic Platonic teaching) possibly lurks behind Eustratios' allegation.[54]

In light of this evidence, the current narrative of the alleged Aristotelian renaissance of the early Komnenian period must be revised, if not abandoned.[55] True, in this period two or more scholars authored commentaries on Aristotelian works. The very nature of this cultural endeavour,

---

[50] See the *testimonia* collected in Sorabji (2005: 37–40). See also Hoffmann (1987), P. Hadot (1990), Baltussen (2008: 147–58).
[51] On Proklos in Eustratios, see Trizio (2009) and (2014: 190–201).
[52] See Giokarinis (1964), Trizio (2014: 194–6). [53] *In Eth. Nic. 1* 45.36–8 ed. Heylbut.
[54] See Atticus, fr. 8.11–12 and 9.7 ed. Baudry. On the *topos* of the agreement between Plato and Aristotle in middle Platonism, see Karamanolis (2006). On the critical reception of Aristotle's works among Church Fathers and Byzantine scholars (with an eye on Atticus' influence), see Bydén (2013).
[55] See the classic study by Browning (1962b).

however, was by no means supportive of Aristotelianism as a philosophical system. Whereas Simplikios (*In Cat.* 7.29–32 ed. Kalbfleisch) invited the commentator to go beyond the letter (*lexis*) towards the real meaning (*nous*) of the lemmata, Eustratios' extensive use of Proklos in his explanation of Aristotle's text suggests that he did something else: he often transcends the text altogether and leads the readers far away from the *lexis*, up to the point where they become inevitably disoriented and confused. While reading these commentaries, they were looking for safe and sound explanations of Aristotle's texts; instead, they encountered a Neoplatonizing commentary in which the author could not help but manifest his fondness of Proklos.

Michael of Ephesus

In recent times, scholars have often relied on the later Sophonias (thirteenth-century) when reconstructing Byzantine commentarian approaches to earlier philosophical texts.[56] In the prologue to his paraphrase of Aristotle's *On the Soul* (1.4–3.9 ed. Hayduck), Sophonias distinguishes between commentaries and paraphrases. According to him, paraphrases differ from commentaries in that (1) the latter are longer than the former; (2) commentaries discuss each lemma of Aristotle's text in sections, whereas paraphrases rewrite the text in a continuous manner; (3) in commentaries, the commentator distances himself from the text, whereas the paraphrast impersonates Aristotle; and (4) though both aim to explain Aristotle's text, commentaries do so by interpreting it, while paraphrases merely break up the text and reassemble it in a more understandable manner.

With regard to these two types of authorial strategies, it has been reasonably argued that Sophonias actually wishes to present his approach as innovative.[57] His approach mostly consists of rephrasing the text for the readers' benefit and, now and then, adding a few additional exegetical notes.[58] When looking at Michael of Ephesus' way of commenting on Aristotle, one cannot help but notice that Sophonias' supposedly new approach is actually quite traditional.[59] In fact, Michael implements it consistently throughout his commentaries on Aristotle's natural works. Just like paraphrasts, he mostly rephrases Aristotle's text in order to make it

---

[56] See e.g. Ierodiakonou (2012). [57] See again Ierodiakonou (2012).
[58] See Ierodiakonou (2012: 202–5). [59] On Michael's life and work, see Golitsis (2018).

more readable; however, unlike them, he does not impersonate Aristotle and adds some personal remarks (often taken from earlier sources) whenever necessary.[60]

Michael has often been regarded as an unoriginal compiler who savagely excerpted earlier material.[61] We might nevertheless reconsider Michael as a commentator if we take into account the huge quantity of work commissioned from him.[62] In fact, Michael's commentaries vastly exceed in number those written by his fellow scholar Eustratios, to such an extent that one would not be wrong in claiming that, within the philosophical circle around Anna Komnene, Michael surely did most of the work. In order to accomplish such an enormous task in such a short time, our commentator relied on earlier material (commentaries or marginal scholia) transmitted in the manuscripts preserving the Aristotelian text. In what follows, I present some evidence of Michael's desperate strategy in those commentaries for which there was no earlier commentary on which to rely.

The case of Michael's commentary on the *Parva naturalia* is telling of Michael's *modus operandi* in extreme conditions. In fact, in Late Antiquity, Aristotle's *Parva naturalia* was excluded from the curriculum of study and, accordingly, no commentary was written by the Neoplatonic commentators active in the fifth and the sixth centuries.[63] Around the middle of the eleventh century, Michael Psellos was still discouraging readers from turning to Aristotle's physiological works, which Psellos considered derivative and inferior to Galen's works.[64] In short, when commenting on *Parva naturalia*, Michael was left on his own by his predecessors. However, though he could not rely on an earlier commentary, he nevertheless survived this ordeal by paraphrasing or quoting from Alexander of Aphrodisias' *On the Soul*, a text which contained plenty of information on physiology. Interestingly, in many instances, Michael relies on a manuscript of Alexander's work which preserved better readings than that in Venice, Biblioteca Nazionale Marciana, gr. Z 258, the oldest known witness preserving the text.[65]

---

[60] Only occasionally does Michael accept the *lexis/theoria* hermeneutics, as in *In Eth. Nic.* 10 593.18–19 ed. Heylbut; *In Parv. nat.* 61.11–12, 66.3–4, 86.27–8, 92.24–6 ed. Wendland; *In de motu an.* 118.15–16, 120.14 ed. Hayduck.
[61] See Ebbesen (1981: 268–85). On Michael as a commentator, see Praechter (1906) and Koch (2015), focusing on Michael's commentary on *Movement of Animals*.
[62] For a list of Michael's works, see Mercken (1990: 431). [63] See Bydén (2018).
[64] Michael Psellos, *Funeral Oration for John Xiphilinos* 160.75–9 ed. Polemis. Nonetheless, Psellos did read Aristotle's *Parva naturalia*. See Trizio (2018: 161–2).
[65] See Donini (1968).

There is more to say on Michael's sources. As Jurgen Wiesner demonstrated, when commenting on *On Divination in Sleep*, Michael relied on some scholia transmitted in one branch of the tradition of the text.[66] Something similar could be said for the scholia to *On Dreams* and *On Memory and Recollection* transmitted in the twelfth-century manuscript Vatican City, Biblioteca Apostolica Vaticana, gr. 260, some of which correspond to the wording of Michael's commentary on these texts.[67] Whereas for some of these correspondences it is not clear whether Michael depends on the scholia or vice versa, for others Michael's dependence on this scholiastic material seems quite obvious. This suggests that, at the time of the composition of Michael's commentary – possibly in the second and third decades of the twelfth century – some earlier exegetical material of unknown origin on Aristotle's *Parva naturalia* was still available in the form of scholia in the margins of Aristotle's text.

Nonetheless, Michael would like to be something more than a mere compiler. Accordingly, he tries to make his commentaries pleasant to read by adding some personal observations or curiosities. For instance, he relates – in his commentary on Aristotle's *Generation of Animals* (149.19–20 ed. Hayduck) – that, according to the dialect spoken in his native Ephesus, 'hyena' corresponds to the word *gannos*, a derivative of the classical form *glanos* used by Aristotle himself (*History of Animals* 594a31). Or he writes in his commentary on *Nicomachean Ethics* 10 (613.4–6 ed. Heylbut) that if a child cannot learn more than thirty verses of Homer by heart, he should not be forced to do so, just as someone who is capable of learning no more than fifty verses by heart should not be forced to learn more than he can. This latter remark may reflect the daily life of grammar teachers in Byzantine schools of the time.

Finally, there is one more reason not to dismiss Michael's commentaries as irrelevant: in the same period as Michael wrote his commentaries on Aristotle's zoological works, a revival of the genre of Greek novels took place. Intriguingly, medieval Greek novels written in those years display a remarkable similarity with Aristotle's *Parva naturalia* that cannot be merely accidental.[68] Clearly, there must be a connection between the Aristotelianism in the Greek novels composed in this period on the one hand and Michael's scholarship on Aristotle's natural philosophy on the other. The exact nature of this connection is not immediately clear, but

---

[66] Wiesner (1981). [67] See Escobar (1990: 122), Trizio (2018: 160).
[68] See MacAlister (1996: 140–64). See also Agapitos in this volume.

hopefully future research will cast further light on this extremely interesting point.

Hidden Treasures: Unknown or Little-Known Philosophical Texts from the Komnenian Period

As previously mentioned, our understanding of the transmission of Byzantine philosophical texts written in the eleventh and twelfth centuries is problematic. However, research shows that fourteenth-century scholars could still access eleventh- and twelfth-century material and manuscripts that are now lost to us.[69] Such material is mostly or entirely unknown to modern scholars. In what follows, I present some case studies of twelfth-century Byzantine philosophical texts that have escaped scholarly attention.

The philosophical commentaries written in this period include not only commentaries proper, paraphrases, *epitomai, synopseis, aposemeioseis* and class exercises, but also short treatises devoted to a single passage or a particular section of an ancient text. For example, in the eleventh century, Michael Psellos authored several short explanatory notes on passages from the writings of Gregory of Nazianzos. Later scholars also display this tendency towards brevity in their treatment of philosophical texts. An interesting example is that of a short text on some passages from Aristotle's *Prior Analytics* 2 transmitted in manuscript Paris, Bibliothèque nationale de France, gr. 1917, fols. 70r–73r under the title of *Scholia by the Metropolitan of Nicomedia on some words from* Prior Analytics *2 which run as follows* (Σχόλια τοῦ μητροπολίτου νικομηδείας εἰς ῥητὰ τινὰ ἀπὸ τῶν δευτέρων ἀναλυτικῶν προτέρων τὰ λέγοντα οὕτως).[70] In this case, the Metropolitan of Nicomedia composed a short set of explanatory notes on specific passages from the Aristotelian work at hand, which, according to him, required special attention because of their intricacy. The author of these notes is Niketas of Nicomedia (fl. mid twelfth century), an important theologian who was known for his commitment to defending the Byzantine view on the procession of the Holy Spirit *ex solo Patre*, and who is mentioned as Anna Komnene's personal mystagogue in the *Funeral Oration* composed for her by George Tornikes.[71]

---

[69] Pérez Martín (2013).
[70] There is a reference to the very first part of this material in Brandis (1836: 189a12–20).
[71] George Tornikes, *Funeral Oration for Anna Komnene* 299.30–301.2 ed. Darrouzès. On Niketas, see Podolak (2016). The identification of the Metropolitan of Nicomedia with Niketas has also been proposed by Nesseris (2014: 271).

Par. gr. 1917 (fols. 17r–45r) also preserves Michael of Ephesus' scholia on Aristotle's *De interpretatione*. This material is little known, possibly because Michael himself does not refer to it in his famous list of his commentaries.[72] Part of the scholia has also been transmitted in the fourteenth-century New Haven, Yale University Library, Beinecke 234 (fols. 114r–127v) in the margin to Aristotle's text and in the well-known ninth-/tenth-century Vatican City, Biblioteca Apostolica Vaticana, Urb. gr. 35 (fol. 55r), where a later hand has copied one of the scholia attributed to Michael. Interestingly, in the Parisian manuscript, Michael's scholia are transmitted as a paratext of Leo Magentinos' commentary on the same work.[73] To the best of my knowledge, this particular feature is very uncommon, the advantage being that readers have access to two distinct exegeses (Michael's and Leo's) on each lemma of the Aristotelian text.

Michael's scholia on the Aristotelian work at hand appear to be a set of unconnected notes which were not intended to form a continuous commentary on the text, but rather a series of marginal, explanatory notes useful for understanding Aristotle's *De interpretatione*. In fact, Michael only produced notes when he considered it necessary, skipping passages which in his view needed no clarification. Furthermore, the scholia are mostly excerpts from earlier commentaries which did not have a separate existence from the corresponding lemma in Aristotle's text. In this regard, Michael's scholia on *De interpretatione* differ slightly from his other commentaries, in that the former reflect a more primitive exegetical strategy. That is the reason why, I believe, Michael avoids referring to his scholia on *De interpretatione* as one of the commentaries penned by him: he probably did not conceive this material as something that could be released or 'published', but rather as notes on the Aristotelian text composed for teaching purposes. Evidently, the scribes of this portion of the text in Par. gr. 1917 had access to these notes and copied them to form the paratext to Magentinos' commentary.

My next case study is that of Milan, Biblioteca Ambrosiana, G 62 sup. (Martini-Bassi 404), a fourteenth-century miscellaneous manuscript preserving, among other ancient scientific works, Nicomachus of Gerasa's *Introduction to Arithmetic*. Interestingly, fols. 65v–66r preserve three scholia on a single passage from this work (1.23.15 ed. Hoche) by Michael of Ephesus (*Inc.*: 'διαζευχθείσης' λέγει τὴν μονάδα. *Expl.*: ὁ πρῶτος τῆς ἀπογεννώσης ἐλάττων τῶν ἀπογεννωμένων), Eustratios of Nicaea

---

[72] Cf. Michael of Ephesus, *In Parva naturalia* 149.8–16 ed. Wendland.
[73] On Leo, see Bydén (2010).

(*Inc.*: Ἀφ' ἧς ἀμφότεραι λέγοιτο. *Expl.*: ὥσθ' ἑκατέρωθεν συνῆκται τὸ ἔλαττον) and an otherwise unknown Nicholas Disypatos, here qualified as *krites* (*Inc.*: Εἰπὼν ὁ Νικόμαχος. *Expl.*: εἰ ἀλλ' ἀντὶ τοῦ μένει εἶπεν τὸ εὑρεθήσεται). This material has been known since Tannery (1888: 453), but has been almost entirely neglected by later scholars.[74] There are at least two reasons for stressing the importance of these short notes. First, the scholia concern the same passage of a single ancient work. Second, they are attributed to authors, such as Eustratios and Michael of Ephesus, who are not otherwise known for having commented on Nicomachus' *Introduction*. Were these scholia part of a full commentary on Nicomachus, or were they conceived as isolated explanatory notes on a difficult passage, composed by these Byzantine scholars for didactic purposes? As the case of Niketas of Nicomedia's short note on a passage from *Prior Analytics* 2 demonstrates, this latter possibility is the more probable: that is to say, Eustratios, Michael and the shadowy Nicholas Disypathos composed notes on a passage from Nicomachus' *Introduction*, which may have circulated in the margin of Nicomachus' text and which were later copied by the scribe of the Ambrosianus.[75] Since Michael, Eustratios and perhaps Nicholas lived in the same period and collaborated with each other, the fact that these scholia have been transmitted together may not be accidental after all and might possibly reflect a collective attempt to clarify an obscure passage of the text.

Between Heaven and Earth: Searching for the Philosophical *Bios* in Eleventh- and Twelfth-Century Byzantium

After Pierre Hadot's path-breaking studies, scholars of ancient philosophy agreed by almost unanimous consensus that philosophy in antiquity was not a mere practice of reason, but rather a *bios*, a way of life.[76] Following in the footsteps of Hadot's approach to ancient philosophy, later scholars adapted Hadot's framework to the Middle Ages and determined that philosophy as a *bios* also applies to several medieval philosophers.[77] In this section, I address the question of the identity and self-representation of the Byzantine philosophers and commentators in this period from the point of view of their *bios*.

---

[74] With the exception of Nesseris (2014: 286–9). The scholia have been transmitted in other manuscripts preserving Nicomachus' *Introduction* as well. See Acerbi and Vitrac (2022).
[75] In this respect, I disagree with Nesseris (2014: 287), who seems more inclined to believe that the scholia are what is extant of commentaries on Nicomachus.
[76] See P. Hadot (1981), (1995), (2001). See also Rabbow (1954), Schmid (1995), Horn (2010), Cooper (2012), Sellars (2003) and (2017).
[77] See e.g. Domanski (1996).

My starting point is Michael Psellos' description of his favoured *bios* as a mixed life, in between the divine life of the philosophers and the earthly life of those who indulge in bodily pleasures.[78] Psellos calls this intermediate *bios* 'political' and characterizes it as a mixture of philosophy and rhetoric.[79] In what follows, I argue that Psellos' depiction of his favoured *bios* became normative for several later intellectuals of the Komnenian period.[80] In order to strengthen my point, I will discuss two texts composed in the first half of the twelfth century.

The first of these is the *Timarion*, a well-known, anonymous twelfth-century satirical dialogue that drew inspiration from Lucian's *Menippus* and appropriated the ancient *topos* of the *katabasis* into Hades.[81] One of the key moments is the meeting of the protagonist and Michael Psellos:

Ἐπὶ τούτοις ἦλθε καὶ ὁ Βυζάντιος σοφιστὴς καὶ τοῖς μὲν φιλοσόφοις προσιὼν ἡδέως ἠσπάζετο παρ' αὐτῶν καὶ τὸ 'χαῖρε, Βυζάντιε', πυκνὸν ἐλέγετο· πλὴν ἱστάμενος ὡμίλει τούτοις, καὶ οὔτ' αὐτοὶ τοῦτον ἐκάθιζον οὔτ' αὐτὸς ἐπεβάλλετο. παριὼν δὲ ἐπὶ τοὺς σοφιστάς, διαφερόντως ἐτιμᾶτο καὶ πάντως αὐτῷ ἐξανίσταντο καὶ ἢ μέσον ἐκάθητο πάντων, ὁπότε αὐτὸς ἀφ' ἑαυτοῦ ὤκλαζεν, ἢ πάντων ὑπερεκάθητο ἐκείνων βραβευσάντων τὸ ἕδρασμα, θαυμαζόντων αὐτοῦ τῆς ἀπαγγελίας τὸ χάριεν, τὸ γλυκύ, τὸ σαφὲς τῆς λέξεως, τὸ κοινόν, τὸ σχέδιον τοῦ λόγου καὶ πρόχειρον, τὸ πρὸς πᾶν εἶδος λόγου ἐπιτήδειον καὶ οἰκεῖον· καὶ 'ὦ βασιλεῦ ἥλιε', συχνάκις αὐτῷ ἐπέλεγον. λόγος δὲ οὗτος ἦν αὐτῷ πρὸς βασιλέα πεπονημένος, ὡς ἔμαθον ἐρωτήσας καὶ περὶ τούτου. (*Timarion* 45.1125–35 ed. Romano)

This scene was interrupted by the arrival of the Byzantine rhetor himself. The philosophers greeted him graciously as he drew near to them, and there was much calling out of 'Hail, Byzantine'. But for all that, he had to talk to them standing up, for they made no move to offer him a seat, and he didn't venture to take one uninvited. When he went over to the rhetors, though, it was a very different story. They rose as one man in his honour and gave him an enthusiastic welcome. He could choose to sit down in the middle of their circle if he wanted to relax, or tower over them all in the chair which they offered him as the reward for the gracefulness of his eloquence, the charm and clarity of his diction, his affability, his gift of instant extemporization, his natural skill in every literary genre. They kept hailing him as 'Sun King', which on enquiry I discovered was an allusion to a speech he had composed in the emperor's honour. (after Baldwin trans.)

---

[78] See Jenkins (2006: 143–5), O'Meara (2012), Miles (2014).
[79] See O'Meara (2012: 165), Papaioannou (2012b).
[80] For texts other than the two discussed in this section, see Papaioannou (2012b: 191–4).
[81] On Lucian in Byzantium, see Marciniak (2016). On the *katabasis topos* in Byzantium, see Nilsson (2016) and (2018).

This text is interesting, though difficult to interpret. A superficial reading might suggest inconsistency with Psellos' aforementioned intermediate *bios* between the divine world, represented by philosophy, and earth, represented by rhetoric. However, a closer inspection of the passage suggests, on the contrary, that the anonymous author of *Timarion* actually is true to Psellos' self-representation as an intellectual who lives in between heaven and earth. In order to clarify my point, I return to Psellos. In his *Chronographia* 6.211a8 (ed. Reinsch) and elsewhere, Psellos distinguishes between two different states of the soul, namely between the soul in and of itself, which is separate from the body, and the embodied soul. Psellos defines the life belonging to the first class of souls as divine, whereas the second type is itself divided into different *bioi*: the life of those who give themselves to bodily pleasures and that of those who, by contrast, are capable of moderating their passions. Psellos' favoured *bios* is the latter state, which he calls 'political', in between the divine life of the separate soul and the beastly existence of those who strive for bodily pleasures alone. As has been said before, within this distinction, rhetoric is identified with the political or mundane *bios*, the earthly condition where each man engages in human affairs and, in Psellos' view, acquires social prestige by performing the most human of all activities, namely to articulate discourse in a speech.[82]

With this in mind, it is not difficult to understand why the anonymous author of *Timarion* depicts Psellos as comfortable among his fellow rhetors, as rhetoric corresponds to Psellos' preferred earthly, mundane and human condition. What then about philosophy? The text's characterization of Psellos' relationship with philosophy is extremely interesting. The philosophers greet Psellos with kind words, but they refuse to give him a seat. The text here also adds an important piece of information: Psellos is neither accepted by philosophers, nor does he seek acceptance among them. In my view, this binary signifies the way Psellos' approach to philosophy was perceived a few decades after his death: in short, *Timarion* depicts Psellos as a scholar and passionate reader of philosophical texts who did not want to be perceived as a pure philosopher. If my interpretation is correct, far from contradicting Psellos' own characterization of his intermediate type of life, *Timarion* is quite faithful to it. As a human being, Psellos is an embodied soul that has learned to place the beastly bodily instincts under the control of reason. In this capacity, Psellos does indeed participate in the divine life of the separate souls of the philosophers, yet without assimilating into a purely philosophical *bios*.

---

[82] See O'Meara (2012: 154–5).

By contrast, he finds himself comfortable with a more down-to-earth form of life, a mundane, 'political' existence that articulates itself through the mastering of rhetoric.

The second text is less cryptic. In the *Funeral Oration for Anna Komnene*, the author, George Tornikes, famously describes Anna's philosophical interests. Tornikes writes:

> Πάντας τοίνυν συναγαγοῦσα λογικῶν ἐπιστημῶν προεξάρχοντας – πολλοὶ δὲ ἦσαν οὗτοι καὶ θαυμαστοί· τῶν γὰρ Ἀλεξίου χρόνων ἐγένετο καὶ τοῦτο κατόρθωμα, τοῖς καθ' ἡμέραν τοὺς περὶ λόγους παιδοτριβοῦντας γυμνάσμασι καὶ βασιλικαῖς τιμῶντος τοὺς εὐδοκίμους καὶ δωρεαῖς καὶ τιμαῖς, ἐξ ὧν ὥσπερ καὶ τοῖς ἄλλοις οὕτω καὶ τοῖς λογίοις αἱ ἐπιδόσεις –, οὓς μὲν φιλοσόφους καὶ τὴν γνῶσιν καὶ τοῦ βίου τὴν αἵρεσιν, τοῦτο τέλος θεμένους ἑαυτοῖς σκοπιμώτερον, οὐ χρηματίζεσθαι, οὐκ ἐμπορεύεσθαι, οὐ τιμήν, οὐκ ἀργύριον, συνάγειν δὲ γνῶσιν ἐκ τῶν βιβλίων καὶ διασπείρειν αὖθις ταῖς τῶν θελόντων ψυχαῖς, ἀκόμψοις ῥήμασι μέγαν νοῦν ταῖς ἀκοαῖς καταχέοντας, οὓς δὲ πολιτικοὺς ἅμα καὶ φιλοσόφους καὶ γλώσσῃ περιτρανοὺς καὶ μετὰ τοῦ πλούτου τῆς γνώσεως καὶ τὴν ἑρμηνείαν κομψευομένους καὶ σοφιστεύοντας καὶ λαμπροὺς τά τ' ἔνδον τοῦ λόγου τά τ' ἔξω ῥέοντα. (George Tornikes, *Funeral Oration for Anna Komnene* 281.4–14 ed. Darrouzès)

> So she gathered together all the most eminent representatives of the logical sciences – and they were numerous and remarkable. For this was one of the achievements of the age of Alexios, that among those who taught the young by daily exercises he honoured the most distinguished by gifts and imperial dignities, which were given to men of letters as to others. First were those who were philosophers by their knowledge and their way of life, making this their prime goal rather than money-making or commerce, wealth or office, but rather gathering knowledge from books and spreading it in turn among the souls of those who desired it, and pouring into their ears great wisdom in simple words. Then came those who were at one and the same time men of the world and philosophers and eloquent of tongue, combining wealth of knowledge with elegance of exposition, teachers as brilliant by the content of their thought as by its outward expression. (trans. Browning)

Here Tornikes alludes to two different classes of philosophers. The author first refers to monks – called 'philosophers' because of their asceticism – who are said to preach and deliver sermons in a simple and unadorned style. Then comes the second class of philosophers, described as worldly or secular scholars, who combine wealth of philosophical knowledge with the capacity of articulating it in elegant exposition. Interestingly, when referring to these philosophers, Tornikes uses the word *politikoi* and, just as Psellos did before him, he understands this *bios* as a mixture between philosophy and rhetoric. As an example of this class of scholars, Tornikes refers to none other than Michael of Ephesus.[83]

The evidence collected in this section suggests three conclusions. First, following the authoritative example of Michael Psellos, eleventh- and twelfth-century Byzantine scholars adopted a peculiar strategy of self-representation consisting in a way of life halfway between heaven and earth, the life of a worldly scholar who, on the one hand, deals with the divine matters of philosophy, without being himself pure philosopher, and, on the other, practises rhetoric as a way to ascend the social ladder.

Second, approaching eleventh- and twelfth-century Byzantine commentators from the point of view of self-representation might prove useful for determining their intellectual profile. In this regard, I would like to point out that, as Dominic O'Meara demonstrates, the political life adopted by the Byzantine scholars of this period must be read against the Neoplatonic ladder of virtues, where the political virtues are only a preliminary lower step in the soul's ascent to purification and knowledge.[84] If this is the case, perhaps the traditional understanding of Psellos as a subversive Neoplatonist should be revised. In fact, Psellos' preferred *bios*, the 'political', intermediate life of a scholar who mixes philosophy and rhetoric, corresponds more to the intellectual profile of a scholar of the Second Sophistic than to that of a late antique Neoplatonist.[85] The advantage of the former view over the latter is that it is strongly rooted in what Psellos himself wrote in his works.

Third, adopting a lifestyle-based approach might help us reconsider the traditional way in which eleventh- and twelfth-century Byzantine scholars are understood. Usually, these scholars are all grouped under the ambiguous category of 'humanism'. Yet, when questioning what they consider to be the most suitable *bios*, we can see significant differences among philosophers and intellectuals of this period. Whereas Psellos and others after him chose an intermediate way of life, Eustratios of Nicaea supported a radically ascetical *bios*, on the basis of Christian and Neoplatonic sources, that clearly does not fit the intellectual type Psellos influentially created.[86]

---

[83] George Tornikes, *Funeral Oration for Anna Komnene* 283.9–12 ed. Darrouzès. On the notion of the 'political' or, perhaps better, 'civic' philosopher in the Middle Byzantine period, see Papaioannou (2013: 29–50).

[84] O'Meara (2012: 156–8).

[85] Literature on the importance of rhetoric in combination with philosophy in the Second Sophistic is vast. See the introductory Whitmarsh (2005: 19–40). For obvious reasons, there is no room here to discuss the crucial issue of Psellos' Neoplatonism. For a useful introduction, see Miles (2017).

[86] See Trizio (2016: 199–223).

The example of Eustratios suggests that, when considered from the point of view of the authors' self-representation, our understanding of the Byzantine intellectual history of this period changes quite significantly. In other words, I believe that, in discussions about the authorial strategies displayed by the Byzantine philosopher and commentators of this period, we should adopt an inclusive notion of authorship that encompasses also the commentators' preferred *bios* and self-representation as scholars.

Conclusion: Wearing Aristotelian Clothes to a Wedding

I conclude my chapter by recalling some memories from a wedding scene. Around 1120 Theodore Prodromos authored a prose *epithalamium* to celebrate the wedding of two of Anna Komnene's sons with foreign princesses. This text has recently been re-evaluated by Leonora Neville in order to show that, contrary to the current narrative, Anna's relationship with her brother, the emperor John II Komnenos, was not as bad as the Byzantine sources suggest.[87] Leaving this issue aside, I believe that Prodromos' description of Anna is important in its own right, because it contains some key allusions to Anna's philosophical interests. The text runs as follows:

> εἴ τί που καὶ ἀληθεύουσιν Ἕλληνες, τετάρτην μὲν ταῖς Χάρισι Χάριτα, δεκάτην δὲ ταῖς Μούσαις Μοῦσαν προσεπιθείημεν, ἢ τὴν μὲν κατ' ἦθος ὅλην φιλοσοφίαν, ἧς οὐ γνῶσις ἀλλὰ πρᾶξις τὸ τέλος, αὐτὴ ἑαυτὴν διὰ τῆς κατ' ἀρετὴν ἐνεργείας ἐμυσταγώγησεν· ἔπειτα γενναιότερόν τε ὁμοῦ φρονήσασα καὶ βασιλικώτερον καὶ κόσμον οἰηθεῖσα ὥσπερ βασιλικοῦ σώματος τὴν πορφύραν, οὕτω καὶ ψυχῆς βασιλικῆς τὴν ἐπιστήμην τῶν ὄντων, τὴν γνῶσιν αὐτῶν ἐτελέσθη καὶ τὴν ἐν τούτοις ἀλήθειαν ἐθηράσατο καὶ προαιρέσεως οὐ γένους ἔδειξεν εἶναι κτῆμα. (Theodore Prodromos, *Epithalamium for the Sons of the Most Blessed Caesar* 347.24–9 ed. Gautier)

And if the Hellenes really spoke some truth, we may add her as a fourth Grace among the Graces and as a tenth Muse among the Muses, for she initiated herself through the forces of virtue to the whole moral philosophy, whose end is not knowledge but action. Then, both more nobly considering and more royally thinking that, just as the colour purple [is the] adornment of the royal body, so too the science of being [is the adornment] of the royal soul, she was introduced into knowledge of these matters and

---

[87] Neville (2016: 118).

she hunted the truth in them. She showed virtue to be an acquisition, not family. (after Neville trans. [2016: 118])

Here Prodromos singles out Anna's character within the broader portrait of the royal wedding and provides readers with two hints about Anna's fondness for Aristotle's *Nicomachean Ethics* as well as her patronage of Eustratios and Michael, the two commentators of books 1, 5, 6, 9 and 10 of this Aristotelian work.[88] These hints are the reference to moral philosophy as a discipline whose goal is *praxis* rather than knowledge and the idea that virtue is not inborn, but is rather something we acquire over time by practising virtuous actions. Since Aristotle discusses those issues in books 1, 2 and 6 of the *Nicomachean Ethics*, when the *epithalamium* was read aloud, the audience undoubtedly must have easily recognized the meaning of these allusions.

With regard to the production of philosophical commentaries written in this period, modern scholars certainly face great challenges. These concern, for instance, the material aspects of the textual transmission of eleventh- and twelfth-century commentaries; the difficulty in determining the intended audience of a given commentary; and, finally, the difficulty in reconstructing in detail the scholarly networks involved in the production of these commentaries. In this chapter, I have isolated these problems and collected the available material required for facing the challenges involved in writing the history of Byzantine philosophical commentaries composed under the Komnenoi.

My first point is that commentaries do not merely attempt to clarify the ancient philosophical texts, but also address contemporary questions of meaning. This is evident, for instance, in Eustratios of Nicaea's commentaries on Aristotle. On the one hand, Eustratios inherits several features of the late antique commentaries written by Simplikios and others; on the other hand, he introduces elements that are not present in the earlier commentary tradition and thus contributes to establishing the Byzantine approach to commenting on Aristotle's works.

My second point concerns the Byzantine commentators' self-representation. Starting with Michael Psellos in the eleventh century, a consistent group of later Byzantine intellectuals pledge allegiance to an intermediate way of life in between the grievous life of those who only pursue bodily pleasures and the extreme asceticism pursued by Byzantine monks. The life of the civic or political philosopher is attributed to

---

[88] On Anna and the *Nicomachean Ethics*, see Frankopan (2009).

Michael Psellos in the early twelfth-century Lucianesque *Timarion* and is attributed to the commentator Michael of Ephesus in the funeral oration for Anna Komnene written after 1153 by George Tornikes. This particular *bios* exemplifies the life of those who combine skills in philosophical literature with rhetoric. Yet, not all Byzantine commentators in this period share this mixed way of life. Eustratios of Nicaea, for instance, identifies the best possible type of life as monasticism and contradicts the general trend initiated by Michael Psellos. This demonstrates that the front of the so-called 'humanists' was far more diversified than has previously been thought.

My third and final point concerns the social impact of philosophical literature on patrons and clients. The case of Anna Komnene's patronage of the Byzantine commentators on Aristotle's *Nicomachean Ethics* is extremely interesting in this regard. Anna is thought to have commissioned the composition of various commentaries on the ten books of this Aristotelian work at the time of her retirement to private life, after 1118. This account has been challenged recently, but no matter what the truth of this is, it is clear that Anna's patronage had an immediate impact on public perception of her. While commenting on the wedding scene, Theodore Prodromos describes Anna's scholarship as a part of her public persona. Anna is portrayed as a living monument of Aristotle's *Nicomachean Ethics*, as if her patronage of Eustratios and Michael were something well known to the wider public. Thus, I believe that Prodromos' portrait of Anna and its implications are a fine summary of the subjects discussed in the present chapter. In my view, the different methodologies employed by Michael Psellos, John Italos, Theodore of Smyrna, Eustratios and Michael of Ephesus do not simply reflect differences in authorial strategies for the composition of philosophical commentaries; on the contrary, they reflect the commentators' and patrons' need to determine their own social and literary identity in an environment where competition must have been cruel.

REFERENCES

Acerbi, F. and B. Vitrac (2022) 'Les mathématiques de Michel d'Éphèse', *RÈB* 80.

Agapitos, P. A. (1998) 'Teachers, Pupils and Imperial Power in Byzantium of the Eleventh-Century', in *Pedagogy and Power: Rhetorics of Classical Learning*, ed. Y. L. Too and N. Livingstone, 170–91. Ideas in Context 50. Cambridge.

(2017) 'John Tzetzes and the Blemish Examiners: A Byzantine Teacher on Schedography, Everyday Language and Writerly Disposition', *MEG* 17: 1–57.

Alexander, L. A. (1990) 'The Living Voice: Scepticism Towards the Written Word in Early Christian and in Graeco-Roman Texts', in *The Bible in*

Three Dimensions: Essays in Celebration of Forty Years of Biblical Studies in the University of Sheffield, ed. D. J. A. Clines, S. E. Fowl and S. E. Porter, 221–47. Sheffield.

Anastasi, R. (1976) 'Sulla tradizione manoscritta delle opere di Psello', in *Studi di filologia bizantina, Siculorum Gymnasium* 2: 61–91.

Baltussen, H. (2007) 'From Polemic to Exegesis: The Ancient Philosophical Commentary', *Poetics Today* 28.2: 247–81.

(2008) *Philosophy and Exegesis in Simplicius: The Methodology of a Commentator.* London–New Delhi–New York–Sydney.

Bardy, G. (ed.) (1952–8) *Eusèbe de Césarée, Histoire ecclésiastique*, 3 vols. Paris.

Baudry, J. (ed.) (1931) *Atticos: Fragments de son œuvre.* Paris.

Benakis, L. (ed.) (2013) *Theodore of Smyrna, Epitome of Nature and Natural Principles according to the Ancients: Editio princeps. Introduction, Text, Indices.* Athens.

Brandis, C. A. (1836) *Aristotelis opera IV: Scholia in Aristotelem.* Berlin.

Bianchi, L. (2013) 'Couper, distinguer, compléter: trois stratégies de lecture d'Aristote à la Faculté des arts', in *Les débuts de l'enseignement universitaire à Paris (1200–1245 environ)*, ed. J. Verger and O. Weijers, 133–52. Turnhout.

Bianconi, D. (2004) 'Eracle e Iolao: aspetti della collaborazione tra copisti nell'età dei paleologi', *ByzZ* 96: 521–58.

(2005) 'La biblioteca di Cora tra Massimo Planude e Niceforo Gregora: una questione di mani', *S&T* 3: 391–438.

(2008) 'La controversia palamitica: figure, libri, testi, mani', *S&T* 6: 337–76.

(2017) 'La lettura dei testi antichi tra didattica ed erudizione: qualche esempio d'età paleologa', in *Toward a Historical Sociolinguistic Poetics of Medieval Greek*, ed. A. M. Cuomo and E. Trapp, 57–83. Byzantios: Studies in Byzantine History and Civilization 12. Turnhout.

Botha, P. J. J. (2012) *Orality and Literacy in Early Christianity.* Eugene, OR.

Bouras-Vallianatos, P., with contributions by S. Xenophontos (2015) 'Galen's Reception in Byzantium: Symeon Seth and His Refutation of Galenic Theories on Human Physiology', *GRBS* 55: 431–69.

(2018) 'Reading Galen in Byzantium: The Fate of *Therapeutics to Glaucon*', in *Greek Medical Literature and Its Readers: From Hippocrates to Islam and Byzantium*, ed. P. Bouras-Vallianatos and S. Xenophontos, 180–229. Abingdon–New York.

Browning, R. (1962a) 'The Patriarchal School at Constantinople in the Twelfth Century', *Byzantion* 32: 167–201.

(1962b) 'An Unpublished Funeral Oration on Anna Comnena', *PCPhS* 188: 1–12.

(1963) 'The Patriarchal School at Constantinople in the Twelfth Century', *Byzantion* 33: 11–40.

(1981) *Church, State and Learning in Twelfth-Century Byzantium.* Friends of Dr. William's Library, Thirty-Fourth Lecture, 5–24. London.

Budelmann, F. (2002) 'Classical Commentary in Byzantium: John Tzetzes on Ancient Greek Literature', in *The Classical Commentary: Histories, Practices, Theory*, ed. R. K. Gibson and C. S. Kraus, 141–69. Mnemosyne Supplements 232. Leiden–Boston–Cologne.

Busse, A. (ed.) (1895) *Ammonius, In Aristotelis categorias commentarius*. Berlin.

(1897) *Ammonius, In librum de interpretatione commentarius*. Berlin.

Bydén, B. (2010) 'Leo Magentenos', in *Encyclopedia of Medieval Philosophy*, ed. H. Lagerlund, 684–5. Dordrecht–Heidelberg–London–New York.

(2013) '"No Prince of Perfection": Byzantine Anti-Aristotelianism from the Patristic Period to Plethon', in *Power and Subversion in Byzantium. Papers from the 43rd Annual Spring Symposium of Byzantine Studies*, ed. D. Angelov and M. Saxby, 147–76. Farnham.

(2018) 'Introduction: The Study and Reception of Aristotle's *Parva Naturalia*', in *The Parva Naturalia in Greek, Arabic and Latin Aristotelianism*, ed. B. Bydén and F. Radovic, 1–50. Cham.

Cacouros, M. (1997) 'Jean Chortasménos, "katholikos didaskalos": contribution à l'histoire de l'enseignement à Byzance', in *Synodia: Studia humanitatis Antonio Garzya septuagenario ab amicis atque discipulis dicata*, ed. U. Criscuolo and R. Maisano, 83–107. Naples.

Cavallo, G. (2000) 'Scritture informali, cambio grafico e pratiche librarie a Bisanzio tra i secoli XI e XII', in *I manoscritti greci tra riflessione e dibattito. Atti del V Colloquio internazionale di paleografia greca, Cremona, 4–10 ottobre 1998*, ed. G. Prato, 219–38. Florence.

(2002) 'Conservazione e perdita dei testi greci: fattori materiali, sociali, culturali', in *Dalla parte del libro: storia di trasmissione dei classici*, ed. G. Cavallo, 49–176. Urbino.

(2010a) 'Sodalizi eruditi e pratiche di scrittura a Bisanzio', in *Bilan et perspectives des études médiévales (1993–1998). Euroconférence (Barcelone, 8–12 juin 1999); Actes du IIe Congrès Européen d'Etudes Médiévales*, ed. J. Hamesse, 645–65. Turnhout.

(2010b) 'Oralità scrittura libro lettura: appunti su usi e contesti didattici tra antichità e Bisanzio', in *Libri di scuola e pratiche didattiche dall'Antichità al Rinascimento. Atti del Convegno Internazionale di Studi Cassino, 7–10 maggio 2008*, ed. L. Del Corso and O. Pecere, vol. I: 11–36. Cassino.

Cesaretti, P. (1991) *Allegoristi di Omero a Bisanzio: ricerche ermeneutiche (XI–XII secolo)*. Milan.

Constantinides, C. N. (1982) *Higher Education in Byzantium in the Thirteenth and Early Fourteenth Centuries, 1204–c. 1310*. Nicosia.

Cooper, J. M. (2012) *Pursuits of Wisdom: Six Ways of Life in Ancient Philosophy from Socrates to Plotinus*. Princeton.

D'Ancona, C. (2001) 'Commenting on Aristotle: From Late Antiquity to the Arab Aristotelianism', in *Der Kommentar in Antike und Mittelalter: Beiträge zu seiner Erforschung*, ed. W. Geerlings and C. Schulze, 200–51. Boston–Leiden–Cologne.

Darrouzès, J. (ed.) (1970) *Georges et Dèmètrios Tornikès, lettres et discours: introduction, texte, analyses, traduction et notes.* Paris.
Del Punta, F. (1998) 'The Genre of Commentaries in the Middle Ages and Its Relation to the Nature and Originality of Medieval Thought', in *Was ist Philosophie im Mittelalter*, ed. A. Speer and J. A. Aertsen, 138–51. Berlin.
Diehl, E. (ed.) (1903) *Procli Diadochi in Platonis Timaeum commentaria.* Leipzig.
Diels, H. (ed.) (1882) *Simplicius, In Aristotelis physicorum libros quattuor priores.* Berlin.
 (ed.) (1895) *Simplicius, In Aristotelis physicorum libros quattuor posteriores.* Berlin.
Dölger, F. (1940) 'Zur Bedeutung von φιλόσοφος und φιλοσοφία in byzantinischer Zeit', in Τεσσαρακοταετηρίς θεοφίλου Βορέα, vol. 1: 125–36. Athens.
Domanski, J. (1996) *La philosophie: théorie ou manière de vivre?* Fribourg.
Donini, P. (1968) 'Il *De anima* di Alessandro di Afrodisia e Michele Efesio', *RFIC* 96: 316–23.
Döring, K. (1979) *Exemplum Socratis: Studien zur Sokratesnachwirkung in der kynisch-stoischen Popularphilosophie der frühen Kaiserzeit und im frühen Christentum.* Wiesbaden.
Droge, A. and J. Tabor. (1992) *A Noble Death: Suicide and Martyrdom among Christians and Jews in Antiquity.* San Francisco.
Ebbesen, S. (1981) *Commentators and Commentaries on Aristotle's Sophistici Elenchi: A Study of Post-Aristotelian Ancient and Medieval Writings on Fallacies*, vol. 1: *The Greek Tradition*, Leiden.
 (2002) 'Late-Ancient Ancestors of Medieval Philosophical Commentaries', in *Il commento filosofico nell'occidente latino (secoli XIII–XV)*, ed. G. Fioravanti, C. Leonardi and S. Perfetti, 1–15. Turnhout.
Edwards, M. (2007) 'Socrates and the Early Church', in *Socrates from Antiquity to the Enlightenment*, ed. M. Trapp, 127–42. Aldershot.
Escobar, A. (1990) 'Die Textgeschichte der aristotelischen Schrift *De insomniis*: Ein Beitrag zur Überlieferungsgeschichte der *Parva naturalia*', unpublished PhD thesis, Free University of Berlin.
Festugiere, A. J. (1969) 'L'ordre de lecture des dialogues de Platon aux Ve/VIe siècles', *MH* 26: 281–96.
Förstel, C. (2011) 'Metochites and His Books between the Chora and the Renaissance', in *The Kariye Camii Reconsidered / Kariye Camii Yeniden, Istanbul Arastirmalari Enstitusu*, ed. H. A. Klein, R. Ousterhout and B. Pitarakis, 241–66. Istanbul.
Frankopan, P. (2009) 'The Literary, Cultural and Political Context for the Twelfth-Century Commentary on the *Nicomachean Ethics*', in *Medieval Greek Commentaries on the Nicomachean Ethics*, ed. C. Barber and D. Jenkins, 45–62. Leiden–Boston.
Fuchs, F. (1926) *Die höheren Schulen von Konstantinopel im Mittelalter.* Leipzig.
Gamillscheg, E. (2006) 'Johannes Chortasmenos als Restaurator des Wiener Dioskurides', *Biblos* 55.2: 35–40.

Garland, L. (2017) 'Mary "of Alania", Anna Komnene, and the Revival of Aristotelianism in Byzantium', *ByzSlav* 75.1–2: 123–63.

Gaul, N. (2011) *Thomas Magistros und die spätbyzantische Sophistik: Studien zum Humanismus urbaner Eliten der frühen Palaiologenzeit*. Wiesbaden.

Gautier, P. (ed.) (1975) *Theodore Prodromos, Epithalamium fortunatissimis caesaris filiis*, in *Nicéphore Bryennios, Histoire*, 341–55. Brussels.

Giannantoni, G. (1986²) *Socrate, tutte le testimonianze: da Aristofane e Senofonte ai padri cristiani*, second revised edition. Rome–Bari.

Giokarinis, K. (1964) 'Eustratius of Nicaea's Defense of the Doctrine of Ideas', *Franciscan Studies* 12: 159–204.

Golitsis, P. (2008) *Les Commentaires de Simplicius et de Jean Philopon à la Physique d'Aristote*. Berlin–New York.

(2010) 'Copistes, élèves et érudits: la production de manuscrits philosophiques autour de Georges Pachymère', in *The Legacy of Bernard de Montfaucon: Three Hundred Years of Studies on Greek Handwriting. Proceedings of the Seventh International Colloquium of Greek Palaeography (Madrid–Salamanca, 15–20 September 2008)*, ed. A. Bravo Garcia and I. Pérez Martín, 157–70. Turnhout.

(2014) 'Trois annotations de manuscrits aristotéliciens au XIIe siècle: les Parisini gr. 1901 et 1853 et l'Oxoniensis Corporis Christi 108', in *Storia della scrittura ed altre storie*, ed. D. Bianconi, 33–52. Rome.

(2018) 'Michel d'Éphèse', in *Dictionnaire des philosophes antiques*, vol. 7, ed. R. Goulet, 609–16. Paris.

Gouillard, J. (1985) 'Le procès officiel de Jean l'Italien: les actes et leurs sous-entendues', *T&MByz* 9: 133–74.

Goulet-Cazé, M.-O. (1982) 'Le programme d'enseignement dans les Écoles néolatonicienne', in *Porphyre, La vie de Plotin*, vol. 1, ed. L. Brisson, M.-O. Goulet-Cazé, R. Goulet and D. O'Brien; preface by Jean Pépin, 277–80. Paris.

Goulet, R. (2007) 'La conservation et la transmission des textes philosophiques Grecs', in *The Library of the Neoplatonists*, ed. C. D'Ancona, 29–62. Leiden–Boston.

Grünbart, M. (2014) 'Paideia Connects: The Interaction between Teachers and Pupils in Twelfth-Century Byzantium', in *Networks of Learning: Perspectives on Scholars in Byzantine East and Latin West, c. 1000–1200*, ed. S. Steckel, N. Gaul and M. Grünbart, 17–31. Zurich–Berlin.

Hadot, I. (1987a) 'Les introductions aux commentaires exégétiques chez les auteurs néoplatoniciens et les auteurs chrétiens', in *Les règles de l'interprétation*, ed. M. Tardieu, 99–122. Paris.

(1987b) 'La division neoplatonicienne des écrits d'Aristote', in *Aristoteles: Werk und Wirkung. Paul Moraux gewidmet*, vol. 2, ed. J. Wiesner, 63–93. Berlin–New York.

(1991) 'The Role of the Commentaries on Aristotle in the Teaching of Philosophy According to the Prefaces of the Neoplatonic Commentaries on the *Categories*', in *Aristotle and the Later Tradition*, ed. H. Blumenthal and H. Robinson, 175–89. Oxford.

(1992) 'Aristote dans l'enseignement philosophique néoplatonicien: les préfaces des commentaires sur les Categories', *RThPh* 124: 407–25.

Hadot, P. (1981) *Exercices spirituels et philosophie antique*. Paris.

(1990) 'The Harmony of Plotinus and Aristotle According to Porphyry', in *Aristotle Transformed*, ed. R. Sorabji, 125–40. Ithaca, NY.

(1995) *Qu'est-ce que la philosophie antique?* Paris.

(2001) *La Philosophie comme manière de vivre*. Paris.

Hayduck, M. (ed.) (1882) *Simplicius, In libros Aristotelis de anima commentaria*. Berlin.

(ed.) (1888) *Asclepius, In Aristotelis metaphysicorum libros A–Z commentaria*. Berlin.

(ed.) (1891) *Alexander Aphrodisiensis, In Aristotelis metaphysica commentaria*. Berlin.

(ed.) (1897) *Ioannis Philoponi in Aristotelis de anima libros commentaria*. Berlin.

(ed.) (1901) *Ioannis Philoponi in Aristotelis meteorologicorum librum primum commentarium*. Berlin.

(ed.) (1904) *Michaelis Ephesii in libros De partibus animalium, De animalium motione, De animalium incessu commentaria*. Berlin.

(ed.) (1907) *Eustratii in analyticorum posteriorum librum secundum commentarium*. Berlin.

Heiberg, J. L. (ed.) (1894) *Simplicius, In Aristotelis de caelo commentaria*. Berlin.

Helmreich, G. (ed.) (1923) *Galeni De alimentorum facultatibus libri III*. Berlin.

Heylbut, G. (ed.) (1889) *Eustratii et Michaelis et Anonyma in ethica Nicomachea commentaria*. Berlin.

Hoffmann, P. (1987) 'Simplicius' Polemics', in *Philoponus and the Rejection of Aristotelian Science*, ed. R. Sorabji, 57–83. Ithaca, NY.

(1998) 'La fonction des prologues exégétiques dans la pensée pédagogique néoplatonicienne', in *Entrer en matière*, ed. B. Roussel and J.-D. Dubois, 209–45. Paris.

(2009) 'What Was Commentary in Late Antiquity? The Example of the Neoplatonic Commentators', in *A Companion to Ancient Philosophy*, ed. M. L. Gill and P. Pellegrin, 597–622. West Sussex.

Horn, C. (2010) *Antike Lebenskunst: Glück und Moral von Sokrates bis zu den Neuplatonikern*. Munich.

Hunger, H. (1957) 'Johannes Chortasmenos, ein byzantinischer Intellektueller der späten Palaiologenzeit', *WS* 70: 153–63.

Hunger, H., O. Kresten and C. Hannick (1984) *Katalog der griechischen Handschriften der Österreichischen Nationalbibliothek 3,2: Codices theologici 101–200*. Vienna.

Ierodiakonou, K. (2002) 'Psellos' Paraphrase on Aristotle's *De interpretatione*', in *Byzantine Philosophy and Its Ancient Sources*, ed. K. Ierodiakonou, 157–81. Oxford.

(2012) 'The Byzantine Commentator's Task: Transmitting, Transforming or Transcending Aristotle's Text', in *Knotenpunkt Byzanz: Wissensformen und*

kulturelle Wechselbeziehungen, ed. A. Speer and P. Steinkrüger, 199–209. Berlin–Boston.
Jenkins, D. (2006) 'Psellos' Conceptual Precision', in *Reading Michael Psellos*, ed. C. Barber and D. Jenkins, 131–51. Leiden–Boston.
Joannou, P. (ed.) (1956) *Quaestiones quodlibetales (Ἀπορίαι καὶ λύσεις)*. Ettal.
Kalbfleisch, K. (ed.) (1907) *Simplicius, In Aristotelis Categorias commentarium*. Berlin.
Kaldellis, A. (2009) 'Classical Scholarship in Twelfth-Century Byzantium', in *Medieval Greek Commentaries on the Nicomachean Ethics*, ed. C. Barber and D. Jenkins, 1–43. Leiden–Boston.
Karamanolis, G. (2006) *Plato and Aristotle in Agreement? Platonists on Aristotle from Antiochus to Porphyry*. Oxford.
Koch, L. (2015) 'Τὸ τῆς λέξεως συνεχές: Michael von Ephesos und die Rezeption der Aristotelischen Schrift *De motu animalium* in Byzanz', unpublished PhD thesis, University of Hamburg.
Kraus, C. S. (2002) 'Introduction: Reading Commentaries/Commentaries as Reading', in *The Classical Commentary: Histories, Practices, Theory*, ed. R. K. Gibson and C. S. Kraus, 1–27. Mnemosyne Supplements 232. Leiden–Boston–Cologne.
Kühn, K. G. (ed.) (1826–7) *Claudii Galeni opera XII–XIII*. Leipzig.
Leclercq, J. (1952) 'Pour l'histoire de l'expression "philosophie chrétienne"', *MSR* 9: 221–6.
Lemerle, P. (1971) *Le premier humanisme byzantin: notes et remarques sur enseignement et culture à Byzance des origines au Xe siècle*. Paris.
 (1977) *Cinq études sur le XIe siècle byzantine*. Paris.
Lilla, S. (1985) *Codices Vaticani Graeci: Codices 2162–2254 (codices Columnenses)*. Vatican City.
MacAlister, S. (1996) *Dreams and Suicides: The Greek Novel from Antiquity to the Byzantine Empire*. London.
Malingray, A. M. (1961) *'Philosophia': étude d'un groupe de mots dans la literature grecque, des Présocratiques au IV siecle après J.C.* Paris.
Marciniak, P. (2007) 'Byzantine *Theatron* – A Place of Performance?', in *Theatron: Rhetorische Kultur in Spätantike und Mittelalter / Rhetorical Culture in Late Antiquity and the Middle Ages*, ed. M. Grünbart, 277–85. Millennium-Studien 13. Berlin–New York.
 (2016) 'Reinventing Lucian in Byzantium', *DOP* 70: 209–24.
Markopoulos A. (2006) 'De la structure de l'école byzantine: le maître, les livres et le processus éducatif', in *Lire et écrire à Byzance*, ed. B. Mondrain, 85–96. Centre de recherche d'Histoire et Civilisation de Byzance: Monographies 19. Paris.
 (2013a) 'In Search for "Higher Education" in Byzantium', *Zbornik Radova Vyzantoloskog Instituta* 50.1: 28–44.
 (2013b) 'Teachers and Textbooks in Byzantium, Ninth to Eleventh Centuries', in *Networks of Learning: Perspectives on Scholars in Byzantine East and Latin*

West, c. 1000–1200, ed. S. Steckel, N. Gaul and M. Grünbart, 3–15. Zurich–Berlin.

Menchelli, M. (2010) 'Cerchie aristoteliche e letture platoniche (Manoscritti di Platone, Aristotele e commentatori)', in *The Legacy of Bernard de Montfaucon: Three Hundred Years of Studies on Greek Handwriting. Proceedings of the Seventh International Colloquium of Greek Palaeography (Madrid–Salamanca, 1–20 September 2008)*, ed. A. Bravo Garcia and I. Pérez Martin, 493–502 and 891–7. Turnhout.

Mercati, G. (1915) 'Fra i commentatori greci di Aristotele', *MEFRA* 35: 191–219.

Mercati, G. and F. de' Cavalieri (1923) *Codices Vaticani Graeci*, Tomus I: *Codices 1–329*. Rome.

Mercken, H. F. P. (1990) 'The Greek Commentators on Aristotle's Ethics', in *Aristotle Transformed: The Ancient Commentators and Their Influence*, ed. R. Sorabji, 407–43. Ithaca, NY.

Mergiali, S. (1996) *L'enseignement et les lettrés pendant l'époque des Paléologues (1261–1453)*. Athens.

Miles, G. (2014) 'Living as a Sphinx: Composite Being and Monstrous Interpreter in the Middle Life of Michael Pellos', in *Conjunctions of Mind, Soul and Body from Plato to the Enlightenment*, ed. D. Kambaskovic, 11–24. New York.

 (2017) 'Psellos and His Traditions', in *Byzantine Perspectives on Neoplatonism*, ed. S. Mariev, 79–102. Berlin–Boston.

Mondrain, B. (2000) 'La constitution de corpus d'Aristote et de ses commentateurs aux XIIIe–XIVe siècles', *CodMan* 29: 11–33.

Mournet, T. C. (2005) *Oral Tradition and Literary Dependency*. Tübingen.

Németh, A. (2014) 'Fragments from the Earliest Parchment Manuscript of Eustratius' Commentary on Aristotle's *Nicomachean Ethics*', *RHT* 9: 51–78.

Nesseris, I. (2014) 'Η Παιδεία στην Κωνσταντινούπολη κατά τον 12° αιώνα', unpublished PhD thesis, University of Ioannina.

Neville, L. (2016) *Anna Komnene: The Life and Work of a Medieval Historian*. Oxford.

Nilsson, I. (2016) 'Poets and Teachers in the Underworld: From the Lucianic katabasis to the *Timarion*', *SO* 90.1: 180–204.

 (2018) 'Hades Meets Lazarus: The Literary *Katabasis* in Twelfth-Century Byzantium', in *Roundtrip to Hades: Visits to the Underworld in the Eastern Mediterranean Tradition*, ed. G. Ekroth and I. Nilsson, 322–41. Leiden.

Nutton, V. (2007) 'Galen in Byzantium', in *Material Culture and Well-Being in Byzantium (400–1453)*, ed. M. Grünbart, E. Kislinger, A. Muthesius and D. Stathakopoulos, 171–6. Vienna.

O'Meara, D. J. (2012) 'Political Philosophy in Michael Psellos: The *Chronographia* Read in Relation to His Philosophical Work', in *The Many Faces of Byzantine Philosophy*, ed. K. Ierodiakonou and B. Bydén, 153–70. Papers and Monographs from the Norwegian Institute at Athens Series 4.1. Athens.

Orsini, P. (2005) 'Pratiche collettive di scrittura a Bisanzio nei secoli IX e X', *S&T* 3: 265–342.
Papadogiannakis, Y. (2013) *Christianity and Hellenism in the Fifth-Century Greek East: Theodoret's Apologetics against the Greeks in Context*. Cambridge, MA.
Papaioannou, S. (2012a) 'Fragile Literature: Byzantine Letter-Collections and the Case of Michael Psellos', in *La face cachée de la littérature byzantine: le texte en tant que message immédiat. Actes du colloque international (Paris, juin 2008)*, ed. P. Odorico, 289–328. Dossiers Byzantins 11. Paris.
  (2012b) 'Rhetoric and the Philosopher in Byzantium', in *The Many Faces of Byzantine Philosophy*, ed. K. Ierodiakonou and B. Bydén, 171–98. Papers and Monographs from the Norwegian Institute at Athens Series 4.1. Athens.
  (2013) *Michael Psellos: Rhetoric and Authorship in Byzantium*. Cambridge.
Penco G. (1960) 'La vita ascetica come "filosofia" nell'antica tradizione monastica', *StudMon* 2: 79–93.
Pérez Martín, I. (1997) 'El *scriptorium* de Cora: un modelo de acercamiento a los centros de copia Byzantinos', in *Epigeios-Ouranos-El cielo en la tierra: estudio sobre el monasterio Byzantinos*, ed. P. Bádenas, A. Bravo and I. Pérez Martín, 203–24. Madrid.
  (2013) 'The Transmission of Some Writings by Psellos in Thirteenth-Century Constantinople', in *Theologica Minora: The Minor Genres of Byzantine Theological Literature*, ed. A. Rigo, 159–74. Turnhout.
Pizzone, A. (2016) 'Emotions and Audiences in Eustathios of Thessaloniki's Commentaries on Homer', *DOP* 70: 225–44.
  (2017) 'Tzetzes' *Historiai*: A Byzantine "Book of Memory"?', *BMGS* 41.2: 182–207.
Podolak, O. A. (2016) 'Nicetas Archbishop of Nicomedia: A Forgotten Figure in the Twelfth-Century Controversy Surrounding the Filioque', *RSBN* 53: 151–72.
Podskalsky, G. (1977) *Theologie und Philosophie in Byzanz: Der Streit um die theologische Methodik in der spätbyzantinischen Geistgeschichte (14./15. Jh.), seine systematischen Grundlagen und seine historische Entwicklung*. Munich.
Polemis, I. (2014) *Michael Psellos, Orationes funebres*, vol. 1. Berlin.
Powell, O. (2003) *Galen, On the Properties of Foodstuffs*. Cambridge.
Praechter, K. (1906) 'Compte rendu de M. Hayduck (éd.), Michaelis Ephesii in Libros De partibus animalium, De animalium motione, De animalium incessu. Commentaria in Aristotelem Graeca XXII 2', *GGA* 168: 861–907.
Protogirou, S.-A. (2014) 'Ρητορική θεατρικότητα στο έργο του Μιχαήλ Ψελλού' (Rhetoric and Theatrality in the Work of Michael Psellos), unpublished PhD thesis, University of Cyprus.
Rabbow, P. (1954) *Seelenführung: Methodik der Exercitien in der Antike*. Munich.
Rabe, H. (ed.) (1896) *Anonymi et Stephani in Artem rhetoricam commentaria*. Berlin.
Reinsch, D. R. (ed.) (2014) *Michaelis Pselli Cronographia*. Berlin–New York.
Richard, M. (1950) 'Ἀπὸ φωνῆς', *Byzantion* 20: 191–222.

Rigo, A. (2006) 'Giovanni Italos commentatore della Gerarchia celeste dello pseudo-Dionigi l'Areopagita', *Nea Rhome* 3: 223–32.
Romano, R. (1974) *Pseudo-Luciano, Timarione: testo critico, introduzione, traduzione, commentario e lessico*. Naples.
Roilos, P. (2005) *Amphoteroglossia: A Poetics of the Twelfth-Century Medieval Greek Novel*. Washington, DC.
Ronconi, F. (2011) 'Le silence des livres: manuscrits philosophiques et circulation des idées à l'époque byzantine moyenne', *Quaestio* 11: 169–207.
Schmid, W. (1995) 'Selbstsorge: Zur Biographie eines Begriffs', in *Zur Grundlegung einer integrativen Ethik*, ed. M. Endreß, 98–129. Frankfurt.
Sellars, J. (2003) *The Art of Living: The Stoics on the Nature and Function of Philosophy*. Aldershot.
  (2017) 'What Is Philosophy as a Way of Life?', *Parrhesia* 28: 40–56.
Ševčenko, I. (1964) 'Some Autographs of Nicephorus Gregoras', in *Mélanges Georges Ostrogorsky*, vol. 2, ed. F. Barišić, 435–50. Belgrade.
  (1975) 'Theodore Metochites, the Chora, and the Intellectual Trends of His Time', in *The Kariye Drami*, vol. 4: *Studies in the Art of the Kariye Djami and Its Intellectual Background*, ed. P. A. Underwood, 19–91. Princeton.
Siniossoglou, N. (2008) *Plato and Theodoret: The Christian Appropriation of Platonic Philosophy and the Hellenic Intellectual Resistance*. Cambridge.
Sorabji, R. (2005) *The Philosophy of the Commentators: A Sourcebook*, vol. 3. Ithaca, NY.
Speck, P. (1974) *Die Kaiserliche Universität von Konstantinopel*. Munich.
Tannery, P. (1888) 'Rapport sur une mission en Italie', in *Archives des Missions Scientifiques et Littéraires* 3e sér. XIV, 405–55.
Temkin, O. (1973) *Galenism: Rise and Decline of a Medical Philosophy*. Ithaca, NY.
Trizio, M. (2007) 'Byzantine Philosophy as a Contemporary Historiographical Project', *RecTh* 74.1: 247–94.
  (2009) 'Neoplatonic Source-Material in Eustratios of Nicaea's Commentary on Book VI of the *Nicomachean Ethics*', in *Medieval Greek Commentaries on the Nicomachean Ethics*, ed. C. Barber and D. Jenkins, 71–109. Leiden–Boston.
  (2012) 'A Neoplatonic Refutation of Islam from the Time of the Komnenoi', in *Knotenpunkt Byzanz: Wissensformen und kulturelle Wechselbeziehungen*, ed. A. Speer and P. Steinkrüger, 71–109. Berlin–Boston.
  (2013) 'Ancient Physics in the Mid-Byzantine Period: The *Epitome* of Theodore of Smyrna, Consul of the Philosophers under Alexios I Komnenos (1081–1118)', *Bulletin de philosophie médiévale* 54: 77–101.
  (2014) 'Eleventh- to Twelfth-Century Byzantium', in *Interpreting Proclus: From Antiquity to the Renaissance*, ed. S. Gersh, 182–215. Cambridge.
  (2016) *Il Neoplatonismo di Eustrazio di Nicea*. Bari.
  (2018) 'The Byzantine Reception of Aristotle's *Parva naturalia* (and the Zoological Works) in Eleventh- and Twelfth-Century Byzantium: An Overview', in *The Parva Naturalia in Greek, Arabic and Latin Aristotelianism*, ed. B. Bydén and F. Radovic, 155–68. Cham.
Tuominen, M. (2009) *The Ancient Commentators on Plato and Aristotle*. Berkeley.

Urbano, A. P. (2013) *The Philosophical Life: Biography and the Crafting of Intellectual Identity in Late-Antiquity*. Washington, DC.
Vitelli, G. (ed.) (1887) *Ioannis Philoponi in Aristotelis physicorum libros tres priores commentaria*. Berlin.
  (ed.) (1888) *Ioannis Philoponi in Aristotelis physicorum libros quinque posteriores commentaria*. Berlin.
  (ed.) (1897) *Ioannis Philoponi in Aristotelis libros de generatione et corruptione commentaria*. Berlin.
Wallies, M. (ed.) (1883) *Alexander Aphrodisiensis, In Aristotelis analyticorum priorum librum 1 commentarium*. Berlin.
  (ed.) (1905) *Ioannis Philoponi in Aristotelis analytica priora commentaria*. Berlin.
Weijers, O. (2002) *La 'disputatio' dans les facultés des arts au Moyen Âge*. Turnhout.
Wendland, P. (ed.) (1901) *Alexander Aphrodisiensis: in librum de sensu commentarium*. Berlin.
  (ed.) (1903) *Michaelis Ephesii in parva naturalia commentaria*. Berlin.
Westerink, L. G. (ed.) (1954) *Proclus, Commentary on the First Alcibiades of Plato*. Amsterdam.
  (1990^2) 'The Alexandrian Commentators and the Introductions to Their Commentaries', in *Aristotle Transformed: The Ancient Commentators and Their Influence*, ed. R. Sorabji, 325–48. Ithaca, NY.
Wiesner, J. (1981) 'Zu den Scholien der Parva Naturalia des Aristoteles', in *Proceedings of the World Congress on Aristotle, Thessaloniki, August 7–14, 1978*, 233–7. Athens.
Wilson, E. (2007) *The Death of Socrates*. Cambridge, MA.
Wilson, N. G. (2008) 'Review of P. Moore, Iter Psellianum', *JHS* 128: 288.
Whitmarsh, T. (2005) *The Second Sophistic*. Cambridge.

CHAPTER 3

Cultural Appropriation and the Performance of Exegesis in John Tzetzes' Scholia on Aristophanes

Aglae Pizzone

Tzetzes' scholia on Aristophanes provide crucial details about his exegetical activity. Not only do they show his engagement with earlier sources, but they also offer valuable information on the exegetical practices of a twelfth-century Constantinopolitan teacher.[1] Like most of the commentaries or paraphrases by Tzetzes, they testify to the author's sustained effort to carve out a personal space within traditional modes of expression. In this respect, Tzetzes' oeuvre is both typical and exceptional: it is typically embedded in well-established teaching practices and methods, while it exceptionally shows how traditional tools, formats, methods and even social rituals linked to education could be stretched out so as to accommodate an original exegetical voice. The particular case of the commentaries on Aristophanes offers added value for our understanding of twelfth-century Constantinopolitan society. If, as stressed in the introduction to this volume, Atticizing Greek was a sociolect that needed to be controlled and mastered by the elite, the language of Aristophanes offered a toolkit that came in handy specifically in the sphere of intellectual/political banter and slander. Mastering Aristophanes' idiolect and its nuances was tantamount to understanding and possibly rebuffing criticism from political and intellectual opponents as well as being in control of light and playful jesting.[2] In other words, it was a useful social skill.

As I have mentioned, the commentaries on Aristophanes are particularly rich in information about the educational setting within which exegetical practices unfolded. This will also be the focus of my contribution. I will first look more closely into the idea of exegesis as performance[3] in order to expand later on how such practices could also open up to cross-linguistic and cross-cultural contaminations/appropriations. Commenting on texts

---

[1] See Benuzzi (2017–18).
[2] See Labuk (2016). On the reception of Aristophanes as a satirist and Atticist in the twelfth century, see also van den Berg (2021). On ridicule and jest in Eustathios' Homeric commentaries, see van den Berg in this volume.
[3] See Gaul (2014: 265–7). On oral exegesis, see also Trizio in this volume.

Cultural Appropriation and Performance of Exegesis

was far from a disembodied act; on the contrary, it required an effort that was both intellectual and physical. Not unlike today, holding a class was an exercise calling for a series of structured bodily and mental practices in order to be successful. I will therefore take into consideration some of these practices, addressing the entanglements between performativity and manuscript culture transpiring from Tzetzes' commentary on Aristophanes.[4] I am interested in what the scholia can tell us about the setting and the execution of the actual exegetical activity. My aim is to show that performative practices and manuscript tradition illuminate each other, thus conveying a fuller picture of twelfth-century Constantinopolitan exegetical culture.[5] After this first part, I will concentrate on *Commentary on Aristophanes' Frogs* 843a,[6] a passage that provides new insights both into Tzetzes' production process and into less obvious but equally important aspects of the engagement with the classics in the capital toward the end of the twelfth century.

Exegesis from Performance to Manuscripts

As with other works by Tzetzes – the *Histories*, the commentary on Hermogenes, the scholia on Lycophron[7] – the manuscripts of the commentary on Aristophanes show traces of multiple stages of dissemination and at least two redactions.[8] These multiple redactions testify to the hybrid nature of Tzetzes' exegesis, suspended between performance and manuscript culture. Leiden, Universiteitsbibliotheek, Vossianus gr. Q 1, for instance, containing the commentary on Aphthonios and on the corpus Hermogenianum, as well as a treatise on the differences and similarities between *staseis* (31v–36r) in political verse, shows us that the material on Hermogenes that Tzetzes used for his teaching was maintained in several versions, subject to many layers of revision and copied upon request for paying patrons.[9] In several instances, Tzetzes describes the setting of his own lectures and his interactions with the public.[10] As Niels Gaul has

---

[4] Cf. for the eleventh century Bernard (2014: 210–28).
[5] On the distinction between orality and performance, see Toth (2018: 46–8).
[6] Pp. 931.15–938.2 ed. Koster (1962).   [7] See Leone (2007: xvi), Scheer (1908: VII–IX).
[8] See Koster (1960: XXV–XXXIX).
[9] See Pizzone (2020: 685). Furthermore, the Viennese manuscript Phil. gr. 300, fols. 81v–111v contains an epitome of the commentary on Hermogenes, complete with diagrams absent in the Vossianus. The manuscript ascribes the authorship of the epitome to Tzetzes. More research will be needed to confirm this, but we cannot exclude the possibility that this is yet another version of the commentary prepared by Tzetzes himself.
[10] See for instance *Scholia on Aristophanes' Frogs* 897a, p. 951.11–955.4 ed. Koster (1962).

shown, books take centre stage as props in such performances.[11] Exegesis, however, was anything but an exclusively bookish enterprise. Tzetzes, who at times seems to have taught in his lodgings,[12] engages the audience with humour, jokes, everyday experiences and even scientific experiments.[13] The scholia on Aristophanes are particularly generous in providing details about the modes of such interactions between the teacher and his listeners.[14] Well beyond the standard framework of questions and answers, a lively and playfully abusive exchange with the audience was common currency.[15] Mutual jesting and joking characterized Tzetzes' teaching, as shown, for instance, by the inclusion in the scholia on Aristophanes of a blasphemous parahymn on famous fools from antiquity – characters through which he often alludes to other grammarians and orators.[16] The hymn follows the *heirmos* of the fourth mode from the canon for the Feast of the Annunciation ἀνοίξω τὸ στόμα μου, composed in the eighth century and still part of the Orthodox liturgy.[17] Though irreverent, the choice appears somewhat fitting, as the *heirmos* is in the dialogic mode – a dialogue between Gabriel and the Virgin – and as such is particularly in tune with a classroom environment. The performance of goliardic-like lines is also testified by the *Histories*, where Tzetzes mentions in the scholia some teasing and salacious verses that were part of the very first redaction of the letter to Lachanas and did not make it into the master copy prepared for 'publication'.[18] Even though the letter to Lachanas does not technically belong to Tzetzes' corpus devoted to the exegesis of ancient texts, it was composed with the purpose of being commented upon within an ideal didactic setting. The lost ἀστεΐσματα ('playful verses') were probably

---

[11] Gaul (2014: 266).

[12] So he says in his commentary on the *Iliad*, complaining about the poor conditions of his accommodation at the time, whose walls were allegedly dripping with water (ad *Il.* 1.352, pp. 325–6 ed. Papathomopoulos). The *Exegesis of the Iliad* is a work from Tzetzes' youth, usually dated to 1143 (see *Prolegomena on Comedy* 1.144–5 ed. Koster [1975]; Papathomopoulos [2007: 19]; Cullhed [2014: 58, n. 42]), that is, before he got lodgings and pension at the Pantokrator (see Grünbart [1994] and Rhoby [2010: 158]).

[13] In the scholion 21 mentioned above, Tzetzes boasts that he alone could prove that everything comes from water and returns to water, as Heraclitus and Homer would argue, by trapping some water coming from his ceiling and observing the formation of mould and lichens (I will expand upon this passage in a forthcoming article in preparation). On banter, see below.

[14] See Benuzzi (2017–18: 369–70).

[15] Bernard (2014: 237–9) has shown that playfulness was particularly connected to the composition of political verse, which, in fact, is one of the verse forms preferred by Tzetzes for his exegetical activity. As Bernard shows, the didactic use of political verse was meant to meet the expectations of aristocratic/courtly audiences and patrons.

[16] See Pizzone (2017: 185, n. 17). [17] See Olkinuora (2015: 163, n. 47).

[18] *Histories* 4.776–9 and *Scholia on the Histories* 5.779, p. 548.2–6 ed. Leone (2007), with Agapitos (2017: 21–2). On the didactic framework behind the *Histories*, see Pizzone (2017).

comparable with another aggressive poem. I refer here to the insulting lines, resulting from improvisation, composed against George Skylitzes and the imperial secretary Gregory, who had dared to criticize Tzetzes' ability to write in verse.[19]

Self-derogatory humour was not unknown to Tzetzes either. The scholia to the *Histories* are revealing in this respect. When glossing on *Histories* 10.358, where he imagines an unlikely encounter with the fourth-century BC author Philoxenus of Cythera, Tzetzes provides the following clarification:[20]

> Τοῦτο ἀστεῖον νόησον· ποῦ γὰρ ὁ Τζέτζης τότε;
>
> Understand this as a witty joke, for where was Tzetzes then?
>
> Τὸ σχῆμα ἀστεϊσμός.
>
> The figure of speech is a witticism.

Verbal abuse and playful banter were in all likelihood integral to the educational setting. This should work as a caveat for any modern reader tempted to take personal attacks at face value, disregarding their actual performative context. The very anecdote from the *Commentary on Aristophanes' Frogs* highlighted by Niels Gaul in the contribution mentioned above might carry a tinge of dry self-deprecation, together with the ruthless teasing of a member of Tzetzes' audience. The story goes as follows:[21] during one of Tzetzes' exegetical performances, a listener keeps claiming that the content presented is not original but is also to be found in a volume in his possession. When, after Tzetzes' protests, the student's book is shown, it turns out that it is not Aristophanes, but 'Euripides or Oppian'. The story is truly amusing only if we assume that the 'Euripides or Oppian' also had notes by Tzetzes, who, while stressing once again the unmistakable peculiarity of his style, then exposes himself as reusing the same exegetical material multiple times.[22] We know from his work on Hesiod that in his teaching Tzetzes actively referred to copies of the authors he commented upon, which he had annotated. The material included in the copies could be used to complement his lectures.[23] More

---

[19] See Petridès (1903), Agapitos (2017: n. 83 and *passim*), Zagklas (2019: 254–5) and (2021: 296–301), Pizzone (2022).
[20] *Scholia on the Histories* 10.851a and b, p. 563.11–12 ed. Leone.
[21] *Scholia on Aristophanes' Frogs* 897a, p. 952.13–954.14 ed. Koster (1962).
[22] It is very easy to find the same material, repeated even verbatim, in different works: see, for instance, the examples mentioned by Mastronarde (2017: 60–88) and Scattolin (2003).
[23] *Scholia on Hesiod's Works and Days* 132 ed. Gaisford: ὑμῖν δὲ τοῖς ἀκροωμένοις φημὶ ὅτι ἐν τῷ ῥηθέντι νῦν χωρίῳ τῶν ἐπῶν οὐκ ἔδει πολυλογίας, λέξεων βραχειῶν τινῶν, καὶ γέγραφα ταύτας

to the point, the manuscript tradition has preserved traces of Tzetzes' hermeneutical work on both Oppian and Euripides[24] together in the same codices.[25] The amusing story, therefore, can be understood better if read against the backdrop of the manuscript tradition, which in turn provides a better grasp of the cultural practices sustaining that tradition. This dialectic between the static character of exegesis 'on paper' and the actual dynamism of exegetical practices evolving over time emerges also in other cases. A somewhat poignant example is provided by Milan, Biblioteca Ambrosiana, C 222 inf. Here, at fol. 218r, there is a copy of a poem revolving around the metric value of the word ὄρνις and the thorny issue of dichrona. The introductory line informs us that the verses were occasional (αὐθωροί) and describes Tzetzes as having already passed away.[26] In the first verse, Tzetzes presents himself as old: πειρᾷ με τὸν γέροντα τοῦ παιδίου τρόπον, 'he tests me, the old man, as the youngsters use to do'. If we are to believe the improvised character of the poem, Tzetzes ironically and jokingly exploited his own elderly persona, turning it into a prop for his teaching practices. This synchronic, phenomenological aspect ends up frozen on the page and becomes an almost nostalgic detail in view of the fact that the teacher is now μακαρίτης, 'blessed', typically used for deceased people.

Performativity is not the only dimension to Tzetzes' exegesis, as already indicated. The scholia on Aristophanes are particularly valuable as they offer glimpses into the process moving from teaching performances to the 'published' work. Such a process, we are informed, takes place when Tzetzes receives a commission. To carry out his task, Tzetzes expects to be able to borrow manuscripts of the work to be commented on (Fig. 3.1):[27]

ἄνωθεν τῶν ἐπῶν, 'I say to you, my listeners, that this passage of the poem does not require many discussions, but only a few remarks and I have written them above the lines'. On Tzetzes' exegesis of Hesiod, see Pietrosanti (2009).

[24] For Euripides, see Mastronarde (2017), mentioned above; for Oppian, see Colonna (1963), Zumbo (1997).

[25] One such manuscript is Vatican City, Biblioteca Apostolica Vaticana, gr. 1345, containing Oppian with scholia by Tzetzes and Euripides with further Tzetzian material (cf. fol. 98v, where one can find political verses on Polydorus that are also in *Histories* 10.314.143–57). Salamanca, Biblioteca Universitaria, Ms. 31, too, (likewise a descriptus from Florence, Biblioteca Medicea Laurenziana, Plut. 31.3, which, however, is missing the part containing Euripides) carries signs of Tzetzes' work on the two authors: see Marzano (2016).

[26] See Mazzucchi (2004: 420) and, for the term related to improvisation, Agapitos (2017: 22, n. 113).

[27] On this passage, in iambs, see Luzzatto (1999: 43–5). Luzzatto believes that Tzetzes sourced the manuscripts from the Imperial Library. This hypothesis seems to be supported also by the fact that some of Tzetzes' followers/pupils were actually living in the palace, as stated by *Histories* 6.40, introductory prose note. The text was appended to the commentary as a personal note and is preserved by Paris, Bibliothèque nationale de France, suppl. gr. 655 (fourteenth century), fol. 7r. Unfortunately, the text is very difficult to read on the digital reproduction (see Fig. 3.1) and would

Fig. 3.1 Paris, Bibliothèque nationale de France, suppl. gr. 655, fol. 7r

Ἐβουλόμην μὲν ἐξανορθοῦν εἰς πλάτος, 1
γράφειν τε πάντα προσφυῶς Τζέτζου τρόποις·
ἐπεὶ δ' ὃς ἡμᾶς ἦν συνωθήσας γράφειν,
πρῶτον παλαιὰν οὐκ ἐφεῦρέ μοι βίβλον
ἢ κἂν δύ' ἢ τρεῖς ἔκ γε τῶν νεογράφων, 5
ὡς ἄλλον ἐξ ἄλλης ἀνορθοίην στίχον·
βίβλους ἐφευρὼν τῶν νεογράφων δύο,
ὧν ἡ μὲν ἦν ἐνοῦσα τοὺς δύο στίχους,
ἄλλη δέ, τετράμετρος εἴπερ ἦν στίχος,
τομαῖς διῄρει τοῦτον εἰς δύο στίχους, 10
εἰς τρεῖς τινάς, ἄλλους <δὲ> καὶ περαιτέρω,
ὤρθουν μὲν ὤρθουν τὸ σκάφος τὸ τοῦ λόγου
ἕως βραχὺ τὸ κῦμα τῆς ἀτεχνίας·
ἐπεὶ [δὲ] πυκνῇ συμμιγὲς τρικυμίᾳ
ἐρροχθίαζε καὶ κατέκαμπτε<το> ζέον, 15
τὰ πηδὰ δ' οὐκ ἦν δεξιῶς ἐμοὶ στρέφειν,
στείλας τὰ λαίφη καὶ παρεὶς τοὺς αὐχένας,
πρὸς κῦμα χωρῶ βαρβαρόγραφα πνέον,
ὅπερ βέβηλοι δυσμαθεῖς βιβλογράφοι
γραφεῖς ἁπασῶν εἰσφοροῦσι τῶν βίβλων. 20
οὕτω τὰ μέτρα τὸ νῦν ἐάσω συγγράφειν
λέξας τινὰ βράχιστα τῇ φύρσει βίβλων·
οὐκ ἀγνοεῖ γὰρ καὶ μετρικοὺς Τζέτζης λόγους,
ὁ σφαῖς διδάξας συγγραφαῖς ἅπαν μέτρον.
(Tzetzes, *Scholia on Aristophanes' Wealth* 137, p. 41.9–42.19 ed. Massa Positano)

I wanted to emend the text in full,
and write everything down as per Tzetzes' method;
Fact is that the person who urged us to write
at first did not find us an ancient manuscript
or at least two or three of the newly copied [ones],
in order for me to restore the one line using another copy.
After finding two of the newly copied manuscripts,
of which one merges the two lines,
while the other, if it had a tetrameter,
would cut it, splitting it into two lines,
or even into three, dividing other verses even more,
time and again I set the vessel of words straight,
when the waves of ignorance were small.
However, when they, intermingled with the thick swell,

benefit from an analysis through multispectral imaging. The text quoted follows the edition by Massa Positano except for line 14, where Massa Positano prints πυκνὴ συμμιγὴς τρικυμία and line 15 where Massa Positano has κατέκαμπτε, which, however, would not provide the correct iambic meter. I warmheartedly thank the anonymous reviewer for suggesting such an elegant solution, which will hopefully be confirmed by a new inspection of the manuscript.

thundered and bent over in rage,
I was not able to manoeuvre the oars skilfully;
giving up on the sails, letting the tiller go,
I proceed toward the swelling wave of barbarisms,
which uncouth and ignorant copyists
bring in while writing all the books.
Thus, I will now give up on writing about meters,
except for a few very short notes on the confusion of the books:
for Tzetzes does know well how to versify,
he who taught all sorts of meter through his own writings.[28]

This passage shows how the manuscript 'publication' of Tzetzes' commentaries worked. It was a complex process that took place over time and in multiple instalments, so to speak. Besides the works designed and penned on commission,[29] Tzetzes also produced written copies of his lectures or teaching material upon request.[30] The material selected for 'publication' would change depending on the targeted audience, as Tzetzes saw fit: at the end of the scholion on *Frogs* 843b, Tzetzes mentions the 'original quire' (πρωτότυπον τετράδιον), which contained the material that was later subject to selection for the individual copies.[31] Paratexts from Voss. gr. Q 1 carrying Tzetzes' commentary on Aphthonios and Hermogenes show the same background and arrangement as the scholia on Aristophanes. There, Tzetzes states that he had produced the relevant copy of the commentaries at the request of a group of 'companions' (ἑταῖροι) and against remuneration.[32] Later, he stresses that the material to be found in that specific copy is different from what can be found in the 'master copy' (πρωτόγραφον) and in the 'drafts' (σχεδίαι) of the book.[33]

Voss. gr. Q 1 is an exceptional case, as it is a copy curated by Tzetzes himself. In addition to the text penned by the professional main copyist, the Vossianus also preserves a large number of interlinear and marginal notes, drafted in a darker ink (varying from light brown to dark brown) and showing a very characteristic, utterly informal handwriting. A comparison with the marginal notes from the Thucydides Heidelberg, Universitätsbibliothek, Pal. gr. 252, ascribed to Tzetzes by Maria Jagoda Luzzatto, leaves little room for doubt: the two hands stem from

---

[28] Tzetzes devoted specific treatises to the subject of ancient meters. As well as the essay on Pindar's meters by Tzetzes' brother Isaac edited by Drachmann (1925), we also have a general overview by John Tzetzes under the title Διδασκαλία σαφεστάτη περὶ τῶν ἐν τοῖς στίχοις μέτρων ἁπάντων edited by Cramer (1836: 302–33), on which see the recent work by Giannachi (2014).
[29] Rhoby (2010).   [30] He mentions this habit in *Histories* 11.364.28.
[31] P. 937, 1–2 ed. Koster (1962).   [32] Fol. 30r.
[33] Fol. 212r. See Pizzone (2020: 685–6) for more details.

the same copyist.³⁴ The authorship of the notes, moreover, is confirmed by their content. At fol. 45v, Tzetzes names himself explicitly as the one who drafted the glosses, and at fol. 73r and fol. 115v he states that he finds himself in his seventieth year of life. As Tzetzes was probably born around 1110–12,³⁵ one can draw the conclusion that the revision of the Vossianus took place in the 1180s, which matches Mazzucchi's dating of Ambrosianus C 222 inf., which is an important witness to the scholia on Aristophanes and where, as we have seen, Tzetzes is mentioned as already deceased – although there is no such notation in the first quires.³⁶ This chronology also squares well with the note to the *Histories*, where we learn that Tzetzes was correcting a copy of his self-commentary for Constantine Kotertzes.³⁷ It might be that, toward the end of his life, when perhaps his position as an intellectual and teacher was more consolidated within the capital's elite circles, Tzetzes reviewed some of his major works for new patrons who desired to have a clean copy of his lectures/material.

Be that as it may, the Vossianus shows once again that the exegetical works originating from Tzetzes' lectures would generate several redactions – all of them authorized by him at different points in time and produced for different addressees/patrons. As I mentioned at the beginning, the manuscript tradition of several works by Tzetzes shows evidence of multiple redactions already circulating during the author's lifetime. The Vossianus is exceptional in that it shows a very early stage of this transmission, allowing us to understand how one of the redactions of the commentaries on Aphthonios and Hermogenes came to be and showing,

---

³⁴ Luzzatto (1999). See also https://cml.sdu.dk/blog/john-tzetzes-in-the-margins-of-the-voss-gr-q1-discovering-autograph-notes-of-a-byzantine-scholar. The autograph notes are currently being edited by myself together with Elisabetta Barili.
³⁵ See Wendel (1948: col. 1961). ³⁶ See Mazzucchi (2004: 420).
³⁷ See the scholion on the *Histories*, published on p. 549 of Leone's edition. The printed edition of this paratext is misleading, as it does not convey the sense of the original layout. In the manuscript Vatican City, Biblioteca Apostolica Vaticana, gr. 1396, dated to the first half of the thirteenth century, containing both the *Histories* and the letters, the verses for Kotertzes (iambs) are to be found at fol. 115v, right after nine political verses in which Tzetzes presents the total number of 'histories' through a sort of mathematical charade. Fol. 115v finds itself just before the third 'block' of histories and after six folia containing the *pinax* of the section, with titles and numbers of the individual histories (fols. 109r–115r). The 'charade', now printed by Leone within the text, as the final part (lines 193–201) of *Historia* 5.23, was clearly designed as a self-standing piece, with the aim of summarizing the *pinax*. Accordingly, the iambs for Kotertzes are not, by design, a scholion to any part of the text, but they are rather a proper book epigram (see Bernard and Demoen [2019]) located at the beginning of the longest part of the *Histories*. Tzetzes warns Kotertzes that the first two parts of the *Letters* plus *Histories* have been revised by him and purged of the copyist's mistakes. Since he is not sure he will be able to complete the task for the third part, he forewarns Kotertzes, who, as intended reader of that copy, is about to go through the relevant text cluster. On Kotertzes and Tzetzes in the late 1140s, see Cullhed (2014).

almost live, Tzetzes' process of revision. A comparable scenario could probably be envisaged also for the scholia on Aristophanes.

The circulation of multiple copies also explains Tzetzes' constant anxiety about intellectual property, as well as the need to define the boundaries of his exegetical production.[38] This is why his 'published' exegetical writings are replete with notes on his own didactic practice, which often inform us about further works that have not survived or are only partially available.[39] The fact that written copies of the lectures were produced on commission is also the reason why Tzetzes feels compelled to account for material constraints preventing him from offering original material. The length of one of the redactions of the scholia on Aristophanes, for instance, was allegedly determined by the lack of paper, which obliged Tzetzes to cut his commentary short.[40]

It is against this backdrop that we must read another significant passage from the commentary on Aristophanes, where Tzetzes explains his reasons for limiting the exegetical notes provided to the reader, while at the same time stressing his ingenuity:[41]

διὰ τὴν περὶ ἡμᾶς ὑμῶν ἀχάριστον γνώμην καὶ τὸ μὴ ἐξ[αρκεῖν] τοὺς χάρτας εἰς ἐπεξήγησιν καὶ ἕτερα δὲ μυρία, καὶ ὅτι τοιαύτας κατατετμημένας ἐννοίας καί, εἰ μὴ φορτικὸν εἰπεῖν, φλυάρους ἐπεξηγεῖσθαι οὐ βούλομαι τζετζικῶς, ὡς εἰ Ὅμηρον νῦν[42] ἦν ἐξηγούμενος ἢ κἂν ἔπη Ἐμπεδοκλέους· ἐῶ δὲ πάμπολλα. μειδιῶ δὲ τὰ τῶν παλαιῶν βλέπων, καὶ τῷ μηδὲν ὁρᾶν ἐπάξιον συγγραφῆς ἀνθρώπων σοφῶν φημι· "ἆρα τοιοῦτοι καὶ τοσοῦτοι ἄνδρες σοφοὶ κοιμώμενοι τοῦτον ἐπεξηγοῦντο;" σὺ δὲ ὁ γενναιότατος, ὁ καὶ παρ' ἄλλοις ἐφευρηκέναι λέγων τὰ ἐμοὶ ἐν ἑβραϊκοῖς καὶ ἄλλοις συγγράμμασιν ἐπεξηγημένα, ἃ οὔτε Ἑβραῖος οὔτε ἄλλος ἀλλογενὴς ἐν βίβλοις οἰκειεθνέσιν οὐδὲ "δαίμων ὀρθῶς ἂν ἴσχυσεν ἐξειπεῖν", αὐτὸς δὲ μόνος δαιμονίως ἐξηγησάμην, πολλῷ μᾶλλον ἐν τοιούτοις συγγράμμασιν οὖσι πανδήμου καὶ κατημαξευμένης ἐννοίας εὑρήσειας.[43] (Tzetzes, *Scholia on Aristophanes' Frogs* 843a, p. 932.7–933.12 ed. Koster 1962)

Because of your unfair opinion about us and also because there is not enough paper for a detailed exegesis and a myriad of other things, since I do

---

[38] See Cullhed (2014: 62–3).   [39] See Benuzzi (2017–18).
[40] See *Scholia on Aristophanes' Frogs* 846a, p. 939.1–6 ed. Koster (1962) with Koster's notes (1962: 939) and 1282, p. 1063.1–3 ed. Koster (1962). Here Tzetzes emphasizes the fact that he is simply reproducing the *scholia vetera*.
[41] The passage transcribed here is isolated between two obeloi, to mark its stand-alone character.
[42] The writing is barely legible here: γάρ is also a possible option.
[43] Koster's text has εὑρήσεται here, but the manuscript Ambr. Gr. C 222 inf. shows the reading εὑρήσειας, which also offers a better syntactical structure.

not want to produce an exegesis in the Tzetzian fashion for these wretched and, if we must speak bluntly, silly notions, as if I were commenting Homer or the sayings of Empedocles, therefore, I leave aside a lot. And I smile when considering the exegetical works of the ancients and, since I do not see anything worthy of the writing of wise men, I say: 'Oh my, were such wise men asleep when they commented on him?' And you, most noble friend, you, who argue that you found elsewhere the exegesis I provided on Jewish works and on other subjects, material that, in fact, no Jew or foreigner [has] in their own books, that no 'evil genius forced me to say', but that I alone ingeniously came up with, much more you would find in such commentaries on trivial and vulgar concepts.

There is a strong emphasis on originality here. Tzetzes describes himself as towering over ancient authors – Aristophanes is not deemed worthy of Tzetzes' exegetical activity – and commentators alike: previous exegeses are seen as void of any ingenious content. While he justifies himself for being more concise than usual, Tzetzes underlines that all the material provided is his as he was deeply unsatisfied by what he had found in the *scholia vetera*. Tzetzes asserts the innate nature of his own inspiration through a wordplay based on δαιμονίως, a term employed in twelfth-century exegetical literature to underline authorial cleverness and artistry.[44] Tzetzes presents his own ingenuity as reaching beyond the boundaries of Hellenism. His commentator's persona is described as at ease and equally proficient in different cultural traditions. In the next section, I will try to understand the facts sustaining Tzetzes' boastful statement.

Appropriating Jewish Culture

Tzetzes provides unique evidence regarding the intersection between Christian/Hellenic and Jewish culture. We know that connections between Hellenism and Hebraism did exist within the Empire, especially in large urban centres, but unfortunately we can perceive only faint fragments, which do not convey any sharp image.[45] The scarcity of information we are confronted with makes Tzetzes' material extremely valuable for retracing

---

[44] Cf. Eustathios, *Commentary on the Iliad* 1026.21 = 3.758.10 and 1235.27 = 4.496.23 ed. van der Valk.

[45] On Jews in Byzantium, see Bonfil, Irshai, Stroumsa and Talgam (2012), Bowman (2014). On the intersection between Hebraism and Hellenism, to which I will return below, see more specifically de Lange (1991) and (1998); Lasker, Niehoff-Panagiotidis and Sklare (2018: 709–10) for linguistic contact points with Tzetzes; Judah Hadassi was a contemporary of Tzetzes showing deep and direct knowledge of Greek texts and language: he wrote a treatise in rhythmic prose on the ten commandments, which tackled also exegesis, grammar and phonetics.

multilingualism among twelfth-century Constantinopolitan intellectuals.[46] Linguistic polyphony, after all, was integral to the city's urban fabric, and the topography of Constantinople itself is likely to have facilitated closer contact between Tzetzes and the Jewish community: the Pantokrator monastery, where Tzetzes had his lodgings from around 1141, was quite close to the Venetian neighbourhood of Perama, from where the ferry to the Jewish quarter of Pera departed.[47]

In this section I will first present the most relevant data suggesting that Tzetzes actively engaged with Hebrew. I will then focus on the way in which such an engagement impacts on his exegetical practice, looking both at his allegorical work on Homer and at the *Histories*. Through this analysis I will try to shed more light on the reference to the 'Jewish books' found in the *scholia* on Aristophanes.

Tzetzes boasts time and again about his knowledge of foreign languages, including Hebrew, which gets a mention in the well-known passage at the end of his *Theogony*, where an ability to greet people in several languages is proudly showcased.[48] This, however, is not an isolated instance. Tzetzes seems to be particularly keen on displaying his knowledge of Hebrew when it comes to etymologies of personal names or place names.[49] One of the most blatant cases comes from the *Histories*, where he goes as far as bluntly appropriating a Jewish (and Arabic) identity, so as to show that he is even more proficient and knowledgeable than native speakers:

Τῇ Κλεοπάτρᾳ τῇ σοφῇ τῇ καὶ ὡραιοτάτῃ,
καὶ τοῖς λοιποῖς δὲ σύμπασι πολλῶν ὑπερφερούσῃ,
πρὸς ἐπιμέλειαν τριχῶν καὶ τῶν ὀνύχων ἦσαν
Χαρμιουνῶ καὶ Τάειρα. Τί δὲ δηλοῦσι τάδε;
Σύρον τὸν Τζέτζην βλέπε νῦν, Ἰσμαηλίτην ἅμα,
καὶ ταῦτα διαρθροῦντα σοι ταῖς γλώσσαις ταῖς ἐκείνων.
Κατὰ Ἑβραίων γλῶσσάν τε καὶ τὴν τῶν Σύρων ἅμα
χαρμὶ δηλοῖ τὴν ἄμπελον, οὐνῶ περιστερὰν δε,
τὴν ἣν φασὶν οἱ Ἕλληνες περιστερὰν οἰνάδα
κατὰ Ἰσμαηλίτας δὲ τοὺς Ἄγαρ γόνους λέγω·

---

[46] Dagron (1994). For the many registers of the Greek spoken and written even within learned circles, see Agapitos (2017).
[47] On the topography of the Jewish neighbourhood in Constantinople, see Jacoby (1967) and Magdalino (2000: 220, n. 76). The Pantokrator monastery would become the headquarters of the Venetians after 1204. Tzetzes himself reports a not very friendly encounter with a Venetian (see *Histories* 4.671–4).
[48] *Theogony* 768–73 (cf. Bekker 1842: 169). On the passage, see Agapitos (2017: 39–41, n. 199) and (2019), Shukurov (2016: 49–51), all with further bibliography. See also Tomadaki in this volume.
[49] Cf. *Histories* 7.126, 8.214.

περιστεράν τὴν Τάειραν σημαίνουσάν μοι νόει.
Αὗται πρὸς ἐπιμέλειαν τριχῶν καὶ τῶν ὀνύχων
τῆς Κλεοπάτρας τῆς σοφῆς ἦσαν τῆς βασιλίδος.
(Tzetzes, *Histories* 6.44.273–285 ed. Leone 2007)

Cleopatra, the wise and most beautiful,
who surpassed many people in every respect,
had, for the care of her hair and nails,
Charmiouno and Tahira. What do these names mean?
Look now at Tzetzes the Syrian, and the Ishmaelite,
he will parse them for you using the language of those people.
In the language of Jews and Syrians
charmi means vine, while *ouno* dove,
so it is what the Greeks call black dove;
and following here the Ismaelites, descendants of Agar, I say:
please, understand Tahira as meaning dove.
These women took care of the hair and the nails
of the wise queen Cleopatra.

The passage is striking. Tzetzes seems to challenge the information found in Greek sources, modifying it according to his own knowledge of foreign languages. Cleopatra's servants are well known from ancient and medieval historical narratives. The two women feature prominently in Plutarch's version of Cleopatra's death and become integral to its later reception, playing significant roles in early modern and modern dramatizations of Cleopatra's life, including the most famous one, Shakespeare's *Anthony and Cleopatra*.[50] Their names, however, are not consistently transmitted. Plutarch's *Life of Anthony*, which we know Tzetzes was acquainted with,[51] mentions Εἰράς and Χάρμιον.[52] Plutarch poignantly describes their death at the queen's feet, with Charmion rearranging Cleopatra's hair seconds before herself collapsing next to her dying mistress. A contemporary source of Plutarch, however, the paroemiographer Zenobius calls the two maidens Νάηρα and Χαρμιόνη,[53] as does Galen.[54] This version is also related by Michael Glykas, who mentions both servants among the people assisting

---

[50] See Jones (2006: 238–46).
[51] In the 1130s, Tzetzes, still young and working as a secretary, had an alleged fall out with his patron at the time, Isaac, eparch of Berroia. As a consequence, he found himself forced to sell his personal library, with the exception of one single book, which he chose to keep, containing Plutarch's *Lives* and some mathematical *excerpta*; the events are recalled as having happened almost eight years before in the *Exegesis of the Iliad* 15.12–19 ed. Papathomopoulos. See also Braccini (2009–10, n. 21) and Xenophontos (2014).
[52] Plutarch, *Life of Anthony* 60.1, 85.4.
[53] Zenobius, *Epitome*, centuria 5, section 24 ed. von Leutsch and Schneidewin.
[54] Galen 14, *On Theriacs* 236.1: Νάειρα καὶ Καρμιόνη.

Cultural Appropriation and Performance of Exegesis 113

Cleopatra during her suicide.⁵⁵ It is highly likely that Tzetzes knew Zenobius' text or at least the tradition the latter drew upon, given that Zenobius is the only author who details the tasks assigned to the servants and mentions nail care next to hairdressing.⁵⁶ From Zenobius, moreover, we learn that the pair was already proverbial in the Graeco-Roman era:⁵⁷

> Εἴρηται δὲ ἡ παροιμία ἐπὶ τῶν μέχρι θανάτου τοῖς εὐεργέταις συγκινδυνευόντων.
>
> The proverb is said about people who share the burden of their masters until their death.

The variation introduced by Tzetzes, then, is all the more remarkable, as it modifies a well-established tradition. Tzetzes emphasizes Cleopatra's exoticism by diversifying the ethnicity of her maidens, whose names allegedly refer – respectively in Hebrew and Arabic – to the 'black dove' or pigeon. Interestingly, the black dove is typically linked to Aphrodite in Byzantium and is associated with sex and prostitutes.⁵⁸ In turn, Aphrodite's iconography is openly evoked by Plutarch in relation to Cleopatra.⁵⁹ The queen herself had historically constructed her own image by exploiting her identification with Aphrodite-Isis.⁶⁰ By wilfully changing the names of her servants based on his knowledge of Arabic and Hebrew, Tzetzes strengthens the internal consistency of the traditional narrative about Cleopatra. We can go as far as to say that, just like Naira and Charmion, foreign languages are ancillary to the Hellenic tradition, reinforcing and sustaining it. Tzetzes in fact does not really challenge his sources about Cleopatra; he uses his knowledge of Arabic and Hebrew to strengthen the aura of exoticism which already surrounded the last Egyptian queen in the Greek tradition.

Tzetzes' para-etymologies show that he most likely had an actual knowledge of the two languages, at least at a lexical level. طائر (tayir) in Arabic is the generic term for bird and remains one of the components of the noun indicating the rock dove or wild pigeon: طائر الحجل (tayir alhajl). Charmion's name, on the other hand, is mapped out on the Greek term for black dove, which literally translates as the 'vine dove'. To establish the analogy, Tzetzes takes Charmion as a compound of כֶּרֶם, kerem, that is, 'vineyard',⁶¹ and יוֹנָה, yonah, that is, 'dove'.⁶²

---

⁵⁵ Michael Glykas, *Annals* 112.10 ed. Bekker (1836): Ναείρας καὶ Χαρμιόνης.
⁵⁶ Zenobius, *Epitome*, centuria 5, section 24, 1–3 ed. von Leutsch and Schneidewin.
⁵⁷ Zenobius, *Epitome*, centuria 5, section 24, 17–19 ed. von Leutsch and Schneidewin.
⁵⁸ See Heckscher (1956) and cf. Artemidorus, *Oneirocriticon* 2.20.
⁵⁹ Plutarch, *Life of Anthony* 26.   ⁶⁰ Heckscher (1956: 17).
⁶¹ See Goor (1966). The term famously occurs in Genesis 20.9 (the first vineyard planted by Noah).
⁶² Tzetzes also mentions the etymology in *Histories* 7.126 ed. Leone (2007).

Needless to say, we cannot ascertain how proficient Tzetzes actually was in these languages. It is possible that his knowledge was limited to some notions of biblical Hebrew or to the vocabulary found in hands-on tools such as the ninth-century fragmentary Mishnaic glossary first published by Athanasios Papadopoulos-Kerameus and later edited by Joshua Starr in 1934.[63] What matters, however, is that he depicts himself as fully in command of Hebrew and Arabic, presenting multilingualism as a distinctive hallmark of his intellectual profile. After all, it is highly likely that some knowledge of foreign languages was required in order to work, as Tzetzes had done in his youth, as a secretary to officers in charge of civil or military administration. We do not have clear sources that can tell us how widespread and deep the knowledge of foreign languages was among secretaries working for the imperial administration, but we do have scattered information in the twelfth century about translators and interpreters active at the chancellery, such as the Italian Mosé del Brolo, Leo the Tuscan and Hugo Etherianus.[64] Moreover, as I have mentioned, the capital was inherently multilingual, and this is also the image Tzetzes wants to convey.

Engagement with Jewish culture also impacts on Tzetzes' exegetical work. A case in point is represented by his interpretation of the Solymi, a tribe mentioned twice in the Homeric poems.[65] In *Iliad* 6, they are recalled by Glaucus in his narrative about Bellerophon, who defeated them after killing the Chimaera. Later, the Solymi would take their revenge, slaying Bellerophon's son Isander.[66] In *Odyssey* 5, Poseidon, on his way back from visiting the Ethiopians, sees Odysseus sailing home, looking down at the Ocean from the distant mountains of the Solymi.[67]

In the *Allegories of the Odyssey*, Tzetzes picks up on a fringe hermeneutic tradition that identified the Solymi with the inhabitants of Jerusalem.[68] Building on such an interpretation, he draws a new chronology in which David and Solomon precede Homer, given that David had founded Jerusalem and Solomon had named it after himself:

σημείωσαι, ὡς Σόλυμοι Ἱεροσολυμῖται,
ἐξ ὧν νῦν Ὅμηρός φησιν, οὐ μὴν δὲ οἱ Μιλύαι,
ὡς ἄλλοι γράφουσί τινες ἄνδρες τῶν νεωτέρων.
καὶ τοῦτο δὲ σημείωσαι περὶ αὐτοῦ Ὁμήρου,

---

[63] See Papadopoulos-Kerameus (1908), Starr (1934).
[64] On these figures, see Dondaine (1952), Pontani (1998), Rodriguez Suarez (2016).
[65] *Iliad* 6.184 and 204; *Odyssey* 5.282.   [66] *Iliad* 6.203–4.   [67] *Odyssey* 5.262.
[68] This tradition has been explored by Whitmarsh (2013: 228–47).

ὡς ὕστερος καθέστηκε Δαβὶδ καὶ Σολομῶντος
ἐκ τοῦ μεμνῆσθαι ὁπωσοῦν ὀνόματος Σολύμων.
Δαβὶδ γὰρ ταύτην ἔθετο καὶ Σολομῶν τὴν κλῆσιν
τῇ χώρᾳ, ἥπερ πρότερον ἦν Ἰεβοὺς ἡ κλῆσις.
λοιπὸν ἀκούων τῶν ἐπῶν ἠκριβωμένως σκόπει.
'Τὸν δ' ἐξ Αἰθιόπων ἀνιὼν κρείων ἐνοσίχθων
τηλόθεν ἐκ Σολύμων ὀρέων ἴδεν· εἴσατο γάρ οἱ'
ἔγνως ἐκ τῶνδε ἀκριβῶς, ἃ σημειοῦσθαι εἶπον.
                    (Tzetzes, *Allegories of the Odyssey* 5.156–65 ed. Hunger 1956)

Note that the Solymi are Jerusalemites,
based on what Homer says here, and not Milyans
as written by certain other men of more recent times.
And note this too about the same Homer,
that he lived after David and Solomon,
given that he mentions in some form the name Solymians.
For David and Solomon gave that name
to the land which had previously been called Jebus.
Listen, then, to his words and consider them carefully,
But the glorious Earth-shaker, as he came back from visiting the Ethiopians,
beheld Odysseus from afar, from the mountain of Solymoi; he saw him.
You learned carefully from these things, which I told you to note well.
                    (trans. Goldwyn and Kokkini 2019, slightly modified)

Following the *scholia vetera*,[69] Tzetzes regards the Solymi mentioned in the *Iliad* and the ones in the *Odyssey* as one and the same people, as is made clear in the *Histories*. There, a few years after the *Allegories of the Odyssey*,[70] he picks up again on the same exegesis, pushing it further. The Solymi now stand for the Jews more broadly:

Ἵππῳ Πηγάσῳ πτερωτῷ δ' ἐποχηθεὶς ὁ νέος
ἤγουν τριήρους ἐπιβὰς ἧσπερ πτερὰ τὰ λαίφη
– καὶ οἱ περὶ Ἀδρίαν δὲ ἵππους φασὶ τὰ πλοῖα –
ἔχων στόλον ἑτέρων τε τριήρεων συμβάλλει,
καὶ νίκην ἀπειργάσατο πρῶτον κατὰ Σολύμων,
τῶν Μυλιῶν, Μυλασσιτῶν, καθὼς φασὶν οἱ ἄλλοι.
Τζέτζης Σολύμους λέγει δὲ τυγχάνειν τοὺς Ἑβραίους,
οὓς Ὅμηρος καὶ λέοντι ὡς ἀναιδεῖς εἰκάζει.
                    (Tzetzes, *Histories* 7.149.825–32 ed. Leone 2007)

---

[69] Scholion ad *Il*. 6.184, p. 163.16–18 ed. Erbse.
[70] The *Allegories of the Odyssey* were authored after the *Allegories of the Iliad*, which were first planned between 1146 (after the *Exegesis*) and the marriage of Bertha of Sulzbach (see Goldwyn [2017: 142, n. 4] and Goldwyn and Kokkini [2019: x–xiii] with previous bibliography). The *Histories* are probably to be dated some twenty years later, after 1166 (see Leone [2007: xvi]) and less than ten years after the *Allegories of the Odyssey*, written after 1158 (see Hunger [1955] and [1956], Braccini [2011]).

> The young man, riding around on Pegasus, the flying horse,
> that is being onboard a trireme, with sails like wings
> – and the people around the Adriatic Sea call the vessels horses –
> and leading his expedition, he engages with the other triremes,
> and first he won over the Solymi,
> or the Milyans, Milassyti, as all the others say.
> Tzetzes, however, argues that the Solymi are the Jews,
> compared by Homer to a lion, as they are shameless.

The Solymi were the offspring of Solymus, a son of Zeus and Chelidonias, according to the *scholia vetera* on the *Odyssey*, which rely on Antimachus. Tzetzes' interpretation challenges the idea that the Solymi were a population from Cilicia who later settled in Pisidia.[71] The passage from the *Histories* implies that this interpretation was also supported by recent scholarship. Not coincidentally, Eustathios comments abundantly on the geographical location of the Solymi. He identifies them with the Minyans, a population in Lycia, who take their name from Minos. In doing so, he slightly modifies the more widespread tradition, going back to Herodotus, according to whom the Solymi were in fact the same tribe as the Milyans – a point mentioned also by Tzetzes.[72] More importantly, Eustathios explicitly mentions the reading found in Tzetzes, if only to refute it:

> Οὐδετέρως μέντοι Σόλυμα πόλις, φασίν, Ἀσσυρίων, κτισθεῖσα μετὰ τὴν ἅλωσιν τοῦ ἐν Ἱεροσολύμοις ἱεροῦ. (Eustathios, *Commentary on the Iliad* 635.33–4 = 2.285.8–9 ed. van der Valk)
>
> And it is absolutely not the city of Solyma, as they say, of the Assyrians, established after the capture of the Temple of Jerusalem.

It is highly likely, therefore, that Eustathios and Tzetzes are in dialogue here and are refuting each other.[73] This would be chronologically plausible, as the first version of Eustathios' commentaries on Homer was

---

[71] Scholion ad *Od.* 5.283, p. 273.16–18 ed. Dindorf.
[72] Van der Valk (1971: 285) believes that Eustathios could rely on a *scholion vetus* that is now lost. Herodotus mentions the Solymi in 1.173.2 (the Lycians were first called Milyans and the Milyans were originally the Solymi). Herodian, on the other hand, distinguishes the Minyans (from Thessaly) and the Milyans (originally Solymi), whose name comes from Milyes, sister and wife of Solymos (3.1.52.30–1). Stephanus of Byzantium relies on Herodian and on a tradition close to the *scholia vetera* on the *Odyssey* (see *Ethnics* 12 lemma 187; *Ethnics* 16 lemma 159 ed. Billerbeck, Lentini and Neumann-Hartmann; *Ethnics* 18 lemma 248 ed. Billerbeck and Neumann-Hartmann).
[73] On the exegetical rivalry between Eustathios and Tzetzes, see also Lovato in this volume.

completed between 1168 and 1175/8 (though they did exist earlier in the form of working material designed for teaching),[74] whereas, as we have seen, the *Allegories of the Odyssey* were written after 1158. Both Tzetzes and Eustathios share a willingness to update Homeric geography so as to make it more palatable to contemporary audiences. Eustathios[75] inserts a remark pointing to the fact that in the rockiest part of Lycia there was still a population called Τζέλυμοι by the locals.[76] On the other hand, the Μυλασσίται mentioned by Tzetzes look like an attempt to update the name of the Mylii by echoing contemporary surnames. This form is not otherwise attested, except for a document from Patmos, dated 1261, mentioning one Mylassites and his children, probably from the city of Mylassa in Caria, modern-day Mylas.[77]

Even though the interpretation of the Solymi as the inhabitants of Jerusalem is not to be found in the *scholia vetera*, the reading is well attested in Imperial times. Tim Whitmarsh has recently explored the reception of the obscure tribe in Graeco-Roman imperial literature.[78] Whitmarsh takes his cue from a passage found in Josephus' *Against Apion*, referring in turn to Choerilus of Samos:[79]

καὶ Χοιρίλος δὲ ἀρχαιότερος γενόμενος ποιητὴς μέμνηται τοῦ ἔθνους ἡμῶν, ὅτι συνεστράτευται Ξέρξῃ τῷ Περσῶν βασιλεῖ ἐπὶ τὴν Ἑλλάδα· καταριθμησάμενος γὰρ πάντα τὰ ἔθνη τελευταῖον καὶ τὸ ἡμέτερον ἐνέταξε λέγων·τῶν δ' ὄπιθεν διέβαινε γένος θαυμαστὸν ἰδέσθαι,
γλῶσσαν μὲν Φοίνισσαν ἀπὸ στομάτων ἀφιέντες,
ᾤκεον δ' ἐν Σολύμοις ὄρεσι πλατέῃ παρὰ λίμνῃ
αὐχμαλέοι κορυφὰς τροχοκουράδες, αὐτὰρ ὕπερθεν
ἵππων δαρτὰ πρόσωπ' ἐφόρουν ἐσκληκότα καπνῷ.
δῆλον οὖν ἐστιν, ὡς οἶμαι, πᾶσιν ἡμῶν αὐτὸν μεμνῆσθαι τῷ καὶ τὰ Σόλυμα ὄρη ἐν τῇ ἡμετέρᾳ εἶναι χώρᾳ, ἃ κατοικοῦμεν, καὶ τὴν Ἀσφαλτῖτιν λεγομένην λίμνην· (Josephus, *Against Apion* 1.172–5)

---

[74] See Cullhed (2012: 447, n. 5, with earlier bibliography) and (2016: 20*–4*). Quarrels between Eustathios and Tzetzes were frequent, also due to Eustathios' foul play and undue appropriation of Tzetzes' material: see Conley (2005: 684), Cullhed (2014: 63, n. 58).
[75] Regarding the Solymi mentioned in the *Odyssey*, Eustathios does not hesitate to say that they were simply a narrative invention of Homer's (πλάττει), along the lines of the tribe mentioned in the *Iliad* (*Commentary on the Iliad* 369.9 = 1.582.14).
[76] Eustathios, *Commentary on the Iliad* 635.35–7 = 2.285.12–14 ed. van der Valk.
[77] *Diploma Joannis Athyboli* 29–30 ed. Nystazopoulou-Pelekidou.
[78] Whitmarsh (2013: 228–47).
[79] Cf. Choerilus fr. 4 ed. Radici Colace. The same tradition – with reference to Choerilus – is recalled in Eusebius, *Preparation for the Gospel* 9.9. See Radici Colace (1979: 41–3 and 45–6).

Choerilus, an older poet, makes mention of our race, specifying that they joined the expedition of Xerxes, the Persian king, against Greece. Having enumerated all the races, he drew up ours last of all, saying that:
They emitted a Phoenician language from their mouths,
They lived in the Solyman mountains by the broad lake,
Squalid of hair, tonsured, and above themselves
They bore the flayed skin of horses' heads, smoke-dried.
It is obvious to anyone, I think, that he is making reference to us, from the fact that the Solyman mountains are in our territory, which we inhabit, as is the so-called asphalt lake, for the latter is broader and larger than the other ones in Syria. (trans. Whitmarsh 2013: 233–4)

In *Jewish Antiquities*, moreover, Josephus subscribes to the identification of the Solymi with the Jews and the inhabitants of Jerusalem in particular, invoking Homer's authority:[80]

> πρῶτος οὖν Δαυίδης τοὺς Ἰεβουσαίους ἐξ Ἱεροσολύμων ἐκβαλὼν ἀφ' ἑαυτοῦ προσηγόρευσε τὴν πόλιν· ἐπὶ γὰρ Ἀβράμου τοῦ προγόνου ἡμῶν Σόλυμα ἐκαλεῖτο, μετὰ ταῦτα δὲ αὐτήν φασί τινες, ὅτι καὶ Ὅμηρος ταῦτ' ὠνόμασεν Ἱεροσόλυμα· τὸ γὰρ ἱερὸν κατὰ τὴν Ἑβραίων γλῶτταν ὠνόμασε τὰ Σόλυμα ὅ ἐστιν ἀσφάλεια. (Josephus, *Jewish Antiquities* 7.67)

> Thus, it was David who first cast the Jebusites out of Jerusalem, and named the city after himself: for at the time of our forefather Abraham it was called Solyma; but afterwards, some say that Homer mentions it as Hierosolyma, for he named the temple Solyma which is safety, according to the language of the Hebrews.

It is worth noting that, when commenting on the story of Bellerophon in the *Allegories of the Iliad*, Tzetzes did not mention the identification of the Solymi with either the inhabitants of Jerusalem or the Jews. Accordingly, the lion simile is interpreted as referring to bravery rather than to shamelessness:[81]

> ἤγουν ὁ τροπωσάμενος ἔθνη τριπλᾶ τῷ πλοίῳ,
> Σολύμους, Ἀμαζόνας τε, τοὺς τῆς ἐνέδρας τρίτους·
> Σολύμους μές, ὡς λέοντας, ὄντας γενναίους ἄνδρας,
> ὡς χίμαιραν, ὡς αἶγα δὲ κρημνοβατοῦσαν πάλιν,
> τῶν Ἀμαζόνων τὸν στρατὸν Ἄρεος θυγατέρων,
> ὡς δράκοντα τὴν ἐνέδραν τῶν ἐλλοχώντων τούτῳ.
> (Tzetzes, *Allegories of the Iliad* 6.53–8 ed. Boissonade)

---

[80] Cf. *Jewish War* 6.438. [81] On this passage, see Goldwyn (2017: 151–3).

(Bellerophon) who put to flight three sets of foreigners with his ship,
the Solymoi, the Amazons, and third those sitting in ambush;
the Solymoi were brave men like lions,
the army of the Amazons, the daughters of Ares,
was like a chimera, like a goat climbing a steep mountain,
and those lying in wait to ambush him were like a serpent.
(trans. Goldwyn and Kokkini 2015)

This discrepancy in Tzetzes' exegetical stance might be due to the rationale informing the *Allegories of the Iliad*, addressed to the future empress Bertha-Irene. The emphasis there is on Hellenism, with less room left for cross-cultural contamination.[82] It might also be that, in the years between the *Allegories of the Iliad* and the *Allegories of the Odyssey*, which are chronologically closer to the *Histories*, Tzetzes acquired new expertise, broadening his knowledge of ancient sources.

In the *Adventures of the Solymi*, Tim Whitmarsh shows how the Jews were first associated with the *Odyssey*'s Solima mountains – a tradition visible in the fragment from Choerilus we have seen above, but probably more widespread.[83] It is only with the Flavian period that the Jews as a whole are 'rebranded' as Solymi, with reference to the passage from the *Iliad*, mainly owing to their heightened visibility during and after the war with Rome, which led to the destruction of the Temple.[84] A similar dynamic, I argue, is probably at stake for Tzetzes.

Jerusalem had already played a very important role in John II's foreign politics during the 1130s and 1140s.[85] When Choniates has the dying emperor speak and retrospectively assess his legacy in the *History*, the conquest of the Kingdom of Jerusalem features among the failed military goals he most poignantly regrets.[86] Later on and closer to the time in which the *Allegories of the Odyssey* and the *Histories* were composed, Manuel I emphasizes time and again his interest in the Holy Land, not least by marrying his niece Theodora to Baldwin III of Jerusalem in 1158, when he also invested a remarkable amount of money in reinforcing the allegiance.[87] This new interest in the Levant, coupled with Tzetzes' willingness

---

[82] See Goldwyn (2017).　　[83] See Whitmarsh (2013: 232–6).　　[84] Whitmarsh (2013: 236–8).
[85] Papageorgiou (2016: 46).
[86] Niketas Choniates, *History* 40.63–77 ed. van Dieten, with Browning (1961), Simpson (2013: 217–18).
[87] Galadza (2018: 127), Magdalino (1993: 69–70).

to prove his knowledge of Jewish culture, might have shaped the exegetical agenda behind the seemingly bizarre interpretation of the Solymi.[88]

Authoritative Models and the Performance of Anti-Judaism

As I have shown in the first section, exegesis was very much subject to performative practices that affected engagement with ancient texts. Such practices also entailed the frequent use of more or less playfully abusive tones. In this section, I will show that the encounter with the otherness of Jewish culture was also shaped by the performative setting of the classroom.

One of the most remarkable features of the passage from the scholia on Aristophanes is the mention of an 'exegesis on the Jewish books'. The reader cannot help but wonder which books Tzetzes is referring to here – provided it is not sheer uncorroborated boasting. Here, I will advance a tentative solution, trying to demonstrate Tzetzes' close engagement with the work of Josephus.

As shown by Bowman,[89] Josephus enjoyed a very rich reception in Byzantium. Photios mentions him in his *Bibliotheca*,[90] and his timeline for Jewish history represents the backbone of many Byzantine chronographies, including Zonaras in the twelfth century. Clear influences are also to be detected in the historiographical work of Niketas Choniates.[91] Appreciation of Josephus is confirmed by manuscript evidence, and here it is worthwhile to point out that between the eleventh and the thirteenth century there is a remarkable increase in the number of manuscripts produced.[92]

Strikingly, Tzetzes is not listed in the few surveys dealing with Josephus' Byzantine readership, and yet Josephus features prominently in Tzetzes' work. Praise for his work is explicit in the *Histories*, where passages from the *Jewish Antiquities* and from the *Jewish War* are commented upon in detail. In his letter collection, Tzetzes also uses the phrase 'unjust destiny', which is only found in *Jewish War* 1.32.2 and then carefully explained in

---

[88] As someone writing on commission, Tzetzes was rather sensitive to contemporary events; we need only think about his only hagiographical piece, the *Life of St. Lucy*, probably written after 1158, which echoes the diplomatic relationships between Constantinople and the Kingdom of Sicily at the time (see Magdalino and Macrides [1992: 153–4]).
[89] Bowman (1987).   [90] Photios, *Library*, cod. 47 ed. Henry.   [91] Bowman (1987: 372).
[92] Schreckenberg (1972: 48–59), Leoni (2016). In the tenth century, the Greek-Jewish community settled in southern Italy and produced a well-known chronicle ascribed to Josephus, the *Sefer Yosippon* (see Dönitz [2016]).

the *Histories*.⁹³ Josephus is generally referred to as a 'wondrous', a 'Jewish historian' or an 'illustrious Jew' with unrestrained praise.⁹⁴

The epithet *hebraios* seems to have been enough to identify Josephus in the twelfth century. In Eustathios' *Inquiry into Monastic Life* the phrase 'sweet Jewish rhetor' probably refers to him:

> ...οὐ φαρισσαϊκῶς μέντοι, ἀλλ' εἰ χρὴ οὕτω φάναι, κατὰ τοὺς περιᾳδομένους Ἐσσαιούς, οὓς ὁ γλυκὺς Ἑβραῖος ῥήτωρ καθιστορεῖ, οἷς μᾶλλον ἀφομοιώσεται τὸ κοινοβιακὸν μοναχικόν. (Eustathios of Thessalonike, *Inquiry into Monastic Life* 195.11–14 ed. Metzler)

> ... surely not like the Pharisees, but, if we must name someone, like the famous Essenes, on whom the sweet Jewish rhetor reports: it is them that the communal lifestyle of the monks most resembles.

The editor of the *Inquiry into Monastic Life* suggests that the reference is to Philo.⁹⁵ Philo, however, never mentions the Pharisees in his work, whereas Josephus begins his excursus on the Essenes – called both Essaioi and Essenoi – by listing the three Jewish sects of Pharisees, Sadducees and Essenes.⁹⁶ The qualification of 'rhetor' for Josephus is not surprising per se, since rhetor can work as portmanteau term for 'author' in Byzantine texts.⁹⁷

To sum up, we have evidence suggesting that, in fact, Tzetzes might have authored commentaries – or at least lectured – on the texts of Josephus, which, as we have seen, were known among twelfth-century Constantinopolitan elites. First, Tzetzes incorporates fragments of such a commentary in the *Histories*, a strategy he also adopts for other works on now-lost ancient authors.⁹⁸ Second, we have seen that he was interested in the intersections between Hellenism and Jewish culture, so much so that he boasted actual knowledge of Hebrew. Third, the curious exegesis he offers on the Solymi is very close to the one provided by Josephus, further reinforcing the hypothesis of an active engagement with the latter's text.

This is not the whole story, though. Again, we must factor in performance and the expectations of the audience. Despite his apparent interest in Jewish culture and his admiring attitude toward Josephus,

---

⁹³ Josephus, *Jewish War* 1.22.1–1.26.3; Tzetzes, *Histories* 6.43: Josephus, *Jewish War* 1.26.3 and *Jewish Antiquities* 16.10.4; Tzetzes, *Ep.* 5, p. 8.16 ed. Leone (1972) and *Histories* 5.12 (significantly, Jerusalem is here called Ἱερὰ Σολύμα).
⁹⁴ See *Historiae* 5.12.513 and 545 ed. Leone (2007).
⁹⁵ Metzler ad loc. (2006: 226): *Hypothetica sive Apologia pro Iudaeis* 11; *Quod omnis probus liber sit* 75.
⁹⁶ *Jewish Antiquities* 18.18–22 with Strugnell (1958). ⁹⁷ See Papaioannou (2014: 22, n. 2).
⁹⁸ One of the most striking cases is represented by a lost verse paraphrasis of Ptolemy's *Geography*, part of which is inserted into *Histories* 11.884–994.

Tzetzes is not immune to anti-Judaic overtones.[99] From the scholia on the *Histories*, we know that his copyist had trouble in understanding the puzzling interpretation of the Solymi offered by Tzetzes, who comments as follows:

> Ἑβραίους
> Ὦ μιαρέ, παμμίαρε καὶ κοπρωτὰ βιβλίων,
> Ἑβραῖε τοὺς Ἑβραίους νῦν Ῥωμαίους ὀνομάζεις.
> (Tzetzes, *Scholia on the Histories* 7.831, p. 558.14–16 ed. Leone 2007)

> *Jews*
> O infamous, totally infamous book-soiler,
> Jew, you call now the Jews Romans.

Tzetzes addresses here the person in charge of producing a clean copy of the draft of the *Histories*. This individual made frequent mistakes in spelling[100] and copying[101] and would leave out entire lines.[102] Since Tzetzes refers to him as 'son' or κόπελος (that is, 'boy' or 'apprentice'), we can hypothesize that he was a youngster in his service. Tzetzes is frankly abusive to him, and the lines quoted above have to be interpreted as a rant due to a mistake, where the scribe wrote the word Ῥωμαίους instead of Ἑβραίους in the text he copied. To express his anger, Tzetzes calls him 'Jew', a purposely thematic insult, which is meant to be as derogatory as the 'son of a cuckold' he throws at the κόπελος in another passage. However, as was discussed at the beginning of the chapter, the violence of these attacks is probably to be read in the performative context of Tzetzes' lecturing and commenting. I would suggest that there might even be a tinge of heavy irony here. The scribe's mistake must have sounded particularly grotesque to twelfth-century audiences, given that Jews were progressively deprived of their rights of free citizens of the Empire.[103]

---

[99] On anti-Judaic polemics in Byzantium, see Déroche (2012).
[100] See e.g. *Scholia on the Histories* 12.140.1, p. 565.1: Δωδεκετηρίδας Κούρβας υἱὲ μιαρέ, δωδεκάκις μετὰ δύο κάππα. Cf. 8.711a.1–2, p. 560.13–14; 12.393.1–3, p. 566.3–5; 12.799.1, p. 567.13–14 ed. Leone (2007).
[101] See e.g. *Scholia on the Histories* 7.941, p. 558.26 (τὸν Σώστρατον ὁ μιαρὸς Σώκρατον, βλέπεις, γράφει).
[102] *Scholia on the Histories* 6.881, p. 555.16–17 (Ζήτει· ὁ μιαρὸς ὁ κόπελος στίχους τῆδε); 8.903.1, p. 560.30 ed. Leone (2007) (Οὐκ οἶδα τί γράφει ὁ μιαρός); 10.933 (Ζήτει στίχον ἢ στίχους· κἄν τι ἀληθὲς γράφῃ ὁ μιαρός, γράφει καὶ τοῦτο ἀπόζον τῆς μιαρᾶς τούτου ψυχῆς· οὐκ οἶδα τί γράφει ὁ μιαρὸς οὐδὲ ὀρθοῦν δύναμαι); and 971, p. 563.17–21 (Κερατᾶ μιαροῦ υἱέ, τίνα εἰσὶ δὲ ἃ γράφεις καὶ ἃ καταλιμπάνεις καὶ κατεκόπρωσάς μου τὴν βίβλον); 12.297.1, p. 565.18 (Ζήτει στίχον. Ὁ μιαρὸς πάλιν ἐμίανε τὸ βιβλίον).
[103] See Linder (2012: 208): 'From its very beginning that state also embarked on a policy of disentitlement in all spheres of life – legal, political, economic, religious, and societal relationships – that rendered that citizenship a largely hollow concept, denuded of most of its practical implications. By 1049, at the latest, that process received official confirmation. An

In conclusion, my reading of *Scholia on Aristophanes' Frogs* 843b against the background of performative teaching practices and Tzetzes' overall exegetical activity has shown that commenting on the classics required meeting the needs and expectations of the student audience. Tzetzes could not avoid addressing the multilayered and multilingual reality of Constantinopolitan society, engaging with cultures that, while being marginalized, had an active role in the economic fabric of the Empire.[104] Yet, when he lectures for the elites of the capital, such an engagement does not take the form of a cultural encounter; rather it is shaped as cultural appropriation. Such an attitude resonates with the more general appropriation of motifs of Jewish history that were incorporated into imperial ideology: from Mosaic Law to the representation of Byzantium as the New Israel and Constantinople as the new Zion, a frequent *topos* during the Middle Byzantine period.[105] On a smaller scale, this dynamic also emerges in the curious exegesis of the Solymi, as well as in the passage from the *Histories* where Tzetzes alleges that he has a better knowledge of Hebrew and Arabic than native speakers. In fact, the figure of Bellerophon had been tightly linked with imperial ideology and power since Roman times. Along these lines, Bellerophon later became a symbol for Christian military strength.[106] In Forum Tauri or Forum Theodosii,[107] moreover, an equestrian statue has been identified with Bellerophon, while a mosaic in the Imperial Palace portrayed Bellerophon killing Chimaera.[108] Tzetzes, therefore, conveys an image of subjugation that is compelling for his listeners, who could map it out on their urban/courtly visual memories. In this respect, when he states that his audience will never be able to find his material in any book of a 'Jew or foreigner', not only does Tzetzes assert his authorial personality, he also reaffirms, more broadly, Hellenism's cultural superiority.

---

eloquent statement of principle on the legal status of the Jews promulgated by Constantine IX Monomachos ignores any claim to Roman citizenship and affirms the concept of their potentially servile status on religious grounds, not unlike the Western institution of the *servitus camerae*.'

[104] See Jacoby (2012). [105] Troianos (2012: 142–3).
[106] On this evolution, see Doblhofer (1983). [107] On the Forum, see Janin (1964: 64–6).
[108] The Bellerophon statue is mentioned by Niketas Choniates in *De Signis* 857.15–858.5. According to others the statue would represent Joshua. It is highly significant that Choniates bases his interpretation on a reading of Homer (see Cutler 1968: 117–18). On the mosaics, see Brett (1942).

REFERENCES

Agapitos, P. (2017) 'John Tzetzes and the Blemish Examiners: A Byzantine Teacher on Schedography, Everyday Language and Writerly Disposition', *MEG* 17: 1–57.

— (2019) 'Vom Aktualisierungsversuch zum kommunikativen Code: Johannes Tzetzes und der Epilog seiner Theogonie für die *sebastokratorissa* Eirene', in *Herbert Hunger und die Wiener Schule der Byzantinistik: Rückblick und Ausblick*, ed. A. Külzer, 271–90. Vienna.

Bekker, I. (ed.) (1836) *Michaelis Glycae annales*. Corpus scriptorum historiae Byzantinae. Bonn.

— (ed.) (1842) 'Die Theogonie des Johannes Tzetzes aus der Bibliotheca Casanatensis (Ms. J. II. 10)', in *Philologische und historische Abhandlungen der Königlichen Akademie der Wissenschaften zu Berlin aus dem Jahre 1840*, 147–69. Berlin.

Benuzzi, F. (2017–18) 'Erudizione, autorità e autorialità: l'esegesi antica alla commedia sulla cattedra di Giovanni Tzetze', *Incontri triestini di filologia classica* 17: 369–86.

Bernard, F. (2014) *Writing and Reading Byzantine Secular Poetry, 1025–1081*. Oxford Studies in Byzantium. Oxford.

Bernard, F. and K. Demoen (2019) 'Byzantine Book Epigrams', in *A Companion to Byzantine Poetry*, ed. W. Hörandner, A. Rhoby and N. Zagklas, 404–29. Brill's Companions to the Byzantine World 4. Leiden–Boston.

van den Berg, B. (2021) 'Playwright, Satirist, Atticist: The Reception of Aristophanes in 12th-Century Byzantium', in *Satire in the Middle Byzantine Period: The Golden Age of Laughter?*, ed. P. Marciniak and I. Nilsson, 227–53. Explorations in Medieval Culture 12. Leiden–Boston.

Bianconi, D. (2010) 'Età comnena e cultura scritta: materiali e considerazioni alle origini di una ricerca', in *The Legacy of Bernard de Montfaucon: Three Hundred Years of Studies on Greek Handwriting: Proceedings of the Seventh International Colloquium of Greek Palaeography (Madrid–Salamanca, 15–20 September 2008)*, ed. A. Bravo García and I. Pérez Martín, vol. 1, 75–96, vol. 2, 668–77. Turnhout.

Billerbeck, M. and A. Neumann-Hartmann (eds.) (2016) *Stephani Byzantii Ethnika*, vol. 4: *Π–Υ*. Berlin–Boston.

Billerbeck, M., G. Lentini and A. Neumann-Hartmann (eds.) (2014) *Stephani Byzantii Ethnika*, vol. 3: *Κ–Ο*. Berlin–Boston.

Boissonade, J. F. (ed.) (1851) *Tzetzae allegoriae Iliadis*. Paris.

Bonfil, R., O. Irshai, G. G. Stroumsa and R. Talgam (eds.) (2012) *Jews in Byzantium: Dialectics of Minority and Majority Cultures*. Jerusalem Studies in Religion and Culture 14. Leiden–Boston.

Bowman, S. (1987) 'Josephus in Byzantium', in *Josephus, Judaism and Christianity*, ed. L. H. Feldman and G. Hata, 362–85. Detroit.

— (2014) 'The Jewish Experience in Byzantium', in *The Jewish-Greek Tradition in Antiquity and the Byzantine Empire*, ed. J. Aitken and J. Carleton Paget, 37–53. Cambridge.

Braccini, T. (2009–10) 'Erudita invenzione: riflessioni sulla Piccola grande Iliade di Giovanni Tzetze', *Incontri Triestini di Filologia Classica* 9: 153–73.
  (2011) 'Riscrivere l'epica: Giovanni Tzetzes di fronte al ciclo troiano', *CentoPagine* 5: 43–57.
Brett, G. (1942) 'The Mosaic of the Great Palace in Constantinople', *JWI* 5: 34–43.
Browning, R. (1961) 'The Death of John Comnenus', *Byzantion* 31: 229–35.
Canart, P. and L. Perria (1991) 'Les écritures livresques des XI et XII siècles', in *Paleografia e codicologia greca. Atti del II Colloquio internazionale Berlino-Wolfenbüttel, 17–20 ottobre 1983*, ed. D. Harlfinger and G. Prato, 67–116. Alessandria.
Colonna, A. (1963) 'Il commento di Giovanni Tzetzes agli "Halieutica" di Oppiano', in *Lanx satura Nicolao Terzaghi oblata: miscellanea philologica*, 101–4. Genoa.
Conley, T. M. (2005) 'Byzantine Criticism and the Uses of Literature', in *The Cambridge History of Literary Criticism*, vol. 2: *The Middle Ages*, ed. A. Minnis and I. Johnson, 669–92. Cambridge.
Cramer, J. A. (ed.) (1836) *Anecdota Oxoniensia*, vol. 3. Oxford.
Cullhed, E. (2012) 'The Autograph Manuscripts Containing Eustathius' Commentary on the *Odyssey*', *Mnemosyne* 65: 445–61.
  (2014) 'The Blind Bard and "I": Homeric Biography and Authorial Personas in the Twelfth Century', *BMGS* 38: 49–67.
  (ed. and trans.) (2016) *Eustathios of Thessalonike, Commentary on the Odyssey*, vol. 1: *On Rhapsodies A–B*. Acta Universitatis Upsaliensis. Studia Byzantina Upsaliensia 17. Uppsala.
Cutler, A. (1968) 'The *De Signis* of Nicetas Choniates: A Reappraisal', *AJA* 72: 113–18.
Dagron, G. (1994) 'Formes et fonctions du pluralisme linguistique à Byzance (XIe–XIIe siècle)', *T&MByz* 12: 234–40.
Déroche, V. (2012) 'Forms and Functions of Anti-Jewish Polemics: Polymorphy, Polysémy', in *Jews in Byzantium: Dialectics of Minority and Majority Cultures*, ed. R. Bonfil, O. Irshai, G. G. Stroumsa and R. Talgam, 535–48. Jerusalem Studies in Religion and Culture 14. Leiden–Boston.
van Dieten, J. (ed.) (1975) *Nicetae Choniatae historia*. Berlin.
Dindorf, W. (ed.) (1855) *Scholia Graeca in Homeri Odysseam*, 2 vols. Oxford.
Doblhofer, E. (1983) 'Bellerophon und Kirke zwischen Heiden und Christen', in *Festschrift für Robert Muth: Zum 65. Geburtstag am 1. Januar 1981*, ed. P. Händel and W. Meid, 73–87. Innsbrucker Beiträge zur Kulturwissenschaft 22. Innsbruck.
Dondaine, A. (1952) 'Hugues Etherien et Léon Toscan', *AHMA* 19: 473–83.
Dönitz, S. (2016) 'Sefer Yosippon (Josippon)', in *A Companion to Josephus*, ed. H. H. Chapman and Z. Rodgers, 382–9. Malden–Oxford–Chicester.
Drachmann, A. B. (ed.) (1925) *Isaac Tzetzes de metris Pindaricis commentarius*. Copenhagen.

Erbse, H. (ed.) (1972) *Scholia Graeca in Homeri Iliadem (scholia vetera)*, vol. 2. Berlin.
Gaisford, T. (ed.) (1823) *Poetae Minores Graeci*, vol. 2: *Scholia ad Hesiodum*. Leipzig.
Galadza, D. (2018) *Liturgy and Byzantinization in Jerusalem*. Oxford.
Gaul, N. (2014) 'Rising Elites and Institutionalization – Ēthos/Mores – Debts and Drafts: Three Concluding Steps towards Comparing Networks of Learning in Byzantium and the "Latin" West, c. 1000–1200', in *Networks of Learning: Perspectives on Scholars in Byzantine East and Latin West, c. 1000–1200*, ed. S. Steckel, N. Gaul and M. Grünbart, 235–80. Zurich–Berlin.
Giannachi, F. (2014) 'Un nuovo manoscritto del *De metris* di Giovanni Tzetzes: Schøyen ms. 1660', *ARF* 16: 133–50.
Goldwyn, A. (2017) 'Theory and Method in John Tzetzes' *Allegories of the* Iliad and *Allegories of the* Odyssey', *Scandinavian Journal of Byzantine and Modern Greek Studies* 3: 141–71.
Goldwyn, A. J. and D. Kokkini (trans.) (2015) *John Tzetzes, Allegories of the Iliad*. Dumbarton Oaks Medieval Library 37. Cambridge, MA.
 (trans.) (2019) *John Tzetzes, Allegories of the Odyssey*. Dumbarton Oaks Medieval Library 56. Cambridge, MA.
Goor, A. (1966) 'The History of the Grape-Vine in the Holy Land', *Economic Botany* 20: 46–64.
Grünbart, M. (1994) 'Tzurichos, ein Häretiker aus der ersten Hälfte des 12. Jhs. (Io. Tzetzes, ep. 55)', *ByzSlav* 55: 15–18.
Heckscher, W. (1956) 'The "Anadyomene" in The Mediaeval Tradition: (Pelagia – Cleopatra – Aphrodite) A Prelude to Botticelli's "Birth of Venus"', *Nederlands Kunsthistorisch Jaarboek (NKJ) / Netherlands Yearbook for History of Art* 7: 1–38.
Henry, R. (ed.) (1959–91) *Photius, Bibliothèque*, 9 vols. Paris.
Hunger, H. (ed.) (1955) 'Johannes Tzetzes, Allegorien zur *Odyssee*, Buch 13–24, kommentierte Textausgabe', *ByzZ* 48: 11–38.
 (ed.) (1956) 'Johannes Tzetzes, Allegorien zur *Odyssee*, Buch 1–12, kommentierte Textausgabe', *ByzZ* 49: 249–310.
Jacoby, D. (2012) 'The Jews in the Byzantine Economy (Seventh to Mid-Fifteenth Century)', in *Jews in Byzantium: Dialectics of Minority and Majority Cultures*, ed. R. Bonfil, O. Irshai, G. G. Stroumsa and R. Talgam, 219–56. Jerusalem Studies in Religion and Culture 14. Leiden–Boston.
Janin, R. (1964) *Constantinople Byzantine*. Paris.
Jones, P. (2006) *Cleopatra: A Source Book*. Oklahoma Series in Classical Culture 31. Norman.
Koster, W. J. W. (1960) 'Prolegomena', in *Jo. Tzetzae Commentarii in Aristophanem, fasc.* I: *Prolegomena et commentarius in Plutum*. Groningen.
 (ed.) (1962) *Jo. Tzetzae Commentarii in Aristophanem, fasc.* III: *Commentarium in Ranas et in Aves; Argumentum Equitum, Commentarii in Ranas et in Aves*. Groningen.

(ed.) (1975) *Prolegomena de comoedia; Scholia in Acharnenses, Equites, Nubes, fasc. I.I.a: Prolegomena de comoedia*. Groningen.

Labuk, T. (2016) 'Aristophanes in the Service of Niketas Choniates – Gluttony, Drunkenness and Politics in the Χρονικὴ διήγησις', *JÖByz* 66: 127–51.

de Lange, N. (1991) 'The Classical Tradition in Byzantium', in *A Traditional Quest: Essays in Honour of Louis Jacobs*, ed. D. Cohn-Sherlock, 86–101. Journal for the Study of the Old Testament Supplement Series 114. Sheffield.

(1998) 'Hebraism and Hellenism: The Case of Byzantine Jewry', *Poetics Today* 19.1: *Hellenism and Hebraism Reconsidered: The Poetics of Cultural Influence and Exchange* 1: 129–45.

Lasker, D., J. Niehoff-Panagiotidis and D. Sklare (2018) *Editing Theology at a Crossroad: A Preliminary Edition of Judah Hadassi's Eshkol ha-Kofer, First Commandment, and Studies of the Book's Judaeo-Arabic and Byzantine Contexts*. Leiden.

Leone, P. L. M. (ed.) (1972) *Ioannis Tzetzae Epistulae*. Leipzig.

(ed.) (2007) *Ioannis Tzetzae Historiae*, second edition. Galatina.

Leoni, T. (2016) 'The Text of the Josephan Corpus: Principal Greek Manuscripts, Ancient Latin Translations, and the Indirect Tradition', in *A Companion to Josephus*, ed. H. H. Chapman and Z. Rogers, 307–21. Malden–Oxford–Chicester.

von Leutsch, E. L. and F. W. Schneidewin (eds.) (1839) *Corpus Paroemiographorum Graecorum*, vol. 1. Göttingen.

Linder, A. (2012) 'The Legal Status of Jews in the Byzantine Empire', in *Jews in Byzantium: Dialectics of Minority and Majority Cultures*, ed. R. Bonfil, O. Irshai, G. G. Stroumsa and R. Talgam, 149–218. Jerusalem Studies in Religion and Culture 14. Leiden–Boston.

Luzzatto, M. J. (1999) *Tzetzes lettore di Tucidide: note sul Codice Heidelberg Palatino Greco 252*. Bari.

Macrides, R. and P. Magdalino (1992) 'The Fourth Kingdom and the Rhetoric of Hellenism', in *The Perception of the Past in Twelfth-Century Europe*, ed. P. Magdalino, 117–56. London.

Magdalino, P. (1993) *The Empire of Manuel I Komnenos, 1143–1180*. Cambridge.

(2000) 'The Maritime Neighborhoods of Constantinople: Commercial and Residential Functions, Sixth to Twelfth Centuries', *DOP* 54: 209–26.

Marzano, T. M. (2016) 'Entre filólogos comnenos y copistas paleólogos: Opiano y Eurípides en el Salmanticensis 31 (con una carta al patriarca de Constantinopla)', *ExClass* 20: 147–62.

Massa Positano, L. (ed.) (1960) *Jo. Tzetzae Commentarii in Aristophanem, fasc. I: Prolegomena et commentarius in Plutum*. Groningen.

Mastronarde, D. J. (2017) *Preliminary Studies on the Scholia to Euripides*. Berkeley.

Mazzucchi, C. M. (2003) 'Ambrosianus C 222 Inf. (Graecus 886): il codice e il suo autore, parte prima: il codice', *Aevum* 77: 263–75.

(2004) 'Ambrosianus C 222 Inf. (Graecus 886): il codice e il suo autore, parte seconda: l'autore', *Aevum* 78: 411–40.

Metzler, K. (ed. and trans.) (2006) *Eustathii Thessalonicensis De emendanda vita monachica*. Corpus Fontium Historiae Byzantinae 45. Berlin.
de Meyïer, K. A. (1955) *Codices Vossiani graeci et miscellanei*. Leiden.
Nystazopoulou-Pelekidou, M. (ed.) (1980) Βυζαντινὰ ἔγγραφα τῆς μονῆς Πάτμου Β' - Δημοσίων λειτουργῶν. Athens.
Olkinuora, J. (2015) *Byzantine Hymnography for the Feast of the Theotokos*. Helsinki.
Papadopoulos-Kerameus, A. (ed.) (1908) 'Glossarion *hebraiohellenikon*', in *Festschrift zu Ehren des Dr. A. Harkavy*, ed. G. von Günzburg and I. Markon, 68–90. Saint Petersburg.
Papageorgiou, A. (2016) 'The Political Ideology of John II Komnenos', in *John II Komnenos, Emperor of Byzantium: In the Shadow of Father and Son*, ed. A. Bucossi and A. Rodriguez Suarez, 37–52. Abingdon–New York.
Papaioannou, S. (2014) 'Voice, Signature, Mask: The Byzantine Author', in *The Author in Middle Byzantine Literature: Modes, Functions, and Identities*, ed. A. Pizzone, 132–40. Berlin–New York.
Papathomopoulos, M. (ed.) (2007) Ἐξήγησις Ἰωάννου Γραμματικοῦ τοῦ Τζέτζου εἰς τὴν Ὁμήρου Ἰλιάδα. Athens.
Petridès, S. (1903) 'Vers inédits de Jean Tzetzès', *ByzZ* 12: 568–70.
Pietrosanti, P. (2009) 'Il prologo dell'ἐξήγησις di Giovanni Tzetzes agli ἔργα καὶ ἡμέραι di Esiodo: polemica letteraria e programma ermeneutico', *I Quaderni del Cairoli* 23: 77–90.
Pizzone, A. (2017) 'The *Historiai* of John Tzetzes: A Byzantine "Book of Memory"?', *BMGS* 41.2: 182–207.
— (2020) 'Self-authorization and Strategies of Autography in John Tzetzes: The *Logismoi* Rediscovered', *GRBS* 60: 652–90.
— (2022) 'Tzetzes and the *prokatastasis*: A Tale of People, Manuscripts and Performances', in Τζετζικαὶ ἔρευναι, ed. E. E. Prodi, 19–73. Bologna.
Pontani, F. (1998) 'Mosè del Brolo e la sua lettera da Costantinopoli', *Aevum* 72: 143–75.
Radici Colace, P. (ed.) (1979) *Choerili Samii Reliquiae*. Rome.
Rhoby, A. (2010) 'Ioannes Tzetzes als Auftragsdichter', *Graeco-Latina Brunensia* 15: 150–77.
Rodriguez Suarez, A. (2016) 'From Greek into Latin: Western Scholars and Translators in Constantinople during the Reign of John II', in *John II Komnenos, Emperor of Byzantium: In the Shadow of Father and Son*, ed. A. Bucossi and A. Rodriguez Suarez, 91–109. Abingdon–New York.
Scattolin, P. (2003) 'Su alcuni codici degli scolii all'Elettra di Sofocle', in *Il dramma sofocleo: testo, lingua, interpretazione*, ed. A. Avezzù, 307–20. Stuttgart–Weimar.
Scheer, E. (ed.) (1908) *Lycophronis Alexandra*, vol. 2: *Scholia continens*. Berlin.
Schreckenberg, H. (1972) *Die Flavius-Josephus-Tradition in Antike und Mittelalter*. Leiden.
Shukurov, R. (2016) *The Byzantine Turks, 1204–1461*. Leiden.
Simpson, A. (2013) *Niketas Choniates: A Historiographical Study*. Oxford.

Starr, J. (ed.) (1934) 'A Fragment of a Greek Mishnaic Glossarium', *Proceedings of the American Academy for Jewish Research* 6: 353–67.
Strugnell, J. (1958) 'Flavius Josephus and the Essenes: *Antiquities* XVIII.18–22', *Journal of Biblical Literature* 77: 106–15.
Toth, I. (2018) 'Modern Encounters with Byzantine Texts and Their Reading Public', in *Reading in the Byzantine Empire and Beyond*, ed. T. Shawcross and I. Toth, 37–54. Cambridge.
Troianos, S. N. (2012) 'Christians and Jews in Byzantium: A Love–Hate Relationship', in *Jews in Byzantium: Dialectics of Minority and Majority Cultures*, ed. R. Bonfil, O. Irshai, G. G. Stroumsa and R. Talgam, 133–48. Jerusalem Studies in Religion and Culture 14. Leiden–Boston.
van der Valk, M. (ed.) (1971–87) *Eustathii archiepiscopi Thessalonicensis commentarii ad Homeri Iliadem pertinentes ad fidem codicis Laurentiani editi*, 4 vols. Leiden.
Wendel, C. (1948) 'Tzetzes Johannes', in *Realencyclopädie der classischen Altertumswissenschaft* VII A 2, 1959–2011. Stuttgart.
Whitmarsh, T. (2013) *Beyond the Second Sophistic: Adventures in Greek Postclassicism*. Los Angeles.
Xenophontos, S. (2014) '"A Living Portrait of Cato": Self-Fashioning and the Classical Past in John Tzetzes' Chiliads', *Estudios Byzantinos* 2: 187–204.
Zagklas, N. (2019) '"How Many Verses Shall I Write and Say?": Poetry in the Komnenian Period (1081–1204)', in *A Companion to Byzantine Poetry*, ed. W. Hörandner, A. Rhoby and N. Zagklas, 237–63. Brill's Companions to the Byzantine World 4. Leiden–Boston.
  (2021) 'Satire in the Komnenian Period: Poetry, Satirical Strands, and Intellectual Antagonism', in *Satire in the Middle Byzantine Period: The Golden Age of Laughter?*, ed. P. Marciniak and I. Nilsson, 279–303. Explorations in Medieval Culture 12. Leiden–Boston.
Zumbo, A. (1997) 'Una misconosciuta ΥΠΟΘΕΣΙΣ ΠΕΡΙ ΑΤΛΑΝΤΟΣ di Giovanni Tzetzes (Schol. Oppian. Hal. 1,622)', *RSBN* 33: 275–8.

CHAPTER 4

Uncovering the Literary Sources of John Tzetzes' Theogony

Maria Tomadaki

John Tzetzes, the well-known Byzantine polymath, teacher, poet and philologist of the twelfth century, had a wide knowledge of the ancient Greek literary tradition, especially of the ancient Greek poets (e.g. Homer, Hesiod, Aristophanes, Lycophron), whose works he used to teach, comment on and imitate. A representative example of his creative engagement with Hesiod is his *Theogony*, a didactic poem in ca. 850 political verses, which is dedicated to the *sebastokratorissa* Irene, one of the most active patrons of the Komnenian aristocracy.[1] The poem usually bears the following title in the manuscripts: Ἰωάννου γραμματικοῦ, τοῦ Τζέτζου ποίημα αὐθωρὸν καὶ ἀμελέτητον διὰ στίχων πολιτικῶν ἔχων πᾶσαν Θεογονίαν ἐν βραχεῖ μετὰ προσθήκης καὶ καταλόγου τῶν ἐπὶ τὴν Ἴλιον ἀρίστων Ἑλλήνων τὲ καὶ Τρώων ('John the grammarian, Tzetzes' poem, immediate and improvised in political verses, containing the whole *Theogony* in brevity along with the addition of a catalogue of Troy's bravest Greek and Trojan <heroes>').[2] Although the poem is said to be improvised, it consists of an elaborate mixture of several ancient sources, the most prominent of which is Hesiod's *Theogony*. This chapter attempts to uncover the main literary sources of Tzetzes' *Theogony*, as well as to examine the poem's function in the context of the patronage relation between Tzetzes and the

---

[*] This chapter is an improved version of my presentation on the same subject at the conference of Byzantine Poetry organized by the editors of the electronic journal *Parekbolai* in Athens (16/12/2016). I sincerely thank Prof. Marina Loukaki for her helpful comments on my presentation, Prof. Ioannis Vassis for his bibliographical support and the editors of the present volume for their remarks. I am grateful to the BOF Research Fund of Ghent University for funding my research on John Tzetzes.

[1] On the *sebastokratorissa* Irene, see E. M. Jeffreys (2012: 177–94), Rhoby (2009: 305–36), Jeffreys and Jeffreys (1994: 40–68), Lampsidis (1984: 91–105), Varzos (1984: 362–79). Among the literary works she commissioned are Constantine Manasses' *Chronicle*, Theodore Prodromos' *Grammar* and many epigrams of both Theodore and Manganeios Prodromos; on her commissions, see especially E. M. Jeffreys (2012: 180–1).

[2] On this title, see one of the *Theogony*'s oldest manuscripts, Vatican City, Biblioteca Apostolica Vaticana, Barb. gr. 30, fol. 145r.

sebastokratorissa Irene. Furthermore, it intends to contribute to the understanding of Tzetzes' attitude towards the ancient poets.

The poem begins with a prologue (vv. 1–47), in which Tzetzes lavishly praises his patroness for her devotion to learning, her physical beauty, her divine favour, her noble origin, her generosity and her wealth.[3] Tzetzes clearly states in the prologue that he received gold from Irene as a reward for composing his *Theogony* (vv. 40–5). This gold, as he characteristically says, broke the bounds of his silence, warmed the nerves of his once talkative tongue and made it again active. Tzetzes' praise of Irene's generosity and his reference to the therapeutic effects of gold should be understood within the system of Komnenian patronage relations and his aim to receive more payment.

The poem continues with a genealogy of mythological deities (vv. 1–377), which reproduces the structure and the themes of Hesiod's *Theogony*, and a genealogy of the heroes of the Trojan War (vv. 378–720). Of particular importance is the epilogue of the *Theogony* (ca. 133 vv.), which testifies to the spoken language of twelfth-century Constantinople and refers to Tzetzes' literary choices. The author implies in the epilogue that he adjusted his style to Irene's level, but that he is adept at writing in every register (Atticizing or vernacular). To support himself against the responses of a critical audience, he quotes relevant sayings of ancient authorities (e.g. Plato, Aristophanes) and presents himself as an imitator of Attic writers such as Aeschines, Demosthenes and Lysias.[4] In addition, he quotes several greeting phrases in Arabic, Latin, Hebrew, ancient Ossetian-Alanic, Cuman, Seljuk Turkish and Russian (all written and translated in his contemporary vernacular) in an attempt to show that he is able to communicate with everyone by adapting his style according to the education and the origin of his addressees.[5] Although Tzetzes' *Theogony* is a poem of great importance

---

[3] All of these elements fit into the broader dominant Byzantine ideology, which prescribed specific images and roles for the imperial woman: cf. Barbara Hill's chapter (1999: 72–93) on 'the creation of the ideal Komnenian woman'. The opening of the *Theogony* recalls the prologue of Manasses' *Synopsis Chronike* and the prologue of his astrological poem: see Rhoby (2010: 167–8).

[4] See *Theogony* 734–65 ed. Agapitos (2017: 40–1). See the quotations on p. 137.

[5] See *Theogony* 766–800 ed. Agapitos (2017: 41–2). This interesting passage indicates the cosmopolitan character of twelfth-century Constantinople and provides evidence of the pronunciation of these languages during the medieval period, at least by a native Greek speaker. On Tzetzes' knowledge of foreign languages, see also Pizzone in this volume.

both for the vernacular and for the reception of the ancient poets in twelfth-century Byzantium, it has not yet been properly studied.[6]

The Poem's Relation to Hesiod and Homer

Tzetzes' *Theogony* does not function as a commentary to Hesiod's *Theogony*, but is rather a work that stands on its own, a paraphrase of Hesiod's *Theogony* enriched with mythological material from other ancient authors, as well as with vocabulary and scenes of Tzetzes' contemporary society.[7] It is also noteworthy that it is not transmitted in the same manuscripts as Hesiod's *Theogony* except for Rome, Biblioteca Vallicelliana, ms. F 016.[8]

Tzetzes' narration follows the narration of Hesiod quite closely until the end of his genealogy of gods (v. 338), which corresponds to Hesiod's *Theogony* 934–7. After these verses, Hesiod continues his narration with Dionysus and Hercules, whereas Tzetzes does not include them. However, at the beginning of Tzetzes' narration about the heroes (vv. 371–2), it becomes clear that he consciously made this omission, since he opposes Hesiod by saying that Hercules and Dionysus should be considered as heroes and not gods.

---

[6] It can be found in several Byzantine manuscripts and in old, incomplete editions; it was first published by Bekker in 1842. His edition is based only on the codex Rome, Biblioteca Casanatense, gr. 306 and contains 777 verses of the *Theogony*, while the complete poem comprises ca. 855 verses. Other incomplete versions of the poem were published in 1850 by Matranga (618 vv.) and in 1915 by Bănescu (767 vv.). The part of the epilogue (35 vv.) that transmits the foreign greetings was first published by Moravcsik in 1930 from the manuscript Vatican City, Biblioteca Apostolica Vaticana, Barb. gr. 30. Some years later, Wendel (1940) published the last 55 verses of the poem from the same manuscript, which were not included in Moravcsik's edition. In 1953, Hunger discovered another manuscript of Tzetzes' *Theogony* in the Austrian National Library, preserving the entire poem (codex Vienna, Österreichische Nationalbibliothek, phil. gr. 118), and he published the important 35 verses with the foreign greetings. An English translation of these 35 verses has been published by Kazhdan and Epstein (1985: 259). The entire epilogue (vv. 719–855) along with an English translation has recently been published by Agapitos (2017: 39–48). Bekker's edition is used as a reference tool in this chapter, as well as Agapitos' text for the verses 719–855. I have been working on a critical edition of the whole poem since 2016. After completing this chapter, I became aware of the new critical edition of the poem by Leone (2019), but I was unable to consult his book.

[7] Other works by Tzetzes which are related to Hesiod are the following: *Commentaries on Hesiod's Works and Days* ed. Gaisford (1823: 10–22), a prose allegorical exegesis *On the Birth of Gods*, ed. Cramer (1841: 101–13), a *Life of Hesiod*, ed. Colonna (1953: 27–39), glosses to the *Theogony* (see Pinakes) and a few epigrams, in which he attacks Proklos for his commentaries on Hesiod; see the *Database of Byzantine Book Epigrams* (DBBE): www.dbbe.ugent.be. On Tzetzes' works that are devoted to the Hesiodic poems, see also Cardin and Pontani (2017: 247). According to the same scholars, Tzetzes' commentaries on Hesiodic works are 'a clear sign that those have been taught at school'.

[8] It is worth noting that some of the *Theogony*'s manuscripts also contain the *Allegories of the Iliad* (Vatican City, Biblioteca Apostolica Vaticana, Barb. gr. 30; Vienna, Österreichische Nationalbibliothek, phil. gr. 118; Paris, Bibliothèque nationale de France, gr. 2705).

It seems that Tzetzes did not have high literary aspirations for his text; his purpose was rather mainly an instructive and informative one. His *Theogony* is characterized by Tzetzes himself as a κατάλογος ('catalogue', vv. 20, 412). In some passages it, indeed, gives the impression of being a catalogue, since Tzetzes simply enumerates gods and heroes without giving them a broad literary representation as Hesiod does. It is quite interesting that in some episodes he either omits mythological names or mentions more than Hesiod.[9] Tzetzes refers in his *Theogony* to approximately 260 mythological deities and 200 heroes. As several of these names can only be found in Tzetzes' *Theogony*, we could suppose that he had access to works that are lost today (such as old scholia on Hesiod and Homer as well as the *Catalogue of Women*).[10]

Although Tzetzes relies on Hesiod for the first part of his poem, namely the genealogy of deities (vv. 1–377), his models for the narration of the heroes' genealogy are not at first sight recognizable (vv. 378–720). At the beginning of my research, I hypothesized that Tzetzes either had access to a longer version of Hesiod's *Theogony*, which also included – after verse 1022 – a genealogy of the heroes of the Trojan War,[11] or that he adopted mythological material from an unidentified lost work called *Heroogony*. The word Ἡρωογονία occurs among the titles of compositions attributed to Hesiod in Proklos' *Prolegomena to Hesiod's Works and Days* and is also mentioned in Tzetzes' *Theogony* 504, indicating a vast genealogy of heroes.[12] However, after a detailed examination of the literary sources that Tzetzes used in his heroic genealogies, it became evident that he draws mythological material from the *Iliad*, Pseudo-Apollodorus' *Bibliotheca* and most possibly from the *Catalogue of Women*, a fragmentary work of genealogies, which is ascribed to

---

[9] For instance, he adds the names of Erinyes (v. 81), Giants (vv. 89–96), Nymphs Meliae (vv. 100–3) and Esperidae (v. 120), but he omits the names of Nereids (vv. 128–31) and several rivers (v. 180).

[10] Dickey (2007: 41) has already pointed out that Tzetzes 'had access to a version of the *Theogony*'s old scholia fuller than has otherwise survived'.

[11] At that stage, I was influenced by Martin West (1966: 49–50), who favoured the idea that an expanded version of Hesiod's *Theogony* could have existed in ancient times, including possibly a genealogy of heroes.

[12] The term *heroogony* is used in Tzetzes' *Theogony* in the context of an invective, where Tzetzes talks about his opponents and explains that, even though they will criticize him, he will omit the superfluous parts of the *heroogony*, derived from the writings of 'monkeys'. Marta Cardin (2009: 247, 249) has pointed out that the title *Heroogony* was actually added in the *Prolegomena* by Tzetzes, but she did not notice that Tzetzes uses the same term in his *Theogony*. Perhaps this term was used as another name for the *Catalogue of Women*.

Hesiod.[13] There is considerable evidence that Tzetzes had access to a version of the *Catalogue of Women*:[14]

- Many female mythological figures of Tzetzes' poem are unattested in other sources.[15]
- There are some passages of Tzetzes' *Theogony* that resemble fragments attributed to the Hesiodic *Catalogue*. For instance, Tzetzes' story about the heroes Eurytus and Cteatus, who are described as Siamese twins with two heads and four hands, is also found in a papyrus fragment of the *Catalogue*.[16] Another piece of evidence comes from the genealogy of the hero Machaon, who appears as child of Asclepius and Xanthe only in Tzetzes and in a fragment of the *Catalogue*.[17]
- There are many similarities between Tzetzes' *Theogony* and Pseudo-Apollodorus' *Library*, a work considered to be closely related to the *Catalogue of Women*.[18]

The poem's connection to the *Iliad* becomes clear in the narration about the Greek heroes (vv. 578–718), in which Tzetzes uses much mythological material drawn from the second book of the *Iliad*, the so-called *Catalogue of Ships*. However, as is the case with his borrowings from Hesiod's *Theogony*, he does not reveal the name of his source, neither does he present the heroes in the same order as Homer.[19] The poem's affinity with the *Iliad* comes as no

---

[13] See its fragments in the edition of Merkelbach and West (1967). Gregory Nagy (2009: 295) has stressed the close relation of Hesiod's *Theogony* to the *Catalogue* by arguing that vv. 1019–20 of Hesiod's *Theogony* function as a 'transition into the narrative that begins with the Catalogue'.

[14] Cardin and Pontani (2017: 257–9) have also argued that Tzetzes knew the *Catalogue of Women* and provide several Tzetzean quotations of Hesiodic fragments of genealogical content from the *Exegesis of the Iliad* and Tzetzes' scholia on Pindar and Lycophron.

[15] E.g. Idaia as the wife of Erichthonius (v. 443), Ielis (v. 446), Eiromene (v. 448), Deityche (v. 688), Melanippe as mother of Elephenor (v. 694), Euande as mother of Sthenelus (v. 701), Polyxene as mother of Menestheus (v. 707).

[16] *Catalogue of Women*, fr. 17a.15–17, ed. Merkelbach and West (1967: 11): see the passage on p. 136. Eustathios of Thessalonike presents Eurytus and Cteatus as monstrous creatures in his *Commentary on the Iliad* and ascribes their myth to Hesiod (882.25–9 = 3.320.3–10 ed. van der Valk).

[17] *Catalogue of Women*, fr. 53, ed. Merkelbach and West (1967: 35): see the passage on p. 136. Cf. also the following less important examples: Tzetzes' *Theogony* 610–11 and 685–6 with the *Catalogue of Women*, fr. 60.7–11 and fr. 204, 56 respectively.

[18] It is not, however, clear if these similarities are due to Tzetzes' acquaintance with Pseudo-Apollodorus' *Bibliotheca* itself. Traces of Pseudo-Apollodorus can also be found in his *Carmina Iliaca* and in his *Scholia on Lycophron*: see Leone (2015: XI), Cardin (2018: 104), Wendel (1948: 1987). Tzetzes is considered the compiler of the so-called *Epitoma Vaticana* of Pseudo-Apollodorus, which is preserved in Vatican City, Biblioteca Apostolica Vaticana, gr. 950: see Wendel (1948: 1987). The question remains whether Tzetzes used for his *Theogony* an expanded version of Pseudo-Apollodorus or a Greek version of Dictys Cretensis, a Latin work derived from a Greek text about the Trojan War, including also genealogies. Tzetzes mentions Dictys in his *Allegories of the Iliad* prolegomena 482 ed. Boissonade (1851), showing he was aware of his work. On the possible influence of Dictys on Tzetzes' *Carmina Iliaca*, see Leone (2015: XI, XIII), Lovato (2017: 138), Cardin (2018: 104).

[19] He also does not refer to the ships of the heroes.

surprise, as several of Tzetzes' works are related to the *Iliad* (*Allegories of the Iliad*, *Exegesis of the Iliad*, *Carmina Iliaca*). Especially his *Allegories of the Iliad*, a didactic poem dedicated to Bertha von Sulzbach (the wife of emperor Manuel I Komnenos),[20] has many similarities with the *Theogony* – mainly in its style, but also in its didactic and mythological character.[21]

List of Indicative Borrowings

Apart from Hesiod and Homer, Tzetzes also adopts elements from Pindar, Aeschylus, Aristophanes, Theocritus, Pseudo-Apollodorus, Pherecydes, Philostratus and other ancient authors.[22] His preference for ancient poets is remarkable. Some notable borrowings are the following:

Theogony 395–8 ed. Bekker
Πρίαμος Τρώων βασιλεὺς ἦν ἐν τοῖς τότε
  χρόνοις,
Ἑκάβην ἔχων σύζυγον, πεντήκοντα δὲ παῖδας.
ἀλλὰ πολλοὺς μὲν ἔσχηκεν ἀπὸ τῶν
  παλλακίδων,
μόνους ἐννεακαίδεκα γεννήσας ἐξ Ἑκάβης,

Iliad 24.495–7 ed. West
πεντήκοντά μοι ἦσαν ὅτ' ἤλυθον υἷες Ἀχαιῶν·
ἐννεακαίδεκα μέν μοι ἰῆς ἐκ νηδύος ἦσαν,
τοὺς δ' ἄλλους μοι ἔτικτον ἐνὶ μεγάροισι γυναῖκες

Theogony 401–4 ed. Bekker
Ἀλέξανδρον τὸν ἅρπαγα τῆς δολερᾶς Ἑλένης,
Ἕλενον καὶ Δηΐφοβον, Ἀγάθωνα, Πολίτην
τὸν Ἀγαυόν, τὸν Αἴσακον, τὸν Πάμμονα σὺν
  τούτοις, Τρωΐλον καὶ Ἀντίμαχον, Ἀντίφονον,
Ἱππόθουν

Iliad 24.249–51 ed. West
νεικείων Ἕλενόν τε Πάριν τ' Ἀγάθωνά τε δῖον
Πάμμονά τ' Ἀντίφονόν τε βοὴν ἀγαθόν τε Πολίτην
Δηΐφοβόν τε καὶ Ἱππόθοον καὶ Δῖον Ἀγαυόν

Theogony 438–9 ed. Bekker
γεννᾷ τὸν Ἐριχθόνιον, ἄνθρωπον ἱπποτρόφον,
ὃς τρισχιλίων ἀριθμὸν ἵππων εἶχε τοκάδων

Iliad 20.219–21 ed. West
Δάρδανος αὖ τέκεθ' υἱὸν Ἐριχθόνιον βασιλῆα,
ὃς δὴ ἀφνειότατος γένετο θνητῶν ἀνθρώπων·
τοῦ τρισχίλιαι ἵπποι ἕλος κάτα βουκολέοντο

Theogony 549–53 ed. Bekker
ὃς χρυσοκόμης Εὔφορβος ὑπάρχων ὑπὲρ φύσιν
καὶ χρυσοκαταδέσμητον εἶχεν αὑτοῦ τὴν κόμην,
καὶ πολεμῶν καὶ καρτερῶν πόνους ἐν τοῖς
  πολέμοις,
ὡς Ὅμηρος παρίστησι τὸν νέον διαγράφων·

Iliad 16.807–11 ed. West
ὤμων μεσσηγὺς σχεδόθεν βάλε Δάρδανος ἀνὴρ
Πανθοΐδης Εὔφορβος, ὃς ἡλικίην ἐκέκαστο
ἔγχεΐ θ' ἱπποσύνῃ τε πόδεσσί τε καρπαλίμοισιν·
καὶ γὰρ δή ποτε φῶτας ἐείκοσι βῆσεν ἀφ' ἵππων
πρῶτ' ἐλθὼν σὺν ὄχεσφι διδασκόμενος πολέμοιο

---

[20] The latter part of this work is dedicated to Constantine Kotertzes, a former pupil of Tzetzes.
[21] Both works are addressed to a woman of the Komnenian dynasty, contain heroic content and are written in *decapentasyllables*. The *Theogony* had been composed before the *Allegories* (namely before the wedding of Manuel I with Bertha in 1146), since Tzetzes refers to his *Theogony* in a scholium on v. 532 of his *Allegories of the Iliad*: see Wendel (1948: 1986).
[22] For an identified fragment from Pherecydes, see *Theogony* 450–3.

Theogony 581-2 ed. Bekker
ἐξ ἧς παῖδες γεγόνασι τρεῖς τούτῳ θυγατέρες,
Χρυσόθεμις καὶ Λαοδίκη καὶ Ἰφιάνασσα

Theogony 659 ed. Bekker
Σχεδίος καὶ Ἐπίστροφος Ἰφίτου τοῦ Ναυβόλου

Theogony 668 ed. Bekker
καὶ Προθοήνωρ, Κλονίος σὺν τῷ Ἀρκεσιλάῳ

Theogony 704-5 ed. Bekker
ἦν συμμαχῶν καὶ Εὔμηλος υἱὸς ὁ τοῦ Ἀδμήτου,
παῖς τῆς κλεινῆς Ἀλκήστιδος, τῆς θυγατρὸς
Πελίαο

Theogony 663-5 ed. Bekker
ὁ δ' Εὔρυτος καὶ Κτέατος ἦσαν διπλοῖ τὴν
φύσιν,
τετρασκελεῖς, τετράχειρες, δικέφαλόν τι τέρας,
υἱοὶ δὲ ἦσαν Ἄκτορος φίλοι καὶ τῆς Μολίνης.

Theogony 682-3 ed. Bekker
Ἀσκληπιοῦ καὶ Ξάνθης τε παρῆσαν δύο παῖδες,
οἱ τῶν Ἑλλήνων ἰατροί, κάλλιστοι κατὰ τέχνην,
ὁμοῦ τε Ποδαλείριος καὶ σὺν αὐτῷ Μαχάων

Theogony 645-6 ed. Bekker
ποθῶ τὸν Ἀμφιάραον, ζητῶ τὸν Ὀικλίδην,
τὸν ὀφθαλμὸν τῆς στρατιᾶς ἁπάσης ἧς περ
ἄρχω

Theogony 400 ed. Bekker
τὸν ἀστραβῆ τὸν κίονα, Πίνδαρος ὥς που λέγει

Theogony 695-7 ed. Bekker
ἦν Διομήδης ὁ κλεινὸς ὁ ἀριστεὺς Ἑλλήνων,
υἱὸς τῆς Δηιπύλου μέν, πατρὸς δὲ τοῦ Τυδέως·
ὁ δὲ Θεόκριτός φησιν Ἀργείας εἶναι παῖδα.

Theogony 289-90 ed. Bekker
δειναῖσι γαμφηλῇσι συρίζων φόνον,
ἐξ ὀμμάτων δ' ἤστραπτε γοργωπὸν σέλας

Theogony 320 ed. Bekker
κατὰ δ' Αἰσχύλον τὸν σοφὸν τὴν κλῆσιν Ἡσιόνη

Iliad 9.286-7 ed. West
τρεῖς δέ οἵ εἰσι θύγατρες ἐνὶ μεγάρωι εὐπήκτωι
Χρυσόθεμις καὶ Λαοδίκη καὶ Ἰφιάνασσα

Iliad 2.517-18 ed. West
αὐτὰρ Φωκήων Σχεδίος καὶ Ἐπίστροφος ἦρχον
υἱέες Ἰφίτοο μεγαθύμου Ναυβολίδαο

Iliad 2.495 ed. West
Ἀρκεσίλαός τε Προθοήνωρ τε Κλονίος τε

Iliad 2.713-15 ed. West
Εὔμηλος, τὸν ὑπ' Ἀδμήτωι τέκε δῖα γυναικῶν
Ἄλκηστις Πελίαο θυγατρῶν εἶδος ἀρίστη.

Catalogue of Women, fr. 17a.15-7
ed. Merkelbach and West
Ἄκτορι κυσαμ]ένη καὶ ἐρικτύπῳι ἐννοσιγαί[ωι,
ἀπλήτω, Κτέα]τόν τε καὶ Εὔρυτον, οἷσι πόδες
[μ]ὲν.[ἦν
τέτορες, κ]εφαλαὶ δὲ δύω̣ ἰδὲ χεῖρες εεισ[..]ν

Catalogue of Women, fr. 53 ed. Merkelbach
and West
Μαχάων δὲ οὗτος υἱὸς Ἀσκληπιοῦ καὶ Ἀρσινόης...
κατὰ δὲ Ἡσίοδον Ξάνθης.

Pindar, *Olympian* 6.16-17 ed. Maehler and
Snell
'Ποθέω στρατιᾶς ὀφθαλμὸν ἐμᾶς
ἀμφότερον μάντιν τ' ἀγαθὸν καὶ
δουρὶ μάρνασθαι.'

Pindar, *Olympian* 2.81-2 ed. Maehler and Snell
ὅς Ἕκτορα σφᾶλε, Τροίας
ἄμαχον ἀστραβῆ κίονα, Κύκνον τε θανάτῳ πόρεν

Theocritus, *Idyll* 17.53 ed. Gow
Ἀργεία κυάνοφρυ, σὺ λαοφόνον Διομήδεα
μισγομένα Τυδῇι τέκες, Καλυδωνίῳ ἀνδρί

Aeschylus, *Prometheus Bound* 355-6 ed. West
σμερδνῇσι γαμφηλῇσι συρίζων φόβον,
ἐξ ὀμμάτων δ' ἤστραπτε γοργωπὸν σέλας

Aeschylus, *Prometheus Bound* 559-60 ed. West
ἄγαγες Ἡσιόναν | πιθὼν δάμαρτα κοινόλεκτρον

Theogony 740 ed. Agapitos
ὥσπερ φησὶν ὁ κωμικός, σκάφην τὴν σκάφην γράφω

Aristophanes, fr. 927 ed. Kassel-Austin
ἄγροικός εἰμι τὴν σκάφην σκάφην λέγων

Theogony 758–9 ed. Agapitos
Ἀριστοφάνης δέ φησιν πάλιν ἐν ταῖς νεφέλαις σὺ μέν μοι ἔλεγες μαμμᾶν, ἐγὼ δ' ἄρτον ἐδίδουν·

Aristophanes, *Clouds* 1383 ed. Wilson
μαμμᾶν δ' ἂν αἰτήσαντος ἧκόν σοι φέρων ἂν ἄρτον·

Theogony 406–7 ed. Bekker
καὶ θυγατέρας τέσσαρας σὺν τούτοις ἐκλοχεύει, Κάσανδραν, Λαοδίκειαν, Κρέουσαν, Πολυξένην.

Pseudo-Apollodorus III 151, 1–2 ed. Wagner
μετὰ τοῦτον ἐγέννησεν Ἑκάβη θυγατέρας μὲν Κρέουσαν Λαοδίκην Πολυξένην Κασάνδραν

Theogony 711–15 ed. Bekker
ὁ δημηγόρος ὁ κλεινός, ὁ Πύλιος ὁ Νέστωρ...
πατὴρ τοῦ Θρασυμήδεος, πατὴρ τοῦ Ἀντιλόχου,
πατὴρ τοῦ Πεισιστράτου τε, Ἐχέφρονος, Στρατίου

Pseudo-Apollodorus I 94.1–5 ed. Wagner
Νέστωρ...Πολυκάστην ἐγέννησε, παῖδας δὲ Περσέα Στράτιχον Ἄρητον Ἐχέφρονα Πεισίστρατον Ἀντίλοχον Θρασυμήδην

Theogony 756–7 ed. Agapitos
καὶ Πλάτων ὁ φιλόσοφος οὕτω φησί που γράφων
"καὶ δὴ ἔλεγόν μοι καλοῦ πατρὸς καλὸς υἱός".

Pseudo-Lucian, *Halcyon* 1.12 ed. Macleod
Κήϋκα τὸν Τραχίνιον τὸν Ἐωσφόρου τοῦ ἀστέρος, καλοῦ πατρὸς καλὸν υἱόν· εἶτα δὴ πτερωθεῖσαν

Theogony 840 ed. Agapitos
τὸ ἀπειρόκαλον ἐν τῷ ἀττικίζειν βάρβαρον.

Philostratus, *The Lives of the Sophists* I 16.4 ed. Kayser
τὸ γὰρ ἀπειρόκαλον ἐν τῷ ἀττικίζειν βάρβαρον

This list reveals what kind of information Tzetzes usually adopts from his favourite models, the way he reshapes them and the level of his imitation. Tzetzes borrows from the ancient authors mythological names, phrases of gnomic content, short genealogies – or he paraphrases descriptive elements and other personal information about the mythical figures. Whenever he mentions the name of the authors before a quotation, he neither praises them, nor ascribes to them encomiastic or descriptive adjectives.[23] He rather makes short references by using stereotypical phrases (e.g. κατὰ δ' Αἰσχύλον, 'according to Aeschylus'; Θεόκριτός φησιν, 'Theocritus says').

It is also noteworthy that Tzetzes often recycles the same mythological material as in his *Scholia on Lycophron*.[24] This serves as additional evidence that these scholia were actually written by Tzetzes himself and not by his brother, Isaac, to whom the work is attributed in the Byzantine manuscripts.

[23] One exception can be found in vv. 761–2, where Tzetzes calls Aeschines, Demosthenes and Lysias σοφούς ('wise') and presents them as examples of the Attic language.
[24] See, for instance, Tzetzes, *Theogony* 435–6, 450–1, 463–4 with Tzetzes, *Scholia on Lycophron* 73.1–2, genus 26–7 and 1232, 7–9 ed. Scheer. Cf. also the scholia's affinity to Pseudo-Apollodorus' *Bibliotheca*. One can find similar mythological information in Tzetzes' *Theogony* and his *Carmina Iliaca*; see, for instance, his account on Hecuba's sons in *Theogony* 395–405 and in *Carmina Iliaca* II 446–54 ed. Leone (1995).

Tzetzes' Authorial Voice

As is clear from the above-mentioned sources, Tzetzes adopts material from ancient authors, mainly poets whose works he had commented on and used for his teaching (Homer, Hesiod, Aeschylus, Pindar, Aristophanes). Although Tzetzes relies so much on authorities, he narrates and structures his genealogy of deities and heroes by highlighting his function as *persona loquens* of the *Theogony*. In contrast to many medieval commentaries on ancient texts, which are usually anonymous, Tzetzes used to sign his works in various ways, trying to protect them from plagiarism. The authorial self-identification is indeed a phenomenon of the twelfth century (e.g. Eustathios of Thessalonike), but Tzetzes' writing style is often distinguished from that of his contemporaries owing to his overconfidence and polemical tone.[25] A noteworthy example of the way he perceived of himself as an author appears at the beginning of his *Theogony* (vv. 26–31), where he audaciously claims that he possesses better knowledge of the subject than a hundred Hesiods, Homers, Musaeuses, Orpheuses, Antimachuses and Linuses.[26] In a similar way, he boasts to the empress Irene in his *Allegories of the Iliad* about his vast knowledge, which he was able to transmit in a compressed manner: 'Thus not even if you had read Homer and Stesichorus, Euripides, Lycophron, Colluthus and Lesches, and Dictys's well-written *Iliad*, Triphiodorus and Quintus, even a hundred books, not even then would you have learned the story in greater detail, since I have incorporated everything in abbreviated form.'[27]

Given this apparent self-confidence, his concerns that he might be criticized by his contemporaries for ignorance of a given subject (e.g. vv. 417–25, 500–3) can appear paradoxical. He is presented as a potential victim of envious people, who are ready to attack him and accuse him of ignorance. In the following passage, for instance, he strongly defends and justifies his literary choices by saying that he always writes in an appropriate style; he uses the Atticizing style for educated people and, if needed, he

---

[25] On the authorial presence and individualism of eleventh- and twelfth-century writers, see Kazhdan (1985: 222–3), Lauxtermann (2003: 37–8), Pizzone (2014: 6–9).
[26] See e.g. M. J. Jeffreys (1974: 149), Budelmann (2002: 152). For Tzetzes' authorial presence in general, see Budelmann (2002: 148–53). Cf. Tzetzes' criticisms against Thucydides in Kaldellis (2015: 65–79) and Proklos (www.dbbe.ugent.be/typ/4023). On the contrary, he presents himself as son of Homer in his *Exegesis of the Iliad* 7.14–17 ed. Papathomopoulos (2007: 7): see Cullhed (2014: 60); or as φιλόμηρος ('fond of Homer') at his first scholium on his *Carmina Iliaca*, ed. Leone (1995: 101). For his self-representation as a living library, see Pizzone (2017).
[27] See Tzetzes' *Allegories of the Iliad* prolegomena 480–5 ed. Boissonade (1851), trans. Goldwyn and Kokkini (2015: 37).

adopts a lower style for the less educated. In this way, Tzetzes assures his patroness and his audience that he is adept at writing texts for every patron and every audience, pointing out only what is appropriate:[28]

> ἡμᾶς δ' οὐκ ἂν νομίσητε τῶν φαύλων συγγραφέων,
> μὴ κομπηροῖς συγγράμμασιν ταῦτα συγγραψαμένους.
> ἐγὼ γὰρ εἴωθα σκοπεῖν καὶ πρόσωπα καὶ τρόπους
> καὶ τοὺς καιροὺς καὶ πράγματα, καὶ γράφειν τὰ πρεπώδη.
> καὶ πρὸς σοφοὺς μὲν γεγραφὼς ἄνδρας καὶ πρὸς λογίους
> τὴν Ἀττικὴν ἁρμόττομαι τότε κιννύραν γλώττης,
> ἐπᾴδων πάνυ λιγυρὰς ἐκείνοις ἁρμονίας·
> εἰ δέ ποτε δεήσει με καὶ πρὸς ἀγροίκους γράφειν,
> ὥσπερ φησὶν ὁ κωμικός, σκάφην τὴν σκάφην γράφω
> (Tzetzes, *Theogony* 732–40)

while you readers will not think of me as being a bad writer,
since I have not written these things in boastful treatises.
For I am accustomed to examine persons and ways of conduct
and occasions and situations, in order to write what is appropriate.
Having written to wise men and learned scholars,
I then fit the Attic lyre to my tongue,
singing for them most sweet harmonies.
Yet should I need to write also to uneducated people,
as the Comic says, I write the trough a «trough».[29]

The passages in which Tzetzes addresses a broader, critical audience indicate the competition and rivalry among the professional poets of the Komnenian court, especially those who struggle to remain under Irene's protection and patronage (e.g. Constantine Manasses, Manganeios Prodromos).[30]

Patronage and Didactic Aspects of the Poem

Tzetzes' relationship to Irene should be understood both as a relationship of a professional poet with a patron and a relationship of a teacher with his student. The *Theogony* is indeed a didactic poem and sometimes gives the

---

[28] Cf. the last verse of the poem: πᾶσι τὰ πρεπωδέστατα γράφοντες κατ' ἀξίαν, 'writing to everyone what is most appropriate according to their dignity', trans. Agapitos (2017: 48). Cf. Theodore Prodromos' comments on low linguistic style and socioeconomic status in Beaton (1987: 10–11). As Beaton (1987: 12) has pointed out, here Tzetzes makes use of the Aristotelian term for 'appropriateness' (τὸ πρέπον). Cf. Agapitos' discussion (2017: 51–7) on Tzetzes' choice of an appropriate style.
[29] English translation by Agapitos (2017: 44).
[30] It is interesting that Tzetzes complains about one of his rivals, who either tries to appropriate his commentaries or harshly criticizes them, in an epistle addressed to the *sebastokratorissa* Irene. See epistle 56 ed. Leone (1972: 77–9). For similar concerns, see also Pizzone in this volume.

impression of a vivid lesson intended to be taught in front of Irene.[31] Specifically, Tzetzes employs several didactic techniques in order to assist Irene to follow his thoughts and also to attract her interest. For instance, he often asks for her attention (e.g. v. 46) or summarizes some mythological episodes that he had already mentioned before, so as to make them more understandable (e.g. vv. 339–52).[32] Moreover, the clear structure of the poem, consisting of certain parts and transitional phrases addressed to Irene, is relevant to the didactic character of the work.[33] Interestingly, in one of these transitional phrases, Tzetzes reveals his mode of writing by saying that his narrative is a mythological one and not an allegorical. Tzetzes, indeed, focuses on mythical genealogies in his *Theogony* and he does not offer allegorical interpretations of mythical figures, as he does in his *Allegories of the Iliad* and *Allegories of the Odyssey*. The choice of metre is also related to the didactic role of the poem; political verse is considered to combine knowledge with play and therefore was well suited for didactic texts.[34] As Tzetzes characteristically says in the *Theogony*, he 'wrote the most important points in a playful way' (v. 722). Thus, his style, metre and language are in line with the poem's didactic purpose.

Despite the heroic content of the *Theogony*, its language is close to Koine. One can also find elements of different linguistic registers in the poem: e.g. mythological vocabulary,[35] Aristophanic words (e.g. v. 727: γρῦ, 'grunt'; v. 803: ἱμονιοστρόφον, 'water-drawer'), several *hapax legomena* (e.g. v. 29: θεογονογράφοι, 'writers of theogonies'; v. 145:

---

[31] As is the case with other didactic poems, the *Theogony* has a strong instructive tone and often resembles a 'lesson in progress'. On the same phenomenon in Psellos' didactic poems, see Bernard (2014: 241–2). On the main characteristics of didactic poetry in Byzantium, see Lauxtermann (2009: 37–46), Hörandner (2012: 55–67), Bernard (2014: 229–35), Hörandner (2019: 459–86).

[32] See, for instance, *Theogony* 20–1, 46, 411–12, 509 ed. Bekker; cf. Rhoby (2010: 168). The second-person narration is a *topos* in didactic poetry in general: see indicatively Hörandner (2012: 67), Bernard (2014: 240–1).

[33] Prologue, vv. 1–47: Tzetzes praises Irene and asks for more money (transitional phrase, v. 47: πλὴν μυθικῶς σοι λέξομεν οὐδ' ἀλληγορημένως, 'but I will tell <these> to you mythologically and not allegorically'); Genealogy of gods, vv. 48–338; Summary, vv. 339–77 (transitional phrase, vv. 339–40: τοῦτο μὲν γένος τῶν θεῶν τῶν πάλαι θρυλλουμένων / ἀλλ' ἤδη καὶ σαφέστερον ἐν κεφαλαίῳ λέξω, 'this is the genealogy of the old well-known gods, but I will say <this> even more clearly in a summary'); Genealogy of Greek and Trojan Heroes, vv. 378–723 (transitional phrase, v. 378–9: ἀλλ' ἐπειδή περ εἴπομεν περὶ θεῶν σοι ταῦτα / φέρε λοιπὸν διδάξωμεν καὶ περὶ τῶν ἡρώων, 'but since I have narrated these things to you about gods, also accept our teaching about the heroes'); Epilogue, vv. 724–855).

[34] See e.g. M. J. Jeffreys (1974: 141–95), Lauxtermann (2009: 45), E. M. Jeffreys (2009: 219–28).

[35] Interestingly, mythological names from Hesiod are often adapted to the pattern of the political verse (e.g. Ἐρινύες instead of Ἐρινῦς) or presented in their most common form (e.g. Θάλειαν instead of Θαλίην, Τυφῶνα instead of Τυφωέα).

κυκνοειδείς, 'swan-shaped'; v. 419: φιλομελαγχίτων, 'fond of black raiment') and many expressions and words from everyday language (e.g. v. 751: βαΐτζας, 'maid servants'; v. 769: καλὴ ἡμέρα, 'good morning'). Tzetzes adopts the spoken language especially in the epilogue of his *Theogony* in an attempt to demonstrate that he is able to use and understand the language of common people as well as of the foreigners living in Constantinople at that time. As he explains in his epilogue, he chose to use a simple linguistic register mainly because of Irene's needs.[36] According to Michael and Elizabeth Jeffreys, Irene was probably of Norman origin, a foreigner in the imperial court; this could explain her desire to learn Greek mythology, so as to become acquainted with the mythology and historical past taught at Byzantine schools.[37] Irene's special interest in Trojan heroes can also be understood in the context of her Norman origin.[38] According to Goldwyn, Norman dynasties had an interest in Trojan genealogical stories and often presented themselves as inheritors of the Roman Empire and descendants of Aeneas.[39]

As regards the function of the poem, it was not only didactic. Apart from a detailed 'lesson' on mythology, the *Theogony* also served Tzetzes' literary *epideixis* for gaining a longer position at the service of his patron. Since Tzetzes expresses concerns about his opponents' reactions to the content and style of the poem, we could suppose that it was intended for a broader audience that could understand its plethora of literary sources. Seen in this light, Tzetzes' *epideixis* could have taken place in the context of the so-called *theatra*, the 'literary salons' of the Komnenian period.[40] Tzetzes was very much dependent on commissions and it was therefore important for him to construct his image as a talented poet not only before the eyes of Irene, but also before the other members of the Komnenian court.[41] Irene, on the other hand, as Elizabeth Jeffreys has pointed out, commissioned literary works of secular content in an attempt to gain prestige among the intellectuals of Constantinople and secure her position during the first years of Manuel I Komnenos' reign.[42] Her eldest son John

---

[36] *Theogony* 748. Other times he adopts the low linguistic register for entertaining his audience: see *Theogony* 751. On Tzetzes' comments on the appropriate use of language, see also Agapitos (2017: 51–5).
[37] See Jeffreys and Jeffreys (1994: 57).
[38] I sincerely thank prof. Ulrich Moennig for this interesting remark.
[39] On Norman interest in the Trojan past in the eleventh–thirteenth centuries, see Goldwyn (2018: 154–74).
[40] On the *theatron*, see Mullett (1984), Marciniak (2004: 33–4) and (2007).
[41] For Tzetzes' social network, see Grünbart (2005: 419–26) and (2014: 27–9).
[42] See E. M. Jeffreys (2012: 192).

was a strong candidate for the imperial throne and, after 1148, a rival of the emperor Manuel I Komnenos; as a result, Irene had to reinforce her power and reputation, establishing her position and role within the imperial family.[43] Furthermore, the epic themes of the *Theogony* correspond to the heroism and military policy of the Komnenian dynasty, as well as to its interest in ancient mythology and Homeric epics.[44]

Lastly, another topic relevant to the didactic character of the poem is the noteworthy transmission of both Tzetzes' *Theogony* and Hesiod's *Theogony* in the Late Byzantine period; Tzetzes' *Theogony* is transmitted in eleven manuscripts and Hesiod's *Theogony* in approximately seventy manuscripts.[45] This might provide an indication that Hesiod was occasionally part of the Byzantine school curriculum and that professional teachers, like Tzetzes, could have used Hesiod's *Theogony* as a textbook. If that is true, Tzetzes' *Theogony* could have also been used by teachers as a manual of mythology, especially during the Palaiologan period.[46] This idea is additionally supported by the content of its manuscripts, which often contain texts used for educational purposes.[47] We could therefore suppose that Tzetzes' *Theogony* had – at a later stage – a broader educational function. A general interest in genealogies as well as in Hesiod can be observed in the twelfth century; apart from Tzetzes, who wrote a biography of Hesiod as well as commentaries on his works, John Galenos wrote an allegorical *Exegesis* of the *Theogony*.[48] The so-called *Anonymous Exegesis* of Hesiod's *Theogony* also probably dates from the same period. In addition to this, authors contemporary to Tzetzes such as Prodromos and Eustathios make several references to Hesiod and his works.[49]

---

[43] Her important role in the court is also evident from the fact that Tzetzes (in the prologue of his *Theogony*, v. 1) as well as other poets in her service (e.g. Theodore Prodromos and Constantine Manasses) address her with the title βασίλισσα ('empress').

[44] Cf. Cullhed (2014: 56).

[45] Approximately sixty manuscripts of Hesiod's *Theogony* are preserved from the Byzantine period (see the *Pinakes* Database).

[46] Tzetzes' epistles were used at school for teaching purposes: see Speck (2003), Grünbart (2005: 426).

[47] See, for instance, the content of Vatican City, Biblioteca Apostolica Vaticana, gr. 895 and 896, which include ancient texts and grammatical, rhetorical and metrical treatises, in Schreiner (1988: 66–76).

[48] Edited by Gaisford (1823: 504–608).

[49] E.g. Prodromos defends Hesiodic poetry against an ignorant grammarian: see Romano (1999: 304–6). I am grateful to Konstantinos Chrysogelos for this reference. It is remarkable that Eustathios refers thirteen times to Hesiod's *Theogony* in his *Commentaries on the Iliad* and the *Odyssey* and 142 times to Hesiod himself. His references to the *Theogony* usually include mythological or grammatical information. For Hesiod's reception in the twelfth century, see also Cardin and Pontani (2017: 245–73).

Conclusion

To conclude, Tzetzes' *Theogony* is a didactic poem of mythology dedicated to the *sebastokratorissa*, which summarizes and simplifies Hesiod's *Theogony*. However, Tzetzes expanded Hesiod's mythical narration, enriching it with a long dedicatory prologue addressed to Irene, a narration of heroic genealogies, several quotations from and allusions to ancient authors and an unusual epilogue offering a vivid image of the cosmopolitan, twelfth-century Constantinople.

Tzetzes teaches mythology to Irene, but at the same time he tries to gain her appreciation, demonstrate his knowledge to a broader audience and portray himself as a specialist in genealogies. The quotations and references to ancient authors provide additional evidence that the poem was addressed not only to Irene, but also to a broader educated audience, which could understand and appreciate their meaning. In short, Tzetzes' borrowings from ancient authors certainly contributed to his own *epideixis*. This work can, therefore, be situated both in the context of the tradition of exegesis of ancient authors and that of literary *epideixis* at the literary gatherings of the Komnenian family. As far as Tzetzes' attitude toward the ancient poets is concerned, he appreciates their work, but does not hesitate to present himself as a better narrator of genealogies due to his ability to combine different sources and present them with brevity and clarity.[50] All the above-mentioned elements make the *Theogony* not just a paraphrase of Hesiod's *Theogony*, but a multidimensional work, indicative of the Tzetzean style.

REFERENCES

Agapitos, P. A. (2017) 'John Tzetzes and the Blemish Examiners: A Byzantine Teacher on Schedography, Everyday Language and Writerly Disposition', *MEG* 17: 39–48.

Bănescu, N. (1915) 'Un ms. inedit al Theogoniei lui Tzetzes', *Convorbiri literare* 49: 747–57.

Beaton, R. (1987) 'The Rhetoric of Poverty: The Lives and Opinions of Theodore Prodromos', *BMGS* 11: 1–28.

---

[50] In several of his works, Tzetzes claims that he aims at brevity, clarity and combination/compression of different sources: see e.g. the *Theogony* 21, 502–6, 747–8; cf. the *Allegories of the Iliad* 492–3 (τὰ πάντα περιέκλεισα τμήματι βραχυτάτῳ / ὁπόσα οὐχ εὑρήσει τις οὐδ' ἑκατὸν βιβλίοις, 'I included everything in a very short section, / containing more than one would find even in one hundred books' (trans. Goldwyn and Kokkini 2015: 39) and the following epigram against Proklos: www.dbbe.ugent.be/occ/9382. On Tzetzes' references to brevity, cf. Cardin (2018: 95).

Bekker, I. (1842) 'Die Theogonie des Johannes Tzetzes aus der Bibliotheca Casanatensis (Ms. J. II. 10)', in *Philologische und historische Abhandlungen der Königlichen Akademie der Wissenschaften zu Berlin aus dem Jahre 1840,* 147–69. Berlin.

Bernard, F. (2014) *Writing and Reading Byzantine Secular Poetry, 1025–1081.* Oxford Studies in Byzantium. Oxford.

Boissonade, J. F. (ed.) (1851) *Tzetzae allegoriae Iliadis.* Paris.

Budelmann, F. (2002) 'Classical Commentary in Byzantium: John Tzetzes on Ancient Greek Literature', in *The Classical Commentary: Histories, Practices, Theory,* ed. R. K. Gibson and C. S. Kraus, 141–69. Mnemosyne Supplements 232. Leiden–Boston–Cologne.

Cardin, M. (2009) '*Heroogonia*: il *Catalogo delle Donne* di Giovanni Tzetze', *Philologus* 153: 237–49.

  (2018) 'Teaching Homer through (Annotated) Poetry: John Tzetzes' *Carmina Iliaca*', in *Brill's Companion to Prequels, Sequels and Retellings of Classical Epic,* ed. R. Simms, 90–114. Leiden–Boston.

Cardin, M. and F. Pontani (2017) 'Hesiod's Fragments in Byzantium', in *Poetry in Fragments: Studies on the Hesiodic Corpus and Its Afterlife,* ed. C. Tsagalis, 245–87. Berlin.

Colonna, A. (1953) 'I Prolegomeni ad Esiodo e la Vita esiodea di Giovanni Tzetzes', *Bollettino del Comitato per la preparazione dell'edizione nazionale dei Classici Greci e Latini* 2: 27–39.

Cramer, J. A. (ed.) (1841) *Anecdota graeca e codd. manuscriptis bibliothecae regiae parisiensis,* vol. 3. Oxford.

Cullhed, E. (2014) 'The Blind Bard and "I": Homeric Biography and Authorial Personas in the Twelfth Century', *BMGS* 38: 49–67.

Dickey, E. (2007) *Ancient Greek Scholarship: A Guide to Finding, Reading, and Understanding Scholia, Commentaries, Lexica, and Grammatical Treatises, from Their Beginnings to the Byzantine Period.* Oxford–New York.

Gaisford, T. (ed.) (1823) *Scholia ad Hesiodum.* Poetae minores Graeci, vol. 2. Leipzig.

Goldwyn, A. J. (2018) 'Trojan Pasts, Medieval Presents: Epic Continuation in Eleventh to Thirteenth Century Genealogical Histories', in *Brill's Companion to Prequels, Sequels and Retellings of Classical Epic,* ed. R. Simms, 154–74. Leiden–Boston.

Goldwyn, A. J. and D. Kokkini (2015) *John Tzetzes, Allegories of the Iliad.* Dumbarton Oaks Medieval Library 37. Cambridge, MA.

Gow, A. S. F. (ed.) (1952) *Theocritus,* vol. 1. Cambridge.

Grünbart, M. (2005) 'Byzantinisches Gelehrtenelend – oder: Wie meistert man seinen Alltag?', in *Zwischen Polis, Provinz und Peripherie: Beiträge zur byzantinischen Geschichte und Kultur,* ed. L. Hoffmann and A. Monchizadeh, 413–26. Wiesbaden.

  (2014) 'Paideia Connects: The Interaction between Teachers and Pupils in Twelfth-Century Byzantium', in *Networks of Learning: Perspectives on*

Scholars in Byzantine East and Latin West, c. 1000–1200, ed. S. Steckel, N. Gaul and M. Grünbart, 17–31. Zurich–Berlin.
Hercher, R. (ed.) (1873) *Epistolographi Graeci*. Paris.
Hill, B. (1999) *Imperial Women in Byzantium 1025–1204: Power, Patronage and Ideology*. New York.
Hörandner, W. (2012) 'The Byzantine Didactic Poem – A Neglected Literary Genre? A Survey with Special Reference to the Eleventh Century', in *Poetry and Its Contexts in Eleventh-Century Byzantium*, ed. F. Bernard and K. Demoen, 55–67. Farnham–Burlington.
  (2019) 'Teaching with Verse in Byzantium', in *A Companion to Byzantine Poetry*, ed. W. Hörandner, A. Rhoby and N. Zagklas, 459–86. Brill's Companions to the Byzantine World 4. Leiden–Boston.
Hunger, H. (1953) 'Zum Epilog der Theogonie des Johannes Tzetzes: Neue Lesungen und Ergänzungen, besonders zu den alt-ossetischen Sprachresten, aus einer bisher unbekannten Handschrift der Österreichischen Nationalbibliothek (Phil. Gr. 118)', *ByzZ* 46: 302–7.
Jeffreys, E. M. (2009) 'Why Produce Verse in Twelfth-Century Constantinople?', in *'Doux remède ...': poésie et poétique à Byzance. Actes du IVe colloque international philologique EPMHNEIA, Paris, 23–25 février 2006*, ed. P. Odorico, P. A. Agapitos and M. Hinterberger, 219–28. Dossiers Byzantins 9. Paris.
  (2012) 'The *sebastokratorissa* Irene as Patron', in *Female Founders in Byzantium and Beyond*, ed. L. Theis, M. Mullett and M. Grünbart, with G. Fingarova and M. Savage, 177–94. Wiener Jahrbuch für Kunstgeschichte 60/61. Vienna.
Jeffreys, M. J. (1974) 'The Nature and the Origins of the Political Verse', *DOP* 28: 141–95.
Jeffreys, M. J. and E. M. Jeffreys (1994) 'Who Was Eirene the *sevastokratorissa*?', *ByzZ* 64: 40–68.
Kaldellis, A. (2015) *Byzantine Readings of Ancient Historians: Texts in Translation, with Introductions and Notes*. Abingdon–New York.
Kassel R. and C. Austin (eds.) (1984) *Aristophanes: testimonia et fragmenta*. Poetae Comici Graeci 3.2. Berlin.
Kayser, C. L. (ed.) (1871) *Flavii Philostrati opera*, vol. 2. Leipzig.
Kazhdan, A. P. and A. Wharton Epstein (1985) *Change in Byzantine Culture in the Eleventh and Twelfth Centuries*. The Transformation of the Classical Heritage 7. Berkeley–Los Angeles–London.
Lampsidis, O. (1984) 'Zur Sebastokratorissa Eirene', *JÖByz* 34: 91–105.
Lauxtermann, M. (2003) *Byzantine Poetry from Pisides to Geometres: Texts and Contexts*, vol. 1. Vienna.
  (2009) 'Byzantine Didactic Poetry and the Question of Poeticality', in *'Doux remède ...': poésie et poétique à Byzance. Actes du IVe colloque international philologique EPMHNEIA, Paris, 23–25 février 2006*, ed. P. Odorico, P. A. Agapitos and M. Hinterberger, 37–46. Dossiers Byzantins 9. Paris.
Leone, P. L. M. (ed.) (1972) *Ioannis Tzetzae Epistulae*. Leipzig.

(ed.) (1995) *Ioannis Tzetzae Carmina Iliaca*. Catania.
(ed. and trans.) (2015) *Giovanni Tzetzes, La leggenda Troiana (Carmina Iliaca)*. Testi e studi di letteratura antica a cura di Onofrio Vox 15. Lecce.
(ed.) (2019) *Ioannis Tzetzae Theogonia*. Lecce–Rovato.
Lovato, V. F. (2017) 'Portrait de héros, portait d'érudit: Jean Tzetzès et la tradition des *eikonismoi*', *MEG* 17: 137–56.
Macleod, M. D. (ed.) (1967) *Lucian*, vol. 8. Cambridge.
Maehler, H. (post B. Snell) (ed.) (1971) *Pindari carmina cum fragmentis*, vol. 1. Leipzig.
Marciniak, P. (2004) *Greek Drama in Byzantine Times*. Katowice.
(2007) 'Byzantine *Theatron* – A Place of Performance?', in *Theatron: Rhetorische Kultur in Spätantike und Mittelalter / Rhetorical Culture in Late Antiquity and the Middle Ages*, ed. M. Grünbart, 277–85. Millennium-Studien 13. Berlin.
Matranga, P. (ed.) (1850) *Anecdota graeca e mss. bibliothecis Vaticana, Angelica, Barberiniana, Vallicelliana, Medicea, Vindobonensi deprompta*. Rome.
Merkelbach, R. and M. L. West (eds.) (1967) *Fragmenta Hesiodea*. Oxford.
Moravcsik, G. (1930) 'Barbarische Sprachreste in der Theogonie des Johannes Tzetzes', *Byzantinisch-Neugriechische Jahrbücher* 7: 352–65.
Mullett, M. 1984. 'Aristocracy and Patronage in the Literary Circles of Comnenian Constantinople', in *The Byzantine Aristocracy, IX to XIII Centuries*, ed. M. Angold, 173–201. BAR International Series 221. Oxford.
Nagy, G. (2009) 'Hesiod and the Ancient Biographical Traditions', in *Brill's Companion to Hesiod*, ed. F. Montanari, C. Tsagalis and A. Rengakos, 271–311. Leiden.
Papathomopoulos, M. (ed.) (2007) Ἰωάννου γραμματικοῦ τοῦ Τζέτζου εἰς τὴν Ὁμήρου Ἰλιάδα. Athens.
Pizzone, A. (2014) 'The Author in Middle Byzantine Literature: A View from Within', in *The Author in Middle Byzantine Literature: Modes, Functions, and Identities*, ed. eadem, 3–18. Boston–Berlin.
(2017) 'The *Historiai* of John Tzetzes: a Byzantine "Book of Memory"?', *BMGS* 41.2: 182–207.
Rhoby, A. (2009) *Byzantinische Epigramme auf Fresken und Mosaiken*. Vienna.
(2010) 'Ioannes Tzetzes als Auftragsdichter', *Graeco-Latina Brunensia* 15: 167–83.
Romano, R. (1999) *La satira bizantina dei secoli XI–XV*. Turin.
Scheer, E. (ed.) (1958) *Lycophronis Alexandra*, vol. 2: *Scholia continens*. Berlin.
Schreiner, P. (1988) *Codices Vaticani graeci: Codices 867–932*. Bibliothecae Apostolicae Vaticanae codices manu scripti recensiti. Vatican City.
Speck, P. (2003) 'Die byzantinische Renaissance und ihre Bedeutung für die byzantinische Literatur', in *Selecta colligere I, Akten des Kolloquiums 'Sammeln, Neuordnen, Neues Schaffen: Methoden der Überlieferung von Texten in der Spätantike und in Byzanz'*, ed. R. M. Piccione and M. Perkams, 17–32. Alessandria.

van der Valk, M. (1971–87) *Eustathii archiepiscopi Thessalonicensis commentarii ad Homeri Iliadem pertinentes ad fidem codicis Laurentiani editi*, 4 vols. Leiden.
Varzos, K. (1984) Ἡ Γενεαλογία τῶν Κομνηνῶν, vol. 1. Thessalonike.
Wagner, R. (ed.) (1894) *Mythographi graeci*, vol. 1: *Apollodori Bibliotheca; Pediasimi libellous de duodecim Herculis laboribus*. Leipzig.
Wendel, C. (1940) 'Das Unbekannte Schlußstück der Theogonie des Tzetzes', *ByzZ* 40: 23–6.
  (1948) 'Tzetzes Johannes', in *Realencyclopädie der classischen Altertumswissenschaft* VII A 2, 1959–2011. Stuttgart.
West, M. (ed.) (2000) *Homeri Ilias: Rhapsodias XIII–XXIV*, Bibliotheca scriptorum Graecorum et Romanorum Teubneriana. Munich–Leipzig.
  (ed.) (2006) *Homeri Ilias: Rhapsodias I–XII*, Bibliotheca scriptorum Graecorum et Romanorum Teubneriana. Munich–Leipzig.
West, M. L. (1966) *Hesiod: Theogony*. Oxford.
  (ed.) (1990) *Aeschylus tragoediae*. Stuttgart.
Wilson, N. G. (ed.) (2007) *Aristophanis fabulae*. Oxford.

CHAPTER 5

Odysseus the Schedographer
Valeria F. Lovato

In his *Parekbolai on the Iliad*, Eustathios of Thessalonike often refers to Odysseus as the Homeric rhetor (*Homerikos rhetor*).¹ Despite sometimes being in competition with Nestor, Odysseus proves able to learn from his mistakes and soon surpasses his rival.² The son of Laertes is such an appropriate embodiment of the rhetor and learned man (*sophos*) that Eustathios opens the very preface to the *Parekbolai on the Iliad* with an Odyssean image: as Odysseus managed to lead his companions past the enticing songs of the Sirens, so Eustathios will guide his readers in their long voyage through the ocean of the Homeric poems.³

This depiction of Odysseus as the epitome of the exemplary rhetor and as a sort of alter ego of the exegete becomes a veritable *Leitmotif* in the *Parekbolai on the Odyssey*. In examining what he considers to be 'the more rhetorical' of the two poems,⁴ Eustathios often uses Odysseus and his adventures as a starting point to meditate upon crucial themes such as the role of poetry and the duties of the exegete, as well as the qualities of the ideal rhetor and teacher of rhetoric.

Part One of this chapter focuses on one such passage, where the analysis of Odysseus' most famous rhetorical exploit leads Eustathios to insert a long excursus on schedography, a rhetorical exercise that was increasingly

---

* I wish to thank Tommaso Braccini, Elizabeth Jeffreys, Aglae Pizzone and Luigi Silvano for discussing various drafts of this chapter with me and for providing crucial insights. I am also grateful to the participants in the *Preserving, Commenting, Adapting* workshop held at the University of Silesia in Katowice (October 2017) for their comments and suggestions. Special thanks go to Kristin Bourassa and Steffen Hope, whose invaluable help extended far beyond the improvement of my English prose.

¹ See e.g. Eust. *in Il.* 96.30–2 = 1.151.13–15 (commenting upon *Il.* 1.247–8). All passages from the *Parekbolai on the Iliad* are quoted from van der Valk's edition. For an overview of Eustathios' life and career, see Cesaretti and Ronchey (2014: 7*–30*) with extensive bibliography.

² Cf. e.g. Eust. *in Il.* 1181.12–15 = 4.317.4–8 and Eust. *in Od.* 1381.62–1382.2 = 1.5.20–4. All extracts from the *Parekbolai on the Odyssey* are quoted from Stallbaum's edition.

³ On the preface of the *Parekbolai on the Iliad*, see the discussion by van den Berg (2017: 32–5).

⁴ Eust. in *Il.* 4.46–5.5 = 1.7.7–12. On Eustathios' remarks about the differences between the *Iliad* and the *Odyssey*, see Pontani (2000: 27–9).

148

popular in twelfth-century Byzantium. More specifically, I will demonstrate that, in Eustathios' eyes, the Homeric text is nothing more than a sort of schedographic display *ante litteram*. I will also show that this interpretation provides Eustathios with an ideal pretext for a lesson on rhetorical 'good taste'.[5]

Part Two examines an extract from John Tzetzes' *Histories* in which Odysseus and his adventures again feature as a starting point for reflecting upon contemporary schedography. In this section, I will show that, despite some similarities with Eustathios' ideas, Tzetzes takes a more dogmatic position.[6] As a matter of fact, Tzetzes' careful depiction of Odysseus might even be interpreted as a subtle criticism of Eustathios' standpoint.

Thus, the texts examined in this chapter perfectly illustrate one of the main concepts underlying the present volume, showing how and why Byzantine commentaries ought to be considered – and studied – as veritable 'bridges' meant to close the gap separating ancient texts and new readerships.[7] In Eustathios' *Parekbolai* and Tzetzes' *Histories*, not only do the Homeric poems become an ideal starting point for discussing contemporary issues, such as the emergence of a controversial form of rhetorical training, but they also provide two of the most prominent Byzantine scholars with a perfect 'battlefield' both to spell out their long-standing rivalry and to articulate their contrasting opinions. In turn, these very opinions end up shaping their respective receptions of Homer and his characters. Before delving further into this inextricable entwinement between past and present, it may be useful to say a few words on the rhetorical exercise that both Tzetzes and Eustathios associated with Odysseus and his famed eloquence, namely the practice of schedography.

---

[5] As will become apparent in what follows, by 'good taste' I mainly refer to the rhetor's ability to compose ingenious and witty pieces while abstaining from an excessive use of rhetorical devices. Therefore, my definition of good taste might seem to overlap with the concept of *asteiotes*, the urbane refinement and wittiness that, combined with education (*paideia*), was an essential requisite for every rhetor aspiring to a successful career in eleventh- and twelfth-century Constantinople. Nevertheless, I decided to abstain from referring directly to the notion of *asteiotes* because it still requires further investigation, something that I am addressing in my current research project, funded by the Swiss National Science Foundation. For an overview of *asteiotes* in eleventh-century Byzantium, see Bernard (2014). On humour and witticisms in Eustathios' Homeric commentaries, see van den Berg in this volume.

[6] For an overview of Tzetzes' life and career, see Wendel (1948), Hunger (1978: 59–63, 117–18) and Wilson (1996: 190–6). For more specific studies, see, among others, Grünbart (1996) and (2005), Rhoby (2010), Braccini (2009–10) and (2011), Cullhed (2014: 58–67), Pizzone (2017), Agapitos (forthcoming). I wish to thank Panagiotis Agapitos for letting me read his forthcoming paper on Tzetzes, as well as Tommaso Braccini, who provided me with his yet unpublished overview of Tzetzes' life and works.

[7] See Introduction, p. 2.

About Schedography

Defining schedography might prove a hard task, as not only did it evolve over the centuries, but it could also take different forms according to the personal tastes and literary agenda of those who engaged in it.[8] For instance, while it is likely that the *schede* mentioned by Michael Psellos had a different form from those composed by his twelfth-century successors, divergent conceptions of schedography could coexist also within the same intellectual environment. Indeed, it has recently been demonstrated that the dazzling *schede* composed by Theodoros Prodromos had little to do with the 'new' and refined schedography proudly advertised by his contemporary and fellow rhetor Nikephoros Basilakes.[9]

This caveat notwithstanding, it is possible to give a general outline of the main features of schedography, especially if we focus on the testimony of twelfth-century literati.[10] Despite the variety of forms they could assume, Byzantine *schede* were generally conceived of as antistoichic riddles or wordplays, originally aimed at helping students to distinguish between homophonic (but not homographic) sequences of words.[11] These short pieces – which stemmed from the tradition of the Homeric epimerisms[12] – were usually composed either in verse or in prose, but sometimes they could be a combination of both.[13]

This kind of exercise became increasingly popular and soon left the classroom for the *theatron*, where public competitions between students and schools were periodically organized and presided over by

---

[8] For schedography as an open genre, see Marciniak (2017: 523). For an overview of the evolution of schedography, see Giannouli (2014: 61–4), Nousia (2016: 59–92).

[9] For a comparison between Basilakes' and Prodromos' conceptions of schedography, see Agapitos (2015a: 8–9).

[10] For a detailed discussion of twelfth-century schedography, see Agapitos (2015a), (2015b), (2017). For a general introduction, see Agapitos (2014).

[11] As observed by Agapitos (2014: 5), the *schede* aimed both at drilling young pupils 'in the complexities of Greek grammar and syntax' and at making them acquainted with different kinds of *progymnasmata*. For a *schedos* based mainly on antistoichic wordplays, see Nousia (2016: 63–4). For a series of *schede* focused mostly on the presentation of different categories of *progymnasmata*, see Marciniak (2017).

[12] See Giannouli (2014: 61–2).

[13] This bipartite structure had become quite common by the middle of the twelfth century: see Agapitos (2015a: 5).

the ruling elite.[14] Being successful in this sort of contest could be an important step towards a career at the imperial court or the patriarchate; consequently, the composition of *schede* acquired a crucial role in school education.

However, as some contemporary writers disapprovingly observe, the growing centrality of schedography generated an excessive concern for rhetorical display, which, in turn, led to linguistic and grammatical distortions.[15] Apparently, for the sake of composing more and more dazzling *schede*, teachers and students of rhetoric alike neglected other essential components, such as the intelligibility and pleasantness of their pieces, which therefore became increasingly intricate and almost impossible to decipher.[16] Moreover, the need for new and surprising riddles led most schedographers to misuse some words, which came to be employed in the wrong context or with an incorrect meaning.[17] Finally, in the case of verse *schede*, many rhetors overlooked the correct alternation between long and short syllables by deliberately ignoring the quantity of the so-called dichrona.

Part One: Odysseus vs. Polyphemus

That Is, When the Proper Use of Schedography Can Save a Rhetor's Life (and Reputation)

As mentioned above, Eustathios himself was concerned with these issues, which he discusses in many passages of his *Parekbolai*. Panagiotis Agapitos has recently analysed an extract from the *Parekbolai on the Odyssey* where the exegete deals extensively with schedography, its origins and its limits.[18] This discussion is prompted by the Homeric text, which Eustathios sees as a source of antistoichic wordplays. As in many other instances, the poet

---

[14] Here, too, it is often impossible to distinguish between *schede* composed only for didactic purposes and *schede* mainly destined for public performance. As school and *theatron* were in constant communication, the same *schedos* could fit both contexts and take up different functions according to the performative occasion. On the multiple layers of meaning that could make up a *schedos*, see Marciniak (2017: 513–14). On schedographic competitions, see e.g. Efthymiadis (2005: 269–70), Gaul (2014: 271–8), Nousia (2016: 74–5).
[15] The earliest evidence is a passage from Anna Komnene's *Alexiad* (15.7.9 ed. Reinsch and Kambylis, to be read along with Agapitos [2013: 92–8]).
[16] In his *Parekbolai on the Odyssey* Eustathios explicitly contrasts the simplicity and pleasantness of earlier *schede* to the excessive complexity of the modern ones: see Agapitos (2015b: 229–30).
[17] These judgements were based on the canon set by widely recognized manuals and authors, Homer *in primis*. For some examples of Eustathios' criticism of such linguistic abuses, see Agapitos (2015b: 230–4).
[18] See Agapitos (2015b: 228–30).

seems to have foreshadowed a practice that would become more and more prevalent in the following centuries, leading to the excesses that Eustathios was well aware of. This long excursus is crucial to our understanding of Eustathios' reception of schedography and it deserves the attention it received in Agapitos' paper. What I want to focus on here, however, is the analysis of the Homeric passage that both precedes and inspires Eustathios' digression. As I intend to show, the exegete's lesson on how to compose tasteful *schede* starts well before his excursus on schedography and informs his whole interpretation of the Homeric text.

We might not be surprised to discover that the passage prompting Eustathios' discussion of schedography is nothing less than the most famous rhetorical exploit of the *Odyssey*, namely the episode where Odysseus saves himself and his comrades by tricking Polyphemus with a clever linguistic stratagem. After having been trapped by the Cyclops, Odysseus persuades his captor that his name is *Outis* (Οὖτις), that is, *Nobody*. This ploy will prove essential to the hero's survival: when the blinded Polyphemus calls his brothers for help, stating that 'Nobody' hurt him, the other Cyclopes think him mad and therefore refuse to come to his aid.[19]

Let us now turn to the section of the *Parekbolai* where Eustathios explains and analyses Odysseus' stratagem and its consequences: reading this passage from the perspective of a Byzantine teacher of rhetoric, Eustathios not only interprets it through the lens of contemporary schedography, but also uses it as a pretext to set a standard of rhetorical good taste.

> Ὅτι ἀκούσας Ὀδυσσεὺς ἐκ τοῦ Κύκλωπος τό, καί μοι τεὸν οὔνομα εἰπὲ [*Od.* 9.355], ... φησίν. Κύκλωψ, εἰρωτᾷς μ' οὔνομα κλυτόν, αὐτὰρ ἐγώ τοι ἐξερέω, σὺ δέ μοι δὸς ξείνιον ὥσπερ ὑπέστης [*Od.* 9.364-5] ... εἶτα ψευδόμενος ἐν καιρῷ συμφερόντως ἑαυτῷ καὶ τοῖς ἑταίροις ἐπάγει. οὖτις ἔμοι γ' οὔνομα [*Od.* 9.366], καὶ ἵνα μὴ ἐπιστήσας τυχὸν ὁ Πολύφημος τῷ παραλογισμῷ γνῷ οὖτις τὸν σύνθετον ἐκ δύο λέξεων τοῦ ου καὶ τοῦ τις ὅπερ οὐ βούλεται Ὀδυσσεύς, ἐπάγει αἰτιατικὴν ἐν ἁπλότητι ἤγουν ἀσύνθετον, λέγων. οὖτιν δέ με κικλήσκουσι μήτηρ ἠδὲ πατὴρ ἠδ' ἄλλοι πάντες ἑταῖροι [*Od.* 9.366-7]. ὡς ἀπὸ εὐθείας τῆς, οὖτις οὖτιδος. οὗ αἰτιατικὴ τὸν Οὖτιν, ὁμοίως τῷ, ὁ Πάρις τὸν Πάριν. τῆς γὰρ ἄλλης εὐθείας τῆς συνθέτου, ἡ αἰτιατικὴ πάντως οὔ τινά ἐστι.[20] διὸ οὐδὲ ἐπάγει μετὰ τοῦ Οὖτιν φωνῆεν, ἵνα μὴ ὑποπτευθῇ ἔκθλιψις ἤγουν κουφισμὸς τοῦ α ἐν τῷ Οὖτιν. ὅπερ ἐπὶ τοῦ λόγου τοῦ Κύκλωπος γίνεται, ἀμειψαμένου νηλέϊ θυμῷ, Οὖτιν ἐγὼ πύματον ἔδομαι [*Od.* 9.369]. ἔνθα ὁ ἀστείως ἀκροατὴς ὑποκινηθεὶς εἰς μειδίαμα, εἰπεῖν δὲ μᾶλλον κατὰ τὸν Ὁμηρικὸν Ὀδυσσέα, γελάσας, συναλείψει τὴν ἀρχὴν

---

[19] *Odyssey* 9.345-414.   [20] Cf. *Etymologicum magnum* s.v. Οὖτις (p. 643.14-20 ed. Gaisford).

τοῦ λόγου, καὶ κατ' ἔκθλιψιν τοῦ α ἐρεῖ ὅτι ἀληθῶς οὔ τινα φάγοις ἂν ἄλλον ἄνθρωπον. ... Οὕτω δὲ θαυμαστή τις τοῦ Οὖτις ὀνόματος, ὥστε καὶ ἐν τοῖς ἑξῆς τριβὴν τῷ λόγῳ χαρίεσσαν δίδωσιν. ... ἔστι δὲ τὸ σόφισμα οὐ παρὰ τὴν ὁμωνυμίαν κατά τινας, ἀλλὰ παρὰ σύνθεσιν μᾶλλον καὶ διαίρεσιν, τοῦ μὲν Κύκλωπος κύριον νοήσαντος καὶ σύνθετον καὶ ἁπλοῦν τὸ Οὖτις ὡς κλινόμενον Οὔτιδος.²¹ ὅθεν καὶ παραπαίζων πρὸς τοὔνομα μετ' ὀλίγα κατὰ παρήχησιν λέγει. ἅ μοι οὐτιδανὸς πόρεν Οὖτις [Od. 9.460]. τῶν δὲ Κυκλώπων εἰς δύο μέρη κατατεμόντων τὴν λέξιν, εἰ μῆτις²² κίνδυνον εἶχε ψυχρεύσασθαι, εἶπεν ἂν ὅτι τό, μῆτις ἀμύμων, πρὸς τὸ Οὖτις πέπαικται. ἢ καὶ πρός, τό, μῆτις σε κτείνῃ [cf. Od. 9.406]. ... ἐκ δὲ τοῦ τοιούτου Ὁμηρικοῦ σοφίσματος οἱ φιλόσοφοι τοὺς παρ' αὐτοῖς οὔτιδας πλέκουσι παραλογισμούς. (Eustathios, *Parekbolai on the Odyssey* 1633.58–1634.5 = 1.348.8–21; 1634.41, 48–52, 55 = 349.18–19, 26–32, 35–6)

Remark that, having heard the Cyclops saying: 'tell me your name straight away' ..., Odysseus replies: 'Cyclops, you ask me of my glorious name, and I will tell it to you; and do give me a stranger's gift, as you promised' ... Then, lying at the appropriate time for his own sake as well as that of his comrades, he adds: 'Nobody is my name.' To prevent Polyphemus from detecting by chance the fallacy and from understanding that *outis* is a compound noun resulting from the combination of *ou* and *tis* – which is exactly what Odysseus wants to avoid – [the hero] uses it again in the accusative as if it were a simplex (that is uncompounded) word and says: 'Nobody do they call me – my mother and my father, and all my comrades as well.' Thus, he implicitly suggests that the word derives from the nominative *Outis, Outidos*, whose accusative would be *Outin*, following the same pattern as *Paris* [nom.], *Parin* [acc.]. Indeed, the accusative of the other nominative [i.e. *outis* indefinite pronoun] is *outina*. This is also the reason why [Odysseus] does not add, after *Outin*, a word with a vocalic beginning, so as to avoid the suspicion that *Outin* is the result of the elision – that is the elimination – of the final alpha. And this is exactly what happens in the Cyclops' speech, when the latter 'answered me with pitiless heart: "Nobody will I eat last among his comrades."' At this point the refined reader, urged to smile, or rather – to follow the example of the

---

²¹ This seems inconsistent with the analysis of the Odyssean σόφισμα adopted so far. However, both Venice, Biblioteca Nazionale Marciana, gr. 460 and Paris, Bibliothèque nationale de France, gr. 2702 read καὶ σύνθετον καὶ ἁπλοῦν. Therefore, the text must be accepted and interpreted as it is. Maybe Eustathios is implying that, in some instances, the incompetent Polyphemus interprets Οὖτις as a compound noun (this would be the case in *Odyssey* 9.460), whereas in others he considers it as an uncompounded proper noun. I would like to thank Eric Cullhed for providing me with the diplomatic transcription of the manuscripts and for suggesting this possible line of interpretation.
²² In both Marc. gr. 460 (fol. 106r) and Par. gr. 2702 (fol. 104r), the space between μητις / μη τις varies and it is difficult to determine whether the two elements are separated or not. Therefore, I decided to adopt, at least provisionally, the text as printed by Stallbaum.

> Homeric Odysseus – urged to laugh, will think of the beginning of the episode and, eliding the final alpha, will declare: 'You will eat nobody... that's for sure!' ... The invention of the name *Outis* is so admirable that it provides further cues for pleasant wordplays also in the following part of the episode. ... This sophism is not based on ambiguity, but rather on composition and resolution. The Cyclops thinks that *Outis* is a proper name, compound and simple, the genitive of which is *Outidos*. This is the reason why, some lines later, playing on the [sound of the] name, he says through alliteration: '[the woes] which good-for-nothing Nobody has brought me'. The other Cyclopes, however, divide the word into two parts. Therefore, were it not for the risk of making a frigid joke, one could say that also *metis amymon* has been made up as a jest echoing *Outis* or even *me tis se kteinei*. ... The philosophers contrive their own nobody-fallacies (*outidas paralogismous*) based on this kind of Homeric sophism.[23]

Eustathios' analysis begins with a thorough explanation of the structure and meaning of Odysseus' rhetorical stratagem, which he repeatedly qualifies as *paralogismos*. This term, generally indicating a logical or linguistic fallacy, had been strictly associated with sophistry since Aristotelian times.[24] This tradition had recently been revived by Psellos, who deals with different types of sophistic fallacies in one of his minor philosophical works.[25] Taking his cue from the Aristotelian classification, Psellos lists six different kinds of linguistic fallacies (*paralogismoi para ten lexin*), namely *homonymia* (equivocation), *amphibolia* (amphibology), *synthesis* (composition), *diairesis* (division), *prosoidia* (accent) and *schema lexeos* (figure of speech). This terminology also features in Eustathios' analysis of Odysseus' ploy, which he defines, significantly, as a clever 'sophism' based on the rhetorical devices of *synthesis* and *diairesis*, rather than on *homonymia* (ἔστι δὲ τὸ σόφισμα οὐ παρὰ τὴν ὁμωνυμίαν κατά τινας, ἀλλὰ παρὰ σύνθεσιν μᾶλλον καὶ διαίρεσιν).[26]

---

[23] Unless otherwise indicated, all translations are my own.

[24] The transmitted title of Aristotle's treatise on *paralogismoi* is Περὶ τῶν σοφιστικῶν ἐλέγχων (*On Sophistical Refutations*). For the environment in which and for which it was produced, see Ebbesen (1981: 2–7).

[25] Aristotle's *Elenchi* enjoyed an immediate and vast success both in the Latin and in the Greek world. However, it was during the twelfth and thirteenth centuries that most Greek scholia on this work were produced: see Ebbesen (1981: 7).

[26] This remark implies that others had tried to interpret Odysseus' stratagem on the basis of the Aristotelian repertoire of *paralogismoi*. I have not yet been able to identify the target of Eustathios' criticism. He might be referring to a scholium on the *Odyssey* or he could be thinking of a more recent treatment of the subject. It is worth noting, in this respect, that the *Souda Lexicon* also devotes a short entry to the *Outis*-stratagem, which is explicitly classified as a *paralogismos* (see *Souda* o 973.1–2 ed. Adler; this source is discussed further *infra*).

Of course, Eustathios was well aware of the long-standing tradition depicting Odysseus as a wily sophist. However, I suggest that Eustathios' association of the hero with sophistry stems also from his personal experience as a Byzantine rhetor and teacher of rhetoric. To be sure, in twelfth-century Byzantium the increasingly popular practice of schedography was often compared to sophistry. Nikephoros Basilakes went as far as to define his own version of the discipline as the 'new sophistry' (*nea sophistike*).[27] Therefore, when he qualifies Odysseus as a sophist devising clever *paralogismoi*, Eustathios is not necessarily alluding to the cynical smooth-talking hero depicted by Sophocles or Euripides, but he is most likely thinking of Byzantine schedographic sophistry and its representatives. In his eyes, being a 'sophist' was not necessarily negative, as long as one was able to follow some fundamental rules.

Indeed, if the Homeric Odysseus could be considered a skilled and refined sophist, the same was not true for other self-declared rhetors, as Eustathios repeatedly implies in his *Parekbolai*. In this respect, the Polyphemus episode was a particularly suitable starting point for discussion: not only did it offer a chance to demonstrate how a good rhetorician should operate, but it also showed the consequences awaiting those who are unable to follow the rules dictated by education (*paideia*) and good taste.

First, as the Homeric passage demonstrates, in order to compose pleasant and effective *schede* one needs to understand the complex mechanisms of language and its inherent ambiguities. The careful way in which Odysseus formulates his riddle shows that the hero was conscious of the dangers posed by a superficially constructed *sophisma*. Being aware that Polyphemus could still have grasped the true meaning of his false name, Odysseus adds a final touch that renders his plan flawless. After stating his pseudonym in the nominative form (*Outis*), the hero repeats it in the accusative (*Outin*). This time, however, he makes sure that *Outin* is immediately followed by a word beginning with a consonant: this prevents the Cyclops from understanding *Outin* as the accusative of the indefinite pronoun (*outina*) having undergone elision before a vowel.

As shown by the subtle strategy informing Odysseus' ploy, being a good sophist requires skill and knowledge, two rare qualities that the uncouth Polyphemus does not share with his refined opponent. What is worse, not only does the uncultured Cyclops not understand Odysseus' riddles, but

---

[27] Nikephoros Basilakes, *Orations and Letters* 3.14–17 ed. Garzya. For further remarks on this passage, see Agapitos (2014: 8–10).

he also inadvertently creates new puns that, ironically, foreshadow the final outcome of his encounter with the wily hero.

Duped by Odysseus' linguistic virtuosities, Polyphemus makes himself ridiculous whenever he tries to be witty or sarcastic. As Eustathios remarks elsewhere,[28] when he mocks his prisoner's apparent weakness by playing on the assonance between *Outis* and *outidanos* ('good-for-nothing'), Polyphemus almost discloses the very ambiguity of Odysseus' pseudonym. However, he is so confident in his superiority that he does not realize that he has failed to grasp the only key that might have saved him from his doom.

Polyphemus' uncouthness is all the more evident in another passage that Eustathios discusses extensively in the extract quoted above. Trying again to be sarcastic, Polyphemus informs Odysseus that, as a reward for his kindness, he will be the last to be eaten (Οὖτιν ἐγὼ πύματον ἔδομαι). Once more, the Cyclops' ignorance turns against him. When he declares that he intends to eat 'Nobody' (*Outin*) after all the other prisoners, not only is he – again – making clear that he did not understand the hidden meaning of Odysseus' pseudonym, but he also unconsciously predicts the denouement of his meeting with the hero. Only someone as well versed in rhetoric as Odysseus can understand the involuntary prophecy uttered by the unaware Polyphemus. While the incompetent rhetor ends up making a fool of himself, a cultured audience can share Odysseus' amusement at his opponent's naivety.[29] What is more, the refined reader can even try to participate in the Homeric and Odyssean game: (correctly) interpreting *outin* as the elided accusative of *outis*, he will sarcastically exclaim: 'you will eat *nobody*, that's for sure!' (οὔ τινα φάγοις ἂν ἄλλον ἄνθρωπον).

If the urbane rhetor can join both Odysseus and Homer in their clever and refined riddles, he should nevertheless be aware that the danger of behaving like the overly self-confident Polyphemus is always lurking, as Eustathios later points out. In the archbishop's opinion, the stratagem described in *Odyssey* 9 is pleasant and could be a source of inspiration for further riddles. Indeed, the pseudonym *Outis* could even be considered as the starting point for a series of wordplays that Homer himself seems to have scattered throughout the episode. However, despite mentioning this possible interpretation, Eustathios warns his audience against the excesses it might lead to. The refined reader should not overinterpret the Homeric text by trying to find puns that would overburden it. Those who do not

---

[28] See the discussion *infra* and cf. Eust. *in Od.* 1638.49 = 1.355.26–7.
[29] On the opposition between 'sagacious' and 'gluttonous' readers in Eustathios' *Parekbolai*, see Pizzone (2016).

listen to Eustathios' warnings and do not prove as careful as Odysseus might end up formulating frigid jokes (*psychreumata*), behaving like the uncouth Polyphemus. Both the terminology and the tone of this passage reveal its didactic scope: contrasting Polyphemus' inadvertent and ridiculous puns with Odysseus' clever riddles, Eustathios shows his audience that there exists a clear – yet tenuous – distinction between a tasteful and a tasteless rhetor.

However, as readers of the *Parekbolai* know, Eustathios is not the sort of teacher who imparts dry lessons to his disciples. On the contrary, he is first and foremost a sophisticated rhetorician ready to show his skills, both to amuse his audience and to give them a further lesson on refined wit and rhetorical urbanity. Indeed, if we look more closely at Eustathios' warning against frigid jokes, we might remark that it is phrased so as to contain a further, encoded, admonition. 'Were it not for the risk of making a lame joke' – Eustathios observes – 'one could say that *metis amymon* has also been made up as a jest echoing *Outis* or even *me tis se kteinei*' (εἰ μήτις κίνδυνον εἶχε ψυχρεύσασθαι, εἶπεν ἂν ὅτι τό, μῆτις ἀμύμων, πρὸς τὸ Οὖτις πέπαικται. ἢ καὶ πρὸς, τό, μήτις σε κτείνῃ). Surprisingly, at the very moment when he cautions against the dangers of *psychreuein*, Eustathios introduces a new antistoichic wordplay playing on the homophony of the expressions μήτις (μή + indefinite pronoun) and μῆτις ('cunning', noun in the nominative singular). If the latter two were already embedded in the Homeric text, the first one has been added by Eustathios himself. Thus, the very sentence cautioning against the dangers of frigid jokes contains the exact definition of one. By using a tasteless pun to further stress the boorishness of such rhetorical games, Eustathios demonstrates not only that he is perfectly aware of the potential for new wordplays offered by the Homeric poems, but also that he deliberately chooses not to go down such a risky path. An urbane rhetor recognizes the limits set by good taste and is able to resist the temptation of crossing them, even when offered the chance to do so. Only thus will he avoid being contaminated by the unruly and unrestrained practices of his 'Polyphemian' colleagues.

The impression that Eustathios is not only teaching his readers a lesson in good taste, but also indirectly criticizing a specific category of vapid 'sophists', is further strengthened by his final comment on the Homeric passage. Immediately after his warnings against frigid jokes, Eustathios observes that the Polyphemus episode inspires the intricate *paralogismoi* concocted by some philosophers (ἐκ δὲ τοῦ τοιούτου Ὁμηρικοῦ σοφίσματος οἱ φιλόσοφοι τοὺς παρ' αὐτοῖς οὔτιδας πλέκουσι παραλογισμούς). The expressions Eustathios uses to describe both the composition of these *paralogismoi* and their content deserve analysis.

For one, the choice of the verb *pleko* ('intertwine'), used to define the activities of these unnamed 'philosophers', is particularly meaningful. The verb *plekein* was closely connected to the rhetorical exploits of twelfth-century schedographers,[30] whose compositions were often depicted as convoluted riddles. This detail, as well as the present tense of the verb (πλέκουσι), seems to indicate that Eustathios is referring to contemporary practices, such as the 'new sophistry' practised by some of his colleagues.[31]

What is more, in this whole section of the *Parekbolai*, the technical term *paralogismos* is constantly and consistently associated with Odysseus' rhetorical exploits. For instance, in another passage on the hero's stratagem,[32] Eustathios defines it as a well-conceived *paralogismos* (παραλογισμὸς τεχνικός). This expression clearly implies that there are different kinds of fallacies, some of which are acceptable (if not commendable) and some of which are not.

Finally, the choice of the rather uncommon expression *outidas paralogismous*[33] seems to hint at one of Polyphemus' jokes that Eustathios had discussed only a few lines before, namely the pun based upon the assonance between the pseudonym *Outis* and the adjective *outidanos* ('good-for-nothing'). As we have seen, when discussing this dull wordplay, Eustathios implied that the Cyclops was wrong to infer that a similarity of sound necessarily entails a similarity in meaning. However, when it comes to the *outides paralogismoi* concocted by the anonymous *philosophoi*, the situation appears to be different. Indeed, Eustathios seems to be suggesting that, in this case, the denomination of these kinds of fallacies perfectly matches their content, which is as empty and meaningless as Odysseus' false name. This interpretation is strengthened by the fact that, apart from the passage at

---

[30] For the use of the verb πλέκω to describe the composition of intricate *schede*, see e.g. Ioannes Mauropous, *Epigrammata* 33.33–4 ed. de Lagarde; Theodoros Prodromos, *Carmina Historica* 71.16 ed. Hörandner; Eust. *in Od.* 1634.13 = 1.348.31. Further examples in Vassis (1994: 9–10), Nousia (2016: 64–5).

[31] Cf. also the extracts from the *Parekbolai* discussed by Agapitos (2015b: 228–30), where past and present tenses are used to contrast the commendable practices of 'traditional education' with the excesses of contemporary schools.

[32] It is worth noting that three of the four instances of παραλογισμός in the *Parekbolai on the Odyssey* occur in the section concerned with the *Outis*-stratagem.

[33] In classical sources, the expression *outides paralogismoi* mostly refers to a specific kind of fallacy that was particularly popular amongst the Stoics, as we learn from Diogenes Laertius' *Life of Zenon*: see e.g. Diogenes Laertius, *Lives of Eminent Philosophers* 7.82.1–9 ed. Long, where the author also establishes a connection between the *outides paralogismoi* and the so-called fallacy of the heap. This same connection also features in the few Byzantine sources that mention the *outides paralogismoi*: see *Souda* o 973.1–2 ed. Adler and Psellos' *Chronographia* 3.15.23–5 ed. Renauld, discussed also *infra*.

hand, the same expression features also in two other texts Eustathios might have been familiar with, namely one of Themistius' orations to the Emperor Constantius[34] and Psellos' *Chronographia*.[35] In both cases, the phrasing *outidas logous* or *outidas paralogismous* denotes a kind of 'philosophy' (equated to sophistry by Themistius) that a wise ruler should not pursue, because of its empty idleness and inapplicability to real life.[36]

On the basis of these observations, we can conclude that Eustathios' closing remark is something more than a passing comment on a rather obscure category of linguistic fallacy. By indirectly pointing out the hollowness of a branch of 'philosophy' devoted to the creation of idle riddles and logical conundrums, Eustathios shows once again that, despite being pleasant and amusing, an excessive focus on this superficial kind of exercise may literally lead to nothing. Those aspiring to acquire a complete and effective *paideia* should refrain from these idle practices and turn to Eustathios: unlike the anonymous *philosophoi*, he is able to use the Homeric model as a starting point for the education of a refined – and, most importantly, successful – *rhetor* and *sophos*.

Part Two: Odysseus vs. Circe

That Is, When the Improper Use of Schedography Can Transform a Rhetor into a Pig

Amongst Eustathios' rivals we can count the less successful John Tzetzes.[37] Their well-attested rivalry notwithstanding,[38] both Tzetzes and Eustathios shared a contempt for the excesses of contemporary schedography. Moreover, they both chose the same Homeric character as a means to

---

[34] Themistius, *Oration* 3, 30b–d ed. Downey and Schenkl: Εἰς Κωνστάντιον τὸν αὐτοκράτορα, ὅτι μάλιστα φιλόσοφος ὁ βασιλεύς, ἢ χαριστήριος. I owe this reference to Elizabeth Jeffreys.
[35] Psellos, *Chronographia* 3.15.23–5 ed. Renauld.
[36] Eustathios often praises Odysseus for his 'practical wisdom' (ἔμπρακτος σοφία), a trait that he connects both with the hero's rhetorical mastery and with his ability to deal effectively even with the most desperate situations. Significantly, he considers the Polyphemus episode to be the perfect demonstration of such a crucial quality (Eust. *in Od.* 1642.40–1 = 1.360.18–19).
[37] For Tzetzes' social position and a comparison with Eustathios' more successful career, see Agapitos (2017: 6–7) and (forthcoming).
[38] Concerning the competition between Tzetzes and Eustathios and their disparaging allusions to one another's works, see e.g. Holwerda (1960: 324–6), Pontani (2000: 41), Conley (2005: 684), Cullhed (2014: 65) and, most recently, D'Agostini (2022), who focuses on the two scholars' contrasting reception of canonical geographical authors, such as Ptolemy and Dionysius Periegetes. See also Pizzone in this volume. On the competitive intellectual environment in general, see Agapitos in this volume.

exemplify the qualities every good rhetor should possess, as opposed to the uncouthness of the incompetent ones.

Indeed, in an extract from Tzetzes' *Histories*,[39] Odysseus plays an extremely positive role. In this passage, the *grammatikos* attacks the practice of schedography, which he labels as 'the New Circe'. In Tzetzes' eyes, the followers of this obnoxious practice are nothing but a bunch of dung-eating pigs, whom only a new Odysseus could bring back to human form. Of course, this new Odysseus is none other than Tzetzes himself, who is ready to redeem his ignorant colleagues by administering to them the divine *moly* of *paideia* that could make them human again. Unfortunately, the pigs Tzetzes is trying to save are unwilling to be rescued: as he remarks, they prefer to revel in their disgusting state, rather than eat the angels' bread they are generously being offered.

> Τανῦν δε τρισεξάγιστα τῶν ἀμαθῶν κνωδάλων
> βίβλους βαρβάρους γράφοντα καὶ τρισεπιβαρβάρους
> ὡς τεχνικοὶ κηρύττονται τοῖς μεθυσοκοττάβοις,
> καὶ τεχνικὸν μὴ γράφοντες μηδέν, μηδὲ εἰδότες,
> τρεφόμενοι κοπρῶνι δε τῆς Κίρκης ἀτεχνίας
> οὐ μόνον οὐκ ἐθέλουσιν ἐᾶν τὸ τρώγειν κόπρον,
> ἀλλὰ καὶ εἴ τις Ὀδυσσεὺς Ἑρμοῦ βαστάζων μῶλυ,
> λόγους κανόνας τε τεχνῶν, ἅπερ κοσμοῦσι βίον,
> ἐκ χοίρων τούτους βουληθῇ τέχναις ἀνθρώπους δρᾶσαι,
> ὅσος ὁ γρύλλος παρ' αὐτῶν, ἡ βόρβορος δὲ πόση,
> χεῖται κατὰ τοῦ θέλοντος τούτους ποιεῖν ἀνθρώπους,
> ἀπόνως κόπρον θέλουσι καὶ γὰρ σιτεῖσθαι πλέον,
> ἢ μετὰ πόνων, ὡς εἰπεῖν, ἄρτον φαγεῖν ἀγγέλων.
> (Tzetzes, *Histories* 10.306.64–76 ed. Leone 1968)

And now the thrice-accursed ignorant beasts | writing barbarous and thrice-barbarous books | are proclaimed experts by a bunch of drunkards, | even though they neither know nor write anything according to the principles of the Art.[40] | Feeding on the dung of Circe's ignorance, | not only do they refuse to stop eating dung, | but even if an Odysseus comes, who yields the *moly* of Hermes | as well as the rules and canons of the Art – indeed these embellish and ordain the life of men – | and wants to make them men again from the pigs they are through the principles of the Art, | their grunts and their filth are such that they swamp the one wanting to

---

[39] The *Histories* or *Chiliades* are a verse commentary to Tzetzes' *Letters*, composed by the *grammatikos* himself. For the nature and aims of this work, see Pizzone (2017).

[40] When he mentions the 'Art' or τέχνη, Tzetzes generally refers to grammar, the art *par excellence*, at least since Dionysius Thrax's Γραμματικὴ τέχνη. Consequently, the term τεχνικοί employed at v. 66 can be read as a synonym for γραμματικοί, 'experts in the Art (of grammar)'.

transform them back into men: | they prefer to keep on eating more and more dung effortlessly | than to make an effort and eat, as they say, the angels' bread.⁴¹

This extract exemplifies the invectives Tzetzes scattered throughout his works. The repertoire of abuses he deploys against his rivals is strikingly consistent: his enemies, generally to be identified with other fellow rhetors or teachers, are debased socially, intellectually and morally through comparison to dubious members of the social spectrum, barbarians or even animals. In this instance, however, the *grammatikos* is especially concerned with the destructive effects of contemporary education. The imagery he employs is clearly reminiscent of other notorious attacks he directs against Byzantine teachers and their questionable methods. Indeed, the New Circe features also in another polemical piece where Tzetzes laments the catastrophic effects of schedography, which, in his opinion, does nothing but prevent the students from learning the canons of the Art of grammar, the *techne par excellence*. In this case, too, contemporary schools are expressly equated to pigsties, breeding generation after generation of incompetent would-be intellectuals.⁴²

If, on the one hand, Tzetzes points to the steady decline of contemporary schools, on the other he constantly depicts himself as the last bastion of true education, which should be based on the books of the ancient authors and not on the barbarous writings of the fake experts infesting the capital. However, as Tzetzes declares in many other instances, not everyone is ready to abandon the easy ways of the New Circe to embark with him on the difficult journey towards education: only those who are prepared to make sacrifices will finally attain the authentic *paideia*, here symbolized by the Homeric *moly* and by the biblical bread of the angels. As Odysseus was the only hope for his comrades, so Tzetzes is the last chance

---

⁴¹ This expression, which Tzetzes sometimes employs to extol his superior knowledge, is a quotation from the *Psalms*: see Psalm 77.25 and Agapitos (2017: 19–20).
⁴² τοὺς βουβάλους δ'ἔασον δυσμαθεστάτους | ἁπανταχοῦ δίφθογγα ταυταὶ γράφειν, | οἱ τὸ σκότος φῶς ὡς τὸ φῶς φασὶ σκότος | Κίρκης τραφέντες χοιρεῶσι τῆς νέας. This short iambic poem features amongst Tzetzes' scholia on Thucydides, reedited and examined by Luzzatto (1999); for the text quoted here, see especially p. 19. Another reference to the pernicious teachings of the New Circe can be found in a passage of the Tzetzean *Logismoi* on the corpus Hermogenianum, which are preserved in Leiden, Universiteitsbibliotheek, Vossianus gr. Q 1 and are currently being edited by Aglae Pizzone. In a preliminary study on the subject, Pizzone convincingly argues that the association between Tzetzes' rivals and the figure of Circe might also hide a reference to the everyday life of the teachers and pupils belonging to the circle of Andronikos Kamateros, who famously attracted Tzetzes' violent criticism (see following footnote). Specifically, the reference to Circe, who was traditionally associated with 'prototypical figures of sorcerous and liminal innkeepers' may be read as an allusion to the dubious boarding houses hosting the young rhetors gathering around Kamateros. For more details on this interpretation, see Pizzone (2021: 669–72).

at redemption for the Constantinopolitan students: those who refuse to follow his example have no alternative but to keep revelling in the repulsive products of their dehumanizing and barbarizing ignorance.

If we return to the extract from the *Parekbolai on the Odyssey* analysed before, we find that Eustathios equally hints at the potentially 'dehumanizing' effects of a severe lack of education. Indeed, apart from its tone, his interpretation of the Polyphemus episode does share commonalities with Tzetzes' outburst against the New Circe. For instance, if in the *Parekbolai* the incompetent rhetor is implicitly compared to the inhuman Cyclops, in the *Histories* the followers of the New Circe are clearly equated to a horde of pigs, equally unaware of their revolting ignorance. Nevertheless, if we compare Odysseus' role in the *Parekbolai* to the part he plays in the *Histories*, we might note a slight difference in the perspective adopted by the two scholars. While Eustathios sympathizes with the sophist Odysseus and even joins him in his display of rhetorical virtuosity, Tzetzes' identification with the wily hero seems to hide a deeper agenda.

First, the Odyssean Tzetzes does not compare himself with the pig-schedographers, nor does he try to propose an alternative (and acceptable) form of schedography. In this extract, as in many others, he makes it clear that he belongs to a different league altogether. He is not a schedographer nor one of the 'ether-walking rhetors'[43] who practise schedography and are therefore prized by the ruling elite. As he asserts elsewhere, he is the *logistes* ('auditor') of the ancients and the moderns.[44] Therefore, he is entitled to chastise his incompetent colleagues, who are not even able to appreciate the angels' bread he offers them. In summary, the Odyssean Tzetzes does not promote a more moderate or refined version of schedography, as was the case in Eustathios' *Parekbolai*. In countless passages of the *Histories*, as well

---

[43] This epithet is often used by Tzetzes to stigmatize the pompousness and ignorance of his unworthy competitors. See e.g. *Histories* 9.278.655–61 ed. Leone (1968), where Tzetzes attacks a rival who had been appointed to a prestigious position by the eparch Andronikos Kamateros. For further details on Tzetzes' falling out with Kamateros, see Agapitos (2017: 22–7), Pizzone (2021: 668–70). For the scholar's repertoire of abuses and the identity of his enemies, see also Luzzatto (1999: 49–55) and *infra*.

[44] Cf. the final *sphragis* of Tzetzes' *Iambi*, published by Leone (1969–70: 146.356–60), where the *grammatikos* presents himself as Τζέτζης λογιστὴς τῶν παλαιῶν καὶ τῶν νέων. This line might be an allusion to the Βίβλος τῶν λογισμῶν, a composite work where Tzetzes exposed all the 'mistakes' made by ancient authors. For more details on the Βίβλος τῶν λογισμῶν, which, until recently, was believed to be entirely lost, see Pizzone (2021), who also expands upon the bureaucratic origin of the term λογιστής and on Tzetzes' exploitation of his own administrative experience as a strategy of self-authorization.

as in his other works, Tzetzes rejects this inacceptable rhetorical practice in favour of the true *techne*, which he alone possesses and truly understands.[45]

What is more, if we consider the entirety of Tzetzes' opus, his identification with the Homeric Odysseus cannot but come as a surprise. Certainly, in the course of his career, Tzetzes has an ambiguous attitude towards Homer[46] and especially Odysseus, whom he considers to be the very embodiment of the dishonest intellectual.[47] Why, then, identify with the Homeric hero he despises the most, especially when it comes to defending the true *paideia* against the dangerous teachings of the New Circe? Of course, we cannot expect absolute consistency in Tzetzes' interpretation of the Homeric poems and their characters, a topic to which he devoted thousands of pages. However, it still is remarkable that, apart from the few passages where he depicts himself as a new Odysseus ready to fight the precepts of the New Circe, his attitude towards the son of Laertes is always rather dismissive, if not blatantly depreciatory.

One reason why Tzetzes might have chosen this particular myth is that Circe's story allowed him to degrade his rivals by comparing them to pigs. Nevertheless, Tzetzes' unexpected choice could also be connected to Eustathios' own interpretation of Odysseus as the perfect rhetor and exegete. As noted, in many passages of his *Parekbolai*, Eustathios identifies with Odysseus, who is sometimes represented as the ideal philosopher, the accomplished rhetor and, most importantly, the perfect teacher, who can guide his disciples through the difficult path leading towards *paideia*. For instance, Odysseus appears as the ideal teacher in a long excerpt from the *Parekbolai of the Odyssey* dealing with the Circe episode.[48] According to Eustathios' interpretation, the divine *moly* that Odysseus receives from Hermes[49] and then uses to free his companions is nothing but the very symbol of *paideia*.[50] Of course, this interpretation was partially hinted at in the Homeric scholia; however, as on many other occasions, Eustathios

---

[45] Tzetzes seems to make a positive comment on schedography only once, in a letter where he praises the compositions of his friend John Ismeniotes: see *ep.* 77.114.3–11 ed. Leone (1972) with Agapitos (2017: 8–10). All the other passages where Tzetzes concerns himself with this rhetorical exercise are extremely derogatory: see again Agapitos (2017: 10–27).

[46] In a recent paper, Eric Cullhed (2014: 61–7) has shown that, in some passages of his works, Tzetzes seems to go as far as to identify with Homer. Cullhed's arguments are rich and persuasive, but they illuminate only one aspect of Tzetzes' reception of Homer. For a preliminary discussion of this rather intricate issue, see Lovato (2016: 335–9).

[47] On Tzetzes' reception of Odysseus, see also Lovato (2017a: 172–239) and (2017b: 148–55).

[48] *Odyssey* 10.135–399.   [49] *Odyssey* 10.302–6.

[50] Eust. *in Od.* 1658.25–6 = 1.381.9–10. On this passage, see also Lovato (2016: 326–7).

expands upon it, adding personal remarks and using them to strengthen his allegorical reading of the poem and its protagonist.

It is well established that Tzetzes and Eustathios knew and indirectly criticized each other's work, sometimes even when it came to tiny details. Moreover, Tzetzes seems to have placed Eustathios in the group of the ether-walking rhetors who did not understand the true meaning of *paideia* and tormented Tzetzes because of their jealousy of his superior talent.[51] Would it not be possible, then, that in presenting himself as a triumphant Odysseus wielding the divine *moly* of *paideia*, Tzetzes is challenging Eustathios' representation of (and identification with) the Homeric hero? In this case, the *grammatikos* would be suggesting that, if the victims of the New Circe really need to be rescued by a new Odysseus, this role should be played by none other than Tzetzes himself, the only rightful bestower of the divine *moly* of *paideia*. As much as he dislikes the wily hero, Tzetzes is ready to take up his mask, especially if this means showing his superiority to his rivals, who deserve to be compared to Odysseus only when it comes to the hero's notorious deceitfulness.

Conclusions

Whatever one is to make of this final suggestion, the texts analysed show that schedography was a central topic of discussion in twelfth-century Byzantium. Indeed, this rhetorical practice was strictly intertwined with – and stimulated reflections upon – crucial issues, such as the meaning and aims of *paideia*. Despite being commonly translated as 'education', the Byzantine concept of *paideia* is a particularly complex one, evolving through time and encompassing moral, cultural and social implications. In the texts examined here, all of these aspects are touched upon, albeit from different perspectives. Certainly, both Tzetzes and Eustathios point out that the schedographers' inaccuracies endanger what we might define as the theoretical and notional aspects of education (i.e. the canons of the Art of grammar so dearly cherished by Tzetzes). However, the two scholars equally remark that the increasing success of schedography threatens to upset also the moral and behavioural norms underlying the very concept of

---

[51] See Tzetzes, *Prolegomena on Comedy* 2.37–47 ed. Koster, where Tzetzes mocks the 'ether-walkers' (αἰθεροβάμονες) for making a blatant chronological mistake concerning the composition of the Homeric poems. As suggested by Cullhed (2014: 65), one of these 'ether-walkers' might well be Eustathios, who adopted the same (erroneous) chronology in his *Parekbolai on the Iliad*.

paideia. For Eustathios, an improper use of rhetorical devices cannot but lead to a dangerous and ridiculous outcome, symbolized by the excesses of the uncultured Polyphemus. Indeed, the Cyclops' attitude is nothing but the very opposite of the elegance and moderation every urbane rhetor should aspire to. Tzetzes is equally concerned with the broader consequences of the schedographers' rising popularity. In his opinion, however, those who follow their example and thus neglect the teachings of the ancient authors are not only vulgar, but also morally and socially repulsive. Their ignorance of the canons of the Art is so devastating that it irreparably compromises their very status as human beings.

Therefore, despite having a common starting point, Tzetzes and Eustathios seem to reach different conclusions regarding the controversial issue of schedography and its effects on educational practices. While warning against the potential dangers of this rhetorical exercise, Eustathios does not reject it completely. Rather, he proposes a moderate, refined use of it: if properly employed, schedographic games can be counted amongst the many resources of the witty and urbane rhetor. Tzetzes, on the contrary, adopts an intransigent stance: his traditional conception of education, as well as his desire to set himself apart from his contemporaries and colleagues, prevents him from recognizing the potentialities hiding behind the teachings of the New Circe. Unfortunately, as in many other occasions, such a dogmatic stance might have contributed to deepening his isolation from the Constantinopolitan elites. Indeed, the most influential families of the capital kept favouring the more moderate Eustathios, who knew how to defend his opinions while at the same time adapting to the trends of his times.

For all their differences of opinion and approach, both Tzetzes and Eustathios chose the Homeric poems, and the figure of Odysseus in particular, to express their stance on contemporary developments that affected crucial sociocultural values such as education and what I have provisionally defined as 'good taste'. No matter their disagreements – or probably because of them – they chose to voice their ideas through the very same references and images, in a constant dialogue with a poetic tradition that, far from being regarded as a remote heritage from a distant past, was seen and used as an inexhaustible source of new meaning(s).

REFERENCES

Adler, A. (ed.) (1928–38) *Suidae lexicon*, 5 vols. Leipzig.
Agapitos, P. A. (2013) 'Anna Komnene and the Politics of Schedographic Training and Colloquial Discourse', *Nea Rhome* 10: 89-107.

(2014) 'Grammar, Genre and Patronage in the Twelfth Century: Redefining a Scientific Paradigm in the History of Byzantine literature', *JÖByz* 64: 1–22.

(2015a) 'New Genres in the Twelfth Century: The *Schedourgia* of Theodore Prodromos', *MEG* 15: 1–41.

(2015b) 'Literary *Haute Cuisine* and Its Dangers: Eustathios of Thessalonike on Schedography and Everyday Language', *DOP* 69: 225–41.

(2017) 'John Tzetzes and the Blemish Examiners: A Byzantine Teacher on Schedography, Everyday Language and Writerly Disposition', *MEG* 17: 1–57.

(forthcoming) '"Middle-class" Ideology of Education and Language, and the "Bookish" Identity of John Tzetzes', in *Ideologies and Identities in the Medieval Byzantine World*, ed. I. Stouraitis. Edinburgh.

Braccini, T. (2009–10) 'Erudita invenzione: riflessioni sulla *Piccola grande Iliade* di Giovanni Tzetze', *Incontri Triestini di Filologia Classica* 9: 153–73.

(2011) 'Riscrivere l'epica: Giovanni Tzetze di fronte al ciclo troiano', *CentoPagine* 5: 43–57.

van den Berg, B. (2017) 'The Wise Homer and His Erudite Commentator: Eustathios' Imagery in the Proem of the *Parekbolai on the Iliad*', *BMGS* 41.1: 30–44.

Bernard, F. (2014) '*Asteiotes* and the Ideal of the Urbane Intellectual in the Byzantine Eleventh Century', *FMS* 47: 129–42.

Cesaretti, P. and S. Ronchey (eds.) (2014) *Eustathii Thessalonicensis exegesis in canonem iambicum pentecostalem*. Supplementa Byzantina 10. Berlin–Boston.

Conley, T. M. (2005) 'Byzantine Criticism and the Uses of Literature', in *The Cambridge History of Literary Criticism*, vol. 2: *The Middle Ages*, ed. A. Minnis and I. Johnson, 669–92. Cambridge.

Cullhed, E. (2014) 'The Blind Bard and "I": Homeric Biography and Authorial Personas in the Twelfth Century', *BMGS* 38: 49–67.

D'Agostini, C. (2022) 'Borders to Cross the Bounds: John Tzetzes and Ptolemy's *Geography* in Twelfth-Century Byzantium', Τζετζικαὶ ἔρευναι, ed. E. E. Prodi, 403–26. Bologna.

Downey, G. and H. Schenkl (eds.) (1965) *Themistii orationes quae supersunt*, vol. 1. Leipzig.

Ebbesen, S. (1981) *Commentators and Commentaries on Aristotle's Sophistici Elenchi: A Study of Post-Aristotelian Ancient and Medieval Writings on Fallacies*, vol. 1: *The Greek Tradition*. Leiden.

Efthymiadis, S. (2005) 'L'enseignement secondaire à Constantinople pendant les XIe et XIIe siècles: modèle éducatif pour la Terre d'Otrante au XIIIe siècle', *Nea Rhome* 2: 259–75.

Gaisford, T. (ed.) (1848, repr. 1967) *Etymologicum magnum*. Oxford.

Garzya, A. (ed.) (1984) *Nicephori Basilacae orationes et epistolae*. Leipzig.

Gaul, N. (2014) 'Rising Elites and Institutionalisation – *Ēthos*/Mores – "Debts" and Drafts: Three Concluding Steps Towards Comparing Networks of Learning in Byzantium and the "Latin" West, c. 1000–1200', in *Networks of Learning: Perspectives on Scholars in Byzantine East and Latin West,*

c. *1000–1200*, ed. S. Steckel, N. Gaul and M. Grünbart, 253–80. Zurich–Berlin.
Giannouli, A. (2014) 'Education and Literary Language in Byzantium', in *The Language of Byzantine Learned Literature*, ed. M. Hinterberger, 52–71. Turnhout.
Grünbart, M. (1996) 'Prosopographische Beiträge zum Briefcorpus des Ioannes Tzetzes', *JÖByz* 46: 175–226.
  (2005) 'Byzantinisches Gelehrtenelend – oder: Wie meistert man seinen Alltag?', in *Zwischen Polis, Provinz und Peripherie: Beiträge zur byzantinischen Geschichte und Kultur*, ed. L. M. Hoffmann and A. Monchizadeh, 413–26. Mainz.
Holwerda, D. (1960) 'De Tzetza in Eustathii reprehensiones incurrenti', *Mnemosyne* 13: 323–6.
Hörandner, W. (ed.) (1974) *Theodoros Prodromos, Historische Gedichte*. Vienna.
Hunger, H. (1978) *Die hochsprachliche profane Literatur der Byzantiner*, vol. 2. Handbuch der Altertumswissenschaft xii.5.2. Munich.
Koster, W. J. W. (ed.) (1975) *Prolegomena de comoedia; Scholia in Acharnenses, Equites, Nubes, fasc. 1.1.a: Prolegomena de comoedia*. Groningen.
de Lagarde, P. (ed.) (1882, repr. 1979) *Joannis Euchaitorum Metropolitae quae in codice Vaticano Graeco 676 supersunt*. Göttingen.
Leone, P. L. M. (ed.) (1968) *Ioannis Tzetzae Historiae*. Naples.
  (ed.) (1969–70) 'Ioannis Tzetzae Iambi', *RSBN* 6–7: 127–56.
  (ed.) (1972) *Ioannis Tzetzae Epistulae*. Leipzig.
Lovato, V. F. (2016) 'Ulysse, Tzetzès et l'éducation à Byzance', in *From Constantinople to the Frontier: The City and the Cities*, ed. N. S. M. Matheou, T. Kampianaki and L. M. Bondioli, 23–44. Leiden.
  (2017a) 'ψεύδεα πολλὰ λέγειν ἐτύμοισιν ὁμοῖα: la ricezione di Odiseo e di Omero presso Giovanni Tzetze e Eustazio di Tessalonica', unpublished PhD thesis, University of Lausanne–University of Turin.
  (2017b) 'Portrait de héros, portrait d'érudit: Jean Tzetzès et la tradition des *eikonismoi*', *MEG* 17: 137–56.
Luzzatto, M. J. (1999) *Tzetzes lettore di Tucidide: note autografe sul Codice Heidelberg Palatino Greco 252*. Bari.
Marciniak, P. (2017) 'A Pious Mouse and a Deadly Cat: The *Schede tou Myos*, Attributed to Theodore Prodromos', *GRBS* 57: 507–27.
Nousia, F. (2016) *Byzantine Textbooks of the Palaeologan Period*. Studi e Testi 505. Vatican City.
Pizzone, A. (2016) 'Audiences and Emotions in Eustathios of Thessalonike's Commentaries on Homer', *DOP* 70: 225–44.
  (2017) 'The *Historiai* of John Tzetzes: A Byzantine "Book of Memory"?', *BMGS* 41.2: 182–207.
  (2021) 'Self-authorization and Strategies of Autography in John Tzetzes: The *Logismoi* Rediscovered', *GRBS* 60: 652–90.
Pontani, F. (2000) 'Il proemio al *Commento all'Odissea* di Eustazio di Tessalonica (con appunti sulla tradizione del testo)', *BollClass* 21: 5–58.

Renauld, É. (ed.) (1926–8, repr. 1967) *Michel Psellos, Chronographie ou histoire d'un siècle de Byzance*, 2 vols. Paris.

Rhoby, A. (2010) 'Ioannes Tzetzes als Auftragsdichter', *Graeco-Latina Brunensia* 15: 155–70.

Stallbaum, J. G. (ed.) (1825–6) *Eustathii archiepiscopi Thessalonicensis commentarii ad Homeri Odysseam ad fidem exempli Romani editi*, 2 vols. Leipzig.

van der Valk, M. (ed.) (1971–87) *Eustathii archiepiscopi Thessalonicensis commentarii ad Homeri Iliadem pertinentes ad fidem codicis Laurentiani editi*, 4 vols. Leiden.

Vassis, I. (1994) 'Graeca sunt, non leguntur: Zu den schedographischen Spielereien des Theodoros Prodromos', *ByzZ* 86/87: 1–19.

Wendel, C. (1948) 'Tzetzes Johannes', in *Realencyclopädie der classischen Altertumswissenschaft* VII A 2, 1959–2011. Stuttgart.

Wilson, N. G. (1996 [1983]) *Scholars of Byzantium*, revised edition. London–Cambridge, MA.

CHAPTER 6

Eustathios of Thessalonike on Comedy and Ridicule in Homeric Poetry

Baukje van den Berg

The twelfth century abounds in satirical and humorous literature. It is the era of Theodore Prodromos and his prose satires, of the Ptochoprodromic poems, the *Timarion*, the *Ananias or Anacharsis*, the *Battle of Cats and Mice* and the *Schede of the Mouse*.[1] It is also the period in which John Tzetzes produced commentaries on Aristophanes' comedies and authors looked to Lucian's dialogues and the sceptic epigrams of the *Greek Anthology* for inspiration.[2] It is the time of back-and-forth invective and satirical polemics between intellectuals: Tzetzes' constant criticism of his colleagues and predecessors is an (in)famous example, but we may also think of Michael Psellos and his polemics against the monk Sabbaïtes and a certain Jacob in the eleventh century.[3] Comedy and satire were found in many other places, too, as 'a general satirical spirit that contaminated other genres', 'a set of rhetorical strategies regulating tone, making satire more a mode than a firmly defined genre', or in the form of 'comic modulations' *qua* discursive textures woven into other genres.[4] We encounter comic and satirical discourse in, for instance, the Komnenian novels, Niketas Choniates' *History* and, in subtle ways, in many letters of the eleventh and twelfth centuries,

---

* A fellowship at the Dumbarton Oaks Research Library and Collection (Spring 2020) made the writing of this chapter possible. I thank Dimiter Angelov, Adam Goldwyn, Anthony Kaldellis, Divna Manolova and Przemysław Marciniak for their valuable comments on an earlier draft. The first version of this chapter was presented at the workshop 'Preserving, Commenting, Adapting: Commentaries on Ancient Texts in Twelfth-Century Byzantium' (Katowice, 20–22 October 2017); it has greatly benefited from the insightful remarks of the workshop's participants.

[1] On satire and humorous literature in the Middle Byzantine period, see the various contributions in Marciniak and Nilsson (2021).

[2] On Tzetzes and Aristophanes: van den Berg (2021), Pizzone in this volume. Lucian: Marciniak (2016a), Messis (2021). *Greek Anthology*: Zagklas (2021: 284–93).

[3] On Tzetzes, see Agapitos (2017); on Psellos, see Bernard (2014: 280–90) with references to earlier bibliography; Labuk (2019).

[4] Kaldellis (2007: 252), Marciniak (2016b: 351), Roilos (2005; for the term modulations, see pp. 14–15). See also Roilos (2021).

which demonstrates 'the importance of elegant banter and playfulness in the behavioral code of this social environment [*scil.* the intellectual elite]'.[5]

Eustathios and his commentaries on the *Iliad* and *Odyssey* may seem an odd place to look for clues on humour, comedy and ridicule in the twelfth century; his analysis of Homeric poetry, however, is firmly grounded in contemporary literary and rhetorical culture and, in this way, shares in the satirical spirit of the time. In the preface of his *Commentary on the Iliad*, Eustathios includes 'acerbic elements of ridicule' (σκωμμάτων δριμύτητες) among the (rhetorical) lessons one can learn from Homer,[6] and throughout the commentaries, he repeatedly reflects on the social dynamics and rhetorical underpinnings of comedy and ridicule in Homeric poetry and beyond.[7] The terms he most frequently uses for such ridicule are σκώπτω and its cognates, which are closely connected with ancient comedy and its satirical potential.[8] Σκῶμμα is also an essential element of the 'comic style' of speaking (κωμικῶς λέγειν), defined by Pseudo-Hermogenes in his *On the Method of Skilfulness* as consisting of bitter elements and jests (πικρὰ καὶ γελοῖα).[9] His twelfth-century commentator Gregory Pardos interprets these bitter elements – grievous and biting as they are – as bitter ridicule (πικρὰ σκώμματα) more specifically. Such ridicule, he explains, serves to keep the audience away from vice, an idea shared by Tzetzes and Eustathios in their respective discussions of the ethical-didactic functions of ancient comedy.[10] While σκῶμμα is thus at the heart of comedy, the term κωμῳδία had by then become a generic term for ridicule and humorous satirical discourse, even if in some contexts it retained its specific connections to Aristophanes' plays.[11]

Eustathios' discussion of ridicule in Homeric poetry addresses its social aspects, its role in narrative and its rhetorical dynamics. An investigation of

---

[5] Novels: Roilos (2005: 225–301); Niketas Choniates: Labuk (2016); letters: Bernard (2015); the quotation is from p. 184. On playful banter in a school context, see Pizzone in this volume; for a humoristic poem from the Palaiologan period that closely engages with ancient literature, see Kubina in this volume.

[6] Eustathios, *Commentary on the Iliad* 1.32 = 1.2.8 ed. van der Valk, with discussion in van den Berg (2022: 36–7). All references to and quotations from the *Commentary on the Iliad* are based on van der Valk's edition. Translations are my own unless indicated otherwise.

[7] See also Pizzone (2017), with a discussion of Eustathios' ideas on the relieving qualities of laughter on pp. 163–5.

[8] See e.g. Tzetzes, *On Differences between Poets* 63–4 ed. Koster and *Prolegomena on Comedy* I, 66–77 ed. Koster, with discussion in van den Berg (2021).

[9] Pseudo-Hermogenes, *On the Method of Skilfulness* 36.9–10 ed. Patillon (2014). On 'comic speaking' in the rhetorical handbooks, see also Pizzone (2017: 147–51).

[10] Gregory Pardos, *Commentary on Pseudo-Hermogenes' On the Method of Skilfulness* 1342.14–17 ed. Walz. For Gregory, Tzetzes and Eustathios on the ethical-didactic value of comedy, see van den Berg (2021); for Eustathios, see also van den Berg (2017a: 17–22).

[11] On the term κωμῳδία, see Roilos (2005: 229), Puchner (2006: 86).

his reflections on ridicule and comic elements in Homer therefore opens a perspective onto the more theoretical or conceptual side of humorous discourse in the twelfth century. I focus primarily on Eustathios' analysis of σκῶμμα (and cognates) and κερτομία (and cognates), the latter being the Homeric term for mockery that Eustathios repeatedly explains in terms of σκῶμμα.[12] With ridicule being connected to humour, we will repeatedly encounter laughter (γέλως) and labels such as laughable (γέλοιος) and funny (ἀστεῖος) in connection with Homeric σκῶμμα throughout the following discussion. Naturally, the breadth of these terms exceeds contexts of ridicule, and a comprehensive discussion of laughter, the laughable and the funny in Eustathios falls outside the scope of this chapter.

Homer, Father of Comedy

For Eustathios, 'Homer is the father of comedy, just as of all other forms of rhetoric, too'.[13] This statement unites two ideas that have ancient origins, mixing critical traditions in a way that is common for Eustathios' Homeric scholarship in general. The idea that poetry belonged to the realm of rhetoric or, put differently, that rhetoric extended to all literary composition, had gained a firm foothold by the Imperial Age. The corollary of this so-called 'literaturization' of rhetoric is the 'rhetoricization' of literature, a phenomenon that is manifest in the literature of the Second Sophistic and would remain a fixture in the literary production of the Byzantine era.[14] Following rhetoricians such as Hermogenes, Eustathios considers Homer the best poet *and* the best orator, with the *Iliad* and *Odyssey* being masterpieces of rhetoric, whose excellent composition and style can be analysed in rhetorical terms – and this is precisely what Eustathios' commentaries set out to do.[15]

---

[12] On κερτομία, see also below (pp. 181–4).
[13] Eustathios, *Commentary on the Iliad* 938.1 = 3.488.17 ed. van der Valk. Tzetzes expresses a similar idea in e.g. *On Differences between Poets* 96–7 ed. Koster: Ὅμηρός ἐστι καὶ πατὴρ κωμῳδίας / καὶ σατυρικῆς ἅμα καὶ τραγῳδίας / ἄλλης τε πάσης ἐν λόγοις εὐτεχνίας, 'Homer is also the father of comedy, and of satyr play and tragedy at the same time, and of every other fine art in literature.'
[14] On the 'literaturization' of rhetoric, see e.g. Kennedy (1999: 3), Pernot (2005: 196–7). For rhetoric as literature and rhetorical theory as literary theory in Byzantium, see e.g. Katsaros (2002), Mullett (2003). A similar process is the 'rhetoricization' of philosophy in late antiquity and Byzantium: see e.g. Papaioannou (2012) and (2015: esp. 276–81), Manolova (2020); for the Palaiologan period, see Amato and Ramelli (2006). On rhetoric and philosophy in the self-representation of twelfth-century commentators, see Trizio in this volume.
[15] Van der Valk (1971–87) was the first to stress the rhetorical nature of Eustathios' commentaries in the preface to his edition (see esp. vol. 2, p. xviii). See also Nünlist (2012), Cullhed (2016: 17*–25*), van den Berg (2022), Lovato in this volume.

Eustathios' statement also ties in with the ancient 'procreative and genealogical fashioning of literary descent' that made Homer the father of all literature, in poetry as well as prose.[16] Aristotle famously traces tragedy and comedy back to Homer when describing the history of mimetic poetry in the *Poetics*. In his view, the earliest poets either discussed elevated subjects and noble characters in epic poetry or wrote iambic invectives on lowly issues and base characters. Homer excelled in both: his serious *Iliad* and *Odyssey* foreshadow the later genre of tragedy, while the *Margites*, a mock epic about the ridiculous adventures of a 'hero', anticipates comedy.[17] Aristotle refers to the *Margites* as an invective (ψόγος) with a strong humorous element (γέλοιον), a combination that resembles the blend of ridicule (σκῶμμα) and the laughable/laughter (γέλοιον/γέλως) that appears in the definitions of comedy in Pseudo-Hermogenes and Gregory Pardos discussed above (see p. 170). Indeed, as Aristotle later explains, comedy draws on the ridiculous but without the malevolence and vituperation that characterize invective.[18]

Comedy is also found embedded within the *Iliad* and *Odyssey*, albeit to different extents. Following ancient critics such as Longinus and Heraclitus, Eustathios describes the nature of the *Iliad* – with its war narrative – as suspenseful, solemn and heroic, while maintaining that the *Odyssey* – with its focus on storytelling – is sweeter in character, its scenes and subject matter closer to everyday life.[19] The latter poem, therefore, provides more starting points for laughter and jests than its more heroic and serious counterpart, whose gloomy battles leave hardly any room for cheerfulness. The sublime Homer, however, 'mixes the unmixable' and creates occasions for entertaining mockery even in the war epic of the *Iliad*, particularly in the form of boastful insults on the battlefield.[20]

---

[16] For an overview of Homer's relationship to subsequent Greek literature and further bibliographical references, see Hunter (2006). The quotation is from p. 237.

[17] Aristotle, *Poetics* 4, 1448b19–1449a6. On Aristotle's discussion of the origins of comedy, see e.g. Rosen (2007: 32–40) with further references. For Homer as the first tragedian, see De Jong (2016), with references to earlier bibliography. While Tzetzes lists the *Margites* among the works authored by Homer (e.g. *Allegories of the Iliad*, prolegomena 80 ed. Boissonade; *Histories* 6.62.587–93 ed. Leone [2007]), Eustathios is more cautious and refrains from discussing the issue (*Commentary on the Iliad* 4.36–7 = 1.6.25–7 and *Commentary on the Odyssey* 1669.48 = 1.395.17 ed. Stallbaum).

[18] *Poetics* 5, 1449a34–7.

[19] See e.g. Longinus, *On the Sublime* 9.15 and Heraclitus, *Homeric Problems* 60. Cf. Aristotle, *Poetics* 23, 1459b14–15. For Eustathios' ideas on the different characters of the poems, see Pontani (2000: 27), Cullhed (2014: 55*–6*). See e.g. Eustathios, *Commentary on the Iliad* 938.1–5 = 3.488.17–23 and *Commentary on the Odyssey* 1837.6–8 = 2.266.45–267.2 ed. Stallbaum.

[20] Mixing the unmixable: Eustathios, *Commentary on the Iliad* 938.1 = 3.488.23 (quoted on p. 181 below). Cf. *Commentary on the Odyssey* 1850.40 = 2.184.5–6. On battlefield insults, see pp. 181–5 below.

For Eustathios, one episode stands out as representing comedy in its purest form: the famous scene with Thersites in *Iliad* 2.[21]

Thersites instigates the whole scene by insulting Agamemnon during the assembly of the army, only to become the target of verbal as well as physical abuse himself: Odysseus tells him to stop his rant and enforces his orders by hitting Thersites on his back and shoulders (*Iliad* 2.244–66). The mood had been rather gloomy before the incident: with Achilles withdrawn from battle, the army, incited by Agamemnon's ill-advised test, had been ready to give up the war and return home. In Eustathios' reading, Homer deliberately created this seemingly hopeless situation, which threatened to lead the *Iliad* into an ahistorical direction – returning home without capturing the city was, of course, not what happened in the actual history of the Trojan War. Homer, however, has an arsenal of strategies at his disposal to steer the narrative back to its historical course: among them, Eustathios lists divine interventions, wise words of elders, threats, blows and laughter. In the *Peira* episode, Homer needs them all: Athena comes down from Olympus, Nestor and Odysseus give speeches, Odysseus threatens and hits Thersites, which makes the Greeks burst into laughter 'according to comic custom' (νόμῳ κωμῳδικῷ).[22] For Eustathios, ridicule and the laughter it causes are thus useful narrative devices to relieve tension and steer the plot in the desired direction.

In the Thersites episode, Eustathios recognizes Homer's excellence in 'lampooning' (σιλλαίνειν), with σίλλοι being a type of comic poetry that the poet also uses in other places, especially in the *Odyssey*. Nowhere, however, is it funnier than here.[23] Eustathios discusses in detail what makes this episode so hilarious: if our antihero unintentionally caused

---

[21] *Iliad* 2.211–78. The Thersites episode dominates modern debates on comedy and ridicule in Homeric poetry: see e.g. Rosen (2007: 67–116, esp. 67–91), with references to earlier bibliography (esp. Nagy [1999 (1979)]: 259–64] and Thalmann [1988]). On the reception of Thersites in antiquity and Byzantium, see e.g. Basilikopoulou-Ioannidou (1971: 110, 128, 134); Jouanno (2005), with references to Eustathios' negative evaluation of Thersites' behaviour on pp. 193, 195–6 and *passim*; Lovato (2022). On the figure of Thersites in an invective exchange between Geometres and Stylianos in the tenth century, see van Opstall (2015: 783–6, 794).

[22] Eustathios, *Commentary on the Iliad* 95.12–28 = 1.149.9–28. On this passage, see also Pizzone (2017: 164–5). The *scholia vetera* point out that Homer uses blows and laughter to bring strife to an end, without connecting this to Homer's directing of the plot at large. Eustathios mentions the laughter at Hephaestus' expense in *Iliad* 1.599–600 as a similar case of tension-relieving laughter that lightens the gloominess of the quarrel between Hera and Zeus.

[23] Eustathios, *Commentary on the Iliad* 204.21–30 = 1.311.20–30. Cf. scholion T ad *Iliad* 2.212b ed. Erbse: ἤδη δὲ οὐ Ξενοφάνει, ἀλλ' Ὁμήρῳ πρώτῳ σίλλοι πεποίηνται, ἐν οἷς αὐτόν τε τὸν Θερσίτην σιλλαίνει καὶ ὁ Θερσίτης τοὺς ἀρίστους. For Homer's excellence in lampooning, see also *Commentary on the Iliad* 206.17 = 1.314.19–20.

laughter while attempting to be serious, then he is completely oblivious to the codes of proper behaviour. If he consciously meant for his disorderly and provocative speech to be amusing, he is the epitome of arrogance and contempt.[24] His deformed body, elongated forehead and lack of eloquence make him a laughing stock.[25] Homer, Eustathios argues, makes the narrative even more laughable and comic at the end of the episode: the very fact that Thersites – disgraceful and ugly as he is – dares to reproach honourable Greeks is comical in the first place,[26] but what makes it even worse is his show of emotion in reaction to Odysseus' abuse. While tears, according to the ancients, do not deform a good-looking face, they make an ugly man even uglier.[27] This altogether shameful figure resorting to even more shameful tears make him even more of a joke than he already was.[28] Often without exact parallels in the ancient scholia, many of Eustathios' observations on the laughable in this episode offer a glimpse into Byzantine (or at least Eustathian) ideas about what is funny and which behaviours are worth ridiculing (see also pp. 187–8 below).

The laughter at Thersites' expense, then, 'takes away the sadness of the Achaeans and by cheering them up, makes them think war is sweeter than returning home'.[29] While gloominess (σκυθρωπότης) and cheerfulness (ἱλαρότης) here concern the mood of the characters within the narrative, more often in Eustathios' analysis they apply to the primary narratees and the narrative itself. Battle scenes tend to be particularly gloomy. By interspersing episodes of fighting with, for instance, beautiful figures of style or more pleasant scenes, such as Hector and Andromache's final goodbye and the friendly meeting of Glaucus and Diomedes in *Iliad* 6, the poet brightens the mood; as a result, the poem 'smiles after being

---

[24] An ancient scholion also proposes two different readings based on two different ways of punctuating Homer's text. Eustathios, however, significantly rephrases and changes the interpretation offered by the scholiast.
[25] Deformed body: Eustathios, *Commentary on the Iliad* 206.43–6 = 1.315.17–20; elongated head: 207.7–9 = 315.29–316.1; lack of eloquence: e.g. 208.21–33 = 1.317.29–318.14 (Homer mocks Thersites for his ἀλογία); 210.28–30 = 1.320.28–321.1 (Homer deliberately makes the syntax of Thersites' speech full of solecisms).
[26] Eustathios, *Commentary on the Iliad* 211.19–20 = 1.322.7–8, following scholion A bT ad *Iliad* 2.135a ed. Erbse.
[27] Cf. scholion bT ad *Iliad* 2.269d ed. Erbse.
[28] Eustathios, *Commentary on the Iliad* 216.14–26 = 1.329.6–21.
[29] Eustathios, *Commentary on the Iliad* 95.21 = 1.149.18–19: ἀπάγει τῆς σκυθρωπότητος τοὺς Ἀχαιοὺς καὶ ἱλαρύνων ποιεῖ γλυκύτερον ἡγεῖσθαι τοῦ νόστου τὸν πόλεμον. Cf. scholion D ad 2.212 ed. van Thiel.

washed clean of the gore of those who have fallen'.³⁰ Striking the right balance between the two moods is the hallmark of the good poet and *summus orator*.

Eustathios' discussion of ridicule in Homer signals that the comic is not wholly unproblematic: there is an underlying sense that it is not completely acceptable for the cultured person to engage in such lowly behaviour and discourse.³¹ Aristotle's distinction between baser and more serious poetry already points to the moral inferiority of invective and comedy, which he extends to its poets: the earliest poets chose their genre in accordance with their moral characters.³² Paraphrasing an ancient scholion, Eustathios passes a similar judgement on different poetic genres: while all poets in one way or another deal with reality, tragedians tend to focus on more solemn and comedians on humbler subject matter. 'For there is nothing heroic in their works, but comedy aims at baseness for the sake of laughter.'³³ He therefore assumes that Homer included the Thersites episode to demonstrate – once and for all – that he was also skilful in the ways of comedy, without wanting to engage too much in such lowly writing or evoke laughter too often. And that is exactly why the poet, through Odysseus, puts a definite end to Thersites' shameful interventions, never to mention the hero again for the remainder of the *Iliad*.³⁴

The idea that Homer deliberately creates opportunities for displaying the breadth of his learning (πολυμάθεια) and skills in various types of writing is recurrent in Eustathios' reading of the *Iliad*.³⁵ This wish to display his prowess is driven by Homer's ambition as a writer as well as his

---

³⁰ Eustathios, *Commentary on the Iliad* 650.11–12 = 2.343.7–8: ἀπονιψαμένη τοῦ λύθρου τῶν πιπτόντων τοῖς ἐπεισοδίοις διεγέλασεν. On *Iliad* 6: 650.5–12 = 342.21–343.8; on 'cheerful' figures of style: e.g. 718.25–7 = 2.599.1–5; 771.6–7 = 2.786.7–9; 959.40–1 = 3.552.23–6. Eustathios' use of 'gloominess' and 'cheerfulness' as qualities of the narrative has no parallels in the ancient scholia.
³¹ Rosen (2007: 32) traces the ancient idea that such hostile joking was 'beneath the dignity of any person aspiring to an aristocratic, "liberal" way of life' back to Plato and Aristotle: see Rosen for further references. See also Freudenburg (1993: 62–72).
³² Aristotle, *Poetics* 4, 1448b23–7, with discussion in Rosen (2007: 34–40). Cf. Aristotle, *Nicomachean Ethics* 4, 1128a20–5, where Old Comedy is associated with bad moral character.
³³ Eustathios, *Commentary on the Iliad* 258.31–2 = 1.394.12–13: οὐδὲν γὰρ ἡρωϊκὸν παρ' αὐτοῖς, ἀλλὰ χάριν γέλωτος εὐτελείας ἡ κωμῳδία στοχάζεται. His discussion is based on scholia AT and b ad *Iliad* 2.478 ed. Erbse.
³⁴ See e.g. Eustathios, *Commentary on the Iliad* 219.12–20 = 1.333.30–334.20.
³⁵ Eustathios argues, for instance, that Homer invented the Greek wall and the battle at the wall to display his skilfulness in composing a *teichomachia*: see *Commentary on the Iliad* 689.56–63 = 2.493.5–16 and 864.10–12 = 3.258.4–7.

desire to teach: by including all these different 'genres', he provides those who wish to write with an abundance of material.[36] That is to say, those who wish to ridicule someone or write something comic can study the Thersites episode and other elements of ridicule throughout the Homeric poems to learn useful methods and techniques. This holds true especially for those who study Homer with the help of Eustathios' commentary, which, among other things, aims to identify the poet's admirable rhetorical methods so that prose authors can imitate them in their writings.[37] Thus, Eustathios discusses comedy and ridicule in Homeric poetry first of all as literary or rhetorical phenomena, with many lessons for Byzantine authors. By projecting his own didactic programme onto the poet, he presents Homer as a teacher of rhetoric like himself. But the Thersites episode has more to offer: through the figure of Thersites, 'Homer teaches that it is nothing strange that, among a large crowd of educated men, some are uncivilized, presumptuous and unreasonable'.[38] It does not seem too farfetched to read into such a statement Eustathios' own experiences in the intellectual world of his time, rather than any lesson intended by Homer.

Ridicule with Dignity

Eustathios' reading of the Thersites episode introduces various recurring aspects of his analysis of ridicule as a rhetorical phenomenon: its narrative function, its effects on characters and primary narratees and its place in the grander scheme of Homer's composition. Eustathios identifies many other instances of ridicule throughout the *Iliad* and *Odyssey* and repeatedly explains how Homer avoids the potential dangers that such ridicule poses to his seriousness and dignity (ἐμβρίθεια) as a poet.[39] Eustathios' intricate interpretation of a passage in *Iliad* 5 gives an interesting example. Wounded in the hand by Diomedes, Aphrodite returns to Olympus and seeks comfort from her mother Dione. Hera and Athena look on and try to provoke Zeus 'with mocking words' (κερτομίοις ἐπέεσσι, 5.419) that

---

[36] See e.g. *Commentary on the Odyssey* 413.45 = 1.395.12–13 ed. Stallbaum. For a more elaborate discussion of this phenomenon, see van den Berg (2022: 82–4).

[37] *Commentary on the Iliad* 2.29–30 = 1.3.14–15, with discussion in van den Berg (2022: 40–1).

[38] Eustathios, *Commentary on the Iliad* 203.41–2 = 1.310.24–6: διδάσκων ὁ ποιητὴς ὡς οὐδὲν καινὸν ἐν πολλῷ πλήθει πεπαιδευμένων ἀνδρῶν καὶ ἀτάκτους εἶναί τινας καὶ ἀτασθάλους καὶ ἀσωφρονίστους.

[39] On such ἐμβρίθεια, see van der Valk (1971–87, vol. 2: LXIV–LXV), who relates it to terms such as σεμνότης ('solemnity') and ὄγκος ('weight', 'grandeur'). All are qualities both of Homer as a poet and of his discourse.

indirectly target Aphrodite. Athena is the first to speak, saying, 'Father Zeus, will you be angry with me at all for what I say?'⁴⁰

> Ὅτι Ἀθηνᾶ καὶ Ἥρα σιλλαίνουσαι ἀστείως καὶ κερτομοῦσαι τὴν τῆς ἀνάλκιδος Ἀφροδίτης πληγὴν κωμικώτερον … Ὁ δὲ Ζεὺς ἐπὶ τῷ σκώμματι οὐ γελᾷ – σεμνῶν γὰρ προσώπων ὁ ἐπὶ τοιούτοις γέλως ἀλλότριον –, ἀλλὰ μειδιᾷ, ὃ πολλῷ τοῦ γελᾶν σεμνότερον, γέλως ὢν ἠρεμαῖος, ἀνακεκραμένος συννοίᾳ. Καὶ σημείωσαι ὅπως ὁ καὶ τὰ τοιαῦτα δεξιὸς ποιητὴς ἐνταῦθα εὐφυῶς τὴν Ἀφροδίτην ἐκωμῴδησεν, οὐκ αὐτὸς ἐκ προσώπου οἰκείου, ἀλλὰ διὰ Ἀθηνᾶς καὶ Ἥρας, αἳ κερτομίοις ἐπέεσσιν ἐπὶ τῇ Ἀφροδίτῃ τὸν Δία ἐρέθιζον. Ὅρα δὲ καὶ τὴν μέθοδον. Ἐπεὶ γὰρ οὐκ ἔδει μὲν τοιούτοις ἐναγωνίοις τόποις παρεντεθῆναι σκώμματος ἱλαρότητα, ἄλλως δὲ πάλιν ἦν ἀνάγκη τοῦτο γενέσθαι διὰ τὴν τῶν προσώπων ποιότητα τῶν μισούντων τὴν Ἀφροδίτην, ποιεῖ ὁ ποιητὴς εὐμεθόδως τὸ πρᾶγμα, καὶ προεπισημηνάμενος ὡς, εἰ καὶ φορτικὸν ἐνταῦθα τὸ σκώπτειν, ὅμως ἀναγκαῖον οὕτως ἐπάγει τὸ σκῶμμα. Φησὶ γὰρ «Ζεῦ πάτερ, ἦ ῥά τί μοι κεχολώσεαι, ὅττι κεν εἴπω» καὶ τὰ ἑξῆς. οἱονεὶ γὰρ πρὸς τὸν πολύνουν ἀκροατὴν ἐνταῦθά φησιν ὁ ποιητὴς ὡς, εἰ καὶ μὴ καιρὸς ἱλαρότητος ἐνταῦθα, ὅμως διὰ τὰ πρόσωπα τὰ ὑποκείμενα χρηστέον λόγῳ κερτόμῳ. συγγνώμην οὖν ζητεῖ τρόπον τινὰ ἐπὶ τῇ κερτομίᾳ καὶ συγγινώσκεται πρός γε Διός, ἤτοι τοῦ ὀρθὰ νοοῦντος.
> (Eustathios, *Commentary on the Iliad* 567.8–28 = 2.115.3–116.5)

> In a witty manner, Athena and Hera insult and mock the blow the feeble Aphrodite suffered in a rather comic way … Zeus does not laugh at the ridicule – for laughter about such things is foreign to solemn characters – but smiles, which is much more solemn than laughing, being gentle laughter mixed with thought. And notice how the poet, skilful also in such things, here cleverly ridiculed Aphrodite, not he himself in his own person, but through Athena and Hera, who teased Zeus with mocking words directed at Aphrodite. Observe also the method. For, since the cheerfulness of ridicule should not be inserted in such battle scenes, whereas in another way it was necessary that this happened because of the disposition of the characters who hated Aphrodite, the poet composes the matter in a well-constructed manner; he indicates beforehand that, even if ridiculing here shows bad taste, he still includes the ridicule in this way as necessary. For he says, 'father Zeus, will you be angry with me at all for what I say?' and so on. For addressing, as it were, the thoughtful listener, the poet here says that, even if this is not the right moment for cheerfulness, he still had to use a mocking speech because of the characters in question. In a way, then, he seeks to be excused for the mockery and is excused in the name of Zeus, i.e. of the one who understands it correctly.

---

⁴⁰ *Iliad* 5.421: Ζεῦ πάτερ, ἦ ῥά τί μοι κεχολώσεαι, ὅττι κεν εἴπω.

Eustathios refers to Athena's ridicule (σκῶμμα, κερτομία) with the verbs σιλλαίνω, σκώπτω, the poetic κερτομέω and the more common κωμῳδέω, which again shows that these terms are closely related or even synonymous. The ridicule is again at someone else's expense and once more its effects are described with words denoting laughter and amusement: Athena's ridicule is witty (ἀστεῖος), rather comic (κωμικώτερος), and leads to cheerfulness (ἱλαρότης) and, potentially, laughter (γέλως).

Zeus does not laugh but shows his amusement at Athena's words with a smile (*Iliad* 5.426). Eustathios explains that this is a more solemn response to such mockery, more suitable for a weighty figure such as the king of gods and men. In the same way, Hera merely smiles at Hephaestus' words in *Iliad* 1 (v. 596), while the other gods burst into 'uncontrollable laughter' (ἄσβεστος γέλως, *Iliad* 1.599) when they see the lame god limping about the palace. Hera, Eustathios explains, thus behaves solemnly, as befits her person, whereas the other gods 'are brought down from such [solemn] grandeur when they suffer uncontrollable laughter'.[41] To say that someone laughs out loud can even be intended as mockery: Homer ridicules Paris by making him 'laugh very merrily' (μάλα ἡδὺ γελάσσας, *Iliad* 11.378) rather than smile heroically as did Ajax and Odysseus (*Iliad* 7.212 and 10.400 respectively).[42] These and many similar examples illustrate the ambiguous nature of laughter and indicate that, even if it has certain narrative and psychological functions, the solemn, heroic and dignified person best avoids uncontrolled and open-mouthed laughter.[43]

But there is also a rhetorical side to the problematic nature of Athena's ridicule. *Iliad* 5 predominantly consists of battle narrative – Eustathios refers to the episode as ἐναγώνιος, 'full of suspense' or 'concerning battle'.[44] While I have discussed above how such gloomy battle scenes can be cheered up with amusing ridicule, the thrust of this passage is slightly different: Eustathios here considers the serious and solemn battle narrative to be an inappropriate place for the cheerfulness of ridicule. In a similar

---

[41] Eustathios, *Commentary on the Iliad* 160.27–30 = 1.248.2–6, quotation from 160.30 = 1.248.5–6: ἄλλοι θεοὶ τοῦ τοιούτου ὕψους ὑποκατέβησαν ἄσβεστον γέλων παθόντες. On smiling as a moderate form of laughter in Byzantine literature, see Hinterberger (2017: 142).

[42] Eustathios, *Commentary on the Iliad* 850.39–42 = 3.215.9–15. Eustathios likewise disapproves of the suitors' laughter at the fight of Irus and the beggar Odysseus in *Odyssey* 18.35 (*Commentary on the Odyssey* 1836.55–1837.1 = 2.166.27–40 ed. Stallbaum).

[43] On ambivalent attitudes toward laughter in Byzantium, see Marciniak (2009), (2011), (2017), with further references. For laughter and its related emotions, see Hinterberger (2017: 136–40). For Eustathios, see Pizzone (2017: 165–7). A more systematic study of laughter in Eustathios' corpus is required to appreciate more fully his position on the matter.

[44] On the semantics of the term in ancient criticism, see Ooms and de Jonge (2013); for Eustathios, see van den Berg (2022: 81).

vein, he argues elsewhere that Homer avoided certain figures of style, as their beauty and the aesthetic pleasure they create do not suit such gloomy scenes.[45] As the consummate poet-rhetorician, Homer is, of course, aware that he is bending rhetorical rules when including cheerful ridicule in the battle scene of *Iliad* 5, which he signals in Athena's question: 'Father Zeus, will you be angry with me at all for what I say?' Here, as elsewhere in Eustathios' interpretation of Homeric poetry, Athena functions as the poet's rhetorical conscience. She represents the 'intelligence' (φρόνησις) *qua* 'rhetorical skilfulness' (δεινότης) that enables the poet to make the best decisions regarding his narrative and its course. When later in *Iliad* 5, for instance, Odysseus deliberates with himself about whether to go after Sarpedon or kill more of the other Lycians first, Athena steers his anger towards the latter. In Eustathios' reading, Odysseus' deliberations are those of Homer: his 'rhetorical' Athena, i.e. 'the skilfulness in himself' (ἡ κατ' αὐτὸν δεινότης), makes him decide that it is better to have Odysseus go after the Lycians. After all, Sarpedon is not fated to be killed by Odysseus.[46] In the same way, Athena/the poet's rhetorical skilfulness is concerned with the course of the narrative when asking for forgiveness for her words of ridicule from Zeus, whom Eustathios interprets as the thoughtful (πολύνους) reader. In many other places throughout the commentaries, he postulates such an ideal reader, a professional *literatus* such as Eustathios himself, who has an expert understanding of Homer's rhetorical strategies and is able to appreciate the poet's narrative choices.[47] Such a reader understands that the tense relations between the goddesses – the lingering result of the judgement of Paris – necessitate some words of mockery at the expense of Aphrodite, even within the context of serious battle.

In his continuous endeavour to reconstruct the poet's composition process and reveal his rhetorical choices, Eustathios points to one further clever (δεξιός, εὐφυής) and well-constructed (εὐμέθοδος) aspect of Homer's handling of ridicule here: rather than presenting the mocking words in his own voice (i.e. the voice of the narrator), the poet distances himself by putting them in Athena's mouth. Homer also uses this technique

---

[45] See e.g. Eustathios, *Commentary on the Iliad* 130.26–30 = 1.200.20–6; 1214.11–16 = 4.426.5–14; 1235.17–20 = 4.495.18–24; 1342.8–11 = 4.878.12–16.
[46] Eustathios, *Commentary on the Iliad* 593.10–18 = 2.169.7–16, on *Iliad* 5.671–6. On Athena as the poet's intelligence, see Cullhed (2014: 70*–1*), van den Berg (2017b: 137–9). For further discussion of Eustathios' interpretation of certain gods as the poet's mental faculties, see van den Berg (2022: 163–74).
[47] On Homer's ideal reader in Eustathios, see Cullhed (2014: 35*–7*), Pizzone (2016). Elsewhere, Eustathios interprets Zeus as the mind of the poet: see van den Berg (2017b: 133–7).

elsewhere: when Patroclus, for instance, ridicules the spear-struck Cebriones for tumbling off his chariot, somersaulting like an acrobat and leaping like an oyster diver, Eustathios explains that Homer could have developed this image into a proper simile, but decided it was better not to do so, as such mockery might be appropriate for Patroclus but is far removed from 'Homeric dignity' (Ὁμηρικὴ ἐμβρίθεια).[48] Another of the poet's concerns is his impartiality: even if, for Eustathios as much as ancient scholars, it was a matter of fact that the poet supported the Greek cause (as did his audience), he still wished to seem impartial.[49] That is why in *Iliad* 3, for instance, Homer refrains from ridiculing Paris in order not to be immediately suspected of philhellenism. Instead, he leaves the insulting to Hector, who can speak freely (παρρησιάζεσθαι) to Paris.[50]

Floris Bernard has recently defined the term παρρησία as 'the available latitude of acceptable speech, as conditioned by social hierarchy', when discussing what seems to have been a misfired joke in a letter by John Tzetzes.[51] In his defence, Tzetzes argues that friendly relationships should allow for some licence to include harmless mockery in (written) conversation.[52] While there is nothing harmless about Hector's insults towards Paris, the same principle of social hierarchy applies: as his older brother, Hector has the παρρησία to criticize Paris for being more interested in women than war. Eustathios gives us a definition of such 'freedom of speech' in his critical essay on contemporary monasticism, explaining that it consists in the courage to say everything to everyone 'according to the rule of virtue and the measure of ethical understanding, with regard to time, person, manner and quantity'.[53] In the context of ridicule, this means that not everyone can say anything to just anyone; social rules must be observed. Eustathios' commentary on *Iliad* 2 provides an example of this: in the guise of Priam's son Polites, the goddess Iris ridicules King Priam for being 'fond of endless words' (μῦθοι φίλοι ἄκριτοι, 2.796). This

---

[48] Eustathios, *Commentary on the Iliad* 1084.51–5 = 3.925.8–13, on *Iliad* 16.745–50.
[49] On Homer and his audience as pro-Greek, see e.g. van den Berg (2022: 84–6) for Eustathios; Stoevesandt (2005) for modern scholarship (with an overview of earlier studies on the partiality of Homer in appendix 1). For ancient criticism, see e.g. scholia b ad *Iliad* 8.274–6a1; bT ad *Iliad* 10.14; bT ad *Iliad* 11.0 ed. Erbse.
[50] Eustathios, *Commentary on the Iliad* 378.29–34 = 1.597.13–18, on *Iliad* 3.39–57.
[51] Bernard (2015: 188).
[52] Bernard (2015: 188). Psellos similarly speaks of the 'audacity of friendship': see Bernard (2015: 186–7).
[53] Eustathios, *Inquiry into Monastic Life* 46.5–6 ed. Metzler (2006a): ἀρετῆς κανόνι καὶ πρὸς μέτρον ἠθικῆς ἐπιστήμης· τὸ κατὰ χρόνον, τὸ προσωπικόν, τὸ κατὰ τρόπον, τὸ ἐν ποσότητι. On the fine line between good and bad παρρησία ('freedom of speech' vs. 'unbridled speech'), see Metzler (2006b: ad loc. and 250–1). For a definition of παρρησία, see also *Souda* π 636 ed. Adler.

phrase recalls the Thersites episode earlier in the same book, where Odysseus addresses our antihero as 'Thersites of reckless speech' (Θερσῖτ' ἀκριτόμυθε, *Iliad* 2.246).[54] The mocking nature of Iris' words, Eustathios suggests, may explain why Homer has Iris say them rather than Polites: it would not be appropriate for Polites to insult his father, while Iris, a goddess, is immune from censure.[55] Homer's choice of having Athena rather than Hera ridicule Aphrodite hinges on a different consideration: as the younger of the two, Athena is more likely to speak her mind, whereas the older, more solemn Hera knows to stay away from dignity-damaging ridicule.[56] In Eustathios' reading, then, ridicule proves to be a complex combination of rhetorical, ethical and social dynamics, which the poet recognizes and navigates with great skill throughout his poems.

Battlefield Abuse

The semantics and pragmatics of the term κερτομία and its cognates, as well as the mocking and insulting speeches they refer to, have prompted much debate in Homeric scholarship. In one of the more recent contributions, Alex Gottesman defines four aspects as central to the pragmatics of Homeric κερτομία: (1) it is an indirect statement, whose target and addressee might not be the same; (2) it is related to a genre of (playfully) aggressive speech favoured by young men at symposia; (3) it serves to assert one's status vis-à-vis others; (4) it may be playful and entertaining.[57] Late antique and Byzantine lexica explain κερτομέω with verbs such as χλευάζω ('scoff', 'jeer'), ἐρεθίζω ('provoke') and, indeed, σκώπτω ('ridicule'),[58] while Eustathios defines κέρτομος λόγος as an expression that 'cuts at the heart, i.e. that bites the soul and bites the heart'.[59] In the *Commentary on the Odyssey*, he further explains the workings of such heart-cutting

---

[54] Cf. *Iliad* 2.246, where Odysseus addresses Thersites as 'confusedly babbling' (ἀκριτόμυθε).
[55] Important for Eustathios' interpretation is that Hector recognizes that 'Polites' is actually Iris (*Iliad* 2.807).
[56] Eustathios, *Commentary on the Iliad* 567.38–42 = 2.116.18–22. That the goddesses are diametric opposites is one further explanation of why Athena should be the one ridiculing Aphrodite: in mythical terms, Athena is a virgin, Aphrodite adulterous; in allegorical terms, Athena stands for rationality, Aphrodite for irrationality.
[57] Gottesman (2008: 11). See also Lentini (2013), Kucharski (2020). Both provide references to earlier bibliography.
[58] See e.g. Hesychios, *Lexicon* κ 2362–5 ed. Latte; Photios, *Lexicon* κ 615–16 ed. Theodoridis; *Souda* ε 2035 ed. Adler.
[59] Eustathios, *Commentary on the Iliad* 214.25 = 1.237.3–4: ὁ κέαρ τέμνων, ὅ ἐστι δάκνων ψυχὴν καὶ θυμοδακής. Cf. *Etymologicum magnum* 506.34 ed. Gaisford: τὸ κέαρ τέμνων τῶν ἀκουόντων, 'biting at the heart of the listeners'.

words: being insolent and insulting, they provoke bitter anger (χόλος), an emotion that resides in the heart (θυμός), as demonstrated in Homeric passages such as *Iliad* 6.326 (δαιμόνι', οὐ μὲν καλὰ χόλον τόνδ' ἔνθεο θυμῷ, 'strange man, it is not good to nurse this anger in your heart').[60]

Patroclus' words of κερτομία directed at the 'acrobat' Cebriones belong to a particular genre of heroic ridicule that takes place on the battlefield: warriors repeatedly address their enemies – especially those they have just killed or are about to kill – with insults and jeering. Such 'flyting' speeches are a type of verbal contest that occurs in traditional heroic narratives from different cultures; it consists of 'an exchange of insults and boasts between two heroes in some public setting' and is often followed by a martial encounter.[61] Even if flyting is not necessarily humorous, Eustathios often recognizes an element of entertaining ridicule in this heroic habit.[62] In fact, he counts such back-and-forth boasts and insults among the poet's strategies for lightening potentially monotonous and all-too-gloomy battle scenes, and he repeatedly stresses their amusing nature. In *Iliad* 14, for instance, he designates a series of four such speeches with various terms denoting humour, calling them 'cases of sarcasm' (σαρκασμοί), 'dignified witticisms' (ἐμβριθεῖς ἀστεϊσμοί) and 'cases of irony' (εἰρωνεῖαι).[63]

Eustathios' formulation suggests that he considers these terms virtually synonymous, which is further underscored by his definition of 'sarcasms' as 'biting cases of irony and heaviness' in his comments on the flyting speeches of *Iliad* 14.[64] Throughout the commentaries, he uses both 'irony' and 'sarcasm' for dissimulation: in *Iliad* 11, for instance, Odysseus boasts over the body of Socus using words that seem full of sympathy. Eustathios warns, however, that they are not spoken sincerely but sarcastically.[65] When the same Socus addresses Odysseus earlier as πολύαινε, Eustathios explains that the word is either meant in a negative sense ('talkative,

---

[60] Eustathios, *Commentary on the Odyssey* 1960.36–7 = 2.322.6–8 ed. Stallbaum.
[61] For the definition of flyting, see Parks (1986: 440–1; quotation from 441). On flyting in traditional heroic narrative, see Parks (1987) and (1990). For Homer, see also the seminal study by Martin (1989), esp. 65–74 and *passim* throughout chapter 3. More recently, see Lentini (2013) with references to earlier studies.
[62] Cf. Eustathios, *Commentary on the Iliad* 940.6 = 3.496.5–6: the heroes have the habit of using sarcasm in the middle of a terrible battle.
[63] Eustathios, *Commentary on the Iliad* 999.1–6 = 3.682.24–683.3, with reference to *Iliad* 14.453–507.
[64] Eustathios, *Commentary on the Iliad* 997.13–15 = 3.677.21–3: ὁ ποιητὴς χρᾶται σαρκασμοῖς, τουτέστι δακνηραῖς εἰρωνείαις καὶ βαρύτησιν, ὡς καὶ ἐν τῇ ν' ῥαψῳδίᾳ, ἡρωϊκῶς καὶ σεμνῶς. On 'heaviness', see below. Eustathios similarly connects sarcasm and irony in 998.34 = 3.681.4.
[65] Eustathios, *Commentary on the Iliad* 855.32–3 = 3.231.9–11, on *Iliad* 11.450–5. Cf. 854.41–3 = 3.227.23–5: Odysseus' words are 'heavy' witticisms.

wordy') or in a positive sense ('much praised'). In the latter case it would mean that Odysseus receives praise even from an enemy – and such praise certainly is the highest one can receive, unless it is intended ironically.[66] Without a clear distinction, Eustathios thus uses both 'irony' and 'sarcasm' for saying the opposite of what is meant.[67] When Menelaus is about to spare Adrastus' life, Agamemnon resolutely kills him and rebukes his brother for being spineless: 'You truly received the best treatment from the Trojans,' he says. Agamemnon means, of course, that the Trojans have treated Menelaus abominably. This, Eustathios explains, is the definition of speaking with heavy irony: to call the best the worst and the worst the best by means of antiphrasis.[68]

Both irony and sarcasm are used effectively in ridicule and insults, and both can be witty (especially sarcasm) and heavy (especially irony). With regard to Acamas' sarcastic and joking flyting in *Iliad* 14 (vv. 476–85), Eustathios once again stresses that Homer in this way 'skilfully cheers up the gloomy episode for the listeners and thus mixes pleasant and sorrowful matters'.[69] The qualification 'for the listeners' is essential: the angry, sad or fearful reactions of Trojans or Greeks clearly demonstrate that, for the addressees within the narrative, the boasts are not funny at all.[70] In his commentary on a similar flyting speech in *Iliad* 13, Eustathios explains more directly how the ridicule affects the characters within the text and the primary narratees in different ways. Idomeneus has just slain Othryoneus, to whom Priam promised his daughter Cassandra as bride in return for valorous deeds in the war. Exulting over the dying Othryoneus, Idomeneus mockingly promises him an Achaean bride and starts dragging his body towards the Greek ships (*Iliad* 13.374–82). Eustathios explains:

---

[66] Eustathios, *Commentary on the Iliad* 854.64–855.1 = 3.228.25–229.1, on *Iliad* 11.430 (following scholion bT ad *Iliad* 11.430a ed. Erbse). On (rhetorical) irony in the *scholia vetera*, see Nünlist (2009: 212–15).

[67] Ancient critics hold different opinions about the relationship between sarcasm and irony. Nünlist (2009: 214) points out, for instance, that Trypho treats the two as separate devices, while Pseudo-Herodian considers sarcasm to be a subcategory of rhetorical irony. Eustathios' position thus seems closer to the latter, while also drawing on Hermogenes' *On Types of Style* for the connection of 'heaviness' and irony: see below. The exact sources of Eustathios' ideas on irony, sarcasm and related concepts require further examination.

[68] Eustathios, *Commentary on the Iliad* 624.23–6 = 2.241.16–18, on *Iliad* 6.52–60. Cf. Hermogenes, *On Types of Style* 2.8.5 ed. Patillon (2012): when a speaker uses irony, he means the opposite of what he says.

[69] Eustathios, *Commentary on the Iliad* 998.36 = 3.681.7–8: τεχνικῶς τὰ σκυθρωπὰ ἱλαρύνοντος τοῖς ἀκροαταῖς, οἷς ἐν ἀστειότητι σαρκάζει, καὶ οὕτω κεραννύντος ἡδέα καὶ λυπηρά.

[70] See e.g. *Iliad* 14.458–9 (the Greeks get angry at Polydamas' flyting); 14.475 (sorrow seizes the Trojans in reaction to Ajax' flyting); 14.486–7 (Acamas' boasts cause sorrow for the Greeks); 14.506–7 (Peneleos' boast fills the Trojans with fear).

> Ὅμηρος μέντοι τεχνικῶς μιγνύων τὰ ἄμικτα παραρρίπτει καὶ ἐνταῦθά τινας ἀστεϊσμοὺς ἐκ μεγαλαυχίας ἡρωϊκῆς, οἳ τοῖς μὲν ἀκροαταῖς ἔξω βελῶν ἑστῶσι παρασύρουσι τὰ χείλη πρὸς μειδίαμα ὑπανοίγοντες, αὐτοῖς δὲ τοῖς τότε μαχομένοις ὑπανῆπτε τὸν θυμὸν ἐπὶ πλέον καί, ὡς ὁ ποιητής φησιν, ἄχος ἐγίνετο καὶ θυμὸν ὄρινεν, ὅ ἐστιν ἐβάρυνε τὴν ψυχήν. (Eustathios, *Commentary on the Iliad* 938.1–7 = 3.488.23–7)
>
> Homer, however, skilfully mixes the unmixable and inserts also here certain witticisms consisting of the heroes' boasting, which draws the lips of the listeners standing beyond the arrows' reach into a smile, but fueled the anger of those fighting at the time even further and, as the poet says, caused sorrow and stirred anger [*Iliad* 13.417–18], i.e. it weighed down their soul.[71]

While the heroes' boasting entertains Homer's audience outside the narrative, it is a heart-cutting and soul-sinking provocation for the bystanders on the Trojan battlefield. Anticipating Gottesman's distinction between the direct target and indirect addressees of Homeric κερτομία, moreover, Eustathios concentrates on its effect on the companions of the dying hero rather than Othryoneus himself: addressing the fallen hero and dragging him by his feet as he does, Idomeneus 'sneers at the Trojan listeners and stings them with his ridicule', so much so that his words provoke a counter-attack by Asius.[72]

Similarly, the slain Lycaon can hardly be the true addressee of the boastful words that Achilles speaks when slinging his victim into the river Scamander (*Iliad* 21.122–35). Again, Eustathios draws attention to the mixture of heaviness and sweetness in this passage, where Achilles 'ridicules [Lycaon] with heaviness' (σκώπτει μετὰ βαρύτητος).[73] This time, however, the mixture does not consist in the insertion of cheerful ridicule into a gloomy battle scene but is found within the ridicule itself: while it provides sweet relief and amusing entertainment for listeners outside the dangers of battle, it fills the addressees in the text, the Trojans, with heaviness and 'weighs down their souls'. Eustathios' consistent connection of this soul-sinking heaviness with irony follows Hermogenes' rhetorical theory. In the influential treatise *On Types of Style*, 'heaviness' is the style used by a speaker who thinks he has been treated unjustly. His speech is therefore full of 'reproachful thoughts' (ἔννοιαι ὀνειδιστικαί) and can

---

[71] On the listeners 'outside the arrows', see also *Commentary on the Iliad* 1.802.11–19 = 506.6–12, with discussion in Cullhed (2014: 71*).

[72] Eustathios, *Commentary on the Iliad* 937.14 = 3.489.3–4: σαρκάζων καὶ δάκνων τοὺς ἀκροατὰς Τρῶας τῷ σκώμματι.

[73] Eustathios, *Commentary on the Iliad* 1227.15–16 = 4.471.12–15.

include ironic statements to express his indignation.⁷⁴ Again, then, it is clear that Eustathios employs rhetorical and critical tools to scrutinize ridicule in Homeric poetry as a rhetorical phenomenon. If we keep in mind that these tools not only assisted the reading of ancient literature but also governed the composition of new texts, we start to see how Eustathios' close reading of Homer's ridicule is, at the same time, a lesson in prose composition.

The Excellent Man Uses Ridicule Sometimes

Homer's poetry also provides instructions of another kind. Throughout his commentaries, Eustathios identifies various Homeric lessons on the (discursive) behaviours appropriate for the cultivated and virtuous person or excellent man (σπουδαῖος ἀνήρ).⁷⁵ In this way, his reading of Homer gives insight into the 'tacit rules of behaviour, manners, pronunciation, and conversation [that] defined a credible member of the elite'.⁷⁶ Odysseus, for instance, suffers many hardships in the *Odyssey* to save his own life and secure his companions' homecoming, which indicates, so Eustathios explains, that the excellent and wise man knows when to take care of himself and his own life without losing sight of his friends in times of danger.⁷⁷ The excellent man is moderate in his emotions rather than lacking in emotions altogether; he pushes sleep away rather than inviting it, because an excellent man does not sleep all night long.⁷⁸ Agamemnon's test of the army in *Iliad* 2 indicates that an excellent man sometimes lies, even though he should only do so at the right time and for the right reasons.⁷⁹ In the same way, he knows when – and when not – to use ridicule, 'and the universe is full of examples'.⁸⁰ Yet when Menelaus hails his archenemy Paris as 'noble' in *Iliad* 3, Eustathios points out that the excellent man should be full of praise and not turn to ridicule when it is not necessary. With an example in *Iliad* 4, where Agamemnon ridicules

---

⁷⁴ Hermogenes, *On Types of Style* 2.8.1, 2.8.4–14 ed. Patillon (2012). For a more detailed discussion of 'heaviness' and of irony as productive of heaviness in Hermogenes and Eustathios, see Lindberg (1977: 254–62).
⁷⁵ On the σπουδαῖος ἀνήρ, see e.g. *Commentary on the Odyssey* 1761.62 = 2.74.39–40 ed. Stallbaum.
⁷⁶ Bernard (2013: 142).
⁷⁷ Eustathios, *Commentary on the Odyssey* = 1383.23–4 = 1.7.33–5 ed. Stallbaum.
⁷⁸ Emotions: Eustathios, *Commentary on the Iliad* 115.36 = 1.180.1; sleep: 162.27–9 = 1.250.28–31.
⁷⁹ See e.g. Eustathios, *Commentary on the Iliad* 1.285.33; van den Berg (2017a).
⁸⁰ Eustathios, *Commentary on the Iliad* 1059.8–9 = 3.848.14–16: καὶ γέμει τῶν εἰς τοῦτο παραδειγμάτων ὁ κόσμος. Cf. Bernard (2013: esp. 131–3, 138–9, 142): a sense of humour and a talent for wit were part of the profile of the ideal urbane intellectual; Bernard (2015): eleventh- and twelfth-century letters show that banter was part of the behavioural code of the educated elite.

Odysseus only mildly, Homer teaches us how to ridicule a friend in times of disagreement without permanently damaging the relationship.[81] Homer's heroes are thus models of the correct way to use ridicule, while the way it is expressed in the Homeric poems teaches the Byzantine σπουδαῖος how to make ridicule part of his eloquence.

But the usefulness of Homer in the context of ridicule goes even further: according to Eustathios, Homeric poetry was a source of serious as well as funny material for the ancients and, as his commentaries demonstrate, for himself and his contemporaries, too.[82] Throughout both commentaries, Eustathios identifies numerous Homeric verses that can be reused by prose authors in specific contexts, thus facilitating the widespread practice of citing from and alluding to Homeric poetry (and other ancient texts) in Byzantine prose.[83] Occasionally, such Homeric citations and allusions are used in mocking or witty ways. In the *Alexiad*, for instance, Anna Komnene refers to the speech of the Franks who come to petition her father, the Emperor Alexios, as 'unbridled scolding', the very words Homer uses when Thersites rails against Agamemnon. She thus associates the uncultivated Westerners with the vulgar and impudent antihero, while Alexios, by consequence, is linked to the great leader of the Greek army.[84] Such subtle ridicule must have elicited a smile from the cultivated audience, who would be able to recognize the allusion and recall its original context. Tzetzes similarly draws on Homer (and Herodotus) to ridicule his addressee – the monk Eliopolos – for loving women and their beautiful buttocks. Floris Bernard has discussed how Tzetzes explains his own joke in the *Histories*, a verse commentary on his letters: through the device of παραγραμματισμός (changing a letter in a word) and by slightly adapting Homer's verses (the technical term is παρῳδία), he has transformed Homer's race of horses into a race of buttocks.[85]

Eustathios' commentaries similarly open up a perspective onto the many citations from and allusions to ancient authors in Byzantine literature. He identifies many Homeric verses that, with or without adaptation, can be used in contexts of ridicule, even when, as in Tzetzes' letter, the

---

[81] Menelaus and Paris: Eustathios, *Commentary on the Iliad* 429.29–31 = 1.666.1–3, on *Iliad* 3.352; Agamemnon and Odysseus: *Commentary on the Iliad* 480.27–35 = 1.759.14–24, on *Iliad* 4.339.
[82] Eustathios, *Commentary on the Iliad* 630.1 = 2.262.15–16.
[83] On this phenomenon, see Nünlist (2012), Cullhed (2016: 17*–25*). For Homeric citations and allusions in Eustathios' sermons, see Perisanidi and Thomas (2021).
[84] Anna Komnene, *Alexiad* 14.4.7 ed. Kambylis and Reinsch; *Iliad* 2.212. For Homeric citations in the *Alexiad*, see Reinsch (1998), with discussion of this specific example on pp. 6–7.
[85] See Bernard (2015: 192–3), with discussion of Tzetzes, *Letter* 67, 96.16–20 ed. Leone (1972) and *Histories* 10.319.234–41 ed. Leone (2007). Tzetzes reuses *Iliad* 9.123–4 and 9.265–6.

original context did not concern ridicule at all. Diomedes' words in *Iliad* 8, for instance, have much potential for mocking reuse. When Diomedes rescues Nestor from the battlefield after the latter's horse had been hit by an arrow, he says to him: 'Old sir, clearly young warriors are wearing you down; but your might is broken and grievous old age attends you, and your attendant is a weakling and your horses slow'.[86] Eustathios identifies different possible contexts for reusing these words: they can be employed to ridicule a man who used to be a skilful craftsman in his younger years but in old age has to yield to his younger colleagues; with a change of 'warriors' into 'disciples' (μαθηταί) the phrase can be used for a teacher who, worn out by age, is inferior to his students. And if one wishes to ridicule a learned old man, one could understand 'the slow horses' as his words, no longer winged but advancing sluggishly, and his 'attendant', i.e. his mind, no longer sharp and sublime but lowly and weak.[87]

Repeatedly, the ridicule – and its amusing effects – are based on changing or inverting the meaning of words in their original context: Homer's famous comparison of Odysseus' rhetorical prowess with snow-flakes on a winter's day could be used for a bad, frigid (ψυχρός) orator; equally ambivalent are the cicadas to which Homer compares Nestor's eloquence.[88] Homer's comparison of generations of men to generations of leaves can be turned into a ridicule of men who look green with sickness.[89] Likewise, the generally positive term θεοειδής, 'godlike (in appearance)', can be taken as ridicule when understood as referring only to a person's beautiful face, to the exclusion of his soul. A beautiful face is, moreover, a description one would tend to apply to women, which means that, when applied to men, the phrase essentially ridicules them as effeminate.[90] The incongruity of the new usage and the original contexts of the expressions in question might have contributed to their amusing effect in the game between author and educated audience, as a display of an author's cleverness and ready wit. In many such notes, Eustathios strays far from the

---

[86] *Iliad* 8.102–4: ὦ γέρον, ἦ μάλα δή σε νέοι τείρουσι μαχηταί, / σὴ δὲ βίη λέλυται, χαλεπὸν δέ σε γῆρας ὀπάζει, / ἠπεδανὸς δέ νύ τοι θεράπων, βραδέες δέ τοι ἵπποι.
[87] Eustathios, *Commentary on the Iliad* 702.6–10 = 2.543.1–8. For similar sceptic reuses of Homer's words, see e.g. 155.10 = 1.239.1–2 (ridicule of a confused old man); 1013.5–6 = 3.723.24–6 (ridicule of an evil ambassador); 1284.5–6 = 4.670.8–11 (ridicule of a rich scrooge); 1290.51–2 = 4.694.8–10 (ridicule of a liar).
[88] Eustathios, *Commentary on the Iliad* 408.14–15 = 1.642.20–2, with references to *Iliad* 3.222 and 3.151.
[89] Eustathios, *Commentary on the Iliad* 630.4–7 = 2.262.21–6, on *Iliad* 6.146.
[90] For Eustathios' discussion of θεοειδής, see *Commentary on the Iliad* 374.15–31 = 1.591.17–36. Cf. 705.5–6 = 2.552.19–20: 'you are like a woman' can be said to ridicule someone for cowardice.

Homeric text, making free associations with Homer's words as starting points. The verb μαίνομαι in *Iliad* 5.185, for instance, prompts a list of various excessive desires referred to with compounds ending in -μανία or -μανής: someone can be ridiculed as mad for gold (χρυσομανής), mad for wine (οἰνομανής), mad for love (ἐρωμανής) and mad for women (γυναιμανής). The term μανιόκηπος, moreover, can be used to make fun of a woman who is mad for sex, as κῆπος refers to the female genitalia.[91]

Eustathios thus offers the Byzantine author much material for ridiculing and jesting, his suggestions displaying a cerebral sense of humour that regularly verges on the salacious. These suggestions reveal the socially deviant behaviours that deserved mockery and elicited laughter and, in this way, shed light on the social values and ideals of the educated elite in twelfth-century Constantinople. Eustathios identifies various bodily features, less-than-perfect intellectual and discursive skills, and other excessive or deviating behaviours as sources of ridicule: the list includes (but is not limited to) eye defects, baldness, paleness, having a large body, dressing in the wrong way, old age, cowardice, babbling and talking nonsense, being a bad orator, simple-mindedness, arrogance, loving sleep, being infatuated with women or men, loving wine, loving gold (like a girl), fickleness, cheating and treachery. Even if a more systematic study of ridicule and wit in Eustathios' scholarly and rhetorical output is required to draw larger conclusions about his sense of humour, social values and ideas on ridicule as a rhetorical and social phenomenon, the behaviours and bodily defects that he identifies as causes for ridicule in the Homeric commentaries seem in line with how the humour of the eleventh and twelfth centuries has been described: Linda Garland, for instance, speaks of humour that is based on the satirical, the obvious and the personal in the context of the historiography of the time; Przemysław Marciniak identifies a penchant for satirical abuse at the expense of individuals and groups as an important part of Byzantine humour; and Barry Baldwin calls 'scurrility but a tool of the Byzantine trade'.[92] Eustathios' commentaries make Homer a writer of Byzantine-style ridicule and aspire to instil in their readership 'a talent to abuse'.

***

---

[91] Eustathios, *Commentary on the Iliad* 536.16–24 = 2.49.18–50.4. Cf. 380.10–18 = 1.600.4–13, where Eustathios discusses words that can be used to ridicule men who are mad for women, paedophiles and women who are mad for men; 211.2–4 = 1.321.22–4: the word χιλίαρχος ('captain of a thousand') becomes a very funny word if one understands ἀρχός in its meaning of 'anus'; 451.2–3 = 1.712.8–10: 'a horn from his head' (*Iliad* 4.109) also applies to the god Pan and in a mocking way can be used for any 'Pan-like' man.

[92] Garland (1990: 4), Marciniak (2014), Baldwin (1982: 28). See also Garland (2007: 184): 'a taste for abuse was an innate part of the Byzantine mentalité and a constituent of most Byzantine humor'.

Eustathios' detailed analysis of ridicule in Homeric poetry is part of his general project to reconstruct the poet's composition process: throughout the commentaries, he reveals Homer's rhetorical choices in order to shed light on the working methods of the consummate orator in constructing his two masterpieces. Homer skilfully mixes ridicule into his narrative for the entertainment of his audience (and sometimes of the characters in the narrative, too). Eustathios considers such episodes of ridicule to belong to the different spices (ἀρτύματα) with which the poet rhetorically seasons his discourse: together with, for instance, duels, historical facts and similes, σκώμματα belong to the poet's repertoire of strategies for adding flavour to potentially monotonous episodes.[93] Eustathios' commentaries offer a wealth of material for the Byzantine author who wishes to season his own writings in the same way with verses adapted from Homer or otherwise. With such material and the minute analysis of the social and rhetorical aspects of ridicule, the commentaries shed light on Eustathios' conception of ridicule in Homeric poetry, Byzantine prose composition and society more generally. In this way, they usefully complement what literary practice teaches about the 'satirical spirit' of the twelfth century. Even if the question of how the ludic character of the twelfth century relates to earlier and later periods remains largely open for now, Eustathios' attention to and interest in comedy and ridicule in Homer seem to have no parallel in pre-modern Homeric criticism.

Eustathios' reading of the Homeric epics further underscores the Byzantine taste for abuse as well as a penchant for cerebral – if sometimes slightly salacious – jokes. While such humour is not always easy for the modern reader to grasp, Eustathios' interpretations of Homer may heighten our awareness of the ways ridicule was employed in Byzantine literary practice. Despite an emphasis on ridicule's corrective function in works of rhetorical theory and classical scholarship, the practice of Byzantine satire suggests that ridicule was meant to damage other people's reputations more than correct their vices, and, as Eustathios' analysis of ridicule in Homeric poetry demonstrates, to entertain the audience of such ridicule at the same time.[94] Eustathios is all too aware that such personal

---

[93] For ridicule as 'spice' of Homeric poetry, see e.g. Eustathios, *Commentary on the Iliad* 1084.9–10 = 3.922.16–18. On such 'spices', see van den Berg (2022: 73–4).

[94] Bernard (2014: 276) reaches a similar conclusion with regard to the satirical poetry of the eleventh century.

ridicule might backfire: when discussing the verbal contest in *Iliad* 14 with its string of verbal abuse on the battlefield, he warns that one should always keep in mind the old maxim: 'Ridicule produces more pain than pleasure. For this is the beginning of verbal abuse: as soon as you say something, you immediately hear it back.'[95]

REFERENCES

Adler, A. (ed.) (1928–38) *Suidae lexicon*, 5 vols. Leipzig.
Agapitos, P. A. (2017) 'John Tzetzes and the Blemish Examiners: A Byzantine Teacher on Schedography, Everyday Language and Writerly Disposition', *MEG* 17: 1–57.
Allen, T. W. and D. B. Monro (eds.) (1902–12) *Homeri opera*, 5 vols. Oxford.
Amato, E. and I. Ramelli (2006) 'Filosofia *rhetoricans* in Niceforo Cumno: l'inedito trattato *Sui corpi primi e semplici*', *MEG* 6: 1–40.
Baldwin, B. (1982) 'A Talent to Abuse', *ByzF* 8: 19–28.
Basilikopoulou-Ioannidou, A. (1971) *Ἡ ἀναγέννησις τῶν γραμμάτων κατὰ τὸν ΙΒ' αἰῶνα εἰς τὸ Βυζάντιον καὶ ὁ Ὅμηρος*. Athens.
Bernard, F. (2013) '*Asteiotes* and the Ideal of the Urbane Intellectual in the Byzantine Eleventh Century', *FMS* 47: 129–42.
  (2014) *Writing and Reading Byzantine Secular Poetry, 1025–1081*. Oxford Studies in Byzantium. Oxford.
  (2015) 'Humor in Byzantine Letters of the Tenth to Twelfth Centuries: Some Preliminary Remarks', *DOP* 69: 179–95.
van den Berg, B. (2017a) '"The Excellent Man Lies Sometimes": Eustathios of Thessalonike on Good Hypocrisy, Praiseworthy Falsehood, and Rhetorical Plausibility in Ancient Poetry', *Scandinavian Journal of Byzantine and Modern Greek Studies* 3: 15–35.
  (2017b) 'Eustathios on Homer's Narrative Art: The Homeric Gods and the Plot of the *Iliad*', in *Reading Eustathios of Thessalonike*, ed. V. Katsaros, F. Pontani and V. Sarris, 129–48. Trends in Classics Supplementary Volume 46. Berlin–Boston.
  (2021) 'Playwright, Atticist, Satirist: The Reception of Aristophanes in Twelfth-Century Byzantium', in *Satire in the Middle Byzantine Period: The Golden Age of Laughter?*, ed. P. Marciniak and I. Nilsson, 227–53. Explorations in Medieval Culture 12. Leiden–Boston.
  (2022) *Homer the Rhetorician: Eustathios of Thessalonike on the Composition of the Iliad*. Oxford Studies in Byzantium. Oxford.
Boissonade, J. F. (ed.) (1851) *Tzetzae allegoriae Iliadis*. Paris.

---

[95] Eustathios, *Commentary on the Iliad* 1312.38–9 = 4.770.21–2: ἡ σκῶψις λυπεῖ πλέον ἢ τέρπει πολύ. τοῦ κακῶς λέγειν γὰρ ἀρχὴ γίνεται. ἂν δ' εἴπῃς ἅπαξ, εὐθὺς ἀντήκουσας. Eustathios quotes Athenaeus, *Learned Banqueters* 10.421ab.

Cullhed, E. (ed. and trans.) (2014) 'Eustathios of Thessalonike, *Parekbolai* on Homer's *Odyssey* 1–2: Proekdosis', PhD thesis, Uppsala University.
  (ed. and trans.) (2016) *Eustathios of Thessalonike, Commentary on the Odyssey*, vol. 1: *On Rhapsodies A–B*. Acta Universitatis Upsaliensis. Studia Byzantina Upsaliensia 17. Uppsala.
Erbse, H. (ed.) (1969–88) *Scholia Graeca in Homeri Iliadem*, 7 vols. Berlin.
Freudenburg, K. (1993) *The Walking Muse: Horace on the Theory of Satire*. Princeton.
Gaisford, T. (ed.) (1967 [1848]) *Etymologicum magnum*. Amsterdam.
Garland, L. (1990) '"And His Bald Head Shone Like a Full Moon …": An Appreciation of the Byzantine Sense of Humour as Recorded in Historical Sources of the Eleventh and Twelfth Centuries', *Parergon* 8: 1–31.
  (2007) '*Mazaris's Journey to Hades*: Further Reflections and Reappraisal', *DOP* 61: 183–214.
Gottesman, A. (2008) 'The Pragmatics of Homeric *Kertomia*', *CQ* 58: 1–12.
Hinterberger, M. (2017) '"Messages of the Soul": Tears, Smiles, Laughter and Emotions Expressed by Them in Byzantine Literature', in *Greek Laughter and Tears: Antiquity and After*, ed. M. Alexiou and D. Cairns, 125–45. Edinburgh Leventis Studies 8. Edinburgh.
Hunter, R. (2006) 'Homer and Greek Literature', in *The Cambridge Companion to Homer*, ed. R. Fowler, 235–53. Cambridge.
de Jong, I. J. F. (2016) 'Homer the First Tragedian', *G&R* 63: 149–62.
Jouanno, C. (2005) 'Thersite, une figure de la démesure? *Kentron* 21: 181–223.
Kaldellis, A. (2007) *Hellenism in Byzantium: The Transformations of Greek Identity and the Reception of the Classical Tradition*. Cambridge.
Kambylis, A. and D. R. Reinsch (eds.) (2001) *Annae Comnenae Alexias*. Berlin.
Katsaros, V. (2002) 'Ἡ ῥητορικὴ ὡς "θεωρία λογοτεχνίας" τῶν Βυζαντινῶν', in *Pour une 'nouvelle' histoire de la littérature byzantine. Actes du colloque international philologique, Nicosie, 25–28 mai 2000*, ed. P. Odorico and P. A. Agapitos, 95–106. Dossiers Byzantins 1. Paris.
Kennedy, G. A. (1999) *Classical Rhetoric and Its Christian and Secular Tradition from Ancient to Modern Times*. Chapel Hill, NC.
Koster, W. J. W. (ed.) (1975) *Prolegomena de comoedia; Scholia in Acharnenses, Equites, Nubes, fasc. 1.1.a: Prolegomena de comoedia*. Groningen.
Kucharski, J. (2020) 'Mocking the Wasps or the Meaning of Homeric *kertomia* Again', *Mnemosyne* 73: 1–24.
Labuk, T. (2016) 'Aristophanes in the Service of Niketas Choniates – Gluttony, Drunkenness and Politics in the Χρονικὴ Διήγησις', *JÖByz* 66: 127–52.
  (2019) 'Gluttons, Drunkards and Lechers. The Discourses of Food in Twelfth-Century Byzantine Literature: Ancient Themes and Byzantine Innovations', unpublished PhD thesis, University of Silesia in Katowice.
Latte, K. (ed.) (1953–66) *Hesychii Alexandrini lexicon*, vols. 1–2. Copenhagen.
Lentini, G. (2013) 'The Pragmatics of Verbal Abuse in Homer', in *The Rhetoric of Abuse in Greek Literature*, ed. H. Tell. *Classics@* 11.
Leone, P. L. M. (ed.) (1972) *Ioannes Tzetzes Epistulae*. Leipzig.

(ed.) (2007) *Ioannis Tzetzae Historiae*, second edition. Galatina.
Lindberg, G. (1977) *Studies in Hermogenes and Eustathios: The Theory of Ideas and Its Application in the Commentaries of Eustathios on the Epics of Homer*. Lund.
Lovato, V. F. (2022) 'From Contentious Hero to Bone of Contention: The Reception of Thersites by John Tzetzes and Eustathios of Thessaloniki', in Τζετζικαὶ ἔρευναι, ed. E. E. Prodi.
Manolova, D. (2020) 'Epistolography and Philosophy', in *A Companion to Byzantine Epistolography*, ed. A. Riehle, 255–78. Brill's Companions to the Byzantine World 7. Leiden–Boston.
Marciniak, P. (2009) '*Homo Byzantinus Ridens*. Byzantine Attitude towards Laughter and Humour: Some General Remarks', in *Homo Byzantinus*, ed. A. Z. Milanova, V. Vatchkova and T. Stepanov, 83–92. Sofia.
  (2011) 'Laughing against All the Odds: Some Observations on Humour, Laughter and Religion in Byzantium', in *Humour and Religion: Challenges and Ambiguities*, ed. H. Geybels and W. Van Herck, 141–55. London–New York.
  (2014) 'Byzantine Humor', in *Encyclopedia of Humor Studies*, ed. S. Attardo, 98–102. Los Angeles.
  (2016a) 'Reinventing Lucian in Byzantium', *DOP* 70: 209–24.
  (2016b) 'The Art of Abuse: Satire and Invective in Byzantine Literature. A Preliminary Survey', *Eos* 103: 349–62.
  (2017) 'Laughter on Display: Mimic Performances and the Danger of Laughing in Byzantium', in *Greek Laughter and Tears: Antiquity and After*, ed. M. Alexiou and D. Cairns, 232–42. Edinburgh Leventis Studies 8. Edinburgh.
Marciniak, P. and I. Nilsson (eds.) (2021) *Satire in the Middle Byzantine Period: The Golden Age of Laughter?* Explorations in Medieval Culture 12. Leiden–Boston.
Martin, R. P. (1989) *The Language of Heroes: Speech and Performance in the Iliad*. Ithaca, NY.
Messis, C. (2021) 'On the Fortune of Lucian in Byzantium', in *Satire in the Middle Byzantine Period: The Golden Age of Laughter?*, ed. P. Marciniak and I. Nilsson. Explorations in Medieval Culture 12. Leiden–Boston.
Metzler, K. (ed. and trans.) (2006a) *Eustathii Thessalonicensis De emendanda vita monachica*. Corpus Fontium Historiae Byzantinae 45. Berlin.
  (2006b) *Eustathios von Thessalonike und das Mönchtum: Untersuchungen und Kommentar zur Schrift De emendanda vita monachica*. Berlin–New York.
Mullett, M. (2003) 'Rhetoric, Theory and the Imperative of Performance: Byzantium and Now', in *Rhetoric in Byzantium. Papers from the Thirty-Fifth Spring Symposium of Byzantine Studies, Exeter College, University of Oxford, March 2001*, ed. E. M. Jeffreys, 151–70. Aldershot.
Murray, A. T. (1999) *Homer, The Iliad*, 2 vols., revised edition by W. F. Wyatt. Cambridge, MA.
Nagy, G. (1999 [1979]) *The Best of the Achaeans: Concepts of the Hero in Archaic Greek Poetry*, revised edition. Baltimore.

Nünlist, R. (2009) *The Ancient Critic at Work: Terms and Concepts of Literary Criticism in Greek Scholia.* Cambridge.
  (2012) 'Homer as a Blueprint for Speechwriters: Eustathius' Commentaries and Rhetoric', *GRBS* 52: 493–509.
Ooms, S. and C. C. de Jonge (2013) 'The Semantics of ΕΝΑΓΩΝΙΟΣ in Greek Literary Criticism', *CPh* 108: 95–110.
van Opstall, E. M. (2015) 'The Pleasure of Mudslinging: An Invective Dialogue in Verse from 10th Century Byzantium', *ByzZ* 108: 771–96.
Papaioannou, S. (2012) 'Rhetoric and the Philosopher in Byzantium', in *The Many Faces of Byzantine Philosophy*, ed. B. Bydén and K. Ierodiakonou, 171–97. Papers and Monographs from the Norwegian Institute at Athens Series 4.1. Athens.
  (2015) 'Sicily, Constantinople, Miletos: The Life of a Eunuch and the History of Byzantine Humanism', in *Myriobiblos: Essays on Byzantine Literature and Culture*, ed. T. Antonopoulou, S. Kotzabassi and M. Loukaki, 261–84. Berlin.
Parks, W. (1986) 'Flyting, Sounding, Debate: Three Verbal Contest Genres', *Poetics Today* 7: 439–58.
  (1987) 'The Flyting Speech in Traditional Heroic Narrative', *Neophilologus* 71: 285–95.
  (1990) *Verbal Dueling in Heroic Narrative: The Homeric and Old English Traditions.* Princeton.
Patillon, M. (ed. and trans.) (2012) *Prolégomènes au De Ideis; Hermogène, Les catégories stylistiques du discourse (De Ideis); Synopsis des exposés sur les Ideai.* Corpus Rhetoricum 4. Paris.
  (ed. and trans.) (2014) *Pseudo-Hermogène, La méthode de l'habileté; Maxime, Les objections irréfutables; Anonyme, Méthode des discours d'adresse.* Corpus Rhetoricum 5. Paris.
Perisanidi, M. and O. Thomas (2021) 'Homeric Scholarship in the Pulpit: The Case of Eustathios' Sermons', *BICS* 64: 81–94.
Pernot, L. (2005) *Rhetoric in Antiquity.* Washington, DC.
Pizzone, A. (2016) 'Audiences and Emotions in Eustathios of Thessalonike's Commentaries on Homer', *DOP* 70: 225–44.
  (2017) 'Towards a Byzantine Theory of the Comic?', in *Greek Laughter and Tears: Antiquity and After*, ed. M. Alexiou and D. Cairns, 146–65. Edinburgh Leventis Studies 8. Edinburgh.
Pontani, F. (2000) 'Il proemio al *Commento all'Odissea* di Eustazio di Tessalonica Tessalonica (con appunti sulla tradizione del testo)', *BollClass* 21: 5–58.
Puchner, W. (2006) 'Zur Geschichte der antiken Theaterterminologie im nachantiken Griechisch', *WS* 119: 77–113.
Reinsch, D. R. (1998) 'Die Zitate in der *Alexias* Anna Komnenes', *Symmeikta* 12: 63–74.
Roilos, P. (2005) *Amphoteroglossia: A Poetics of the Twelfth-Century Medieval Greek Novel.* Washington, DC.

(2021) 'Satirical Modulations in 12th-Century Greek Literature', in *Satire in the Middle Byzantine Period: The Golden Age of Laughter?*, ed. P. Marciniak and I. Nilsson, 254–78. Explorations in Medieval Culture 12. Leiden–Boston.

Rosen, R. M. (2007) *Making Mockery: The Poetics of Ancient Satire*. Oxford–New York.

Stallbaum, J. G. (ed.) (1825–6) *Eustathii archiepiscopi Thessalonicensis commentarii ad Homeri Odysseam ad fidem exempli Romani editi*, 2 vols. Leipzig.

Stoevesandt, M. (2005) *Feinde – Gegner – Opfer: Zur Darstellung der Troianer in den Kampfszenen der Ilias*. Basel.

Thalmann, W. G. (1988) 'Thersites: Comedy, Scapegoats, and Heroic Ideology in the *Iliad*', *TAPhA* 118: 1–28.

Theodoridis, C. (ed.) (1998) *Photii patriarchae lexicon (E–M)*, vol. 2. Berlin–New York.

van Thiel, H. (ed.) (2014) *Scholia D in Iliadem: Proecdosis aucta et correctior*. Elektronische Schriftenreihe der Universitäts- und Stadtbibliothek Köln 7. Cologne.

van der Valk, M. (ed.) (1971–87) *Eustathii archiepiscopi Thessalonicensis commentarii ad Homeri Iliadem pertinentes ad fidem codicis Laurentiani editi*, 4 vols. Leiden.

Walz, C. (ed.) (1834) *Rhetores Graeci*, vol. 7.2. Stuttgart.

Zagklas, N. (2021) 'Satire in the Komnenian Period: Poetry, Intellectualism and the Ancients', in *Satire in the Middle Byzantine Period: The Golden Age of Laughter?*, ed. P. Marciniak and I. Nilsson, 277–303. Explorations in Medieval Culture 12. Leiden–Boston.

CHAPTER 7

Geography at School
Eustathios of Thessalonike's Parekbolai on Dionysius Periegetes

Inmaculada Pérez Martín

Although geographical information appears here and there in many texts that were studied at Roman and Byzantine schools, the *Periegesis* or *Description of the Known World* of Dionysius of Alexandria is the only Greek poem 'intended as an effective tool to engrave in the spirit of its readers a coherent image of the world'.[1] Composed in the time of Hadrian (AD 117–38), the image of the world transmitted in the 1187 verses of this didactic poem was marked by the new order imposed by Rome,[2] while the *Periegesis* belonged, by virtue of its content, to the Greek periegetical tradition (which began with the lost work of Hecataeus)[3] and, on account of its metre and language, to that of Homeric poetry. In terms of its genre, the *Periegesis* was one of the didactic poems from the Alexandrian and Roman periods that would be most widely disseminated in Byzantium,[4] becoming the most common point of access for the Byzantine student to an organized vision of the known world. The preserved copies, particularly those from the thirteenth century onward (when a variety of circumstances would result in the greatest number of Byzantine books being preserved), confirm that in Byzantium such didactic poems were used in schools and transmitted together, rather than with other texts that dealt with the same topics. Thus, the works of Nicander (the second-century BC author of the *Theriaka* and *Alexipharmaka*, both of which address the issue of poisons)

---

* Instituto de Lenguas y Culturas del Mediterráneo y del Oriente Próximo (ILC-CSIC). This research has been funded by the Ministry of Economics and Competitivity of Spain (Project 'The Byzantine Author (III)', PID2019-105102GB-I00).
[1] Jacob (1990: 12). The most recent edition of the poem is by Lightfoot (2014), but it is based only on the text of the oldest manuscript, Paris, Bibliothèque nationale de France, suppl. gr. 388. The latest critical edition, which was widely criticized, is by Tsavari (1990); see also Reeve (1994).
[2] Jacob (1991), Bowie (2004).
[3] Despite being Alexandrian, Dionysius can be placed within an eclectic geographical tradition, which does not mention either the earth as a sphere or the *sphragides* of Eratosthenes; see Lightfoot (2014: 13, 16).
[4] On didactic poetry, see Kneebone (2017); on Byzantine didactic poetry, see e.g. Lauxtermann (2009).

were not copied in collections of medical texts; nor do the *Phaenomena* of Aratus (ca. 276–4 BC, which describe the constellations) usually figure in books of specialized astronomical works, but instead appear together with Lycophron or Pindar.[5] It seems, therefore, that the content of such poems was only a secondary reason for their being read in a school context.

Similarly, the *Periegesis* was not copied into geographical miscellanies such as Mount Athos, Mone Batopediou, 655,[6] an ambitious volume that sought to compile all the geographical texts accessible in Constantinople at the end of the thirteenth century. Rather, its transmission largely took place together with other, non-technical poems, which were didactic either due to their content or because they were commented upon in a school context: in a collection of hexametric poetry in the oldest preserved codex of the *Periegesis*, Par. suppl. gr. 388 (tenth century); with Oppian and Sophocles in Paris, Bibliothèque nationale de France, gr. 2735 (thirteenth century); with Hesiod in Paris, Bibliothèque nationale de France, gr. 2771 (tenth century) and Milan, Biblioteca Ambrosiana, C 222 inf. (end of the twelfth century, see below); and with Euripides in Venice, Biblioteca Nazionale Marciana, gr. 471 (eleventh/twelfth centuries).[7] This textual environment confirms that the transmission of the poem took place on the periphery of most geographical literature and in combination with other scholastic texts; however, as we shall see, the Byzantine reader was interested in the *Periegesis* not only for its form but for its geographical content as well.[8]

While there are no papyri or other pieces of fragmentary evidence preserved from ancient copies of the poem, Latin translations and various specimens of indirect transmission confirm its success with the public, which was due to its ability to draw the reader into a fast-paced, systematic presentation of Alexandrian cartographic discoveries that created the illusion of mastering space and revealing the confines of the world.[9] The subsequent and widespread dissemination of Dionysius' poem (ca. 150

---

[5] Planoudes, however, paired Aratus with Cleomedes' *Caelestia* (an introduction to astronomy written by a stoic) in Edinburgh, National Library of Scotland, Adv. 18.7.15 (from 1290), while contemporaneously John Pediasimos would, indeed, include Aratus' poem, along with its commentary, in a somewhat eclectic scientific miscellany, the Vatican City, Biblioteca Apostolica Vaticana, gr. 191 (from c. 1296). Aratus was also copied into the beautiful astronomical miscellany Vatican City, Biblioteca Apostolica Vaticana, gr. 1087, in the circle of Nikephoros Gregoras around the 1320; see Guidetti and Santoni (2013).

[6] Only the main part of the former volume is preserved at the Monastery of Vatopedi; other folia and quires are now in London, British Library, Add. 19391; Paris, Bibliothèque nationale de France, suppl. gr. 443A; Saint Petersburg, Rossijskaja Nacional'naja Biblioteka, Ф. № 536 (according to Pinakes: https://pinakes.irht.cnrs.fr/notices/cote/66822/).

[7] Reeve (2004: 368–9).   [8] On the ubiquitous concept of 'utility' in the *Parekbolai*, see below.

[9] Jacob (1990: 12).

manuscripts, six prior to the thirteenth century and around fifty from the thirteenth and fourteenth centuries)[10] is in strong contrast to the limited diffusion of Stephanus of Byzantium's geographical dictionary;[11] the *Periegesis* was also much more read than Strabo's *Geography*, whose seventeen books were the main reference work of ancient geography in Byzantium, that is to say, the work which could satisfy the curiosity about any given region of the known world. Indeed, it was Strabo and Dionysius who would shape the worldview and geographical thought of the Byzantines. In his commentary to the *Periegesis*,[12] Eustathios of Thessalonike relies heavily on Strabo, who was himself one of the authorities used by the Periegetes.[13] Geographical treatises in prose that vulgarized the advances of Alexandrian cartography were too stark to be able to compete with the mythical geography that had such a strong hold on the Byzantine imagination. Such treatises were schematic introductions to the known world and shared with the *Periegesis* the 'virtue' of brevity, while reflecting a more updated vision of Alexandrian cartographic discoveries; but their circulation was limited to a few copies of geographical miscellanies.[14] Maximos Planoudes, whose maps for the *Geography* of Ptolemy were reviewed or designed under the patronage of Emperor Andronikos II and caused a cultural stir, recommended that his contemporaries ignore

---

[10] On the transmission of the text, see Tsavari (1990a), Counillon (1991), Marcotte (2009).

[11] This work, composed in the mid-sixth century, has been transmitted only in abridged form, except for the fragment of the unabridged version preserved in Paris, Bibliothèque nationale de France, Coislin 228, fols. 116–22v, from the eleventh century, with only the end of Book 10 and the beginning of Book 11. Ed. Billerbeck (2008–16); see Bouiron (2012) and Billerbeck (2015) on the version of Stephanus used by Eustathios.

[12] Eustathios of Thessalonike, *Commentarius in Dionysii orbis descriptionem*, ed. Müller (1861: 2.201–407); hereafter: *in Dion. Per.* The previous edition by Bernhardy (1828: 65–316 and 833–975, with Bernhardy's notes to the *Parekbolai*) should not be overlooked. On the copy of Strabo used by Eustathios, see Diller (1975: 86–7), Leroy (2013: 51–4).

[13] According to Lightfoot (2014a: 162–7), Strabo influenced the *Periegesis*, while Ilyushechkina (2011–12) considers it unlikely that Dionysius made use of Strabo. For a discussion of Dionysius' geographical sources, see Göthe (1875) and Sakellaridou-Sotiroudi (1993), (1994), (1995). On the textual transmission of Strabo in Byzantium, see Diller (1975).

[14] Particularly the Ὑποτύπωσις γεωγραφίας ἐν ἐπιτομῇ, a text based on Ptolemy and Strabo which has received very little attention; ed. Müller (1861: 2.494–509); see Marcotte (2000: xl–xlii). A second work half the length, the *Hypotyposis* of Agathemeros, is dated to the first–second centuries AD by Diller (1975a), according to whom the text is a collection of excerpts from Eratosthenes and other geographers; it nevertheless has the virtue of providing measurements and a range of theories on the shapes and limits of the *oikoumene*. Fragments of this text appear among Dionysius' scholia and through these in Eustathios; see Diller (1952: 36–7), Diller (1975a: 72). A third text, the *Diagnosis*, ed. Müller (1861: 2.488–93), is different in nature, offering a small number of descriptions taken from Ptolemy and accompanied by four diagrams; see Marcotte (2000: xli–xlii). Finally, it must be mentioned that a section of Strabo's Book 2 (5.18–33) constitutes an authentic *hypotyposis* in its own right.

Dionysius' vision of an *oikoumene* surrounded by the ocean and replace it with Ptolemy's.[15] We do not know, however, if Planoudes' recommendation achieved much impact beyond the small circles who read scientific works. Indeed, Ptolemaic cartography, despite the attractiveness of these maps, was up against a formidable adversary, given the intensity with which Homer and the other poets were read. At least some of Planoudes' disciples, who were teachers of rhetoric and imperial officials, decided to take on the task of copying the voluminous work of Strabo, an author Planoudes himself championed in his *Synagoge*.[16]

The *Parekbolai*

The archaic vocabulary and convoluted, mannered expression that we find in the *Periegesis*, the issues of toponymy and cartography it raises, its innumerable mythological allusions and the extreme concision of its verse all suggest that the poem was accompanied from the beginning by exegetic scholia.[17] However, not only is the date of the scholia preserved in the margins of Byzantine codices of the *Periegesis* still uncertain, but so too is the date of a paraphrase which shares these margins and whose purpose was to allow a faster reading avoiding linguistic difficulties.[18] This version of the *Periegesis* in prose and in Koine is a key element in the poem's transmission and confirms that it was also approached and studied as a source of specific and organized knowledge about the world.[19] Thanks to the prose version, which turned away from the original words with their endless literary echoes and made the content of the poem more immediate and accessible, the

---

[15] Planoudes, epigram 5, ed. Taxidis (2017: 90.23–7).
[16] This copy of Strabo is now the ms. Venice, Biblioteca Nazionale Marciana, gr. XI.6, see Skalli-Cohen and Pérez Martín (2017). On Planoudes' *Synagoge*, see Diller (1975: 89–90).
[17] The poem has traditionally been placed within the scholastic context by Jacob (1981: 62 and 65). Leo (2001–2: 156–7, 161) has argued that it was composed to be read in public, perhaps to celebrate the arrival of Hadrian in Alexandria in AD 130.
[18] The scholia are published in Müller (1861: 2.427–57) and Ludwich (1885: 2.575–87), the paraphrase in Müller (1861: 2.409–25) and Ludwich (1885: 2.556–74). The scholia are both interpretative, i.e. explaining the meaning of Dionysius' lines, and historical-geographical, expanding upon information about seas, cities, rivers and nations mentioned in the poem. The paraphrase was partly based on the preliminary interpretative scholia. According to Tsavari (1990a: 58–60), the paraphrase would have been composed in the tenth–eleventh centuries, but Counillon (1991: 370) is more cautious and advocates a precise analysis of the textual transmission of the scholia and paraphrase before reaching any conclusions.
[19] In some manuscripts (Vatican City, Biblioteca Apostolica Vaticana, gr. 117 and 121, among others), the correspondence between groups of verses and their respective paraphrases is made precise by the use of consecutive numbers that appear together with the poem and at the beginning of each prose section. In Vatican City, Biblioteca Apostolica Vaticana, gr. 999, the paraphrase interrupts the copied verses, which are grouped by units of meaning.

student was not forced to delve deeper into the grammatical and lexical peculiarities of the poem's hexametric form before understanding what Dionysius was actually saying.[20] Given that the *Periegesis* achieved such a broad dissemination, the fact that the poem was made into a geographical essay or treatise in the margins of the verses presents us with an interesting paradox: the prose version was, for the Dionysian worldview, the means of finding a place within the genre of *hypotyposeis* or 'geographical sketches' composed by Byzantines with selections from Strabo.[21]

Among many other sources such as Strabo, Stephanus of Byzantium or Ptolemy,[22] Eustathios of Thessalonike used the marginalia I have described to compose his *Parekbolai* ('explanatory notes taken from different sources'), the only commentary on the *Periegesis* by a known author.[23] This is essentially a scholastic work on another scholastic work, in which the *maistor ton rhetoron*, the great *exegetes* of Homer, revealed and amplified the meaning of Dionysius' verses.[24] In effect, his geographical commentary forms part of an inseparable whole together with the other two commentaries by Eustathios that have been preserved, his *Parekbolai* on the *Iliad* and on the *Odyssey*.[25] The three are the result of a complex and lengthy study of a range of sources, the product of which (the citations, the links between words, the linguistic evidence of variation, and so on) would probably find their way into the resulting *parekbole* through the reworking of index cards, as is suggested by the not uncommon repetition of the same pieces of information in different places.

---

[20] On the inverse transposition of prose into didactic poetry, see Hutchinson (2009). Dionysius' *Periegesis* does not seem to be based on an earlier prose handbook but on the author's own readings of Eratosthenes and Posidonius (perhaps through Strabo), among other Alexandrian geographical texts; see Jacob (1981: 25) and (1990: 50). On the literary and scientific Alexandrianism of Dionysius, see Lightfoot (2014a).
[21] On the anthologies of Strabo in Byzantine manuscripts, see Diller (1975: 80–96).
[22] Cassella (2003).
[23] The scholia attributed in a later specimen (Paris, Bibliothèque nationale de France, suppl. gr. 36) to Demetrios Lampsakenos were reported by Müller (1861: 2.xxxi) and Diller (1936) as an invention by Konstantinos Palaiokappa (mid-sixteenth century). Jacob (1981: 26) implicitly considers them to be Byzantine.
[24] See Eust. *in Dion. Per.* 205.10–11 and 35–6 ed. Müller. As Jacob (1990: 14) has pointed out, Eustathios' commentary perfects the pedagogical efficiency of the Roman poem; cf. Hunter (2017: 17–18).
[25] *Commentarii ad Homeri Iliadem*, ed. van der Valk (1971–87); *Commentarii ad Homeri Odysseam*, ed. Stallbaum (1825–6); see the new edition of the commentary on the first two books of *Odyssey* by Cullhed (2016); see also van den Berg (2017) and Lovato and van den Berg in this volume. Eust. *in Dion. Per.* 206.41–207.2 alludes to the common features of Homer and Dionysius: 'And so, if the material in this commentary serves as an aid to the reading of Dionysius, it is natural for it to share its warm reception. This is, indeed, the case of the wise and good Homer and the one who explains his work: he shares with him both the virtue of being beneficial and his goal. And the same is true for Dionysius and the other sages as well.'

In this light, the order in which these commentaries were composed does not seem to be a crucial issue, especially if we remember that all three were later revised by the author, who would continue to add short supplements.[26] Nonetheless, some passages of the *prooimion* to the commentary on Dionysius provide a degree of self-criticism (or anticipate later criticism) about the 'lesser' character of the work, which can be better understood in the context of the *magnum opus* of Eustathios' Homeric *parekbolai*.[27] As a matter of fact, Eustathios alludes to various earlier-composed notes in his Homeric commentaries to avoid repeating information, which demonstrates that Eustathios worked on the *Periegesis* after finishing some of the Homeric notes. Although the different commentaries frequently share quotations from poets as well as orthographic developments, the mention of the earlier Homeric commentaries allows Eustathios to avoid some explanations about fabulous peoples such as the eastern Ethiopians, Troglodytes and Eremboi and, thus, to adapt the content of the *Parekbolai on Dionysius* to geographical knowledge subsequent to that reflected by Homer.[28] Eustathios, we know, had studied other ancient poets (and the *Iambic Pentecostal Canon*) in great depth, even if his commentaries on Pindar, Aristophanes and Oppian have not survived (with the exception of his preface to Pindar);[29] whether any of the material that appears in the margins of the Palaiologan manuscripts was based on his exegesis is largely unknown.[30]

---

[26] Diller (1975: 181–3), Cullhed (2012).

[27] Eust. *in Dion. Per.* 203.29–36: 'I know that for many this work, for its lack of pretensions, will not be judged as generally well constructed, as more than a few have shown themselves to be vain, severe and arrogant in this respect; for me, however, these criticisms are not convincing, as I consider it necessary for anyone who takes on a commission to do it well and not suffer facile criticisms of any such commission, be it great or small.' The author's concern over finishing the text is clear at the beginning of the preface; see Eust. *in Dion. Per.* 202.18–204.3. Eustathios seems to have initially planned a less ambitious commentary, and then later to have begun writing a more complex set of notes.

[28] See e.g. Eust. *in Dion. Per.* 248.31–249.22 (179–80), where he refers to *Od.* 4.84 and *in Od.* 1484.33–1485.5 = 1.149.21–150.19 ed. Stallbaum; Eust. *in Dion. Per.* 269.18–32 (302), where he refers to *Il.* 13.5 and *in Il.* 916.7–51 = 3.425.11–427.27 ed. van der Valk. On the traditional chronology of Eustathios' commentaries, which considers the Homeric *Parekbolai* to be the last ones, see Pontani (2000: 14, n. 11).

[29] *Canon iambicus pentecostalis*: ed. Cesaretti and Ronchey (2014); preface to Pindar: ed. Kambylis (1991).

[30] Pontani (2010: 188–9) has detected some scholia from the *Parekbolai* on Dionysius in the commentary on Oppian. In *in Dion. Per.* 208.2–9, Eustathios echoes the proverb that speaks of the impossibility of drawing the world on a fingernail, while a considerable number of codices of Oppian (see Marcotte [2010], Cariou [2014]) include in the commentary on the *Halieutika* a drawing of the *oikoumene* in which the Gulf of Nicomedia is oversized and framed in a square with one curved side, precisely in the shape of a fingernail. On the quotations from Oppian in Eustathios, see Benedetti (1976–7: 431–41); on the hypothetical commentary on Oppian, see Dyck (1982).

The Audience of the *Parekbolai*

Even if Eustathios continued his teaching practice after being transferred to Thessaloniki in 1175/8, the prefatory letter of the *Parekbolai on Dionysius* proves that his notes date back to the time when he was *maistor ton rhetoron*, the leading professor of rhetoric in Constantinople as well as an official court orator. The commentary to the *Periegesis*, then, sheds light on Byzantine education and culture in the mid-twelfth century, that is to say, to the field of rhetorical studies in the time of Manuel I Komnenos and to the value of geographical knowledge in Constantinopolitan education.[31] At that time, the podium from which Eustathios would have spoken had maximum visibility, so his words would certainly have transcended the confines of the classroom and also have addressed the members of the court.[32] He compares his own audience to that of the poem as follows:

> This commentary of mine works with these qualities of Dionysius towards the things which a student of literature wishes to know. If Dionysius sometimes addresses well-advanced students in a condensed way, then this commentary serves as a reminder by expatiating on what is necessary for the sake of beginners who are less sophisticated. If, on the other hand, Dionysius elsewhere speaks to beginners, then the present work speaks at greater length for those who enjoy learning. (Eustathios, *Parekbolai on Dionysius Periegetes* 205.26–33, trans. Hunter 2017: 18)

A distinctive feature of the *Parekbolai* to the *Periegesis* is the fact that it opens with a prefatory letter addressed to John Doukas, the son of Andronikos Kamateros, in which Eustathios claims to have repaid the debt he owed to John (by writing the commentary) and describes the nature of his labour.[33] After the letter, the reader finds a proper introduction and it is in this second part of the *prooimion* that we meet Eustathios' teachings on geography and cartography,[34] naturally developed in the *Parekbolai* in accordance with Dionysius' verses themselves.

In the prefatory letter, John Doukas is presented as a student of Eustathios who has made great progress in his studies, and this has urged the master to deliver his commentary without further delay.[35] John is

---

[31] On Eustathios, see Magdalino (1993: 335–56), Kaldellis (2009), Nesseris (2014, 1: 91–104 and 2: 162–87).
[32] Eustathios alludes to the audience of his commentary with words that have a double meaning: ἀκροατής and ἀκροώμενος 'listener or pupil', but also ὁμιλητής 'disciple, scholar'. In *in Dion. Per.* 205.27–8, he is more specific: ἀκροατὴς φιλόλογος, 'a student of literature'. He also uses φιλακροάμονας, 'the attentive audience' (205.33). On the various types of audience in Eustathios' Homeric *parekbolai*, see Pizzone (2016).
[33] Eust. *in Dion. Per.* 201.6–207.33.   [34] Eust. *in Dion. Per.* 207.34–216.37.
[35] Eust. *in Dion. Per.* 202.4–203.14.

Eustathios' Achilles but, unlike Achilles, he 'has not only one virtue, that of quickness, but excels in all; he is rich in everything that really matters, imperial in lineage and noble of soul, erudite; his carriage is illustrious and his body like a statue of the Graces, but inwardly he is what could be described as a wise human being'.[36] A second version of the title (probably due to Eustathios himself) indicates that Doukas was later appointed *epi ton deeseon* ('in charge of petitions'), and adds that Eustathios was promoted later to the Thessalonian see; a complete rethinking of the textual tradition would be required in order to establish if the longer title corresponds to a revised edition of the text.[37]

That it was this commentary of Eustathios', and not another, which had a specific addressee must be understood in light of the numerous mentions of the utility of the poem and its commentary,[38] especially at the end of the preface, where we read:

> The ancients also make it clear that the knowledge obtained from geographical descriptions has other guaranteed benefits, claiming, among other things, that the *Periegesis* is useful for living (βιωφελής), awakens the understanding of the expert and is undoubtedly of great utility for military officers and emperors. (Eustathios, *Parekbolai on Dionysius Periegetes* 214.30–5)[39]

This is an unusual mention of the utility of studying geography for Byzantine political life, one that illuminates a cultural reality which is sometimes blurred: the extent to which the ancient scientific and technical, and in this case geographical, tradition was studied in Byzantium.[40] In another passage from the work, where the meaning of vv. 170–4 is developed, Eustathios insists on the social outreach of this knowledge:

---

[36] Eust. *in Dion. Per.* 204.28–33.

[37] Ed. Diller (1975: 182): Πρὸς τὸν πανσέβαστον <σέβαστον> Δοῦκα κύριον Ἰωάννην <τὸν μετὰ ταῦτα ἐπὶ τῶν δεήσεων>, τὸν υἱὸν τοῦ πανσεβάστου σεβαστοῦ καὶ μεγάλου δρουγγαρίου, κῦρ Ἀνδρονίκου τοῦ Καματηροῦ, Εὐσταθίου διακόνου ἐπὶ τῶν δεήσεων καὶ μαΐστωρος τῶν ῥητόρων τοῦ καὶ <ὕστερον γεγονότος ἀρχιεπισκόπου> Θεσσαλονίκης ἐπιστολή . . .. On the career of this John Doukas, see Angelov (2022). The first approach to the transmission of the *Parekbolai* can be found in Diller (1975: 181–207).

[38] According to Eust. *in Dion. Per.* 206.11–25, the reader of the poem, on finding only brief mentions of peoples, regions and cities, will be avid for more information, and this curiosity will be satisfied by the commentary. A bit later (206.31–4), the *maistor* claims that his work will bring together what is most beautiful in the poem with what is good for both use and knowledge (ἀγαθὸν εἰς χρῆσιν εἴτε καὶ γνῶσιν).

[39] It is difficult to ascertain if Eustathios is speaking about Dionysius' poem or the genre itself; in my view, *periegesis* may sometimes be translated as 'geographical description'.

[40] I believe that this is what Eustathios is referring to *in Dion. Per.* 204.4–8: 'Do not forget that you yourself ordered me to select for you the most beautiful verses of the *Periegesis* of Dionysius, those which may provide a *complementary knowledge* (τὴν ἄλλην γνῶσιν), a necessary amplification, a style proper to oratory and a collection of *experiences* (ἐμπειρίας συναγωγήν).' On the political utility of geography, see Bazzaz, Batsaki and Angelov (2013).

'that the aim of the *Periegesis* is the student's learning, as well as his teaching to other people who lack the knowledge, and their aim is, again, the honour granted by the learners'.[41] This affirmation prepares the ground for the preface, where he writes: 'For in just a few verses at the beginning of the work, [Dionysius] states his purpose and then goes on to describe the usefulness of the *Periegesis*, saying that it transmits knowledge to the student and at the same time it is a lesson from the one who has learnt for those who do not know it and a source of honour for the one who teaches.'[42] Acquiring knowledge, then, has the aim of receiving recognition from the circle to which one belongs. Since the privileged recipient is in this case John Doukas, who would rise to a lofty position in the court, his ability to exhibit his geographical knowledge in a courtly setting that included members of his own family would confer upon him a corresponding level of prestige.[43]

Indeed, John's father, the *megas droungarios* Andronikos, was the author (in 1172) of the Ἱερὰ Ὁπλοθήκη (*Sacred Armoury*), which formulated Emperor Manuel's religious policy toward the Roman and Armenian churches, a subject not entirely unrelated to geographical knowledge.[44] His uncle, John Kamateros, who was a close friend of Manuel I, was the author of an Εἰσαγωγὴ ἀστρονομίας (*Introduction to Astronomy*) and an orator of renown;[45] he knew the *Periegesis*, as a note to fol. 339 of Ambros. C 222 inf. indicates:[46]

> For Kamateros said that, among all the poetical books, two poets require to be illustrated and copied, Dionysius Periegetes and Aratus, since the first describes the map and the second the celestial sphere; without them, the young people interpreting these materials would not understand anything but strictly the words. And the map cannot be given without a text in order to allow to see with the senses and to comprehend what is written. The same goes for the sphere. Out of the two authors, the most difficult is Aratus. Thus I was told by the rhetor.[47]

---

[41] Eust. *in Dion. Per.* 246.36–40 (Pk. 170).   [42] Eust. *in Dion. Per.* 214.25–30.
[43] On this, Bourbouhakis (2017: 185*) comments: 'His [Eustathios'] erudition, shared with peers through learned commentaries and "bookish" writings, as well as through more direct instruction, made him a likely candidate to serve as a "source" for the kind of *recherché* expressions and historical allusions prized by Byzantine audiences.'
[44] See Angelov (2013: 48); the text is edited by Bucossi (2014). On the text, see also Agapitos in this volume.
[45] Ed. Weigl (1908); see Magdalino (1993: 259), Bucossi (2014: xxi).
[46] This manuscript refers to a cultural context similar to that of the *Parekbolai*, as it is a codex from the second half of the twelfth century and, in fact, the only preserved copy of Dionysius which is contemporary to John Tzetzes and Eustathios. It is a compilation of extra-Homeric poetry and is filled with all manner of short notes. It has been the subject of extensive research by Mazzucchi (2003) and (2004), who considers its copyist and owner to have been a disciple of Tzetzes; he identifies, however, the Kamateros of the note as the patriarch John Kamateros (1198–1206); see Mazzucchi (2004: 420–2). The manuscript also contains Tzetzes' scholia on Aristophanes' *Frogs*: see Pizzone in this volume.
[47] Ed. Mazzucchi (2004: 421).

Eustathios draws the same parallel between Aratus and Dionysius in his preface:[48]

> Aratus, the perfect interpreter of Hermes who soars through the heavens, in his introduction addresses and beautifully describes the celestial phenomena in verse, while it is Dionysius, Hermes' assistant, who now spreads his wings rapidly around the earth, whom the intellect of the Muses, as he himself boasts in his preface, guides over the entire earth without ever letting him stray or lose his way. (Eustathios, *Parekbolai on Dionysius Periegetes* 211.7–13)

We lack sufficient information about the exact relationship of Eustathios with the other members of the Kamateroi family to determine whether this was also a master–disciple relationship or if they were simply individuals with whom he interacted at court. The familiarity with geography possessed by some members of the imperial circles does not seem coincidental, however, and may well have been the product of reading Dionysius (and Strabo?) at the instigation of Eustathios. Whatever the case, in settings such as imperial or civil administration or the military, in which students of the *maistor* would come to hold outstanding positions, the fact that geographical knowledge was considered an important asset is not surprising, even if the link to some specific teaching is unclear. Although the administrative geography of the Empire has little to do with the *Periegesis*, a succinct periplus of the Black Sea with distances measured in *stadia* and *milia* is included in some manuscripts of Dionysius at the beginning or end of the poem's marginalia,[49] this being a type of administrative document which has other preserved examples and whose utility is obvious.[50]

Eustathios' Decisions as Exegete

The eclecticism that characterizes the *Periegesis* seems at odds with the concise information on distances in works like the *hypotyposeis* or the peripli that I have already mentioned. The Roman poem is quite different: a reading of the ancient mythical universe organized in the form of a 'bird's-eye view', combined with a linear or circular exploration of some of

---

[48] On the influence of Aratus on Dionysius, see Aujac (1993: 66–8).
[49] Ed. Müller (1861: 2.457.19–43). The data it contains should be compared with those of the so-called *Periplus Ponti Euxini*, ed. Müller (1861: 1.402–23), actually a compilation of extracts from Arrian and other authors updated to an administrative setting of ca. 540–60, according to Marcotte (2007: 171).
[50] This periplus is not unlike the famous *stadiodromikon* from 949, transmitted as an appendix to *De Cerimoniis* (2.45); see Haldon (2000: 235, 301–2), Pryor and Jeffreys (2006: 547–70). On the dissemination of geographical knowledge in Byzantium, see Pérez Martín and Cruz Andreotti (2020).

its elements, such as continents, islands or rivers.⁵¹ Any challenge to this vision of the world, not in relation to our present knowledge but to the scientific knowledge available to the Byzantines, was potentially explosive in that it could jeopardize the entire tradition. For this reason, in his *prooimion*, Eustathios clarifies again and again the principles and objectives of his commentary and, throughout, his specific and systematic referencing of sources (by proper name or with the professional attribution of γεωγράφος or ἐθνογράφος) suggests that the exegete had no intention of changing or criticizing the image of the world projected in the poem.⁵² What is more, Eustathios argues that the poem leads us to the truth:

> Its value is made clear in all possible ways: by composing his song in verse, by varying the dialect, by not avoiding the measured use of mythical stories, by exploiting the persuasiveness of its inventions, by elaborating with descriptions wherever it was suitable, by inserting stories and, as we have stated earlier, by guiding us towards the truth by means of geographical law, and presenting his thoughts in order to teach, for example, in the passages where he discusses the Kronios Ocean (the North Sea), the celebrated island of Thoule and the climate below Cancer, as well as by occasionally turning his attention to nature itself. (Eustathios, *Parekbolai on Dionysius Periegetes* 214.4–13)

Eustathios' commentary, therefore, does not seek to correct errors or ambiguities,⁵³ nor to argue against the validity of Dionysius' global vision:

> Dionysius was concerned to produce a general description of the earth and a review of its peoples; he was not very concerned in every case to set down where or among whom names arose or the characteristics of places and peoples. We have respected that as far as it was convenient for the pieces of information he gave. (Eustathios, *Parekbolai on Dionysius Periegetes* 206.1–7; after Hunter 2017: 18 trans.)

---

⁵¹ Jacob (1981: 27–9), Lightfoot (2014: 120–6). In *in Dion. Per.* 210.9–211.3, Eustathios defines with great beauty the various perspectives adopted by the voice which describes the world in the poem.
⁵² On the conservatism that characterizes many geographical texts, see Jacob (1981: 64), Hunter (2017: 17).
⁵³ However, Eustathios points out that Homer changes the location (ἐκτοπίζειν) of some populations in the context of his mythification of Odysseus' wanderings; see Eust. *in Od.* 1379.29–31 = 4.13–16 ed. Cullhed; on the ancient debate about the truthfulness of the Homeric narrative of those wanderings, see Pontani (2000: 15). It seems clear that not criticizing Dionysius' mistakes allowed Eustathios to avoid a massive revision of the information transmitted by the poem. Counillon (1991: 370) thinks that Eustathios' aim in using several copies of the *Periegesis* was to correct the text ('se livrer à une véritable *diorthôsis* du texte'). It is true that the exegete often mentions several copies (πολλὰ τῶν ἀντιγράφων τοῦ Διονυσίου), but his purpose was usually to create a sounder text from the point of view of orthography, rather than to correct Dionysius' cartography.

Actually, it was a question of seasoning the poem without adulterating it, 'by adding a kind of sauce taken from other places and selected so as to give a certain balance as this was felt to be necessary and opportune'.[54] Eustathios, in any case, does not avoid explaining the poem's difficulties or shedding light on what was 'careless and obscure'.[55] The exegete is thus obliged to gather together and add complementary material, because Dionysius' text offers a very general vision within the narrow limits of *periegesis*.[56] To elucidate this general vision, Eustathios employs a variety of methods: he sometimes transforms the words of Dionysius into a paraphrase that explains or expands upon the poem; at other times, he maintains the verses and adds more information where necessary.[57] The 'prosification' of the poem is thus a necessary recourse:

> And so may this be a gift with which we honour your excellence, so worthy of reverence [John Kamateros], a Dionysius no longer a poet but rather liberated from metre and telling in prose many more things; not speaking concisely but exposing and revealing himself with greater breadth, as it is possible to do when most things are set free from metrical composition to prose; not only singing but reciting, in those places where song seems to us inopportune, and becoming double-voiced instead of having only one voice; without expressing in an elevated style nor always corseted by metre, but in some places also advancing with the narrative step by step; nor reciting everything from a metrical stage, but treating many themes without the poetic mask; not 'needing someone to explain it all', as would say the Theban lyre (Pi. *O.* 2.85–6) but, having now acquired the appropriate clarity, without the need for an interpreter. (Eustathios, *Parekbolai on Dionysius Periegetes* 207.2–17)

His intervention has a limit, however; although the *Periegesis* is 'in need of development',[58] Eustathios feels obliged to accept the poem's concision without correcting its insufficiencies, without 'filling in the map':[59]

> [My commentary] does not fill in gaps as though what Dionysius has said is incomplete, but rather it expands at greater length on his own topics, as is appropriate for a prose work, and so to speak, by extracting the substance of what he tells, it enriches it even further in a different way, and develops

---

[54] Eust. *in Dion. Per.* 204.36–205.2. On the culinary metaphor with which Eustathios explains his exegetic work, see Jacob (1981: 63–8), van den Berg (2017: 40–3).
[55] Eust. *in Dion. Per.* 204.14: ἀργὸν καὶ ἀπόθετον.
[56] Eust. *in Dion. Per.* 204.10–11: πάνυ ἐπελευστικὸν καὶ ἐν στενῷ περιηγήσεως κείμενον.
[57] Eust. *in Dion. Per.* 205.9–16.   [58] Eust. *in Dion. Per.* 204.6–7: πρὸς ἀνάπτυξιν δέουσαν.
[59] Eustathios' amplification is largely linguistic, through the etymological study of toponyms; cf. Jacob (1981: 63–5).

plainly and simply its words and fulfils the audience's appetite.[60] ... In writing like this, I do not correct the Periegete, nor do I fill in what has been unnecessarily omitted, as I noted above, but I follow my audience's wishes in softening what is imposed by the metrical nature of the lecture. (Eustathios, *Parekbolai on Dionysius Periegetes* 205.34–9 and 206.7–11; after Hunter 2017: 18 trans.)

Displaying the *Parekbolai*

Eustathios' preface is inspired in part by the additional materials which usually take up several pages of the manuscripts before the beginning of the *Periegesis* itself.[61] These appear in every copy with commentary and are its natural development; given that their volume far exceeded the margins of the verses, they would eventually 'have grown' into the space preceding the poem, which some forward-thinking scribes would arrange for this purpose before copying the *Periegesis*. However, some of these materials (such as Dionysius' *Vita* or the list of winds) do not originate in the margins of the text but genuinely belong to this preliminary space, offering the rudiments of geographical learning. Conversely, since Dionysius offers in the first lines of the *Periegesis* a worldview of the *oikoumene* which is susceptible to commentary and development, the preliminary concentration of accompanying texts may be considered as scholia to the first lines of the poem and as such are found in the margins. These texts address general issues about the known world and, for Byzantine readers, they were probably a suitable, if elementary, introduction to this particular worldview.

I have already referred to the *Periplus of the Euxine Sea*, which Eustathios does not mention, just as he does not include in his commentary the lists of winds, seas, gulfs or islands which constitute the most elementary mnemotechnic material of geography.[62] He does, however, reproduce and amplify a short note on Dionysius and his works (the most common additional text found in the manuscripts),[63] as well as a definition of

---

[60] On the audience's appetite (τὸ λίχνον), see Pizzone (2016: 226–34).
[61] He introduces them in this way: 'But before the work, I want to add a few things by which I will indicate to you the disposition of Dionysius, honour the subject of the description, explain what is notable about it and tell what the *Periegesis* is capable of, what is the objective of geography, what is the meaning of chorography, and some other appropriate things, if there are any, before turning to the work itself' (Eust. *in Dion. Per.* 207.34–208.2).
[62] Müller (1861: 2.457a.12–18 and 457b.5–46).
[63] Müller (1861: 2.427a.1–15); Eust. *in Dion. Per.* 215.6–17 includes it with almost no changes. Eustathios did not know the so-called *Vita Chisiana*, preserved in two manuscripts from the fourteenth century; see Kassel (1985).

geography as opposed to chorography whose ultimate source is Ptolemy's introduction to the *Geography*.[64] In the preface, these are made into a short essay on the genre of *periegesis* and the types of geographical texts,[65] followed by some notes of literary criticism on the poem, part of which I have already mentioned here.[66]

I have also alluded to one of the features of Eustathios' working method, that of creating index cards that gathered together information on certain terms and may be considered the embryo of his commentary. The *Parekbolai* themselves appear in the oldest preserved copy (Vatican City, Biblioteca Apostolica Vaticana, gr. 1910)[67] in blocks of text separated by ':-' and a space. These are designed to be read independently from the poem, without the need for the verses to precede the comments, since the *Parekbolai* may be understood without referring to the actual verse or already include the passage in question in either verse or prose.[68] Even so, a transmission of the commentary separated from the verses is less than effective, and the general tendency is to bring together both poem and *Parekbolai* in some way, although this may make redundant some of the exegetic scholia or paraphrases found in the margins and incorporated and amplified by Eustathios.[69] In the same Vat. gr. 1910, we find a copy of the poem, in two columns and surrounded by paraphrases, which is more recent than the copy of the *Parekbolai* and therefore was not necessarily conceived with this accompaniment in mind. In other codices, poem and commentary, whether copied by the same scribe or not, are contemporary and were probably intended to complement each other in an independent volume, as both texts could be fitted into a small-format book that would be too reduced in size without either one.[70] Commentary and text thus found their own corner of the book universe, one in which they could comfortably interact in the hands of any Byzantine poetry lover curious to know about the world.

---

[64] Müller (1861: 2.428a.1–6). [65] Eust. *in Dion. Per.* 211.14–213.25.
[66] Eust. *in Dion. Per.* 213.26–216.37.
[67] See Diller (1975: 184–5). On the manuscript, see now Pérez Martín (2021).
[68] If, for example, the *parekbole* addresses a specific people or place, it is superfluous to copy the verse. When the commentary deals with one or more verses, however, Eustathios does mention them, as he announces in the preface: 'we have searched out and carefully selected all that is useful for those who take on the reading of the work in prose and also for those purist readers of Dionysius' original' (Eust. *in Dion. Per.* 204.14–16). Cf. the proem of the commentary on the *Iliad* for similar claims (2.23–36 = 1.3.8–22; 3.2–5 = 1.3.35–1.4.2 ed. van der Valk).
[69] Still to explore in this sense are the copies of Dionysius which combine the commentary of Eustathios with earlier marginalia, as in the case of the sophisticated copy of Par. gr. 2723.
[70] This is the case of Paris, Bibliothèque nationale de France, gr. 2852 (thirteenth/fourteenth century) and 2855 (thirteenth century). In Vatican City, Biblioteca Apostolica Vaticana, gr. 922, Oppian is added to the volume; in Rome, Biblioteca Casanatense, 356, it is Aratus.

Epilogue

Compared to his Homeric commentaries, Eustathios' *Parekbolai* to the *Periegesis*, the geographical poem written by Dionysius of Alexandria, are a modest contribution, but not without interest. The commented-upon poem provides a referential ensemble of geographical information that attracted different kinds of supplementary materials, some of which found their way to the pages preceding the verses. For the Byzantines, these materials, which probably originated from a school environment, formed the main way of accessing elementary knowledge about the inhabited world. Secondly, this is the only Eustathian commentary preceded by a prefatory letter dedicating the work to a specific individual, John Doukas Kamateros. This circumstance must be linked with Eustathios' assertion about the ways geographical knowledge may spread from his students to other people, a forecast that becomes true if we pay attention to a note preserved by Ambros. C 222 inf., where John's uncle, also named John Doukas, expresses his opinion on Dionysius as geographical reference text. We understand the meaning of geographical knowledge for this family belonging to the inner circle of Emperor Manuel I better when, in the *Parekbolai*, we encounter Eustathios' insistence on the practical character of his commentary, which also points to the political and administrative context of his teaching. A deeper reading of the entire text will shed further light on how the Byzantines learned geography and how their worldview was shaped.

REFERENCES

Angelov, D. (2013) '"Asia and Europe Commonly Called East and West": Constantinople and Geographical Imagination in Byzantium', in *Imperial Geographies in Byzantine and Ottoman Space*, ed. S. Bazzaz, Y. Batsaki and D. Angelov, 43–52. Cambridge, MA–London.

   (2022) 'Repurposing Ancient Knowledge: Eustathios of Thessaloniki and His Geographical Anthology', in *Imagined Geographies in the Mediterranean, Middle East, and Beyond*, ed. D. Kastritsis, A. Stavrakopoulou and A. Stewart. Washington, DC.

Aujac, G. (1993) *La Sphère, instrument au service de la découverte du monde: d'Autolycos de Pitanè à Jean de Sacrobosco*. Caen.

Bazzaz, S., Y. Batsaki and D. Angelov (eds.) (2013) *Imperial Geographies in Byzantine and Ottoman Space*. Cambridge, MA–London.

Benedetti, F. (1976–7) 'De Eustathii grammatici studiis Oppianeis', *AFLPer* 14: 431–41.

van den Berg, B. (2017) 'The Wise Homer and His Erudite Commentator: Eustathios' Imagery in the Proem of the *Parekbolai on the Iliad*', *BMGS* 41.1: 30–44.
Bernhardy, G. (1828) *Dionysius Periegetes Graece et Latine*. Leipzig.
Billerbeck, M. (2008–16) *Stephani Byzantii Ethnica (A–Y)*, 4 vols. Berlin.
  (2015) 'Eustathios und die *Ethnika* des Stephanos von Byzanz', in *Lemmata: Beiträge zum Gedenken an Christos Theodoridis*, ed. M. Tziatzi, M. Billerbeck, F. Montanari and K. Tsantsanoglou, 418–30. Berlin–Boston.
Bouiron, M. (2012) 'Du texte d'origine à l'*Épitomé* des *Ethnika*: les différentes phases de réduction et la transmission du lexique géographique de Stéphane de Byzance', *Rursus* 8: 1–42.
Bourbouhakis, E. C. (2017) *Not Composed in a Chance Manner: The Epitaphios for Manuel I Komnenos by Eustathios of Thessalonike*. Acta Universitatis Upsaliensis. Studia Byzantina Upsaliensia 18. Uppsala.
Bowie, E. L. (2004) 'Denys d'Alexandrie: un poète grec dans l'empire romain', *REA* 106: 177–85.
Bucossi, A. (2014) *Andronici Camateri Sacrum armamentarium*. Turnhout.
Cariou, M. (2014) 'La géographie en marge des *Halieutiques*, inventaire et étude des cartes préservées dans les scholies à Oppien', *RSBN* 51: 281–310.
Cassella, P. (2003) 'Sul commentario di Eustazio a Dionigi Periegeta', in *L'erudizione scolastico-grammaticale a Bisanzio. Atti della VII Giornata di Studi Bizantini, Salerno 2001*, ed. P. Volpe Cacciatore, 27–36. Naples.
Cesaretti, P. and S. Ronchey (eds.) (2014) *Eustathii Thessalonicensis exegesis in canonem iambicum pentecostalem*. Supplementa Byzantina 10. Berlin.
Counillon, P. (1991) 'À propos de l'Histoire du texte de Denys le Périégète', *REA* 93: 365–71.
Cullhed, E. (2012) 'The Autograph Manuscripts Containing Eustathius' Commentary on the Odyssey', *Mnemosyne* 65: 445–61.
  (ed. and trans.) (2016) *Eustathios of Thessalonike, Commentary on the Odyssey*, vol. 1: *On Rhapsodies A–B*. Acta Universitatis Upsaliensis. Studia Byzantina Upsaliensia 17. Uppsala.
Diller, A. (1936) 'Two Greek Forgeries of the Sixteenth Century', *AJPh* 57: 124–9.
  (1952) *The Tradition of the Minor Greek Geographers*. Oxford.
  (1975) *The Textual Tradition of Strabo's Geography with Appendix: The Manuscripts of Eustathius' Commentary on Dionysius Periegetes*. Amsterdam.
  (1975a) 'Agathemerus, *Sketch of Geography*', *GRBS* 16: 59–76.
Dyck, A. R. (1982) 'Did Eustathius Compose a Commentary on Oppian's *Halieutica*?', *CPh* 77: 153–4.
Göthe, A. (1875) *De Fontibus Dionysii Periegetae*. Göttingen.
Guidetti, F. and A. Santoni (eds.) (2013) *Antiche stelle a Bisanzio: il codice Vaticano greco 1087*. Pisa.
Haldon, J. (2000) 'Theory and Practice in Tenth-Century Military Administration: Chapters II, 44 and 45 of the *Book of Ceremonies*', *TM* 13: 201–352.
Hunter, R. (2017) 'Eustathian moments', in *Reading Eustathios of Thessalonike*, ed. F. Pontani, V. Katsaros and V. Sarris, 9–76. Trends in Classics Supplementary Volume 46. Berlin–Boston.

Hutchinson, G. O. (2009) 'Read the Instructions: Didactic Poetry and Didactic Prose', *CQ* 59: 196–211.
Ilyushechkina, E. (2011–12) 'Zur Quellenfrage der Erdbeschreibung des Dionysius Periegetes: Die *Geographika* Strabons als eine der Quellen?', *Geographia Antiqua* 20–1: 111–18.
Jacob, C. (1981) 'L'œil et la mémoire: sur la *Periégèse de la Terre habitée* de Denys', in *Arts et légendes d'espaces: figures du voyage et rhétoriques du monde*, ed. C. Jacob and F. Lestringant, 21–97. Paris.
— (1990) *La description de la terre habitée de Denys d'Alexandrie ou la leçon de géographie*. Paris.
— (1991) 'Θεὸς Ἑρμῆς ἐπὶ Ἁδριανοῦ: la mise en scène du pouvoir impérial dans la *Description de la terre habitée* de Denys d'Alexandrie', *CCG* 2: 43–53.
Kaldellis, A. (2009) 'Classical Scholarship in Twelfth-Century Byzantium', in *Medieval Greek Commentaries on the Nicomachean Ethics*, ed. C. Barber and D. Jenkins, 1–43. Leiden–Boston.
Kambylis, A. (ed.) (1991) *Eustathios von Thessalonike, Prooimion zum Pindarkommentar: Einleitung, kritischer Text, Indices*. Veroffentlichung der Joachim Jungius-Gesellschaft der Wissenschaften 65. Göttingen.
Kassel, R. (1985) 'Antimachos in der Vita Chisiana des Dionysius Periegetes', in *Catalepton: Festschrift für Bernhard Wyss zum 80. Geburtstag*, ed. C. Schäublin, 69–76. Basel.
Kneebone, E. (2017) 'The Limits of Enquiry in Imperial Greek Didactic Poetry', in *Authority and Expertise in Ancient Scientific Culture*, ed. J. König and G. Woolf, 203–30. Cambridge–New York.
Lauxtermann, M. (2009) 'Byzantine Didactic Poetry and the Question of Poeticality', in *'Doux remède ...': poésie et poétique à Byzance. Actes du IVe colloque international philologique EPMHNEIA, Paris, 23–25 février 2006*, ed. P. Odorico, P. A. Agapitos and M. Hinterberger, 37–46. Dossiers Byzantins 9. Paris.
Leo, A. (2001–2) 'La *Periegesi* di Dionigi d'Alessandria e il viaggio di Adriano in Egitto', *Rudiae* 13–14: 145–74.
Leroy, P.-O. (2013) 'Deux manuscrits vaticans de la *Géographie* de Strabon, et leur place dans le *stemma codicum*', *RHT* 8: 37–60.
Lightfoot, J. L. (2014) *Dionysius Periegetes, Description of the Known World, with Introduction, Text, Translation, and Commentary*. Oxford.
— (2014a) 'Between Literature and Science, Poetry and Prose, Alexandria and Rome: The Case of Dionysius' *Periegesis of the Known World*', in *The Alexandrian Tradition: Interactions between Science, Religion, and Literature*, ed. L. A. Guichard, J. L. García Alonso and M. P. de Hoz, 157–74. Bern.
Ludwich, A. (1885) *Aristarchs Homerische Textkritik nach den Fragmenten des Didymos*. Leipzig.
Magdalino, P. (1993) *The Empire of Manuel I Komnenos, 1143–1180*. Cambridge.
Marcotte, D. (2002 [2000]) *Géographes grecs*, vol. 1: *Introduction générale; Circuit de la Terre, Ps.-Scymnos*, second edition. Paris.

(2007) 'Le corpus géographique de Heidelberg (Palat. Heidelb. gr. 398) et les origines de la Collection philosophique', in *The Libraries of the Neoplatonists*, ed. C. D'Ancona, 167–75. Leiden–Boston.

(2009) 'La *Periegesi* di Dionigi tra Bisanzio e l'Italia nel sec. XII', *QS* 35: 89–104.

(2010) 'Une carte inédite dans les scholies aux *Halieutiques* d'Oppien: contribution à l'histoire de la Géographie sous les premiers Paléologues', *REG* 123: 641–59.

Mazzucchi, C. M. (2003) 'Ambrosianus C 222 inf. (Graecus 886): il codice e il suo autore. Parte prima: il codice', *Aevum* 77: 263–75.

(2004) 'Ambrosianus C 222 inf. (Graecus 886): il codice e il suo autore. Parte seconda: l'autore', *Aevum* 78: 411–40.

Müller, K. (1861) *Geographi Graeci minores*, 2 vols. Paris. (repr. Hildesheim 1965)

Negri, M. (2000) *Eustazio di Tessalonica, Introduzione al commentario a Pindaro*. Antichità classica e cristiana 32. Brescia.

Nesseris, I. (2014) 'Ἡ παιδεία στην Κωνσταντινούπολη κατά τον 12° αἰώνα', unpublished PhD thesis, University of Ioannina.

Pérez Martín, I. (2021) 'El manuscrito Vat. gr. 1910, la copia más antigua de las *Parekbolai a Dionisio Periegeta* de Eustacio de Tesálonica', *Φιλόδωρος εὐμενείας. Miscellanea di studi in ricordo di Mons. Paul Canart*, ed. M. D'Agostino and L. Pieralli, 577–90. Vatican City.

Pérez Martín, I. and G. Cruz Andreotti (2020) 'Geography', in *A Companion to Byzantine Science*, ed. S. Lazaris, 231–60. Brill's Companions to the Byzantine World 6. Leiden–Boston.

Pizzone, A. (2016) 'Audiences and Emotions in Eustathios of Thessalonike's Commentaries on Homer', *DOP* 70: 225–44.

Pontani, F. (2000) 'Il proemio al *Commento all'Odissea* di Eustazio di Tessalonica (con appunti sulla tradizione del testo)', *BollClass* 21: 5–58.

(2010) 'The World on a Fingernail: An Unknown Byzantine Map, Planudes, and Ptolemy', *Traditio* 65: 177–200.

Pryor, J. H. and E. M. Jeffreys (2006) *The Age of the Dromon: The Byzantine Navy ca. 500–1204*. Leiden–Boston.

Reeve, M. D. (1994) 'Some Manuscripts of Dionysius the Periegete', *ICS* 19: 209–20.

(2004) 'Dionysius the Periegete in Miscellanies', in *Il codice miscellaneo: tipologie e funzioni. Atti del Convegno internazionale (Cassino, 14–17 maggio 2003)*, 365–78. Segno e testo 2. Cassino.

Sakellaridou-Sotiroudi, A. (1993) 'Ὁ Ἡρόδοτος στις *Παρεκβολές* του Εὐσταθίου Θεσσαλονίκης, στον Διονύσιο τον Περιηγητή', *Hellenika* 43: 13–28 and 415–17.

(1994) and (1995) 'Ὁ Στράβωνας στις *Παρεκβολές* του Εὐσταθίου Θεσσαλονίκης στον Διονύσιο τον Περιηγητή', *Epistemonikê Epeterida tês Philosophikês Scholês Thessalonikês. Tmema Philologias* ser. v, 4: 173–93 and 5: 141–50.

Skalli-Cohen, A. and I. Pérez Martín (2017) 'La *Géographie* de Strabon entre Constantinople et Thessalonique: à propos du Marc. gr. XI.6', *Scriptorium* 71: 175–207 and Pl. 23–6.

Stallbaum, J. G. (1825–6) *Eustathii archiepiscopi Thessalonicensis commentarii ad Homeri Odysseam ad fidem exempli Romani editi*, 2 vols. Leipzig.

Taxidis, I. (2017) *Les épigrammes de Maxime Planude: introduction, édition critique, traduction française et annotation*. Berlin–Boston.

Tsavari, I. O. (1990) Διονυσίου Ἀλεξανδρέως Οἰκουμένης περιήγησις. Ioannina.

(1990a) *Histoire du texte de la Description de la terre de Denys le Périégète.* Ioannina.

van der Valk, M. (ed.) (1971–87) *Eustathii archiepiscopi Thessalonicensis commentarii ad Homeri Iliadem pertinentes ad fidem codicis Laurentiani editi*, 4 vols. Leiden.

Weigl, L. (1908) *Johannes Kamateros, Eisagôgê astronomias: Ein Kompendium griechischer Astronomie und Astrologie, Meteorologie und Ethnographie in politischen Versen*. Leipzig–Berlin.

CHAPTER 8

Painting and Polyphony
The Christos Paschon *as Commentary*

Margaret Mullett

Of all twelfth-century texts which show engagement with classical literature, the *Christos Paschon* seems the most unlikely to appear in a volume on commentary. On the spectrum of Byzantine texts dealing with the classics, from transmission, through *sylloge*, schedography, gloss, book review, to *metaphrasis*, popular paraphrase, parody, mimesis and generic revival, it appears to be at the opposite end from anything we would conventionally consider as 'commentary'.[1] It is literary, experimental, creative; it implies performance not private reading.[2] It is a problem play, one of the problems being whether it is a play at all. It is certainly debated whether it was in any sense performed, whether it is generically tragedy or cento, and whether it is predominantly secular or sacred. Its date is contested and its authorship ascribed variously. I believe it to be a Byzantine tragedy with included lament, which uses Euripidean cento in counterpoint with gospel narrative and was performed rhetorically or noetically in schoolroom or *theatron* in twelfth-century Constantinople. I justify these answers elsewhere,[3] but here I am concerned to consider the precise nature of its engagement with ancient texts.

The Text

The *Christos Paschon* is regarded as anonymous, though the manuscript tradition ascribes it to Gregory of Nazianzos.[4] Herbert Hunger and

---

[1] See the definitions offered in Most (1999a), Gibson and Kraus (2002), Kraus and Stray (2016a).
[2] It may be wrong to think of commentary as entirely visually received; on commentary as a quintessentially teaching mode, see Budelmann (2002: 155), Sluiter (1999: 173): 'The existence of a commentary on any given text is evidence that that text was used in teaching.' See also Pizzone in this volume.
[3] For lament, see Mullett (forthcoming a); for cento, Mullett (2021); for its religious positioning, Mullett (forthcoming b); for performance, Mullett (forthcoming c).
[4] Brambs (1885), Tuilier (1969).

Wolfram Hörandner convincingly resited it in the twelfth century,[5] and authorship has been variously ascribed to Constantine Manasses, John Tzetzes and Theodore Prodromos.[6] Twenty-five manuscripts survive from the middle of the thirteenth century on.[7]

It comprises 30 + 2602 iambic lines on the subject of the passion and resurrection of Christ. It is a tissue of lines and half-lines from *Medea*, *Hippolytus*, *Rhesus* and *Bacchae* plus rather fewer from *Hecuba*, *Orestes* and *Troades*; there are some quotations from *Prometheus Bound* and the *Agamemnon*.[8] But the vast majority of the quoted lines (954/1123 lines) is drawn from the first four plays.

It has been studied by Byzantinists trying to prove the existence or otherwise of a Byzantine drama,[9] by Margaret Alexiou on the Virgin's Lament,[10] and by Elizabeth Bolman on the Galaktotrophousa.[11] But until recently,[12] it has not been studied as a Byzantine reading of Euripides to supplement what little we know about Byzantine appreciation of tragedy:[13] classicists have been more concerned with using the text to understand the manuscript tradition of the *Bacchae* than with seeing it as a work in its own right.[14]

It takes us from the Theotokos surrounded by the chorus of women of Galilee during the night of Maundy Thursday to the events of Easter Sunday. In his 1969 edition André Tuilier suggested that it is not one but

---

[5] Since Hunger (1968a: 63–5) the text has been redated to the twelfth century, though Gregory had his adherents through the 1970s and 1980s, countered by Hörandner (1988). Although the contextual argument for the twelfth century may seem overwhelmingly persuasive, revisiting the issue is a desideratum to set a sure foundation for further work.
[6] Respectively Horna (1929), Dübner (1846: iv–v), Hilberg (1886).
[7] For the manuscripts, see Tuilier (1969: 75–116).
[8] The quotations are identified with varying levels of persuasiveness in both Brambs' and Tuilier's editions; also quoted are *Alcestis*, *Andromache*, *Helen*, *Iphigenia at Aulis* and *Tauris*, *Phoenissae* and Lycophron's *Alexandra*, as well as biblical and apocryphal texts. It is by no means a complete cento, and some, possibly including Terése Nilsson of Uppsala University, would argue that it is not a cento at all.
[9] For a judicious treatment, see Marciniak (2004: 89–95). See also Kazhdan and Wharton Epstein (1985: 140–1).
[10] Alexiou (1975: 122–4).
[11] Elizabeth Bolman quoted it at the Theotokos conference, Oxford, August 2006, in a paper which will form part of a book on the middle and late Galaktotrophousa.
[12] Alexopoulou (2013: 123–37), Bryant Davies (2017: 1–25). For lament, see Bernier-Farella (2015). Bryant Davies in particular requires detailed response for which there is no space here.
[13] See the rather puzzling *synkrisis* of Psellos in Dyck (1986) and the anonymous treatise in Barocci 131 published by Robert Browning (1963). See Agapitos (1998: 137–41), Wojtylak-Heszen (2004) probes the use of Euripidean material, but in a fifth-century context; Vakonakis (2011) grounds the text in the issue of a Byzantine theatre, the reception of tragedy and Byzantine cento technique; the last pages, 153–62, look at the implications for textual criticism, especially of *Bacchae* and *Medea*.
[14] An early exception was Dostálová (1982).

three plays: first the Crucifixion (lines 1–1133), second the story from Deposition through Lamentation to Entombment (lines 1134–1905) and third the Resurrection (lines 1906–2531), and I adopt this suggestion here.[15]

Play I The Crucifixion (lines 1–1133)

It begins at daybreak on Friday a few paces from a vantage point on the road to Golgotha. The Virgin stands majestically, upright and static like the Virgin of Torcello, centre stage throughout the text. She is surrounded by shock after shock as three messengers make their way to her one after another, the first announcing the betrayal in the garden (lines 130–266), the second describing the trial by the Sanhedrin (lines 360–418) and the third (639–81) taking us to the Crucifixion. The women react and comment and support her, but as the messengers leave, she is alone until the words of Christ to her at line 727. By then, she and the women have gone to witness the Crucifixion, where she finds her son and John the Theologian and remains for the rest of the play, lamenting throughout, interceding for Peter, and left bereft at the end, abandoned by her son and helpless as to what to do next.

Play II The Burial (lines 1134–1905)

The second play begins with an exchange between John the Theologian and Joseph of Arimathea before the Theotokos enters, and it is focused on the short journey between the cross and Joseph's rock-cut tomb. The actors (the Theotokos, John the Theologian and Joseph of Arimathea plus Nicodemus as a non-speaking fourth) make that journey through ritual acts of deposition (lines 1269–1308), *threnos* (lines 1309–1406), entombment (lines 1434–88) and *teleutaios aspasmos* (lines 1489–1609), almost claustrophobically confined in that space and by the fear of discovery. At the end, Joseph sets out for exile, the women are taken by John to his house where the Theotokos and chorus of women lament, and then a fourth messenger arrives to announce that a guard has been set at the tomb.

Play III The Resurrection (lines 1906–2531)

The third play includes a high proportion of the resurrection episodes in an attempt at performed gospel harmony. It moves between the house of John where the women have spent the night, the tomb where they go in the

---

[15] Tuilier (1969: 20). For further discussion, see Mullett (forthcoming c).

morning, and the house of Mary where the disciples are based and where all the women go to join the disciples (and Cleopas of the Emmaus episode) at the end for the epiphany of Christ. It begins with a discussion by the women of what they should do, and Mary Magdalen's offer to scout out the tomb before they all set out (lines 1906–91). The Magdalen tries to wake the women, and the Virgin performs one last lament (lines 1992–2030). At 2031, they see that the guards are not there and at 2045 the empty tomb. At 2054–83, they come across an angel in the tomb, and (lines 2084–2115) Christ himself greets them. At 2116, the women join them and they see a young man dressed in white in the tomb. While the chorus is recovering and the Magdalen goes to tell the disciples, a fifth messenger (lines 2174–2388) comes to tell the story of the guard's report to the priests and Pilate, which develops into a subplot. The chorus then announces the arrival of Peter and John (offstage) with the Magdalen, and the Theotokos begins to report to the women events before they arrived, continued by the Magdalen (lines 2437–79) as they head back to the house of Mary and (lines 2480–2503) the chorus narrate their arrival at the house and the appearance of Christ, who addresses them (lines 2504–31).

In what follows, I attempt an analysis of the use of the four main source texts not by selecting key passages or modes of handling, but by proceeding source text by source text through the three plays to indicate what is used and why. After considering each source text, I compare the reading of the text in the *Christos Paschon* with more modern interpretations. The aim is to give a clear sense of the interrelationship of *Paschon* and source texts and its development over the plot of the trilogy.

Have Some Medea, M'dear

If we take the use of the *Medea* in the first play, it can be seen as considered. The quotations are not random or mechanical, but there is no attempt at a simple equivalent transfer of text from character to character, a point well made by Karla Pollmann.[16] It does not smack of parody.[17] Nor is this a juvenile school exercise concerned to show off skills, self-conscious and boasting. The author has thought carefully about his source plays, has identified speeches with the strongest emotional punch and has reminded his audience of them and their relevance to the ultimate drama of the Passion. Occasionally there is a self-referential word for the

---

[16] Pollmann (1997).
[17] Unlike Housman (1901); Theodore Prodromos, *Katomyomachia*, ed. Hunger (1968b).

audience: the use at 1014–15 of *Medea* 1224–30, the sting in the tail for 'crafters of polished speeches' in the description of the death of Creon and his daughter, quoted at greater length than usual, could be a wry remark intended for the *theatron* in Constantinople.[18]

The quotations can be whole lines, half-lines, short chunks of 5–6 lines, and sometimes they bow to the sense of a speech rather than specific words. Sometimes a series of individual words or syntactical patternings suggest a continuing reference which could be picked up by the audience. An example is the use made of the nurse's opening speech on might-have-beens (M1–45) echoed in the Theotokos' speech on the Fall (1 1–90). There is flexibility in who voices the lines. The Theotokos voices Medea (e.g. M765 at II 1247), but also Jason (e.g. M1323 at 1 283), and the horror of Medea's crime is used to underline the Theotokos' implacable opposition to Judas and to the threatening crowd.[19] The chorus does voice the chorus (e.g. M1306 at 1 120) but also the nurse (e.g. M43 at 1 493); the messengers voice the messengers (e.g. M1187 at 1 235) but also Medea (e.g. M365 and 368–9 at 1 253–5 and 1 205–6) and Creon (the first messenger at 1 226–51 uses four lines in M348–55); John the Theologian voices the nurse (e.g. M27–8 at 1 972) and Christ voices Jason (e.g. M922 at 1 730), Medea (e.g. M872 at 1 739), the paedagogus (e.g. M1012 at 1 731), Aegeus (M719 at 1 766) and the messenger (e.g. M1222 at 1 824). Much of the source play goes unused (only 310 lines out of 1419 are brought across). Our author chooses moments of high emotion or horror or dramatic tension: Medea's farewell to the children (M1069–80), the death of Jason's wife (M1156–1203), Medea weeping once the die is cast and she cannot go back on her actions (M1004–5). He uses these moments to heighten the emotional content of his text. It is highly likely that he knew what he was doing: Euripides was famous in Byzantium for his portrayal of emotion as much as for the beauty of his poetry.[20] Some lines are used three or four times,[21] sometimes two sides of a question (for

---

[18] On *theatra*, see Mullett (1984), Marciniak (2007), Gaul (2018) and (2020).

[19] Much of the Virgin's curse, 1 267–357, esp. 290–304, is built on two passages of confrontation between Medea and Jason: in M465–75 Medea confronts Jason for his betrayal; in 1323–30, signalled in 1294, Jason confronts Medea for her murder.

[20] Michael Psellos in Dyck (1986: 44) puts it thus: 'Euripides, who wrote eighty or more dramas is always full of grace and charm, not in the charms of diction alone, but even in the sorrowful events themselves.' On Euripides, 'the lamenting one', in Theodore Prodromos' *Sale of Poetical and Political Lives*, see Marciniak (2013: 231). See now also Marciniak (2022).

[21] M37, 38, 101, 145, 340–1, 947–8 (in all three plays), 1219, 1271, 1397 are used three times; M712, 743, 1008, 1042, 1076, 1079, 1187, 1202, 1234 are used four times; M1071 is used five times and M930 is used seven times: ἔτικτον αὐτοὺς. In addition, thirty-three lines from *Medea* are used twice in the trilogy.

example Jason and Medea on parenting) are combined to add texture (M1377 at II 1273; M1244 at II 1275). Occasionally a whole block is lifted wholesale (M516–19 at I 347–50, M1224–30 at I 1012–18). Both the first line and the last (I 1133) of the first play are taken from *Medea*, the former referring to the first line, the latter being the penultimate line (M1418; the formulaic 1419 could not be used).

In the second (II **Burial**) and third (III **Resurrection**) plays, the *Medea* takes a back seat. In II 1134–62, the first three speeches are bare of *Medea*, then from 1163 Joseph and John the Theologian use nurse and paedagogus, then the Theologian (II 1206–9, 1223–5, 1230–3) quotes the messenger on Creon's discovery of his daughter dead (M1218, 1204–6, 1211–13) and at II 1240 Joseph comes back with the nurse (M80). At II 1247, the Theotokos enters voicing Medea (M765), then Joseph (at II 1259 and 1266) the nurse (M38) and Creon (M321–2), then at II 1269 the Theotokos evokes both Jason on the dead children (II 1273, M1377) and Medea psyching herself up to kill them (II 1275, M1244) in a debate over whether the Theotokos will hold Christ in her arms. As the issue is resolved, line 1275 is repeated at 1306. From II 1309 in the *threnos*, the ritual lament familiar from Byzantine wall-paintings from the twelfth century on, a great deal is made of the farewells to the children by Jason and Medea (M1349–50, M1069–80), plus the bride's cry of pain (M1183) and her father's agony (M1204–21); thereafter use of the *Medea* tails off.

In the third (III **Resurrection**) play, the Theotokos opens at 1906, as she considers setting out for the tomb, and there is a sequence of speeches by chorus, Magdalen, chorus, Magdalen, Theotokos without any *Medea* material. *Medea* returns at III 1973–4 with the Theotokos promising presents to the Magdalen, using M947–8, the gift to the bride. The Magdalen replies at III 1976, where she sets out to the tomb on the Theotokos' business (reflecting M460, Jason on consulting Medea's interests); the next three speeches (III 1981–8) of Theotokos and Magdalen, discussing their shared desire to see the risen Christ, evoke Medea to Aegeus (M688), Medea sending the children with gifts (M974) and Jason on his return to Medea (M866). The section from III 1989–2022 is bare of *Medea* references, then at 2023 the Theotokos, in addressing Christ, uses the words of Medea to her children (M1071) in farewell. After another gap, III 2024–2101, at 2102 the Theotokos uses the reported death of the bride (M1195) to dramatize the prosternation of the myrrophores after Christ's *chairete*. At 2104, the response of Christ, the reaction of Magdalen, the youth, Magdalen, the chorus, Theotokos, messenger, Theotokos, messenger are all without reference to *Medea*. Lines III

2181–2, the arrival of the final messenger, are M663–4, Aegeus' first couplet, a cheerful omen. The Pilate subplot from 2184 to 2400 has no *Medea* references, except for 2235 when the priests offer a bribe to the guard in the words of Medea (M947) promising gifts to Jason's bride – not a cheerful omen for the guard. Then at III 2402, in her response to the messenger, the Theotokos says ἔτικτον αὐτόν ('I gave birth to him'), recalling Medea at M930, then the text is bare to the end of III at 2531. There is nothing in the prayer to Christ, but 2602 (the last line in Tuilier's text, praise to the Virgin as salvation) is M14 on safety lying in harmony with one's husband. So I is rich in *Medea*, II and III not so, but the trilogy ends with a reference to *Medea*.

As a reading of *Medea*, the *Christos Paschon* emphasizes not the witch or the monster or the *xene*,[22] but the weeping mother, bereft of any family support as she makes up her mind to sacrifice a child. It shows a strong woman outraged by betrayal: Judas' behaviour affects Mary emotionally as Jason's does Medea, though clearly the logic of the situation develops differently. Parts of the 'Women of Corinth' speech (M214–66) are used (at I 755–7), not to hammer home a feminist message, though there is sympathy for the lot of women, but to signal how Mary is different from other women: her maternity did not involve the pain of childbirth. But in other ways it is a Theotokos who has absorbed the torments of Medea (and, we shall see, of Agave and Phaedra) as she voices them, a mother of God built of the strongest stuff, no milk-and-water Western Virgin or supplicating Byzantine mediatrix. This strong Theotokos reflects the Middle Byzantine Virgin who micromanages punishments and rescues her true adherents in danger.[23] It is a Theotokos strangely sympathetic to the concerns of the twenty-first century, in a play which also suggests that the twelfth century's understanding of the workings of tragedy was not so very far from our own.[24]

---

[22] For modern readings of *Medea*, see Stuttard (2014); Hall, Macintosh and Taplin (2000). M. Carr (2002), first performed at the Abbey Theatre Dublin, 7 October–14 November 1998; on it, see Sihra (2005) and Wilmer (2005); in general, Lauriola and Demetriou (2015).

[23] For this 'scary Mary', see Baun (2011).

[24] The playwright understands technical features such as messenger speeches, stichomythia, laments, the three-actor rule, and has some awareness of the possibilities of the chorus, while not flagging up entrances and exits as a fifth-century dramatist would, and shows no awareness of masks. The author is also tuned into *anagnorisis* and *peripeteia* and supremely alert to tragic emotion, though he is constrained in emotional trajectory by his plot, in a different way from the constraints and freedoms of myth. He knows that 'tragedy essentially arouses powerful emotions' (Taplin and Billings [2010]).

Hyping *Hippolytus*

The use of the source play starts when lines 1 101–3 use the beginning of *Hippolytus*: Aphrodite on the *theologeion* (H1–57) informs the first interchange of chorus and Theotokos, and at 1 109–12/H498 the Theotokos, responding to the first suggestion from the chorus that Christ is going to die, voices Phaedra shocked by the nurse's forthright embrace of her lovesickness. At 1 128/H 857–8, this is reinforced by the Theotokos' not wanting to hear that Christ will die being expressed in terms of Theseus steeling himself to look at the suicide note; again here the same quotation is used when the issue is first raised and when it is settled (1 109, 129). At 1 130–7, the exchange between Theotokos, chorus and First Messenger opens with the chorus's reactions to Phaedra hearing the nurse berated by Hippolytus behind closed doors (H595, 575, 571); we shall hear this exchange evoked six more times over the three plays, a clearly crucial moment for the playwright. At 1 142, the horror of the Theotokos at the messenger's news recalls the horror of Theseus reading the suicide note (H874). A similar pitch of emotion – though not the same emotion – matches at 1 233 Theseus' mourning for Phaedra (H829) with the messenger addressing Judas. At 1 419, the Theotokos' response to the Second Messenger uses Theseus on Phaedra (H881) again, and at 1 423–5 the Theotokos on the Jews echoes Theseus' (mistaken) revulsion from Hippolytus (H936–8). At 1 522–4, we are told that the Theotokos, like Hippolytus (at H1004–6), is a virgin, and at 1 605 and 609 the Theotokos voices Phaedra hearing the nurse berated (H570, 569); it is the first time she realizes that her passion is a public as well as a private problem, a threat as well as a sickness. At 1 606, the Theotokos voices Hippolytus (at H1091): he knows more than he can tell; she has to watch her son die on the cross. At 1 610–12 the Theotokos voices Phaedra at H598–600, seeing only death as a way out. At 1 650, the messenger on Christ uses the messenger on Hippolytus (H1162) – both are by now as good as dead. At 1 714–15, the Theotokos voices Theseus' grieving for Phaedra (H845–6), and at 1 723 the Theotokos' musings on herself reflect those of the nurse on women who lose through love (H458). At 1 714–15, just before Christ speaks to her, the Theotokos quotes Theseus describing his grief (H845–6), and at 1 802 Theseus saying goodbye to Hippolytus (H1454). At 1 803, the Theotokos on Christ voices Artemis to Hippolytus (H1389) on nobility of mind. The Theotokos' intercession for Peter (1 812–24) makes use of the chorus noting Hippolytus' sad arrival (H1342), Artemis offering pardon to Theseus for his injustice to Hippolytus (H1325) and the nurse's urging of forgiveness for human frailty (H615).

Then we come at I 848–59 to the Virgin's moment of realization as she sees and accepts that Christ is dead. She once more uses Phaedra's reaction to the nurse (H565), Artemis reporting that Hippolytus is about to die (H1439) and Hippolytus' words to Artemis on leaving a long friendship (H1441); the definitive moment at I 853 uses Hippolytus seeing Phaedra dead (H905–7) and also, we shall see, Agave realizing that Pentheus is dead. In the Virgin's lament which follows, nature joins in as with the death of Hippolytus (H1215–17), and Hippolytus finding Phaedra (H907–10, 912), Theseus' words as Hippolytus dies (H1408–10), Hippolytus' own realization that he is dying (H1444) and Theseus' lament for Phaedra (H839–46) all come into play.

In II **Burial,** 1283–8 and again at 1290–4, Joseph voices the messenger speech on Hippolytus' accident (H1261–4, 1250–4), and, like the Messenger, Joseph cannot believe Christ guilty. When at II 1301 and 1303 the Theotokos asks Joseph to get Christ down she echoes Artemis telling Theseus to take Hippolytus in his arms and embrace him (H1431–2, 1445). When at II 1309 the Theotokos has Christ in her arms, she uses Hippolytus' farewell to Troezen (II 1316, H1097), and his sensing of Artemis' presence (II 1326, H1391–2). The discovery of Judas' hanging (I 244) evokes the discovery of Phaedra (H802), Theseus when he heard of Hippolytus' accident (III 1434, H1169, III 1436, H1172) and Hippolytus' berating of the nurse (III 1447, H614) to underline the Theotokos' opposition to Judas. When at 1453 the Theotokos orders the burial, she uses Hippolytus' last words, asking for his face to be covered (H1458), and at II 1478 Theseus asking for Hippolytus to be brought in (H1265) is the model for the Theotokos asking for Christ's body to be brought to the tomb. At II 1481, the Theotokos' grieving for Christ involves the whole community like the last speech of the chorus (H1345) in *Hippolytus* as the broken Hippolytus enters. The Virgin's *teleutaios aspasmos* at II 1486, 1498 reflects Hippolytus' words to his peers as he leaves Troezen (H1099–1100, 1101); Joseph's last word (II 1636) is the same. At 1818, the Theotokos' last speech in II at the house uses the exclamation of Phaedra listening to her downfall (H569) plus Theseus on the death of Phaedra (H845). At 1863–5, the Messenger who tells of troops set at the tomb uses the speech of the Messenger who brings the news of Hippolytus' accident (H1153–6), maintaining the tragedy.

In III **Resurrection**, at 1920–1, the Theotokos voices Artemis to Hippolytus (H1416, 1418), at 2122–3 the Magdalen vies with Hippolytus in a desire to find out what has happened (H1416, 1418) and at 2179 the Angel at the tomb speaks the words of Artemis on

Hippolytus' virtues to extol Christ's: his miracles and goodness. In the **Prayer to the Virgin,** line 2572 addresses her as Hippolytus and the chorus do Artemis; it uses the speech of Hippolytus to Artemis at H73–87, 62–72.

The source play, much admired in the last hundred years, is seen to balance the fate of two noble and principled heroes, while two goddesses either engineer their fall or try to repair the damage. The power of emotion to defeat principle is usually emphasized, and Phaedra tends to usurp centre stage.[25] In the hands of the playwright of the *Christos Paschon*, a chaste hero, who died tragically young through machination, is understood in the mould of the many heroes of Byzantine literature who fought off personifications of *porneia* from Romanos' Joseph II to the desert fathers to the lives of Meletios, all in the name of *sophrosyne*.[26] Phaedra and her torments are hardly considered, though her intelligence in instantly foreseeing her downfall is a model for the Theotokos' growing understanding of what unfolds before her eyes.

Rhesus Derivative

Here the use of the source play begins late in the first play I **Crucifixion**. At I 90, as day dawns, the Theotokos is persuaded to wait as Hector, wisely, is persuaded to wait for dawn (R66). But much of our text makes use of the farcical aspect of Hector and Aeneas trying to figure out what's going on in the dark (I 91–4/R90–3; I 95–6/R41–5; I 98/R85). Elsewhere in the Virgin's curse (I 275), the Theotokos blaming Judas uses the driver blaming Hector (R835), and the Muse's promise that Odysseus will be punished at the beginning of her first speech (R894) prefigures the comeuppance of Judas (I 277). The parallel of a leader being persuaded by his or her comrades enables the Theotokos, in agreeing to retire to a little hill for safety, to voice Hector agreeing to send a volunteer. The account by the Theotokos (I 1080–5) of the piercing of Christ's side voices the driver's narration of the damage to Rhesus' side (R790, 794). And at 1125, the Theotokos' suspicions derive from those of the driver at R873: how can I trust you, Hector? But there is very little *Rhesus* in I.[27]

In II **Burial**, however, the first words are from *Rhesus*: at 1134, John the Theologian on Joseph's entrance uses the chorus on Aeneas' entrance, and

---

[25] Mills (2013), McKee (2017). [26] See the recent treatment by Nilsson (2017: 244–8).
[27] 29/1133 lines in I use *Rhesus*, as against 72 *Bacchae*, 166 *Hippolytus* and 298 *Medea*. In II 102/772 lines use *Rhesus*, in III 125/626 lines.

we know that an ally has appeared. ll 1159–60/R904–5 Joseph to John the Theologian voices the chorus to the Muse just before her lament, signalling that lamentation will follow their conversation. At ll 1213–15, John the Theologian echoes the Theotokos on the piercing of the side of Christ, and 1341–1426 the Theotokos launching into the *threnos* with Christ in her arms uses R915–50, the Muse's first speech, and Hector's reply in R952–61. When she instructs the men at ll 1446 to take the body and entomb it, she uses Hector urging his men to take the driver and look after him (R877), reinforcing it at ll 1455 with the words of the chorus introducing the Muse carrying the body of Rhesus (R888). At ll 1629, the offer of John the Theologian of a bed for the night recalls Hector's offer to Rhesus of a space to spend the night at R519, in so doing creating a whiff of danger (it did not turn out well). At ll 1637, 1639 John the Theologian on the divinity of Christ voices the chorus on the charioteer's news of the death of Rhesus at R754–5.

From line ll 1715, the use of *Rhesus* becomes a great deal richer: from now on, the text is mostly about *Rhesus* and *Bacchae*. There is also play with separate blocks of lines, for example, six blocks of Hector/Rhesus form the foundation for the speech of John the Theologian at ll 1715 to 1749: at 1715–26, we learn that the reluctance of Jews to declare for Christ is like Rhesus turning up late for the Trojan War (R399–403, 406–18), and at 1727–37 we get Rhesus to Hector (R443–50) in response; 1740–5 loops back to the first group of lines and 1747–9 to the second group then back to the first. So Rhesus defending himself is interspersed with Hector accusing him, a virtuoso performance. At ll 1766–9 John the Theologian's conversation with Joseph mirrors Hector's with the chorus at R330–1; both are confident, whether in resurrection or victory, and yes, for both, tomorrow will bring clarity. At ll 1770–82, Joseph's speech of faith uses the Muse's second speech (R962–82): 'he will not go down'. The resurrection trope specifically is not quoted directly, but six lines of the Muse's speech are used by Joseph, as well as the three lines of the chorus that follow (R983–5): the chorus and Joseph urge the others to leave the Muse/Theotokos to mourn (that's her job). As John the Theologian at ll 1783–4 repeats Hector's confidence in victory at R991–2, Joseph at ll 1785 expresses the chorus's hope in Rhesus as incoming saviour at R464: 'may I see that day'. At ll 1806–7, Joseph voices Paris at R663–5 to say that John the Theologian, like Athena, has persuaded him not to fear. Here the switch to *Bacchae* at ll 1810 may be an indicator that Joseph exits here. From here to the end of the play we see night draw on. At ll 1813–15, John the Theologian leads the women to where they can spend the night just as Hector shows Rhesus at

R518–19. At II 1819, the Theotokos' lament echoes the charioteer at R770, but effects become more atmospheric as we see the use at II 1820 of the sleepy chorus at R555, and at 1831, the end of the Theotokos' speech, the sleepy chorus again, suggesting that the women will now sleep. At II 1840, we hear the chorus claim they didn't sleep (R824–5), followed at 1850 by the sleepy chorus (R547–55) and at 1851 the half-chorus quotes the driver, 'my worrying heart woke me up' (R770), then again (with extra words) at 1852. We go back to the chorus at II 1853, who neither slept nor slumbered (R825), and at 1855 the Theotokos' call to wake echoes the chorus on the changing of watch near dawn (R532). The messenger at II 1872–83 uses Paris' report to Athena on Greek spies (R653–60) to paint the posting of sentries at the tomb.

Rhesus immediately sets up the third play, III **Resurrection**, with the Theotokos at 1908 expressing the need to take unguents to the tomb, while echoing Odysseus to Diomedes on the need for caution (R587), and we begin to see that it will be necessary to send a volunteer to the tomb. After scattered references to Aeneas and Hector and Dolon, at III 1941 we meet the Magdalen and realize she is that volunteer and that the reward she claims is to be the first to see the resurrection. This is reinforced by the Theotokos' speech warning the Magdalen at III 1980 not to bump into the guard, as Odysseus does to Diomedes at R570. Diomedes' mission is recalled with III 1995 the Magdalen's demand that the women wake, voicing the chorus at R532, and R8, the waking of the change of the guard, the sleepy chorus R554–5 and the driver's worrying heart (R770) plus the wakeful chorus (R825), 'we are fully alert'. At III 2004 the Magdalen is cautious, like Odysseus at R582–4 with Diomedes, and we realize the danger of her secret mission. At III 2009, the Theotokos picks up Odysseus' caution (R582) three times in five lines, but at III 2010 the use of Hector the confident (R991–2) lets us believe that the women will prevail. At III 2019, the Virgin has her last chance to lament her son – when shall I see you? – which might suggest doubt. At III 2031, the Magdalen cries out like Odysseus to Diomedes, spots the absence of the guard as at R574, and the Theotokos picks up Diomedes' part at R578 – is this a trap for us? When, like Diomedes at R580, the Magdalen asks, 'so what will we do?', and the Virgin replies at III 2038 'have confidence and advance', we see a positive spin on the cautious retreat of Diomedes and Odysseus. At III 2058, the Theotokos sees a figure in white like snow, just as Athena spots the white horses of Rhesus looking like a swan's wing (R618). The Theotokos at III 2025–30 again recalls the chorus awaiting Rhesus (R369–70), and at 2095 before Christ's *chairete* and at 2098 after it she voices the messenger telling of the arrival of Rhesus (R284) and Rhesus greeting Hector (R388). There is then a dearth of *Rhesus* references until the announcement of the arrival of Christ's army from Hades (III 2186–90) through the messenger announcing the arrival of Rhesus (R280, 282). The Theotokos asks for proof at III 2193, as Aeneas does of Hector at R94, and the dispersal of the guard uses R41–7 when the chorus brings word to Hector of Greek activity, as well as R88–9, Aeneas' scepticism. The Pilate subplot, III 2205–2379, uses a great deal of *Rhesus* (messing about in the dark), but when we return to the main resurrection plot, *Rhesus* recedes. At III 2386, the *angelos* in conversation with the Theotokos voices the chorus to Hector at the beginning of the play (R50), and at 2389 the Theotokos echoes the chorus to Hector at R52 on timeliness – the fifth use of the line in the trilogy. At III 2411, the Theotokos voices Odysseus at R582: let's go back now – let's have a good look and report. At 2443, the Magdalen beards the danger at the tomb as the messenger does the Thracians at R297, and can report through Hector and the messenger at R280–95 that Rhesus has arrived and that Jesus is back. The **Prayer to the Pantanax** at III 2538 quotes Rhesus' first address to Hector (R388), and the **Prayer to the Theotokos** at III 2601 Paris to Athena at R653–4.

The *Rhesus*, no longer considered to be by Euripides, when studied or performed today, is often seen in terms of ambush, of ambivalent helpers, of late arriving allies, a grey world of mistrust and espionage in which it is difficult to distinguish friend from foe.[28] The author of the *Paschon* uses that atmosphere of mistrust to create a world of threat not unlike Colm Tóibín's *The Testament of Mary*,[29] but also focuses on the natural descriptions of darkness and light to create stunningly lovely evocations of the women fighting off sleep, as the weekend's events demand wakefulness at night and enforced rest during the day. The comic potential of the blundering about in the dark or semi-light is fully realized in the Pilate subplot, but the arrival of a long-awaited saviour, teamed with the presence

---

[28] Opinion appears to be swinging against Euripides as author of the *Rhesus*: see Liapis (2011: Introduction, v); the editors of *Brill's Companion to the Reception of Euripides* declined to include it on the basis of the authenticity issue and minimal evidence for reception independent of the *Iliad* (our text might fill that gap). See now Fries (2018) with a convincing argument for the fourth century.

[29] Tóibín (2012). This Booker-shortlisted novella was first trialled as a monologue at the Dublin Theatre Festival in 2011 and then rewritten as a play, in which Fiona Shaw played Mary in the Broadway run of April 2013. It is a version of the passion story told through the reactions of Mary: fear in the face of the crowd as in the *Paschon*, but also of the regime more generally (Judaea as a police state) and most of all of the disciples, who have enforced on her an official narrative of events.

Painting and Polyphony

of the Muse, the only innocent mother allowed to grieve in all four source plays, offers a more spiritual reading.

Back to the *Bacchae*

The thinner use of this source text sometimes enables a more powerful message as the horror of the story of the *Bacchae* is applied to the passion. In the first play, I **Crucifixion**, at 161 the first messenger on the betrayal uses Agave's proud report to Cadmus beginning at B1233. At I 373, the Theotokos wonders to the women how her son will die, built upon the women's chorus that asks the second messenger at B1041 how Pentheus died. The chorus comments on the Theotokos' response to the second messenger's news at I 438 with the announcement of the death of Pentheus at B1030 and the Theotokos at I 444 uses Agave's moment of *anagnorisis* at B1280. Richer use of the source text from I 567 reflects Teiresias on Dionysus (B280, 284–5, 288–91), the third messenger (I 657–81) uses the chorus responding to the death of Pentheus (B1041–4), then the second messenger on the death of Pentheus (B1046–50). At I 853–4 the Theotokos realizes that Christ is dead as Agave realizes that her slaughtered lion is her son (B1280–1). At I 1046–62, the Theotokos, after the death of Christ, picks up Cadmus grieving for Pentheus (B1244, 1247) and Cadmus' conversation with Agave during the horror of the bits of Pentheus being reassembled (B1259–62). At I 1075, the Theotokos on the bloody wounds of Christ uses the maenads on the mountain and the damage they wrought (B742).

The second play, II **Burial,** begins strongly. At II 1263–5, Joseph's practical handling of ladder and nails recalls Agave's desire to see her trophy nailed up (B1213–15); Joseph (II 1295) urges the Theotokos to stretch out her hand to Christ as Dionysus (B973) urges the women to stretch theirs towards Pentheus. At II 1309–25, the *threnos* includes Cadmus' lament over Pentheus at B1314. At II 1455, the Theotokos reflects Cadmus' speech bringing Pentheus into the palace (B1226). Joseph at II 1473 on the wounding of Christ reflects the *sparagmos* of Pentheus (B1135) and on entombment (II 1485–8) reflects Cadmus taking the reassembled body of Pentheus into the palace (B1216–21). Joseph says goodbye to the dead Christ at II 1634–5 in Cadmus' words at B1316–17, and in facing exile (II 1700–11) quotes the exile of Cadmus (B1352–6); at the end he echoes Cadmus and Teiresias (II 1788–91, B360–3): let's go and pray. At II 1890–3, the Theotokos with the exhausted women quotes Agave and Cadmus (B1260–2) in a daze.

In the third play, III **Resurrection**, the women on the loose at the tomb (III 1994) are compared to the maenads on the mountain (B692); Christ escaping the tomb (III 2070–5) is like the bacchantes escaping prison (B445–8); the Theotokos' statement of faith at III 2100, 'King, you are god indeed', echoes the chorus to Dionysus on the death of Pentheus at B1031. At III 2194–2224 (before the subplot kicks in), the messenger telling of Christ leaving Hades makes good use of the first messenger on the women on the mountain (B667, 712, 713, 716). In the subplot (III 2194–2388), dialogue between guard and priests reflects the threats of Dionysus to Pentheus (for example III 2277 and 2286 use B787–91). Both the **Prayer to the Pantanax** (at III 2542) and the **Prayer to the Theotokos** (at III 2564) pick up the affirmation of the chorus (B1031) and the desperate plea of Pentheus to Agave (B1118–20) respectively. This is a terrible world that the trilogy paints.

The fortunes of the play from Victorian times have progressed from the privileging of a gentlemanly Pentheus, through an ecstatic dithyrambic Gilbert Murray evoked memorably in Shaw's *Major Barbara*, to an equation of the mass hysteria of fascist rallies with dionysiac frenzy. More recently, however, the play has spoken memorably to hippies, feminists and rebels of all shades with the Schechner interactionist production of *Dionysos in 69* in New York as a watershed (on one occasion the audience decided to rescue Pentheus); Maureen Duffy's focus on the women; Wole Soyinka's counter-cultural, racially mixed liberationist rebellion; Shared Experience's physical theatre treatment of where the line should be drawn in women's liberation; more recent treatments of what is true masculinity, as the shape-changing, play-acting, androgynous aspects of the play have been more fully understood, and productions demanded relevance to the Iraq war. All have seen the play as a conflict between radicalism and oppression.[30] The *Paschon* through *Bacchae* however considers the nature of religious experience, faith and defiance and, above all, the horror of violent death.[31]

I have only touched on the deployment of the four most frequently used source texts and the analysis needs to be complete in order to make the

---

[30] Stuttard (2016), and two dissertations: Powers (1999), Sampatakakis (2005).
[31] It has been understandably common for classicists (Pollmann [1997], Alexopoulou [2013]) to look for one-to-one correspondences between religious aspects of *Bacchae* and the *Paschon*. As Bryant Davies (2017) demonstrates, this search is illusory, not least because a close parallel with a pagan god would have been a hard sell in Byzantium. But this is not to deny a concentration on aspects of religion, e.g. cult and discipleship, expressed through *Bacchae*. More striking is the way horror is channelled through the story of Agave and Pentheus as well as Phaedra and Hippolytus and Medea and her children.

case complete. Much work remains to be done on this text, which engages with the gospel narrative in intertextuality with ancient drama. But we have seen enough to draw some very tentative conclusions.

Painting and Polyphony

The use of source texts in the *Christos Paschon* can be seen as painting: pointilliste[32] or sloshed on.[33] It is traditional, of course, in terms of its etymology to think of cento in terms of textile, whether weaving or patchwork.[34] But this assumes a complete cento in which every line is made up of earlier text. The source texts in the *Paschon* are used with care and intelligence, but not always in keeping with the stated aims of cento composition.[35] Complete lines taken over exactly are fewer than one might imagine, as are direct importations of half-lines. And there are long tracts of originally composed material, which is why painting is a better metaphor than textile.[36] Chunks of up to five or six lines are also common, sometimes starting fully followed by strategically placed odd words, sometimes starting with fragments and working up to a fuller quotation. Sometimes the substitutions are not caused by gender or number or tense but are more significant, and sometimes the reader is expected to remember the original formulation, as when θυμός is replaced by λύπη, βούλευμα by ἐλπίς.[37] Comparisons are important, but contrasts are also; we are asked

---

[32] For pointillism, see for example I 322–5, in the Virgin's Curse, using H1250–4, the messenger on the death of Hippolytus, which has two lines with only two syllables apiece. I 569–87, the Virgin with the chorus before the third messenger, using B285–312, Teiresias on Dionysus, offers odd words and no whole lines. II 1521–65, the *teleutaios aspasmos*, using Dionysus' appearance as a human in Thebes at B960–7, sometimes uses one word per line, sometimes four in a line but from different lines. I 598–604, the chorus's *chairetismoi* to the Virgin, uses all but *Rhesus*, with odd words rather than lines or half-lines. III 2389–2405, the Theotokos speaking after the fifth messenger has finished, uses all four major source texts but very sparsely.

[33] Broad-brush examples are I 347–50, which lifts M515–19 wholesale, Medea invoking Zeus, the Theotokos her Son, or III 1872–83, where the fourth messenger telling of the watch set on the tomb uses the speech of Alexander telling of the arrival of Achaean spies at R656–60. Longer blocks which at first sight are similar may turn out to be intricately assembled, like I 896–901, the fifth lament just after the death of Christ, which combines H839, H1408–10 and H1444–7, Hippolytus on the death of Phaedra, the dying Hippolytus to Theseus and Theseus on Hippolytus.

[34] There are examples, such as the first part of the Virgin's curse, I 267–88, where all but *Bacchae* are used with only 3/21 new lines.

[35] On cento technique, the fundamental locus is Ausonius' prose letter to Axius Paulus, prefatory to his *Cento nuptialis*, ed. Green (1991: 145–8), given with translation and good discussion in McGill (2005: 1–30). On the nature of cento in the *Paschon*, see Mullett (2021).

[36] For an alternative comparison, to the embedment of spolia in new architecture, see Mullett (2021).

[37] M1079 at I 744.

to read how different the Theotokos is from Medea as well as to consider their points of similarity. Sometimes two lines are combined into one, sometimes one is spread out into two, or one into three.[38] Sometimes change appears to be made for its own sake, to prove that it can be done;[39] sometimes very few words over several lines point out the source passage in a way that only the keenest ear could have detected.[40] Sometimes paraphrase rather than textual mimesis is found;[41] sometimes the same quotation appears at the beginning and end of an argument;[42] sometimes a shift in source text indicates stagecraft.[43] Doubling is another technique: using both Medea and Jason on parenting in the Theotokos' voice may say something about her as a mother.

Alternatively, the use of the source texts can be seen as polyphony: play I starts with *Medea*, *Hippolytus* enters at 50, *Rhesus* at 87, *Bacchae* at 161. We then see play by play accommodated politely with occasional themes from others. At times of the greatest emotion, polyphony is richest: at I 848, when the Theotokos realizes that Christ is dead, Agave's realization that she has killed her child (I 853–4, cf. B1280) is interwoven with Hippolytus seeing his stepmother dead (H902–12, cf. I 843–65), and Artemis realizing that Hippolytus is close to death (H1439, cf. I 850). At 1020–85, *Medea*, *Rhesus* and *Bacchae* combine to evoke a bloody sight.[44] In II, the moment of deposition (II 1298–1305) has all four texts conveying the shock of Medea's outrageous response to the messenger (M1127–8), Agave on Dionysus in the second messenger speech (B1147), Artemis telling Theseus to take Hippolytus inside (H1431–2) and a wake-up call for Hector from *Rhesus* (R7). At II 1340, the sixth lament passage uses the first part of the Muse's lament (915–49) and Cadmus' lament over Pentheus (B1314–15). Later (II 1453–6) it combines all four with the moment of Hippolytus' death (H1458), the introduction to the Muse's lament (R888), Cadmus bringing Pentheus' body into the palace (B1226) and Jason prevented from burying or

---

[38] E.g. R535–6 is combined into III 998; R555 spreads over III 2000–1; M1010 is stretched over I 1036, 1037 and 1038.

[39] R300 πάντ' for III 2455 τοῦδ' and R105 εὔβουλος for III 2367 πρόβουλος are possible cases.

[40] For example, III 2070–5 uses B445–8. The first line borrows half a word, the second none, the third half a word, the fourth one word, the fifth 2½ words and the sixth two words.

[41] For example, B1041 at I 373. [42] E.g. the use of M1244 at II 1275 and II 1309.

[43] As when a shift from *Rhesus* to *Bacchae* at 1809/1810 may signal Joseph's exit.

[44] At M37, 43 the nurse's fears of what Medea will do; at M1202 the sight of the poisoned bride; at M1252 the chorus after Medea has gone into the house to kill the children; at R790, 794 the driver on the death of Rhesus and his own bloody dream; at B1244, 1161–2, 1259–63, 1144 the death of Pentheus; B333–5, cf. I 1032, leads into the evocation of the death of Actaeon. The discovery of the body of Hippolytus at H1342 is not used.

mourning his boys (M1412). In III, which predominantly leans on *Rhesus*, Christ shocks with his one-word line *chairete* at 2097, and the Theotokos responds as Rhesus does to Hector on his first appearance (R388), as the chorus does to Dionysus acclaiming his power (B1031) and the horrible death of Jason's bride (M1195).

Contributing both to painting and polyphony is which parts of the source texts are chosen, the passages of highest emotion or horror.[45] Passages of high density[46] of quotation are, in *Medea*, the nurse's opening (M1–48), the nurse's exchange with the paedagogus (M49–95), Medea's speech as suppliant to Aegeus (M708–18), parts of the women of Corinth speech (M225–31, 250–8), the paedagogus and Medea at 1002–18, Medea awaiting the messenger (M1116–20) and Jason and Medea at the killing of the children (M1293–1316). In *Hippolytus*, his questioning of his father about the death of his stepmother (H902–15) and his farewell to his friends and home (H1090–1103); in *Rhesus*, Hector, Aeneas and the chorus (R34–165), Hector blaming the guards (R808–15) are densest. In *Bacchae*, Dionysus' opening (B1–63), Cadmus' speeches to Teiresias (B177–88, 210–14) and parts of the confrontation between Pentheus and Dionysus (B775–95) as well as everything from Agave's entrance at 1202 are very dense.

Source Texts and Trilogy

It might be argued, and I think the supposition underlies much puzzlement about the text, that the author would have been better off using the odd quotation if need be, but not weaving the complex web of intertext that we have seen. Less often condemned is the imperfection of the text as a cento: we have seen that quite a small proportion of lines from Euripides or other sources are used, and it is by no means completely stitched. What I think we can see is the rich impact of the intertext in terms of emotion and gore. It doubly shocks, it horrifies, it illuminates, it demands reflection. We have seen a steely and determined Theotokos who is also Artemis, the Muse and all the grieving parents (Creon, Theseus, Cadmus, Agave, the Muse), an ambitious and danger-courting Magdalen compared to Dolon, Odysseus and Diomedes, a Christ who is the shape-shifting Dionysus in his incarnation, the long-awaited saviour Rhesus who will not remain dead, Hippolytus the ascetic hero and Pentheus, the inert

---

[45] For further examination of tragic emotion in the text, see Mullett (2022).
[46] I.e. where around or slightly more than 50 per cent of the source text is used.

damaged hero in deposition and entombment. John the Theologian is the confident Hector; Joseph, who grows spiritually over the second play, is Medea's nurse.

It is, for our purposes, more important to ask what the trilogy tells us about the Byzantine reception of Euripides. We know that Euripides was probably more popular in Byzantium than at any time before the past thirty-five years in the late twentieth and early twenty-first centuries: for Anna Komnene, he was the Tragedian as Homer was the Poet, and it is Euripides that Michael Psellos chooses to compare (oddly to us) with George of Pisidia.[47] His plays, or at least those of the selection, were key to the school syllabus.[48] A Katowice PhD has indicated that Euripides appears in the *Katomyomachia* at moments of heightened emotion,[49] and the same goes for the *Christos Paschon*. We have seen a different Medea from the witch, the feminist, the monster of European reception, a *Bacchae* which focuses on horror rather than liberation or civil disobedience, a Hippolytus who is the protagonist of his own play, a truly Byzantine hero of the wars against *porneia* and a *Rhesus* of light and dark, sleep and wakefulness. Taken together, they cast light on Byzantine views of motherhood.[50]

But it is not just a Euripidean tragedy, it is a Komnenian one. It is important to understand not just the intertextual relationship between the core text and its intertexts, but also the intertextual relationships of our core text with its contemporaries, interaural as well as intervisual. There is a twist in that we have to decide between two possible reception milieux:

---

[47] The popularity of Euripides had increased over the Roman period; see Cribiore (2001a: 244): 'Euripides was by far the most popular of the tragedians in the Greco-Roman world.' As for the present day, see, in the context of a revival of interest in Greek tragedy since the 1970s, Hall (2004: 5): 'In the first half of 1995 more Euripides was performed in London than any other playwright, including Shakespeare.'

[48] Zuntz (1965: 255). With Cribiore (2001b) we begin to understand how this might have worked in the schoolroom rather than on the manuscript page, and with Woods (2019) the implications for performance.

[49] Warcaba (2017).

[50] The Theotokos of our text is, of course, no ordinary mother of the kind sought by Hatlie (2009), nor does she reflect perfectly his cardinal virtues of learning, nurturing, unwavering piety and indomitable spirit. Nor is she a politically astute and powerful Komnenian mother like Barbara Hill's empresses (1999). Nor is she a typical holy woman of Byzantium (not a battered housewife or cross-dressing jet-setter or competent abbess) or even a standard representation of the mother of God, if such a thing exists (Brubaker and Cunningham [2011]). What she mostly shows us is sacrifice and loss and her slow coming to terms with a long-dreaded, clearly projected and deeply suffered bereavement, experienced through grief, anger, self-control, eloquence, hope, all set against an overwhelming fear. We briefly see her through John's eyes as more vulnerable and less controlled than in the trilogy as a whole; throughout she takes on both the maternity and the losses of the strong women of her source texts (see e.g. Easterling [2003], Given [2009]) and her *pathos* is deepened and sharpened accordingly.

the Cappadocian milieu of Gregory of Nazianzos in the late fourth century or the Constantinople of the mid-twelfth century. I am firmly on the side of a twelfth-century date, and probably a date in the 1140s or 1150s, the high point of literary innovation in Byzantium.[51]

It is accepted that Byzantium at this time was a highly performative culture which pervaded the streets and public places of Constantinople with spectacle and ceremony, the churches with homilies and hymns, lawcourts with dicanic rhetoric, schoolrooms with *progymnasmata*, private houses with funerary rhetoric. On the page, monologue, stichomythia and dialogue were increasingly current, together with direct speech in narrative. The revival of Lucianic satire produced small dialogues, *dramatia*, which are very close to our text. Even closer are two parodic texts of the period, both with included lament: the narrative *semeioma* on the cannibal Maria told by the *protekdikos* Andronikos, and Theodore Prodromos' *Katomyomachia*, again centonic, tragic as well as mock-epic, learned and funny. Writing of all these kinds, for schoolroom or *theatron*, made the creation of something like our text possible.[52]

But these contexts of performative text which depends on classical forms or authors need to be supplemented by the context of commentary in the twelfth century. What has our text to do with Tzetzes or Eustathios or Anna Komnene's stable of commentators on Aristotle? One thing that must not be forgotten is that commentaries are themselves literary texts, and as much a boom genre in twelfth-century Byzantium as rhetoric or fiction or dialogue.[53] But at first sight, the picture is less cheerful. So many of the criteria arrived at to define commentary are absent in our text. It is not a systematic series of comments; it does not follow the order of the source text(s)[54] (quite the reverse in fact); it is not separate from the text in the margin or at the end[55] but integrated after *sparagmos*; it is not complete[56] or overtly problem-solving[57] or keyed to an agenda set by the text.[58] It shares a literary format with the source texts,[59] so cannot, according to some, be a commentary. We might add that it is not a commentary on a single text, or more than one in sequence, but on several interlaced.

---

[51] On the innovative literary milieu of the Komnenian period, see also Agapitos in this volume.
[52] Further on these literary contexts, see Mullett (2020).
[53] Cameron (2014) and (2016), Cameron and Gaul (2017). On the literary nature of commentary and self-commentary, see the important ongoing project of Aglae Pizzone, 'Exegesis and the Medieval Self'; see also Pizzone (2017).
[54] Budelmann (2002: 142), Kraus and Stray (2016b: 1).   [55] Kraus and Stray (2016b: 1).
[56] Murgia (1984: 314).   [57] Most (1999b: xiii).   [58] Kraus and Stray (2016b: 2).
[59] Kraus and Stray (2016b: 3).

But, fortunately, not all commentators on commentaries require these characteristics: Felix Budelmann insists on room for variation in commentary style[60] and Glenn Most explicitly rejects formal criteria in favour of a more cultural-historical approach.[61] Our text can fit into his commentary universe. His emphasis on empowerment fits well with what we have seen of the text, and his determined inclusion of poetic production would add a third column to Kraus's diagram distinguishing commentary from monograph: are there poetic texts which are not commentaries, he asks.[62] The *Paschon* has to do with canon:[63] the inclusion of *Rhesus* is intriguing, the other texts unsurprising. But it also fits some of Kraus's concerns: it is deeply concerned with segmentation, tralaticiousness (it needs to be determined whether the densest usages are precisely those which prevailed during Roman performances of the source texts) and parallels with the introduction of other tragedies in polyphony.[64] It is clearly a vehicle for the commentator's own views,[65] and without doubt preserves, comments on and adapts the ancient dramatic heritage;[66] note its appearance in all commentaries on *Bacchae*, for example.

We should remember that we are dealing with three things, only one of which have I considered here in any depth. They are plot, form and texture.[67] Plot gives us the story of the four gospels and the apocryphal gospels already worked over by hymns and sermons: the choice of episodes, the arrangement of dramatis personae, the spatial arrangements of the text are in themselves a commentary on the gospel harmony current in the author's day.[68] Form gives us the mimesis of tragedy, a kind of macro-commentary, in which the author highlights what features he sees as most important in tragic form: we might single out messenger speeches and laments. Texture gives us the microcommentary on specific speeches, passages, lines and half-lines of the source texts: by selection, density, voicing, painting and polyphony.

These approaches to the original texts empower the source texts, emphasizing their most eloquent and emotional passages, allowing them to be voiced by holy figures of the holiest of narratives, allowing that story to shine forth in

---

[60] Budelmann (2002: 143). [61] Most (1999b: i).
[62] Most (1999b: xiii). Kraus (2002: 2) opposes 'empirical', 'objective', 'common-sense', 'wissenschaftlich', 'positivist', 'useful' as attributes of commentary to 'subjective', 'transient', 'rhetorical', 'coherent' as attributes of monographs; attributes for creative mimesis might begin with 'ludic', 'evaluative', 'selective', 'affirmative', 'celebratory'.
[63] Most (1999b: xiii). [64] Kraus (2002: 10–22). [65] O'Donnell (2000).
[66] See above, Introduction, p. 25.
[67] I am not attempting here a narratological commentary, though I hope to, and use here different vocabulary from any currently accepted school.
[68] On biblical exegesis in the Komnenian period, see Agapitos in this volume.

full Euripidean glory. But they also emulate the ancient authors both at micro and macro levels. And this leads to the contemporary purposes of the text: I cannot (yet?) see anything as clear as a theological or political purpose to the text; what is clear is ludic and agonistic display in a demonstration of mastery of the source texts and also a desire to take tragedy further, to innovate and show the inventive experimentation of the mid-twelfth century at its best. These are often the elements which have most puzzled scholars: the comic subplot with Pilate, the priests and the guard, and the mixture of diegesis and mimesis in moments of greatest horror like the piercing of the side. The anonymous author (in Most's words)[69] attaches his own easily forgettable name to the immortal name(s) of the author(s) – in fact it could be argued that he might have done it twice: Euripides and Gregory of Nazianzos were a powerful combination in the twelfth century. It is didactic, and possibly designed for schoolroom as well as *theatron*; like many commentaries it may have been dictated and held together by oral delivery.[70] That it relates to the literary production of the time is quite clear; despite its status as unicum, it is patently close to some of the most innovative texts of the period (the *Life of Cyril Phileotes* in its handling of syllogistic material, the letters of James of Kokkinobaphos as cento, the cannibal poem in its generic hybridism and high emotional content, the *Katomyomachia* in its classical mimesis).[71]

Whether this text represents appropriation or emulation or both is a question for elsewhere,[72] but it is certainly reception, an earlier reception of Euripides than is customarily discussed in modern studies: the Theotokos in 1140 might turn out to be just as interesting as Dionysus in 69.[73] And it is Laird's 'hermeneutic reconstruction' (after deconstruction), exegesis more 'flexible, fluid, adventurous'.[74] Flawed, puzzling, troubling, unequal to its source texts though it may be, the *Christos Paschon* is never dull; this commentary is not 'duller than the text(s) on which it is based'.[75]

REFERENCES

Agapitos, P. A. (1998) 'Narrative, Rhetoric and "Drama" Rediscovered: Scholars and Poets in Byzantium Interpret Heliodorus', in *Studies in Heliodorus*, ed. R. Hunter, 125–56. Cambridge Philological Society, Supplementary Volume 21. Cambridge.

---

[69] Most (1999b: xiv).
[70] Budelmann (2002: 155); cf. Woods (2019: 10), who suggests how this can happen in the classroom.
[71] Sargologos (1964), Hunger (1968b), Macrides (1985: 137–68), Jeffreys and Jeffreys (2009).
[72] I deal with this question in Mullett (2021). [73] Zeitlin (2004). [74] Laird (2002: 178, 198).
[75] Robin Nisbet quoted in Henderson (2002: 205, n. 3).

Alexiou, M. (1975) 'The Lament of the Virgin in Byzantine Literature and Modern Greek Folk-Song', *BMGS* 1: 111–40.

Alexopoulou, M. (2013) '*Christus patiens* and the Reception of Euripides' *Bacchae* in Byzantium', in *Dialogues with the Past 1: Classical Reception. Theory and Practice*, ed. A. Bakogianni, 123–37. Bulletin of the Institute of Classical Studies Supplements 126.1. London.

Baun, J. (2011) 'Apocalyptic Panagia: Some Byways of Marian Revelation in Byzantium', in Brubaker and Cunningham (eds.), 199–218.

Bernier-Farella, H. (2015) 'Ritual Voices and Social Silence: Funerary Lamentations in Byzantium', *Voice and Voicelessness in Medieval Europe*, ed. I. R. Kleiman, 47–63. Basingstoke–New York.

Brambs, J. G. (ed.) (1885) *Christus Patiens: Tragoedia quae inscribi solet CHRISTOS PASCHON Gregorio Nazianzeno falso attributa*. Leipzig.

Browning, R. (1963) 'A Byzantine Treatise on Tragedy', in *Geras: Studies Presented to George Thomson on the Occasion of His 60th Birthday*, ed. V. Varcl and R. F. Willetts, in collaboration with B. Borecký, J. Burian, J. Frel and J. Pečírka, 67–81. Acta Universitatis Carolinae. Prague.

Brubaker, L. and M. B. Cunningham (eds.) (2011) *The Cult of the Mother of God in Byzantium: Texts and Images*. Birmingham Byzantine and Ottoman Studies. Farnham.

Bryant Davies, R. (2017) 'The Figure of Mary Mother of God in *Christus patiens*: Fragmentary Tragic Myth and Passion Narrative in a Byzantine Appropriation of Euripidean Tragedy', *JHS* 137: 1–25.

Budelmann, F. (2002) 'Classical Commentary in Byzantium: John Tzetzes on Ancient Greek Literature', in Gibson and Kraus (eds.), 141–69.

Cameron, A. (2014) *Dialoguing in Late Antiquity*. Cambridge, MA.

(2016) *Arguing It Out: Discussion in Twelfth-Century Byzantium*. Budapest.

Cameron, A. and N. Gaul (eds.) (2017) *Dialogues and Debates from Late Antiquity to Late Byzantium*. Abingdon.

Carr, M. (2002) *By the Bog of Cats*. New York.

Cribiore, R. (2001a) 'Euripides' *Phoenissae* in Hellenistic and Roman Education', *Education in Greek and Roman Antiquity*, ed. Y. L. Too, 241–59. Leiden.

(2001b) *Gymnastics of the Mind: Greek Education in Hellenistic and Roman Egypt*. Princeton–Oxford.

Dostálová, R. (1982) 'Die byzantinische Theorie des Dramas und die Tragödie Christos Paschon', *JÖByz* 32: 73–82.

Dübner, F. (1846) *Christus patiens, Ezechieli et christianorum poetarum reliquiae dramaticae*. Paris.

Dyck, A. R. (ed. and trans.) (1986) *Michael Psellus, The Essays on Euripides and George of Pisidia and on Heliodorus and Achilles Tatius*. Byzantina Vindobonensia 16. Vienna.

Easterling, P. E. (2003) 'The Infanticide in Euripides' *Medea*', in *Oxford Readings in Classical Studies: Euripides*, ed. J. Mossman, 177–92. Oxford.

Fries, A. (2018) 'The *Rhesus*', in *Greek Tragedy after the Fifth Century: A Survey from ca. 400 BC to ca. AD 400*, ed. V. Liapis and A. K. Petrides, 66–89. Cambridge.

Gaul, N. (2018) 'Performative Reading in the Late Byzantine *Theatron*', in *Reading in the Byzantine Empire*, ed. T. Shawcross and I. Toth, 215–33. Cambridge.
  (2020) 'The Letter in the *Theatron*: Epistolary Voice, Character, and Soul (and Their Audience)', in *Companion to Byzantine Epistolography*, ed. A. Riehle, 353–73. Brill's Companions to the Byzantine World 7. Leiden–Boston.
Gibson, R. K. and C. S. Kraus (eds.) (2002) *The Classical Commentary: Histories, Practices, Theory*. Mnemosyne Supplements 232. Leiden–Boston–Cologne.
Given, J. (2009) 'Constructions of Motherhood in Euripides' *Medea*', in *Text and Presentation 2008*, ed. S. Constantinidis, 42–54. Jefferson, NC.
Green, R. P. H. (1991) *The Works of Ausonius*. Oxford.
Hall, E. (2004) 'Introduction: Why Greek Tragedy in the Late Twentieth Century?', in Hall, Macintosh and Wrigley (eds.), 1–46.
Hall, E., F. Macintosh and O. Taplin (eds.) (2000) *Medea in Performance 1500–2000*. Oxford.
Hall, E., F. Macintosh and A. Wrigley (eds.) (2004) *Dionysus since 69: Greek Tragedy at the Dawn of the Third Millennium*. Oxford.
Hatlie, P. (2009) 'Images of Motherhood and Self in Byzantine Literature', *DOP* 63: 31–57.
Henderson, J. (2002) 'The Way We Were: R. G. Austin, *In Caelianam*', in Gibson and Kraus (eds.), 205–34.
Hilberg, I. H. (1886) 'Kann Theodoros Prodromos der Verfasser des Χριστός Πάσχων sein?', *WS* 8: 282–314.
Hill, B. (1999) *Imperial Women in Byzantium, 1025–1204: Power, Patronage and Ideology*. London.
Hörandner, W. (1988) 'Lexikalische Beobachtungen zum *Christos Paschon*', in *Studien zur byzantinischen Lexikographie*, ed. E. Trapp, J. Diethart, G. Fatouros, A. Steiner and W. Hörandner, 183–202. Vienna.
Horna, K. (1929) 'Der Verfasser der *Christus patiens*', *Hermes* 64: 429–31.
Housman, A. E. (1901) 'Fragment of a Greek Tragedy', *Cornhill Magazine* 10: 443–5.
Hunger, H. (1968a) 'Die byzantinische Literatur der Komnenenzeit', *Anzeiger der philologisch-historischen Klasse der österreichischen Akademie der Wissenschaften* 105: 63–5.
  (ed.) (1968b) *Der byzantinische Katz-Mäuse-Krieg: Theodoros Prodromos, Katomyomachia. Einleitung, Text und Übersetzung*. Byzantina Vindobonensia 3. Graz–Vienna–Cologne.
Jeffreys, E. M. and M. J. Jeffreys (2009) *Iacobi Monachi Epistulae*. Corpus Christianorum, Series Graeca 68. Turnhout.
Kazhdan, A. P. and A. Wharton Epstein (1985) *Change in Byzantine Culture in the Eleventh and Twelfth Centuries*. The Transformation of the Classical Heritage 7. Berkeley–Los Angeles–London.
Kraus, C. S. (2002) 'Introduction: Reading Commentaries/Commentaries as Reading', in Gibson and Kraus (eds.), 1–27.

Kraus, C. S. and C. A. Stray (eds.) (2016a) *Classical Commentaries: Explorations in a Scholarly Genre*. Oxford.
Kraus, C. S. and C. A. Stray (2016b) 'Form and Content', in Kraus and Stray (eds.), 1–18.
Lauriola, R. and K. Demetriou (eds.) (2015) *Brill's Companion to the Reception of Euripides*. Brill's Companions to Classical Reception 3. Leiden–Boston.
Laird, A. (2002) 'Juan Luis de la Cerda and the Predicament of Commentary', in Gibson and Kraus (eds.), 171–203.
Liapis, V. (2011) *A Commentary on the Rhesus Attributed to Euripides*. Oxford.
McGill, S. (2005) *Virgil Recomposed: The Mythological and Secular Centos in Antiquity*. Oxford.
McKee, T. L. (2017) 'A Rich Reward in Tears: Hippolytus and Phaedra in Drama, Dance, Opera and Film', unpublished PhD thesis, The Open University.
Macrides, R. (1985) 'Poetic Justice in the Patriarchate: Murder and Cannibalism in the Provinces', in *Cupido Legum*, ed. L. Burgmann, M. T. Fögen and A. Schminck, 137–68. Frankfurt am Main.
Marciniak, P. (2004) *Greek Drama in Byzantine Times*. Katowice.
 (2007) 'Byzantine *Theatron* – A Place of Performance?', in *Theatron: Rhetorische Kultur in Spätantike und Mittelalter / Rhetorical Culture in Late Antiquity and the Middle Ages*, ed. M. Grünbart, 277–85. Millennium-Studien 13. Berlin–New York.
 (2013) 'Theodore Prodromos' *Bion Prasis*: A Reappraisal', *GRBS* 53: 219–39.
 (2022) 'Sophocles, Euripides and the Unusual Cento', in *After the Text: Byzantine Enquiries in Honour of Margaret Mullett*, ed. L. James, O. Nicholson and R. Scott, 167–75. Birmingham Byzantine and Ottoman Studies. Abingdon.
Mills, S. (2013) *Euripides, Hippolytus*. Duckworth Companions to Greek and Roman Tragedy. London.
Most, G. W. (ed.) (1999a) *Commentaries = Kommentare*. Aporemata: Kritische Studien zur Philologiegeschichte 4. Göttingen.
 (1999b) 'Preface', in Most (1999a), vii–xv.
Mullett, M. (1984) 'Aristocracy and Patronage in the Literary Circles of Comnenian Constantinople', in *The Byzantine Aristocracy, IX to XIII Centuries*, ed. M. Angold, 173–201. BAR International Series 221. Oxford.
 (2020) 'Contexts for the *Christos Paschon*', in *The Eloquence of Art: Studies in Honour of Henry Maguire*, ed. A. Olsen Lam and R. Schroeder, 204–17. Abingdon.
 (2021) 'Spoiling the Hellenes: Intertextuality, Appropriation, Embedment', in *Spoliation as Translation: Medieval Worlds in the Eastern Mediterranean*, ed. I. Jevtic and I. Nilsson, 99–115. *Convivium*, Supplementum 2021.2. Brno.
 (2022) 'Tragic Emotions? The *Christos Paschon*', in *Emotions through Time: From Antiquity to Byzantium*, ed. D. Cairns, M. Hinterberger, A. Pizzone and M. Zaccarini, 281–302. Tübingen.
 (forthcoming a) 'Performability, Lament, and the Tragedy *Christos Paschon*', in *Lament as Performance in Byzantium*, ed. N. Tsironi. Abingdon.
 (forthcoming b) '*Christos Paschon*: Sacred or Secular?', ed. N. Tsironi.
 (forthcoming c) 'Performance Issues in the *Christos Paschon*', ed. N. Tsironi.

Murgia, C. E. (1984) 'Tacitus auctus', *CP* 79: 314–26.
Nilsson, I. (2017) 'To Touch or Not to Touch: Erotic Tactility in Byzantine Literature', in *Knowing Bodies, Passionate Souls: Sense Perceptions in Byzantium*, ed. S. Ashbrook Harvey and M. Mullett, 239–57. Washington, DC.
O'Donnell, J. (2000) Review of Most (1999a), *BMCR* 2000.05.19.
Pizzone, A. (2017) 'The *Historiai* of John Tzetzes: A Byzantine "Book of Memory"?' *BMGS* 41.2: 182–207.
Pollmann, K. (1997) 'Jesus Christus und Dionysos', *JÖByz* 47: 87–106.
Powers, M. (1999) 'The Reception of Euripides' *Bacchae* in Performance from 1960 to the Present', unpublished MSt thesis, University of Oxford.
Sampatakakis, G. (2005) 'Bakkhai-Model: The Re-Usage of Euripides' *Bakkhai* in Text and Performance', unpublished PhD thesis, University of London.
Sargologos, E. (ed.) (1964) *La vie de saint Cyrille le Philéote, moine byzantine (+1110)*. Subsidia Hagiographica 39. Brussels.
Sihra, M. (2005) 'Greek Myth, Irish Reality: Marina Carr's *By the Bog of Cats ...*', in *Rebel Women: Staging Ancient Greek Drama Today*, ed. J. Dillon and S. Wilmer, 115–35. London.
Sluiter, I. (1999) 'Commentaries and the Didactic Tradition', in Most (ed.), 173–205.
Stuttard, D. (ed.) (2014) *Looking at Medea*. London.
  (ed.) (2016) *Looking at Bacchae*. London.
Taplin, O. and J. Billings (2010) 'What Does Tragedy Do for People?', podcast (Oxford) http://podcasts.ox.ac.uk/what-does-tragedy-do-people 1 March 2010, accessed 27 December 2019.
Tóibín, C. (2012) *The Testament of Mary*. London.
Tuilier, A. (ed.) (1969) *Grégoire de Nazianze, La Passion du Christ, Tragédie: introduction, texte critique, traduction, notes et index*. Sources Chrétiennes 149. Paris.
Vakonakis, N. (2011) *Das griechische Drama auf dem Weg nach Byzanz: Der euripideische Cento Christos Paschon*. Classica monacensia 42. Tübingen.
Warcaba, K. (2017) *Bizantyński epos dla średnio zaawansowanych: Katomyomachia Teodora Prodromosa jako tekst trzeciego stopnia (Byzantine Epic Poetry for Intermediate Students: The Katomyomachia by Theodore Prodromos as an Example of Genette's 'Literature in the Third Degree')*. Katowice.
Wilmer, S. E. (2005) 'Irish Medeas: Revenge or Redemption (An Irish Solution to An International Problem)', in *Rebel Women: Staging Ancient Greek Drama Today*, ed. J. Dillon and S. Wilmer, 136–48. London.
Wojtylak-Heszen, A. (2004) *Tragedia Póżnoantyczna ΧΡΙΣΤΟΣ ΠΑΣΧΩΝ a jej źródła klasyczne*. Biblioteka Tradycji 29. Krakow.
Woods, M. C. (2019) *Weeping for Dido: The Classics in the Medieval Classroom*. Princeton–Oxford.
Zuntz, G. (1965) *An Inquiry into the Transmission of the Plays of Euripides*. Cambridge.
Zeitlin, F. I. (2004) 'Dionysus in 69', in Hall, Macintosh and Wrigley (eds.), 49–75.

CHAPTER 9

Parodying Antiquity for Pleasure and Learning
The Idyll *by Maximos Planoudes*

Krystina Kubina

Maximos Planoudes is well known for his engagement with classical literature, including his collection of epigrams, the *Planoudean Anthology*, his critical editions of and scholia for classical texts and his translations of Latin literature.[1] His own poetic production is less well known. Some thirty-six poems have come down to us under his name, the majority of which are epigrams on secular and religious topics rooted in ancient tradition but clearly Byzantine in subject and style.[2] In addition to Planoudes' epigrams, some of his translations of Latin secular literature also include metrical components, most notably his rendering of Boethius' *Consolation of Philosophy*, where he imitates the prosimetric form of the original, employing twenty-seven different metres in his translation.[3] Entirely different from the rest of his work is a dialogic poem of 270 hexameters usually referred to as an idyll, which has been neglected in scholarship.[4] It is a humorous piece drawing on numerous ancient sources, especially bucolic poetry in the

---

* I am grateful to my friends and colleagues Andreas Rhoby and Nikos Zagklas as well as to the editors of this volume for their insightful comments on earlier versions of this chapter. I also thank Zachary Rothstein-Dowden for his help that by far exceeded language proof. An earlier draft was presented at a lecture for the Austrian Byzantine Society and I am grateful for the critical remarks of the audience. I thank M. Lauxtermann, C. Messis and N. Zagklas for sharing their unpublished work with me. This article was written as part of the project 'Late Byzantine Poetry from the Fourth Crusade until the End of the Empire', funded by the Austrian Science Fund (FWF project no. T1045–G25).

[1] For an introduction to the life and work of Planoudes, see Wendel (1950); now with further literature, Taxidis (2012: 17–29); on Planoudes' engagement with classical learning, see, among others, Constantinides (1982: 66–89), Wilson (1996: 230–41), Mergiali (1996: 34–42), Pérez Martín (1997) and (with caution) Fryde (2000: 226–67).

[2] Recently edited with commentary by Taxidis (2017); on epigrams in the middle and late Byzantine period including a discussion of Planoudes, see Drpić (2016).

[3] Planoudes' translation of the *Distichs of Cato* is entirely in verse, while his translation of Ovid's *Metamorphoses* and *Heroides* are almost entirely written in prose with only few metrical parts. On his translations, see, among others, Anagnostou-Laoutides (2017), Fisher (2004), Fisher (2002/2003) and (with caution) Fodor (2004).

[4] Ed. Pontani (1973: 12–26) and earlier Holzinger (1893: 12–20), first partial edition (vv. 78–141) by Cyrillo (1832: 148–55). For some text-critical remarks, see Kurtz (1893), Schneider (1894). I cite Pontani's edition. See also Wendel (1950: 2219–20) and the (mostly unconvincing) article by Nissen

tradition of Theocritus and on Lucian's satires. In the first part of this article, I will offer a close reading of the text with regard to the topics of love and homoeroticism, the alterity of otherworlds and magic and the marvellous. I will then investigate the connection of this *Idyll* to other literary traditions and to Planoudes' scholarship as a whole, as well as the reception of the poem in Byzantium. I will close with some considerations on its nature as a parody. The *Idyll* will be analysed in its manifold relations with ancient literature or, in other words, its hypertextuality.[5] As a parody, the *Idyll* creatively comments on ancient texts by using topics, motifs and other literary borrowings drawn from these, while at the same time transgressing the limits of a commentary proper. As I will show, Planoudes creates with his *Idyll* a parody of ancient texts and authors that is both entertaining and instructive while being unique in its setting and context.

The plot of the *Idyll* is as follows: Kleodemos visits his friend Thamyras, a peasant like himself, who reproaches him for his long absence. The former informs his friend of the tragic death of his ox, which had caused him great misery. To buy a new ox, Kleodemos had gone to the city of Aithra at Mount Olympus, where he met an Egyptian sorcerer amongst a crowd of feasting people. This sorcerer announced that he wanted to know what Zeus was doing at that very moment and so performed a miraculous show, sending first two apples and finally his young attendant to heaven so that he might learn from them about the gods. When they return, the young man reports that the gods are celebrating the wedding of Ares and Aphrodite. Kleodemos continues his narrative, explaining that he then purchased a strong ox from the sorcerer. However, when he had brought the animal home and washed it, it turned into a mouse and immediately began eating all the food stored in the house. Thamyras promises his friend a mousetrap and invites him over for dinner.

As this summary shows, the poem consists of three main parts (greeting scene, report about Aithra, problems with the mouse) in which four different speakers are featured (Thamyras, Kleodemos, the Egyptian, his attendant) and which includes three narrative spaces (the rural sphere including Thamyras' and Kleodemos' houses, the city of Aithra and Mount Olympus).

(1936). Pontani (1973: 6, n. 13) cites an MA thesis by M. Burei, 'L'idilio di Massimo Planude', Padua 1968, which was not available to me.

[5] The term hypertextuality was coined by Genette, who defines it as 'any relationship uniting a text B (which I shall call the hypertext) to an earlier text A (I shall, of course, call it the hypotext), upon which it is crafted in a manner that is not that of commentary' (Genette [1997: 5]).

Content	vv.	Speakers	Space
Greeting scene	1–52	Thamyras, Kleodemos	Thamyras' house
Report about visit to Aithra	53–174	Kleodemos	Aithra
Description of Aithra	53–77	Kleodemos	Aithra
Magic performance	78–174	Kleodemos; direct speeches from Egyptian (102–13, 144–9) and attendant (155–73)	Aithra; Olympus (report from attendant)
Problems with the mouse	175–270	Thamyras, Kleodemos	Kleodemos' house; Thamyras' house

The poem is preceded by a short summary (*hypothesis*), which starts: ἡ τοῦ παρόντος εἴδους ὑπόθεσίς ἐστιν αὕτη ('The content of the present idyll is the following'). This kind of introduction is well known from Byzantine manuscripts transmitting Theocritus' *Idylls*. Additionally, the term *eidos* as an alternative to *eidyllion* explicitly refers to this first most relevant context, namely ancient bucolic poetry.[6] The poem's form and length fit this scheme, especially Planoudes' choice of the hexameter, as well as the dialogue and the linguistic borrowings from Theocritus.[7] The bucolic setting of two friendly peasants in conversation and the extended references to the ox and Kleodemos' household also create a pastoral environment. Secondly, the poem alludes to Lucian of Samosata and in particular to his *Symposium*. The key for the identification of this hypotext is the name of the protagonist Kleodemos, which is also found in Lucian, namely in the *Symposium* and in the *Lover of Lies*. Throughout the whole poem, there is a strong connection to the *Symposium* both in its motifs and structure. The *Idyll* as a parody of classical texts thus has a strong and complex hypertextual relationship with Theocritus, Lucian and other ancient authors and texts.

Love and Homoerotic Elements

Maximos Planoudes is certainly not the first Byzantine author who comes to mind when thinking about love in Byzantine literature. In his *Idyll*,

---

[6] Εἰδύλλιον is a diminutive of εἶδος, as is noted in the scholia to Theocritus (see scholium *Prolegomena E*, ed. Wendel [1914: 5]). See also *Prolegomena* VII, ed. Dübner (1849: 2), which is preserved in Naples, Biblioteca Nazionale 'Vittorio Emanuele III', II.F.9, fol. 215, a manuscript that also transmits Planoudes' *Idyll* (see below).

[7] For Theocritean expressions, see the critical apparatus by Pontani.

however, he plays with erotic and especially homoerotic discourse in a subtle way that requires careful reading.

Homoeroticism in Planoudes' *Idyll* is chiefly connected to the protagonists, Thamyras and Kleodemos on the one hand, the Egyptian and his attendant on the other. In the expanded salutatory scene between the two peasants, the Theocritean setting and the playful dealing with love are clear (vv. 1–44). The friends refer to a dinner at the house of their friend Aristaios during a feast honouring Demeter (see vv. 7–9).[8] Demeter is the goddess of agriculture *par excellence* and hence omnipresent in bucolic idylls, and Aristaios is the name of a rustic god with the epithet *Nomios* ('pastoral').[9] However, the name also connects the *Idyll* with Lucian's *Symposium*, which tells the story of a wedding feast in the house of a certain Aristainetos. The similarity between the names Aristaios and Aristainetos underlines the importance of the satirical hypotext. The use of the name Aristaios thus combines Theocritean and Lucianic elements. The initial tone between the two friends, when Thamyras starts by assuring Kleodemos of his heartfelt love, is well known from idylls:

(*Thamyras*) ὡς ἐρατός, Κλεόδημε, τεῷ παρ' ἑταίρῳ ἱκάνεις,
ὡς φίλιος φιλέοντι καὶ ὡς ποθέων ποθέοντι.
τίς τίνι γὰρ πεφίλητο τοσαῦτα, τίς ὡς σὺ ἔμοιγε;
τίς τίνι τόσσ' ἀγαπάζεται ὡς σὺ φιλῇ παρ' ἐμεῖο; (vv. 1–4)

Like a lover to his beloved, Kleodemos, you come to your companion, like a friend to a friend and like one yearning (for his friend) to another so yearning. Who was ever loved by whom as much as you by me? Who is so much treated with affection by someone as you are loved by me?

The words he uses can be connected to a discourse among friends prevalent in Byzantine literature and especially in epistolography,[10] but their intensity also points to (homo)erotic love, as this is a common theme in bucolic poetry (see esp. ἐρατός, ἑταῖρος, φίλιος, ποθέω, ἀγαπάζω). That Thamyras sees his friend as a lover becomes all the more obvious from his name. In Greek mythology, Thamyras was a singer who haughtily offended the Muses and who was, more relevantly,

---

[8] Theocritus' *Idyll* 7 begins in a similar setting where the protagonists speak about a reunion at the Thalysia, a feast honouring Demeter.
[9] On Aristaios Nomios, see e.g. Nonnos, *Dionysiaka* 5.215 and 29.180–1 ed. Keydell.
[10] See below p. 254.

considered to be the inventor of homoerotic love amongst men.[11] Kleodemos in Lucian's *Symposium*, on the other hand, is described as an adulterer and a paederast who had an affair with a cupbearer.[12]

Although Kleodemos in the *Idyll* states that he feels the same passionate love for Thamyras as the latter does for him, he soon changes the topic and becomes upset because his best ox has died. In his negation of Thamyras' erotic advances through his grieving for the ox, Planoudes' Kleodemos deviates from the known lascivious nature of Lucian's character. The scene has the effect of exaggerating the worth of the animal and ridiculing the affection of Thamyras. Making the clash of Thamyras' love for his friend and Kleodemos' love for his ox even more obvious, Kleodemos uses the same words and thoughts to describe his ox that Thamyras uses for his friend.[13] The humour of the situation is further enhanced through the elaborate description of the ox and his death. Planoudes uses two *hapax legomena* (v. 18: ἀμφοκλάσσας, 'twisting [his ankle] all around'; v. 22: παρπροθέων, 'run before on the side') and the attribute ἀελλήεις ('storm-swift', v. 23) for the ox (a Nonnian epithet certainly not suitable for a yoked ox). Keeping in mind that Lucian's Kleodemos is a philosopher of the peripatos, a philosophical school known for its emphasis on restraint of the passions, his unrestrained lament renders him even more ridiculous. The same holds true for a passage at the end of the poem where Kleodemos voices his fear of being transformed into an animal by the Egyptian, should he ever see him again. He is specifically afraid of being transformed into a billy goat (τράγος, see v. 252). That it is the billy goat of all animals is another pun in line with the erotic undertone of the *Idyll*, as billy goats, both in ancient Greece and in Byzantine satires, were traditional symbols of stupidity and, more importantly in this context, of lasciviousness.[14]

---

[11] The more common form of the name is Thamyris; see on homoerotic love *Souda* s.v. Θάμυρις ἢ Θαμύρας ed. Adler and Pseudo-Apollodorus 1.16–17 ed. Wagner.

[12] See Lucian, *Symposium* 15 and 32 ed. MacLeod.

[13] See ἀγαπάζω v. 4 about Kleodemos: *(Kleodemos)* τίς τίνι τόσσ' ἀγαπάζεται ὡς σὺ φιλῇ παρ' ἐμεῖο; ('Who is so much treated with affection as you are loved by me?') and v. 17 about the ox: ..., ὃν ἐκ θυμοῦ ἀγάπαζον ('whom I loved from the bottom of my heart'). Furthermore, Thamyras bemoans Kleodemos' forgetfulness towards him (see vv. 38–9), while Kleodemos, although claiming not to have forgotten his friend (see v. 15), focuses on the fact that he will never forget the ox (see vv. 24 and 26: *[Kleodemos]* μήποτε μήποτε τοῖο κίχησιν ἐμὴν φρένα λήθη, 'May forgetfulness of this never ever overtake my mind').

[14] Richter (1972: 420–1 and 429).

Kleodemos and Thamyras are thus characterized through their erotic desires in an unflattering way and ridiculed from the beginning.

The erotic discourse returns to the stage with the Egyptian and his assistant. The latter is called ἠίθεος several times (vv. 91, 137, 141, 146), denoting an unmarried youth who is on the verge of passing from childhood to manhood, thus being of an ideal age for a paederastic relationship.[15] On the other hand, the attendant calls the sorcerer an ἀμφίπολος which, although occasionally used in the masculine, usually means 'handmaid' or 'priestess'[16] and thus characterizes the Egyptian as an effeminate priest. The sorcerer and his attendant in their boyish and effeminate character thus mirror Kleodemos and Thamyras in the homoerotic tone and allusions.

The sorcerer declares that he is interested in Zeus. The motif of an individual who wishes to learn about the gods can be found in Lucian's *Icaromenippus* among other texts, in which the protagonist constructs wings for himself and flies to heaven from Mount Olympus, where he, too, takes part in a divine banquet. Yet, while Menippus, the protagonist of Lucian's text, wants to know about philosophical issues, Planoudes' Egyptian is eager to learn about the activities of Zeus and his love life:

> *(the sorcerer)* αὐτὰρ ἐγὼν ἐθέλω μαθέειν τί ποτ' ἔλλαχεν ἔρδων
> ὑψιμέδων Κρονίδης νῦν ὄμβριμος, ἢ ὅ γε κεῖνος
> ἐσθίει ἢ λέκτροισι παρήμενος αἰετὸς ὄρνις
> δὴν γάνυται Γανυμήδεος ἠὲ θεῶν ἄπο μοῦνος,
> ὄφρα κε μὴ νοέῃ ζηλήμων ἔξοχον Ἥρη,
> λῦσαι παρθενικῆς τινος ἵεται ἅμμα κορείης. (vv. 108–13)

> But I wish to know what the mighty son of Cronos, ruling on high, does now; whether he eats, or whether, lying in bed as an eagle, takes protracted pleasure in [the company of] Ganymede, or whether he, by himself away from the gods, lest his most jealous wife, Hera, take notice, is eager to loosen the knot of some virgin maiden.

The erotic discourse continues when the sorcerer throws two apples, one after another, to heaven to report on the gods. The apple traditionally was an erotic symbol in Byzantine literature which was often (but not

---

[15] See LSJ s.v. ἠίθεος. The term is often used in the *Greek Anthology* in connection to paederasty; see e.g. *Anthologia Graeca* (ed. Beckby) XII 54.2, 91.4, 96.5 and many more.
[16] See LSJ s.v. ἀμφίπολος and in the same vein *Souda* (ed. Adler) s.v. and Photios, *Lexicon* (ed. Theodoridis) s.v.

exclusively) connected with weddings.[17] Moreover, in several texts, the apple was connected with magic, or more precisely love magic, which links the apple to the witchcraft of the sorcerer – the most famous parallel being, of course, the apple of discord thrown by Eris.[18] When neither of the apples comes back to earth, the Egyptian loses his temper and throws his young assistant up to heaven (vv. 114–41). When he comes back from Olympus, he brings a chicken leg that Zeus gave him as a gift for the Egyptian (vv. 151–2 and 172–4):

> (the attendant) αὐτίκα τὸν πόδα τὸν καθορᾷς μοὶ χερσὶν ὄρεξε
> καί σε φῆ ἀντιγεγηθέναι, ἀμφιπόλων τὸν ἄριστον. (vv. 172–4)
>
> Immediately, he placed the leg which you can see into my hands and said that you yourself should rejoice in turn, you, the best of priests.

The passage relates to certain epigrams in the *Greek Anthology*, where a man promises to offer a cock to Apollo if the latter will bring him back his adolescent lover Polemon, who was on a long journey.[19] Yet, when his lover comes back, he has grown a beard and is thus no longer erotically desirable company, so that the speaker refrains from his sacrifice. The epigrams are not included in Planoudes' edition of the *Anthology*, but one can assume that he knew them from other sources. Secondly, the strange gift can be explained through the hypotext of Lucian's *Symposium*. There a brutal and bloody fight between philosophers breaks out over a chicken (*Symp.* 42–3). The chicken leg thus reintroduces the comic tone, which, however, is only understandable for readers familiar with the *Symposium*.

Although love outside marriage is prevalent in both the bucolic setting and Aithra, the gods provide an unexpected counterpart. The Egyptian first prophesies (and the attendant later confirms) that in Olympus they are celebrating the wedding of Ares and Aphrodite (vv. 142–74).

> (the attendant) ἀλλὰ θεοὶ τέρποντο διαμπερὲς ἐς Διὸς οἶκον
> ἀμφὶ γάμοις Ἄρεος καὶ Κύπριδος ἀφρογενείης,
> Ζεὺς δὲ πατὴρ προκάθητο μέγας μεγάλου ἐπὶ θώκου,
> πὰρ δ' Ἥρη τῷ ἕζετο πότνια δῖα θεάων,

---

[17] Littlewood (1974: 34–52).
[18] Littlewood (1993: 83–4) and Grünbart (2020: 82–4). Cf. also the proverb μήλῳ βάλλειν: ἐπὶ τῶν εἰς ἔρωτα ἐπαγομένων τινάς ('hit with an apple: on those who induce others to fall in love', Leutsch and Schneidewin [1839–51, vol. 1: 279 and vol. 2: 39]).
[19] *Anthologia Graeca* XII.24–7 ed. Beckby.

ἐν δ' Ἄρης, ἐν δ' Ἀφροδίτη Διὸς ἄγχι καὶ Ἥρης,
ἑξείης δ' ἑτέρων μακάρων ἱερὸς χορὸς ἧστο. (vv. 158–63)

But the gods were feasting continuously in the house of Zeus at the wedding of Ares and the foam-born Kypris. Zeus, the great father, presided on a great throne, next to him sat Hera, the divine queen of the goddesses, next to Zeus and Hera were Ares and Aphrodite, and the holy choir of the other blessed ones was seated there in a row.

In mythology, Ares and Aphrodite are, indeed, lovers, but Aphrodite is married to Hephaestus. Aphrodite and Ares are known for their erotic passion, but not for legitimate marriage. Planoudes himself included a passage in his collection of excerpts saying that Aphrodite presides over sexual intercourse solely for pleasure.[20] The story in Homer of Ares and Aphrodite being caught red-handed was famous in Byzantium.[21] By describing a formal wedding feast of the two gods, Planoudes subverts the myth. He plays with the expectation of the audience concerning Aphrodite and Ares and their lustful relationship by 'correcting' the myth and thus creating a new, astonishing story. In contrast to variations, corrections change the core of the myth. At the same time, corrections only make sense if the recipient knows the original or standard story.[22] As is common when myths are 'corrected', the narrator, in this case the Egyptian, underlines how remarkable his story is by insisting on the truth of his prophecies (v. 144: εἴ τι ἐγὼ ἀψευδὴς τελέθω καὶ μάντις ἀληθής, 'if I am an unerring and true seer').[23] The subversion of the myth is underscored by the references to Lucian's *Symposium* as a hypotext, which recounts the events at a wedding feast. The Egyptian's attendant describes the seating arrangements at the feast with Zeus at the throne and Hera next to him, while Ares and Aphrodite and the other guests follow according to their rank (vv. 160–3). Ganymede, as cupbearer, brings them nectar (vv. 164–6). In the *Symposium*, too, seating arrangements are described (*Symp.* 8–9) and cupbearers feature prominently (*Symp.* 14.19–21 and 15). Lucian also refers to the famous apple of discord

---

[20] Excerpt no. 70 ed. Piccolomini (1874: 160): "Ὅτι γάμων μὲν τῶν κατὰ νόμον Ἥρην φασὶν ἐπιστατεῖν, μίξεως δὲ καθ' ἡδονὴν μόνην, Ἀφροδίτην· Ἄρτεμιν δέ, τοκετοῦ καὶ λοχείας, 'because one says that Hera presides over marriages according to law, Aphrodite over intercourse solely for pleasure, but Artemis over childbirth and delivery'.
[21] *Odyssey* 8.266–366. The story is also used in Aphthonios, *Progymnasmata* 2 ed. Patillon.
[22] See the concept of 'Mythenkorrektur' in Vöhler and Seidensticker (2005), especially Vöhler, Seidensticker and Emmerich (2005).
[23] See Vöhler, Seidensticker and Emmerich (2005: 8–9).

(*Symp.* 35.14–20), of which the apples in Planoudes' *Idyll* are reminiscent. Ganymede, finally, brings with him the reintroduction of the homoerotic discourse at Olympus as he is the mythological example *par excellence* for paederastic and same-sex relationships:

> *(the attendant)* ἀθανάτοις δὲ θεοῖσι πόσιν μακάρων, γλυκὺ νέκταρ,
> ἐς δέπας ἀμφικύπελλον ἐῳνοχόει Γανυμήδης
> γραπτὸν ἐνὶ χλαίνῃσιν ἔχων μέγαν αἰετὸν ὄρνιν. (vv. 164–6)
>
> For the immortal gods Ganymede poured the beverage of the blessed, sweet nectar into the double cup, (Ganymede) who had inscribed on his mantle a great eagle.

The eagle on Ganymede's mantle (v. 166) alludes to the myth of Zeus's rapture of Ganymede in the guise of an eagle, while at the same time the eagle is a ubiquitous symbol of imperial power in Byzantium to be worn on garments by the emperor and high officials.[24] That a boy well known for his (same-sex) affair with Zeus wears an imperial symbol creates a funny effect. There is no need to believe that this is a direct criticism of the reigning emperor or one of his attendants, but by intermingling spheres that usually would not be talked about in the same breath – namely gay love and the imperial court – it produces a symbolic pun to comic effect.

The Alterity of Otherworlds

The second part of the *Idyll* contains Kleodemos' report of his strange experiences in Aithra at Mount Olympus (vv. 59–174), where he had gone to buy a new ox. However pragmatic the reason for his journey is, what he witnesses there differs greatly from what one expects of a market town. Aithra, the city of Zeus (v. 63), is constructed as a place of alterity clearly separated from the pastoral landscape in which Thamyras and Kleodemos meet, situated at the uppermost part of the mountain, close to the clouds and hidden by snow storms (vv. 64–6). The name Aithra also appears in Nonnos' *Dionysiaka* as the city of Helios in the very eastern parts of the known world.[25] In the *Dionysiaka*, however, the city is not surrounded by clouds, but clear skies, as the name ('clear sky') suggests. Planoudes

---

[24] Cf. Macrides, Munitiz and Angelov (2013: 342–3).
[25] Nonnos, *Dionysiaka* 26.85–6 ed. Keydell.

subverts Aithra by describing a concealed place and thus creates a strong boundary between the pastoral sphere and the otherworld. Yet, far from being dark and gloomy, Aithra is described as a *locus amoenus*, where the people rejoice in singing, dancing and sporting, where milk and honey gush out of the earth and the sheep give birth to twins, the latter being a *topos* especially in Theocritus for fat sheep giving a lot of milk (see vv. 67–77 and 103–7).[26] The description of Aithra is ambivalent in its character, but, both in its dark and its paradisiac aspect, it is clearly different from Kleodemos' home.

When the Egyptian is first mentioned, he is described in detail:

(Kleodemos) τοῖσι δὲ τερπομένοισιν ἐφίκετο δαιμόνιός τις
ἄγριος ἀνήρ, θηρὸς ἔχων ὄπα, θηρὸς ὀπωπήν,
ἀμφιλαφὴς πλοκάμοισιν ἀμαυροτέροισι κοράκων
οἷον ἐχιδναίῃσι τιταινομένοις πλέον οὐρῆς
καὶ σκολιῆς ἑλίκεσσιν ἑλισσομένοις ὑπὲρ ὤμων,
μηκεδανὸν τὸ γένειον ἀπὸ στομάτων προϊάλλων
καὶ μέλας ἅψεα πάντα, πρόσωπα, χέρας τε πόδας τε. (vv. 78–84)

To these feasting people came a marvellous, wild man with the voice and the appearance of a beast, full all around with curls blacker than ravens, writhing more like serpents' tails and coiling down over his shoulders in winding spirals. A long beard came forth from his mouth and all his limbs were black: his face, his hands and his feet.

The Egyptian's black complexion and his viper-like curled hair, which resembles the Gorgon, create a counterpart to the paradisiac situation described before. He is said to come from Egypt as a wandering priest performing miracles at feasts of Zeus, Aphrodite or Apollo, joined by a young assistant carrying two pouches (see vv. 85–92). His origin does not come as a surprise to the reader, as Egyptians were frequently described as black in literature[27] and Egypt was considered to be the homeland of sorcery and magic.[28] In Lucian's *Symposium*, too, an Egyptian-speaking man appears (18.22: αἰγυπτιάζων τῇ φωνῇ), while in his *Lover of Lies* one of the dialogue partners describes how he was trained by Pankrates, an Egyptian sorcerer (33–4). The nature of the witchcraft of Planoudes' Egyptian is hinted at when the pouches that the assistant carries are described as μέγα Παλλάδος ἔργον ('a great work of Pallas Athena', v. 92). The passage alludes to the *Odyssey*, where Athena transforms

---

[26] Cf., among others, Theocritus, *Idylls* 1.25 and 3.34 ed. Gow; on their special value, cf. the scholion 1.23–6 b and c, ed. Wendel.
[27] *Locus classicus* is Herodotus, *Histories* 2.104.2.   [28] Cupane (2014: 493).

Odysseus into a beggar and gives him a shabby pouch,[29] and thus refers to the power of metamorphosis. The Egyptian transgresses the laws of nature, thereby adding to the otherworldly character of Aithra.

Kleodemos further strengthens the alterity of the city when he says about his return that he travelled back 'coming from the feast from above from below' (καί τε πανηγύρεως ὑπένερθεν ὕπερθεν ἰόντα, v. 191). His journey is an *anabasis* ('ascent') in that he travels to an otherworld,[30] in the same sense as its counterpart, the *katabasis* ('descent'), describes the journey to an otherworld. The *Idyll* thus stands in the tradition of the experience of otherness as found in Greek literature from Odysseus' descent into Hades described by Homer and the otherworldly texts by Lucian to Byzantine texts such as the *Timarion* or the later *Mazaris*.[31] The journey to an otherworld is also part of storytelling in different genres and contexts such as the fairy tale and hagiographic texts describing journeys to paradise. The most important stages of the journey are the question or demand by the future traveller that initiates the journey, the way to the underworld, the description of the wonderful places and the return to the world, sometimes together with a magical object.[32] While the journey itself is hardly relevant in Planoudes' *Idyll*, the general structure of the visit to the otherworld fits well with it. Kleodemos' journey starts with his desire to buy a new ox, yet this stays in the pastoral realm of his daily life. Only the description of Aithra makes the otherworldly character of the journey clear and introduces the miraculous events that follow. On his return, Kleodemos brings the ox to his home believing it to be a 'normal' animal before discovering its magic and disastrous retransformation into a mouse.

In addition to the pastoral sphere and Aithra, a third place, Olympus, is described briefly and likewise separated from the other realms. The journey to Olympus is even more closely linked to other otherworld stories than that to Aithra, since all of the above-mentioned elements feature prominently. It is initiated by the Egyptian's question about Zeus. The journey of the apples and the attendant to Olympus as well as the wonderful venue, namely the wedding feast at Olympus, are described. Finally, the traveller brings back a

---

[29] *Odyssey* 13.429–38.
[30] Nissen (1936) argued that the *Idyll* presents a journey to the underworld. Although he is right concerning the alterity of Aithra, the city is no underworld and the connection he draws with ancient shamanism is not valid.
[31] On *katabasis* in Byzantine literature, see Lampakes (1982), Nilsson (2016) and (2018), Marciniak (2018).
[32] Penskaya (2018).

gift, the chicken leg, as proof of his journey. The alterity of Aithra and Olympus creates an opposition to the bucolic world of the *Idyll* and links it especially to satirical texts, while Planoudes does not write a satire *stricto sensu*. Rather, the setting enforces the character of the *Idyll* as a parody playing with literary traditions and turning them – as in the case of the myth of Ares and Aphrodite – upside down.[33]

Magic and the Marvellous

After the report about Olympus, the narration leaves both the home of the gods and Aithra. The poem continues with the story of the ox that was magically transformed into a mouse by the Egyptian who, although not present, has a high level of influence over Kleodemos' pastoral world.

As mentioned above, the first description of the sorcerer is found in the report about Aithra (quoted above). The Egyptian is called δαιμόνιος ('marvellous', v. 78, cf. also v. 90), τερατουργός ('wonder-worker', v. 132 and hypothesis to the *Idyll* ll. 4–5), ἀλλόκοτόν τι θέαμα καὶ οὐκ ἔθιμον ('a strange sight and unusual', v. 94) and ἀήθης ('unwonted', v. 99). Introducing him, Kleodemos states that the sorcerer miraculously changes the world (κόσμον ἀμειβόμενος τεράτων τελετῆς, v. 88), foreshadowing the story of the mouse transformed into an ox and back. His deeds, too, are described as miraculous (θαῦμα, vv. 122 and 138). The words derived from τέρας in particular have a negative connotation, and the characterization of the sorcerer by Kleodemos is ambivalent to unflattering. The description of his wondrous nature, however, is not confined to the alterity of Aithra. Although the sorcerer acts in the otherworldly city of Aithra, he is also present in the pastoral sphere of Kleodemos' and Thamyras' everyday life. Thamyras' first reaction to Kleodemos' account is to praise the Egyptian:

> (*Thamyras*) δαιμόνιός τις ἐκεῖνος ἔην καὶ ἐπήβολος ἀνήρ,
> ἀθανάτων παίδευμα δίδαγμά τε οὐρανιώνων,
> ὃς τοιαῦτα τέτευχε· θεῶν νύ τοί ἐστιν ἀπορρώξ.

> He was a marvellous and skilled man, a pupil of the immortals and [thus] a [living] instruction on the heavenly gods, who did such things. He is surely broken off of the gods.

Thamyras also twice wishes to see him (vv. 178–9 and 245–7). His image of the sorcerer is thus entirely positive. This fits well with Lucian's *Lover of Lies*

---

[33] On the importance of parody in the *katabasis* included in the *Timarion*, see Nilsson (2016).

as a hypotext, the theme of which is the superstitiousness of philosophers.[34] In contrast to Thamyras, Kleodemos emphatically states that not even in a dream or in a dream inside a dream would he wish to see the sorcerer again (vv. 180–2), who deceives men with his tricks (v. 220) and whom he fears even in his absence (vv. 250–1). The different reactions to the Egyptian by Kleodemos and Thamyras echo, on a literary level, the ambivalent attitude towards magic in Byzantium in general.[35] Although here it is not connected to Christianity and is confined to the archaizing world of the *Idyll*, magic appears as both a positive force and at the same time a threat to the life of the figures in Planoudes' poem. Despite this ambivalence, Kleodemos and Thamyras believe in the power of magic and its existence is never questioned.

Back in the pastoral sphere, Kleodemos describes how he brought the ox home (vv. 189–96). He explains in detail the everyday actions of bringing the ox home and washing it with the help of his wife (vv. 201–10). Then, suddenly, unnatural forces re-enter when the ox is transformed into a mouse because the water washed off a magical salve that the Egyptian had smeared on it (vv. 211–20). The motif of a magic ointment with transformative power is well known in storytelling in various cultures.[36] It links Planoudes' *Idyll* with a narrative tradition that is not limited to highbrow literature but includes folktale elements. After the ox's retransformation into its muroid shape, it beats up the cat of the house, assembling around it an army of mice and finally eating up whatever they find in the storeroom (vv. 221–40). The battle of cats and mice is a *topos* in Byzantine literature, for instance in the *Katomyomachia* by Theodore Prodromos (see below). The personification of the animals and the ridiculed cat are in line with the comic tone that prevails in the *Idyll*. Following this report, Thamyras counsels Kleodemos go to a friend who will give him a mousetrap and utters his wish to see the sorcerer on their way there, while Kleodemos vehemently states that he never wants to see the latter again (vv. 249–51). Thamyras finally assures his friend that, indeed, they shall never see the sorcerer again. In his last words, he instructs a boy at his house to take care of his oxen:

(*Thamyras*) παῖ, σὺ δὲ βόσκε τὰ βοίδια καὶ ποτὶ ἕσπερον αὐτά
ἐν μεγάροισι κόμισσον ἐπὶ σταθμοῖσί τε δῆσον,
κρῖ τε δόμεν τοῖς ἄργυφον, ὥς κε καμόντα φάγῃσιν. (vv. 268–70)

---

[34] Holzinger (1893: 4–5) argues that Thamyras is a rational counterpart to the superstitious Kleodemos, but his vivid interest in the sorcerer's deeds proves the opposite.
[35] Cupane (2014), Greenfield (1995: 118–19).
[36] See the motif index of folk-literature no. D1244, Thompson (1956). In a Byzantine context, Pseudo-Lucian's *The Ass* is an important text in which the motif appears.

Feed the oxen, child, and towards evening bring them inside the house and bind them to their standing-places, and give them silver-white barley so that they can eat when they are exhausted.

Thamyras leaves the sphere of magic and comes back entirely to the everyday life of the two peasants. The last section of the *Idyll* thus connects to the first two by uniting the pastoral environment and common problems of peasants with the otherworldly story of the scene at Aithra.

Literary Traditions and Planoudes' Scholarship

As shown in the close reading of the *Idyll* above, the text is heavily influenced by various hypotexts from ancient authors, most importantly Theocritus and Lucian. In the following, I shall give a more detailed account of the *Idyll* in the context of Byzantine literature and Planoudes' work as a scholar.

Planoudes was the first Byzantine author to write an idyll and he was succeeded only by one anonymous author of the fifteenth century, whose poem does not seem to be connected with Planoudes'.[37] However, Theocritus' poetry influenced many late antique and Byzantine authors, such as Nonnos, Kyros, Agathias Scholastikos, John Geometres, the twelfth-century novel writers and, among those, most prominently Niketas Eugeneianos, who shows a strong interest in the homoerotic aspect of bucolics.[38] The first extant manuscripts containing Theocritus' works date to the thirteenth century, showing that he appealed to learned men of that period. Planoudes knew Theocritus well from a philological standpoint, as attested through his text edition, his commentaries and the use of the idylls in his *Dialogue on the Construction of Verbs* in which he refers to them multiple times.[39] Planoudes also expresses the close connection of Theocritus' poetry and the theme of love in his translation of the *Dicta Catonis*. In the introduction to Book II, he states: Εἰ δέ γ' ἐρᾶν βούλει τοῦ ἐρᾶν τε τέχνην ἐπιγνῶναι, | στεῖχε Θεόκριτον ἀμφὶ γυναιμανῆ ('but if you wish to love and to learn the art of loving, approach Theocritus who is mad for women').[40] Planoudes here changes the Latin original, where a number of authors are mentioned and connected to various topics,

---

[37] Sturm (1901).
[38] See Burton (2006) on various authors and Burton (2003) and (2012) particularly on Eugeneianos, with earlier literature.
[39] 106.10–13, 106.20–4, 107.31–5 ed. Bachmann. On scholarly interest in Theocritus in Late Byzantium, see also Caballero Sánchez in this volume.
[40] Recensio α II.prol.6–7 ed. Papathomopoulos.

among them Ovid as the proponent of love. In the scholia to the passage, Planoudes explicitly points to his change, noting that the original says Ovid instead of Theocritus.[41] However, it is the desire for women that characterizes the works of Theocritus who is called 'mad for women' (γυναιμανής). Bearing in mind that the opposite, ἀρρενομανής, denotes a gay man,[42] and considering that in the Latin original there is no such attribute for Ovid, it becomes clear that Planoudes wishes to reject Theocritus' homoerotic side explicitly. What holds true for a collection of moral sayings such as the *Dicta Catonis*, however, is not relevant for Planoudes' *Idyll*, which clearly stands in a different tradition.

Erotic, and especially homoerotic,[43] literature is not widespread in Byzantium, yet interesting examples do exist.[44] Homoerotic discourse can be found where one might not expect it, namely in the hymns of Symeon the New Theologian, directed to God, and in religious epigrams, again directed to God, the Theotokos or Saints.[45] Although not sexual in their content, these texts employ a language which clearly evokes eroticism. Furthermore, in Byzantine letters dealing with friendship, there are no strict boundaries between friendly and erotic discourse.[46] In this way, the ambivalence of the relationships between men in the *Idyll* resembles the situation in epistolography.

The most important collection of erotic poetry in the Byzantine period is without doubt the *Greek Anthology*, which consists mainly of ancient and late antique texts. The history of the *Anthology* is complex.[47] Most important for our context, however, is the collection that Maximos Planoudes himself assembled. The most famous codex is the autograph manuscript Venice, Biblioteca Nazionale Marciana, gr. 481, which contains the *Planoudean Anthology* as a whole.[48] In as early as the ninth century, scholars around Leo the Philosopher collected ancient epigrams that later became part of the *Palatine Anthology*, and their reading of ancient erotic

---

[41] Scholia II.prol. ed. Papathomopoulos.   [42] Laiou (1992: 77).
[43] Erotic same-sex relationships were generally seen as problematic in Byzantium, yet close homosocial bonds existed, see Rapp (2016: 40–4) with further literature. Planoudes, however, does not speak about gay acts, but plays with homoeroticism as found in literature.
[44] As an introduction, see Beck (1986).
[45] On Symeon, see Krueger (2006); on epigrams, see, among others, Drpić (2016: 296–331).
[46] Fundamentally, see Mullett (1999); most recently, with further literature, see Masterson (2018), whose monograph on the topic (*Between Byzantine Men: Desire, Brotherhood, and Male Culture in the Medieval Empire*) is forthcoming; on Psellos specifically, Papaioannou (2011).
[47] See Cameron (1993), Lauxtermann (2003–19, vol. 1: 83–128).
[48] For a description of the Laurentianus, see Bandini (1768: 140–6); for the Marcianus, see Mioni (1985: 276–83). On the *Planoudean Anthology*, see Beckby (1965, vol. 1: 70–3), Fryde (2000: 244–6), Lauxtermann (2003–19, vol. 1: 115–16).

epigrams inspired them to compose similar ones themselves.[49] Planoudes' *Idyll* exemplifies a similar phenomenon, whereby Planoudes' preoccupation with the *Anthology* provided inspiration for his own classicizing works.[50] References to the *Anthology* in the *Idyll* are mainly on the lexical level, but also include elements of erotic symbolism (see above, p. 246, on the cock). How the *Anthology* directly influenced Planoudes' literary production is further illustrated by a scoptic epigram on a stepmother that he wrote in the tradition of the *Greek Anthology*.[51] Apart from being an inspiring source for erotic literature, it also connects Planoudes' *Idyll* to the tradition of satirical literature. In this way, he follows a tradition of the twelfth century in which authors modelled their satires on the *Anthology*.[52]

The satirical tone in the *Idyll* mainly depends on Lucian. The latter was enormously popular in Byzantium with more than 180 manuscripts transmitting his oeuvre.[53] However, his reception was ambivalent. On the one hand, he was rebuked for the abusive language and the blasphemous content in his work, especially concerning Christianity. On the other hand, he was perceived as a true master of the Attic language and an important stylistic model and was, as such, used for classroom instruction.[54] What is more, he also stirred the Byzantines to write their own texts in the tradition of his satires. The heyday of these compositions was the twelfth century. In Palaiologan times, too, Lucian was a matter of debate not predominantly as a source of imitation but rather in terms of literary criticism.[55] The fame of Lucian in Byzantium leaves no doubt that Planoudes was familiar with his work.

The magical story about the ox does not seem to have any direct connection to ancient authors. It rather draws on Byzantine attitudes towards magic and widely known motifs such as the magic ointment or the myth of Icarus. The appearance of a sorcerer and the connection of a highbrow text with magic is not without predecessors. Magicians play a role in the Bible and early Christian literature as well as in hagiography and historiography.[56] What is more, magic is often connected with

---

[49] Lauxtermann (1999) and (2003–19, vol. 1: 98–107).
[50] The influence of the *Planoudean Anthology* on Palaiologan authors can be traced in the work of Manuel Philes (see Pietsch-Braounou [2010]) as well as in the romance *Kallimachos and Chrysorrhoe* (see Agapitos [1990: 270–3]).
[51] Epigram 1, ed. and commented by Taxidis (2017: 71–2); see also Valerio (2018: 277–80).
[52] Zagklas (2021). On verse satire up to the tenth century, see Lauxtermann (2003–19, vol. 2: 119–44).
[53] Marciniak (2016: 210).   [54] Marciniak (2016), Messis (2021).
[55] Marciniak (2016: 221–3), Messis (2021).
[56] Cf. e.g. Simon the Sorcerer in *Acts* 8.9–24. On magicians from the eighth to the eleventh centuries, see extensively Vlavianos (2013).

metamorphosis and love. Niketas Choniates in his *History* reports that a sorcerer by the name of Seth Skleros used an apple to cast a love spell on a maiden and eventually deflower her, thus combining the motif of sorcery with the apple in an erotic context.[57] In the romance *Libistros and Rhodamne*, which is roughly contemporary to Planoudes, magic features prominently. Here we find a witch at one of the crucial turning points in the plot.[58] Her magic is connected to the art of metamorphosis and miraculous journeys with flying horses and interferes with the struggle of Libistros to find his beloved Rhodamne. Similarly, in the romance *Kallimachos and Chrysorrhoe*, at a key point in the narration, a witch appears, who even uses an apple bearing an inscription to aid in casting her spell.[59] Yet, in these texts, witches and sorcerers are accompanied by demons and clearly perform black magic. In Planoudes' *Idyll*, in contrast, magic is morally neither good nor bad. Only the impact of the sorcerer's deeds on the protagonists in the bucolic sphere gives them a positive or negative character. Outside the literary tradition, a prohibition against magic was instituted by the patriarchate, as demonstrated by a document from the register of the patriarchate dating to the early fourteenth century.[60] Apparently, Planoudes was taking up a fraught topic in Byzantine society, especially in the early Palaiologan period, and so included it in his poem without references to a specific text.

The hypotext of the battle of cats and mice remains uncertain. However, the motif is widespread in Byzantine sources.[61] The story of the *Idyll* calls to mind Theodore Prodromos' *Katomyomachia*, a poem in the form of an ancient drama in which mice fight a battle against cats.[62] The leader of the mice is called λοχαγός ('commander') both in Planoudes (v. 228) and in Prodromos (v. 119, ed. Hunger). As Venice, Biblioteca Nazionale Marciana, gr. 524, the most important manuscript of the *Katomyomachia*, may be a product of the Planoudes school,[63] one is tempted to see it as a hypotext for the *Idyll*. However, in the absence of further intertextual references and as λοχαγός is not an uncommon word, a relationship between the two texts cannot be proven. It might well be

---

[57] Niketas Choniates, *History* 148.86–95 ed. van Dieten; see Grünbart (2020: 84).
[58] Cupane (2009), (2014: 493–4). [59] Cupane (2014: 494–5) with references.
[60] Cupane (1980). [61] Kislinger (2011).
[62] Ed. with introduction Hunger (1968); for the latest studies, see Lauxtermann (forthcoming) and Marciniak and Warcaba (2018). The editors of Planoudes' *Idyll* likewise drew the connection to the *Katomyomachia* (see Holzinger [1893: 35] and Pontani [1973: 24] in the apparatus).
[63] See Rhoby (2010: 200) with further literature. But see Spingou (2021: 41–3), who is reluctant about the issue.

that they have a common point of reference, namely one of Aesop's fables which also deals with a battle between cats and mice.[64] Planoudes may have been responsible for a schoolbook version of the fables including a commentary, which were often used for the first stages of education and the instruction of younger students.[65] Even though the relevant fable is missing in the selection ascribed to his editorship,[66] one might suspect that Planoudes knew of it. The Pseudo-Homeric *Batrachomyomachia* tells of a battle of frogs and mice and is a further possible inspiration, although the *Idyll* does not reference it clearly. Furthermore, the awful character and deeds of mice are a popular theme in Byzantine literature, as can be seen, for example, in a poem by Christopher of Mytilene, in which he describes how they eat up his books (and, ironically, the most important codex transmitting his poems has suffered great damage from mice).[67] None of these texts tells the same story, but they show that Planoudes used Byzantine literature the way he used ancient texts, namely by picking known topics and modes of expression and transforming them by placing them in a new context.

Love, alternate places of a threatening or comic character and magic are well-known topics in literature. However, the appearance of homo-eroticism, humorous passages built on satire and playful variations of superstition in a poem by Maximos Planoudes may come as a surprise for a modern reader who is used to seeing Planoudes as a severe, earnest scholar and pious monk. This picture of him stems in particular from the part he supposedly played in editing the *Greek Anthology*. The common narrative is that, while working on the *Anthology*, he was piqued by its erotic content and acted as a kind of Byzantine 'Dr Bowdler', leaving out the most vulgar epigrams.[68] Indeed, when collecting the epigrams for his *Anthology*, he excluded some epigrams because of their indecent and shameful character, as he explains in a famous note

---

[64] Fable no. 174 ed. Hausrath.
[65] The question is whether the so-called *Accursiana* version of Aesop's fables, which was ascribed to Planoudes from the fifteenth century onwards, is indeed a work by this scholar. See fundamentally Hausrath (1901) arguing against and Perry (1936: 217–28) for Planoudes' editorship; Karla (2003) reconsiders the question on the basis of more recent scholarship and follows Perry's conclusion.
[66] See the manuscript Naples, Biblioteca Nazionale 'Vittorio Emanuele III', II D 22, which contains Planoudes' edition with comments, but does not include fable 174 (ed. Hausrath); on the manuscript, see Formentin (1995: 25–7). However, the exact relationship between Planoudes and this manuscript is a matter of debate: see Canart (2011: 325–7).
[67] Christopher of Mytilene, poem 103 ed. de Groote. On mice in Byzantine literature, see Marciniak (2017: 507–8 and *passim*) with further literature, and Carpinato (2005).
[68] See Karla (2006) for a longer discussion of the issue and for further literature; a peculiar form of 'bowdlerization' is the transliteration of an objectionable word into Latin letters: see Valerio (2011).

in his autograph manuscript Marc. gr. 481.⁶⁹ However, he by no means excluded all such epigrams.⁷⁰ By changing our perspective on his collection, we must adjust this picture of him: he included a high number of erotic and satirical epigrams, thereby showing vivid interest in reading and disseminating these texts. When he collected and rendered into prose excerpts from the novel by Constantine Manasses, he also chose many passages connected with love.⁷¹ The *Idyll* also changes our perspective on Planoudes' scholarly work on Theocritus and Aesop's fables, as it presents a Planoudes who uses allusions to ancient authors not only as a means of linguistic and rhetorical training but also for fun. This fits well with his version of the *Life of Aesop*, a novelistic, humorous and fictional work. Although raising the language register to a learned Atticizing Greek and despite some omissions in the text, Planoudes, by writing the metaphrasis, demonstrates his love of entertaining narratives.⁷² His translations of Ovid's erotic works and *Metamorphoses* prove his interest in love stories and storytelling in a broader sense.⁷³ Planoudes' *Idyll* fits well with his wide knowledge of and his eager passion for ancient literature.⁷⁴ It shows that Planoudes had a sense of learned humour and was able to play with the ancient tradition. This erudite context allowed him to deal wittily with topics such as homoeroticism or magic that were otherwise problematic or even taboo in Byzantine society. It goes without saying that these were literary games, the details of which can by no means be referred to Planoudes himself. Making jokes about homoerotic love does not mean that Planoudes was gay, nor does his treatment of magic mean that he was a practising sorcerer. Yet, it shows his openness to many different and comical topics; or perhaps more generally, the openness of Byzantine literature to such topics, as the many parallels mentioned above show.

---

⁶⁹ Fol. 68v ed. Mioni (1985: 280): Ἐν τῷδε τῷ ἑβδόμῳ τμήματι περιέχεται ἑταιρικά τινα ἀποφθέγματα ... ὅσα μὴ πρὸς τὸ ἀσεμνότερον καὶ αἰσχρότερον ἀποκλίνεται, τὰ γὰρ τοιαῦτα πολλὰ ἐν τῷ ἀντιγράφῳ ὄντα παρελίπομεν, 'in this seventh section, some erotic poems are included ... that do not tend towards the overly undignified and shameful. For we left out many such poems that were included in the original'.
⁷⁰ Karla (2006: 216–21). ⁷¹ See the edition by Mazal (1967: 163–209).
⁷² Karla (2016: 315 and 329–32).
⁷³ His translation of the *Metamorphoses* was edited by Papathomopoulos (2002); on the amatory poems, see Easterling and Kenney (1965).
⁷⁴ In his letters, by contrast, his scholarly activities seem not to have left any literary traces; see Schneider (2009: 70–1).

Reading the *Idyll* in Byzantium

The *Idyll* is transmitted in four manuscripts, of which only two were known to the editors: Ravenna, Biblioteca Classense 183 (*R*) and Naples, Biblioteca Nazionale 'Vittorio Emanuele III', II.F.9 (*N*). The Ravenna manuscript was written by an unknown scribe of the second half of the fourteenth century.[75] It includes *Idylls* 1–8 by Theocritus, Hesiod's *Works and Days* and Pindar's *Olympian Odes* 1–13. These texts are accompanied by scholia and glossae of Manuel Moschopoulos.[76] Planoudes' *Idyll* is copied directly after Theocritus (fols. 42r–48v) and ends with v. 238 without any punctuation mark. The reason for this abrupt ending is unclear. The Naples codex is a famous manuscript written by the monk Gabriel and containing mostly ancient texts with numerous scholia from the school of Planoudes and Moschopoulos.[77] Its main contents are a collection of excerpts by Planoudes, four plays by Euripides (*Hecuba, Orestes, Phoenician Women, Trojan Women*), the triad of Sophocles (*Ajax, Electra, Oedipus Tyrannus*), Hesiod's *Works and Days* and Theocritus' *Idylls*. Planoudes' *Idyll* is found at the beginning on fols. 3r–4v after some short miscellaneous texts and before a large section of Planoudes' excerpts from various authors.[78]

Vatican City, Biblioteca Apostolica Vaticana, gr. 1721 (*V*) is the third manuscript containing the *Idyll* and was unknown to its editors. The manuscript consists of two main codicological units, one going back to the fourteenth, the other to the sixteenth century. The latter was inserted to supply a section missing from the original manuscript. The codex contains the *On the Soul and the Resurrection* by Gregory of Nyssa and a section with works mainly by Maximos Planoudes, namely the *Comparison of Winter and Spring*, a letter, the *Idyll* and another spurious letter. An anonymous scribe from the milieu of Planoudes and Gregoras wrote the section with the main part of Planoudes' works. In contrast to *R* and *N*, *V* does not contain any classical literature. Instead of being grouped with Theocritus, here the *Idyll* is found as part of a small collection of Planoudes' rhetorical works.[79] The text is directly dependent on *N*.

---

[75] According to Anna Gioffreda, the same scribe copied Vienna, Österreichische Nationalbibliothek, phil. gr. 48 (on the manuscript, see Hunger 1961: 170–1). I thank her for sharing this information with me.
[76] See Mioni (1965: 359–60).
[77] Formentin (1995: 124–31); on the scribe, see Pérez Martín (1997: 83–8).
[78] On the excerpts, see Piccolomini (1874).
[79] The most recent description including a discussion of the hands is found in Gioffreda (2020), with earlier literature.

Hence, the readings of the *Idyll* that the manuscript offers do not add to the critical text of Pontani's edition.[80]

A fourth manuscript, Berlin, Staatsbibliothek zu Berlin, Hamilton 555 (*B*) includes on pp. 1 and 214–17 the vv. 53–231 of the *Idyll*. This codicological unit was written in the fourteenth century and is now split into two parts flanking a collection of technical texts (dialectic, rhetoric, philosophy, astronomy) written in the fifteenth century.[81] The origins of the pages that contain the *Idyll* are unclear and hence it is impossible to trace its original context. Its readings do not add to the critical edition by Pontani.

The two codices *R* and *N* are scholarly manuscripts suitable for school instruction as well as more advanced learning and scientific exchange. In fact, no borders between these levels of instruction and no distinction between manuscripts for various forms of scholarship can be drawn.[82] Placed in this context, the *Idyll* is likely to have been used in the scholarly circle of Planoudes and Moschopoulos and should be seen as an instructive text to be read together with ancient literature. It was copied in the manuscripts *R* and *N* in the immediate vicinity of Theocritus, which suggests a parallel reading of his and Planoudes' idylls. Codex *V*, on the other hand, shows interest in the *Idyll* as a rhetorical text as part of Planoudes' oeuvre. What makes the poem especially suitable for educational purposes is its multifaceted character, which allows for many different readings.

On a linguistic level, readers (from student to teacher) could enjoy and possibly analyse the hexameter and archaizing language. The hexameter, however, is decidedly not a pure Homeric or Nonnian one, but exhibits clear signs of Byzantine usage.[83] Most characteristic is the use of the medial caesura in about 20 per cent of the verses, a caesura that never occurred in ancient hexameters, but was introduced in Late Antiquity. Although it became popular in Byzantine literature, Planoudes seems to have a special inclination to it in his *Idyll*.[84] In terms of the vocabulary,

---

[80] *V* shares all variants with the former including obvious errors (e.g. ὑψικομκίντα instead of ὑψικομῶντα v. 32 and the genitive Κίρκου instead of Κίρκης v. 253), but offers some new variants itself. The most important peculiarities of the manuscript are the following: at the end of the hypothesis, we find a remark, unknown to the other manuscripts: Τὰ πρόσωπα γοῦν Θαμύρας καὶ Κλεόδημος ('the characters [of the *Idyll*] are Thamyras and Kleodemos'). The *Idyll* proper is transmitted from vv. 1–197 (first half) and 204 (second half)–270. The reason for the omission must be the similarity between the beginnings of vv. 197 and 204.

[81] De Boor (1897: 237–8); the manuscript was already mentioned in Wendel (1950).

[82] Bianconi (2010: 476 and *passim*).

[83] On the meter of the *Idyll* in detail, see Pontani (1973: 8–10), Holzinger (1893: 9–10); on the hexameter in Planoudes' other poetic works, see Taxidis (2017: 32–4).

[84] On the medial caesura, see Lauxtermann (2003–19, vol. 2: 359–61); in Planoudes' other hexameter poems this caesura occurs in about 8 per cent of the verses (Taxidis [2017: 32]).

the most important models for Planoudes are Nonnos, Homer, Theocritus and the *Greek Anthology*, all of which were important school authors and texts.[85] Gnomic expressions and comparisons could also be learnt from the *Idyll*, as indicated by the few marginal notes in the manuscripts (gnomic expressions vv. 48 and 49 in *RNV*, vv. 185 and 231 in *RNBV* and comparisons v. 30 in *R*, v. 95 in *RNBV*).[86] Some passages can be used as examples of *progymnasmata*, a type of text which Planoudes himself collected and edited with commentary.[87] The description of the sorcerer, in particular, is a fine example of an *ekphrasis* bringing the person vividly before the reader's eyes (vv. 78–84, see above). As expected in the *progymnasmata*, e.g. by Pseudo-Hermogenes and Aphthonios, it is written in a lively style using varied rhetorical figures.[88] Planoudes makes ample use of metaphors and comparisons, includes rare, especially Nonnian words and employs various rhetorical devices.[89] His *ekphrasis* also follows the principle of describing from head to toe by starting with his face and ending with his feet. In general, the essential prerequisite for a full understanding of the poem and the true callenge for students and literati when analysing the text is the complex disentanglement of the literary tradition and the relationship of the *Idyll* with its hypotexts.[90]

Although unique in its form and literary structure, the *Idyll* can be compared to other Byzantine texts in a broader educational context. The study of ancient authors throughout Byzantine history, but especially from the twelfth century onwards, moved writers to compose new forms of rhetorical texts. The *schedos*, originally a school exercise building on

---

[85] See the critical apparatus of Pontani (1973) and, particularly on Nonnos, Schneider (1894: 617–19). That the *Anthology* was used in the classroom is proven by the *Sylloge Vaticana*, a collection of epigrams stemming from the *Greek Anthology*, which was used as a schedographic school collection (see Mioni [1971–2: 90–5]).

[86] *R* additionally has a gloss on the word ἧκεν in v. 169, which is commented upon with the easier synonym ἔπεμψεν.

[87] On his edition of and commentary to Aphthonios' *progymnasmata*, see Hock (2012: 277–302) with literature.

[88] See Pseudo-Hermogenes, *Progymnasmata* 10 ed. Patillon; Aphthonios, *Progymnasmata* 12 ed. Patillon, who both stress the ideal of *enargeia* (vividness).

[89] For rare words, see e.g. μηκεδανός, 'long' (v. 83), μεταναστάσιος, 'wandering' (v. 85), ἰκμαλέος, 'damp' (v. 87). For rhetorical devices, see e.g. metaphor (v. 80), comparison (v. 81), *polysyndeta* (vv. 84 and 89), alliteration (v. 88).

[90] The *Idyll* thus evoked exactly the reading that I presented above. There is certainly more work to be done on this front as well. Nonnos, in particular, was a point of reference for Planoudes since there are many linguistic references to him in the *Idyll* (see the critical apparatus in the editions by Holzinger and Pontani).

antistoichic sound plays, evolved to be a self-standing literary genre, valued not only in school but also for the pleasure of members of the upper class. The most important author of such *schede* is Theodore Prodromos.[91] Planoudes, too, composed some antistoichic sentences although he does not seem to have written literary *schede*.[92] Furthermore, Byzantine authors composed very learned *progymnasmata* that by far exceeded elementary rhetorical education and rather constituted complex literary pieces. Famous are, for instance, the *progymnasmata* by the twelfth-century author Nikephoros Basilakes.[93] In Palaiologan times, this tradition was continued and *meletai* and *progymnasmata* kept being produced, as for example those of George of Cyprus, George Pachymeres or Nikephoros Gregoras.[94] Planoudes' *Comparison of Winter and Spring* can be seen in this light as an example of one type of *progymnasmata*, the *synkrisis*, and a rhetorical showpiece.[95] *Schede*, *progymnasmata* and *meletai* are alike in that they are instructive in their rhetorical guise, their linguistic finesse and their reference to ancient literature, while at the same time they were self-standing literary products. In this light, Planoudes' *Idyll* is yet another example of how rhetorical training instigated original literary production.

However important the instructive merits of the *Idyll* were, one can be sure of its entertaining quality, although the nuances of humour are perhaps more inextricably tied to the moment of their composition than any other form of human expression. For this reason, humour in ancient and medieval texts can be difficult to recognize and more difficult still to appreciate in its social context.[96] There can be no doubt that the unexpected twists in the plot as well as the hidden hints to homoerotic discourse and satirical hypotexts were funny to Planoudes and his peers. What is more, Planoudes himself stresses the combination of the instructive and the entertaining qualities of hexametric poetry. In his autograph manuscript Florence, Biblioteca Medicea Laurenziana, Plut. 32.16, which includes the most important textual witness of Nonnos' *Dionysiaka* as well as an important version of his *Paraphrase of the Gospel of John*, he writes about the latter:[97]

---

[91] Vassis (1994; 2002); Agapitos (2013), (2014), (2015a), (2015b), (2015c), (2017); Nousia (2016: 49–92). See also Agapitos in this volume and Lovato in this volume.
[92] Ed. Treu (1896).   [93] See Beneker and Gibson (2016).   [94] Constantinides (2003: 48–50).
[95] Ed. Treu (1878).   [96] Bernard (2015: 179–80).
[97] On the manuscript tradition of Nonnos' works, see De Stefani (2016).

ἰστέον δὲ ὅτι αἰεὶ πρόσεστι τοῖς φιλομάθεσι ποθεινὸν καὶ ἐράσμιον ἡ τῶν ἑλληνικῶν συγγραμάτων ἀνάγνωσις, καὶ μάλιστα ἡ τῶν Ὁμηρικῶν, διὰ τὸ εὐφραδὲς καὶ ποικίλον τῶν λέξεων· οὗ ἕνεκεν καὶ ἡ παροῦσα μετάφρασις ἐμμέτρως ἐν ἡρωϊκοῖς ἐγεγράφει στίχοις πρὸς τέρψιν τοῖς φιλομάθεσι καὶ φιλολόγοις·[98]

> It must be known that reading Hellenic texts is always something longed for and beloved by those fond of learning, especially the works of Homer because of his eloquent style and varied lexicon. For this reason, the present metaphrasis has also been composed metrically in heroic verses for the pleasure of those fond of learning and of literature.

Byzantine erudition was no dry enterprise of studying grammar and rhetoric alone. On the contrary, classical texts, both secular (Homer) and religious (Nonnos' *Paraphrase*), were also read for pleasure. Indeed, pleasure and learning stood not contradiction but rather were interlaced in one and the same text – a tradition that, of course, goes back to antiquity and for which Horace's *dictum* of *prodesse et delectare* (cf. *Ars poetica* 333–4) constitutes the prime example. Planoudes' *Idyll* with its both instructive and entertaining character fits perfectly into this context.

What exactly this meant – who read or performed this text, when, where, to whom and how – is hard to tell. The *Idyll* should certainly be put in the context of the *theatron*, the literary gathering of Byzantine intellectuals and members of the upper class, where rhetorical texts were virtuosically performed, appreciated and discussed.[99] Yet, the precise nature of the *theatron* is as elusive as it is essential. Who was the audience for a text like the *Idyll*? Only well-educated persons could understand the subtle humour and wit of the piece. At the same time, not every reader was necessarily supposed to understand all the layers of the text. A student probably learned other things from it than a mature intellectual.[100] In any case, one should chiefly imagine a group of literati around Maximos Planoudes and his successors who read the *Idyll* in tandem with classical texts, as indicated by the manuscript tradition. One could call this a school environment, but teaching and erudition go hand in hand with no clear boundaries in between.[101] In this sense, the gathering of intellectuals who read and discuss the *Idyll* is none other than a *theatron*.

---

[98] Ed. Gallavotti (1959: 30). In Marc. gr. 481, another autograph of Planoudes, he left a similar note on the same text: ἡρωϊκὸν ἔμμετρον τουτὶ τὸ δρᾶμα εἰς τέρψιν νύττον τοὺς φιλοσόφους νέους ('this is a story in heroic verse spurring the wisdom-loving young men to pleasure', ed. Mioni [1985: 283]).
[99] On *theatra*, see as an introduction Marciniak (2007), Gaul (2011: 17–53) and (2018).
[100] The same holds true for other Byzantine texts; see on Eustathios of Thessalonike, Pizzone (2016) and van den Berg (2018: 221–6).
[101] Extensively Bianconi (2010); see also Bianconi (2017: 57–9).

Planoudes' *Idyll* is a parody of ancient texts and contemporary practices or discourses with complex hypertextual relationships.[102] One must note that parody does not necessarily polemicize the hypotexts, but that it can draw on one or more hypotexts to criticize or playfully refer to contemporary discourses.[103] The *Idyll* is certainly not a satire that attacks either ancient literature or Planoudes' contemporaries. It belongs to the rather lighthearted parodies that poke fun at a variety of topics without employing fierce sarcasm. However, it is in the essence of humour that it allows us to transgress social taboos and voice opinions or refer to discourses otherwise not socially accepted[104] – especially not in highbrow literature. This holds especially true for the playful allusions to homoerotic relationships and the ambivalent references to magic. In general, parody can be understood in its *verbatim* sense, but only the detection of the relationship with its hypotexts makes a full understanding of the often ambiguous and funny meaning possible.[105] Although explaining jokes may lessen the enjoyment, as immediate understanding may not be possible, there is an interesting example of how jokes could be used for instruction in twelfth-century literature. In the *Histories*, John Tzetzes' verse commentary to his own letters, the author refers explicitly to one of these and explains the joke as it functions through allusions to classical authors and the use of various rhetorical figures.[106] The commentary was at least partly written for didactic purposes.[107] The example shows how didactics, in the broadest sense of explaining and interpreting given texts, were used to facilitate the understanding of humour and, indeed, to compose comic wordplay. It is precisely this combination of fun and learning that exemplifies these two qualities of the *Idyll*. On the one hand, the plot and, more importantly, the references to other texts, which often create a double entendre, make the *Idyll* great fun to read. On the other hand, only the detection of these references, made possible by a careful and literarily informed reading, allows for a full understanding of the text. The pace at which the recipients understood its humour, of course, depends on their literary knowledge and certainly differed greatly between various readers. In a way, the *Idyll* both equals and transgresses the more straightforward comments on ancient literature as found in scholia and commentaries

---

[102] I understand parody as 'any cultural practice which provides a relatively polemical allusive imitation of another cultural production or practice' (Dentith [2000: 9]).
[103] Dentith (2000: 9). [104] Bernard (2015: 179–80). [105] Genette (1997: 397).
[106] John Tzetzes, *Histories* 10.307–24 ed. Leone; on this passage, see Bernard (2015: 192–3). See also van den Berg in this volume.
[107] Pizzone (2017: 198).

proper. The latter explicitly explain ancient texts and, in the layout of the manuscript, stand *beside* it. In other words, they are metatexts.[108] The *Idyll*, as a parody, on the other hand, builds *on* the classical tradition as a hypertext, making it a kind of 'criticism in action', to use Gérard Genette's words.[109] The poem thus equals a metatext, but goes beyond it. Its relationship with the hypotexts is more complex than that of a metatext.[110] The *Idyll* is a self-standing literary piece to be read for its own sake. The literary tradition that one must know to fully understand it disappears and only gleams from behind the text like the underscript of a palimpsest. In this sense, understanding the *Idyll* requires a higher level of education than understanding the classics with the help of commentaries. And, indeed, reading the *Idyll* might have been much more entertaining.

REFERENCES

Adler, A. (ed.) (1928–38) *Suidae lexicon*, 5 vols. Leipzig.
Agapitos, P. A. (1990) 'The Erotic Bath in the Byzantine Vernacular Romance *Kallimachos and Chrysorrhoe*', *C&M* 41: 257–73.
  (2013) 'Anna Komnene and the Politics of Schedographic Training and Colloquial Discourse', *Nea Rhome* 10: 89–107.
  (2014) 'Grammar, Genre and Patronage in the Twelfth Century: A Scientific Paradigm and Its Implications', *JÖByz* 64: 1–22.
  (2015a) 'Learning to Read and Write a *Schedos*: The Verse Dictionary of Par. Gr. 400', in *Pour une poétique de Byzance: hommage à Vassilis Katsaros*, ed. S. Efthymiadis, C. Messis, P. Odorico and I. D. Polemis, 11–24. Dossiers Byzantins 16. Paris.
  (2015b) 'Literary *Haute Cuisine* and Its Dangers: Eustathios of Thessalonike on Schedography and Everyday Language', *DOP* 69: 225–41.
  (2015c) 'New Genres in the Twelfth Century: The *Schedourgia* of Theodore Prodromos', *MEG* 15: 1–41.
  (2017) 'John Tzetzes and the Blemish Examiners: A Byzantine Teacher on Schedography, Everyday Language and Writerly Disposition', *MEG* 17: 1–57.
Anagnostou-Laoutides, E. (2017) 'A Web of Translations: Planudes in Search of Human Reason', in *Byzantine Culture in Translation*, ed. A. Brown and B. Neil, 155–76. Leiden.
Bachmann, L. (ed.) (1828) *Anecdota Graeca*, vol. 2, 105–66: *Maximi Planudae Tractatus ineditus Περὶ συντάξεως*. Leipzig.

---

[108] Genette (1997: 4).   [109] Genette (1997: 397).
[110] See also Mullett in this volume on the intricate relations of the *Christos Paschon* to its Euripidean source texts.

Bandini, A. M. (1768) *Catalogus codicum manuscriptorum Bibliothecae Mediceae Laurentianae*, vol. 2. Florence.
Beck, H.-G. (1986) *Byzantinisches Erotikon*. Munich.
Beckby, H. (ed.) (1965) *Anthologia Graeca*, 4 vols., second revised edition. Munich.
Beneker, J. and C. A. Gibson (2016) *The Rhetorical Exercises of Nikephoros Basilakes: Progymnasmata from Twelfth-Century Byzantium*. Cambridge, MA.
van den Berg, B. (2018) 'Homer and the Good Ruler in the "Age of Rhetoric": Eustathios of Thessalonike on Excellent Oratory', in *Homer and the Good Ruler in Antiquity and Beyond*, ed. J. Klooster and B. van den Berg, 219–38. Mnemosyne Supplements 413. Leiden–Boston.
Bernard, F. (2015) 'Humor in Byzantine Letters of the Tenth to Twelfth Centuries: Some Preliminary Remarks', *DOP* 69: 179–95.
Bianconi, D. (2010) 'Erudizione e didattica nella tarda Bisanzio', in *Libri di scuola e pratiche didattiche: dall'antichità al Rinascimento. Atti del Convegno Internazionale di Studi, Cassino, 7–10 maggio 2008*, vol. 2, ed. L. Del Corso and O. Pecere, 475–512. Cassino.
  (2017) 'La lettura dei testi antichi tra didattica ed erudizione: qualche esempio d'età paleologa', in *Toward a Historical Sociolinguistic Poetics of Medieval Greek*, ed. A. M. Cuomo and E. Trapp, 57–83. Byzantioς: Studies in Byzantine History and Civilization 12. Turnhout.
de Boor, C. (1897) *Verzeichnis der griechischen Handschriften der königlichen Bibliothek zu Berlin*, vol. 2. Berlin.
Burton, J. B. (2003) 'A Reemergence of Theocritean Poetry in the Byzantine Novel', *CPh* 98: 251–73.
  (2006) 'The Pastoral in Byzantium', in *Brill's Companion to Greek and Latin Pastoral*, ed. M. Fantuzzi and T. Papanghelis, 549–79. Leiden–Boston.
  (2012) 'From Theocritean to Longan Bucolic: Eugenianus' *Drosilla and Charicles*', *GRBS* 52: 684–713.
Cameron, A. (1993) *The Greek Anthology from Meleager to Planudes*. Oxford.
Canart, P. (2011) 'Les anthologies scolaires commentées de la période des Paléologues, à l'école de Maxime Planude et de Manuel Moschopoulos', in *Encyclopedic Trends in Byzantium? Proceedings of the International Conference Held in Leuven, 6–8 May 2009*, ed. P. van Deun and C. Macé, 297–331. Leuven.
Carpinato, C. (2005) 'Topi nella letteratura greca medievale', in *Animali tra zoologia, mito e letteratura nella cultura classica e orientale. Atti del convegno, Venezia, 22–23 maggio 2002*, ed. E. Cingano, A. Ghersetti and L. Milano, 175–92. Padua.
Constantinides, C. N. (1982) *Higher Education in Byzantium in the Thirteenth and Early Fourteenth Centuries (1204–ca. 1310)*. Nicosia.
  (2003) 'Teachers and Students of Rhetoric in the Late Byzantine Period', in *Rhetoric in Byzantium. Papers from the Thirty-Fifth Spring Symposium of Byzantine Studies, Exeter College, University of Oxford, March 2001*, ed. E. M. Jeffreys, 39–53. Aldershot.

Cupane, C. (1980) 'La magia a Bisanzio nel secolo XIV: azione e reazione dal registro del patriarcato costantinopolitano (1315–1402)', *JÖByz* 29: 237–62.
  (2009) 'Itinerari magici: il viaggio del cavallo volante', in *Medioevo romanzo e orientale: sulle orme di Shahrazàd: le 'Mille e una notte' fra Oriente e Occidente. VI Colloquio Internazionale, Ragusa, 12–14 ottobre 2006*, ed. M. Cassarino, 61–79. Soveria Mannelli.
  (2014) 'Désirs interdits: témoignages de magie malveillante dans la littérature byzantine', in *Les savoirs magiques et leur transmission de l'Antiquité à la Renaissance*, ed. V. Dasen and J.-M. Spieser, 477–96. Florence.
Cyrillo, S. (1832) *Codices graeci manuscripti regiae bibliothecae Borbonicae*, vol. 2. Naples.
Dentith, S. (2000) *Parody*. London.
van Dieten, J. (ed.) (1975) *Nicetae Choniatae historia*. Berlin.
Drpić, I. (2016) *Epigram, Art and Devotion in Later Byzantium*. Cambridge.
Dübner, F. (ed.) (1849) *Scholia in Theocritum*. Paris.
Easterling, P. E. and E. J. Kenney (1965) *Ovidiana graeca: Fragments of a Byzantine Version of Ovid's Amatory Works*. Cambridge.
Fisher, E. A. (2002/2003) 'Planoudes, Holobolos, and the Motivation for Translation', *GRBS* 43: 77–104.
  (2004) 'Planudes' Technique and Competence as a Translator of Ovid's *Metamorphoses*', *ByzSlav* 62: 143–60.
Fodor, N. (2004) 'Die Übersetzungen lateinischer Autoren durch M. Planudes', unpublished PhD thesis, Heidelberg University.
Formentin, M. R. (1995) *Catalogus codicum Graecorum Bibliothecae Nationalis Neapolitanae*, vol. 2. Rome.
Fryde, E. (2000) *The Early Palaeologan Renaissance (1261–c. 1360)*. Leiden.
Gallavotti, C. (1959) 'Planudea', *BollClass* 7: 25–50.
Gaul, N. (2011) *Thomas Magistros und die spätbyzantinische Sophistik: Studien zum Humanismus urbaner Eliten in der frühen Palaiologenzeit*. Wiesbaden.
  (2018) 'Performative Reading in the Late Byzantine *Theatron*', in *Reading in the Byzantine Empire and Beyond*, ed. T. Shawcross and I. Toth, 215–33. Cambridge.
Genette, G. (1997 [1982]) *Palimpsests: Literature in the Second Degree*. Trans. C. Newmann and C. Doubinsky. Lincoln–London.
Gioffreda, A. (2020) *Tra i libri di Isacco Argiro*. Transmissions: Studies on Conditions, Processes, and Dynamics of Textual Transmission 4. Berlin–Boston.
Gow, A. S. F. (ed.) (1952) *Theocritus*, second edition. Cambridge.
Greenfield, R. P. (1995) 'A Contribution to the Study of Palaeologan Magic', in *Byzantine Magic*, ed. H. Maguire, 117–53. Washington, DC.
de Groote, M. (ed.) (2012) *Christophori Mitylenaii versuum variorum collectio Cryptensis*. Turnhout.
Grünbart, M. (2020) 'Das Parisurteil im griechischen Mittelalter', in *Mythen und Narrative des Entscheidens*, ed. M. Wagner-Egelhaaf, B. Quast and H. Basu, 73–92. Kulturen des Entscheidens 3. Göttingen.

Hausrath, A. (1901) 'Die Äsopstudien des Maximus Planudes', *ByzZ* 10: 91–105.
  (ed.) (1970) *Corpus fabularum aesopicarum*, vol. 1: *Fabulae Aesopicae soluta oratione conscriptae*, fourth edition by H. Hunger. Leipzig.
Hock, R. F. (2012) *The Chreia and Ancient Rhetoric: Commentaries on Aphthonius's Progymnasmata*. Atlanta, GA.
von Holzinger, C. (1893) *Ein Idyll des Maximus Planudes*. Vienna.
Hunger, H. (1961) *Katalog der griechischen Handschriften der Österreichischen Nationalbibliothek, Erster Teil: Codices historici; Codices philosophici et philologici*. Vienna.
  (1968) *Der byzantinische Katz-Mäuse-Krieg: Theodoros Prodromos, Katomyomachia. Einleitung, Text und Übersetzung*. Byzantina Vindobonensia 3. Graz–Vienna–Cologne.
Karla, G. (2003) 'Die Redactio Accursiana der *Vita Aesopi*: Ein Werk des Maximos Planudes', *ByzZ* 96: 661–9.
  (2006) 'Maximos Planoudes: Dr. Bowdler in Byzanz? Zensur und Innovation im späten Byzanz', *C&M* 57: 213–38.
  (2016) 'The Literary Life of a Fictional Life: Aesop in Antiquity and Byzantium', in *Fictional Storytelling in the Medieval Eastern Mediterranean and Beyond*, ed. C. Cupane and B. Krönung, 313–37. Brill's Companions to the Byzantine World 1. Leiden–Boston.
Keydell, R. (ed.) (1959) *Nonni Panopolitani Dionysiaca*, 2 vols. Berlin.
Kislinger, E. (2011) 'Byzantine Cats', in Ζώα και Περιβάλλον στο Βυζάντιο (7ος–12ος αι.) / *Animals and Environment in Byzantium (7th–12th c.)*, ed. I. Anagnostakis, T. G. Kolias and E. Papadopulu, 165–78. Athens.
Krueger, D. (2006) 'Homoerotic Spectacle and the Monastic Body in Symeon the New Theologian', in *Towards a Theology of Eros: Transfiguring Passion at the Limits of Discipline*, ed. V. Burrus and C. Keller, 99–118, 399–403. New York.
Kurtz, E. (1893) 'Review of Holzinger (1893)', *Neue Philologische Rundschau* 22: 338–40.
Laiou, A. E. (1992) *Mariage, amour et parenté à Byzance aux XIe–XIIIe siècles*. Paris.
Lampakes, S. (1982) Οι καταβάσεις στον κάτω κόσμο στη βυζαντινή και στη μεταβυζαντινή λογοτεχνία. Ioannina.
Lauxtermann, M. D. (1999) 'Ninth-Century Classicism and the Erotic Muse', in *Desire and Denial in Byzantium. Papers from the 31st Spring Symposium of Byzantine Studies, Brighton, March 1997*, ed. L. James, 161–9. Brookfield.
  (2003–19) *Byzantine Poetry from Pisides to Geometres: Texts and Contexts*, 2 vols. Vienna.
  (forthcoming) 'Of Cats and Mice: The *Katomyomachia* as Drama, Parody, School Text, and Animal Tale', in *Byzantine Poetry in the 'Long' Twelfth Century (1081–1204)*, ed. B. van den Berg and N. Zagklas.
Leone, P. L. M. (ed.) (2007) *Ioannis Tzetzae Historiae*, second edition. Galatina.
von Leutsch, E. L. and F. W. Schneidewin (1839–51) *Corpus Paroemiographorum Graecorum*, 2 vols. Göttingen.

Littlewood, A. R. (1974) 'The Symbolism of the Apple in Byzantine Literature', *JÖByz* 23: 33–59.
  (1993) 'The Erotic Symbolism of the Apple in Late Byzantine and Meta-Byzantine Demotic Literature', *BMGS* 17: 83–103.
MacLeod, M. D. (ed.) (1972–89) *Luciani opera*, 4 vols. Oxford.
Macrides, R., J. Munitiz and D. Angelov (2013) *Pseudo-Kodinos and the Constantinopolitan Court: Offices and Ceremonies*. Farnham.
Marciniak, P. (2007) 'Byzantine *Theatron* – A Place of Performance?', in *Theatron: Rhetorische Kultur in Spätantike und Mittelalter / Rhetorical Culture in Late Antiquity and the Middle Ages*, ed. M. Grünbart, 277–85. Millennium-Studien 13. Berlin–New York.
  (2016) 'Reinventing Lucian in Byzantium', *DOP* 70: 209–24.
  (2017) 'A Pious Mouse and a Deadly Cat: The *Schede tou Myos*, Attributed to Theodore Prodromos', *BMGS* 57: 507–27.
  (2018) '"Heaven for Climate, Hell for Company": Byzantine Satirical *Katabaseis*', in *Round Trip to Hades in the Eastern Mediterranean Tradition: Visits to the Underworld from Antiquity to Byzantium*, ed. G. Ekroth and I. Nilsson, 342–55. Leiden–Boston.
Marciniak, P. and K. Warcaba (2018) 'Theodore Prodromos' *Katomyomachia* as a Byzantine Version of Mock-Epic', in *Middle and Late Byzantine Poetry: Texts and Contexts*, ed. A. Rhoby and N. Zagklas, 97–110. Turnhout.
Masterson, M. (2018) 'Desire, Dreams, and Visions in the Letters of Emperor Konstantinos VII Porphyrogennetos and Theodoros Kyzikos', in *Dreams, Memory and Imagination in Byzantium*, ed. B. Neil and E. Anagnostou-Laoutides, 136–59. Leiden–Boston.
Mazal, O. (1967) *Der Roman des Konstantinos Manasses: Überlieferung, Rekonstruktion, Textausgabe der Fragmente*. Vienna.
Mergiali, S. (1996) *L'enseignement et les lettrés pendant l'époque des Paléologues (1261–1453)*. Athens.
Messis, C. (2021) 'The Fortune of Lucian in Byzantium', in *Satire in the Middle Byzantine Period: The Golden Age of Laughter?*, ed. P. Marciniak and I. Nilsson, 13–38. Explorations in Medieval Culture 12. Leiden–Boston.
Mioni, E. (1965) *Catalogo di manoscritti greci esistenti nelle biblioteche italiane*, vol. 2. Rome.
  (1971–2) 'Nuovi contributi alla Silloge Vaticana dell'Antologia Planudea', *RSBN* 8–9: 87–107.
  (1985) *Bibliothecae Divi Marci Venetiarvm codices Graeci manvscripti*, vol. 2: *Thesaurus antiquus; Codices 300–625*. Rome.
Mullett, M. (1999) 'From Byzantium, with Love', in *Desire and Denial in Byzantium. Papers from the 31st Spring Symposium of Byzantine Studies, Brighton, March 1997*, ed. L. James, 3–22. Brookfield.
Nicholas, N. and G. Baloglou (2003) *An Entertaining Tale of Quadrupeds: Translation and Commentary*. New York.
Nilsson, I. (2016) 'Poets and Teachers in the Underworld: From the Lucianic katabasis to the *Timarion*', *SO* 90: 180–204.

(2018) 'Hades Meets Lazarus: The Literary *Katabasis* in Twelfth-Century Byzantium', in *Round Trip to Hades in the Eastern Mediterranean Tradition: Visits to the Underworld from Antiquity to Byzantium*, ed. G. Ekroth and I. Nilsson, 322–41. Leiden–Boston.

Nissen, T. (1936) 'Die Aristeas-Legende im Idyll des Planudes', *ByzZ* 36: 291–9.

Nousia, F. (2016) *Byzantine Textbooks of the Palaeologan Period*. Studi e Testi 505. Vatican City.

(2017) 'The Transmission and Reception of Manuel Moschopoulos' *Schedography* in the West', in *Teachers, Students, and Schools of Greek in the Renaissance*, ed. F. Ciccolella and L. Silvano, 1–25. Leiden–Boston.

Papaioannou, S. (2011) 'Michael Psellos on Friendship and Love: Erotic Discourse in Eleventh-Century Constantinople', *Early Medieval Europe* 19: 43–61.

Papathomopoulos, M. (1979) Τοῦ σοφωτάτου κύρου Θεοδώρου τοῦ Προδρόμου τὰ Σχέδη τοῦ μύος', *Parnassos* 21: 376–99.

(2002) Ὀβιδίου Περὶ μεταμορφώσεων ὃ μετήνεγκεν ἐκ τῆς λατίνων φωνῆς εἰς τὴν ἑλλάδα Μάξιμος Μόναχος ὁ Πλανούδης. Athens.

(ed.) (2009) Κάτωνος γνῶμαι παραινετικαὶ δίστιχοι ἃς μετήνεγκεν ἐκ τῆς Λατίνων φωνῆς εἰς τὴν Ἑλλάδα διάλεκτον Μάξιμος Μόναχος ὁ Πλανούδης. Athens.

Patillon, M. (ed. and trans.) (2008) *Anonyme, Préambule à la rhétorique; Aphthonios, Progymnasmata; Pseudo-Hermogène, Progymnasmata*. Corpus Rhetoricum 1. Paris.

Penskaya, D. (2018) 'Hagiography and Fairytale: Paradise and the Land of the Blessed in Byzantium', in *Byzantine Hagiography: Texts, Themes & Projects*, ed. A. Rigo, M. Trizio and E. Despotakis, 141–55. Turnhout.

Pérez Martín, I. (1997) 'La "escuela de Planudes": notas paleográficas a una publicación reciente sobre los escolios euripideos', *ByzZ* 90: 73–96.

Perry, B. E. (1936) *Studies in the Text History of the Life and Fables of Aesop*. Haverford, PA.

Piccolomini (ed.) (1874) 'Intorno ai Collectanea di Massimo Planude', *RFIC* 2: 101–17, 149–63.

Pietsch-Braounou, E. (2010) 'Ein Aspekt der Rezeption der *Anthologia Planudea* in Epigrammen des Manuel Philes auf Bilder', in *Imitatio, aemulatio, variatio. Akten des internationalen wissenschaftlichen Symposions zur byzantinischen Sprache und Literatur (Wien, 22.–25. Oktober 2008)*, ed. A. Rhoby and E. Schiffer, 217–30. Vienna.

Pizzone, A. (2016) 'Audiences and Emotions in Eustathios of Thessalonike's Commentaries on Homer', *DOP* 70: 225–44.

(2017) 'The *Historiai* of John Tzetzes: A Byzantine "Book of Memory"?', *BMGS* 41.2: 182–207.

Pontani, F. M. (ed.) (1973) *Maximi Planudis Idyllium*. Padua.

Rapp, C. (2016) *Brother-making in Late Antiquity and Byzantium: Monks, Laymen, and Christian Ritual*. Oxford.

Rhoby, A. (2010) 'Zur Identifizierung von bekannten Autoren im Codex Marcianus graecus 524', *MEG* 10: 167–204.

Richter, W. (1972) 'Ziege', in *Pauly's Real-Encyclopädie der classischen Altertumswissenschaft: Neue Bearbeitung*, Zweite Reihe: vol. 10/1, ed. G. Wissowa, W. Kroll, K. Mittelhaus and K. Ziegler, 398–433. Munich.

Schneider, J. (2009) 'Une correspondance érudite: les lettres de Maxime Planude', *Eruditio Antiqua* 1: 63–85.

Schneider, M. (1894) 'Review of Holzinger (1893)', *Berliner philologische Wochenschrift* 14: 615–21.

Spingou, F. (2021) *Words and Artworks in Byzantium: Twelfth-Century Poetry on Art from MS. Marcianus Gr. 524*. Tolworth, Surrey.

de Stefani, C. (2016) 'Brief Notes on the Manuscript Tradition of Nonnus' Works', in *Brill's Companion to Nonnus of Panopolis*, ed. D. Accorinti, 671–90. Leiden–Boston.

Sturm, J. (1901) 'Ein unbekanntes griechisches Idyll aus der Mitte des xv. Jahrhunderts', *ByzZ* 10: 433–52.

Taxidis, I. (2012) Μάξιμος Πλανούδης: Συμβολή στη μελέτη του corpus των επιστολών του. Thessaloniki.

  (ed.) (2017) *Les épigrammes de Maxime Planude: introduction, édition critique, traduction française et annotation*. Berlin–Boston.

Theodoridis, C. (ed.) (1982–) *Photii patriarchae lexicon*, 3 vols. Berlin.

Thompson, S. (1956) *Motif-Index of Folk-Literature: A Classification of Narrative Elements in Folktales, Ballads, Myths, Fables, Mediaeval Romances, Exempla, Fabliaux, Jest-Books and Local Legends*, vol. 2: *D–E*, second revised and enlarged edition. Bloomington.

Treu, M. (ed.) (1878) *Maximi Planudis Comparatio hiemis et veris*. Ohlau.

  (1896) 'Antistoichien', *ByzZ* 5: 337–8.

Valerio, F. (2011) 'Planudeum', *JÖByz* 61: 229–36.

  (2018) 'Tre epigrammi di Massimo Planude', in *Il calamo della memoria* VII: *raccolta delle relazioni discusse nell'incontro internazionale di Trieste, Biblioteca statale, 29–30 settembre 2016*, ed. L. Cristante and V. Veronesi, 271–91. Trieste.

Vassis, I. (1994) 'Graeca sunt, non leguntur: Zu den schedographischen Spielereien des Theodoros Prodromos', *ByzZ* 86/87: 1–19.

  (2002) 'Των νέων φιλολόγων παλαίσματα: Η συλλογή σχεδών του κώδικα Vaticanus Palatinus gr. 92', *Hellenika* 52: 37–68.

Vlavianos, S. (2013) *La figure du mage à Byzance: de Jean Damascène à Michael Psellos, VIIIe – fin XIe siècle*. Paris.

Vöhler, M. and B. Seidensticker (eds.) (2005) *Mythenkorrekturen: Zu einer paradoxalen Form der Mythenrezeption*. Berlin–New York.

Vöhler, M., B. Seidensticker and W. Emmerich (2005) 'Zum Begriff der Mythenkorrektur', in *Mythenkorrekturen: Zu einer paradoxalen Form der Mythenrezeption*, ed. M. Vöhler and B. Seidensticker, 1–18. Berlin–New York.

Volk, R. (ed.) (2006–9) *Die Schriften des Johannes von Damaskos VI: Historia animae utilis de Barlaam et Ioasaph (spuria)*, 2 vols. Berlin.

Wagner, R. (ed.) (1926) *Mythographi graeci*, vol. 1: *Apollodori Bibliotheca; Pediasimi libellus de duodecim Herculis laboribus*. Stuttgart–Leipzig.

Wendel, C. (1950) 'Planudes, Maximos', in *Paulys Real-Encyclopädie der classischen Altertumswissenschaft: Neue Bearbeitung*, vol. 20.2, ed. G. Wissowa, W. Kroll, K. Mittelhaus and K. Ziegler, 2202–53. Stuttgart.
Wendel, K. (ed.) (1914) *Scholia in Theocritum vetera*. Leipzig.
Wilson, N. (1996 [1983]) *Scholars of Byzantium*, revised edition. London–Cambridge, MA.
Zagklas, N. (2021) 'Satire in the Komnenian Period: Poetry, Satirical Strands, and Intellectual Antagonism', in *Satire in the Middle Byzantine Period: The Golden Age of Laughter?*, ed. P. Marciniak and I. Nilsson, 279–303. Explorations in Medieval Culture 12. Leiden–Boston.

CHAPTER 10

Teaching Poetry in the Early Palaiologan School
Manuel Holobolos' and John Pediasimos' Commentaries on Theocritus' Syrinx

Paula Caballero Sánchez

The aim of this chapter is to show how, from the year 1265 on, the Palaiologan school would engage with the newly rediscovered Hellenistic pattern-poem *Syrinx*, traditionally attributed to Theocritus. Two scholar-teachers who made use of this text in their classes were Manuel/Maximos Holobolos (1243–1310/14) and John Pothos Pediasimos (ca. 1240–1310/14), both of whom produced commentaries on the poem. Their work on this text and their study of it in a scholastic context have so far received little notice. I hope, therefore, to shed light on the various ways in which these educators approached their commentaries on this highly unusual work in its cultural context, so as to understand how they used and adapted it to their didactic needs.

The *Syrinx*: A Hellenistic Pattern-Poem

The *Syrinx* is one of the six compositions that comprise the corpus of what have been designated *technopaegnia* or *carmina figurata*. The peculiar characteristic common to these poems is their form, as they are in effect visual poems that reproduce a silhouette of the object to which they are dedicated.

Neither their ancient nor their Byzantine commentators referred to these poems as *technopaegnia* (pattern-poems). This label, which means 'game of ingenuity', is found in Latin (*technopaegnion*) in the homonymous work by

---

* This article was funded by a contribution from the research project group 'The Byzantine Author' (MICINN, FFI2015-65118-C2-2-P) of the CCHS-CSIC (Spain) and research group HUM 312 of the University of Málaga. I thank I. Pérez Martín for her critical reading and the editors of this volume for their recommendations.
Abbreviated works:
  Br. = Briquet, C. M. (1907) *Les filigranes. Dictionnaire historique des marques de papier dès leur apparition vers 1282 jusqu'e en 1600*. Geneva. 4 vols.
  ODB = Kazhdan, A. P. et al. (1991) *The Oxford Dictionary of Byzantium*. New York–Oxford. 3 vols.
  PLP = Trapp, E. et al. (1976–95) *Prosopographisches Lexicon der Palaiologenzeit*. Vienna. 15 vols.

Ausonius (fourth century AD).[1] Ausonius' compositions, however, have few similarities to the Greek *technopaegnia*, as they do not create any particular silhouette. Nevertheless, in the seventeenth century, the Italian humanist Fortunio Liceti, who wrote commentaries to five of the *technopaegnia*,[2] would introduce the term in its modern philological sense by taking it from Ausonius.

We know very little about the history of these poems. Chronologically, except for the *Ionic Altar*, they date from the Hellenistic period. Simmias of Rhodes might have been the inventor of the genre,[3] as he is the author of the three earliest pattern-poems (third century BC) *Egg*, *Axe* and *Wings*,[4] according to the grammarian and poet Hephaestion.[5] The *Syrinx* of Theocritus would have been contemporary to this series, if, that is, we accept the Theocritean paternity of the poem.[6] The *Ionic Altar* is a work by Dosiadas and shows the influence of Lycophron's *Alexandra*, to which it must therefore be contemporary or slightly posterior.[7] The latest of these compositions is thought to be the *Altar* of Besantinus (second century AD),[8] as its acrostic 'Ὀλύμπιε, πολλοῖς ἔτεσι θύσειας' ('Olympian, may you sacrifice for many years') probably refers to the emperor Hadrian,[9] who adopted the title of 'Olympian' among others. In a broad sense, this type of visual poetry has had a long tradition throughout history ranging from Ausonius and Optatianus Porfirius in the Latin context and the writers and scholars of Byzantium[10] to the experimental calligrammes of Apollinaire in the twentieth century. The peculiarity of the Greek pattern-poems

---

[1] Peiper (1886).   [2] Liceti (1630), (1635), (1637), (1640), (1655).
[3] On Simmias of Rhodes and visual poetry in Greek and Latin contexts, see Kwapisz (2019). See also Kwapisz (2013) for an exhaustive study of the Greek *technopaegnia* with an edition and translation of and commentary on the poems.
[4] Fränkel (1915: 10–11).   [5] Fränkel (1915: 9–10).
[6] Philologists still debate his authorship. Gow (1914: 128–38) did not believe that Theocritus was the author, as in the poet's time the syrinx did not have a triangular but rather a rectangular shape, with all of its reeds having the same length. See West (1992: 111) for the same opinion on the shape of the syrinx. The debate on the authorship of the poem has since remained open; among the sceptics, we may also cite Guichard (2006: 84, n. 6), who feels that the question was resolved with Gow's thesis, or Palumbo Stracca (2007: 120–6), for whom the poem, conceived in homage to Theocritus, cannot be attributed to him. Meanwhile, Gallavotti (1993³) does not doubt Theocritus' authorship, nor do Fantuzzi and Hunter (2002: 40–1) or Männlein-Robert (2007: 150, n. 144) view it as improbable.
[7] The *terminus post quem* for the *Altar* of Dosiadas is considered to be Lycophron's *Alexandra*, while the *terminus ante quem* is Lucian, who quotes from the *Altar*: see Fantuzzi and Hunter (2002: 40, n. 161).
[8] This Besantinus would be a corruption of the name of Lucius Julius Vestinus, a Roman sophist and official at Hadrian's court: see Haeberlin (1890: 283–4) and Bowie (2002: 185–9).
[9] Haeberlin (1887: 65–6).   [10] On visual poetry in Byzantium, see Hörandner (1990: 1–42).

(except for Simmias' *Axe*, *Egg* and *Wings*) lies also in their obscure and enigmatic content, rendered in an ornate style based on cryptic wordplays that challenge the erudition of even the most scholarly reader. This is especially true of the *Syrinx* and the *Doric Altar*.

The Greek pattern-poems had a double transmission: through the *Corpus Bucolicorum* (in miscellanies composed in the Palaiologan period) and the *Palatine Anthology* (now the codex Paris, Bibliothèque nationale de France, suppl. gr. 384), to whose Book IV they were added around the year AD 900.[11] In any case, one only needs to read them to see that these compositions are not in fact bucolic in character. They fall, rather, within the genre of epigrams and this is precisely, with the exception of the *Ionic Altar*, what they appear to be.

The *Syrinx* was supposedly conceived as a dedicatory inscription engraved on a bucolic panpipe;[12] it is a hymn as well as a dedication. In the poem, Theocritus, the 'judge of gods' according to the etymology of his name (*theos* and *krites*), offers his pipe (*syrinx*) to the god Pan, so that the latter may play sweet melodies on them to one of his beloved nymphs, Echo. This dedication, however, only appears in verses 11–12,[13] while the rest of the poem is an erudite and highly mannered hymn to the god himself, to his life, loves and achievements, which are never alluded to explicitly, but rather through continuous riddles or *griphoi*. Thus, by unravelling these enigmas, the reader is able to trace nearly the entire mythical and literary tradition of the god. What is more, to create the graphic effect of the instrument itself, the poet employs distichs that are gradually reduced in length (with each progressive distich losing a half-foot) to produce the visual image of a panpipe:

Οὐδενὸς εὐνάτειρα, Μακροπτολέμοιο δὲ μάτηρ,
μαίας ἀντιπέτροιο θοὸν τέκεν ἰθυντῆρα,
οὐχὶ Κεράσταν ὅν ποτε θρέψατο ταυροπάτωρ,
ἀλλ' οὗ πειλιπὲς αἶθε πάρος φρένα τέρμα σάκους,

---

[11] *A.P.* 15.21, 22, 24–7 in this order respectively: *Syrinx, Axe, Wings, Ionic Altar, Doric Altar* and *Egg*. All of these poems were accompanied by scholia except for *Doric Altar*. On the manuscript transmission of the Greek figure poems, see Strodel (2002), Kwapisz (2013: 50–6, with bibliography).

[12] According to Wilamowitz (1906: 243), these compositions were not intended to be published; Fränkel (1915: 56–62), more cautiously, does not believe they were ever inscribed on real objects.

[13] ᾧ τόδε τυφλοφόρων ἐρατόν / πᾶμα Πάρις θέτο Σιμιχίδας ('to him Paris son of Simichus dedicated the lovely possession of the carriers of blindness') where the Greek πᾶμα ('item', 'possession') is the possession of Theocritus: the syrinx.

οὔνομ᾽ Ὅλον, δίζων, ὃς τᾶς μέροπος πόθον   5
κούρας γηρυγόνας ἔχε τᾶς ἀνεμώδεος,
ὃς Μοίσᾳ λιγὺ πᾶξεν ἰοστεφάνῳ
ἕλκος, ἄγαλμα πόθοιο πυρισμαράγου,
ὃς σβέσεν ἀνορέαν ἰσαυδέα
παπποφόνου Τυρίας τ᾽ ἐ<ξήλασεν>,   10
ᾧ τόδε τυφλοφόρων ἐρατὸν
πᾶμα Πάρις θέτο Σιμιχίδας·
ψυχὰν ᾇ, βροτοβάμων,
στήτας οἶστρε Σαέττας,
κλωποπάτωρ, ἀπάτωρ,   15
λαρνακόγυιε, χαρεὶς
ἁδὺ μελίσδοις
ἔλλοπι κούρᾳ,
Καλλιόπᾳ
νηλεύστῳ.   20

1–2 The bedfellow of Nobody and mother of Far-war gave birth to the swift director of the nurse who stood in for a stone, **3** not the Horned One who was once nurtured by a bull father, **4** but he whose mind was once set on fire by the p-lacking shield rim, **5–6** Whole by name, double in nature, who loved the voice-dividing girl, swift as the wind and with human speech, **7–8** him who put together a shrill wound for the violet-crowned Muse to represent his fiery love, **9–10** who extinguished the might that sounded like a man who murdered his grandfather, and drove it out of the Tyrian girl. **11–12** To him Paris son of Simichus dedicated the lovely possession of the carriers of blindness. **13–16** May it please your soul, man-treading gadfly of the Lydian woman, son of a thief and son of no one, coffer limbed, **17–18** and may you play it sweetly **19–20** to a girl who has no voice of her own but is an unseen Calliope.[14]

These ingenious devices did not go unnoticed by either the ancients or the Byzantines. It is evident that, from the earliest times, the cryptic nature and visual aspect of these poems aroused the interest of commentators, who struggled to decipher and explain the text.[15]

In the eleventh century, Michael Psellos left us a testimony of his reading of the *Syrinx* in a fragment of a didactic poem he dedicated to his student, the future emperor Michael VII Doukas. In it, Psellos refers to the limitations of grammar in explaining some of the poem's intricate wordplay and in finding equivalents in the common language. In particular, he mentions the epithet which alludes indirectly to Zeus in the *Syrinx* (v. 2): ἀντίπετρον ('of the nurse who stood in for a stone'):

---

[14] For the *Syrinx* I use the edition and translation in the Loeb collection: Hopkinson (2015: 572–3).
[15] The *scholia vetera* were edited by Wendel (1914: 336–52).

Οὐ πάντων ἡ γραμματικὴ πέφυκεν ἐμπειρία· τῶν πολιτευομένων γὰρ
λέξεων ἐπιστήμη, οὐ τῶν ἐν παραβύστῳ δέ τισι συμπεπλασμένων. τὰς
γὰρ ἐν τῷ Λυκόφρονι 'εὐῶπας κόρας', κώπας, καὶ τὸν παρὰ τῇ Σύριγγι
'ἀντίπετρον' οὐκ οἶδεν·[16]

> Grammar does not provide experience on every kind of topic, as it is the science of common words, but not those that might be invented in some elaborate text; in effect, grammar does not know that the 'beautiful maidens' (εὐῶπας κόρας) in Lycophron are oars (κώπας) nor 'of the nurse who stood in for a stone' (ἀντίπετρον) in the *Syrinx*.

In the twelfth century, we find mentions of the *Syrinx* in the works of John Tzetzes and the bishop Eustathios of Thessalonike. The former alludes occasionally to the poem in his commentary to Lycophron's *Alexandra*, citing words or verbal structures employed by the bucolic poet to elucidate the text.[17] The latter, meanwhile, mentions it in his commentaries to the *Iliad* and the *Odyssey*,[18] where he often references the Theocritean *Idylls* as his lexical and literary source. One such instance is particularly interesting, as it shows that the bishop not only read the *Syrinx*, but was also interested in its meaning. In a lexical scholion, he presents the various meanings of the word σύριγξ (*sic*), which occurred in *Iliad* 19.387:

> Σύριγξ δὲ ὀπή τις ἐπιμήκης δοράτων φυλακτική, ἡ καὶ δουροδόκη. Σημείωσαι δὲ τὴν ὁμωνυμίαν τῆς σύριγγος. οὐ μόνον γὰρ σύριγξ ποιμενική, ἔτι δὲ καὶ ποδὸς ἕλκος, ὡς ὁ Θεόκριτος, καὶ ἐκ πόλεως κρυπτὸς ὑπόνομος κατάγων εἰς ὕδωρ, ἀλλ' ἰδοὺ καὶ αὕτη σύριγξ δουρατοδόχος. (Eustathios, *Commentary on the Iliad* 1189.45–7 = 4.346.15–18 ed. van der Valk)

> 'Syrinx' is a type of long sheath, with an opening, for carrying spears and thus it also means 'a case for spears' (δουροδόκη). Note the homonymy of the word 'syrinx'. That 'syrinx' is not only [the instrument] used by shepherds, as well as an ulcer of the foot, to which Theocritus refers, and an urban underground canal through which water flows, but, mind you, this syrinx is also a spearholder.

There is no doubt that the *Syrinx* and the *technopaegnia* were read and copied in the Macedonian and Komnenian periods, as shown by their

---

[16] Westerink (1992: 6.168–71).
[17] See, for example, schol. in Lyc. 558.7 regarding ἐγκορύψεται (charge, *Id.* 3.5).
[18] *Iliad*: van der Valk (1971–87); *Odyssey*: Stallbaum (1825–6).

transmission in manuscripts and their *scholia vetera*. Thirty-six extant manuscripts from the twelfth to fifteenth centuries contain at least one of these compositions. However, it was not until the Palaiologan period that a renewed interest in these peculiar works would arise. In the context of restoring teaching in Constantinople after the recapture of the city from Latin domination (1261), Greek poetry was studied again in the capital. Hellenistic bucolic poetry played an important role in the education of Byzantine intellectuals, as reflected by the numerous scholastic manuscripts which date from this period (for example, Florence, Biblioteca Medicea Laurenziana, Plut. 32.16, thirteenth-cent. ex., copied by Maximos Planoudes). In fact, the only Byzantine exegetical commentaries that exist on the *technopaegnia* are from this early Palaiologan period.[19]

We owe the renewed interest in the *technopaegnia* to two scholars who re-introduced the study of these works in school by penning exegetical commentaries on the poems. These authors were Manuel Holobolos, who devoted commentaries to at least four of the six *technopaegnia*, and his student, John Pediasimos, who commented solely on the *Syrinx*.

The *Syrinx* in the Palaiologan School: The Commentary of Manuel Holobolos

Manuel/Maximos Hololobos (mid-thirteenth century–ca. 1296/1310)[20] prepared a *recensio* and commentaries to, at least, the *Doric Altar*, the *Ionic Altar*, the *Syrinx* and the *Axe*. If the same is true of *Egg* and *Wings*, these writings have not been preserved, although Carl Wendel maintains that Holobolos edited those poems and even accompanied them with an illumination that would have been exclusively Palaiologan in creation.[21] More recently, Silvia Strodel has argued that there are indications of the existence of a commentary to *Wings* by Holobolos in the anonymous exegesis contained in fol. 110v of Moscow, Gosudarstvennyj Istoričeskij

---

[19] On bucolic poetry in the Palaiologan period, see also Kubina in this volume.
[20] *PLP* 21047 and *ODB* 2, 940. On Holobolos, see e.g. Treu (1896: 538–54), Hannick (1981), Hörandner (1970: 116–19). On his pedagogical and intellectual work, Constantinides (1982: 26–7, 50–65) and Mergiali (1996: 30–1).
[21] Wendel (1907: 460–7), (1910: 331–7). It is true that we do not now have any of these poems with illumination from before the Palaiologan period, although this does not mean that they did not exist. On the other hand, it is difficult to know for certain whether the Holobolos edition contained drawings: Kwapisz (2019: 128) presents his doubts in this respect. Bernabò and Magnelli (2011: 219–21), however, do not completely reject the hypothesis that this edition could have included drawings. On the Byzantine and later iconography that accompanies the *technopaegnia* in Palaiologan manuscripts, see also Bernabò and Magnelli (2011: 189–232).

Musej, Sinod. gr. 501 (Vlad. 480), from the fifteenth/sixteenth centuries,[22] which is edited for the first time[23] by Strodel, together with Holobolos' commentaries on the preserved pattern-poems.[24]

Holobolos' philological and exegetical work on the *technopaegnia* happened in the context of reintroduction of education for future dignitaries and functionaries, which was implemented by Emperor Michael VIII in Constantinople (1261). In fact, Holobolos, in one of his propagandistic panegyrics dedicated to Michael VIII,[25] for whom he served as imperial secretary, speaks of the emperor's efforts to reinstitute in the capital subjects such as grammar, poetry, rhetoric, philosophy (Aristotelian and dialectical logic), arithmetic, geometry and harmony. His exegetical production reveals that Holobolos taught classes in some of these areas, specifically philosophy and poetry, for which subjects we have extant commentaries[26] and scholastic exercises of a grammatical nature.[27] His exegeses correspond to a basic and generalized teaching of the subjects of the *trivium*, but was strongly influenced by the political circumstances of the imperial and patriarchal policy of the Union of Catholic and Orthodox Churches, as can be observed in his Greek translation of Boethius.[28] It is likely that his scant exegetical production was due to the difficult circumstances of his life, which prevented him from working continuously and systematically in the capital, falling out of the emperor's favour on at least two occasions: first, for his support of the legitimate emperor, John IV Laskaris; and second, for his fierce opposition to the Union of Churches.[29]

---

[22] I here follow Strodel's dating, as I have not been able to consult the codex, which is not found in digitized or microfilmed format in the IRHT.

[23] Strodel (2002: 148–50). On the commentaries of Holobolos, see Strodel (2002: 131–56). Holobolos' commentary on the *Syrinx* was edited previously by Dübner (1849: 111–13).

[24] Strodel (2002: 131–56). Prior to this, Holobolos' commentary on the *Axe* of Simmias was edited by Sbordone (1951: 169–77), and his commentary on the *Doric Altar* of Dosiadas by Ferreri (2006: 317–54).

[25] Treu (1906: 95.34–97.7). For their chronology and role in imperial propaganda, see Angelov (2007: 68, n. 150).

[26] Apart from his commentaries on the Hellenistic *carmina figurata*, Holobolos is the author of some cursory exegetic notes on Aristotle's *Prior Analytics*, preserved in Vatican City, Biblioteca Apostolica Vaticana, gr. 1141 (first quarter of the fourteenth century) under the title Τοῦ Ὀλοβόλου (sic) εἰς τὰ τρία σχήματα (*Holobolos on the three figures*). These notes were identified by Treu (1896: 552–3). On the same notes, see also Pérez Martín (1997: 86–9), Bydén (2004: 133–57).

[27] See his solutions to the enigmas attributed to Eustathios Makrembolites, edited by Treu (1893).

[28] On the historical/cultural context and the motives that might have led Holobolos to undertake his translation, see Bydén (2004: 143–6). On his Greek version of the *On Topical Differences* and *On Hypothetical Syllogisms* of Boethius, for which he wrote accompanying commentaries, see Fisher (2002/3: 77–104), (2012: 210–22).

[29] On the bloody persecution of anti-unionist intellectuals by the emperor, see Constantinides (1993: 86–93), Pérez Martín (1995: 411–22).

But why did he choose these poems for his classes? What is the contribution of his commentaries to the Palaiologan school? The reading and study of this type of composition is related to the Byzantine taste for erudite, mannered works, as they pose a challenge to the reader by presenting a complex and obscure literary puzzle to be decoded. From a scholastic perspective, the study of pattern-poems was striking and attractive for the instructor as much as for his students owing to their enigmatic content, non-Attic language and peculiar graphic form. They did not only introduce students to completely new and different compositional techniques, but also allowed a complete study of some of their aspects: metrics, lexicon (wordplay, synonymy, homonymy, metonymy, etc.) and mythology. These poems offer a host of didactic possibilities from the perspective of both language and content, as well as an interesting visual experience based on an intricately crafted metrical structure. In the specific case of the *Syrinx*, the poem constitutes an enigmatic gloss on the god Pan, as it condenses into only a few verses a great part of the mythical and literary tradition of one of the more remarkable and extravagant divinities in the Greek pantheon.

Holobolos' exegetical work on the *technopaegnia* consisted of a *recensio* of these poems accompanied by brief, simple commentaries, sometimes paraphrastic, as in the case of *Axe*, whose principal, and we might say almost exclusive, source were the *scholia vetera*. As we will see, for the *Syrinx*, Holobolos wrote a commentary divided into two sections (on metrics and on content) that was shorter than this earlier material (it was in fact a synopsis, as he himself called it), in which he is especially concerned with lexicon and etymology, and disregards the mythological aspects present in the *scholia vetera*. Holobolos was also the author of two epigrams on the *Syrinx* which are found in the margins of the poem. However, in some Palaiologan manuscripts, these epigrams are frequently found with no mention of their authorship. This, and the fact that no pre-Palaiologan manuscripts of the bucolic corpus are preserved, does not permit us to know for certain whether this is completely original material.[30]

The epigram reads as follows:

Τοῦ σοφωτάτου ῥήτορος Ὁλοβόλου ἐπίγραμμα εἰς τὴν Σύριγγα:
Ἤχημα Μουσῶν ἡ Θεοκρίτου Σύριγξ.
Τοῦ αὐτοῦ ῥήτορος Ὁλοβόλου:
Σύριζε τὴν σύριγγα τήνδε συντόνως,

---

[30] The manuscripts of the bucolic tradition contain an ancient epigram that Holobolos probably read (see p. 286 below) and that he seems to have confused with the poem: σῦριγξ οὔνομ' ἔχεις, ᾄδει δέ σε μέτρα σοφίης ('syrinx, you are notable, so he sings you metres of wisdom').

Εἴ τις λόγων πέφυκας ἔννουν τεκνίον,
Καὶ γάλα Μουσῶν ἐξαποθλίβειν θέλεις.³¹

Epigram to the *Syrinx* of the all-wise rhetor Holobolos: the *Syrinx* of Theocritus is a melody of the Muses. From the same rhetor Holobolos: play this syrinx with vehemence / if you are somehow a sane boy of words, / and want to squeeze all the milk out of the Muses.

By means of this epigram, a literary amusement dedicated to Pan, Holobolos not only leaves his own authorial stamp as scholar, editor, transmitter and commentator of the text, but is probably seeking to emulate the enigmatic content of the poem itself. The epigram alludes to the tiny Pan, who, a goatherd, milks his goats. In the same way, as goatherd-musician, he will now be able to obtain the milk of the Muses by playing the sweetest melodies to them on the syrinx. For Holobolos' students, these epigrams are an exhortation to read the *Syrinx*, a poetic form that they must master just as Pan masters the instrument.

The commentaries are noteworthy for providing a new generation of scholars with a *recensio* of these poems with their corresponding exegeses, which must have enjoyed a certain popularity, as they were widely transmitted. Indeed, more than twenty manuscripts from the thirteenth to seventeenth centuries that contain exegeses by Holobolos of one or other of the pattern-poems have been preserved. In the particular case of the *Syrinx*, there are four that transmit his commentary (fourteenth–sixteenth centuries). These are Paris, Bibliothèque nationale de France, gr. 2832 (second quarter of the fourteenth century)[32] and its direct apographs for the text of the *Syrinx*,[33] which were produced in Italy in the fifteenth century: Milan, Biblioteca Ambrosiana, gr. B 75 sup. (fifteenth century);[34] Florence, Biblioteca Medicea Laurenziana, Asburnham 1174 (second quarter of the fifteenth century);[35] and Uppsala, University Library, gr. 21 (second quarter of the fifteenth century).[36] It was perhaps the uniqueness of these poems, together with their peculiar graphic form, that

---

[31] Strodel (2002: 144).
[32] Watermark: 'Lion', sim. to Mošin 6119 (a. 1348) and 6122 (a. 1353) in the first codicological unit. For a description of this manuscript, see Omont (1904: 189–97), (1905: 155–8) and (1929: 60, pl. 130 a–b).
[33] Sbordone (1951: 172), Gallavotti (1993³: 310–11).
[34] Not having access to this manuscript, I have followed here the dating given in the Martini–Bassi catalogue (1906: 116–17).
[35] Watermarks: 'Balance', sim. to *Br.* 2448 (Treviso, a. 1433) and 'Aigle', sim. to *Br.* 80 (Ferrara, a. 1434).
[36] Not having the opportunity to study the manuscript *in situ*, I have followed here the dating of the exhaustive description available online at: www.manuscripta.se/ms/100021.

led to their presentation in an illustrated edition in the Palaiologan period.³⁷ The most detailed testimonies of this (Par. gr. 2832, Ambros. gr. B75 sup. and Laur. Ashb. 1174) show that the poem occupied the central part of a folio, within a syrinx with orifices, to the sides of which are polychrome figures of Pan and Theocritus, while in its more modest version (Uppsala gr. 21) the space in which these figures appear is occupied by marginal commentary, with the poem itself situated within a silhouette barely recognizable as a syrinx.

For the sake of brevity, I will not attempt to explain the transmission of the commentary and the manuscripts, but I would like to examine the oldest of these testimonies more closely, as it is the archetype of the tradition and the model of the first edition of the commentary. Par. gr. 2832 is a *recueil factice*, whose first codicological unit contains the Triklinian *recensio* of a selection of bucolic poems (fols. 1r–45r),³⁸ including the *Idylls*, and two elegant illustrated versions of the *technopaegnia* and their Palaiologan commentaries. These include the *Syrinx* of Theocritus with the two epigrams by Holobolos (fol. 46r); Holobolos' synopsis (fol. 46v); the commentary of Pediasimos (fols. 46v–47r); the *Altar* of Dosiadas, with figures of the poet and Apollo on either side of an altar with the two epigrams by Holobolos (fol. 47v); and, once again, the *Syrinx*, accompanied by Holobolos' two epigrams, figures of Theocritus and Pan on opposite sides of the poem and glosses from Holobolos' commentary between the lines (fol. 48v) (see Fig. 10.1).

This manuscript was the only one used by Dübner for the first edition of Holobolos' synopsis, to which he assigned the letter G.³⁹ However, just after this, Dübner would edit another more detailed and orderly commentary on the *Syrinx*, this one anonymous and untitled, which is included in Paris, Bibliothèque nationale de France, gr. 2781 (last quarter of the fifteenth century)⁴⁰ and which he gave the letter M. This has led some researchers to attribute this commentary unconsciously to Holobolos. This same exegesis, similarly anonymous, is found in other manuscripts contemporary to Holobolos: Vatican City, Biblioteca Apostolica Vaticana, gr. 915 (fol. 39r),⁴¹ gr. 1825 (fol. 160v)⁴² and gr. 42 (fol. 49v).⁴³ A careful reading of this detailed

---

³⁷ See n. 21.   ³⁸ Sbordone (1951: 172), Gallavotti (1993³: 310–11).
³⁹ Dübner (1849: 111–12).   ⁴⁰ Watermark 'Main', Harlfinger 21 (a. 1491).
⁴¹ Schreiner (1988: 126). The handwriting of the scholia to the *Syrinx* can be dated to the third quarter of the thirteenth century.
⁴² Canart (1970: 240). The codicological unit that contains this exegetic material dates from the first quarter of the fourteenth century: watermark *Br.* 5396 (Bologna, a. 1316).
⁴³ Mercati and Franchi de' Cavalieri (1923: 37). Vat. gr. 42, on oriental paper, can be dated to the last quarter of the thirteenth century, according to palaeographic criteria.

Teaching Poetry in the Early Palaiologan School

Fig. 10.1 Paris, Bibliothèque nationale de France, gr. 2832, fol. 48v

commentary reveals that it is, in fact, a selection of ancient exegetic material that was transmitted in complete form in the margins of the *Palatine Anthology*. This leads one to wonder whether Holobolos had access to this text, which seems very likely. On the one hand, the palaeographic evidence of codices contemporary to Holobolos which transmit this exegesis, such as Vat. gr. 915, dating from the third quarter of the thirteenth century and traceable to Constantinople, informs us that this text was circulating in the capital when Holobolos was teaching (from 1265 on). From a textual point of view, his commentary reveals a reading and reworking of this ancient material. These dates, therefore, indicate that he must have worked on the *Syrinx* in the third quarter of the thirteenth century; that is, after 1265, in the capacity of *rhetor ton rhetoron* (literally, 'rhetor of rhetors', a post appointed by the emperor in which he would train the future ecclesiastics of the capital), given that we find this position indicated in the manuscript transmission of his exegesis of the poem, and perhaps before 1283, when he was named *protosynkellos* (deputy of the patriarchy of Constantinople), a title which does not appear in any of the *inscriptiones* of his exegesis of the *Syrinx*. Thus, Holobolos would have been working on this exegesis during the first phase of his teaching career in Constantinople (1265–73), before his second fall into disgrace.

Perhaps the key word for understanding Holobolos' work on the *Syrinx* is to be found in the title of his commentary. Two titles are used in the manuscripts: one opens the first section of the commentary, on the metrics of the poem, while the second precedes the commentary dedicated to the content of the poem. Thus, the structure of the commentary follows that of the *scholia vetera*:

> 1. Τοῦ σοφωτάτου ῥήτορος τῶν ῥητόρων κύρου Μαξίμου τοῦ Ὀλοβόλου εἰς τὴν Θεοκρίτου Σύριγγα σύνοψις τῶν μέτρων.
> 2. Τοῦ αὐτοῦ σύνοψις ἐννοίας καὶ σύνταξις καὶ ἀνάπτυξις τῶν λέξεων.[44]

> 1. A summary of the metrics of the *Syrinx* of Theocritus by the all-wise rhetor of rhetors, the honourable Maximos Holobolos.
> 2. A summary of the meaning, syntax and an explanation of the words by the same author.

The term σύνοψις informs us that Holobolos' exegetic text is neither a commentary *stricto sensu* (exegesis) nor a series of exegetic notes (scholia),

---

[44] Strodel (2002: 139). The modern edition of Holobolos' exegesis of the *Syrinx* by Strodel (2002: 139–44) considers the four manuscripts that transmit his commentary. This is the edition I have followed for the present study.

but rather a brief general exposition, an exegetic epitome of the most notable aspects of the poem, which deserve clarification. What is more, the term suggests that Holobolos has been working with broader exegetic material, the *scholia vetera*, which he has adapted to his didactic purposes.

How exactly did Holobolos use his exegetic synopsis? How did he read, interpret and adapt those sources to his didactic needs? His commentary on the *Syrinx* closely follows the ancient material. Strodel has carefully studied this aspect and has identified notable similarities between Holobolos' work and the ancient commentary.[45] Despite its brevity, his synopsis explores the poem's didactic possibilities (especially metrics and lexicon), with his own explanations of its metrical structure (first section) and its lexical and grammatical content (second section). In effect, as we will see, Holobolos focuses primarily on metrics and semantics, examining the latter in even more depth than do the *scholia vetera*. On the other hand, with respect to the mythical elements of the poem, Holobolos does not seem particularly interested in these even if his source is. His fundamental interest is in words, their meanings and etymology and the mechanisms by which the poem's obscure riddles are generated.

In the first section, the metrical synopsis, the commentator addresses his students and readers directly:

> Τὸ ἐπιγραμμάτιον ἡ σύριγξ τοῦ Θεοκρίτου, ἔστι μὲν ἐννεάφωνος ὡς ὁρᾷς· ὅπας γὰρ ἔχει ἐννέα· συνέστηκεν δὲ ἐκ μέτρων μὲν ὅλων δακτυλικῶν ποσότητι δέκα· διαφερόντων δὲ ἀλλήλοις.[46]
>
> The epigram *Syrinx* of Theocritus, as you can see, is comprised of nine sounds, just as there are nine orifices. It is made up entirely of dactylic verses, ten in total, all different from each other.

This brief introduction to the metrics of the poem gives us an idea of how the poem was probably taught in class. First, the presence of the expression 'as you can see', followed by the physical description of the pipe of Pan, suggests that the instructor was showing his students an illustrated copy of the poem,[47] with a design similar to what we find in the most artistic of the manuscripts, in which a drawing of a panpipe with its orifices can be seen

---

[45] Strodel (2002: 139–44).
[46] Strodel 2002.139.1. Along with the reference to the edition of his synopsis, I provide in each instance the source of the *scholia vetera* employed by Holobolos, in this case, schol. vet. 336c.
[47] Regarding the expression ὡς ὁρᾷς, Wendel (1907: 461) suggests that the image of the instrument could have been created according to the commentary of Holobolos, while Bernabò and Magnelli (2011: 219–20) speculate that Holobolos might have introduced the expression *a posteriori* as he was working from an illustrated edition.

and the poem framed within it. The metrical synopsis goes on to analyse the meters that comprise each distich, with specific explanations by Holobolos himself of some metrical aspects:

> ἤτοι τὸ μὲν πρῶτον, τρίστιχον ἐξάμετρον ἀκατάληκτον· ἤγουν δὲ μὴ δεόμενον καταλήξεως· μετρούμενον ὡς ἡρωϊκόν.[48]
>
> Therefore, the first is an acatelectic hexametric tristich, that is to say, it lacks a syllable at the end; it is measured as a hexameter.

As the *scholia vetera* have this as δίστιχον (distich) rather than τρίστιχον (tristich), Holobolos seems to interpret this as meaning that the ancient epigram that accompanies the *Syrinx* in manuscripts of the bucolic tradition forms part of it, given that it has the same metrical structure as the poem's first distich: σῦριγξ οὔνομ' ἔχεις, ᾄδει δέ σε μέτρα σοφίης ('syrinx, you are notable, so he sings you metres of wisdom'). This fact thus reveals that Holobolos was working from a manuscript of the bucolic tradition and not from the *Palatine Anthology*, and that Holobolos himself corrected δίστιχον to τρίστιχον.

In the second section of his commentary, on the poem's content, his synopsis is even more synthetic than for the first section, if that is possible, as it does not include some of the lemmata commented upon in the ancient exegetic tradition.[49] In this second section, his exegesis is dedicated essentially to the poem's lexicon. Holobolos reveals a special interest for popular etymologies, which, in many cases, are based on metonyms and homonyms (as he himself declares). These etymological explanations are an aspect that the *scholia vetera* do not explore, but which Holobolos does not hesitate to address. We see an example of this interest in v. 9:

> v. 9. ὃς ὁ Πὰν ἔπαυσε **τὴν ἠνορέαν**[50] καὶ τὴν ἀνδρίαν· **τὴν ἰσαυδέα**· τὴν ὁμώνυμον **τοῦ παπποφόνου** ἤγουν τοῦ Περσέως· ἤγουν τῶν Περσῶν μετωνυμικῶς·[51]
>
> He, Pan, extinguished their **might** and **homonymous** manhood: the homonym of **who murdered his grandfather**, that is, of Perseus, that is, a metonym for the Persians.

This verse refers to the might of the Persians, against whom Pan fought alongside the Greeks in the battle of Marathon. It plays on the phonetic similarity between 'Persian' and 'Perseus' (words which are nearly

---

[48] Strodel 2002.139.2 [= schol. vet. 336c.17–18].
[49] These are: ἀνεμώδεος (v. 6), ὃς Μοίσᾳ λιγὺ πᾶξεν ἰοστεφάνῳ (v. 7) and νηλεύστῳ (v. 20).
[50] Lemmata in bold.   [51] Strodel 2002.143.4 [= schol. vet. 339.9/10c].

homonyms), the hero who would kill his grandfather Acrisius by accidentally striking him with a discus, thereby fulfilling the prophecy of an oracle. Holobolos highlights the etymological relationship between 'Persian' and 'Perseus', which is justified in the verse by means of a metonym.

V. 10, which refers to Pan's participation in the battle of Marathon, adds that the god saved 'the Tyrian woman', that is to say, Europe, in this case understood as the continent. Here, Holobolos paraphrases the verse without referring to the ancient material:

> v. 10: **παπποφόνου Τυρίας τ' ἐξήλασεν**· καὶ ἀφείλετο καὶ ἐξέβαλεν ἐκείνην τῆς εὐρώπης δηλονότι.[52]
>
> **A man who murdered his grandfather, and drove it [the might] out of the Tyrian girl**: and so kept at bay and expelled that [*scil.* might] from Europe.

Vv. 11–12 capture the essence of the poem: the item most appreciated by the shepherds is the syrinx, which Theocritus offers to the god Pan and upon whose reeds the poem is inscribed. The semantic complexity of this distich, loaded with lexical and phonetic enigmas, undoubtedly required an etymological exegesis. However, Holobolos does not enter into details about dialectal particularities, which are also not addressed in the ancient commentary:

> vv. 11–12. ᾧ **τόδε** ἤγουν τὴν σύρριγγα τὸ κτῆμα τῶν **τυφλοφόρων** καὶ σακκουλοφόρων· ἤγουν τῶν ποιμένων· πήρα γὰρ τὸ σακκούλιον καὶ πηρὸς ὁ τυφλός, ἀνέθηκεν ὁ **Πάρις** ἤγουν ὁ Θεόκριτος. ὁ γὰρ Πάρις διὰ τὸ κρῖναι τὰς θεὰς ὠνόμασται Θεόκριτος.[53]
>
> **To him**, Paris, or rather Theocritus, dedicated the syrinx, belonging to **the carriers of blindness** and to the carriers of bags; that is, the shepherds, as 'rucksack' (σακκούλιον) is 'bag' (πήρα) and 'lame' (πηρός) is 'blind' (τυφλός). Paris is called Theocritus because he judged the goddesses.

Holobolos does not go deeper into the mythological and literary tradition of the god, which the *scholia vetera* address in somewhat more detail. His exegesis, being a synopsis, does not allow him to further explore these aspects, which perhaps are less relevant to his purpose, as he is concerned above all with semantics. The myth of Pan is only succinctly touched upon in his scholion to vv. 13–16, once again in reference to the intricate lexicon used to speak of the god:

---

[52] Strodel 2002.143.4.   [53] Strodel 2002.143.5 [= schol. vet. 339.11/12.18–21].

vv. 13–16. **ὦ βροτοβάμων** καὶ πετροβάμων ἐκ πετρῶν γὰρ οἱ βροτοὶ ὡς ὁ μῦθος· **οἴστρε** καὶ ἐραστὰ **τῆς στήτας** καὶ τῆς γυναικὸς τῆς δέτας καὶ τῆς Λυδίας· ἤγουν τῆς νυμφάλης· **κλωποπάτωρ**· ἤγουν τοῦ κλεπτοῦ Ἑρμοῦ υἱέ· **ἀπάτωρ**· πολυπάτωρ ἤτοι τῶν μνηστήρων υἱέ.[54]

Man-treading and clay-treading, as mortals are born from the clay, according to the myth. **Gadfly**, lover **of the woman**, of the passion and of the Lidian woman, that is, of the nymph [Omphale]. **Son of a thief**, that is, the son of the thief Hermes. **Son of no one**, of many fathers, that is, you son of the suitors.

The epithets of Pan 'man-treading' and 'clay-treading' are references to the myth of Deucalion, the Greek Noah, which Holobolos does not explain but which he had read in the ancient material.[55] In it, the god falls hopelessly in love with the Lydian queen Omphale, although the manuscript used by the Byzantine author must have read νυμφάλης, or else Holobolos himself misread the term.[56] Pan, the son of Hermes, was given the epithet of 'son of a thief' and, as the son of Penelope, of 'son of no one'; that is, his father is unknown as he is the son of Odysseus' wife and all her suitors.

As we have seen, Holobolos draws upon the *scholia vetera* for his terse synopsis, selecting from it those semantic aspects which enable him to decipher the enigmatic meaning of the words that comprise the poem. Holobolos is not interested in the myth; he is interested in the words themselves, in their meaning and their etymology in the context of this obscure poem and in the linguistic mechanisms that generate the poem's riddles. He remains ever faithful to the synoptic format of his exegesis. In his synopsis, there is no place for the digressions and reflections that we find in many commentaries, where the work commented upon is used as a pretext or departure point for discussing other aspects not directly related to the text under discussion.

The Commentary of John Pediasimos

The exegetic work of Manuel Holobolos on these poems had a clear influence on the following generation of scholars and, in particular, on the Thessalonian John Pediasimos (ca. 1250–1310/14).[57] Pediasimos is

---

[54] Strodel 2002.143.6 [= schol. vet. 340.13–15a]. [55] Schol. vet. 340.13.
[56] Schol. vet. 340.14.
[57] *PLP* 22235 and *ODB* 3, 1615. Pediasimos' biography and work have been reconstructed by Constantinides (1982: 117–25). For more details of his life and work, see the introductory chapters of recent editions by Levrie (2018) and Caballero Sánchez (2018) of his commentaries

the author of a more extensive and detailed commentary on the *Syrinx* which also had greater repercussions, as it was transmitted in at least fifteen manuscripts dateable to between the thirteenth and late seventeenth centuries. Along with writing his own commentary to the *Syrinx*, he also took on an exegesis of Hesiod's *Shield of Heracles*, for which he composed a *technologia*.[58] This interest in Heracles and mythology is reflected in a mythographical tract he wrote entitled *On the Labours of Heracles*, a paraphrase of the second book of the *Bibliotheca* of Pseudo-Apollodorus (2.72–126),[59] an author that he read, knew and used as a source on various occasions. It is in fact probable that his study of and commentary on the *Syrinx* was motivated by his interest in Greek mythology and by mythography as a genre; his commentary on the *Syrinx*, more extensive, detailed and original than Holobolos', is lexical and mythological in nature, and draws regularly upon Pseudo-Apollodorus as a source.

When and in what context could Pediasimos have composed his commentary on the poem? It would be realistic to think that it was during his time as *hypatos ton philosophon* (consul of philosophers), which began in 1274. The Palaiologan testimonies mention only his position as *chartophylax* of Justiniana Prima and all of Bulgaria, which he held during his stay in the archbishopric of Ohrid (ca. 1280).[60] Pediasimos indeed taught classes in Bulgaria, as evidenced by a letter (ca. 1283) sent to him by George of Cyprus,[61] which speaks of a young man, Doukopoulos, a student of Pediasimos in Ohrid, who had been transferred to the capital to continue his studies with the Cypriot. This letter is also important as it mentions the subjects that Pediasimos taught in Bulgaria: grammar, poetry, rhetoric, logic and geometry. Therefore, according to the *inscriptiones* of the Palaiologan manuscripts and his activities in Bulgaria, it would be plausible to think that Pediasimos composed his commentary in Ohrid for his classes in poetry. Such a chronology would take us to the decade of the 1380s and would correspond perfectly with the circulation of both the corpus of ancient scholia and the synopsis of Holobolos, which, as we will see, the scholar used as sources for his commentary. Pediasimos, then, would have composed his exegesis in Ohrid and had access to a copy of the *scholia vetera* as well as the synopsis of Holobolos. However, as there is presently no critical edition of the text that considers all testimonies

---

on the *On the Labours of Heracles* of Pseudo-Apollodorus and the *Caelestia* of Cleomedes, respectively. His handwriting has also been identified by Pérez Martín (2010: 109–19).
[58] Gaisford (1823: 609–54).   [59] Levrie (2018).
[60] For Pediasimos' stay in Ohrid, see Constantinides (1982: 117).
[61] Treu 1899: 48.25.30. George of Cyprus: *PLP* 4590.

(only that of Dübner,[62] based on Par. gr. 2831), I prefer to take a cautious stance on this hypothesis, which I will need to explore in greater depth in a study of the transmission of the text, based on a critical edition that has yet to be compiled.

In any case, the title of Pediasimos' commentary on the *Syrinx* provides us with some clues to interpreting the work:

> Τοῦ σοφωτάτου χαρτοφύλακος τῆς πρώτης Ἰουστινιανῆς καὶ πάσης Βουλγαρίας, κύρου Ἰωάννου τοῦ Πεδιασίμου, ἐξήγησις εἰς τὴν τοῦ Θεοκρίτου Σύριγγα.[63]

> Exegesis on the *Syrinx* of Theocritus by the all-wise *chartophylax* of Justiniana Prima and of all of Bulgaria, the honourable John Pediasimos.

Unlike Holobolos, Pediasimos conceives his commentary as an exegesis *stricto sensu*, more extensive, didactic and detailed. Indeed, as in his other commentaries, he presents the lemmata at length, in this case verse by verse.

His commentary is structured in two parts. The first is an introduction to the nature of the poem, and it provides the guidelines to reading the poem. The second is the commentary proper, focused on the lexical aspects and content of the poem. Pediasimos seems uninterested in the metrical characteristics that are emphasized by Holobolos and the *scholia vetera*. His only metrical reference is to the poem's dactylic rhythm:

> οὐ γὰρ ἐμπνευστὴ αὕτη ἡ σύριγξ, ἵνα καὶ ᾠδὰς ἔχῃ, ἀλλὰ μετρουμένη τῷ καλλίστῳ τῶν μέτρων δακτυλικῷ.[64]

> This syrinx, then, is not a real wind instrument to make music with, but it is measured by that most beautiful of metres, the dactylic.

This exegesis refers precisely to the second part of the ancient epigram that accompanies the *Syrinx* in manuscripts of the bucolic tradition: σῦριγξ οὔνομ' ἔχεις, ᾄδει δέ σε μέτρα σοφίης ('syrinx, you are notable, so he sings you metres of wisdom').[65] Like Holobolos, Pediasimos also views it as being part of the poem, functioning as a sort of title: Ὁ πρῶτος στίχος ἀποκεκομμένην ἰδίως ἔχει τὴν ἔννοιαν. ἔστι γὰρ ἐπιγραφὴ τῆς Σύριγγος,[66] 'the first verse contains, in a peculiar manner, the abbreviated meaning, as it is the title of the *Syrinx*'.

Before this, however, Pediasimos familiarizes his students with the poem by means of an introduction of his own creation, in which he describes it as an *ainigma* (enigma), a term not used by earlier commentators. In effect,

---

[62] Dübner (1849: 110–11). [63] Dübner 1849.110a.15–18. [64] Dübner 1849.110a.37–9.
[65] See p. 286 above. [66] Dübner 1849.110a.30–2.

Pediasimos is aware that the entire poem constitutes a kind of riddle behind which is hidden the complete mythological and literary tradition of the god Pan. This great poetic enigma also represents attractive content for his classes, by which his students could deepen their knowledge of Greek mythology as they reflected upon the lexicon and etymology of Pan's epithets. By using the word *ainigma*, Pediasimos probably wanted not only to capture the attention of his students, but also to define the poem's literary essence: a guessing game or riddle. In his introduction, Pediasimos reflects on the characteristics of this poem-enigma. Despite its non-Attic language, the scholar does not hesitate to comment on it, although, like his predecessors, he does not analyse its dialectal particularities. The objective of his commentary is, rather, to decipher the meaning of the *griphoi* that are produced by means of a continuous metalepsis, a variant of metonymy which consists of expressing a term or idea with the name of another to which it is semantically related (semantic exegesis), and next, to present the poem's mythical content (exegesis of mythological content):

> ... διά τε τὴν τῶν μεταλήψεων πύκνωσιν καὶ διὰ τὸ ἀκροθιγῶς τῶν μνημονευθεισῶν ἱστοριῶν ἔχεσθαι, καὶ τὸ ἐλλειπὲς τῆς συντάξεως, καὶ ταῦτα μὴ κατὰ τὴν Ἀττικὴν συνήθειαν, ἀλλά τινα ἔκφυλον, πολλὴν ἐμποιοῦσαν ἀσάφειαν.[67]

> ... through the accumulation of metalepsis and with stories that are mentioned only superficially, and an inadequate syntax, and all of this contrary to Attic usage, but rather as something foreign which generates a great obscurity.

His semantic explanations, as in Holobolos' synopsis, are supported by explanations that illustrate the rhetorical mechanics of the *Syrinx*. Thus, along with the poem's use of homonymy[68] and metonymy,[69] Pediasimos focuses on metalepsis. Although this term was not found in the earlier exegeses, it is in fact a fundamental one, since, as Pediasimos well knows, it is the poem's principal rhetorical device. Alongside the introduction, it is used throughout the entire commentary.[70] We see it here in a specific example in reference to a lemma also commented on by Holobolos:

> vv. 11–12. Ὦ τόδε τυφλοφόρων] Ὧτινι Πανὶ τὸ πᾶμα καὶ κτῆμα τόδε τῶν τυφλοφόρων, ἤγουν τῶν ποιμένων κατὰ μετάληψιν, τουτέστι πηροφόρων καὶ σακκοφόρων (πηροφόρος γὰρ καὶ ὁ τυφλοφόρος), τὸ ἐρατὸν καὶ ἐπιθυμητὸν κατὰ ψυχὴν ὁ **Πάρις**, ἤγουν ὁ Θεόκριτος κατὰ μετάληψιν,

---

[67] Dübner 1849.110a.23–8. [68] Dübner 1849.110a; 111a.1; 111b.1.
[69] Dübner 1849.111b.9. [70] Dübner 1849.111a.16; 111a.33; 111b.11; 111b.14 y; 111b.26.

διὰ τὸ καὶ τὸν Πριαμίδην Πάριν κρῖναι τὰς τρεῖς θεὰς περὶ τοῦ μήλου καὶ τῆς Ἔριδος, καὶ δύνασθαι καλεῖσθαι θεόκριτον, **θέτο** καὶ ἀνέθηκεν ὁ Σιμιχίδης, καὶ ὁ υἱὸς τοῦ Σιμιχίδου.[71]

To him, Paris son of Simichus dedicated the lovely possession of the carriers of blindness: proper to Pan are the ownership and belongings of a bag-carrier, or rather, the shepherds are referred to through a metalepsis, as they carry bags and rucksacks ('carrier of leather bags' means also 'wearer of the blind man's skin'). The **lovely** and desired is **Paris**, or rather, by metalepsis, Theocritus, as the son of Priam, Paris, judged the three goddesses in the trial of the apple; therefore, it is possible to call him 'Theocritus'. The Simichides, that is, the son of Simichus, **dedicated (θέτο)** and devoted (ἀνέθηκεν) [it to him].

We can see here that Pediasimos has read the *scholia vetera*, but, unlike Holobolos, he gives a more detailed explanation of those lexical and grammatical aspects which do not conform to Attic Greek: thus, for the adjective ἐρατὸν he presents ἐπιθυμητὸν as a synonym, and for the verb θέτο (Homeric aorist of τίθημι) the corresponding and more adequate ἀνέθηκεν, with a preverb.

On other occasions, along with his minute explanations of the elements of a particularly enigmatic verse, Pediasimos also chooses to paraphrase:

v. 9. **ὃς σβέσεν ἀνορέαν ἰσαυδέα**] ὅς, ἤγουν ὁ Πάν, ἔσβεσε τὴν Περσικὴν ἀγερωχίαν, ὅτε συνεστρατήγει τοῖς Ἕλλησι. ἣν καὶ **ἰσαυδέα**, ἤγουν ὁμώνυμόν φησι τοῦ **παππoφόνου**, τοῦ Περσέως δηλαδή. ἀπὸ γὰρ Περσέως, Πέρσης, ἐξ οὗ τὸ Περσῶν γένος. παππoφόνος δὲ ὁ Περσεύς, καθὼς ἱστορεῖ καὶ Λυκόφρων. τὸν γὰρ πάππον Ἀκρίσιον μετὰ τὸν κατὰ Γοργόνων ἆθλον ἀπέκτεινε. καὶ ἀφείλετο, ἀπὸ κοινοῦ, τὴν ἠνορέαν καὶ τὴν Περσικὴν ἀλαζονείαν, ἀπὸ τῆς **Τυρίας**, ἤγουν τῆς Εὐρώπης μετωνυμικῶς. ἐν γὰρ τῇ Τύρῳ τῇ Εὐρώπῃ ὁ Ζεὺς ἐμίγη.[72]

Who extinguished the might that sounded like a man: who, or rather Pan, put an end to the arrogance of the Persians when he fought alongside the Greeks; which sounded like a man who murdered his grandfather or rather Perseus. From Perseus comes 'Persian' and from him the lineage of the Persians. Perseus was a man who murdered his grandfather, as told by Lycophron, as he killed his grandfather Acrisius in the games held in honour of the Gorgon. He drove jointly the Persian manliness and the vanity **from the woman of Tyre**, i.e. a metonym for Europe, as Zeus had relations with Europa in Tyre.

---

[71] Dübner 1849.111b.9–17 [= Hol. in *Syr.* 143.5 and schol. vet. 339.11/12.20–1].
[72] Dübner 1849. 111a.53–b.9 [= Hol. in *Syr.*143.4. 44–7 and schol. vet. 339.9/10c].

It should be noted that, unlike other commentators, Pediasimos cites the source of the myth of Acrisius (Lycophron). The principal mythographical source for this myth is Pseudo-Apollodorus 2.4.47–49,[73] whom Pediasimos had very probably read. The specific mention of Lycophron, however, may also suggest a reading of John Tzetzes' commentary on the *Alexandra*, *schol. in Lyc.* 838.69–73 to be precise,[74] which in turn draws upon Pseudo-Apollodorus. However, Pediasimos quoted only a small part of it. It is, in any case, the commentator who explains the myth and not the Hellenistic author. As mentioned earlier, the primary mythographical source for Pediasimos' explanations of mythology is the *Bibliotheca*, and so we see him here expanding upon the ancient scholia with an allusion to Telegonus, the illegitimate son of Circe and Odysseus, of whom Pseudo-Apollodorus speaks in the epitome of his *Bibliotheca* (Ep. 7.17):

> v. 1 Οὐδενὸς εὐνάτειρα, Μακροπτολέμοιο δὲ μᾶτερ], ἤγουν τοῦ Τηλεμάχου. Τῆλε γὰρ τὸ μακράν, καὶ μάχη ὁ πόλεμος. ἐκ μὲν γὰρ Κίρκης Τηλέγονος, ἐκ δὲ Πηνελόπης τῷ Ὀδυσσεῖ γεννᾶται Τηλέμαχος.[75]
>
> **The bedfellow of Nobody, and mother of Far-war**: that is, of Telemachus, as τῆλε (tele) is 'far' and μάχη 'war'. And so, from the union of Odysseus and Circe was born Telegonus, and from Penelope and Odysseus, Telemachus.

In other cases, however, when Pseudo-Apollodorus does not offer clarification of some mythological element, Pediasimos turns to Hellenistic bucolic poetry and its scholia as a source. Thus, in v. 3, his source for the detailed ἱστορία on the shepherd Comatas is the ancient commentary on *Idyll* 7.78–88,[76] which mentions the story of Comatas (*schol. vet. in Theoc.* 99.79c),[77] while in v. 4, which speaks of Pan's passion for weapons (and, by metonymy, for war), it is the *Dionysiaka* of Nonnos of Panopolis. Pediasimos' *scholium* to v. 4 is interesting not only for showing his knowledge of the work of Nonnos (the principal source for the campaign of Dionysus in Asia, narrated in Books 13–40), but also for his critical evaluation of this mythic tale:

> v. 4. ἀλλ' οὐ πειλιπὲς αἴθε πάρος φρένα τέρμα σάκους] ... ἀλλ' αὐτὴ ἡ ἴτυς, τουτέστιν ἡ ἀσπίς, ἀπὸ μέρους τὸ ὅλον. μᾶλλον δὲ ἀπὸ μόνης τῆς ἀσπίδος καὶ πᾶν ὅπλον· ἵν' ᾖ ἡ ἔννοια, ὅτι ἔρωτα εἶχε τῶν ὅπλων, ἤγουν τῶν πολεμικῶν ἔργων. ἱστόρηται γὰρ ὁ Πὰν συστρατεῦσαι τῷ Διονύσῳ

---

[73] Scarpi and Ciani (2004). [74] Scheer (1958).
[75] Dübner 1849.110b.7–9. [= Hol. *in Syr.*142.1 and schol. vet. 337.1/2a.16–18].
[76] Gow (1950). [77] Wendel (1914).

παρ' Ἰνδοὺς καὶ ἔργα ποιῆσαι πολεμικά. τὸ δὲ πάρος, ἤγουν πρότερον, οὐκ ἐναντιοῦται τῷ λόγῳ. οὐ γὰρ ἀεὶ ὁ Πὰν περὶ τὰ πολεμικὰ ἠσχολῆσθαι ἱστόρηται, ἀλλ' ὅτε ὁ Διόνυσος κατὰ τῆς Ἀσίας ἐστράτευσεν.[78]

He whose mind was once set on fire by the p-lacking shield rim: ... but this shield rim, that is, understood as the part for the whole, is the shield itself. And, by referring to the shield only, this refers by extension to all weapons; from this the meaning is that he felt love for weapons, that is, for acts of war. And it is told that Pan took part in a campaign together with Dionysus against the Indians and performed acts of war. This does not contradict the tale [*scil.* about Pan]. For it is not said that Pan always took part in war, but only when Dionysus fought in Asia.

Likewise, with respect to the mythical origin of the shepherd Comatas (v. 3), Pediasimos opened a window onto Western geography by his critical analysis of a possible incoherence in the mythological tradition of this figure:

v. 3. **οὐχὶ Κεράσταν ὅν ποτε θρέψατο ταυροπάτωρ**] τὸ δὲ λέγειν ὡς καὶ Κομάτας Πηνελόπης υἱός, μὴ καὶ ταῖς ἀληθείας ἀνάρμοστον εἴη, σκοπεῖν ἄξιον. Πηνελόπη μὲν γὰρ εἰς Ἰθάκην, Κομάτας δὲ Σικελός· καὶ ἡ μὲν ἐπὶ τῶν Ἰλιακῶν, ὁ δὲ ἐπὶ τῶν Ῥωμαϊκῶν. μεταξὺ δὲ τοῖν τόποιν καὶ χρόνοιν τούτοιν χάσμα μέγα ἐστήρικται.[79]

Not the Horned One, who was once nurtured by a bull father: To affirm that Comatas is also the son of Penelope would not be incongruent with the truth, but it merits examination, as Penelope is from Ithaca and Comatas a Sicilian. And she is from the time of the Trojans and he of the Romans. Between the two there is a great gap of both space and time.

Pediasimos' critical observations are interesting from a mythographical point of view. He does not dismiss the idea that Comatas was the son of Penelope, as he has read this in the ancient scholia.[80] His contribution, however, goes further when he makes an interesting geographical and chronological observation, for which he does not hesitate to display his erudition to get his students' attention, using the dual τοῖν τόποιν καὶ χρόνοιν. His observation is not entirely correct, however. The tradition presents Comatas as a shepherd of the Sicilian forests, which is undoubtedly prior to the Roman domination of the island. Indeed, we find it mentioned for the first time in the Theocritean *Idylls*. Pediasimos, however, not knowing Theocritus' chronology, seems to associate the island with a concept of the Romans as the inhabitants of the Italic territories in

---

[78] Dübner 1849.110b.54–111a.1–8.   [79] Dübner 1849.110b.47–50.   [80] Schol. vet. 338.3.

general, when, in fact, between the period when Comatas lived and the Roman presence on the island, there was a gap in time. Even so, his observation confirms his critical sense regarding the text, as well as his great interest in mythology.

Pediasimos, as educator and commentator, cannot resist using elements of the text as starting points for embarking on small *excursus*. Ultimately, as a teacher, although he does not specify this in his commentary, his aim is to use this content in class to stimulate his students and to digress from it. A good example of this is found in his scholion to parts of v. 5 and v. 6, where the poem speaks of Pan's overriding passion for the nymph Syrinx and, by metonymy, for his own pipe.

> vv. 5–6. ὃς τᾶς μέροπος πόθον / κούρας γηρυγόνας] εἰ γὰρ μονόφθογγος, εἴτουν μονόφωνος ἦν ἡ σύριγξ, ἦν ἂν ἀνάρμοστος, καὶ μηδὲ ψυχὴν ἀνθρωπίνην κηλεῖν οἷα τε. ἡ γὰρ ψυχὴ ἐξ ἁρμονιῶν συνέστηκε, καὶ ἐκ μόνων τῶν συγγενῶν ἁρμονιῶν κηλεῖσθαι πέφυκεν. ἁρμονία δέ ἐστι πολυμιγέων καὶ δίχα φρονεόντων ἕνωσις.[81]

> **Who loved the voice-dividing girl, swift as the wind and with human speech**: as, if it were uni-tonal, if the syrinx only emitted one note, it would be inadequate, and would not cause so much fascination in the human soul, as the soul is composed of various parts and it can be charmed only by compositions of the same kind. Harmony is the union of multiple elements and of two parts well balanced.

In this way, the syrinx served as a starting point to remind his students of the unique composition of the soul and the literal definition of the Pythagorean concept of harmony. These are concepts with which scholars such as Pediasimos were well familiarized and which they transmitted to their students.

From v. 13 of the poem, Pediasimos' explanations follow the *scholia vetera* very closely, and there is no place for mythological explanations or digressions. He comments on each of the verses until the very last (v. 20). It is precisely in his scholion on this last verse (not commented upon by Holobolos), that we can observe an interesting etymology of his own, which differs from that of the ancient commentary:

> v. 20. **νηλεύστῳ**] τῇ ἀλιθοβολήτῳ, ἤγουν ἀθανάτῳ· ἀπὸ τοῦ νη στερητικοῦ, καὶ τοῦ λεύω τὸ λιθοβολῶ.[82]

> **Unseen**: that which was not stoned, that is, immortal; [it is derived] from νη indicating negation and from λεύω ('to stone'), i.e. to pelt with stones (λιθοβολῶ).

---

[81] Dübner 1849.111a.20–4. [82] Dübner 1849.111b.35–7.

For the term νελεύστῳ, the ancient commentary had proposed the etymology νη + λεύσσειν ('not see').[83]

The Influence of Holobolos on Pediasimos

As Constantinides has pointed out, there is good reason to believe that John Pediasimos studied under Manuel Holobolos in Constantinople.[84] Indeed, the fact that both wrote commentaries on the *Syrinx* constitutes an argument to this effect. What is more, research reveals similarities between the two commentaries that support the idea that Pediasimos had read Holobolos' exegesis.[85] The Thessalonian, moreover, was also the author of commentaries on Aristotle, specifically on *De interpretatione*[86] and the *Analytics* (a paraphrastic reworking of John Philoponos' exegesis),[87] and may have begun his study of Aristotle under the guidance of Holobolos in Constantinople. At the same time, there exist several epistolary testimonies from which one can infer a possible master–disciple relationship between Holobolos and Pediasimos. One such letter,[88] from George of Cyprus to Pediasimos, states that he and Pediasimos were both students of George Akropolites[89] and of another teacher whom Constantinides identifies as Holobolos.[90]

From this, the question is therefore to what extent Holobolos' synopsis influenced Pediasimos' commentary and, especially, to what extent Pediasimos drew from his own reading of it. Constantinides' cursory study does not consider the fact that the second commentary edited by Dübner (112b), from manuscript G, cannot be attributed to Holobolos, as it does not present him as author. For this reason, our comparative study deals only with Holobolos' synopsis.

The comparative table that follows presents some of the examples already discussed, with the aim of determining the use that Pediasimos made of both the ancient scholia and Holobolos' synopsis:

---

[83] Schol. vet. 341.17–20.   [84] Constantinides (1982: 119).
[85] Constantinides (1982: 119, n. 33).
[86] Constantinides (1982: 122), although this work does not appear in the *Pinakes* database, nor is it mentioned by Bassi (1898: 1399–1417).
[87] De Falco (1926: 3–120) and (1928: 251–69). On Aristotelian commentators in the eleventh and twelfth centuries, see Trizio in this volume.
[88] Treu 1899.49.4–6.   [89] *PLP* 518.   [90] Constantinides (1982: 118).

Scholia vetera	Holobolos	Pediasimos
vv. 9–10: ἀντὶ τοῦ ὁμώνυμον τοῦ Περσέως, ὃς τὸν πάππον αὐτοῦ τὸν Ἀκρίσιον ἀπέκτεινεν· Ἀκρισίου δὲ Δανάη, ἀφ' ἧς Περσεύς. τὴν δὲ Εὐρώπην Τυρίαν εἶπεν, ἐπειδὴ ἡ Εὐρώπη ὑπὸ Διὸς ἁρπασθεῖσα ἐκεῖθεν ἦν.[91]	ὃς ὁ Πὰν ἔπαυσε τὴν ἠνορέαν καὶ τὴν ἀνδρίαν· τὴν ἰσαυδέα· τὴν ὁμώνυμον τοῦ παπποφόνου ἤγουν τοῦ Περσέως· ἤγουν τῶν Περσῶν μετωνυμικῶς· καὶ ἀφείλετο καὶ ἐξέβαλεν ἐκείνην τῆς εὐρώπης δηλονότι.[92]	ὅς, ἤγουν ὁ Πάν, ἔσβεσε τὴν Περσικὴν ἀγερωχίαν, ὅτε συνεστρατήγει τοῖς Ἕλλησι. ἣν καὶ ἰσαυδέα, ἤγουν ὁμώνυμόν φησι τοῦ παπποφόνου, τοῦ Περσέως δηλαδή. ἀπὸ γὰρ Περσέως, Πέρσης, ἐξ οὗ τὸ Περσῶν γένος. παπποφόνος δὲ ὁ Περσεύς, καθὼς ἱστορεῖ καὶ Λυκόφρων. τὸν γὰρ πάππον Ἀκρίσιον μετὰ τὸν κατὰ Γοργόνων ἆθλον ἀπέκτεινε. καὶ ἀφείλετο, ἀπὸ κοινοῦ, τὴν ἠνορέαν καὶ τὴν Περσικὴν ἀλαζονείαν, ἀπὸ τῆς Τυρίας, ἤγουν τῆς Εὐρώπης μετωνυμικῶς. ἐν γὰρ τῇ Τύρῳ τῇ Εὐρώπῃ ὁ Ζεὺς ἐμίγη.[93]
v. 11: Τυφλοφόρους δὲ εἶπε τοὺς ἀγροίκους, ἐπειδὴ πήρας φοροῦσι· πήρα δὲ καὶ τυφλὴ συνώνυμα. πᾶμα δὲ τὸ κτῆμα. Θεόκριτος δὲ Πάριν ἑαυτὸν εἶπεν, ἐπειδὴ ὁ Πάρις τὰς Θεὰς κρίνων ὑπό τινων Θεόκριτος ὠνομάσθη.[94]	ᾧ τόδε ἤγουν τὴν σύριγγα τὸ κτῆμα τῶν τυφλοφόρων καὶ σακκουλοφόρων· ἤγουν τῶν ποιμένων· πήρα γὰρ τὸ σακκούλιον καὶ πηρὸς ὁ τυφλός, ἀνέθηκεν ὁ Πάρις ἤγουν ὁ Θεόκριτος. ὁ γὰρ Πάρις διὰ τὸ κρῖναι τὰς θεὰς ὠνόμασται Θεόκριτος.[95]	Ὧτινι Πανὶ τὸ πᾶμα καὶ κτῆμα τόδε τῶν τυφλοφόρων, ἤγουν τῶν ποιμένων κατὰ μετάληψιν, τουτέστι πηροφόρων καὶ σακκοφόρων (πηροφόρος γὰρ καὶ ὁ τυφλοφόρος). τὸ ἐρατὸν καὶ ἐπιθυμητὸν κατὰ ψυχὴν ὁ Πάρις, ἤγουν ὁ Θεόκριτος κατὰ μετάληψιν, διὰ τὸ καὶ τὸν Πριαμίδην Πάριν κρῖναι τὰς τρεῖς θεὰς περὶ τοῦ μήλου καὶ τῆς Ἔριδος, καὶ δύνασθαι καλεῖσθαι Θεόκριτον, θέτο καὶ ἀνέθηκεν ὁ Σιμιχίδης, καὶ ὁ υἱὸς τοῦ Σιμιχίδου.[96]

[91] Schol. vet. 339.9/10c. [92] Strodel 2002.143.4. [93] Dübner 1849.111a.53–b.9.
[94] Schol. vet. 339.11/12.20–4. [95] Strodel 2002.143.5. [96] Dübner 1849.111b.9–17.

(cont.)

Scholia vetera	Holobolos	Pediasimos
v. 13: βροτοβάμονα δὲ εἴρηκε τὸν Πᾶνα ὡς πετροβάτην, ἀπὸ τῶν λαῶν καὶ τοῦ κατὰ Δευκαλίωνα μύθου. Φασὶ γάρ, ὅτι μετὰ τὸν κατακλυσμὸν σπανιζόντων τῶν ἀνθρώπων λίθους λαβὼν ὁ Δευκαλίων ἀνθρώπους ἐποίει, ὅθεν αὐτοὺς καὶ λαοὺς κεκλῆσθαι λέγουσιν.[97]	ὦ βροτοβάμων καὶ πετροβάμων ἐκ πετρῶν γὰρ οἱ βροτοὶ ὡς ὁ μῦθος.[98]	ὦ Πὰν βροτοβᾶμον, ἤγουν πετροβᾶμον. ἐκ πετρῶν γὰρ οἱ βροτοὶ κατὰ τὸν παλαιὸν μῦθον.[99]
v. 16: λαρνακόγυιον δὲ τὸν Πᾶνα, ἐπεὶ χηλόπυς ἐστί. λάρναξ δὲ ἡ χηλὸς καὶ ἡ κιβωτός· ταὐτόν δ' ἐστί.[100]	λαρνακόγυιε, ὁ ἔχων χηλὰς εἰς τὰ γυῖα· ὁμωνύμως καὶ τοῦτο· χηλὴ γὰρ ἡ λάρναξ καὶ τὸ κιβώτιον.[101]	λαρνακόγυιε, ἤγουν χηλόπου κατὰ μετάληψιν. χηλός γὰρ τὸ κιβώτιον, καὶ ἡ λάρναξ, καὶ χηλὴ ὁ ὄνυξ.[102]
v. 20: νήλευστον δὲ τὴν ἀόρατον· τὸ γὰρ νη στερητικόν, τὸ δὲ λεύσσειν ἐστὶν τὸ ὁρᾶν.[103]		νηλεύστῳ, τῇ ἀλιθοβολήτῳ, ἤγουν ἀθανάτῳ· ἀπὸ τοῦ νη στερητικοῦ, καὶ τοῦ λεύω τὸ λιθοβολῶ.[104]

These passages exemplify the reworking of reference sources in the respective commentaries and the adaptation of these to the specific didactic needs of the respective authors. Holobolos follows the *scholia vetera* very closely, adapting them with an emphasis on the poem's semantic and etymological aspects. Pediasimos, for his part, employs several different sources: the ancient scholia, Holobolos' synopsis, and mythographical sources. I will here break down the various sources used by Pediasimos for the examples given in the previous table:

(1) Schol. vv. 9–10: use of ancient material + Holobolean material with reference to another exegetic source (Tzetzes' commentary on Lycophron) for the myth of Perseus and Acrisius;
(2) Schol. v. 11: use of ancient material + Holobolean material;
(3) Schol. v. 13: use of exclusively Holobolean material;

---

[97] Schol. vet. 340.13.5–9. [98] Strodel 2002.143.6. [99] Dübner 1849.111b.18–20.
[100] Schol. vet. 340.16. [101] Strodel 2002.143.6. [102] Dübner 1849.111b.25–7.
[103] Schol. vet. 341.17–20. [104] Dübner 1849.111b.35–8.

(4) Schol. v. 16: use of exclusively ancient material;
(5) Schol. v. 20 (not commented on by Holobolos): partial use of ancient material with commentator's own interpretation.

It seems, therefore, credible to posit a direct intellectual relationship between Holobolos and Pediasimos, as Constantinides has already pointed out.[105] In addition, the reading of Holobolean material by Pediasimos does not contradict the chronology of the respective commentaries. Holobolos' synopsis, which, as argued above, may have been written during the first period of his teaching in Constantinople (1265–73), would have been available in the 1280s, when Pediasimos was teaching in Bulgaria, and where he may have written his own commentary.

The work of these two commentators on the *technopaegnia* left its mark on the scholars who came after Pediasimos. In the fourteenth century, the circle of Demetrios Triklinios in Thessalonike studied these poems using the exegeses of both Holobolos and Pediasimos. This is confirmed by Paris, Bibliothèque nationale de France, gr. 2832 (Fig. 10.1),[106] a manuscript linked to the Triklinian circle,[107] which is the oldest manuscript to contain Holobolos' synopsis of the *Syrinx*. It was also the first codex to transmit the exegeses of Holobolos (fol. 46v) and Pediasimos (fols. 46v–47r) on the *Syrinx* in the same volume, and so it is plausible that the two commentaries were grouped together by the Triklinian circle itself. Thus, it is certain that both were well known and highly regarded, and became the exegeses of reference for the study of the *Syrinx* beyond Constantinople.

Conclusions

Several insights have emerged from the present study into the intellectual labours of Manuel Holobolos and John Pediasimos, the products of complex personal and historical contexts. Holobolos, educated during the years of the Nicaean Empire, demonstrated an interest and inclination toward the study of the Greek legacy and its transmission, which won him such prestige that he would be recommended for one of the most important positions of his time, that of *rhetor ton rhetoron*. However, the circumstances of his life, shaped by the precarious historical climate in which he lived and, without doubt, a scarcity of material means, perhaps did not allow him to carry out

---

[105] Constantinides (1982: 117, n. 33).   [106] On this manuscript, see pp. 281–3.
[107] See p. 282.

the type of exhaustive and orderly study that Pediasimos achieved in Ohrid and as *hypatos ton philosophon* in Constantinople after 1274.

Thanks to Holobolos, the study of the *technopaegnia* was revived during the Palaiologan period with his *recensio* and commentaries, which, by their reworking of the *scholia vetera*, focused on metrical and lexical aspects, while leaving aside other aspects such as the dialectal or mythological. For reasons of space, it has not been possible to address his work on the other pattern-poems. His work on the *Syrinx*, however, is more relevant for its influence on the generation of scholars who came immediately after him, particularly Pediasimos. My study has shown that his primary didactic interest was in lexical study and in the meaning of words in the context of this obscure poem.

While it is not possible to affirm categorically that Holobolos and Pediasimos were master and student, as there are no documents which attest to this directly, all indications seem to point in this direction. It is likely that Pediasimos, following in his master's footsteps, devoted himself to commenting on texts that he would have studied under him, but he did this in a way which bore his own personal stamp, a characteristic recognizable in the rest of his exegetic production as well. In fact, Pediasimos' style is remarkable for its profound didacticism, which is manifested in his detailed lexical and mythographical explanations, and his broad knowledge of the earlier exegetic and mythographical sources. Unusual for the Palaiologan period in which he lived, Pediasimos showed a unique interest in mythography. Above all, however, his exegesis on the *Syrinx* is marked by imagination and critical acumen. In this sense, he exemplifies the attributes of the experienced commentator.

REFERENCES

Angelov, D. (2007) *Imperial Ideology and Political Thought in Byzantium, 1204–1330*. Cambridge.

Bassi, D. (1898) 'I manoscritti di Giovanni Pediasimo: appunti del dottore Domenico Bassi', *RIL* 31: 1399–1417.

Bernabò, M. and E. Magnelli (2011) 'Il codice laurenziano plut. 32.52 e l'iconografia bizantina del *carmina figurata*', *RSBS* 2: 189–232.

Bowie, E. L. (2002) 'Hadrian and Greek Poetry', in *Greek Romans and Roman Greeks: Studies in Cultural Interaction*, ed. E. N. Ostenfeld, 172–97. Aarhus.

Bydén, B. (2004) 'Strangle Them with These Meshes of Syllogisms!', in *Latin Philosophy in Greek Translations of the Thirteenth Century: Interaction and Isolation in Latin Byzantine Culture*, ed. J. O. Rosenqvist, 133–57. Stockholm.

Caballero Sánchez, P. (2018) *El Comentario de Juan Pediásimo a los 'Cuerpos celestes' de Cleomedes: estudio, edición crítica y traducción*. Madrid.

Canart, P. (1970) *Codices Vaticani Graeci: Codices 1745–1962*. Vatican City.

Constantinides, C. N. (1982) *Higher Education in Byzantium in the Thirteenth and Early Fourteenth Centuries (1204–ca. 1310)*. Nicosia.
  (1993) 'Byzantine Scholars and the Union of Lyon (1274)', in *The Making of Byzantine History: Studies Dedicated to Donald M. Nicol*, ed. R. Beaton and C. Roueché, 86–93. London.
De Falco, V. (ed.) (1926) *Ioannis Pediasimi in Aristotelis Analytica scholia selecta*. Naples.
  (1928) 'Altri scholii di Giovanni Pediasimo agli *Analitici*', *ByzZ* 28: 251–69.
Dübner, F. (ed.) (1849) *Scholia in Theocritum, Nicandrum et Oppianum*. Paris.
Fantuzzi, M. and R. Hunter (2002) *Muse e modelli: la poesia ellenistica da Alessandro Magno ad Augusto*. Rome–Bari.
Ferreri, L. (2006) 'Il commento di Manuele Olobolo all'*Ara Dorica* di Dosiada: storia della tradizione ed edizione critica', *Nea Rhome* 3: 319–21.
Fisher, E. (2002/3) 'Planoudes, Holobolos and the Motivation for Translation', *GRBS* 43: 77–104.
  (2012) 'Manuel Holobolos and the Role of Bilinguals in Relations between the West and Byzantium', in *Knotenpunkt Byzanz: Wissensformen und kulturelle Wechselbeziehungen*, ed. A. Speer and P. Steinkrüger, 210–22. Berlin–Boston.
Fränkel, H. (1915) *De Simia Rhodio*. Leipzig.
Gaisford, T. (ed.) (1823) *Hesiodi Carmina*. Leipzig.
Gallavotti, C. (ed.) (1993³) *Theocritus quique feruntur Bucolici Graeci*. Rome.
Gow, A. S. F. (1914) 'The Σῦριγξ technopaegnium', *AJPh* 33: 128–38.
  (1950) (ed.) *Theocritus*, 2 vols. Cambridge.
Guichard, L. A. (2006) 'Simias' Pattern Poems: The Margins of the Canon', in *Beyond the Canon*, ed. M. A. Harder, R. F. Regtuit and G. C. Wakker, 83–104. Leuven–Paris–Dudley, MA.
Haeberlin, C. (ed.) (1887) *Carmina figurata Graeca*. Hannover.
  (1890) 'Epilegomena ad figurata carmina Graeca', *Philologus* 49: 271–84; 649–61.
Harlfinger, J. (1974–80) *Wasserzeichen aus griechischen Handschriften*, 2 vols. Berlin.
Hannick, C. (1981) *Maximos Holobolos in der kirchenslawischen homiletischen Literatur*. Vienna.
Hopkinson, N. (ed.) (2015) *Theocritus, Moschus, Bion*. Cambridge, MA.
Hörandner, W. (1970) 'Miscellanea epigrammatica', *JÖByz* 19: 109–19.
  (1990) 'Visuelle Poesie Byzanz: Versuch einer Bestandsaufnahme', *JÖByz* 40: 1–42.
Kwapisz, J. (ed.) (2013) *The Greek Figure Poems*. Leuven.
  (2019) *The Paradigm of Simias*. Berlin.
Levrie, K. (2018) *Jean Pédiasimos, Essai sur les douze travaux d'Héraclès: édition critique, traduction et introduction*. Leuven–Paris–Bristol.
Liceti, F. (1630) *Encyclopaedia ad Aram mysticam Nonarii Terrigenae anonymi vetustissimi*. Padua.
  (1635) *Ad Aram Lemniam Dosiadae poetae vetustissimi & obscurissimi encyclopaedia*. Paris.

(1637) *Ad Epei securim encyclopaedia*. Bologna.
(1640) *Ad Alas Amoris divini a Simmia Rhodio compactas... enclyclopaedia*. Padua.
(1655) *Fortunii Liceti ... ad Syringam, a Theocrito Syracusio compactam & inflatam, encyclopaedia*. Udine.
Männlein-Robert, I. (2007) *Stimme, Schrift und Bild: Zum Verhältnis der Künste in der hellenistischen Dichtung*. Heidelberg.
Martini, E. and D. Bassi (1906) *Catalogus codicum graecorum Bibliothecae Ambrosianae 1*. Milan.
Mercati, G. and P. Franchi de' Cavalieri (1923) *Codices Vaticani Graeci*, vol. 1: *Codices 1–329*. Vatican City.
Mergiali, S. (1996) *L'enseignement et les lettrés pendant l'époque des Paléologues (1261–1453)*. Athens.
Mošin, V. A. and S. M. Traljić (1957) *Filigranes des XIII et XIV ss.*, 2 vols. Zagreb.
Omont, H. (1904) 'Notice sur le manuscrit grec 2832 de la Bibliothèque Nationale', *RPh* 28: 189–97.
(1905) 'Dosiades et Théocrite offrant leurs poems à Apollon et à Pan', *MMAI* 12: 155–8.
(1929) *Miniatures des plus anciens manuscrits grecs de la Bibliothèque Nationale du VIe au XIVe siècle*. Paris.
Palumbo Stracca, B. M. (2007) 'La dedica di "Paride Simichida" (*Syrinx, A.P.* XV 21 = XLVII Gallavotti): aspetti metaletterari di un *carmen figuratum*', in *L'epigramma greco: problemi e prospettive*, ed. G. Lozza and S. M. Tempesta, 120–6. Milan.
Peiper, R. (ed.) (1886) *Decimi Magni Ausonii Burdigalensis Opuscula*. Leipzig.
Pérez Martín, I. (1995) 'Le conflit de l'Union des Églises (1274) et son reflet dans l'enseignement supérieur de Constantinople', *ByzSlav* 56: 411–22.
(1997) '*El libro de actor*: una traducción bizantina del *Speculum Doctrinale* de Beauvais (Vat. gr. 12 y 1144)', *REByz* 55: 81–136.
(2010) 'L'écriture de l'hypatos Jean Pothos Pédiasimos d'après ses scholies aux *Elementa* d'Euclide', *Scriptorium* 64: 109–19.
Sbordone, F. (1951) 'Il commento di Manuele Olobolo ai Carmina figurata graecorum', in *Miscellanea Giovanni Galbiati* II, 169–77. Milan.
Scarpi, P. and M. G. Ciani (ed.) (2004) *Apollodoro, I miti greci (Biblioteca)*. Trans. M. G. Ciani. Milan.
Scheer, E. (ed.) (1958) *Lycophronis Alexandra*, vol. 2: *Scholia continens*. Berlin.
Schreiner, P. (1988) *Codices Vaticani Graeci: Codices 867–932*. Vatican City.
Stallbaum, J. G. (ed.) (1825–6) *Eustathii archiepiscopi Thessalonicensis commentarii ad Homeri Odysseam ad fidem exempli Romani editi*, 2 vols. Leipzig.
Strodel, S. (2002) *Zur Überlieferung und zum Verständnis der hellenistischen Technopaignien*. Frankfurt am Main–Berlin.
Treu, M. (ed.) (1893) *Eustathii Macrembolitae quae feruntur aenigmata*. Breslau.
(1896) 'Manuel Holobolos', *ByzZ* 5: 538–59.
(ed.) (1899) *Theodori Pediasimi eisque amicorum quae exstant*. Potsdam.
(ed.) (1906) *Manuelis Holoboli orationes*, vol. 1. Postdam.

van der Valk, M. (ed.) (1971–87) *Eustathii archiepiscopi Thessalonicensis commentarii ad Homeri Iliadem pertinentes ad fidem codicis Laurentiani editi*, 4 vols. Leiden.
Wendel, C. (1907) 'Die Technopägnien-Ausgaben des Rhetors Holobolos', *ByzZ* 16: 460–7.
⎯⎯ (1910) 'Die Technopägnien-Scholien des Rhetors Holobolos', *ByzZ* 19: 331–7.
⎯⎯ (ed.) (1914) *Scholia in Theocritum vetera*. Leipzig.
West, M. L. (1992) *Ancient Greek Music*. Oxford.
Westerink, L. G. (ed.) (1992) *Michaelis Pselli poemata*. Stuttgart.
von Wilamowitz, U. (1906) *Die Textgeschichte der griechischen Bukoliker*. Berlin.

CHAPTER 11

Late Byzantine Scholia on the Greek Classics
What Did They Comment On? Manuel Moschopoulos on Sophocles' Electra

Andrea M. Cuomo

To the beloved memory of Ingrid Weichselbaum

The Moschopoulean comments on Sophocles are among the many materials for the teaching of high-register Medieval Greek that emerged from the well-regarded school of Maximos Planoudes and Manuel Moschopoulos in Constantinople between the end of the thirteenth and the beginning of the fourteenth centuries. The aim of my contribution is to explore this material, questioning what its focus was and what this can tell us about Medieval Greek education in Byzantium. In order to do so, I will take as a case study the Moschopoulean scholia on Sophocles' *Electra*. First, it will be necessary to explain the context in which these scholia were produced and briefly discuss how the tragic plot of *Electra* develops. I will then present a few previously unpublished passages from the prologue of *Electra* alongside some critical notes of my own. This will enable me to compare the medieval and modern interpretations of these passages, which offer especially interesting Sophoclean material. In the final discussion, I will contextualize the analysis of these passages to consider how a close reading of this kind can illuminate the broader questions of Byzantine education.

The Moschopoulean Comments on Sophocles as Textbooks for the Teaching of Greek: The Context

Grammar studies constituted the basic cultural requirement for beginning a career in the complex bureaucratic system of the Eastern Roman

---

* I want to thank Klaas Bentein, Donald Mastronarde and Georgios Xenis for sharing with me their comments on an earlier draft of this paper, as well as Nicola Wood and Lauren Stokeld for the English proofreading. This chapter, first drafted during my fellowship at Dumbarton Oaks in 2016, benefited from Project 30775 'Greek Scholia, and Medieval Greek' funded by the Austrian Science Fund (2018–21).

Empire.¹ Boys attended grammar schools between the ages of ten and thirteen with the aim of mastering high-register Medieval Greek.² Also known as Atticizing Greek, this variant of Medieval Greek was not a self-referential, stereotyped imitation of the historically attested Attic Greek, as it also changed throughout the centuries and was influenced by other variants of Greek (e.g. the vernacular and Koine).³ Unfortunately, it is not clear to us how the Greek medieval school actually worked, how a normal lesson was carried out, what the teacher-pupil relationship was, or what the role of orality and books was in the classroom.⁴

Nevertheless, we see that in order to develop the necessary linguistic skills and related cultural competencies, key textbooks were prepared, to which, over the centuries, teachers added comments, corollaries, etc. The basis of Byzantine grammar teaching originates from the philological endeavours of Alexandrine and late antique grammarians. These texts circulated throughout the Greek Middle Ages: the *Techne* by Dionysius Thrax in the second-first centuries BC (alongside its various scholia and medieval comments);⁵ the *Canons* by Theodosius in the fourth century AD;⁶ the treatise *On Syntax* by Apollonius Dyscolus (first-second century AD),⁷ the *Katholike Prosodia* by Herodian (first-second century AD).⁸

---

¹ Various studies have emphasized the relationship between education and belonging to cultural elites: see e.g. Cavallo (1995), Maltese (2001), Constantinides (2003: 39–42), Gaul (2011: 121–5), Ronconi (2012: 92). However, mastering the required linguistic and cultural competencies was not in itself an unmistakable sign of belonging to the cultural elite, but rather the gateway to it (Cuomo [2017a]).

² Private teachers taught the girls of the aristocracy the *enkyklios paideia* at home. On this, see Chrysostomides (1994: 1–20, at 12), Mavroudi (2012).

³ See Horrocks (2007) and (2014); and, for examples, Horrocks (2017a) and (2017b).

⁴ Interesting studies on this subject help us get an idea of the complexity of these issues; an overview thereof can be found in Markopoulos' studies quoted in the bibliography section below. Furthermore, Cavallo (2010: 16–21) argues that textbooks are the tip of the iceberg and that oral teaching, not attested, was the true basis of the Byzantine school system. Cavallo's thesis seems to be perfectly demonstrated by scholia. As we will see from the examples below, the scholia cannot be properly understood by simply grasping the meaning of each word. A correct understanding depends on their interaction with the text they refer to, on the layout and on a varying series of conjectures that the reader has to undertake. On oral teaching as a complement to written exegesis, see also Trizio in this volume.

⁵ Ed. in *Grammatici Graeci* vol. 1. See also Lallot (1998), Ciccolella (2008: 106, n. 98), Dickey (2007: 78–9) and Callipo (2011).

⁶ Ed. *Grammatici Graeci* vol. 4, 1–2 (ed. Hilgard).

⁷ See also Householder (1981), Lallot (1994), (1997), (2015), Fuchs (1997), Brandenburg (2005), Matthaios (2015: 257–66).

⁸ The *Katholike Prosodia* survives in epitomes. The two major epitomes have recently been edited by Xenis (2015); Roussou (2018). See also Dyck (1993), Schneider (1999: 772), Dickey (2007: 76–7).

These were continuously commented on and readapted.⁹ In fact, the grammatical *auctoritates* could not have been used in schools as such, both because they needed explanations to be didactically effective and because didactical needs changed throughout the centuries. The production of textbooks for the teaching of Greek was not limited to adaptations of the fundamental grammar books. In order to improve students' high-register Greek vocabulary and compositional skills, teachers also wrote comments on reference authors and produced collections of terms for students to use in their own compositions.¹⁰ The focus of these textbooks (grammar books, lexica, comments on reference authors, anthologies) was on morphology, lexicography and micro-syntax. In sum, we can say that the Byzantine schooling system remained coherently unchanged throughout the centuries.¹¹

In every Byzantine era, teachers composed and adapted textbooks. Here for example, we can mention John Charax (sixth century)¹² and Sophronios of Jerusalem (ninth century)¹³ alongside the better-known George Choiroboskos, Gregory Pardos, Eustathios of Thessalonike, John Tzetzes and Theodore Prodromos. However, the Palaiologan era stands out.¹⁴ After the 1261 Byzantine reconquest of Constantinople, the City and other civil and cultural centres such as Thessalonike and Trebizond flourished admirably. The study of law, theology, literature, philosophy and the natural sciences thrived, and studies on grammar followed a similar trend. Particularly in the capital, at the schools linked to the monasteries of Akataleptos and Chora, intellectuals such as Maximos Planoudes, Manuel Moschopoulos, Theodore Metochites and Nikephoros Gregoras produced textbooks whose impact was felt even during the Western Renaissance.¹⁵

---

⁹ See Callipo (2011: 26–7), Lallot (1998: 33–5), Lallot (2012: 6), Schneider (2000). In the Byzantine millennium, many grammatical works arose, became popular and influenced subsequent works. For an overview of the most significant treatises, see Nuti (2014: 8–72) and on linguistic correctness (*hellenismos*), Sandri (2020).
¹⁰ See Cuomo (2017b), Valente (2017), Tribulato (2019), Ucciardello (2019).
¹¹ Of course, it is necessary to keep in mind that, for example, the readings of the reference authors could vary. This variation depended on many factors: the context, the skill and/or interests of the master and the availability of books. This emerges from research on the curriculum of studies in southern Italy, for which see Arnesano and Sciarra (2010), Ronconi (2012: 99–102), Silvano (2014). But there are also differences between Tzetzes, Prodromos, Eustathios, Gregoras and Triklinios. For example, in the Palaiologan era, Synesios and particularly Aelius Aristides played a more prominent role as reference authors compared to earlier ages. On Aristides, see Nousia in this volume. Interesting observations on the reception of grammatical theories in the Palaiologan era can be found in Nousia (2019a) and Rollo (2019) about Calecas and Moschopoulos, respectively.
¹² See Hilgard (1889/1904: cxxiiiff.), Schneider (1999: 73–109)   ¹³ See Schneider (1999: 767).
¹⁴ See Constantinides (1982), Fryde (2000). On Holobolos' and Pediasimos' scholia on Theocritus' *Syrinx* as Palaiologan textbooks, see Caballero Sánchez in this volume.
¹⁵ See Förstel (1992), Maisano and Rollo (2002), Ciccolella (2008), (2009), (2010), Nuti (2014), Ciccolella and Silvano (2017), Rollo (2019).

Among the most influential textbooks of the Palaiologan era are: Manuel Moschopoulos' *Erotemata* ('Ερωτήματα),[16] and his *Schedographia* (Περὶ σχεδῶν).[17] The most popular lexica of the period are Manuel Moschopoulos' *Collection of Attic Words*,[18] Thomas Magistros' *Lexicon*,[19] the *Lexicon Hermanni*[20] and the *Lexicon Vindobonense*.[21]

The Moschopoulean Comments on Sophocles and the Teaching of Syntax

In order to understand better the Moschopoulean comments on Sophocles – and other, similar compositions more broadly – we eventually have to consider a difficult aspect pertaining to the Byzantine teaching of grammar, namely the teaching of syntax.

Regular readings of the canonical authors evidently gave students the opportunity to learn the vocabulary (e.g. the correct context in which to use a certain word, the proper [κυρίως] use of a term vs. its figurative meaning [μεταφορικῶς/ποιητικῶς]) and micro-syntax (such as the syntax of individual verbs and prepositions) necessary to write in the high-register variety of Medieval Greek on their own. Thus, reference authors were regarded as sets of examples of good Attic usage of vocabulary and phrases to be imitated. Earlier grammatical explanations handed down the lexicographic, morphological and related knowledge of the construction of prepositions and verbs in a summarized way. The material was not systematically organized, as it rather followed the order imposed by the

---

[16] This work presents traditional grammatical material (e.g. Dionysius' *Techne* and Theodosius' *Canons*) in a new way (Pertusi [1962], Rollo [2019]) in the form of questions (hence, *Erotemata*). This method of teaching grammar might have been borrowed from the Lombard school (Pertusi [1962: 330], Cavallo [1980: 180]). The *Erotemata* were introduced by a series of questions and explanations about the eight parts of speech, according to the structure of Dionysius' *Techne*. Moschopoulos relied upon previous material from the Komnenian and Nicene ages (see Nuti [2014: 19–20]). On Moschopoulos' *Erotemata*, see Rollo (2019), Nousia (forthcoming).

[17] On the practice of teaching grammar by means of *schede*, see Ciccolella (2008: 114). On the Komnenian era, see Agapitos' 2015 studies and Lovato in this volume. For the composition of his *Schedographia*, Moschopoulos probably took schedographic material dated to the age of the Komnenian dynasty (from 1081 to about 1185) and rearranged it into a canon of twenty-two *schede*. This work enjoyed a large circulation, as the numerous copies dated to the fourteenth and fifteenth centuries are witness. On Moschopoulos' *Schedographia*, see Nousia (2016), (2019b), (forthcoming).

[18] The first edition appeared in 1524 (Venetiis, In aedibus Aldi, et Andreae Asulani Soceri). In the most recent scholarship, I found only the 1532 Paris edition referred to (see below, *abbreviations*, s.v. CVA). See Guida (1999: 22), Gaul (2008: 168), Canart (2011: 301–5).

[19] Ed. Ritschl (1832). See Gaul (2007), Villani (2012), Conti Bizzarro (2013), Ucciardello (2018).

[20] See the edition by Hermann (1801: 319–52). See also Ucciardello (2018: 107–14).

[21] Ed. Guida (2018).

commented-upon text. Occasionally, the comments also provided paraphrases and rephrases,[22] which allowed students to compare an alternative example of word order in a sentence to that of the canonical author.

However, there is something missing in these explanations and in other surviving textbooks, which prevents us from fully understanding how medieval students could end up mastering the art of composition necessary to write good Atticizing Greek texts. In fact, other, less tangible factors than the surviving scholia and glossae must have contributed to the acquisition of syntax. Among such factors, at least two played a fundamental role. The first factor has to do with the vernacular Greek substrate that the students spoke or to which they were at least exposed. This everyday Greek influenced the perception of what was acceptable in high-register Greek, as recent studies have demonstrated[23] and the 2019 *Grammar of Medieval and Early Modern Greek* indicates.[24] The second factor concerns the actual readings of reference authors. The assiduous dealing with this material occurred in many ways, e.g. through direct extensive readings, lexica, anthologies and sylloges of model sentences collected according to various principles (e.g. collections of *sententiae* organized alphabetically).[25] These two factors were predominant in creating a 'sense of language', a 'feeling of what is linguistically correct' in the students and, in turn, in making them authors capable of compositions that could bear comparison with those of the model authors. For these reasons, I believe that the comments on the writings of model authors should also be seen as tools for learning syntax and can help us understand the method followed by medieval scholars to acquire such important skills, even if this requires some audacious speculation. The comments, which we can still read today, evidently did not replace the actual reading of the model authors that each student undertook, either on his own or with a teacher's guidance. While we can carry out more and more targeted studies on the surviving glossae and scholia, when considering the individual reading habits of medieval students, we can largely only make assumptions, with perhaps some empirical observations from reading the classics ourselves with the surviving medieval reading guides. Of course, one should remember that medieval reading guidance, partially given in written form (e.g. in the scholia), was mainly presented orally by teachers.

---

[22] See below comments 31m, 38f, 47f–h, 47i.
[23] O'Sullivan (2011) and (2013), Horrocks (2017a) and (2017b).
[24] Holton, Horrocks, Janssen, Lendari, Manolessou and Toufexis (2019).
[25] See Canart (2010) and (2011), Mazzon (forthcoming).

In any case, our observations would be mere speculations because the practice of reading itself always comprises individual, unique and thus unrepeatable processes.

In scholarship, the (absence of) syntax in Greek grammars from the Hellenistic to the medieval period is a burning topic.[26] In recent years, an increasing number of studies have given deserved attention to the subject.[27] My suggestion is that such absence looks less striking if we also take the Byzantine comments on the reference authors into consideration, a perspective which achieves a better understanding of Byzantine methods of teaching syntax. Indeed, studying only the most popular treatises on syntax available in Byzantium (e.g. Apollonius Dyscolus,[28] Michael Synkellos,[29] Gregory Pardos,[30] John Glykys,[31] Maximos Planoudes[32]) would leave the modern linguist unsatisfied.[33]

The Comments on Sophocles Preserved in the Moschopoulean Manuscripts

The comments on Sophocles presented here were written within this context. They are transmitted by the so-called Moschopoulean manuscripts of Sophocles. Throughout my chapter, the adjective 'Moschopoulean' does not mean that Moschopoulos is the author of all these comments. It rather

---

[26] Lallot (1994) and (2015), Sluiter (1997: 209–10), Schenkeveld (2000), Swiggers and Wouters (2003). For the Byzantine period, a good overview is in Robins (2000: 417–23).

[27] See e.g. Bentein (2020, with bibliography) and the extensive section on this topic, particularly the part pertaining to the Byzantine era, in the *International Handbook on the Evolution of the Study of Language from the Beginnings to the Present*.

[28] See above, n. 7.

[29] Ed. Donnet (1982). See also Donnet (1979), Cunningham (1991), Nuti (2014: 24–7).

[30] Ed. Donnet (1967). See Nuti (2014: 27–30).

[31] Ed. Jahn (1839). In his treatise on syntactical correctness (Περὶ ὀρθότητος τῆς συντάξεως), dedicated to his pupil Gregoras, Glykys offers a Platonic-Christian view of language, which is perceived as a gift donated by God to human beings in order for them to build communities, become aware of reality and understand the divine mind. Any decline of, and detriment to language must be condemned and avoided. Throughout the work, it is clear that the aim is to preserve and renew the linguistic features of the Greek classics. Like Gregory Pardos, Glykys aims to teach his students how to avoid solecisms (grammatical mistakes) and barbarisms (words that do not belong to the lexicon of the 'canonical' authors). Unlike Gregory, Glykys structured his works as a treatise rather than as a reference handbook. Picciarelli (2003: 263–6) analyses the theory expounded by Glykys. Donnet (1981) offers a new overview of the manuscripts. See also Nuti (2014: *passim*).

[32] Planoudes' *Dialogue on Grammar* (ed. Bachmann [1828: 2:3–101]) and the treatise *On the Syntax of Verbs* (ed. Hermann [1801: 391–421]) are important for their original speculations on the nominal cases and on the relationship between the temporal and aspectual value of Geek verbs. Also important are the observations in Murru (1978) and (1979), Lallot (1985: 76–8), Robins (1993: 220–32). On Planoudes' textbooks for the teaching of grammar, see Nuti (2014: 33–6 and *passim*).

[33] See, for example, Ucciardello (2018) and (2019).

indicates the comments that are found in the Moschopoulean manuscripts of Sophocles. These are a subset of manuscripts that hand down, wholly or partially, the Byzantine triad of Sophocles, sometimes with the addition of *Antigone*, together with a set of scholia and glossae. The appellation 'Moschopoulean' was attributed to the manuscripts by Turyn (1949) in his description of them. From Dawe's collation (1973) onwards, it has been commonly accepted that Sophocles' text was not the result of a critical edition by Planoudes and Moschopoulos, but rather a vulgate that the two grammarians used as a basis for their lessons.[34] As Turyn had already noted,[35] the Moschopoulean manuscripts do not only contain comments authored by Moschopoulos. In fact, each manuscript, to a greater or lesser extent, contains comments by Planoudes, Magistros, Triklinios and even comments of dubious origin. That is to say, alongside a more or less coherently transmitted set of comments, each manuscript contains notes added due to contingent didactic needs. I will here present a few examples.

The copyist of D, Gabriel the Monk,[36] kept adding glossae and scholia over the years, some of which have great affinity with Na (ca. 1335), Xr (ca. 1412) and Mc (mid-fourteenth century). Other manuscripts – Mq, Mt, Mx, Mz, Td – explicitly declare that they transmit notes from both Moschopoulos and Magistros, and distinguish them by putting a cross before the former. Mz and Td, alongside the scholia, also distinguish Thoman glossae from the Moschopoulean ones. These two manuscripts are important because, when they agree against the rest of the tradition (presuming that the manuscripts do not all depend on other sources),[37] they enable us to suppose that the scholion or gloss in question is Thoman and thus we can identify the author of the comment, should it appear in another manuscript anonymously. Manuscript D and manuscript Br (first half of the fourteenth century) label some scholia and longer glossae with the initials μαξ (= τοῦ Μαξίμου τοῦ Πλανούδη, 'by Maximos Planoudes'), though they do not always agree.[38]

These data suggest an important methodological observation, necessary for approaching this material with awareness. When we talk about Moschopoulean comments on Sophocles, we must not imagine a text such as, say, an oration by Demosthenes. Rather, we must imagine the existence of as many 'Moschopoulean commentaries' as there are manuscripts that transmit them, and each manuscript's peculiarities must be taken into account. Consequently, our efforts in respect of this material should be

---

[34] See Pontani (2015: 417).   [35] Turyn (1949: 102–24).   [36] See Pérez Martín (1997).
[37] See 64g.   [38] See Cuomo (2020: 396–403).

aimed at understanding its reception and use and not at reconstructing the Urtext, which probably never existed as such and for which the famous words of Seneca apply perfectly.[39] Hence, the way in which each manuscript passes down the comments is important. In this chapter, I have therefore decided to present the excerpts relevant to our discourse in the form of a critical collation (see below).

While the editing of Greek scholia and their relevance for linguistic analysis are topics for other studies, familiarity with these problems is essential to the argument of the present chapter. Having explored the composition context, we can now consider how late Byzantine comments on the Greek classics actually focused on the language of the canonical authors and tended to neglect other aspects such as the plot, dramaturgical devices, allusions and quotations. Thus, I will present five key passages of the prologue of *Electra* and show how these have been commented on in the Moschopoulean manuscripts.

Dramaturgical Highlights in Sophocles' *Electra*: The Themes of *Kairos* and *Kerdos* in Medieval and Modern Readings

In order to emphasize Electra's isolation and make her reach the abyss of her despair and torment, Sophocles adopts a cruel dramaturgic device. First, he depicts Orestes as shallow and one-dimensional relative to Electra. Orestes, in fact, does not measure up to his sister in terms of tenderness, pity and compassion.[40] He is solely focused on accomplishing his task – killing his mother and her lover and bringing about justice – in the most convenient way possible.[41] One can see this already at the beginning of the tragedy, in the prologue, where Orestes explains his plan to the paedagogus

---

[39] *De brevitate vitae* 13.2: Graecorum iste morbus fuit quaerere, quem numerum Ulixes remigum habuisset, prior scripta esset Ilias an Odyssia, praeterea an eiusdem essent auctoris, alia deinceps huius notae, quae sive contineas, nihil tacitam conscientiam iuvant sive proferas, non doctior videaris sed molestior. 'This was the *idée fixe* of the Greeks, to seek out how many rowers Ulysses had, whether the *Iliad* or the *Odyssey* was written first and whether these are by the same author and other such things. Things which, if you keep them to yourself, will not bring you any advantage apart from covertly knowing them, and if you publish them, you will not appear more cultured but more fastidious.' Ed. Bourgery (1994 [1923]); trans. mine.

[40] Even in the ἀναγνώρισις, the recognition scene that happens at vv. 1217ff. (at the end of the tragedy!), Electra's expressions of joy do not find an equivalent counterpart in Orestes' lines: he only asks her to be quiet and focus on the revenge. On this peculiar ἀναγνώρισις, see Di Benedetto (1988: 188).

[41] By contrast, the character of Electra has greater substance. As a member of a noble family, as a daughter of Agamemnon, she always expresses feelings of nobleness and a sense of duty, and her targets are justice, glory and honour, all values opposed to the less noble *kerdos*. See Di Benedetto (1988: 161–4).

with remarkable coldness. As far as Orestes is concerned, nothing should disturb the opportune moment/favourable occasion (*kairos*). For him, nothing seems to count more than profit/advantage (*kerdos*). In order to fulfil the prophecy of the oracle, he is even ready to let the false news of his death spread: 'How can it distress me, namely to die in word, if in fact I am safe and win glory? I maintain that a word that brings advantage cannot be ill-omened. I have already seen many, even wise men dying in false stories and then, after returning to their houses, being held in even greater honour. And so, for myself, I trust that as a result of this rumour I, too, shall live, shining down like a star upon my enemies.'[42] So, Orestes appears to be chiefly interested in realizing the prophecy of the oracle of Apollo and carrying out revenge, even if his plan calls for tricks, disguising himself, spreading fake news of his own death, etc.

Even the spectators are set apart from Orestes' plan, but not Electra. And yet it is precisely with this dramaturgical choice that Sophocles can tragically isolate and enhance the figure of Electra. She will remain alone, fighting for justice for her father's murder. She will reach the peak of solitude and despair when she is told that Orestes has passed away, all in accordance with her brother's ruthless plan. Indeed, from the point of view of Orestes' plan, it was pointless to keep Electra in the dark. The fact that Orestes decides not to let Electra know about the prophecy of the oracle of Apollo, that he allows her to believe that he himself, her sole hope for redemption, has died and that he does not then tell her that he is alive and back, ready to vindicate his father, seems an avoidable cruelty to Electra. Indeed, when a few lines later (v. 77), Electra's lamenting appears for the first time, both the paedagogus and Orestes, despite having correctly supposed that the voice they were hearing was Electra's, decide to leave the scene (vv. 80–5), so as not to impede the plan, the *kairos* (v. 75). Of course, from the dramatic point of view, Sophocles needed, as we have seen, a completely isolated Electra, who can thus reach the deepest point of her sorrow when she learns that Orestes has died (vv. 676–822), culminating in the line 'I desire life no more'.

Comments in Comparison

Having highlighted these concepts, I would like to look at how the manuscripts comment on the above-mentioned passages of the prologue. I will proceed as follows. Firstly, I will provide extracts from the most relevant manuscripts for seventeen verses of the prologue here published

---

[42] Sophocles, *Electra* 59–66, after Jebb and Dugdale trans.

for the first time, and accompany these passages with some critical, explanatory notes and translations where needed. This should allow us to compare the modern understanding of key concepts such as *kairos* and *kerdos* to that of the medieval manuscripts with greater ease. The presence of the medieval comments below is indispensable to this chapter, as we cannot discuss the nature of these comments abstractly nor by quoting decontextualized scholia or glossae.

The passages to be considered are the following. Excerpt 1, vv. 29–31: Orestes takes the floor and decides to explain his plan for revenge to the paedagogus so that he will help him. Excerpt 2, vv. 38–41 & Excerpt 3, vv. 47–8: Having reported the prophecy of Apollo's oracle, according to which Orestes is allowed to avenge his father's death, Orestes invites the paedagogus to enter the royal palace 'when the time is right' and to begin the plan by announcing that Orestes has died. Excerpt 4, vv. 59–64: Orestes comments on the opportunity to let this false news spread. Excerpt 5, vv. 75–6 offers another reference to the concept of *kairos*.

In the Greek texts below, I defer to the manuscripts in matters of punctuation and orthography.[43] The upper dot, the *teleia* (α·), works as our full stop. The *mesai*, middle dots (α·), have the function of modern commas. Note that I write all the *hypostigmai* (the lower dots of the manuscripts, α.) as commas (α,) because I find that the lower dot may disturb modern readers, despite the fact that this makes the *hypostigmai* in my edition look like *hypodiastolai* (manuscripts commas). The *hypodiastole* resembles our comma (α,) but its function is different, as it indicates that two (or more) elements in the microsyntax belong together. The *hypostigme*, by contrast, indicates that what follows is the main clause, which completes the phrase.

The glossae and scholia do not exist without the main text. Hence, for each passage, I will firstly provide the text of Sophocles alongside its translation and an *apparatus criticus*. This apparatus will indicate how the Moschopoulean manuscripts of Sophocles behave both with respect to each other and with respect to the rest of the manuscript tradition. Secondly, I will provide an edition of the comments preserved in the Moschopoulean manuscripts of Sophocles, based on the best and more complete manuscripts. The glossae and scholia are accompanied by an *apparatus criticus*, my commentary and a translation where needed. Finglass (2007) is my reference edition: I collated my manuscripts with his apparatus and with Dawe's collation (1973). I also include the text of

---

[43] Cuomo (2016: xlviii–l), with further bibliography.

the scholia, as edited by Brunck/Dindorf and Capperonnier, because I want to show (a) how freely previous editors presented this material and (b) how much has so far remained unedited.

List of Manuscripts and Abbreviations

For the purposes of this article, I referred to the manuscripts listed below. Unless otherwise noted, these mss. are dated or datable to within the 1360s.

D = Naples, Biblioteca Nazionale 'Vittorio Emanuele III', II.F.9
Ba = Milan, Biblioteca Ambrosiana, B 97 sup.
Br = Bremen, Staats- und Universitätsbibliothek, b. 0023
Ga = Milan, Veneranda Biblioteca Ambrosiana, G 43 sup.
La = Milan, Veneranda Biblioteca Ambrosiana, L 39 sup.
M = Florence, Biblioteca Medicea Laurenziana, Conv. Sopp. 172
 However, M only transmits carries a single scholion, on the καιρός of v. 75 (fol. 97v), written by the first hand, and a few glossae, twenty or so, along with a γραπτέον added by a later hand. The scholion partially depends on *Souda* κ 1189 (καιρός) and ε 2615 (and a few glossae, twenty or so, along with a γραπτέον added by a later hand. Τερ ἀνδράσι μέγιστος (i.e. ἔργου, as in Suid. ε 2615) ἤτοι ἐπωφελής.
Mc = Madrid, Biblioteca Nacional de España, 4617
Md = Modena, Biblioteca Estense, α.U.9.19
Mh = Paris, Bibliothèque nationale de France, gr. 2805
Mi = Paris, Bibliothèque nationale de France, gr. 2820
Mo = Vatican City, Biblioteca Apostolica Vaticana, gr. 40
Mp = Vatican City, Biblioteca Apostolica Vaticana, gr. 44
Mq = Vatican City, Biblioteca Apostolica Vaticana, gr. 47
Mt = Venice, Biblioteca Nazionale Marciana, gr. 470[44]
 Mt^m = The scholion or glossa marked with Mt^m was ascribed to Manuel Moschopoulos by the copyist of Mt. Similarly, Mt^t indicates a scholion ascribed to Thomas Magistros.
Mx = Paris, Bibliothèque nationale de France, gr. 2884
Mz = Vienna, Österreichische Nationalbibliothek, phil. gr. 163
 Mz^m = The scholion or glossa marked with Mz^m was ascribed to Manuel Moschopoulos by the copyist of Mt. Similarly, Mz^t indicates a scholion ascribed to Thomas Magistros.

---

[44] Tessier (2015 [2005]: XXIII–XXV).

Na = Milan, Veneranda Biblioteca Ambrosiana, N 166 sup.
　　　Mid-fourteenth cent., with a few extra-Moschopoulean scholia on Sophocles' *Ajax* by Michael Lygizos[45]
Td = Vienna, Österreichische Nationalbibliothek, phil. gr. 209, fifteenth cent. See Tessier (2015 [2005]: xxii–xxiii). Td^m = The scholion or glossa marked with Td^m was ascribed to Manuel Moschopoulos by the copyist of Td. Similarly, Td^t indicates a scholion ascribed to Thomas Magistros.

X　= Florence, Biblioteca Medicea Laurenziana, Conv. Sopp. 71
Xa = Vatican City, Biblioteca Apostolica Vaticana, gr. 50
Xc = Florence, Biblioteca Medicea Laurenziana, Conv. Sopp. 98
Xd = Vatican City, Biblioteca Apostolica Vaticana, Urbin. gr. 140
Xe = Vatican City, Biblioteca Apostolica Vaticana, gr. 48
Xh = Venice, Biblioteca Nazionale Marciana, gr. 617[46]
Xr = Vienna, Österreichische Nationalbibliothek, phil. gr. 161, a. 1412
Xs = Vienna, Österreichische Nationalbibliothek, suppl. gr. 71
Xu = Florence, Biblioteca Medicea Laurenziana, Plut. 31,9
Xv = Florence, Biblioteca Medicea Laurenziana, Plut. 32,51
Xz = Florence, Biblioteca Medicea Laurenziana, Plut. 32,34

Other Sophoclean Manuscripts[47]
Ma = Leipzig Universitätsbibliothek Rep. 1 44a
Mb = Leipzig Universitätsbibliothek Rep. 1 44b
　　　Ma and Mb are Moschopoulean; but I only used them on a few occasions as they display a more predictable text, comparable to X, Xc, Xh, and Xs.
g　= Florence, Biblioteca Medicea Laurenziana, Conv. Sopp. 152, a.1282
N　= Madrid, Biblioteca Nacional de España, 4677, end of the thirteenth cent.
P　= Heidelberg, Universitätsbibliothek, Pal. gr. 40
V　= Venice, Biblioteca Nazionale Marciana, gr. 468
A　= Paris, Bibliothèque nationale de France, gr. 2712, beginning of the fourteenth cent.

---

[45] On these scholia, see Cuomo (2020). On Lygizos, see RGK 1 nr. 282; *PLP* 15914.
[46] Mioni (1982: 209–16). Note that the section containing the Sophoclean triad dates back to the mid-fourteenth century, whereas the rest was written later.
[47] Finglass (2007: 20–2).

t = Consensus codicum T (= Paris, Bibliothèque nationale de France, gr. 2711) & Mt
l = Consensus codicum L (= Florence, Biblioteca Medicea Laurenziana, Plut. 32,9), Λ (= Leiden, Universiteitsbibliotheek, gr. 60A), K (= Florence, Biblioteca Medicea Laurenziana, Plut. 31,10)

Brunck = *Sophoclis quae extant omnia cum veterum grammaticorum scholiis. Superstites tragoedias* VII, ed. R. F. P. Brunck, 2 vols. (Strasbourg, 1786)
Capperonnier = *Sophoclis Tragoediae septem, cum interpretatione latina et scholiis veteribus ac novis*, ed. J. Capperonnier and J.-F. Vauvilliers (Paris, 1781). I refer to the 'scholia inedita', published on the basis of L(aud 54), B(odl. Auct.F.3.25). I use Capperonnier (1781) instead of Johnson (1746), as the former is a reprint of the latter.[48]
Dindorf = W. Dindorf, *Scholia in Sophoclis tragoedias septem ex codicibus aucta et emendata*, 2 vols. (Oxford, 1852)
Dindorf 1863 = Schol. in Eur.
Finglass = P. Finglass, *Sophocles:* Electra (Cambridge, 2007)
Xenis = G. A. Xenis, *Scholia vetera in Sophoclis Electram*, Sammlung griechischer und lateinischer Grammatiker 12 (Berlin and New York, 2010)
Schol. in Eur. = W. Dindorf, *Scholia in Euripidis tragoedias*, 4 vols. (Oxford, 1863)
CVA = Manuelis Moschopuli, *Collectio Vocum Atticarum e libro de arte imaginum Philostrati et scriptis poetarum.* Lutetiae 1502.
ThMag. *Ecl.* = F. Ritschl, *Thomae Magistri sive Theoduli Monachi Ecloga Vocum Atticarum* (Leipzig, 1832; repr. Hildesheim, 1970)

Excerpt 1

τοιγὰρ, τὰ μὲν δόξαντα, δηλώσω· σὺ δὲ (29)
ὀξεῖαν ἀκοὴν τοῖς ἐμοῖς λόγοις διδούς, (30)
εἰ μή τι καιροῦ τυγχάνω, μεθάρμοσον· (31)
31 μεθάρμοσον] -ωσον Mh, R

So, I will reveal to you what I have in mind, and you give acute listening to my words: If I happen not to get the right moment, correct me. (after Jebb and Dugdale trans.)

---

[48] See Johnson (1746).

29a τοιγάρ] διὸ DBrGaLaMaMbMcMdMhMiMoMpMqMtMzNaTdXXaXc XdXeXhXsXrXuXvXz
    29a διό] διά Mb || no comments on this word in MpMx
    This glossa points to a problem to which I have not yet found any solution: When Mz puts a cross before a gloss, it means that the marked gloss is Moschopoulean. How should we interpret the origin of those glossae without any distinctive mark?

29b τὰ μὲν δόξαντα] om. BrMaMoMpXs ||¹ ἤγουν τὰ ἀρεστὰ φανέντα DGaLaMbMdMhMiMqMtMxMzNaTd^{m}XXaXcXdXeXdXhXuXv ||² τὰ φανέντα McXr ||³ κυρωθέντα Mp
    29b¹ ἤγουν GaMbMdMhXXaXcXdXeXhXuXv] om. cett. | post φανέντα habent ἐμοί Na sive μοί MqMxMzTd^m
        The origin of the (ἐ)μοί is unknown. Generally, Mq, Mt, Mx, Mz and Td together against the others render a note by Thomas Magistros; and here only Mt disagrees with the rest of the subgroup. Hence, (ἐ)μοί should be a Thoman glossa. Unlike Mz, Td explicitly attributes the entire glossa, μοί included, to Moschopoulos.
    29b3: For examples of κυρόω glossing δοκέω in scholia, see the TLG online.

29c δηλώσω] σοί MqMtMxMzTdXr
    29c post σοί habet δηλονότι Xr
Probably, this note has to be ascribed to Magistros.

30a ὀξεῖαν] om. Mx || ἤγουν ταχεῖαν DBrGaLaMaMbMcMdMhMiMoMqMtMz^{m}NaXXaXcXdXeXhXsXrXuXv
    30a ἤγουν BrGaMaMbMdMhMoXXaXcXdXhXuXv] om. cett.

30b ὀξεῖαν] προσεκτικὴν D
    While the rest of the Moschopoulean mss. only explain ὀξεῖαν, 'sharp', as ταχεῖαν, as in (30a), ms. D also suggests that listening to Orestes' words has to be προσεκτικὴν, 'careful'. The most common gloss (ταχεῖαν s. 30a) is a standard one, applied almost automatically. The minority gloss (προσεκτικὴν) is a more skillful one, in the sense that it tries harder to show the precise nuance of the adjective in this context. In the scholia on Euripides, Moschopoulos and/or Magistros tend to use a more accurate glossa that reflects the subtlety of this particular passage, as kindly confirmed to me by Donald Mastronarde via email.

30c ὀξεῖαν] σύντονον MtMxTd
    Probably, this note has to be ascribed to Magistros. It is suggested that the adjective here takes on the nuanced meaning of 'intense, of perceptions and feelings'.

30d ἀκοὴν] om. MpMxMt || τὴν ἀκουστικὴν δύναμιν DBrGaLaMaMbMcMdMhMiMoMqMz^{m}NaTd^{m}XXaXcXdXeXhXsXrXuXv
    30d τὴν] om. Mc
        Concerning the subgroup that renders Thoman glossae, it is common that Mt disagrees with Mz by Mt omitting a note marked as Moschopoulean by Mz.

30e ὀξεῖαν – διδούς] ἀκούων μετὰ προσοχῆς, σπουδαίως τοὺς ἐμοὺς λόγους· D

Verses 31 to 62 are not visible in the images of Mh at my disposal.

31a τί] κατά τι MqMtMzTd
31b εἰ - τυγχάνω] ἤγουν εἰ κατά τι μὴ ἐπιτυγχάνω καιροῦ· εἰ μὴ κατὰ καιρὸν λέγω
DBrGaMaMbXs
  31b (ἤγουν) εἰ κατά] : εἰ μή τι καιροῦ ἤγουν Ga | εἰ μὴ κατὰ καιρὸν λέγω D] om. cett.

31c εἰ - τυγχάνω] εἰ κατά τι μὴ ἐπιτυγχάνω καιροῦ· ἤγουν εἰ μὴ ἐγκαίρως λέγω κατά τι Mi¹&², Brunck/Dindorf
  31c εἰ κατά - καιροῦ] om. Brunck/Dind. | In hac hac nota codicis Mi, Mi¹ tantum scripsit "κατά", ut vid.

In Mi, a second hand, contemporary to the first, seems to have read the entire tragedy, provided it with new comments (as in this case) and suggested a new colometry.

31d εἰ - τυγχάνω] εἰ μὴ ἔστιν ὁ ἐμὸς λόγος καίριος· εἰ μὴ ἐγκαίρως λέγω Na
31e εἰ - τυγχάνω] κατά τι μὴ ἐπιτυγχάνω Mc
31f εἰ - τυγχάνω] ἤγουν εἰ κατά τι μὴ ἐπιτυγχάνω καιροῦ· MdMoXXaXcXhXv
  31f post εἰ habet μὴ sic Md

31g εἰ μὴ κατά τι καιροῦ ἐπιτυγχάνω Mt
  The Mt glossa is merely a variation of the previous one.

31h εἰ - τυγχάνω] εἰ μὴ κατὰ καιρὸν λέγω Xe
31i εἰ - τυγχάνω] ἤγουν ἐὰν κατά τι μὴ ἐπιτυγχάνω, καιροῦ Na
  Underneath the previous note, Na¹ later added καλοῦ (sic).

31j εἰ - τυγχάνω] τοῦ πρέποντος ἐπιτυγχάνω ἐν τῷ λέγειν MqMxTd
  31j ἐπιτυγχάνω] om. Mq

31k τυγχάνω] ἐπιτυγχάνω MtXe² (cf. supra)
31l εἰ - τυγχάνω] κατά τι Mz
31m μεθάρμοσον] om. NaMcMpMxXu ‖ ἐπὶ μουσικῆς λέγεται κυρίως τὸ μεθαρμόζειν· ἤγουν τὸ μετατιθέναι τὴν ἁρμονίαν: DBrGaMaMbMdMiMo MqᵐMtᵐMzᵐTdᵐXXaXcXdXeXhXsXrXv, Brunck/Dindorf
  31m τὸ²] om. Xe | post ἁρμονίαν: habent τὸ δὲ ὅλον, εἰ κατά τι μὴ ἐπιτυγχάνω, καιροῦ· μεθάρμοσον ἤγουν ἐπανόρθωσον MtᵐMzᵐTdᵐ

  Actually, in Mc, the margins are severely damaged. Hence, this scholion might have appeared in this ms. as well. If so, however, it was written in an unconventional place, i.e. far from the Sophoclean passage. Na also has this same note, though with minor changes (see 31n). At the end of the scholion 'ἐπὶ μουσικῆς…', MtᵐMzᵐTdᵐ alone provide a paraphrasis of the entire verse, introduced by the words τὸ δὲ ὅλον. It is difficult to state whether the copyists or their source(s) added this comment, which actually summarizes the glossae on v. 31. There Mt comments as follows: after μή, it adds κατά. Before τυγχάνω, it writes ἐπι- (scil. ἐπιτυγχάνω). Then it glosses μεθάρμοσον with ἐπανόρθωσον, which is, in turn, taken from the corresponding ancient scholion. In my view, this is good evidence for how this material might also have been transmitted. The material that one is used to seeing as interlinear glossae might also have been contained in a scholion. In music, the verb means 'to change the mode'.

31n μεθάρμοσον] τὸ μεθαρμόζειν κυρίως, ἐπὶ μουσικῆς λέγεται· ἤγουν τὸ
μετατιθέναι τὴν ἁρμονίαν:- Na¹
31o μεθάρμοσον] ἀντὶ τοῦ ἐπανόρθωσον·
DBrLaMaMbMcMdMiMoMqMtMzXXaXcXdXeXhXsXrXv
  31o ἀντὶ τοῦ MaMbMdMoXXaXcXhXsXv] om. cett.

31p μεθάρμοσον] ἐπανόρθωσον· μεταβαλοῦ Na ||² μεταβοθλεύων, παανορθῶσ..
  non liquet Mp
31q μεθάρμοσον] ἐπανόρθωσον· μετάστησον D ||² μετάστησον· ἀντὶ τοῦ
ἐπανόρθωσον GaXe
  31q, 31r, and 31s transmit the same note, ἐπανόρθωσον, either with a different word order
  or accompanied by an additional explanation.
31r μεθάρμοσον] μετάβαλε καὶ τὰ βέλτιστα, αὐτὸς συμβούλευσον MxMz^mTd
  Unlike Mz, Td does not explicitly ascribe this note to Moschopoulos. MqMt do not have the
  note. Mx also transmits a scholion on vv. 30–1, of which only a few letters are now visible.
  However, it does not seem to be any of those I just transcribed.

Excerpt 2

ὅτ' οὖν τοιόνδε χρησμὸν εἰσηκούσαμεν, (38)
σὺ μὲν μολών, ὅταν σε καιρὸς εἰσάγῃ, (39)
δόμων ἔσω τῶνδ', ἴσθι πᾶν τὸ δρώμενον, (40)
ὅπως ἂν εἰδώς, ἡμῖν ἀγγείλῃς σαφῆ· (41)
  41 σαφῆ] σαφῶς P (= Heidelberg Pal. gr. 40), et O s.l., et O^gl. (= Leiden, Voss. gr. Q 6)⁴⁹

Now, this being the prophecy that we have heard, you must go into that house,
learn all that is being done, so that, having found it out, you can
clearly report it to us. (after Jebb and Dugdale trans.)

38a ὅτε] ἀντὶ τοῦ ἐπεὶ· ἐπίρρημα ἀντὶ συνδέσμου·
DBaBrLaMaMbMdXdXuNaTdXXaXcXeXhXsXv, Brunck/Dindorf,
  Capperonnier, only
  38a ἀντὶ τοῦ BrMaMbMdMoNaXXaXcXdXeXhXsXuXv, Capp.] ὅτε ἀντὶ τοῦ Ga : om. cett. |
  ἐπίρρημα ἀντὶ] ἐπίρρημα ἀντὶ τοῦ GaMoTd

38b ὅτε] ἀντὶ τοῦ ἐπεὶ ἐπίρρημα ἀντὶ [τοῦ] συνδέσμου Mi
  38b ἀντὶ τοῦ add. Mi²| ἐπεὶ] -εὶ p.c. Mi²
    38a and 38b actually mean the same. Nonetheless, I want to keep them separate to show that
    two hands were involved in the copying of Mi. To be more precise, in Mi, there is a second,
    slightly later hand (Mi²) that oversees the entire work of Sophocles. In the lyrical parts, it
    changes the colometry. Overall, it adds new and modifies extant glossae and scholia.

38c ὅτ' οὖν] ἐπεὶ οὖν ἐπίρρημα ἀντὶ συνδέσμου· D
38d ὅτ' οὖν] ὅτε οὖν· ἐπίρρημα ἀντὶ συνδέσμου· ὡς ἐν τῷ· ὅτ' ἄλλοτ'
ἄλλον· ἀντὶ τοῦ δέ: D
  38d ὅτ' ἄλλοτ' ἄλλον] Soph. Aj. 58.

---

⁴⁹ See Dawe (1973, vol. 2: *passim*).

38e ὅτε] ἐπεί McMtMxMzXr
The omission of previous glossae and the sole ἐπεί must be Thoman characteristics, unless one considers ἐπεί and ἐπίρρημα ἀντὶ συνδέσμου as two separate glossae. In fact, Td, which generally transmits Thoman glossae, has both.

38f ὅτ' οὖν - εἰσηκούσαμεν] ἤγουν ὡς δεῖ τὸ ἔργον σὺν δόλῳ μεταχειρίσασθαι Mq ||² ἤγουν ὡς δεῖ σὺν δόλῳ τὸ ἔργον μεταχειρίσασθαι MxMzTd
    38f² δόλῳ τὸ ἔργον MzTd] δόλῳ τὸν ἔργον Mx
    Transl.: 'i.e. that it is necessary to treat the thing with deceit'.
    This glossa comments on τοιόνδε, as it specifies the content of the prophecy that Orestes heard.

38g εἰσηκούσαμεν] ἀντὶ τοῦ ἠκούσαμεν· DBaBrGaLaMaMbMcMdMiMoMqNaXXaXcXdXhXsXuXv, Brunck/ Dindorf
    38g ἀντὶ τοῦ DBaBrMaMbMoNaGXXaXcXhXsXv

38h εἰσηκούσαμεν] τὸ πρόσωπον, γενικῇ· πρὸς δὲ τὸ πρᾶγμα, αἰτιατικῇ: D
Contemporary users of the manuscripts were expected to be able to supply something like εἰσακούω συντάσσεται πρὸς μὲν at the beginning. Hence, the sense of the glossa should be as follows: The verb εἰσακούω ('to hear something from someone') is constructed with the person in the genitive and the thing in the accusative.

39a μολών] εἰς τὸ δῶμα ἐλθών DNa
    39a ἐλθὼν εἰς τὸ δῶμα Na

39b μολών] ἐλθών BrGaLaMaMbMcMdMiMoMqMtTdXXaXcXdXeXhXsXr XuXv

39c καιρός] ὁ (scil. καιρός) Na

39d καιρός] ὁ πρέπων MqMtMxMzTd
This note must have a Thoman origin.

39e καιρὸς εἰσάγῃ] νῦν γὰρ ἔτι νύξ MqMxTd
Trans.: 'for now it is still night'. In the ms. La, a much later hand adds the glossa "νύξ" as a comment on "καιρός".
The note explains the key term καιρός by simply underlining the fact that, as it is still night, the moment is not yet opportune for entering the palace and embarking upon the plan.

39f εἰσάγῃ] εἰσκαλῇ DMqNaTd^m Mz^m
Cf. Schol. in Aristophanis Plutum (406a) εἰσαγαγεῖν] εἰσκαλέσασθαι. Ed. M. Chantry, Scholia in Thesmophoriazusas, Ranas, Ecclesiazusas et Plutum [Scholia in Aristophanem 3.4b. Groningen 1996].
Mt, which transmits both Moschopoulean and Thoman comments, tends to disagree with Td and Mz as it omits many glossae marked there as Moschopoulean. So, the fact that Mt does not have this glossa does not surprise.

40a ἴσθι] ἀντὶ τοῦ μάνθανε DBrGaMaMbMcMiMoNaXXaXcXeXhXsXrXv, Brunck/Dindorf, Capperonnier
    40a ἀντὶ τοῦ MaMbMoNaXXaXcXe] ἴσθι ἀντὶ τοῦ Ga : ἤγουν Xs : om. cett.

Late Byzantine Scholia on the Greek Classics   321

40b ἴσθι] γίνωσκε MqMtMx
    Apparently, γίνωσκε is the Thoman glossa against μάνθανε, which is Moschopoulean. However, see the following glossa, 40c. Γίνωσκω and its forms provide a commonplace gloss for forms of οἶδα and some other verbs; here it is also needed to differentiate ἴσθι from εἰμί (where the gloss ἔσο or ὕπαρχε might be used).

40c ἴσθι] γίνωσκε· μάνθανε Td^m
40d τὸ δρώμενον] ἤγουν τὸ πραττόμενον ἐκεῖσε DBrLaMaMbMcMdMiMoMtMz^{m}NaTd^{m}XXaXcXdXeXhXsXrXuXv ||^2
τὸ ἀφ' ἐκείνης πραττόμενον Mq
    40d^1 ἤγουν MaMbMoNaXXaXcXeXhXsXv | τὸ πραττόμενον] πραττόμενον MiMoMz^{m}Td^m, -όμενος Xe | ἐκεῖσε Na] om. cett.
    Clearly mistakenly, Xe reads πραττόμενος. Mx and Td do not agree with Mq, but see their glossa below (40f).

40e τὸ δρώμενον] τὸ δρώμενον· ἤγουν τὸ πραττόμενον· Ga, Capperonnier
    Ga differs from other sources in the layout only, by having the note as a glossa.

40f τὸ δρώμενον] ὑπὸ Κλυταιμνήστρας καὶ Αἰγίσθου· καὶ τῶν ὑπ' ἐκείνης (scil. Ἠλέκτρας?) MxTd
    40f ὑπὸ Td] ἀπὸ Mx | καὶ^2 Td] om. Mx | ὑπ' Td] ἀφ' sic Mx
    After Αἰγίσθου, given the omission of the second καὶ, Mx considers this glossa as two separate notes, though it does not punctuate after Αἰγίσθου. The second part of the glossa expands on τὸ δρώμενον and includes τῶν (δρωμένων), i.e. the actions undertaken by Electra. The reference to Electra puzzles me, because Orestes actually seems only interested in knowing how Clytemnestra and Aegisthus are acting. However, alluding to Clytemnestra (ὑπ' ἐκείνης = 'by that woman') again would be too much. Alternatively, if we consider 40f as two separate glossae, which happened to have merged, the second glossa may well then refer to Clytemnestra only. This would imply putting a *teleia* after Αἰγίσθου and rejecting Td's reading (καὶ^2).
    Another question arises from the use of τῶν instead of τὸ, as I did not find any Moschopoulean manuscript reading τῶν δρωμένων in v. 40. This must be a Thoman glossa.
    The mss. which chiefly transmit Moschopoulean scholia do not comment on v. 41.

41a εἰδώς] γνῶσιν εἰληφὼς τοῦ πράγματος· ἀκριβῶς γινώσκων· D, only | ἀκριβῶς γινώσκων· γνῶσιν εἰληφὼς τοῦ πράγματος· Na
    In their respective first and second phrases, D and Na must imply that εἰδώς, being here γνῶσιν, is simply an accusative.

41b σαφῆ] φανερῶς DMt
41c σαφῆ] σημεῖα δηλονότι Xr
41d σαφῆ] οὐκ ἀντὶ τοῦ σαφῶς Mq
41e σαφῆ] τοῦτο οὐκ ἀντὶ τοῦ· σαφῶς ἀλλ' ὄνομά ἐστι MxMzTd
    41e ἐστι] -ιν TdMz
    41e must be a Thoman glossa.
    41d and 41e do not explain the text of Sophocles. They rather seem to be debating a possible *varia lectio*, σαφῶς (cf. app. crit. ad loc.). Hence, the note should be interpreted as follows: 'σαφῆ is the correct reading, σαφῶς is not'. Glossa 41e, in particular, by adding ὄνομά ἐστι, seems to point out explicitly that σαφῆ here is an internal accusative connected

with ἀγγείλης (ἀγγείλης σαφῆ ἀγγέλματα), and not an adverb. In other words, the glossa warns against taking the word as equivalent to the adverb and advises that it is better taken as substantival.

41f] As a general comment on Orestes' plan:
ἐπειδὴ ὁ Ὀρέστης παρὰ τῷ Στροφίῳ ἐτρέφετο, ὁ μὲν Πυλάδης καὶ ὁ
Ὀρέστης μέλλουσιν εἰπεῖν· ὅτε τὸ ἄγγος πρὸς Κλυταιμνήστραν ἄξουσιν,
ὡς παρὰ Στροφίου ἐπέμφθησαν· τῷ δὲ Παιδαγωγῷ ὑποτίθενται εἰπεῖν,
ὡς παρὰ Φανοτέως ἥκει προμεμηνυκότος ὡς φίλου, τὸν τοῦ Ὀρέστου θάνατον:-
MtMxTd

1 ὁ³ MtTd] om. Mx || **2** εἰπεῖν] om. Td | ὅτε codd.] ubi -ε ex -ι Mx¹ | ἄγγος MtTd] ἄγγους Mx || **3** ὡς παρὰ MtTd] παρὰ Mx

Trans.: 'Since Orestes had been raised by Strophius, Pylades and Orestes will find themselves saying, when they bring the urn before Clytemnestra, that they were sent by Strophius. Also, they suggest that the paedagogus says that he has come from Phanoteus, who, being a friend, had informed <the Paedagogus> about Orestes' death.'

This appears to be a Thoman scholion, despite its absence in Mq, and Mz. Mt and Td, consequently, do not mark it with a cross.

The note comments on the plan expounded by Orestes in vv. 38–50: 'Accordingly, since I received this divine declaration, you must go into that house there when opportunity gives you entrance, and learn all that is happening, so that you may report to us out of sure knowledge. Your age and the lapse of time will prevent them from recognizing you; they will never suspect who you are with that silvered hair. Let your story be that you are a Phocian stranger sent by Phanoteus, since he is the greatest of their allies. Tell them, and affirm it with your oath, that Orestes has perished by a fatal chance, hurled at the Pythian games from his speeding chariot. Let that be the substance of your message' (after Jebb and Dugdale trans.). In order to get the right meaning of προμεμηνυκότος ὡς φίλου, one should probably bear in mind vv. 670 and 673 of the rhesis, where the paedagogus, pretending to be an emissary from Phanoteus, ruthlessly announces that Orestes is dead. The scholion also mentions Pylades, Orestes' inseparable friend and a non-speaking character.

Excerpt 3

ἄγγελλε δ' ὅρκῳ προστιθείς, ὅθ' οὕνεκα (47)
τέθνηκ' Ὀρέστης ἐξ ἀναγκαίας τύχης· (48)

47 ὅρκῳ codd.] ὅρκον Finglass (Reiske/ Erfurdt) sed cf. glossas ad 47b, d, f–h. | ὅθ' οὕνεκα codd.] ὁθούνεκα edd.

Then, adding an oath (i.e. to the announcement), do announce that Orestes died because of a necessity of fate. (after Jebb and Dugdale trans.)

47a ἄγγελλε] λέγε· διηγοῦ Na
47b ὅρκῳ προστιθείς] ἀντὶ τοῦ ὅρκον X

This is one of the cases in which one wonders whether the commentator is providing a *varia lectio* rather than a comment on the poetic text. See also 47d, 47f–h, and above, 41d–e.

47c ὅρκῳ προστιθείς] ἀντὶ τοῦ ὅρα προστιθείς sic Xe
47d ὅρκῳ προστιθείς] om. MxTd || ἀντὶ τοῦ ὅρκον προστιθείς·

DBrGaLaMaMbMdMc³MiMoMqMtMzXXcXdXhXsXrXuXv
  47d ἀντὶ τοῦ] ἤγουν MiMqMtMz : om. Mt | ὅρκον] ὅρκῳ DXs
47e προστιθεὶς] τὴν ἀγγελίαν δηλονότι DLa²MqMxMzNaXr
  47e τὴν ἀγγελίαν] τῇ ἀγγελίᾳ Na | δηλονότι Xr] om. cett.
  Different layout: Mq has τὴν ἀγγελίαν either as a gloss to ἄγγελλε or at the beginning of the scholion τοῦτο
  ἀντιστρόφως etc.

47f ἄγγελλε δ' ὅρκῳ προστιθείς] om. DMcMiMqMtMxMzTdX || ἄγγελε δὲ προστιθεὶς τὴν ἀγγελίαν δηλονότι ὅρκῳ· λέγεται δὲ ἀντιστρόφως, ἀντὶ τοῦ προστιθεὶς ὅρκον τῇ ἀγγελίᾳ:· BrGaLaMaMbMoNaXaXcXdXeXhXsXrXuXv
47g ἄγγελλε δ' ὅρκῳ προστιθείς] τὴν ἀγγελίαν δηλονότι ὅρκῳ. λέγεται δὲ ἀντιστρόφως, ἀντὶ τοῦ προστιθεὶς ὅρκον τῇ ἀγγελίᾳ. Dindorf
47h ἄγγελλε δ' ὅρκῳ προστιθείς] τοῦτο ἀντιστρόφως λέγεται, ἀντὶ τοῦ· προστιθεὶς ὅρκον τῇ ἀγγελίᾳ MiMqTd, Brunck
  47f ὅρκον] ὅρκῳ Xu
  47h προστιθεὶς MqTd, Brunck] προτιθεὶς sic Mi
  Generally, Mx and MqMtMzTd form a subset of mss. that transmit Thoman scholia, i.e. when they are in agreement against the others, and when Mz and Td do not mark the comment with a cross, the text they transmit is likely to be Thoman. Here we can only count on Td, as Mz does not transmit this scholion.

47i] ὅρκῳ προστιθεὶς ἀντιστρόφως καὶ τοῦτο λέγει· λέγει προστιθεὶς τὴν ἀγγελίαν δηλονότι τῷ ὅρκῳ· ὀφείλων λέγειν· τῇ ἀγγελίᾳ προστιθεὶς ὅρκον· ὅμοια καὶ ταῦτα· λύπη δίδωμι τινὰ καὶ ἡδονῇ· καὶ τοῖς τοιούτοις ἀντὶ τοῦ· λύπην παρέχω τινὶ καὶ ἡδονήν:· D
  47i: ἡδονῇ scripsi] ἡδονὴ sic D

47j ὅθ' οὕνεκα] om. Mq ||¹ ἀντὶ τοῦ ὅτι· ἐκ παραλλήλου· DBrGaLaMaMbMdMoXXcXdXeXhXsXuXv ||² ἐκ παραλλήλου· ἤγουν ὅτι Na ||³ ἀντὶ τοῦ ὅτι McMx^{al}Xr ||⁴ ἐκ παραλλήλου MiMtMzTd, Brunck/Dindorf
  47j¹ ἀντὶ τοῦ] om. DLa || 47j³ ἀντὶ τοῦ McXr] om. Mx^{al}
  The manuscripts acknowledge the meaning of this conjunction, 'ὅτι/that', which introduces the declarative phrase. However, they should have spelled it ὁθούνεκα (i.e. ὅτου + ἕνεκα = ὅτι) instead of ὅθ' οὕνεκα (i.e. ὅτι + ἕνεκα).

48a ἀναγκαίας] ἤγουν βιαίας DBrGaLaMaMbMcMdMiMqMoMtMxMz NaTdXXcXdXhXsXrXuXv
  48a ἤγουν BrGaMaMbMdMoXXcXeXhXsXv] ἤτοι Xd : om. cett. | βιαίας] θηβαίας sic Xe
  Probably, the curious mistake in Xe was due to the copyist mishearing the word βιαίας. Xe also carries another remarkable phonetic error in 47c.

48b τύχης] τουτέστιν τῆς εἱμαρμένης Na ||² δυστυχοῦς ut vid. Mp
  Scholia on the Greek classics also gloss τύχη with ἡ εἱμαρμένη (μοῖρα) destiny, i.e. the lot assigned by fate. Here, only Na does so.

48c: πάντα γὰρ τὰ ἐξ ἀνάγκης βίαια· θάνατος ἡ μετὰ δουλείας αἰχμαλωσία· D

Excerpt 4

τί γάρ με λυπεῖ τοῦθ'· ὅταν λόγῳ θανών, (59)
ἔργοισι σωθῶ κἀξενέγκωμαι κλέος; (60)
δοκῶ μὲν οὐδὲν ῥῆμα, σὺν κέρδει, κακὸν (61)
ἤδη γὰρ εἶδον πολλάκις καὶ τοὺς σοφοὺς, (62)
λόγῳ μάτην θνῄσκοντας· εἶθ' ὅταν δόμους (63)
ἔλθωσιν αὖθις, ἐκτετίμηνται πλέον· (64)

    59 τοῦθ'· ὅταν] τοῦτο, ὅταν X
    61 μέν codd. nostri, ubi Na^{rpc}, G^{pc}AZrHN^{ac}PV, t] μὲν ὡς McNa^{rac}XcXs, lr CFOZc et Suid. iii. 300.14, iv. 546.24
    63 δόμους K, ap] -οις L^{ac}ΛZc, r et Suidas ii 552,9

And why should this hurt me, being dead in a tale if in reality I am safe and winning glory? I believe that any word, if it brings advantage, is not ill-omened. I have already often seen even wise men dying in false stories and then, after making return to their houses, being held in even greater honour. (after Jebb and Dugdale trans.)

59a τί] κατά (*scil.* κατὰ τί) D
59b λυπεῖ] βλάπτει DNa
59c τοῦθ'] κατά (*scil.* κατὰ τοῦτο) Xr
59d λόγῳ] ἤγουν διὰ λόγου DBrGaLaMaMbMcMdMiMoMqMtMx NaTdXXaXcXdXeXhXsXrXuXv

    59d ἤγουν Mb] om. cett. | διὰ] om. Xr | διὰ λόγου] διαλόγου Na

    None of the notes on this verse is now visible in Mz, if they ever were.

59e λόγῳ] τῇ φήμῃ Na
59f λόγῳ] ὑπό (*scil.* ὑπὸ λόγῳ) D
59g θανών] ἐγώ D

Verse 60 is labelled as γνωμικόν by McMiXaXv.

60a ἔργοισι] διὰ τῶν ἔργων DBrGaLaMaMbMcMdMiMoMxNaXXaXcXd XeXhXsXrXuXv ||² ἤγουν δι' ἔργων MqMtMz^{m}Td^{m} ||³ καὶ πράγμασι Mp
    60a² ἤγουν Mz^{m}] om. cett. | δι' MqMz^{m}Td^{m}] διὰ Mt
60b κἀξενέγκωμαι] ἐπενέγκωμαι λάβω DMc
    60b λάβω DMc, ubi postea in mg. add Mc²
60c κἀξενέγκωμαι] ἀντὶ τοῦ ἐπενέγκωμαι GaLaMaMbMdMiMoMqMx MzTdXXaXcXdXeXhXsXrXuXv
    60c ἀντὶ τοῦ BrGaMaMbMdMoMqXaXcXdXeXhXsXv] om. cett. | ἐπενέγκωμαι BrMaMbMdMiMoMxXXcXdXeXhXsXu] ἀπενέγκωμαι MqMzTdXaXr | post ἀπενέγκωμαι add. καὶ λάβω Xr
    In lexica and scholia, it is more frequent to find ἀποφέρω glossing λαμβάνω (or vice versa) than ἐπιφέρω.

60d κάξενέγκωμαι] ἀπενέγκωμαι· ἀντὶ τοῦ ἐπενέγκωμαι Na
   Considering the ink employed, ἀντὶ τοῦ ἐπενέγκωμαι seems to have been added at a later stage, always by Na¹. Na¹ reads his copy over and over again and adds notes at different times.

60e κάξενέγκωμαι κλέος] ἐξήνεγκα τὸ ἔξω τοῦ ἔργου, ἐνεργητικὸν· ἀπηνέγκατο ὃ ἔλαβε, παθητικόν· D
60f κλέος] τιμή X
   It also seems that another hand is involved here.

60g κλέος] δόξαν MqMtMx
   This must be a Thoman glossa.

Verse 61 is marked as ὡραῖον by Mb²Na and labelled as γνωμικόν by Mi

61a δοκῶ] νομίζω DMqMtMzTd
   This must be a Thoman glossa.

61b δοκῶ] μοι Xe
61c δοκῶ μὲν οὐδὲν] ὅτι BrGaLaMaMbMcMdMiMoMqMxNaTd XXaXcXeXhXsXrXuXv
   In Xc and Xs, ὡς, which probably happened to be a glossa, was inserted into the text. Na^rac also wrote it as part of the verse and glossed on it 'ὅτι'.

61d οὐδὲν ῥῆμα] ἐστὶ δηλονότι Xr
61e κέρδει] καὶ ὠφελείᾳ τινι Na
61f σὺν κέρδει κακόν] ἀφαιρεῖται γὰρ τὴν ἐκ τοῦ κακοῦ ἀηδίαν τὸ κέρδος MqMzTd
   61f τὴν ut vid. Mq] om. MzTd

62a ἤδη] ἦν ὅτε DBrGaLaMaMbMcMdMiMoMqMtMxMzNaTdXXa XcXdXeXhXsXrXuXv
   62a ὅτε] ὅτε sic Mi : τότε· McXr : om. Mt
62b εἶδον πολλάκις] ἐθεασάμην MxX
62c καὶ τοὺς σοφοὺς] φρονίμους Xr
62d σοφοὺς] φιλο- (scil. φιλοσόφους) Na
62e καὶ τοὺς σοφοὺς] ὁ λόγος πρὸς τὸν Πυθαγόραν τείνει· DNa
62f ἤδη] ἤδη ποτὲ ἐγένετο τόδε ἀντὶ τοῦ ἦν ὅτε· ἤδη δὲ γίνεται ἀντὶ τοῦ ἰδοὺ γίνεται δεικτικῶς· ἤδη δὲ βαδιοῦμαι πρὸς τὴν ἐξέτασιν ἀντὶ τοῦ ἀποτουνῦν: D
62g ἤδη] ἤδη βαδιοῦμαι· ἀντὶ τοῦ ἀπάρτι ἤδη ποιῶ, ἀντὶ τοῦ ἰδού:- Xr
   There is no other Moschopoulean ms. that transmits either of these two scholia. One would expect Mc and Xr to agree here as well. They may actually agree, but the margins in Mc at this point are severely damaged: the lost portion of text might, therefore, have contained this note.
   Vv. 31–62 were not visible in my photo reproduction of Mh. From now on, I can report Mh's readings again.

63a λόγῳ] διὰ λόγου διηγήσ(εως) φήμη D
63b λόγῳ] om. Td || διὰ λόγου BrGaLaMaMbMcMdMhMiMoMqMt
MxMzNaXXaXcXdXeXhXsXrXuXv
  63b διὰ] om. Xr | λόγου] om. Mz
63c μάτην] ἤγουν ψευδῶς
DBrGaLaMaMbMcMdMhMiMoMqMtMxMz^{m}NaTd^{m}XXaXcXdXeXhXs
XrXuXv, Brunck/Dindorf
  63c ἤγουν BrGaMaMbMdMhMoXaXcXdXeXhXuXv] ἤτοι Mz^{m}Td^m : om. cett.
63d δόμους] om. XeXs || εἰς DBrGaLaMaMcMdMhMiMoMqMtMxMzNaTd
XXaXcXdXhXrXuXv
  63d εἰς δόμους Xv
63e δόμους] ἐπανέλθωσι D

64a ἔλθωσιν] om. Mz ||^1 ἐπανῆλθον ἤκωσι D ||^2 ἀντὶ τοῦ ἐπανῆλθον
BrGaLaMaMbMc^{2}MdMhMiMoMqMtMxNaTdXXaXcXdXeXhXsXrXuXv
  64a^2 ἀντὶ οὗ BrGaMaMbMc^{2}MdMoMhNaXaXcXdXeXhXsXrXuXv] om. cett. | ἐπανῆλθον]
  ἀπανῆλθον sic Xe
64b ἐκτετίμηνται] om. DMiMtMx, non liquet Mc || ἀντὶ τοῦ τετίμηνται·
BrGaLaMaMdMbMhMoMqMzNaTdXXaXcXdXeXhXsXrXuXv
  64b ἀντὶ τοῦ] om. LaMiMqMtMxTd | τετίμηνται] τεμίμηται sic Na
  Two of these glossae in Mc are illegible to me. The first one was written by Mc^1, the second one
  by Mc^3.

64c ἐκτετίμηνται] τιμῶνται Mx
64d ἐκτετίμηνται πλέον] περισσὴ   πλείονα τιμὴν λαμβάνουσι D
64e ἐκτετίμηνται πλέον] ἀργ(όν) MiMqMx$^?$Td
  64d and 64e: In scholia, the feminine gender of περισσὴ generally indicates that ἡ
  πρόθεσις is to be understood. Similarly, the masculine form means that ὁ σύνδεσμος is
  intended, whereas the neuter (more common) refers to a word or phrase normally
  introduced by a τὸ. Therefore, both 64d and the ἀργὸν in 64e are saying that the
  preposition ἐκ- has no function in the understanding of the verb, which is just a poetic
  variation on the simple verb.

64f πλέον] ἢ πρόσθεν MqMtMz
  'I.e.: more than before.'
  This must be a Thoman glossa.

64g] Comment on vv. 62–4.
Ἱστορία· Πυθαγόρας καθείρξας ἑαυτὸν ἐν ὑπογείῳ, λογοποιεῖν ἐκέλευσε τὴν
μητέρα, ὡς ἄρα τεθνηκὼς εἴη· καὶ μετὰ ταῦτα ἐπιφανείς, περὶ παλιγγενεσίας
καὶ τῶν καθ' Ἄδου τινὰ ἐτερατεύετο· διηγούμενος πρὸς τοὺς ζῶντας περὶ τῶν
οἰκείων· οἷς ἐν Ἅδου συντετυχήκει, ἔλεγεν· καὶ πολλάκις τοῦτο ποιήσας,
ἑαυτῷ δόξαν περιέθηκε ταύτην, ὡς πρὸ μὲν τῶν Τρωϊκῶν Αἰθαλίδης ἦν ὁ
Ἑρμοῦ· εἶτα Εὔφορβος· εἶτα Ἑρμότιμος ὁ Σάμιος· εἶτα Πύθιος ὁ Δήλιος· εἶτ' ἐπὶ
πᾶσι, Πυθαγόρας: εἰς τοῦτον οὖν ἔοικεν ἀποτείνεσθαι ὁ Σοφοκλῆς:- MtMxTd
  64g 1 Ἱστορία Td] non habent cett. cum ScholVet : περὶ Πυθαγόρου· ἤδη γὰρ εἶδον πολλάκις
  καὶ τοὺς σοφοὺς λόγῳ μάτην θνῄσκοντας· εἶθ' ὅταν δόμοις ἔλθωσι πάλιν, ἐκτετίμηνται πλέον
  Suid. | Πυθαγόρας] ὡς Πυθαγόρας Suid. | ἑαυτόν] αὑ- Mt || 2 ἄρα ScholVet, Suid.] non
  habent MtMxTd || εἴη MtMxTd, Suid.] ἔοι ScholVet || 4 συντετυχήκει MtMxTd] -ηκέναι
  ScholVet, Suid. | ἔλεγεν] om. MtMxTd || 4 καὶ - ποιήσας MtMxTd] ἐξ ὧν τοιαύτην ScholVet,

Suid. ‖ 5 περιέθηκε ταύτην MtMxTd] περιέθηκεν ScholVet, Suid. ‖ 5 Αἰθαλίδης] θαλίδης MtMxTd | ἥν MtMxTd] ὧν ScholVet, Suid. | Εὔφορβος Mx] Ἔ- Mt, Ἤφορφος ut vid. Td. | ὁ¹] non habent ScholVet, Suid. ‖ 6 Σάμιος] non habent ScholVet ‖ 6 ὁ²] non habent ScholVet, Suid. ‖ εἶτ' ἐπὶ MtMxTd] εἶτα ἐπὶ ScholVet, Suid. ‖ 6 εἰς τοῦτον - Σοφοκλῆς Td, ScholVet] non habent MtMx, Suid. | τοῦτον ScholVet] -το Td | οὖν ScholVet] γὰρ Td
  Paralleli loci sive fontes: ScholVet = Scholia Vetera on Soph. El., v. 62, ed. Xenis 2010.
  Suid. = η (88) ll. 5sqq.

  Trans.: 'Mythological tale. As Pythagoras locked himself in the basement, he ordered his mother to spread the false news of him being dead. Then he appeared again, and he would talk marvels about reincarnation of souls and things pertaining to Hades. Recounting in detail to the living ones, he would narrate about the relatives whom he had come across in Hades. And having done so many times, he created around himself this reputation, that he, before the times of Troy, had been Aethalides, the son of Hermes, then Euphorbus, Hermotimus of Samos, then Pyrrhus of Delos and at last Pythagoras. So, Sophocles seems to refer to him.'

  Overall, MtMxTd agree on a few passages against *scholia vetera* and *Souda*, as is evident in the apparatus. We can give the translation 'mythological tale', because the manuscripts employ the term ἱστορία, 'tale', 'story', to introduce a mythological account. I prefer the reading εἰς τοῦτον of the *scholia vetera* (ed. Xenis) against εἰς τοῦτο of Td, bearing in mind 62e: ὁ λόγος πρὸς τὸν Πυθαγόραν τείνει, 'the text refers to Pythagoras'.
  Cf. A. Nauck, *Porphyrii philosophi Platonici opuscula selecta*, Leipzig 1886² (repr. Hildesheim: Olms, 1963) § 45; H.S. Long, *Diogenis Laertii vitae philosophorum*, 2 vols., Oxford: Clarendon Press, 1964 (repr. 1966), book 8, § 5; F. Wehrli, *Herakleides Pontikos* [Die Schule des Aristoteles vol. 7, Basel 1969²], fragment 89; H. Diels and W. Kranz, *Die Fragmente der Vorsokratiker*, vol. 1, Berlin 1951⁶, fragment 8. Cf. Ovid., Met. XV, 160–4.

Excerpt 5[50]

νῷ δ' ἔξιμεν· καιρὸς γάρ, ὅσπερ ἀνδράσι (75)
μέγιστος ἔργου παντός ἐστ' ἐπιστάτης· (76)
  75 νῷ
    BrMiXcXs^ac

We will now depart. In fact, this is the right moment, the greatest tutelary god of every human action. (after Jebb and Dugdale trans.)

75a νῷ δ'] ἡμεῖς DBrGaLaMaMbMcMdMhMiMoMqMtMxMzNaTdXaXc XdXeXhXsXrXuXv
  75a post ἡμεῖς habent δὲ MhMq
75b ἔξιμεν] non liquet Mz ‖ ἀντὶ τοῦ ἐξίωμεν ἐξερχώμεθα· BaBrGaLaMaMbMdMhMiMoNaXaXcXdXeXhXsXuXv
  75b ἀντὶ τοῦ] om. LaMhMiNa | ἐξερχώμεθα] om. Mh
75c ἔξιμεν] ἐξερχώμεθα McMqMtMxTdXr
  75c ἐξερχώμεθα McXr] -όμεθα MqMtMxTd
75d ἔξιμεν] ἀντὶ τοῦ ἐξίωμεν· ἐρχώμεθα· ὡς τὸ ἵνα εἴδομεν, ἀντὶ τοῦ εἰδῶμεν: D
  75d ἵνα εἴδομεν] Hom. A, 316 et in Homero *passim*

---

[50] No comments on these verses in X.

Schol. in Eur. Phoen. 93: ...ὡς παρ' Ὁμήρῳ ἵνα εἴδομεν ἀντὶ τοῦ εἰδῶμεν. (ed. Dindorf 1863); Schol. in Eur. Phoen. 736: καὶ παρ' Ὁμήρῳ ἵνα εἴδομεν ἄμφω, ἀντὶ τοῦ εἰδῶμεν. (ed. Dindorf 1863). These scholia are edited by Dindorf from Gr, the 'Moschopoulean' hand of Wolfenbüttel, Herzog August Bibliothek, cod. Gud. gr. 15; see Günther (1995: 30, 54–5). Donald Mastronarde kindly confirmed to me that these glossae, edited by Dindorf from Gr, are actually Moschopoulean.

75e ἔξιμεν καιρὸς] ὁ ἐνεστώς· ἀντὶ ὑποτακτικοῦ DNa
    75e ὁ D] om. Na

75f καιρὸς] ὑπάρχει McNa, only ‖ ἐνθένδε ἐστὶ Mi²MqTd
    75f ἐστί] om. Td

75g ὅσπερ] ὅς τις sic DMcNa

75h καιρὸς - ἀνδράσιν] ἤγουν ὁ καιρὸς ἐν ἡμῖν δηλονότι· Xr

75i καιρὸς] καιρός ἐστιν ὃς ποιεῖ τοῖς ἀνδράσι ποιεῖν ἀγαθόν· ἀλλ' ὁ καιρὸς ὁ ἐπιτήδειος· οἷον καιρός ἐστιν ἐνδεχόμενος λουθῆναι· εἰ μὲν ἔνι νύξ, κοιμηθῆναι: D

    Trans.: '"Opportunity" is the thing that makes it good for people to do (something). But "opportunity" is also the "appropriate time", as the moment when one should wake up, or, if it is night, sleep.'
    The phrase οἷον καιρός ἐστιν ἐνδεχόμενος λουθῆναι can be translated as: 'such as: *kairos* is when it is possible to/when one can wash'. The translation 'should wake up' is justified by the following phrase that mentions the night and sleeping.

76a μέγιστος] ὁ πρωϊνὸς καιρὸς DNa
    'The morning *kairos*.'

76b ἔργου] ἔστι D

76c ἐστ'] καὶ ἐστὶ DBrGaLaMaMbMdMcMiMoNaTdXaXcXdXeXhXuXs
    76c καὶ Na] om. cett. | ἐστί] -ὶν LaMaMcMdMiNaXaXcXdXhXu

76d ἐπιστάτης] παρακλήτωρ Td

76e ἐπιστάτης] om. MxX ‖¹ ἤγουν ἔφορος ἡγεμών· DNa ‖² ἤγουν ὁ ἡγεμών· BrGaLaMaMbMcMdMhMiMoMqMtMz^mTdXaXcXdXeXhXsXrXv
    76e¹ ἤγουν Na | ἔφορος ἡγεμών D] ἡγεμὼν ἔφορος Na ‖ 76e² ἤγουν BrGaMaMbMhMoMqXaXcXe
XhXs] om. cett. | ὁ MoXs] om. cett.
    D and Na should be viewed as agreeing against the others.

76f] Comment on verses 73–6: ... σοὶ δ' ἤδη, γέρον, τὸ σὸν μελέσθω βάντι φρουρῆσαι χρέος. – ἐπιστάτης] om. MxX ‖ σοὶ δὲ ἀποτουνῦν ὦ γέρον, μελέτω τὸ σὸν χρέος, ἤγουν ὅπερ ἐτάχθης· καὶ χρεωστεῖς πληρῶσαι· λέγω τὸ, (*scil.* σοὶ) πορευθέντι φρουρῆσαι (*scil.* μελέτω χρέος)· τουτέστι κατασκοπῆσαι: καιρὸς γὰρ νῦν δηλονότι· ὅς ἐστι τοῖς ἀνδράσι μέγιστος, ἐπιστάτης· ἤγουν ἡγεμὼν ἔργου παντός:-DBrMaMbMcMhMiMoMq^mMt^mMz^mNaTd^mXaXcXeXhXsXrXv
    76f 1 σοὶ] σὺ Mq^m | ἀποτουνῦν DMb] ἀπὸ τοῦ νῦν cett. | γέρον] o ex ω D¹ et Xs¹ ‖ 2 χρέος] om. Mq^mMt^mMz^mTd^m | ἤγουν¹] om. BrMcTd^mXs | λέγω τὸ] λέγω τῷ DMcTd^mXr ‖ 3 φρουρῆσαι· τουτέστι] om. MiMq^mMt^mMz^mTd^m ‖ 4 ὅς ἐστι] ὅς ἐστι BrMaMbMhMoXaXcXeXhXv : ἐστὶ Xs
    Edd. Brunck/Dindorf: see below.

    Trans.: 'This, o old man, you should take to heart: your task, i.e. what you have been appointed to do, and what you must complete. I say this to you, who are on your way, take care to accomplish your mission, that is, to spy. Clearly, now is the right moment, the *kairos* who is the greatest tutelary god of men, i.e. the origin of every (human) action.'
    The κατασκοπῆσαι is a more sophisticated glossa to φρουρῆσαι χρέος, because it eventually explains what the mission to be completed is.

It is worth noticing that MtMqMzTd depend on a common source. When witnessing a scholion alongside other mss., they present characteristic features that do not accord with the others. They also agree in attributing the scholion to Moschopoulos.

As the colon after κατασκοπῆσαι suggests, these are two distinct notes. For the manuscripts, these two notes comment on the same concept: the fact that the paedagogus is now old, and hence he would not likely be recognized, indicates that this is the right moment to act.

Xr and Brunck/Dindorf split the two notes and explicitly refer καιρὸς – παντός to v. 75. This is appropriate, but it does not illustrate well, I think, the way the medieval reader looked at this passage. See Brunck/Dindorf on: v. 73 σοὶ δ' ἤδη γέρον] σοὶ δὲ ἀπὸ τοῦ νῦν, ὦ γέρον, μελέτω τὸ σόν· ἤγουν ὅπερ ἐτάχθης καὶ χρεωστεῖς πληρῶσαι· λέγω τό, πορευθέντι κατασκοπῆσαι. And on 75 καιρός] καιρὸς γάρ, νῦν ἐστὶ δηλονότι, ὅς ἐστι τοῖς ἀνδράσι μέγιστος ἐπιστάτης, ἤγουν ἡγεμὼν ἔργου παντός:-

D numbers the following words in this way: καιρὸς¹ ὅσπερ² ἀνδράσι³ μέγιστος⁴ ἔργου παντός ἐστι⁵ ἐπιστάτης⁶. What surprises me is that the mss. commonly assign a number to the words with the aim of indicating the most natural word order, particularly in cases of hyperbata. Here, there would not have been the need for such indications. Also, the numbers above the words do not link to any scholion in the margin. Gabriel the Monk, the copyist of D, had already employed this system of *signes-de-renvoi* to help the reader find the corresponding notes in a very crowded page.

Observations

I would like to start with an important fact that catches our attention when examining the so-called Moschopoulean manuscripts of Sophocles. An original and homogeneous commentary on Sophocles never existed. Instead, there are manuscripts – each with its own characteristics due to its context of production and educational needs – that transmit the set of scholia and glossae to Sophocles that originated from the school of Planoudes, Moschopoulos and Magistros (and more rarely Triklinios), although these three names are not mentioned here as individual authors, but as a brand.[51]

If the aim of our research on this material is to understand what these scholia and glossae are, what they comment on, what their didactic efficacy is and what those who use them can learn, then the way forward is to consider each manuscript as a world unto itself. This implies leaving aside (a) the relationships between the manuscripts and (b) any attempt to distinguish the Urtext from subsequent additions and alterations. Thus, in drawing our conclusions on the basis of a certain scholion, for example, we must always bear in mind which manuscript transmits it and take into account its history. In this final part, I will expand on these concepts, which arose during the course of the chapter.

From the examples presented above, we see that the only concern of the Moschopoulean comments is to explain the meaning and syntax of almost every word and phrase of Sophocles' text. The meaning is explained by providing a synonym in high-register Greek, sometimes

[51] See Gaul (2008: 177).

alongside a synonym in Koine. The syntax is sometimes explained by adding a pronoun to the verb (e.g. 29c δηλώσω σοί) to indicate which case the analysed verb takes, or, as in 60e, by explaining when compounded forms of a certain verb (φέρω in the example) take the passive or the active voice. Neither morphology/lexicography nor syntax are treated systematically. The notes aim, as in the example above, to explain Sophoclean words as well as the syntax of verbs and prepositions as they appear in the commented-upon text. It is the reading of the authors of reference itself that instils the 'sense of language' in students and familiarizes them with the Attic word order and the use of subordinate conjunctions typical of Attic Greek. Even if rare, there are paraphrases of passages (e.g. 31m, 38f, 47f–h, 47i) and more general discussions about the semantic range of a word (e.g. 31m–n, 75i).

In the introduction to the present chapter, I stressed the importance of the concept of *kairos*, i.e. the right moment, in the *Electra*. In no manuscript do we find a comment that highlights this concept and exposes its dramaturgical characteristics. Whenever the term appears, it is treated as if it were the first and sole time it has occurred. In addition, *kairos* is never contextualized and its symbolic meaning for the tragedy remains obscure to the readers. So, in 31j and 39d we simply have a synonym to explain the word *kairos*. These two notes seem to be Thoman, as they are transmitted by (some of) the mss. of the Thoman subgroup: MqMtMxMzTd. In 31b, 31c, 31d, 31h and 31j, we have a paraphrase of the passage. There, the generic expression 'if I happen not to be appropriate' pronounced by Orestes, is expanded on by adding '. . . in my speech'/ 'if I do not speak appropriately'. Similarly, comment 39e explains that this is the right time to act, for 'now in fact it is still night'. And comment 75h explains that 'the right moment' is 'the right moment to act, to start the revenge'. In 75i, the term *kairos* is de-contextualized and used for a semantic exercise.

The same happens to the concept of *kerdos*, the 'advantage'. Unlike Electra, driven by noble and moral ideals, what moves Orestes to action is the search for advantage, the achievement of the goal, that is, only revenge. No comment highlights this feature of Orestes when the term *kerdos* appears. Yet through this feature, Sophocles can enhance the character of Electra and make her stand out in isolation even in terms of moral calibre. Consequently, in 61c, Na alone says that the advantage is also a gain, while Mq, Mz, Td (perhaps a Thoman gloss) say that '*kerdos* takes away the unpleasantness from what is bad'.

So, in answering the question in the title of this chapter, it can be said that the Moschopoulean comments on Sophocles are notes of lexicography and micro-syntax that aim at facilitating the learning of high-register Medieval Greek for pupils engaged in the readings of the canonical authors. Sophocles' language is only a pretext for achieving that goal. If we relied only on the known Moschopoulean scholia, we would learn very little about the plot of the tragedy, the psychology of the characters, their relationships and, in general, everything that pertains to the meaning of the tragedy and Attic theatre. Moschopoulean observations concerning language and grammar are well-rooted in the millennia-long Greek grammar tradition. Some of them, now scattered, were later organized alphabetically in the *Collection of Attic Words* attributed to Moschopoulos (see above n. 18).

One last thing has yet to be observed. If we want to conduct a study on medieval commentaries on ancient authors today, we must take into account their transmission. Regarding texts such as the commentaries on Homer by Eustathios, Moschopoulos' *Technologia*,[52] or Manuel Gabalas' *Introduction to Homer's* Odyssey,[53] it is clear that we are faced with a text like any other, whose critical edition and study do not differ much from those of any other Byzantine text. If, instead, we consider the comments transmitted in the form of scholia and glossae, then things change. Their understanding and editing must take into account: (a) the relationship between the comment and the text it comments upon, as it appears in the various manuscripts (e.g. layout, any discrepancies between the comment and the given Sophoclean *lectio*) and (b) that each manuscript is a world unto itself, where even the particular notes characterizing a single manuscript are to be taken into consideration. In fact, when quoting a glossa or scholion, I often referred to the *sigla* of manuscripts. One could say that Moschopoulos' comments on Sophocles do not exist anymore. Rather, it is the comments preserved in the so-called Moschopoulean manuscripts of Sophocles that exist. And each manuscript transmits a customized and particular version of the comments, worth studying in itself.

Some manuscripts more than others, such as D, Na, Xr (and less frequently Mc), frequently add scholia of doubtful origin against the rest of the tradition. Others, such as Mq, Mt, Mx, Mz and Td, also more or less explicitly insert comments authored by Thomas Magistros. The reason for these additions, evidently, is to fill some exegetical gaps in the Moschopoulean comments and to address specific didactic needs related to the composition of the particular manuscript. Consequently, we have 40f and 41f, which offer additional information concerning the relationships between characters and their background, or 64g, which offers a story related to Pythagoras, to which Sophocles' text seems to refer in vv. 62–4 (previously D and Na had noted that with 'the wise men' mentioned in

---

[52] Grandolini (1980–1: 5–22) and (1982: 131–49).   [53] See Silvano (2017: 217–37).

v. 62, Sophocles refers to Pythagoras [see 62f]). Again, commenting on τὸ δρώμενον ('the actions', 'what has been accomplished'), Mx and Td explain that these are the actions performed by Clytemnestra and Aegisthus in the royal palace (40f). In other words, they give the context and explain to whom Orestes is alluding in that particular verse.

***

The study of this type of commentary on ancient texts, therefore, carried out as I mentioned above, opens up two worlds to us. First, it reveals how the Byzantines learned high-register Medieval Greek. Second, it contributes to giving us an idea of how the Byzantines read the Greek classics. The study of these two aspects, i.e. linguistic and cultural skills acquired through comments on reference authors, promises to modify the way we conceive the concept of grammar and its teaching in the Middle Ages. Furthermore, it allows us to understand which images, which associations certain quotations from classical authors could potentially evoke in the minds of the Byzantines. This would enable us to react to those quotations and allusions in the same way as the Byzantines did. The 2017 workshop that gave rise to the present collected volume bore the title 'Preserving, Commenting and Adapting'. To summarize, we can say that the Moschopoulean comments on Sophocles did not preserve and adapt Sophocles as much as they preserved and adapted the millennia-long Greek grammatical tradition.

REFERENCES

Agapitos, P. A. (2015a) 'New Genres in the Twelfth Century: The *Schedourgia* of Theodore Prodromos', *MEG* 15: 1–41.
  (2015b) 'Literary *Haute Cuisine* and Its Dangers: Eustathios of Thessalonike on Schedography and Everyday Language', *DOP* 69: 225–41.
  (2015c) 'Learning to Read and Write a *Schedos*: The Verse Dictionary of Par. Gr. 400', in *Pour une poétique de Byzance: hommage à Vassilis Katsaros*, ed. S. Efthymiadis, C. Messis, P. Odorico and I. D. Polemis, 11–24. Dossiers Byzantins 16. Paris.
Arnesano, D. and E. Sciarra (2010) 'Libri e testi di scuola in Terra d'Otranto', in *Libri di scuola e pratiche didattiche: dall'antichità al Rinascimento. Atti del convegno internazionale di studi, Cassino, 7–10 maggio 2008*, vol. 2, ed. L. Del Corso and O. Pecere, 425–73. Collana scientifica. Studi archeologici, artistici, filologici, filosofici, letterari e storici 26. Cassino.
Bachmann, L. (1828) *Anecdota Graeca e codicibus Bibliotecae Regiae Parisiensis*. Leipzig.
Bentein, K. (2020) 'The Distinctiveness of Syntax for Varieties of Post-Classical and Byzantine Greek: Linguistic "Upgrading" from the Third Century BCE

to the Tenth Century CE', in *Varieties of Post-Classical and Byzantine Greek*, ed. K. Bentein and M. Janse. Berlin–New York.

Bourgery, A. (1994 [1923]) *Sénèque Dialogues*, vol. 2: *De la Vie heureuse; De la Brièveté de la vie*. Paris.

Brandenburg, P. (2005) *Apollonios Dyskolos, über das Pronomen: Einführung, Text, Übersetzung und Erläuterungen*. Munich.

Callipo, M. (2011) *Dionisio Trace e la tradizione grammaticale*. Rome.

Canart, P. (2010) 'Pour un répertoire des anthologies scolaire commentées de la période de Paléologue', in *The Legacy of Bernard de Montfaucon: Three Hundred Years of Studies on Greek Handwriting: Proceedings of the Seventh International Colloquium of Greek Palaeography (Madrid–Salamanca, 15–20 September 2008)*, ed. A. Bravo García and I. Pérez Martín, 449–62. Turnhout.

(2011) 'Les anthologies scolaires commentées de la période des Paléologues, à l'école de Maxime Planude et de Manuel Moschopoulos', in *Encyclopedic Trends in Byzantium? Proceedings of the International Conference Held in Leuven, 6–8 May 2009*, ed. P. van Deun and C. Macé, 297–331. Leuven–Paris–Walpole.

Cavallo, G. (1980) 'La trasmissione scritta della cultura greca antica in Calabria e in Sicilia trai secoli X–XV', *Scrittura e civiltà* 4: 157–245.

(1995) 'I fondamenti culturali della trasmissione dei testi a Bisanzio', in *Lo spazio letterario di Grecia antica* II: *la ricezione e l'attualizzazione dei testi*, ed. G. Cambiano, L. Canfora and D. Lanza, 265–306. Rome.

(2010) 'Oralità scrittura libro lettura: appunti su usi e contesti didattici tra antichità e Bisanzio', in *Libri di scuola e pratiche didattiche: dall'antichità al Rinascimento. Atti del convegno internazionale di studi, Cassino, 7–10 maggio 2008*, vol. 2, ed. L. Del Corso and O. Pecere, 11–36. Collana scientifica. Studi archeologici, artistici, filologici, filosofici, letterari e storici 26. Cassino.

Chrysostomides, J. (1994) *Byzantine Women: Lecture Delivered to the Lykeion tôn Hellinidôn in London, 18 October 1993*. Camberley.

Ciccolella, F. (2008) *Donati Graeci: Learning Greek in the Renaissance*. Leiden.

(2009) 'Tra Bisanzio e l'Italia: grammatiche greche e greco-latine in età umanistica', *Studi Umanistici Piceni* 29: 397–410.

(2010) 'Greek Grammars and Elementary Reading in the Italian Renaissance', in *Libri di scuola e pratiche didattiche: dall'antichità al Rinascimento. Atti del convegno internazionale di studi, Cassino, 7–10 maggio 2008*, vol. 2, ed. L. Del Corso and O. Pecere, 577–605. Collana scientifica. Studi archeologici, artistici, filologici, filosofici, letterari e storici 26. Cassino.

Ciccolella, F. and L. Silvano (eds.) (2017) *Teachers, Students, and Schools of Greek in the Renaissance*. Leiden–Boston.

Constantinides, C. N. (1982) *Higher Education in Byzantium in the Thirteenth and Early Fourteenth Centuries (1204–ca.1310)*. Nicosia.

(2003) 'Teachers and Students of Rhetoric in the Late Byzantine Period', in *Rhetoric in Byzantium. Papers from the Thirty-Fifth Spring Symposium of Byzantine Studies, Exeter College, University of Oxford, March 2001*, ed. E. M. Jeffreys, 39–53. Aldershot.

Conti Bizzarro, F. (2013) *Ricerche di lessicografia greca e bizantina*. Alessandria.
Cunningham, M. (1991) *The Life of Michael the Synkellos*. Belfast.
Cuomo, A. M. (2016) *Ioannis Canani de Constantinopolitana Obsidione Relatio: A Critical Edition, with English Translation, Introduction and Notes of John Kananos' Account of the Siege of Constantinople in 1422*. Byzantinisches Archiv 30. Berlin–Boston.
  (2017a) 'Historical Sociolinguistics – Pragmatics and Semiotics, and the Study of Medieval Greek literature', in Cuomo and Trapp (eds.) (2017), 9–31.
  (2017b) 'Medieval Textbooks as a Major Source for Historical Sociolinguistic Studies on (High-Register) Medieval Greek', *Open Linguistics* 3: 442–53.
  (2020) 'Sui manoscritti moscopulei di Sofocle: il Vindobonense *Phil. gr.* 161 di Konstantinos Ketzas e i suoi scolii all'*Electra*', in *Griechisch-byzantinische Handschriftenforschung: Traditionen, Entwicklungen, neue Wege*, ed. C. Brockmann, D. Deckers, D Harlfinger, and S. Valente, vol. 1, 397–419 (with 14 plates in vol. 2). Berlin–Boston.
Cuomo A. M. and E. Trapp (eds.) (2017) *Toward a Historical Sociolinguistic Poetics of Medieval Greek*. Βυζάντιος: Studies in Byzantine History and Civilization 12. Turnhout.
  (eds.) (forthcoming) *Medieval Textbooks: Their Editing and Their Understanding*. Byzantinisches Archiv. Boston–Berlin.
Dawe, R. D. (1973) *Studies on the Text of Sophocles*, vol. 2: *The Collations*. Leiden.
Di Benedetto, V. (1988) *Sofocle*. Florence.
Dickey, E. (2007) *Ancient Greek Scholarship: A Guide to Finding, Reading, and Understanding Scholia, Commentaries, Lexica, and Grammatical Treatises, from Their Beginnings to the Byzantine Period*. Oxford–New York.
Donnet, D. (1967) 'La place de la syntaxe dans les traités de grammaire Grecque, des origines au XIIe siècle', *AC* 36: 22–48.
  (1979) 'La tradition imprimée du traité de grammaire de Michael le Syncelle de Jérusalem', *Byzantion* 49: 441–508.
  (1981) 'Jean Glykys, *De la correction syntactique*: inventaire préalable à l'histoire du texte', *RHT* 11: 81–97.
  (1982) *Le traité de la construction de la phrase de Michel le Syncelle de Jérusalem*. Brussels–Rome.
Dugdale, E. (2008) *Sophocles, Electra: A New Translation and Commentary by Eric Dugdale. Introduction to the Greek Theatre by P. E. Easterling*. Cambridge.
Dyck, A. R. (1993) 'Aelius Herodian: Recent Studies and Prospects for Future Research', in *Aufstieg und Niedergang der römischen Welt: Geschichte und Kultur Roms im Spiegel der neueren Forschung* 33.6, ed. W. Haase and H. Temporini, 772–94. Berlin.
Finglass, P. (2007) *Sophocles, Electra*. Cambridge.
Förstel, C. (1992) *Les grammaires grecques du XVe siècle: étude sur les ouvrages de Manuel Chrysoloras, Théodore Gaza et Constantin Lascaris*. Paris.
Fryde, E. (2000) *The Early Palaeologan Renaissance (1261–c.1360)*. Leiden–Boston.
Fuchs, C. (1997) 'Apollonius Dyscole, *De la construction (syntaxe)*', *Lingvisticæ Investigationes* 21: 422–6.
Gaul, N. (2007) 'The Twitching Shroud: Collective Construction of *Paideia* in the Circle of Thomas Magistros', *Segno e Testo* 5: 263–340.

(2008) 'Moschopulos, Lopadiotes, Phrankopulos (?), Magistros, Staphidakes: Prosopographisches und Methodologisches zur Lexikographie des frühen 14. Jahrhunderts' in *Lexicologica byzantina: Beiträge zum Kolloquium zur byzantinischen Lexikographie (Bonn, 13.–15. Juli 2007)*, ed. E. Trapp and S. Schönauer, 163–96. Göttingen.

(2011) *Thomas Magistros und die spätbyzantinische Sophistik: Studien zum Humanismus urbaner Eliten in der frühen Palaiologenzeit*. Wiesbaden.

Grammatici Graeci recogniti et apparatu critico instructi. Leipzig 1867–1910.

Grandolini, S. (1980–1) 'La parafrasi al secondo libro dell'*Iliade* di Manuel Moschopulos', *AFLPer* 18: 5–22.

(1982) 'La parafrasi al primo libro dell'*Iliade* di Manuel Moschopulos', in *Studi in onore di Aristide Colonna*, 131–49. Perugia.

Guida, A. (1999) 'Sui lessici sintattici di Planude e Armenopulo, con edizione della lettera A di Armenopulo', *Prometheus* 25: 1–34.

(2018) *Lexicon Vindobonense*. Biblioteca dell'*Archivum Romanicum*, Series 11: Linguistica, v. 63. Florence.

Günther, H.-C. (1995) *The Manuscripts and the Transmission of the Paleologan Scholia on the Euripidean Triad*. Stuttgart.

Hermann, G. (1801) *De emendanda ratione Graecae grammaticae, pars prima*. Berlin.

Hilgard, A. (1889/1904) *Theodosii Canones et Choerobosci Scholia in canones nominales*, vols. 1 and 2. Leipzig. = *Grammatici Graeci*, vol. 4.1–2.

Holton, D., G. Horrocks, M. Janssen, T. Lendari, I. Manolessou and N. Toufexis (2019) *The Cambridge Grammar of Medieval and Early Modern Greek*, 4 vols. Cambridge–New York.

Horrocks, G. (2007) 'Syntax: From Classical Greek to the Koine', in *A History of Ancient Greek*, ed. A. F. Christidis, 618–31. Cambridge.

(2014) 'High-register Medieval Greek', in *Storia e storie della lingua greca*, ed. C. Carpinato and O. Tribulato, 49–72. Venice.

(2017a) 'High and Low in Medieval Greek', in *Variation in Ancient Greek Tense, Aspect and Modality*, ed. K. Bentein, M. Janse and J. Soltic, 219–41. Leiden–Boston.

(2017b) 'Georgios Akropolitis: Theory and Practice in the Language of Later Byzantine Historiography', in Cuomo and Trapp (eds.) (2017), 109–18.

Householder, F. W. (1981) *The Syntax of Apollonius Dyscolus*. Amsterdam.

Jahn, A. (1839) *Joannis Glycae Patriarchae Constantinopolitani, Opus de vera syntaxeos ratione*. Bern.

Jebb, R. (1894) *The Electra of Sophocles*. Cambridge.

Lallot, J. (1985) 'La description des temps du verbe chez trois grammairiens grecs (Apollonius, Stephanos, Planude)', *Histoire, Épistémologie, Langage* 7: 47–81.

(1994) 'Les fonctions syntaxiques chez Apollonius Dyscole', in *Florilegium Historiographiae Linguisticae*, ed. J. De Clerq and P. Desmet, 131–41. Louvain-la-Neuve.

(1997) *Apollonius Dyscole, De la construction (syntaxe)*. Paris.

(1998) *La grammaire de Denys le Thrace*, second revised edition. Paris.

(2012) *Études sur la grammaire alexandrine*. Paris.

(2015) 'Syntax', in *Brill's Companion to Ancient Greek Scholarship*, vol. 2: *Between Theory and Practice*, ed. F. Montanari, S. Matthaios and A. Rengakos, 850–95. Leiden–Boston.

Matthaios, S. (2015) 'Greek Scholarship in the Imperial Era and Late Antiquity', in *Brill's companion to Ancient Greek Scholarship*, vol. 1: *History; Disciplinary Profiles*, ed. F. Montanari, S. Matthaios and A. Rengakos, 184–296. Leiden–Boston.

Maisano, R. and A. Rollo (eds.) (2002) *Manuele Crisolora e il ritorno del greco in Occidente. Atti del convegno internazionale, Napoli, 26–29 giugno 1997*. Naples.

Maltese, E. V. (2001) 'Atene e Bisanzio: appunti su scuola e cultura letteraria nel Medioevo greco', in *La civiltà dei greci: forme, luoghi e contesti*, ed. M. Vetta, 357–87. Rome.

Markopoulos, A. (2006) 'De la structure de l'école byzantine: le maître, les livres et le processus éducatif', in *Lire et écrire à Byzance*, ed. B. Mondrain, 85–96. Centre de recherche d'Histoire et Civilisation de Byzance: Monographies 19. Paris.

(2008) 'Education', in *The Oxford Handbook of Byzantine Studies*, ed. E. M. Jeffreys, 785–95. Oxford.

(2015) 'Teachers and Textbooks in Byzantium, Ninth to Eleventh Centuries', in *Networks of Learning: Perspectives on Scholars in Byzantine East and Latin West, c. 1000–1200*, ed. S. Steckel, N. Gaul and M. Grünbart, 3–16. Zurich–Berlin.

(2017) 'L'éducation à Byzance aux IXe–Xe siècles', in *Mélanges Jean-Claude Cheynet*, ed. B. Caseau, V. Prigent and A. Sopracasa, 53–73. Paris.

Mavroudi, M. (2012) '*Learned Women of Byzantium and the Surviving Record*', in *Byzantine Religious Culture: Studies in Honor of Alice-Mary Talbot*, ed. D. Sullivan, E. A. Fisher, S. Papaioannou, 53–84. Leiden–Boston.

Mazzon, O. (forthcoming) 'The Use of Anthologies of Excerpts as Textbooks in the Early Palaeologan Period: Two Case Studies from the School of Planudes', in Cuomo and Trapp (eds.) (forthcoming).

Mioni, E. (1982) 'Il codice di Sofocle Marc. gr. 617', in *Studi in onore di Aristide Colonna, 209–16*. Perugia.

Murru, F. (1978) 'A proposito della teoria localistica: un excursus storico', *Vichiana* 7: 366–83.

(1979) 'Alla riscoperta dei grammatici dimenticati: Massimo Planude', *Rivista di studi classici* 27: 217–24.

Nousia, F. (2016) *Byzantine Textbooks of the Palaeologan Period*. Studi e Testi 505. Vatican City.

(2019a) 'Manuel Calecas' Grammar: Its Use and Contribution to the Learning of Greek in Western Europe', in *Making and Rethinking the Renaissance between Greek and Latin in 15th–16th Century Europe*, ed. G. Abbamonte and S. Harrison, 51–66. Trends in Classics Supplementary Volumes 77. Berlin–Boston.

(2019b) 'A Byzantine Comprehensive Textbook: Moschopoulos' Περὶ σχεδῶν', *AION(filol)* 41: 253–66.

(forthcoming) 'Teaching Ancient Greek in Late Byzantium: Manuel Moschopoulos' *Schedography* and His Scholia to Homer's *Iliad* and Hesiod's *Works and Days*', in Cuomo and Trapp (eds.) (forthcoming).

Nuti, E. (2014) *Longa est via: forme e contenuti dello studio grammaticale dalla Bisanzio paleologa al tardo Rinascimento veneziano*. Alessandria.

O'Sullivan, N. (2011) '"It would be the time to discuss the optatives": Understanding the Syntax of the Optative from Protagoras to Planudes', *Antichthon* 45: 77–112.

(2013) 'The Future Optative in Greek Documentary and Grammatical Papyri', *JHS* 133: 93–111.

Pérez Martín, I. (1997) 'La "escuela de Planudes": notas paleográficas a una publicación reciente sobre los escolios euripideos', in *ByzZ* 90: 73–96.

Pertusi, A. (1962) 'Ἐρωτήματα: per la storia e le fonti delle prime grammatiche greche a stampa', *IMU* 5: 321–51.

Picciarelli, M. (2003) 'Les réflexions sur le cas chez les grammairiens byzantins', in *Syntax in Antiquity*, ed. P. Swiggers and A. Wouters, 255–82. Leuven–Paris–Dudley, MA.

Pontani, F. (2015) 'Scholarship in the Byzantine Empire (529–1453)', in *Brill's Companion to Ancient Greek Scholarship*, vol. 1: *History; Disciplinary Profiles*, ed. F. Montanari, S. Matthaios and A. Rengakos, 297–455. Leiden–Boston.

Ritschl, F. (1832) *Thomae Magistri sive Theoduli Monachi Ecloga Vocum Atticarum* Leipzig. (repr. Hildesheim 1970)

Robins, R. H. (1993) *The Byzantine Grammarians: Their Place in History*. Berlin–New York.

(2000) 'Greek Linguistics in the Byzantine Period', in *History of the Language Sciences / Geschichte der Sprachwissenschaften / Histoire des sciences du langage: An International Handbook on the Evolution of the Study of Language from the Beginnings to the Present / Ein internationales Handbuch zur Entwicklung der Sprachforschung von den Anfängen bis zur Gegenwart / Manuel international sur l'évolution de l'étude du langage des origines à nos jours*, 3 vols., ed. S. Auroux et al., 1: 417–23. Berlin–New York.

Rollo A. (2019) 'Gli Erotemata di Manuele Moscopulo e i suoi precedenti', *AION(filol)* 41: 235–52.

Ronconi, F. (2012) 'Quelle grammaire à Byzance? La circulation des textes grammaticaux et son reflet dans les manuscrits', in *La produzione scritta tecnica e scientifica nel medioevo: libro e documento tra scuole e professioni*, ed. G. De Gregorio and M. Galante, 63–118. Spoleto.

Roussou, S. (2018) *Pseudo-Arcadius' Epitome of Herodian's De Prosodia Catholica*. Oxford.

Sandri, M. G. (2020) *Trattati greci su barbarismo e solecismo: introduzione, edizione critica*. Untersuchungen zur antiken Literatur und Geschichte 135. Berlin–New York.

Schenkeveld, D. M. (2000) 'Why No Part on Syntax in the Greek School Grammar? Solecisms and Education', *Histoire, Épistémologie, Langage* 22: 11–22.

Schneider, J. (1999) *Les traités orthographiques grecs antiques et byzantins*. Corpus Christianorum, Lingua Patrum 3. Turnhout.

(2000) 'Une collection grammaticale de la haute époque byzantine', in *Manuscripts and Tradition of Grammatical Texts from Antiquity to the Renaissance. Proceedings of a Conference Held at Erice, 16–23 October 1997*, 2 vols., ed. M. De Nonno, P. De Paolis and L. Holtz, 1: 89-131. Cassino.

Seaford, R. (1985) 'The Destruction of Limits in Sophocles' *Electra*', *CQ* 35: 315-23.

Silvano, L. (2014) 'Schedografia bizantina in Terra d'Otranto: appunti su testi e contesti didattici', in *Circolazione di testi e scambi culturali in Terra d'Otranto tra tardoantico e Medioevo*, ed. A. Capone, with F. Giannachi and S. J. Voicu, 212-67. Vatican City.

(2017) 'Perché leggere Omero: il prologo dell'Odissea di Manuele Gabala nelle due redazioni autografe', in *JÖByz* 67: 217-37.

Sluiter, I. (1997) 'The Greek Tradition', in *The Emergence of Semantics in Four Linguistic Traditions: Hebrew, Sanskrit, Greek Arabic*, ed. W. van Bekkum, J. Houben, I. Sluiter and K. Versteegh, 147-224. Amsterdam Studies in the Theory and History of Linguistic Science. Series 3: Studies in the History of the Language Sciences 82. Amsterdam–Philadelphia.

Swiggers, P. and A. Wouters (2003) 'Réflexions à propos de (l'absence de?) la syntaxe dans la grammaire gréco-latine', in *Syntax in Antiquity*, ed. P. Swiggers and A. Wouters, 25-41. Leuven–Paris–Dudley, MA.

Tessier, A. (2015 [2005]) *Demetrii Triclinii scholia metrica in Sophoclis tetradem*, second edition. Alessandria.

Tribulato, O. (2019) 'Making the Case for a Linguistic Investigation of Greek Lexicography: Some Examples from the Byzantine Reception of Atticist Lemmas', in *The Paths of Greek: Literature, Linguistics and Epigraphy. Studies in Honour of Albio Cesare Cassio*, ed. E. Passa and O. Tribulato, 241-70. Berlin–Boston.

Turyn, A. (1949) 'The Sophocles Recension of Manuel Moschopulus', *TAPhA* 80: 94-173.

Ucciardello, G. (2018) 'Insegnamento della sintassi e strumenti lessicografici in epoca paleologa: alcuni esempi', in ΛΕΞΙΚΟΝ ΓΡΑΜΜΑΤΙΚΗΣ: *Studi di lessicografia e grammatica greca*, ed. F. Conti Bizzarro, 97-124. Naples.

(2019) '"Atticismo", excerpta lessicografici e prassi didattiche in età paleologa', *AION(filol)* 41: 208-34.

Valente, S. (2017) 'Old and New Lexica in Palaeologan Byzantium', in Cuomo and Trapp (eds.) (2017), 45-55.

Villani, E. (2012) 'Le sezioni 'lambda' e 'rho' dell'*Ecloga vocum atticarum aucta* di Tommaso Magistro nel codice Ambrosiano M 51 sup.', *Aevum* 86: 713-58.

Xenis, G. (2010) *Scholia vetera in Sophoclis Electram*. Sammlung griechischer und lateinischer Grammatiker 12. Berlin–New York.

(2015) *Iohannes Alexandrinus, Praecepta Tonica*. Berlin–Munich–Boston.

CHAPTER 12

Theodora Raoulaina's Autograph Codex Vat. gr. 1899 and Aelius Aristides

Fevronia Nousia

This chapter explores Theodora Raoulaina's contribution to the reception and preservation of Aelius Aristides in the early Palaiologan period through her famous autograph volume Vatican City, Biblioteca Apostolica Vaticana, gr. 1899.[1] The codex has been extensively used as a key manuscript in palaeography courses for teaching the minuscule scripts known as *Fettaugen-mode* and *Beta-Gamma*.[2] Its philological value, however, has not attracted the attention it deserves. The main reason is the fact that Vat. gr. 1899 has long been considered an apograph of A, i.e. Paris, Bibliothèque nationale de France, gr. 2951 and Florence, Biblioteca Medicea Laurenziana, Plut. 60.3, owned and annotated by Arethas.[3] In 1976, Charles Behr refuted this view and asserted that 'it is clear from the addition of the Prolegomena at the beginning and *Oration* XVI in the middle that this manuscript is not a copy of A, but either has borrowed the new material from another source or was copied from an exemplar which did so'.[4] My intention is to test his view by examining the scholia to the two Platonic discourses, Ὑπὲρ Ῥητορικῆς Λόγος Α' & Β', which in Behr's edition constitute *Oration* 2.[5]

---

* I would like to thank Przemysław Marciniak, Divna Manolova and Baukje van den Berg for their kind invitation to contribute to the present volume. I would also like to thank Costas N. Constantinides, Charalambos Dendrinos and Inmaculada Pérez Martín for their advice on various aspects of this chapter.
[1] For Aelius Aristides' reception in Byzantium, see Quattrocelli (2008: 432–55), Jouanno (2009: 113–44), Raïos (2009: 237–51), Pérez Martín (2012: 213–38), Quattrocelli (2012: 239–61), Fontanella (2013: 1–37), Pérez Martín (2017: 85–107).
[2] For the scripts, see Hunger (1961: I, 101–2, fig. 22) and (1972: 105–13), Wilson (1977: 263–7), De Gregorio and Prato (2003: 59–101), Zorzi (2019: 262, 276–7).
[3] Quattrocelli (2008: 206–26).
[4] Behr (1976: XXXVIII–XXXIX). For a description of the manuscript tradition of the Aristidean manuscripts, see Behr (1976: IX–LXVI), and Pernot (1981: 437–40) for a comprehensive and supplementary list.
[5] *Platonic Oration* II has been edited by Dindorf (1829, vol. 2: 1–155) and by Behr (1978: 145–289). For an English translation of the work, see Behr (1986); the work has recently been edited and translated by Trapp (2017: 336–659).

339

Theodora Palaiologina Kantakouzene Raoulaina

The available information about Theodora amounts to very little.[6] Some biographical information about her can be retrieved from the histories of George Akropolites, George Pachymeres and Nikephoros Gregoras as well as the correspondence from the scholars with whom she was associated.[7] Theodora was born during the exile of Nicaea around 1240 as the daughter of John Kantakouzenos Komnenos Angelos and Irene-Eulogia Palaiologina, a sister of the later emperor Michael VIII Palaiologos. We have no knowledge of her education or her teachers.[8] Most probably, as a young member of the aristocracy, she would have been instructed at home with private teachers to the level of the *enkyklios paideia*. In 1256, she married the *protovestiarios* George Mouzalon (ca. 1220–25 August 1258), on the order of the Emperor Theodore II Laskaris (1222–18 August 1258), even though Mouzalon was not of noble origin. After Mouzalon's murder in 1258 and in the wake of the reconquest of Constantinople, this time following the demand of her uncle Michael VIII, in 1261 Theodora married the aristocrat and *protovestiarios* John Raoul Komnenos Doukas Angelos Petraliphas.[9] Once again, she became a widow in 1274.

Theodora was on good terms with her uncle the emperor until 1273, when, along with her mother, Manuel Holobolos and others, she vigorously objected to Michael VIII's efforts and plans for the Union of the Churches. As a result, she was punished and finally exiled with her mother and sister Anna to the fortress of St. Gregory in Nicomedia.[10] Theodora returned to Constantinople sometime after Michael VIII's death in December 1282, associating herself with the salient scholars of her time, George of Cyprus, Manuel Holobolos, Constantine Akropolites, Nikephoros Choumnos and

---

[6] On Theodora, see Lambros (1913: 347–8), Talbot (1983: 605–7, 611–12, 615, repr. 2001, art. XVIII), Hoffmann (1985: 279–81), Nicol (1994: 33–47), Agati (2001: 390–4), Kotzabassi (2011: 115–70), Riehle (2014: 299–315), Quattrocelli (2019: 113–52), Zorzi (2019: 259–82).

[7] Only the letters by Constantine Akropolites, George of Cyprus, Nikephoros Choumnos and Maximos Planoudes addressed to Raoulaina have survived. So far, her own letters to them seem to be lost.

[8] Cf. Nicol (1994: 41).

[9] This is the reason Theodora introduces herself as the niece of the Roman Emperor, the descendant of the Kantakouzenoi, the imperial dynasties of Angeloi, Doukai and Palaiologoi, as well as the wife of John Raoul Doukas Komnenos, the *protovestiarios*. See also below, p. 342 with n. 25.

[10] Pachymeres, VII, 2 ed. Failler (vol. 3: 23.23–5). Cf. George of Cyprus' comments on Theodora's sufferings as a result of her anti-unionist stance, *Ep.* 6.7 ed. Kotzabassi: ταῖς ἡμέραις τῶν ὀδυνῶν σου; and Planoudes, *Epigram* 1.15 ed. Lambros (1916: 415–16): δόγματος ὀρθοτόμοιο χάριν πάθεν ἄλγεα πολλά.

Maximos Planoudes, who praised her for her literary ability and education, which she further cultivated, most probably in Constantinople under the guidance of her spiritual father George of Cyprus.[11] We know that Theodora authored the *Life of Saints Theophanes and Theodoros the Graptoi* (*BHG* 1793), the two iconophile brothers and saints of the ninth century.[12] Having restored the monastery of St Andrew in Κρίσει[13] in Constantinople, she retired there until her death on 6 December 1300. Theodora was a true bibliophile and assembled a rich collection of books.[14] She copied manuscripts and seems to have been connected with a *scriptorium* and a group of some twenty-five deluxe manuscripts containing biblical and liturgical texts, which in all probability she commissioned.[15] Apart from those manuscripts, which bear common features in script and decoration, eight further manuscripts are mentioned in the epistles sent to Theodora by famous scholars, which are connected with her and formed part of her collection, including codices containing Demosthenes and other orators,[16] harmonics,[17] a mathematical treatise,[18] Basil of Caesarea's *Ethics*,[19] Thucydides (Munich, Bayerische Staatsbibliothek, gr. 430),[20] Theophylact of Ohrid's *Commentary to the Four Gospels* (Paris, Bibliothèque nationale de France, Coisl. 128)[21] and, more importantly, her two autograph manuscripts, Moscow, Gosudarstvennyj Istoričeskij

---

[11] See George of Cyprus, *Ep.* 7 ed. Kotzabassi: μὴ μόνον τῶν πάλαι γυναικῶν ὑπεράνω φαίνῃ τῶν ἐπὶ λογικῇ παιδεύσει γνωριζομένων, ἀλλὰ καὶ τοὺς πλείους τῶν ἄλλων ὅσοι ἐπὶ μέγα σοφίας ἀρθέντες εἰσίν, and 27 (ed. Kotzabassi): ἐν λόγοις εὐδοκιμοῦσα; Constantine Akropolites, *Ep.* 60 ed. Romano: εὐγενεστάτη καὶ σοφωτάτη κυρία μου; Nikephoros Choumnos, *Ep.* 76 ed. Boissonade (1844, repr. 1962: 91–2): πρὸς σὲ τὴν σοφωτάτην καὶ διακριτικωτάτην ἅμα ψυχήν; Maximos Planoudes, *Epigram* 1.5 ed. Lambros (1916: 416): ἡ πάσαις ἐνὶ θηλυτέρῃσι σοφὴ Θεοδώρα; and Nikephoros Gregoras, *History of the Romans* 1.178.22–3 ed. Schopen (= vi, 4): φιλολόγος γὰρ ἦν ἡ γυνὴ καὶ τὰ πολλὰ τῆς γλώττης τοῦ πατριάρχου ἐξεχομένη.
[12] For the edition of Theodora's hagiographical work, see Papadopoulos-Kerameus (1897: 185–223) and (1898: 397–9). See also Talbot (1983: 611 and 615), Rizzo-Nervo (1991: 147–61, esp. 152–61), Nicol (1994: 44–5).
[13] See Janin (1964: 348).
[14] See George of Cyprus, *Ep.* 17 ed. Kotzabassi; 227 ed. Lameere; Talbot (1983: 611).
[15] Apart from the seminal work of Buchthal and Belting (1978), see also Fonkich (1980: 113–16), Maxwell (1983: 47–58), Nelson (1986: 79–134), Nelson and Lowden (1991: 59–68), Prato (1991: 138–9), Nicol (1994: 45–6) and Gaul (2015), who mentions Theodora and her 'atelier' in passing (see pp. 4–5, 258, 262).
[16] See George of Cyprus, *Ep.* 18 ed. Kotzabassi; 228 ed. Lameere.
[17] See George of Cyprus, *Ep.* 68 ed. Kotzabassi; Nicol (1994: 41).
[18] See Constantinides (1982: 109, 140), Nicol (1994: 42).
[19] See Planoudes, *Ep.* 68; cf. Constantinides (1982: 140).
[20] See Kougeas (1907: 588–609), Nicol (1994: 47).
[21] See Nicol (1994: 46), Zorzi (2019: 281–2).

Musej, Mus. sobr. 3649 containing Simplicius' *Commentary to Aristotle's Physics*,[22] and Vat. gr. 1899 containing the works of Aelius Aristides, on which I shall concentrate.

Vat. gr. 1899 (= G in Pernot, A in Keil and Behr)

The codex measures 243 × 175 mm, was copied in two columns on oriental paper and contains II 423 (+213a) folios, presently split into two parts (I = 1–192, II = 193–423).[23] It was produced in the intellectual context of the early Palaiologan period, meeting the needs of the scholarly circle to which Theodora belonged, attesting to a special interest in rhetoric, in particular in Aelius Aristides. This reveals her personal study of and effort for the preservation of Aristides' work along with the *scholia vetera* of the text, as well as her ownership of this manuscript as part of her personal book collection. Regrettably, virtually nothing is known about the history of the codex through the centuries, its former and later possessors and how and when it found its way to the Vatican Library, where it is housed at present.[24]

Another intriguing question concerns the timeframe of the copying of the codex. Theodora's eight-line autograph inscription in dodecasyllabic verse on fol. 9r is helpful in this respect. Addressing the future reader of the codex she underscores (ἴσθι) that this Aristidean manuscript, too, was copied by her with the utmost diligence. She also introduces herself as the child of the sister of the Emperor of New Rome, the descendant of the Kantakouzenoi, of the imperial dynasties of Angeloi, Doukai and Palaiologoi and the wife of the illustrious *protovestiarios* Raoul Doukas Komnenos.[25] The fact that she refers to her husband but also designates herself as wife (δάμαρ) rather than widow of John Raoul led Nicol to date

---

[22] See Fonkich (1974: 134 with Pl. I), Harlfinger (1987: 267–86), Nicol (1994: 45), Zorzi (2019: 265, 270–3, 277–80, with fig. I–IV).

[23] For the description of the codex, see Turyn (1964: 63–5 with pl. 36), Follieri (1969: 60–2 with pl. 40), Canart (1970: 578–81) and Pernot (1981: 198–200, 248, 474). Digital images of the codex are accessible at: https://digi.vatlib.it/view/MSS_Vat.gr.1899.pt.1 and https://digi.vatlib.it/view/MSS_Vat.gr.1899.pt.2.

[24] Lilla (2004: 61–3, at 63): Theodora's codex belongs to a group of forty-two codices of uncertain direct provenance.

[25] Vat. gr. 1899, fol. 9r: καὶ τὴν Ἀριστείδου (δὲ) τήνδε τὴν βίβλον / γραφεῖσαν **ἴσθι** (my emphasis) παρὰ τῆς Θεοδώρας / καλῶς εἰς ἄκρον γνησίως ἐσκεμμένην / Ῥώμης νέας ἄνακτ(ος) ἀδερφῆς τέκους / Καντακουζην(ῆς) ἐξ ἀνάκτων Ἀγγέλω(ν) / Δουκῶν φυείσης Παλαιολόγ(ων) φύτλης / Ῥαοὺλ δάμαρτος Δούκα χαριτωνύμου / Κομνηνοφυοῦς πρωτοβεστιαρίου. See also Lambros (1913: 348), Turyn (1964: 64 with Pl. 168c), Follieri (1969: 60), Canart (1970: 580), Fonkich (1974: 134 with Pl. I), Talbot (1983: 606) and Nicol (1994: 45), Zorzi (2019: 265–70).

the copying of the manuscript to the untroubled times before her husband's death in 1274. If we also take into consideration that she prides herself on being the niece of the Emperor Michael VIII Palaiologos, we could conceivably predate the copying of the manuscript further, to a period sometime before 6 October 1273, when Holobolos and Theodora along with eight other anti-unionists were publicly humiliated and punished by the emperor.[26] If this hypothesis is correct, the copying of Theodora's Aristides should be placed before George of Cyprus copied his own Aristides codex for his teaching activities, sometime between March 1274 and 1283, when he ascended the Patriarchal throne,[27] and clearly before Planoudes' Aristides.[28]

Exemplar

A question is therefore raised concerning the exemplar Theodora used for copying her manuscript. Undoubtedly, Theodora's Aristides is not an *apographon* of Arethas' codex, as not only does the latter not contain the *Prolegomena*,[29] but, more importantly, Arethas' codex also includes *Orations* missing in Theodora's Aristides, i.e. *Orations* 26, 35, 36, 42, 43. Furthermore, the arrangement is quite different: the order of *Orations* 1–11 is the same as in Par. gr. 2951. Then follows *Oration* 16, and after that Theodora follows the order of the first part of Arethas' codex, Laur. Plut. 60.3: *Orations* 12–15, 47–52, 34, 18, 22, 19, 20, 24, 23, 33, 28. Theodora's codex continues with *Orations* 21 and 17, reversing the order found in Laur. Plut. 60.3, before finally reverting to Arethas' order for *Orations* 36, 29, 27, 30, 37, 38, 41, 40, 39 and 53.[30]

The scholia copied in both manuscripts constitute another important factor which differentiates the two codices. These differences between them demonstrate that a direct relationship cannot be ascertained. However, there is a clear connection between Vat. gr. 1899 and Vatican

---

[26] Pachymeres, v, 20 (ed. Failler and Laurent, II, 503.20–505.7).
[27] For George of Cyprus' Aristidean manuscripts, among which Paris, Bibliothèque nationale de France, gr. 2953 and 2998, see Pérez Martín (1992: 73–84), (1996: 32–50).
[28] For Maximos Planoudes' Aristides (Florence, Biblioteca Medicea Laurenziana, Plut. 60.8 [= T]), see Quattrocelli (2006: 206–26) and (2009: 145–62), Wilson (2009: 253–61).
[29] See Lenz (1959).
[30] For the *Orations* preserved in Vat. gr. 1899, Par. gr. 2951, Par. gr. 2953, Laur. Plut. 60.3 and Laur. Plut. 60.8, see Appendix 1. In Vat. gr. 1899 Theodora started copying *Or.* 12 twice on fol. 419r, but she quickly noticed the duplication and copied only the first ten lines of the *Oration*. *Or.* 16 is copied in a different place than in Arethas' codex. In Vat. gr. 1899 on fols. 420v–423v, a later hand copied *Or.* 44 and part of *Or.* 25.

City, Biblioteca Apostolica Vaticana, gr. 1298 (**R**). The latter is a parchment volume from the end of the tenth to the beginning of the eleventh century. This relationship is testified by the scholia to the two *Platonic Orations*. **R** was revised and completed by a later hand in the first decades of the fifteenth century, which replaced folios missing in the original codex.[31] An important characteristic of this codex is that it is linked with the intellectual milieu of Emperor Manuel II Palaiologos (1390–1425), as evidenced by its binding,[32] meaning that the codex was considered very important and was still in Constantinople before 1421. This date appears on fol. 1r in an Italian note by a later possessor.[33] Even though there are few variations between the two Vatican codices and the selection of the orations in Theodora's codex is far more extensive, the existence of an intermediary copy in the transmission is quite clear.

For the copying of the scholia, then, Theodora had at her disposal a rare codex of the same family to which Vat. gr. 1298 belongs. Another feature that points towards this exemplar is the fact that Theodora follows a practice common in the Komnenian codices: the title of each work is copied twice, first to open the text and then to denote its end. Sometimes the end of a work is also indicated by a decorative band or by τέλος τοῦ...[34] Another distinctive feature of Vat. gr. 1899 is its *mise-en-page*: it has been copied in two columns. None of the other known Aristidean manuscripts share this characteristic, which makes Vat. gr. 1899 unique.

It is important to turn briefly to the place of Theodora's work in the transmission history of Aristides. According to Laurent Pernot, Vat. gr. 1899 belongs to the ε family of Aristidean manuscripts.[35] However, for her exemplar, which remains a *desideratum*, no definite conclusions can be reached so far.[36] Hopefully, the new catalogue of Aristidean manuscripts, currently being prepared by Pernot and his research team at the University of Strasbourg, will shed further light on this question.

Theodora at Work

Reading through the massive Vat. gr. 1899, we have the opportunity to see Theodora at work, determined to copy a handsome volume which

---

[31] For the description of the codex, see Pernot (1981: 197–8).
[32] Grosdidier de Matons and Förstel (2008: 375–86).
[33] Cf. Grosdidier de Matons and Förstel (2008: 380).
[34] For this practice, see Pérez Martín (2017: 87).   [35] Pernot (1981: 231–8).
[36] Undoubtedly, the evidence presented here confirms Behr's view that Theodora's codex was not an *apographon* of Arethas'.

included most of Aelius Aristides' works, an indispensable author for the Byzantine student's classical training in the Palaiologan period and before, as the vast manuscript tradition corroborates. Theodora handled the copying of the Aristidean corpus, occupying no fewer than 419 folios, with great aplomb.

Among the Aristidean works, she copied the two *Platonic Orations*[37] (fols. 184r–234r) along with their scholia.[38] Theodora was not a trained philologist, an active teacher with students, and thus she could not compose the scholia.[39] She faithfully drew them from an earlier codex to which she had access. The scholia in Theodora's codex are linked to the text either through Greek numbers or graphic signs marked with red ink in the interlinear space of the main text. In most cases, the passage of the text to which the scholion refers is also copied in the upper or lower margin at the beginning of the scholion itself. In this way, the user of the codex could be autonomous, indulging himself in the reading of Aristides without any further help.

Theodora was not only the copyist of the codex, but also the editor, who, collating her manuscript from her exemplar, carefully went through the codex and traced errors, omissions of the main text, or misplacements of the scholia on wrong folios: e.g. on fol. 234r she wrote in red ink above the line γρ(άφεται) (καὶ) θοἰμάτιον (with reference τὸ ἱμάτιον in the text); on fol. 209v on the lower margin, she wrote ζή<τει> ἔμπροσθεν σχόλιον ἕν, drawing attention to the fact that the scholion was erroneously copied on the following folio (fol. 210r); on fol. 222r, she wrote ζή<τει> τὸ κεί<μενον> ἔμπροσθεν, indicating that she copied on fol. 222r scholia which refer to a passage that is preserved on the following folio (fol. 222v); on fol. 219r, she added into the margin ὥσπερ ὧν σὺ μέμνησαι τῶν κιθαρῳδῶν, ἀλλ' ἐπεγείροντες, a sentence that she had inadvertently omitted when copying the text.

---

[37] In the *Orations*, Aristides defends rhetoric against philosophy. For the difference between rhetoric and philosophy and their contribution to learning according to Psellos, see his *Chronographia* 6.41. On rhetoric and philosophy in the self-representation of eleventh- and twelfth-century commentators on Aristotle, see Trizio in this volume.

[38] The scholia to these two *Platonic Orations* correspond to Dindorf's edition, vol. 3 (1829; repr. 1964: 356–432).

[39] Theodora Raoulaina could be compared with Anna Komnene as far as her secular education is concerned. They were both trained at home and they distinguished themselves in secular learning. Other learned imperial or aristocratic women in the Late Byzantine period include Irene-Eulogia Choumaina Palaiologina, although she became more known for her involvement in religious matters. Furthermore, Theodora acquired a rich collection of manuscript books with important secular texts, which famous scholars of her time could borrow and use. See also Mavroudi (2012).

However, Theodora also introduced a number of errors (which she failed to correct): errors due to **iotacism**, e.g. fol. 187v at sch. να: ἠδηκημένων (instead of ἠδικημένων); fol. 189v at sch. οζ: ἀδιαλήπτως (instead of ἀδιαλείπτως); errors in **accentuation**, e.g. fol. 188v at sch. ξε: ἴαται (instead of ἰᾶται); fol. 185v at sch. κη: εἴπεν (instead of εἶπεν); **spelling**, e.g. fol. 188r at sch. νγ: μένεσθαι (instead of μαίνεσθαι); fol. 194v at sch. μζ: φιλανθροπία (instead of φιλανθρωπία), **misinterpretation of letters**, e.g. fol. 192v at sch. κστ: ψιγουμένου (instead of ἡγουμένου); fol. 230v, at the third scholion εἴδη λόγων ἀρκοῦντες (instead of ἀσκοῦντες). She also corrected an omission (here underlined) in the text due to **homoioteleuton**, e.g. fol. 233r: ... ὅτι εἰ μὲν θεῶν παῖδες, <u>οὐ φιλοχρήματοι· εἰ δὲ φιλοχρήματοι, οὐ θεῶν παῖδες</u> ... which she completed in the lower margin.

Apart from Theodora's interventions, other hands, hitherto unidentified, likewise made corrections.[40] One of them belongs to George of Cyprus, as already identified by Inmaculada Pérez Martín in the oration of *Panathenaikos*.[41] We can similarly trace corrections by George of Cyprus' hand in the *Orations* studied here, e.g. on fol. 191v. col. a (left column of the main text), seven lines from the bottom of the column, the interlinear (καὶ) φροντίζει and elsewhere on other folios.[42] If this manuscript is indeed the one referred to in George of Cyprus' *Epistle* 17, it was in his possession; he clearly stated that he wanted to revise it and correct its errors (φαύλως ἔχουσαν τῆς γραφῆς) wherever he could.[43] In this case, Theodora's copy led George of Cyprus to prepare his own copy of Aristides for his teaching. In fact, a comparison between Theodora's and George of Cyprus' copies of Aristides shows that the former is a reference book while the latter is a teacher's personal textbook.[44]

Considering the difficulties presumably involved in copying manuscripts of this size, we must appreciate Theodora's conscientious work on Vat. gr. 1899. Although it is, for the moment, hard to gauge precisely both Theodora's role and the value and position of her codex in the branches of

---

[40] Canart (1970: 580). [41] Pérez Martín (1996: 36 with n. 78).
[42] I would like to thank Inmaculada Pérez Martín for confirming the identification of George of Cyprus' hand.
[43] George of Cyprus, *Ep.* 17 ed. Kotzabassi.
[44] Theodora's deluxe paper volume was prepared as part of a wider collection of reference books intended to be consulted as a precious exemplar by those who, for various reasons, had an interest in Aelius Aristides. George of Cyprus' paper codex, rather humble and modest, without decorative features or different colours for the titles of the works etc., is a textbook; after being copied, it was subsequently used and consulted primarily by George himself, who kept notes, wrote scholia in the margins and used the codex in order to prepare his classes.

the Aristidean tradition, she nevertheless contributed to the preservation, dissemination and propagation of Aelius Aristides and the *scholia vetera* to his works which were re-introduced in the curriculum, most probably by George Akropolites in the early Palaiologan period, after the reconquest of Constantinople and the re-establishment of advanced learning in Late Byzantium. It was George of Cyprus' editions of Aelius Aristides that kindled the Palaiologan scholars' interest in and attention to the ancient orator, who was highly regarded as a model for students to imitate.[45] Theodora was not strictly a scholar or, indeed, a teacher, but rather a wealthy, educated patron who fostered scholars in her circle, while also copying texts and gathering manuscripts which she managed to trace, collect and re-edit. It seems, therefore, that her manuscript was prepared as a model edition for future generations. This is substantiated not only by her determination to name herself as the copyist in her inscription on fol. 9r, but also by the guidance she provides through her manuscript in phrases such as ζήτει ἔμπροσθεν σχόλιον ἕν or ζήτει τὸ κείμενον ἔμπροσθεν, clearly addressing the future reader of the manuscript and using the imperative ἴσθι. In this sense, Theodora and her codex Vat. gr. 1899 represent an important link in the transmission history of Aelius Aristides, reflecting the place of ancient texts and traditions in the 'Palaiologan Revival'.[46]

Edition of the Unedited Scholia to Ὑπὲρ Ῥητορικῆς Λόγος Aʹ & Bʹ (Vat. gr. 1899, fols. 184r–234r)

Of the marginal scholia to the *Platonic Orations* Ὑπὲρ Ῥητορικῆς Λόγος Aʹ & Bʹ, copied by Theodora Raoulaina in Vat. gr. 1899 (**G**), I edit in this chapter only those which were previously unedited or which are entirely different from the scholia published by Dindorf,[47] e.g. 1. **Dindorf:** ἀντὶ τῆς ἀρετῆς] **Theodora:** ἀντὶ τοῦ τῆς ἀρετῆς. 2. **Dindorf:** τῶν σεμνοτέρων· τουτέστι τῶν πολιτικωτέρων] **Theodora:** τῶν σεμνοτέρων λέγει τουτέστι τῶν πολιτικῶν. 3. **Dindorf:** λέγειν αὐτὸν ... Ἀργείαν εὐπρεπεστάτην] **Theodora:** αὐτὸν λέγειν... Ἀργείαν ἱέρειαν εὐπρεπεστάτην: simple variants or simple completions from Theodora's codex to Dindorf's edition are not recorded.

G follows the same tradition of the scholia as **R** (Vat. gr. 1298), sharing, however, a small number of variants and different forms of the same word.

---

[45] See Constantinides (1982: 153).
[46] On the 'Palaiologan Revival', see Runciman (1970). Constantinides (1982).
[47] Dindorf (1829, vol. 3: 356–432).

In such cases I have adopted the readings in **G** in the text, indicating the correct readings in **R**. Words completed or omitted by Theodora in **R** appear in *italicized* characters.

The following symbols are used in the edition:

⌜αβγ⌝ additions of words and phrases in **R** completing Dindorf's edition (only in cases where a lacuna is marked by an asterisk [*] in Dindorf's edition have I included the scholion below. Otherwise, only the previously unedited scholia or those entirely different from Dindorf's edition are given in my edition)

[*leg.* αβγ] correct readings in **R**

Spelling or accentuation errors have been tacitly corrected. Mute iota has also been tacitly supplied.

fol. 184r:
ζ· καὶ κιθαριστάς] κιθαρῳδὸς κιθαριστοῦ διαφέρει· ὁ μὲν κιθαρῳδός, τῇ φωνῇ μετὰ τῆς κιθάρας κέχρηται, ὁ δὲ κιθαριστής, κρούει [*leg. κρούειν*] μόνον ἐπίσταται.

fol. 185v:
κδ· εἰ γὰρ ἐκεῖνος Ὁμήρῳ] ...⌜πολλὰ φιλονεικεῖ αὐτὸς δὲ⌝ ...⌜ἔστιν αὐθαδέστερον⌝...

fol. 186r:
λη· εἰσὶ δὲ οἱ καὶ τῶν ἐκείνους] τὸ νόημα τοῦτο εἰσί τινες φιλόσοφοι, οἱ τὰ Πλάτωνος θαυμάζουσι, καὶ οὐ μόνον πάντα αὐτοῦ, ἀλλὰ πλείω πάντων τὰ γνωρικότατα [*leg.* γνωριμώτατα], ἀλλ᾽ ὅμως καὶ τῶν γνωρίμων προτιμῶσι Γοργίαν τὸν διάλογον· τοῦτο δὲ εἶπεν, ἵνα δείξῃ τὸν ἀγῶνα μέγαν.

λθ· θείας δεῖν τῆς βοηθείας] πάλιν αὔξησίς ἐστι τῶν ἰδίων λόγων· ἐξάρας γὰρ τὴν κατηγορίαν, ἀκολούθως τὴν ἀπολογίαν θείαν καλεῖ.

fol. 186v:
μ· τὰς τῶν παρανόμων γραφάς] οἱ γὰρ τῶν ψηφισμάτων καλῶς περιλαμβανόμενοι, οὕτως ποιοῦνται τὴν κατηγορίαν· πρῶτον ἀναγινώσκουσι τὰ ψηφίσματα· καὶ μετὰ ταῦτα τοὺς νόμους, καὶ οὕτως δεικνύουσι τὸ διάφορον· τοῦτο δὲ ποιοῦσι θαρροῦντες τῇ ἀληθείᾳ. ἐνταῦθα οὖν ὁ Ἀριστείδης δεῖξαι βουλόμενος ὅτι καὶ αὐτὸς θαρρεῖ τῇ ἀποδείξει ἑαυτὸν μὲν τῷ τοιούτῳ κατηγόρῳ περιβάλλει, ἵνα δείξῃ ὅτι κηδόμενος τῶν ὅλων πραγμάτων, ὥσπερ ἐκεῖνοι τῶν νόμων, ποιεῖται τοὺς λόγους· λεληθότως δὲ τοὺς μὲν ἑαυτοῦ λόγους νόμοις εἰκάζει· τοὺς δὲ Πλάτωνος ψηφίσμασι.

μα· ἀπ᾽ αὐτῶν ὧν εἴρηκε] ἀντὶ τοῦ ἀπὸ τοῦ ἀγῶνος αὐτοῦ.

μγ· ψυχῆς στοχαστικῆς] στοχαστικῆς τῆς τὰ ἡδέα μᾶλλον αἰσθανομένης· τὸ δὲ ἀνδρείας ἐνταῦθα πρὸς ψόγον. εἴρηται δὲ καί τινων ἰσχυόντων πρὸς κακίαν· τὰ τέσσαρα δὲ μόρια τῆς κολακείας ἐνταῦθα δηλοῖ. ἐκ μὲν τοῦ εἰπεῖν τεχνησομένου τὴν μεγαρικήν [*leg.* μαγειρικήν]. ἐκ δὲ τοῦ στοχαστικοῦ τὴν ῥητορικήν. ἐκ δὲ τοῦ ἀνδρείου τὴν σοφιστικήν· ἐκ δὲ τοῦ φύσει δεινῆς τὴν κομμωτικήν.

μδ· ἐν δὲ καὶ ὀψοποιητική [*leg.* ὀψοποιική] ἵνα καὶ τὰ ἄλλα τρία δηλώσῃ.

με· ἐπὶ τέτταρσι πράγμασιν] πάλιν ἀντὶ τοῦ εἰπεῖν τέχναις.

μϛ· ἔστι γὰρ ῥητορική] τοῦ [*leg.* οὕτως] ὁ ὅρος ἑρμηνεύεται. πολιτικῆς μόρια [om. G] δύο νομοθετική καὶ δικαστική· εἴδωλον δὲ τῆς μὲν νομοθετικῆς, ἡ σοφιστική· τῆς δὲ δικαστικῆς, ἡ ῥητορική· τοῦ οὖν μορίου τῆς πολιτικῆς εἴδωλον γίνεται ἡ ῥητορική.

fol. 187r:
ὀψοποιόν τε καὶ ἰατρόν] ἐνταῦθα δεικνύει ὁ Πλάτων, τὴν κολακείαν· περὶ μὲν τοῖς εὐήθεσιν εὐδοκιμοῦσαν· παρὰ δὲ τοῖς φρονίμοις ἐκβαλλομένην.

καὶ πονηρῶν] ὡς ἐπὶ τὸ πλεῖστον οἱ ἰατροὶ ἀσιτεῖν προστάττουσιν.

ἐμπειρίαν] ὁ μὲν Πλάτων τὴν κοινωνίαν ἐν τῷ τὴν ἀναλογίαν κατὰ τὴν ἰσότητα [*leg.* κατὰ τὴν ἀναλογίαν καὶ ἰσότητα] λέγει εἶναι· ὁ δὲ μεταφέρει τὸν νοῦν αὐτοῦ· ὡς κατὰ τὴν φύσιν λέγοντος κοινωνεῖν.

fol. 187v:
μζ· ἐνταῦθα ἀπόδειξις μὲν] καὶ τί διαφέρει ἔλεγχος ἀποδείξεως· λέγομεν δὲ ὅτι ἀπόδειξιν ... πράξεις ⌜καὶ ἀπὸ τῶν μερικῶν τούτων⌝ πράξεων ... ἀντιλέγοντας· ⌜ἐπίτηδες δὲ οὐ προσέθηκε τὰ λοιπὰ τῆς χρήσεως ἐπειδὴ καὶ ἀπόδειξιν ἔχουσιν⌝.

μη· καὶ μηδεὶς μήτ' ἀγροικίαν] ... ἀπαιδευσίαν, ⌜ἀπὸ μεταφορᾶς τῶν ἐν ἀγροῖς διαμενόντων καὶ ὅλως μὴ παιδευθέντων τὰ τοιαῦτα· ψυχρότητα δὲ τὴν ἀτελῆ ἀπαιδευσίαν⌝ ἀπὸ μεταφορᾶς ...

μθ· δυοῖν ἐπιστήμαιν] ... λέγεται· ἐπίτηδες δὲ κοινὰ δέδωκεν ἀμφοτέραις τὰ ὀνόματα, ἵνα τὴν κοινωνίαν αὐτῶν δείξῃ· ἢ γὰρ καὶ ἡ φιλοσοφία δύναμίς ἐστι καὶ ἡ ῥητορικὴ ἐπιστήμη.

ν· τοῖς μὲν τὴν ἑτέραν] νῦν πειρᾶται καὶ μείζονα δεῖξαι [*leg.* δεικνύναι] τὴν ῥητορικήν· βλασφημεῖ γάρ τις διαβάλλων τοὺς κρείττους. ὅθεν ἐπὶ θεῶν ἡ λέξις ἀεὶ τάττεται, τῶν ὁμολογουμένων μειζόνων, ἢ καθ' ἡμᾶς.

να· οὐδὲ τοῖς αὐτοῖς] οἷς διεβλήθησαν καλῶς δὲ τὸ ἀμύνεσθαι ὡς ἐπὶ ἠδικημένων ὑπὲρ τὸ δίκαιον ἔχουσι.

νβ· οὐ τοῦ φορτικοῦ] ἀντὶ τοῦ οὐχ ἕνεκα τοῦ κατὰ ἀλήθειαν διαβάλλει φιλοσοφίαν· ὅρα δὲ πῶς φορτικὸν καλεῖ τὴν διαβολήν· δεικνὺς ὅτι καὶ Πλάτων φορτικῶς διέβαλε τὴν ῥητορικήν.

fol. 188r:

νγ· ἀλλ' οὔτε τοῦτο ὑγιαίνοντος οἶμαι] δοκεῖ μὲν τὸ πλεῖον παρέχει [leg. παρέχειν] τῇ φιλοσοφίᾳ διὰ τὸ τὴν μανίαν τάξαι ἐπὶ τῶν τολμώντων διαβάλλειν αὐτήν. τὸ γὰρ μὴ δύνασθαι ἀποδεῖξαι· τοῦ μὴ ὑγιαίνειν ἔλαττον· λεληθότως δὲ ἀμφότερα αὐτῷ περιάπτει καὶ τὸ μένεσθαι [leg. μαίνεσθαι] καὶ τὸ ἀπόδεικτον [leg. ἀναπόδεικτον]· εἰ γὰρ μόνης τῆς ἐπωνυμίας τῆς ῥητορικῆς μεταβεβλημένης εἰς τὴν φιλοσοφίαν· χώραν ἔχουσιν οἱ κατὰ τῆς φιλοσοφίας λόγοι· μαινομένων δὲ ἀνθρώπων ἐστί, τὸ τὰ οὕτως ἄτοπα τολμᾶν λέγει [leg. λέγειν] τοὺς ῥήτορας κατὰ τῶν φιλοσόφων, οὐκ οὖν ἄρα μαινομένων ἀνθρώπων ἐστί· τὸ ἄτοπα οὕτως λέγει [leg. λέγειν] τοὺς φιλοσόφους κατὰ τῆς ῥητορικῆς.

νε· ὡς οὐχ ὑβρίζοντός ἐστιν] τὸ ὑβρίζειν μὲν ὀψοποιΐαν ἀπεικάζειν δὲ αὐτὴν ῥητορικῇ· ἀποδείξεως ἐκτός· οὐδὲν ἄλλό ἐστιν, ἢ ἀναγκάζεσθαι ἡμᾶς τῶν ὁμολογουμένων ἀποδείξεις φέρειν, ὅσον κεχώρισται ῥητορικῆς [leg. ῥητορικὴ] ὀψοποιΐας· οὐδεὶς γὰρ ἑκὼν τὰ λίαν ὁμολογούμενα κατασκευάζει.

νϛ· ὑποστήσομαι τοῦτο] τὸ ἀπαιτῆσαι ἡμᾶς δεῖξαι τὰς διαφορὰς ὀψοποιητικῆς καὶ ῥητορικῆς.

fol. 188v:

ξβ· ἐπειδὰν ἐκστῶσιν] ... μάντεις ⌜δὲ οἱ ἀπὸ γνώμης⌝ οἷος ...

ξγ· λόγους ἀνθρωπίνους] ἢ τοὺς παρὰ τοῦ [om. G] σώματος λέγει· ἢ πρὸς ἀντιδιαστολὴν τῶν θείων εἶπεν ἀνθρωπίνους.

ξδ· κρείττων ὀψοποιικῆς] εὐκαίρως ἐνταῦθα ταύτης ὁ ῥήτωρ ἐμνήσθη, ἐπειδή γε Πλάτων ἐζήτησε δεῖξαι τὴν μὲν ἰατρικὴν καλὴν τὴν δὲ ὀψοποιητικὴν φαύλην· ῥητορικὴν δὲ ταύτῃ ὁμοίαν. Ἀριστείδης ὁ ῥήτωρ δείκνυσιν· ὡς εἰ καὶ ἡ ῥητορικὴ μὴ τέχνη, ἀλλ' ἐκ θεῶν· μικρὸν ἰατρικὴ πρὸς ῥητορικὴν καταφαίνεται· ἡ τῆς ὀψοποιητικῆς ἀμείνων ὑπάρχουσα· κἂν γὰρ μὴ τὸ τῆς ῥητορικῆς ἐνταῦθα τίθησιν ὄνομα, ἀλλ' οὖν ἃ περὶ μαντικῆς λέγει τῆς ἔξω τέχνης τυγχανούσης· ταῦτα καὶ περὶ ῥητορικῆς λεκτέον, ὅτι δὲ τοῦτό ἐστιν. ὅρα πῶς πάντα ὅσα ὁ Πλάτων ἐπιτηδεύματα τέθεικεν, ὡς ἄριστα ταῦτα δεικνύειν ἀπολυπόμενα [leg. ἀπολειπόμενα] τῶν ἔξω τέχνης πραγμάτων.

ξε· ἡ κατ' αὐτὴν ἑστηκυῖα] ἡ ἐξ ἐναντίας αὐτῆς τῆς ἰατρικῆς οὖσα. ὃ γὰρ ἐν σώματι ἰατρική· τοῦτο ἐν ψυχῇ δικαιοσύνη, ὥσπερ γὰρ ἰατρικὴ ἴαται [leg. ἰᾶται] τὰ συμβαίνοντα πάθη, οὕτω δικαστικὴ ἰᾶται τὰ τῆς ψυχῆς ἁμαρτήματα.

fol. 189r:

ξη· ὁ δὲ τῷ παρὰ τὴν Πυθίαν] ...τοῦ θεοῦ ⌜ἔδο⌝ξαν...τέχνης ⌜μεγάλην⌝...

fol. 189v:

οϛ· πλέον ἐλείπομεν τοῦ σωφρονεῖν] οὐ μόνον φησὶ τὸ διάφορον ἐκ τοῦ γένους συμβῆναι [leg. συμβαίνει], ἀλλὰ καὶ ἐκ τοῦ πλήθους.

οζ· ὅσον δ' αὖ καὶ καθάπερ] ... εἶπεν περὶ ⌜τῶν Πυθίων⌝ ... λέγει περὶ τῶν ἀδια⌜λείπτως⌝ μαινομένων ...

οθ· εἰ δὲ μὴ πολλοί] ⌜ἐπειδὴ οὐκ εἶχεν⌝ ἄλλον εἰπεῖν ...

πδ· εἰ ὁ μὲν ποιητής] ἀποδείξας ὅτι ἡ ποιητικὴ ὁμοία ἐστὶ τῇ μαντικῇ· θεῖαι γὰρ ἀμφότεραι καὶ ἄνευ τέχνης· εἶτα ἀποδείξας ὅτι ἡ μαντικὴ τῶν τεσσάρων ἀρετῶν περιγίνεται νομοθετικῆς δικαστικῆς γυμναστικῆς ἰατρικῆς· νῦν ἀποδείκνυσιν ὅτι ἡ πολιτικὴ [leg. ποιητικὴ] μιμεῖται τὴν ῥητορικὴν κατὰ τὸν αὐτοῦ Πλάτωνος λόγον· ἵνα μὴ μόνον μέρος οὖσαν τῶν ἀρετῶν ῥητορικὴν ἀποδείξῃ, ἀλλὰ καὶ κρεῖττον ἢ κατ' ἐκείνας, καὶ αὐτὸς δὲ Πλάτων ὁμολογεῖ τὴν ποιητικὴν δύνασθαι εἶναι ῥητορικήν, εἴ τις αὐτῆς περιέλοι τὸ μέτρον.

fol. 190r:
πε· φιλόδωρον τὸν Ἑρμῆν] διὰ τὸ ἐριούνιος· ὁ γὰρ δωρούμενός τι, καὶ ὠφελεῖ.

πη· καταφεύγοντα] εἰ γάρ τις μὴ σὺν τέχνῃ κακίζει ἄνευ δὲ τέχνης αὗται λέγουσι· καταφεύγει δὲ πολλαχοῦ τῶν νόμων ἐπ' αὐτὰς τρόπον τινὰ ὑπὸ τῶν οἰκείων λόγων ἐξελεγχόμενος.

fol. 191r:
δ· καὶ μὴν εἰ μαντικὴν μέν] ... ἐπειδὴ τὰ ⌜ἡγούμενα τῶν ἑπομένων, ἐπεκράτει⌝ τοῦ οὖν Ἀπόλλωνος ...

ε· καὶ οὐδὲ περὶ ἓν γράμμα] ἐπειδήπερ ἐν τῇ μανίᾳ ὄντες οἱ νέοι προσθέντες μαντικὴν ἐκάλεσαν· ἐν δὲ τῷ καλεῖν αὐτοὺς λογίους οὐδὲν προστίθησιν.

fol. 191v:
η· εἰ δ' οὐδὲν τοῦτό τις συγχωρεῖ] τὸ εἶναι Πλάτωνα ἀξιόπιστον· καλῶς δὲ τοῦτο, ἵνα μὴ αὐτὸς δόξῃ ὑβρίζειν.

ι· ἐκ τοῦ αὐτοῦ γυμνασίου] ... Σωκρατικὸν ⌜ὥσπερ ἦν ὁ Πλάτων⌝ διὰ τοῦτο λέγει ...

fol. 192v:
ιθ· καὶ ὅσοι τῶν κατ' Αἴγυπτον] τινὲς λέγουσιν αὐτὸν λέγει [leg. λέγειν] πάλιν τὸν Ἀσκληπιόν, τὸν εἰς Μέμφιν τιμώμενον· κακῶς δὲ λέγουσιν· εἰ γὰρ ἤμελλε τὸν αὐτὸν ἐπάγειν ἀνάγκη ἄνω διέστελλε καὶ ἔλεγε τὸν [leg. αὐτὸν] ἐν Περγάμῳ. ἔστι δὲ αὕτη πόλις τῆς Ἀσίας ἀλλ' ἴσως ἄλλον θεόν τινα λέγει ἐν Αἰγύπτῳ τιμώμενον.

κ· ἐπὶ τοὺς θεοὺς σχεδόν] ... ἀλλὰ ⌜ὡς καὶ ὡς ἄξια⌝ [leg. καὶ ὡς ἄξιοι].

κε· οὐδὲν κωλύει φρίττειν] διὰ τὸ παράδοξόν τι προστάττειν τὸν θεόν· οἷον τὸν ἀλγοῦντα τοὺς ὀφθαλμοὺς γάρον ἀπονίπτεσθαι.

fol. 193r:
κζ· ὦ μεγίστη σὺ γλῶττα τῶν Ἑλληνίδων] τοῦτο Κρατῖνος περὶ τοῦ Περικλέους εἶπεν.

fol. 194r:
λθ· ἀλλὰ μὴν εἰ μηδετέρως] . . . αἰσχρὸν γὰρ τὸ ψεύδεσθαι. ⌜εἰ τοίνυν φησὶ κατὰ ἀμφότερα οὐ σοφός⌝, καὶ κατὰ ἀμφότερα σοφὸς . . .

fol. 194v:
μζ· τὸν δὲ τῶν Φαιάκων] πάλιν κατασκευάζει· ὅτι καὶ ἡ φιλανθρωπία καὶ ἡ εὐσέβεια τὰ μέγιστα τῶν ἀνθρώπων· οὐκ ἐκ τέχνης, ἀλλ' ἐκ τοῦ θεοῦ τυγχάνουσιν.

fol. 195r:
να· οὐδ' εἰκῇ προσθεὶς] . . . ἡ κατασκευὴ τῶν ⌜ἐπαίνων καὶ ἡ πίστις· ἐπειδὴ δὲ⌝ ἐφόλκιόν . . . ⌜τὴν πίστιν τῶν ἐπαίνων⌝· διὰ τοῦτο . . .

fol. 195v:
νδ· αὐτοδίδακτος δ' εἰμί] . . . πολλὰ τέθεικεν, ἀλλὰ ⌜ἐγγύς⌝, ὥστε εἶναι γνώριμον. . .

fol. 196r:
ξα· πρῶτος τότε ῥητορεύων] ἵνα δείξῃ ὅτι οὐ προέμαθεν.

fol. 197r:
οε· εὑρεῖν οὖν φησίν] . . . καλῶς ὡς παρὰ Ἡσιόδου τὸν λόγον ἐποίησεν· ⌜τὸ γὰρ φησὶ πρὸς τὸν Ἡσίοδον⌝.

fol. 198r:
ἄκραντα γαρύετον] ἀντὶ τοῦ φλυαροῦσιν, ἀπὸ τῆς γήρυος.

fol. 200r:
ἀρχῇ τοῦ προστάξαι] ἀντὶ τοῦ πρέποντος τῇ ἀρχῇ [*leg.* ἡ ἀρχὴ] τοῦ προστάξαι.

fol. 200v:
εἰ δέ τις μὴ] ἡ παρὰ ἀντὶ τῆς διά· καθὼς [*leg.* καλῶς] δὲ προσέθηκεν· εἰκὸς γὰρ ὡς εἰρήκαμεν ἄνω κατά τι ἄλλο διαφέρει [*leg.* διαφέρειν].

fol. 201v:
χειρὸς ἔχοντα] οὐκοῦν τὰ καθέκαστα.

δι' ὧν εἰσιν ἡ ναῦς] λιμένος ἐπιτηδείου.

βιβλίου] ἀντὶ τοῦ διὰ ῥημάτων καὶ παραινέσεων καὶ προσταγμάτων.

εἰ δὲ δὴ] μικρὸν ἀνωτέρω εἶπεν· διατί ποῦ θαλάττης εἰσὶ πυνθάνονται, ἵνα στοχάσωνται τοῦ σκοποῦ· εἶτα ὥσπερ ἐν ἀντιθέσει ἔλαβεν, ἀλλ' οὐχ' οἵ γε ἀκριβεῖς ἐρεῖς· καὶ λύσας τοῦτο καὶ διὰ μέσου ἄλλα τινὰ βραχέα εἰπών· ἀναλαμβάνει πάλιν καὶ λέγει, ὅτι εἰ δὲ δεῖ κἀκείνους τοὺς κυβερνήτας τοὺς παρ' ἄλλων πυνθανομένους ἀνθρώπων, καὶ οὐ παρὰ θεῶν εἰδότας οὐδὲν ὅμως τέχνην αὐτοὺς λέγειν [*leg.* λέγεις] ἔχειν· ἴσθι ὅτι, καὶ οὗτοι τεχνίται ὄντες, κατὰ δὲ [*leg.* σὲ] στοχάζονται.

fol. 202r:
φθήσονται πάντων] ἀντίστροφος ἰατρική σοι.

Πίνδαρον γίγνεται] ἐπειδὴ πρώτην εἶναι λέγει τὴν νομοθετικήν, ὡς καὶ ἐν τῇ κοινῇ ἀπολογίᾳ ἔγνωμεν.

fol. 203v:
κ· ἀλλὰ τὰς πίστεις τοῖς σημείοις] ὁ εἰδὼς πολλάκις καὶ ⌜ἀφ' ἑαυτοῦ λέγει· ὁ δὲ εἰκάζων, ἔκ τινων⌝ εἰκάζει ἑτέρων...

fol. 208v:
τῆς μαρτυρίας] καὶ αὐτό φησι τὸ γεγράφθαι μέρος ἐστὶ τῶν λογικῶν πρακτικόν.

fol. 209r:
λέγει δικαιῶν τὸ βιαιότατον] ... ὁ νόμος ⌜φησὶ⌝ τῶν θεῶν...

fol. 209v:
ζήτει ἔμπροσθεν σχόλιον ἕν.

fol. 210r:
γ· πρώτη καὶ μέση] ... ἐδεήθη καὶ ⌜αὐτὴ ῥητορικῆς· καὶ ὕστερον⌝ ... ἀμφοτέρας ἡ ῥητορική· ⌜καὶ οὕτως λοιπὸν ἡ ῥητορικὴ εὑρίσκεται συνεχομένη καὶ συνέχουσα⌝.

δ· ὁμοῦ μὲν γὰρ] ἀντὶ τοῦ ἑαυτήν· ἀπὸ κοινοῦ δὲ τὸ καθιστᾶσα.

fol. 211v:
νομισθεῖσαν] τὴν ῥητορικὴν λέγει.

fol. 213αr:
ζήτει ἔμπροσθεν σχόλιον ἕν.

fol. 215r:
εἰ δὲ τις μήδ' ὅσον] ἡ σύνταξις αὕτη· εἰ δέ τις δέον τινὰ σῶσαι τοὺς ἑαυτοῦ μηδαμοῦ αὐτὸν κινηθέντα τὴν ἐπὶ τούτῳ μεταχειρίζεται δύναμιν· οὐκ ἐπαινεῖς αὐτόν.

fol. 218r:
ζήτει ἔμπροσθεν σχόλιον ἕν.

fol. 222r:
ζήτει τὸ κείμενον ἔμπροσθεν.

fol. 230v:
οἱ δὲ πολλοὶ μορίοις] οἱ [om. G] τοιοῦτοί φησι Ὁμήρου δέονται, καλοῦντος αὐτοὺς οὕτως· ὥσπερ ἐκεῖνος καλεῖ τοὺς εὐτελεῖς καὶ λοιπὸν λέγει [ἔχει G] πῶς καλεῖ Ὅμηρος.

καὶ ὅσα τοίνυν εἴδη] δοκεῖ τὸ αὐτὸ περὶ τοῦ αὐτοῦ εἶναι· οὐκ ἔστι δὲ ἀλλὰ τὸ μὲν ἄνω περὶ τῶν προσώπων εἶπεν· τοῦτο δὲ περὶ τῶν αὐτῶν εἰδῶν· ἀμέλει καὶ τὸ ἐπιφερόμενον τοῦτο δηλοῖ· εἶπεν γὰρ ὅτι τὸν Ὅμηρον ἐπαινοῦμεν καθόλου ὡς ῥητορικῆς μετέχοντα· καὶ τῆς ποιήσεως δὲ ὁμοίως αὐτοῦ πάσης ἐκεῖνα τὰ χωρία θαυμάζομεν πλέον, ἔνθα ῥητορεύει· ὁμοίως καὶ ἐπὶ Σοφοκλέους.

οὗτοι μάλιστα εὐδοκιμοῦσιν] οὗτοι μάλιστα εὐδοκιμοῦσι τῶν ἀρχαίων, ὅσοι ἕτερα εἴδη λόγων ἀρκοῦντες [*leg.* ἀσκοῦντες] ῥητορικὴν ἐν αὑτοῖς πολλὴν εἰσήνεγκαν.

καὶ τοιοῦτος ἐγγένοιτο] περὶ ἑαυτοῦ λέγων· ὁ γὰρ Ἀριστείδης, οὐκ εὐχερῶς ἐδείκνυτο [*leg.*

ἐπεδείκνυτο] ἐν θεάτροις, ἀλλὰ ἐξεδίδου τοὺς λόγους.
ὁρῶν ἑτέρως ἔχοντα τὰ πράγματα] ἐπειδὴ Ῥωμαῖοι νῦν εἶχον τὴν ἀρχήν, τοῦτο δὲ λέγει, ἵνα μὴ νομισθῇ ὑπὸ ἀσθενείας φεύγειν τὸ συμβουλεύειν.

καὶ θεὸν ἡγεμόνα] τὸν Ἀσκληπιὸν λέγει· εἰρήκαμεν γὰρ ὅτι περὶ ἑαυτοῦ λέγει· καὶ πόθεν δῆλον; ἐπειδὴ εἶπεν ὅτι ἡγεμόνα θεὸν ἔχων τοῦ βίου καὶ τῶν λόγων· *τοῦ μὲν γὰρ τῶν λόγων* [om., homoioteleuton G] ἁρμόζει καὶ ἐπὶ τοῦ Σωκράτους τοῦ σοφιστοῦ· τὸ δὲ τοῦ βίου, ἐπὶ μόνου τοῦ Ἀριστείδου, οὐδὲν γὰρ ἔπραττεν ἐκτὸς τοῦ Ἀσκληπιοῦ.

fol. 231r:
λόγους καλοὺς ἐργάζομαι] λόγους λέγει καλοὺς τοὺς ῥητορικοὺς πρὸς ἀντιδιαστολὴν φιλοσοφίας· τουτέστιν τοὺς κακῶν αἰτίους γενομένους ταῖς πόλεσιν.

οὐδὲ γὰρ εἰ μὴ θαυμασθήσομαι] οἱ γὰρ δημοσίᾳ ἐπιδεικνύμενοι διὰ τοῦτο λέγουσιν, ἵνα παρὰ τῶν πολλῶν ἐπαινῶνται.

καὶ τούτοις ἀνθ' ἑτέρων] διὰ πραγμάτων· τινὰ δὲ τῶν ἀντιγράφων ἔχουσι διὰ τῆς διφθόγγου καὶ περισπωμένης, ἵν' εἴη *ἐπὶ* [om. G] γυναικῶν.

κἂν τὰ αὐτοῦ πράττων] τὸν καθ' ἑαυτὸν φησὶ τὴν τέχνην [*leg.* τῇ τέχνῃ] χρώμενον· σοὶ πλέον οὐ πρέπει [*leg.* πρέπει πλέον τοῦ] μὴ καλέσαι ῥήτορα, ἢ ἐμοί· τὸ δὲ διὰ ταῦτα, ἀντὶ τοῦ διὰ τὰ παρὰ σοῦ εἰρημένα περὶ ἰατρικῆς καὶ πολιτικῆς· ἐλέγχει γάρ σου τὴν κατηγορίαν τὴν περὶ τούτους τοὺς ῥήτορας, ἡ ἐκείνων διάνοια.

κολακείαν γε] ὅρα πῶς λεληθότως συλλογίζεται τὸν Πλάτωνα ἐκ τῆς αὐτοῦ φωνῆς· ὅτι μὲν γάρ φησι καθ' ἑαυτὸν τῇ τέχνῃ χρώμενος συμμαρτυρεῖς· ὅτι δὲ οὐ κόλαξ, δῆλον ἐκ τοῦ φεύγειν τὸν παρὰ τῶν πολλῶν ἔπαινον· ὅτι μὴ [*leg.* δὲ] καὶ τῶν αἰσχρῶν ἐκτός, δῆλον ἐκ τοῦ μὴ δύνασθαι αὐτὸν ἄλλως περιγενέσθαι τῆς τῶν λόγων δυνάμεως, εἰ μὴ τῷ πάντων ἀπέχεσθαι τῶν αἰσχρῶν.

fol. 232r:
ἀλλὰ δύο οὐσῶν] οὐ τὴν ὄντως ῥητορικὴν ἐλέγχει Πλάτων· πῶς γὰρ ἦν διὰ παντὸς αὐτὸς τῶν λόγων ἐξυμνεῖν [*leg.* ἐξυμνεῖ], ἀλλὰ τὴν δοκοῦσαν, ἥτις ἐν Γοργίᾳ καὶ Πώλῳ, περὶ παντὸς τοῦ προτεθέντος διατεινομένη τὸ ἱκανὸν εὑρεῖν, κἂν θεολογικόν, κἂν φυσικόν, κἂν γεωμετρίας ἐχόμενον, κἂν περὶ τοὺς φθόγγους καὶ τὰ τῆς μουσικῆς διαστήματα, ὁρῶ τοι ἐνευδοκιμοῦν [*leg.* τὸ ἐνευδοκιμεῖν].

fol. 233r:
μᾶλλον δὲ] ἐπειδὴ ἐν μέσῳ τῶν παραδειγμάτων, ἐμνήσθη ῥητορικῆς.

fol. 233v:
πανταχῇ] ἀντὶ τοῦ πάντες ψηφίζονται καλῶς ποιεῖν.

ἕλξειν] ἐπειδὴ φησὶ μαθὼν τὴν ῥητορικὴν καλλωπίζεται δι' αὐτῆς.

πρὸς δὲ Πλάτωνα] αὐτὸς γάρ φησι Πλάτων ἐστὶν ὁ συμβουλεύων τὸν ἀρξάμενον βάλλειν, ἀντιπάσχει [*leg.* ἀντιπάσχειν] κακῶς.

ἐξαιρεῖται] καὶ αὐτός φησι ὁ Ἀσκληπιὸς ψηφίζεται, ὅτι καλῶς ποιοῦμεν, ἀντιλέγοντες Πλάτωνι· εἰ γὰρ ἀπήρεσκεν αὐτῷ τὸ πρᾶγμα, πάντως δι' ὀνείρων ἐμήνυέ μοι, εἴ γε καὶ περὶ τῆς ὑγείας καὶ περὶ τῶν ἄλλων ἐμήνυσέ μοι δι' ὀνείρων.

Appendix 1

	Vat. gr. 1899	Par. gr. 2951	Laur. Plut. 60.3	Par. gr. 2953	Laur. Plut. 60.8
	Raoulaina	Arethas		George of Cyprus	Planoudes
		(B. Keil's Numbering)			
1	*Prolegomena*	–	–	*Prolegomena*	–
2	I	I	XII	I	I
3	III	III	XIII	III	II
4	II	II	XIV	II	III
5	IV	IV	XV	IV	IV
6	V	V	XLVII	XXI	V
7	VI	VI	XLVIII	V	VI
8	VII	VII	XLIX	VI	VII
9	VIII	VIII	L	VII	VIII
10	IX	IX	LI	VIII	IX
11	X	X	LII	IX	X
12	XI	XI	XXXIV	X	XI
13	XVI	XXVII	XVIII	XII	XII
14	**XII**	XII	XXII	XIII	XIII
15	XIII	XIII	XIX	XIV	XIV
16	XIV	XIV	XX	XV	XV
17	XV	XV	XXIV	XVIII	XVI
18	XLVII	XXVIII	XXIII	XXII	XVII
19	XLVIII	XXX	XXXIII	XIX	XVIII
20	XLIX	XXXIII	XXVIII	XX	XIX
21	L	XVIII	XVII	XXIV	XX
22	LI	XIX	XXI	XXVII	XXI
23	LII	XX	XXXVI	XXX	XXII
24	XXXIV	XXI	XXIX	XXXIX	XXIII

(*cont.*)

	Vat. gr. 1899	Par. gr. 2951	Laur. Plut. 60.3	Par. gr. 2953	Laur. Plut. 60.8
25	XVIII	XVII	XXVII	XXXIV	XXIV
26	XXII	XXII	XXX	XVI	XXV
27	XIX	XXXIV	XXXVII		XXVI
28	XX	XXIX	XXXVIII		XXVII
29	XXIV	XXXIX	XLI		XXVIII
30	XXIII	XXIII	XL		XXIX
31	XXXIII	XVI	XXXIX		XXX
32	XXVIII	XXXVII	LIII		XXXI
33	XXI	XXXVIII			XXXII
34	XVII	XL			XXXIII
35	XXXVI	XLI			XXXIV
36	XXIX	XXVI			XXXV
37	XXVII	XXXV			XXXVI
38	XXX	XLII			XXXVII
39	XXXVII	XLIII			XXXVIII
40	XXXVIII	XLVII			XXXIX
41	XLI	XLVIII			XI
42	XL	XLIX			XLI
43	XXXIX	L			XLII
44	LIII	LI			XLIII
45	XII [EXTRACT]				XLIV
46	XLIV				XLV
47	XXV				XLVI
48					XLVII
49					XLVIII
50					XLIX
51					L
52					LI

REFERENCES

Agati, M. L. (2001) 'Una Dotta Copista e Bibliofila: Teodora Raulena', in *La Civiltà Bizantina: donne, uomini, cultura e società*, ed. G. Passarelli, 390–4. Milan.

Behr, C. A. (ed.) (1976) *P. Aelii Aristidis opera quae exstant omnia*, vol. 1, fasc. 1. Leiden.

(ed.) (1978) *P. Aelii Aristidis opera quae exstant omnia*, vol. 1, fasc. 2. Leiden.

(ed.) (1986) *P. Aelius Aristides, The Complete Works*, vol. 1: *Orations I–XVI*. Leiden.

Boissonade, J. F. (ed.) (1844) *Anecdota Nova*. Paris. (repr. Hildesheim 1962)

Buchthal, H. and H. Belting (1978) *Patronage in Thirteenth-Century Constantinople: An Atelier of Late Byzantine Book Illumination and Calligraphy*. Washington, DC.

Canart, P. (1970) *Codices Vaticani Graeci: Codices 1745–1962*. Vatican City.
Constantinides, C. N. (1982) *Higher Education in Byzantium in the Thirteenth and Early Fourteenth Centuries (1204–ca. 1310)*. Nicosia.
De Gregorio, G. and G. Prato (2003) 'Scrittura arcaizzante in codici profane e sacri della prima età paleologa', *Römische Historische Mitteilungen* 45: 59–101.
Dindorf, W. (1829) *Aristides*, vol. 2. Leipzig. (repr. Hildesheim 1964)
   (1829) *Aristides*, vol. 3. Leipzig. (repr. Hildesheim 1964)
Failler, A. (ed.) (1999) *Georges Pachymérès Relations historiques*, vol. 3: Books VII–IX. Paris.
Failler, A. and V. Laurent (eds.) (1984) *Georges Pachymérès Relations historiques*, vol. 2: Books IV–VI. Paris.
Follieri, E. (1969) *Codices Graeci Bibliothecae Vaticanae Selecti . . . (= Exempla Scripturarum. . ., Fasciculus IV)*. Vatican City.
Fonkich, B. (1974) 'Заметки о греческих рукописях советских хранилищ. I Московский автограф Феодоры Раулены', *Visantisjkij Vremennik* 36: 134 with pl. 1.
   (1980) 'Scriptoria bizantini: risultati e prospettive della ricerca', *RSBN* 17–18: 73–119.
Fontanella, F. (2013) 'Aspetti di storia della fortuna di Elio Aristide nell'età moderna', in *Elio Aristide e la legittimazione greca dell'impero di Roma*, ed. P. Desideri and F. Fontanella, 1–37. Bologna.
Gaul, N. (2015) '"Writing with Joyful and Leaping Soul": Sacralization, Scribal Hands and Ceremonial in the Lincoln College Typikon', *DOP* 69: 243–71.
Grosdidier de Matons, D. and C. Förstel (2008) 'Quelques manuscrits grecs liés à Manuel II Paléologue', in *Actes du VIe Colloque International de Paléographie grecque (Drama, 21–27 septembre 2003)*, ed. B. Atsalos and N. Tsironi, 375–86. Athens.
Harlfinger, D. (1987) 'Einige Aspekte der handschriftlichen Überlieferung des Physikkommentars des Simplikios', in *Simplicius, sa vie, son oeuvre, sa survie. Actes du Colloque international de Paris (28 Sept.–1 Oct. 1985)*, ed. I. Hadot, 267–86. Berlin–New York.
Hoffmann, P. (1985) 'Une nouvelle reliure byzantine au monogramme des Paléologues (Ambrosianus M 46 SUP. = gr. 512)', *Scriptorium* 39: 274–81.
Hunger, H. (1961) 'Antikes und mittelalterliches Buch- und Schriftwesen', in *Geschichte der Textüberlieferung der antiken und mittelalterlichen Literatur*, vol. 1: 72–107. Zurich.
   (1972) 'Die sogenannte Fettaugen-Mode in griechischen Handschriften des 13. und 14. Jahrhunderts', *ByzF* 4: 105–13. (= H. Hunger (1973) *Byzantinische Grundlagenforschung*. London. Nr. 11.)
Janin, R. (1964) *Constantinople byzantine: development urbain et repertoire topographique*. Paris.
Jouanno, C. (2009) 'Les Byzantins et la seconde sophistique: étude sur Michel Psellos', *REG* 122: 113–44.
Kotzabassi, S. (2011) 'Scholarly Friendship in the Thirteenth Century: Patriarch Gregorios II Kyprios and Theodora Raoulaina', *Parekbolai* 1: 115–70.

Kougeas, S. (1907) 'Zur Geschichte der Münchener Thukydides-Hs. Augustanus F', *ByzZ* 16: 588–609.
Lameere, W. (1937) *La tradition manuscrite de la correspondance de Grégoire de Chypre patriarche de Constantinople (1283–1289)*. Brussels–Rome.
Lambros, S. (ed.) (1913) 'Δύο Ἑλληνίδες βιβλιογράφοι', *Νέος Ἑλληνομνήμων* 10: 346–9.
  (ed.) (1916) ''Ἐπιγράμματα Μαξίμου Πλανούδη', *Νέος Ἑλληνομνήμων* 13: 415–21.
Lenz, F. W. (1959) *The Aristeides Prolegomena*. Leiden.
Lilla, S. (2004) *I manoscritti vaticani greci: lineamenti di una storia del fondo*. Vatican City.
Mavroudi, M. (2012) 'Learned Women of Byzantium and the Surviving Record', in *Byzantine Religious Culture: Studies in Honor of Alice-Mary Talbot*, ed. D. Sullivan, E. Fisher and S. Papaioannou, 53–84. Leiden–Boston.
Maxwell, K. (1983) 'Another Lectionary of the "Atelier" of the Palaiologina, Vat. gr. 352', *DOP* 37: 47–58.
Nelson, R. (1986) 'Byzantine Miniatures at Oxford: CBM 1 and 2', *Byzantine Studies/Études byzantines* 13: 79–134.
Nelson R. and J. Lowden (1991) 'The Palaeologina Group: Additional Manuscripts and New Questions', *DOP* 45: 59–68.
Nicol, D. M. (1994) *The Byzantine Lady: Ten Portraits 1250–1500*. Cambridge.
Papadopoulos-Kerameus, A. (1897) and (1898) 'Βίος καὶ πολιτεία τοῦ ὁσίου πατρὸς ἡμῶν Θεοφάνους τοῦ Ὁμολογητοῦ καὶ τοῦ αὐταδέλφου αὐτοῦ Θεοδώρου συγγραφεὶς παρὰ Θεοδώρας Ῥαουλαίνης Κατακουζηνῆς τῆς Παλαιολογίνης (e cod. Metochii S. Sepulcri 244, f. 130–154)', *Ἀνάλεκτα Ἱεροσολυμιτικῆς Σταχυολογίας* 4: 185–223 and 5: 397–9.
Pérez Martín, I. (1992) 'À propos des manuscrits copies par Georges de Chypre (Grégoire II) Patriarche de Constantinople (1283–1289)', *Scriptorium* 46: 73–84 with pl. 9.
  (1996) *El Patriarca Gregorio de Chipre (ca. 1240–1290) y la transmisión de los textos clásicos en Bizancio*. Madrid.
  (2012) 'Elio Aristides en el Monasterio de Cora', in *La tradición y la transmisión de losoradores y rétores griegos = Tradition and Transmission of Greek Orators and Rhetors*, ed. F. Hernández Muñoz, 213–38. Berlin.
  (2017) 'Aristides' *Panathenaikos* as a Byzantine Schoolbook: Nikephoros Gregoras' Notes on Ms. Escorial Φ.Ι.18', in *Toward a Historical Sociolinguistic Poetics of Medieval Greek*, ed. A. Cuomo and E. Trapp, 85–107. Byzantios: Studies in Byzantine History and Civilization 12. Turnhout.
Pernot, L. (1981) *Les Discours Siciliens d'Aelius Aristide (Orr. 5–6): étude littéraire et paléographique, édition et traduction*. New York.
Prato, G. (1991) 'I manoscritti greci dei secoli XIII e XIV: note paleografiche', in *Paleografia e codicologia greca. Atti del II Convegno Internazionale*, vol. 1: 131–49. Alessandria.

Quattrocelli, L. (2006) 'Ricerche sulla tradizione manoscritta di Elio Aristide: per la nuova datazione del Laur. 60,8', *Scriptorium* 60: 206–26.
  (2008) 'Aelius Aristides' Reception at Byzantium: The Case of Arethas', in *Aelius Aristides between Greece, Rome and the Gods*, ed. W. H. Harris and B. Holmes, 432–55. Leiden–Boston.
  (2009) 'Maxime Planude éditeur d'Aelius Aristide', *REG* 122: 145–61.
  (2012) 'Le Vat. gr. 914: un autographe d'érudit dans la tradition manuscrite d'Ælius Aristide', in *Tradición y transmisión de losoradores y rétores griegos = Tradition and Transmission of Greek Orators and Rhetors*, ed. F. G. Hernández Muñoz, 239–61. Berlin.
  (2019) 'Théodora Rhaoulaine: une femme érudite et philologue entre Nicée et Byzance', in *Femmes de savoir et savoirs des femmes: littérature et musique religieuses entre l'Antiquité tardive et le Moyen Âge*, ed. G. Aragione and B. Föllmi, 113–52. Turnhout.
Raïos, C. (2009) 'Du nouveau sur les manuscrits athonites d'Aelius Aristide', *Scriptorium* 63: 237–51.
Renauld, É. (1926–8; repr. 1967) *Michel Psellos, Chronographie ou histoire d'un siècle de Byzance (976–1077)*, 2 vols. Paris.
Riehle, A. (2014) 'Καί σε προστάτιν ἐν αὐτοῖς τῆς αὐτῶν ἐπιγράψομεν σωτηρίας: Theodora Raulaina als Stifterin und Patronin', in *Female Founders in Byzantium and Beyond*, ed. L. Theis, M. Mullett and M. Grünbart, with G. Fingarova and M. Savage, 299–315. Wiener Jahrbuch für Kunstgeschichte 60/61. Vienna.
Rizzo-Nervo, F. (1991) 'Teodora Raulena: tra agiografia e politica', in Σύνδεσμος: *Studi in onore di Rosario Anastasi*, vol. 1, 147–61. Catania.
Romano, R. (ed.) (1991) *Costantino Acropolita, Epistole*. Naples.
Runciman, S. (1970) *The Last Byzantine Renaissance*. London.
Schopen, L. (ed.) (1829) *Nicephori Gregorae historia Byzantina*, vol. 1. Bonn.
Talbot, A.-M. (1983) 'Bluestocking Nuns: Intellectual Life in the Convents of Late Byzantium', *Harvard Ukrainian Studies 7. Okeanos: Essays Presented to Ihor Ševčenko on His Sixtieth Birthday by His Colleagues and Students*, 604–18. (repr. in A.-M. Talbot (2001) *Women and Religious Life of Byzantium*. Variorum Collected Studies Series 733. Aldershot)
Trapp, M. (ed. and trans.) (2017) *Aelius Aristides Orations 1–2*. Cambridge, MA.
Turyn, A. (1964) *Codices Graeci Vaticani saeculis XIII and XIV scripti annorumque notis instructi*. Vatican City.
Wilson, N. G. (1977) 'Nicaean and Palaeologan Hands: Introduction to a Discussion', in *La paléographie grecque et byzantine (Paris, 21–25 octobre 1974). Actes du Colloque international sur la paléographie grecque et byzantine*, 303–21. Paris.
  (2009) 'Maximus Planudes, the Codex Laurentianus 60.8, and Other Aristidean Manuscripts', *REG* 122: 253–61.
Zorzi, N. (2019) 'Una copista, due copisti, nessuna copista? Teodora Raulena e i due codici attribuiti alla sua mano', *MEG* 19: 259–82.

CHAPTER 13

The Reception of Eustathios of Thessalonike's Parekbolai *in Arsenios Apostolis' and Erasmus' Paroemiographic Collections*

Lorenzo M. Ciolfi

For Alessia
ἦλθες, † καὶ † ἐπόησας, ἔγω δέ σ' ἐμαιόμαν,
ὂν δ' ἔψυξας ἔμαν φρένα καιομέναν πόθωι.
(Sappho, fr. 48 Lobel-Page)

Homerus omnem poesin suam ita sententiis farsit ut singula eius ἀποφθέγματα vice proverbiorum in omnium ore fungantur ... et alia innumerabilia, quae sententialiter proferuntur.
(Macrobius, *Saturnalia* 5.16.6–7 ed. Kaster)

Homer crammed all of his poetry with *sententiae* to such an extent that every single one of his sayings functions like a proverb on everyone's lips . . . and there are countless other examples that are cited as proverbs.

As highlighted by this famous statement from Macrobius' *Saturnalia*, from Late Antiquity onward, many Homeric verses and formulas were given the status of proverbs worthy of being employed as independent witty sayings. This tendency, which is probably rooted in the practices of Hellenistic philology, seems to be confirmed by the common and widespread presence of the sign 'γν' (to be understood as γνώμη, 'proverb/maxim', or γνωμικόν, 'proverbial') in the margins of Homeric manuscript witnesses. From the point of view of the study of proverbs, and with the aim of better understanding these rich Homeric materials as well as their reception, it thus seems important to plumb the efforts of Eustathios of Thessalonike, who dedicated his energies to the composition of two extensive *Parekbolai* on the *Iliad* and the *Odyssey*.[1] This approach is even more valuable when we realize that such twelfth-century commentaries, whose contents were read and reused in the post-Byzantine era, offer us a glimpse of the future paroemiographic innovations of the Renaissance.

---

[1] For an overview on the author and these works, see Cullhed (2016: 1*–34*) and Kolovou (2018). On Eustathios, see also the chapters by Lovato, van den Berg and Pérez Martín in this volume.

At first glance, these works could appear as simple exegetical compilations, but behind their lines lay a veritable and practical *repertorium* for the erudite of the time:[2] in fact, in order to comment on the poems, Eustathios summarized and re-elaborated the best examples from his source(s), offering readers an easily accessible and handy inventory of rhetorical materials. According to the scholar's own words, 'the wish of our friends was to pass through the *Iliad* and provide useful tools to those who undertake this trip'.[3] With these volumes in their hands, authors preparing compositions would not have to browse for a long time in their personal books or, in the worst case, in scattered libraries and markets.[4] Moreover, these materials could help authors cope with the changes that had occurred in the new cultural era emerging between the eleventh and the twelfth centuries, an intense 'age of literacy', when political and social reforms had slowly caused – among other phenomena – an unexpected interruption in the copying of codices containing classics.[5]

When considering proverbs, we may note that, in the *Parekbolai*, Eustathios not only went through Homer's poems, listing possible maxims and lingering on their detailed exegesis; he also suggested how his audience

---

[2] According to his own testimony (*Proem on Pindar* 38.4 ed. Kambylis), Eustathios' work was conceived for τοῖς καὶ γράφειν καὶ ἄλλως δέ πως νοεῖν ἐθέλουσι, 'those who want to write and think in some other way'.

[3] In *in Il.* 2.21 = 1.3.5–6 ed. van der Valk: ἦν δὲ τὸ φιλικὸν θέλημα διὰ τῆς Ἰλιάδος ἐλθεῖν καὶ ἐκπορίσασθαι τὰ χρήσιμα τῷ διεξοδεύοντι. On the functionality of the *Parekbolai*, see Cullhed (2016: 2*–4*).

[4] See *in Od.* 1380.10–12 = 10.13–16 ed. Cullhed, where the following translation is found: ἔσται δὲ ἡμῖν κἀνταῦθα, ὡς καὶ ἐν τῇ Ἰλιάδι, τῆς μεταχειρίσεως ἡ ἐπιβολὴ οὐ κατὰ ἐξήγησιν, ἧς ἄλλοις ἐμέλησεν, ἀλλὰ κατ' ἐκλογὴν τῶν χρησίμων τοῖς ἐπιτρέχουσι καὶ μὴ <ἐν> εὐχερεῖ ἔχουσιν ἑαυτοὺς ἐπαφιέναι τῷ τῆς ποιήσεως πλάτει σχολαίτερον, 'here, just as in the *Iliad*, our method of handling the subject matter will not be through exegesis, which others have concerned themselves with, but through collecting useful passages for those who run through the work and cannot easily permit themselves to go leisurely into the breadth of the poem'. Similar ideas are also stated in Patriarch Photios' *Bibliotheca* (codex 167 ed. Henry) about Stobaios' *Anthology*, a model for following collections: κοινὸν δ' ἀμφοτέροις ἡ τῶν ζητουμένων, ὡς εἰκός, ἀταλαίπωρος καὶ σύντομος εὕρεσις, ἐπειδάν τις ἀπὸ τῶν κεφαλαίων εἰς αὐτὰ τὰ πλάτη ἀναδραμεῖν ἐθελήσειε, 'both categories [i.e. of readers] will be helped in locating with little effort and quickly what they are looking for, whenever they might wish to return from these chapters [i.e. of Stobaios' *Anthology*] to the full works themselves'. For a commentary on this passage, see Ciolfi (2018: 382–4).

[5] The quote is from Browning (1964: 13). An analysis of this particular phenomenon was carried out – but unfortunately has not yet been published – on the textual traditions of Herodotus, Thucydides, Xenophon, Apollonius of Rhodes and Lucian in G. Cavallo's Greek Palaeography seminar at Sapienza University of Rome (academic year 2008/9). When dealing with the script change of that period, Cavallo offered the following explanation: 'at the advent of the Komnenian dynasty, the liquidation of this scholarly class and the breakdown of the intense scholarly activity that was connected to it – during the twelfth century, as we know, education will pass under the control of the Patriarchal Academy – explains perhaps the subsequent contraction in book production' (2000: 237, n. 108).

could insert and reuse them in the composition of new literary pieces. After all, Homer was traditionally and unanimously renowned as ὁ τῶν ποιητῶν γονιμώτατος ('the most fecund of poets').[6] Moreover, the aforementioned scheme was put into practice by Eustathios, who tended, on the one hand, to use several proverbs to explain Homeric figures or passages and, on the other, to highlight the proverbial verses of the *Iliad* and the *Odyssey*.[7] In these two volumes, there are thousands of such references to proverbs, as other scholars have already highlighted, and this chapter takes their studies as its starting point.[8]

Exploring two of the greatest European Renaissance collections of proverbs, the work by Aristoboulos/Arsenios Apostolis (1465/69–1535) for Greek and that by Erasmus of Rotterdam (1466–1536) for Latin, this paper will firstly consider some 'new' Homeric findings in a codex of Arsenios' Ἰωνιά. On the basis of a selection of those entries, it will demonstrate how Eustathios was a source for *interpretamenta* and a forerunner in the development of sixteenth-century paroemiology. Secondly, through reading selected passages from Erasmus' *Adagia*, the chapter will discuss the appropriation of Eustathios' ideas in the Renaissance and their consequent adaptations to new needs and tastes.

New Homeric Marginalia in Arsenios and Erasmus

Arsenios Apostolis is responsible for codex Paris, Bibliothèque nationale de France, gr. 3058 (hereafter **P**), one of the three surviving autograph examples of the new Ἰωνιά, probably copied during the pontificate of Leo X (Giovanni de' Medici, 1513–21), to whom this collection

---

[6] See Browning (1975: in particular 18). This description is from the preface to Theodore Prodromos' *Battle of Cats and Mice*, whose *editio princeps* was prepared by Arsenios Apostolis and published by Aldus Manutius in Venice between 1494 and 1495 (see Legrand [1885: 18–19]).

[7] Homer himself reused his own verses in the *Iliad* and the *Odyssey*, thus demonstrating the versatility of such poetry. For this reason, it is not surprising that Eustathios, while giving instruction on how to adapt a Homeric utterance into a maxim (see *in Il.* 210.34–5, to quote one example), employed the same practice while composing his works and often bent the verses to his current purpose. This also allowed Byzantine rhetors to reuse Homer's verses in witty ways in contexts of ridicule: see van den Berg in this volume.

[8] Other than Cullhed (2016: 17*–25*), see also Nünlist (2012) and Andersen (2014), the latter a still-unpublished doctoral thesis, which, unfortunately, I had the possibility to read only when finishing this paper. In composing his commentaries, Eustathios must have taken advantage of a reference book, a 'school' tool, which included entries not only from ancient and well-known sources, but also from the popular tradition, as Tosi (2017: 229–30) argues.

was dedicated.⁹ Arsenios' work is a development of the Συναγωγή, a collection of both classical and Christian proverbs put together by his father, the scribe Michael, who most likely had the idea to produce such a text after leafing through an ancient manuscript of Stobaios.¹⁰ As we might imagine for a challenge of this kind, the result was an 'open' compilation on which Michael never stopped working, motivated as much by cultural curiosity as by the ambition of completing an enterprise never attempted before. He never finished the work, as becomes apparent in the working codex Rome, Biblioteca Angelica, gr. 27, into which new folia – sometimes even new quires – were inserted and where every available surface was used to juxtapose new paroemiographic types to the παροιμίαι.¹¹ In the end, the task of perfecting the collection and sending it for printing was inherited by his son Arsenios.

When leafing through the folia of **P**, tidily organized in a one-column layout and with a clear division into paragraphs (first alphabetically and then according to the typology of the proverbial entries), the reader's attention is immediately captured by the incredible number of notes, once again in Arsenios' own hand, filling the margins of nearly every page of the manuscript, as if they were meant to serve as an elegant frame. It is surprising that, although this Parisian volume has been at the centre of paroemiographic studies since the publication of the *CPG – Corpus paroemiographorum Graecorum* in the mid-nineteenth century and was used to establish the modern – although partial – critical edition of Apostolis' collection, these notes have not so far received attention.¹²

On a few occasions, these marginalia consist of a simple upgrade and amendment to parts of the collection, as well as corrections of possible mistakes, as might be expected in a handwritten book. Nevertheless, in most cases, the notes represent an ample selection of Homeric scholia.¹³ When putting these additions into the context of Arsenios' corpus, this material

---

⁹ The others are Florence, Biblioteca Medicea Laurenziana, Plut. 4.26 and Moscow, Gosudarstvennyj Istoričeskij Muzej, Sinod. gr. 10. On the life of Arsenios and for relevant bibliography, see the short note by Flamand in Ferreri et al. (2017: 211–13).
¹⁰ The Συναγωγή survives in two autograph editions: the first and more complete on fols. 23r–143r of the codex Paris, Bibliothèque nationale de France, gr. 3059, dedicated to Lauro Quirini; the second on fols. 1r–102r of the codex Paris, Bibliothèque Mazarine, Ms. 4461, promised in the 1470s, during a meeting in Rome, to the Bishop of Osimo and former secretary of Cardinal Bessarion, Gaspare Zacchi. On the different editorial phases of Michael's collection, see now Villa (2021).
¹¹ See Di Lello-Finuoli (1971), Ciolfi (2014).
¹² See Leutsch (1851) and the preparatory studies for the upgrade of the *CPG* (Leutsch [1856], [1857], [1859], [1862]).
¹³ For a general introduction to Homeric scholia, see Dickey (2007: 18–28). The prolific copyist Arsenios was also very active as exegete of the classics generally, not only of Homer. This is apparent

turns out to be part of an enormous mass of exegetical comments that he had collected and copied into various manuscripts and which he had already organized in the hopes of printing an edition soon thereafter.[14] Unfortunately, he did not succeed in completing this ambitious project, to which the codex Vatican City, Biblioteca Apostolica Vaticana, gr. 1321 (to be attributed to the years 1519–28) is an important witness. The Vaticanus is the prototype of an exegetic manuscript, elegant and orderly, containing only the notes to the poems in a continuous, full-page format – a volume that can certainly be considered the first modern 'edition' of scholia on Homer.[15]

In order to retrace the origins of this Homeric 'contamination' of the Ἰωνιά, it is necessary to follow Arsenios during his stay in Venice. The Homeric influence was undoubtedly shaped by his meeting with Erasmus on the lagoon, which we know about from a note that Arsenios wrote to his Dutch friend on 30 September 1521 to accompany a gift copy of his Ἀποφθέγματα φιλοσόφων καὶ στρατηγῶν ῥητόρων τε καὶ ποιητῶν / *Praeclara dicta philosophorum, imperatorum oratorumque et poetarum* ('Apophthegms of philosophers, commanders, orators and poets').[16] He remained fascinated by this encounter and certainly was inspired by the varied contents of the *Adagia*, Erasmus' monumental 'encyclopedia *sub*

---

from several pieces of evidence. Firstly, this can be seen from the 1525 Aristophanes with scholia, printed in Florence by Filippo Giunti's heirs and edited by Antonio Francini, who admitted the great importance of Arsenios in determining the Greek text of the comedies, as we read in the preface of the volume [fol. A2]: *ad hoc Arsenii Cretensis Archiepiscopi Monembasiae magna eruditione viri acerrimo iudicio usi*, 'for this goal [i.e. the edition of Aristophanes' comedies] I resorted to the most acute judgment of Arsenios of Crete, Archbishop of Monemvasia, a man of vast erudition'. We can also consider the evidence of Arsenios' scholia on seven Euripidean tragedies (*Hecuba, Orestes, Phoenissae, Medea, Hippolytus, Alcestis* and *Andromache*) printed in Venice in 1534 by Lucantonio Giunti and dedicated to the newly elected Pope Paul III (see Legrand [1885: 219–24]).

[14] On the advanced phase of the Homeric project, see the promises made by Arsenios himself in the preface of the aforementioned edition of Euripides' tragedies and especially in a letter probably addressed to the influential Cardinal Niccolò Ridolfi (Manousakas [1958: n. 10]). This letter mentions a Ὁμηρικὴ σειρά, a work to be printed – if considered worthy – by the recipient of the epistle; moreover, in close connection to such work, we also have a Παροιμιακὴ σειρά. It is worth noting that, in presenting his efforts to the cardinal, Arsenios described the books with the same metaphorical image (i.e. sons of Paideia and Homer's and Penelope's suitors), which was later employed in the preface to the 1532 edition of Michael Psellos (printed in Venice by Stefano Nicolini da Sabbio; see Legrand [1885: 2012–15]).

[15] On the history of Homeric exegesis, with particular attention to the *Odyssey*, see Pontani (2005).

[16] This little volume was released by the press of the Roman Greek College most likely in 1519 (the date has been proposed by Legrand [1885: 166, n. 3; see also 169–71]). A new study on this work, within the framework of Arsenios' activities, is found in Ferreri et al. (2017: 269–80). Here, it is important to point out that two of the manuscript witnesses of these Ἀποφθέγματα, London, British Library, Harley 5542 and Oxford, Bodleian Library, Canon. gr. 30, were copied by Christophoros Kondoleon (*RGK* I 383, II 526 and III 615), who was from the city of Monemvasia (where, even if controversially, Arsenios was elected archbishop) and shared with Arsenios a deep interest in Homer (see Piasentin and Pontani [2018]).

specie proverbii, in which a section concerning the *Homerici versus proverbiales* ('proverbial Homeric verses') held a crucial place starting with the edition printed by Aldus Manutius in 1508, as we shall see.

From the very start of his study of Greek, in fact, Erasmus was interested in the Homeric poems, one of the tools for so many who desired to learn the 'new' language: they were canonical and privileged texts that carried great weight for the didactic practices of humanism from its early stages onwards, with Homer perceived as θάλασσα τῶν λόγων, 'an ocean of learning'.[17] Therefore, while reading and learning Homer, Erasmus sought to put together into a compilation all of the verses that seemed to him to have proverbial or didactic value.[18] The mass of this material grew over the years and, when Erasmus was ready to proceed to the new and expanded edition of the *Adagia*, those verses came to occupy an organic, coherent and well-defined section within the work, solidified, moreover, by a brief introduction which emphasized Macrobius' authoritative and paradigmatic quoted above. In almost three hundred examples devoted to this particular type of entry, Erasmus provided the Homeric verses with a Latin translation and succinctly indicated the meaning of the expression as well as its primary suggested context of use.[19]

This was the first time that Homer's work had been systematically reemployed for other purposes, if we exclude the poetic 'Homeric centos' and the prose versions dating from the fourteenth century.[20] It is easy to understand, then, why Arsenios, having at his disposal a huge number of exegetic materials on the Homeric epic, decided to follow in Erasmus' footsteps and import such an innovation into his own collection, especially since he had a better access to Eustathios' *Parekbolai* than Erasmus.[21]

---

[17] As John Tzetzes wrote in his *Allegories of the Iliad* (in *Prolegomena* 51 ed. Boissonade [1851]).

[18] The proverbs also served as a starting point for elaborating articulated speeches on the moral concept of the maxim itself, as was prescribed in the widespread textbook of *progymnasmata* by Aphthonios of Antioch. Their importance and value in the study of a new language is nowadays accepted (see Fiedler [2014]).

[19] They are now nn. 2701–2975 of the *Adagia*: possibly following a literary *topos*, Erasmus claimed that this was just a small part of all the materials he had gathered (see the edition by Heinimann and Kienzle [1981: 481–574]).

[20] On the 'Homeric centos', see Schembra (2006); on the prose rewriting of Homer, see Browning (1992a). Moreover, it is worth remembering that, soon after the Venetian publication of the *Adagia*, Erasmus' Homeric section enjoyed public success in an independent volume, but without any Greek and without commentary: *Proverbia quaedam Homerica D. Erasmi Roterodami labore exquisitissimo e Graeco in linguam Latinam versa, ingenii ac eruditionis plenissima*, 'Some Homeric proverbs, absolutely full of ingeniousness and erudition, translated from Greek to Latin by D. Erasmus of Rotterdam with the highest attention to detail' (the book was published in Antwerp, 1529, probably without Erasmus' consent).

[21] In the final version of the *Adagia*, Erasmus explicitly mentions Eustathios and/or quotes passages from his *Commentaries* in fifty-four entries without giving him any special attention or treatment. Moreover, according to his own statement in the maxim *Festina lente*, 'Make haste slowly' (*adagium*

Thus, Arsenios integrated a fifth section, the 'Homeric proverbs', into the four sections already delineated in former versions: παροιμίαι ('proverbs'), γνῶμαι ('maxims'), ἀποφθέγματα ('apophthegms') and ὑποθῆκαι ('proverbial anecdotes'), making a final update to his collection of proverbs. Such a move, only visible in the margins of codex **P**, had not been attempted in earlier Greek paroemiographic works since the weak endeavours by the Alexandrian scholars. However, the fact that the 'Homeric proverbs' section does not appear in later manuscript versions of the Ἰωνιά suggests that it was not successful.

The interventions in the Parisian codex would appear to suggest that Erasmus influenced Arsenios, even if there is no unequivocal evidence of this relationship. Nevertheless, when we directly compare entries from the two collections, the similarities in structure and in content are so substantial that it seems highly likely that the two scholars influenced each other in terms of the arrangement of their exegetical material on Homer. While Arsenios' work is still *in nuce*, Erasmus' final printed version shows a refined scheme and offers precise explanations, paying particular attention to the translations of the Greek quotations into Latin for his multicultural audience. This difference, however, does not undermine the above-mentioned hypothesis: the *lemmata* are interpreted by both authors firstly by introducing the relevant Homeric passages and then by explaining their meanings within and outside of the original context, so as to help readers – explicitly or implicitly – understand all their possible metaphorical uses:[22]

Adagia 2708	Par. gr. 3058, fol. 203r
Inanis conatus. Ubi sentiemus frustra sumi operam neque quicquam promoveri diutinis laboribus, non inepte quadraverit illud ex eodem libro: Ἄπρηκτον πόλεμον πολεμίζειν ἠδὲ μάχεσθαι (*Il.* 2.121), id est *Pugnam infrugiferamque et inutile ducere bellum*.	Ἵπποι δ' οὐ παρέασι καὶ ἅρματα τῶν κ' ἐπιβαίην· / ἀλλά που ἐν μεγάροισι (*Il.* 5.192–3). Κερτομεῖ τὸ ἑαυτοῦ φιλάργυρον ὡς ἀμελοῦντος τῆς ἰδίας σωτηρίας χρημάτων φειδοῖ.

---

n. 1001), Erasmus revealed he had held a copy of Eustathios' *Parekbolai* in his hands only once in Venice. There, he also had the opportunity to meet Markos Mousouros and discuss Homer with him: in fact, Mousouros gave public lectures on Homer between 1507 and 1508 in the city of Padua, leaving his autograph notes in the margins of the incunabulum Inc. 1.50 of the Biblioteca Apostolica Vaticana (on the life and deeds of Mousouros, see Speranzi [2013]). This volume was used by Arsenios between 1519 and 1521, when he was in Rome as the head of the Greek College and preparing his edition of Homeric scholia.

[22] A general overview of the question has been presented in Ciolfi (2016: 149–52), from which the following example is drawn.

A vain attempt. When we realize that labour is being expended in vain and that nothing has been achieved despite persistent efforts, this saying from the same book would be appropriate: 'to engage in fruitless war and battle'.

I have neither horses nor chariots on which to ride; but somewhere in the palace. He blames his own avarice, inasmuch as, in cutting costs, he has taken no care to preserve his own safety.

Importing and Reusing Eustathian Materials

Among these Homeric additions included in the project of codex **P**, some were passages chosen by Arsenios himself, while others were derived – more or less directly – from Eustathios' *Parekbolai* on Homer.[23] Arsenios knew these works very well, having also copied them in the codices Paris, Bibliothèque nationale de France, gr. 2696 and gr. 2698, and Vatican City, Biblioteca Apostolica Vaticana, Rossianus 961 (*olim* Angelicanus, showing the same *mise-en-page* as the aforementioned Vat. gr. 1321). Let us examine here a few of the additions listed under the letter iota, which has been at the centre of my preparatory studies for a new edition of Apostolis' Ἰωνιά.

First of all, we have the cases in which Arsenios simply accepted Eustathios' explanations of Homeric verses without giving further details on why and how we should consider the *lemmata* as proverbs. He also adopts entries which were original creations by Eustathios and not derived from another source – at least, this is the judgement made by the Eustathian editor Van der Valk on the first of the following five examples:

a Ἱεροῖο δόμοιο (*Il.* 6.89). Ταὐτὸν κατὰ πολυωνυμίαν ναὸν εἰπεῖν καὶ ἱερὸν δόμον. Εἰπὼν γοῦν Ἕλενος 'νηὸν Ἀθηναίης' ἐπάγει 'οἴξασα κληῗδι θύρας ἱεροῖο δόμοιο'.[24]

Of the sacred enclosure: through polyonymy, to say 'temple' and 'sacred enclosure' is the same. Helenus, then, mentioning 'Athena's temple', continues with the words 'having opened by the key the doors of the sacred enclosure'.

---

[23] It is worth recalling that Arsenios had a personal method for elaborating his exegetic corpus: he commonly used different sources and mixed together their data. Concerning the Homeric scholia, the result of his operation is clearly visible in the folia of codex Paris, Bibliothèque nationale de France, gr. 2766 (the following *sigla* are those used by the editor Erbse [1969]). Here Apostolis added a personal selection drawn from Eustathios' work, scholia from the classes D and E⁴, as well as some excerpts from the ancient philosopher Porphyry and the thirteenth-century scholar Michael Kakos Senacherim, a teacher of rhetoric and poetry at the Nicaean school of St. Tryphon (all this most likely from another manuscript, the Leiden, Universiteitsbibliotheek, Vossianus gr. 64) to the h class of scholia proper to this particular Parisian manuscript.

[24] *Apparatus fontium*: EUST. *in Il.* 626.58–60 = 2.251.5–7 ed. van der Valk.

b **Ἱερὸν κνέφας** (*Il.* 11.194). Τὸ μέγα ἐπὶ μεγάλου πολλάκις τὸ ἱερὸν τίθεται.[25]

Sacred darkness: often, as emphasis, he defines what is big as sacred.

c **Ἴν' ἀπέλεθρον ἔχοντας** (*Il.* 5.245). Δύναμιν πολλὴν ἔχοντας. Ἀπὸ τοῦ πέλεθρον, ὅ ἐστιν εἶδος μέτρου, ἔστι δὲ πλέθρον τὸ δίμοιρον τῶν Ρ' πηχῶν καὶ μετὰ τοῦ "α" ἐπιτατικοῦ ἀπέλεθρον τὸ ὑπὲρ τὸ μέτρον καὶ διὰ τοῦτο μέγα.[26]

Those who have the strength of a plethron: those who have great strength. From *pelethron*, which is a unit of measurement; the *plethron* is half of one hundred cubits and, with the intensive alpha, *apelethron* means 'beyond measure' and therefore 'large'.

d **Ἱπποκορυσταί** (*Il.* 2.1). Ἱπποκορυστὰς ἐνόησάν τινες τοὺς ἔχοντας ἱππείας τρίχας ἐν ταῖς κόρυσιν. Ἀλλ', εἰ τοῦτο ἦν, ὤφειλεν ἱπποκόρυθας εἰπεῖν ἢ οὕτω πως, ὁμοίως τῷ κορυθάϊκες καὶ κορυθαιόλος. Ἔστιν οὖν ἱπποκορυστὴς ὁ καὶ ἱππιοχάρμης ἢ ὁ ἱππότης πολεμιστής.[27]

Arrangers of chariots: some interpreted *hippokorystas* as 'those who have horsehair on their helmets'; however, if this were the case, the poet should have said *hippokorythas* or something analogous. [It is] similar to *korythaikes* ('who shake the crest') and *korythaiolos* ('with a streaked crest'). *Hippokorystês*, then, means 'lord of chariots' or 'warrior on horseback'.

e **Ἴσας δ' ὑσμίνη κεφαλὰς ἔχον** (*Il.* 11.72). Τοῦτο μετηνέχθη τροπικῶς ἀπὸ ἀνθρώπων ἐχόντων ἰσότητα μεγέθους. Ἔστι δὲ ῥητορικὴ ἀλληγορία καὶ δηλοῖ, ὡς οὐδεὶς τῷ τέως ὑπερεῖχε μαχόμενος, ἀλλ' ἰσοκέφαλος οἷον μέχρι τινὸς ἡ μάχη ἦν διὰ τὸ ἀνυπέροχον καὶ ἰσοπαλές. Τὸ δὲ σχῆμα κατὰ ἄρσιν καὶ θέσιν ἐστί ἢ ὁμοίας εἶχον τὰς τάξεις μετὰ τὸν πόλεμον.[28]

They had equal strength in the battle: this has been said metaphorically about men who are the same size. It is a rhetorical allegory and it indicates that, up to this time, no one had prevailed while fighting, but the battle had been, as it were, equal-headed until now, because it was undecided and even. Or, by arsis and thesis, the figure could mean they had similar ranks after the battle.

Furthermore, direct access to the work of Eustathios is demonstrated by another entry where, while taking his cue from a *scholium vetus*, Arsenios

---

[25] *Apparatus fontium*: Eust. *in Il.* 839.29 = 3.180.10 (post μέγα, σκότος om. P || post ἐπεί, καί om. P).
[26] *Apparatus fontium*: Eust. *in Il.* 545.17–20 = 2.67.7–11 ed. van der Valk.
[27] *Apparatus fontium*: Eust. *in Il.* 163.45–7 = 1.253.11–14 ed. van der Valk (ἤ: ἤγουν **Eustath.**).
[28] *Apparatus fontium*: μετηνέχθη – ἰσοπαλές Eust. *in Il.* 832.1–3 = 3.154.15–18 ed. van der Valk (ante τροπικῶς, μέν om. P || ῥητορικὴ et ἀλληγορία trps. P).

added a final remark directly inspired by what he could read in the *Parekbolai*:

> **f Ἰόμωροι** (*Il.* 4.242). Ἀργεῖοι ἰόμωροι· ἰῶν φύλακες. Ἐπονείδιστον δὲ τὸ μόνον τοξεύειν· ἀμέλει δὲ εἰδότες οὐ τοξεύουσιν. Οἱ δὲ περὶ ἰοὺς πεπονημένοι· τετάρακται δὲ τῇ Μενελάου λύπῃ, ἢ ὑπὸ βελῶν φονευθησόμενοι.[29]
>
> ***Arrow-fighters***: Argives, guardians of arrows: 'those who shield from arrows'. Yet it would be dishonourable to use only the bow: even if they are actually skilled, they do not rely on it. 'Those who are trained in archery': he is upset by the suffering of Menelaus, otherwise 'being about to be killed by arrows'.

Within these examples, it is possible to trace some common denominators: a 'translation' of the terms on the basis of etymology, the indication of grammatical or stylistic particularities and parallels with possible variants. Against this background, the παροιμίαι were developed, or at least became distinguished as a trope, which in the Byzantine literary tradition served a twofold function: firstly, they contributed to the understanding and comprehension of obscure passages of texts; secondly, they provided pre-prepared materials and variants to enrich new texts. We have previously pointed out this function as one of the main features of medieval and Renaissance anthologies such as those of Eustathios, Arsenios and Erasmus.

On the other hand, an interesting shift from παροιμίαι to another paroemiographic genre can be found in the following entry, the only one in the iota section dealing with the *Odyssey*:

> **Ἱστὸν ἀμαιμάκετον νηὸς κυανοπρῴροιο** (*Od.* 14.311). Πρὸς διαστολὴν τοῦ ὑφαντικοῦ. Ἐκ γὰρ τῆς ὁμωνυμίας τῆς λέξεως λόγος ἐνέπεσέ τοι ἀστεῖος παρὰ τοῖς παλαιοῖς. Λέγεται γὰρ ἐν Κορίνθῳ ἑταίρας τινὸς ἐπαινουμένης ὡς ἐργατικῆς εἰπεῖν τὸν ἀκούσαντα "καὶ πῶς οὐκ ἂν εἴη ἐργατική, ἥτις ἐν μιᾷ ἡμέρᾳ δύο ἱστοὺς καθεῖλε;" Καὶ δοκεῖ μὲν ὁ λόγος δηλοῦν δύο ἱστάρια· τὸ δ' ἦν ἄλλως, ὅτι ταχὺ δύο ναυκλήρους ἀπήγαγεν ἐκείνη τοῦ εὐπορεῖν, φοιτῶντας ἐπ' αὐτήν.[30]
>
> ***The firm mast of the dark-prowed ship***: to distinguish it [i.e. the mast] from the one used in weaving. Because of the homonymy of the term *histos*, a witticism came about among the ancients. It is said that, in the city of

---

[29] *Apparatus criticus*: ἰόμωροι² – λύπη Schol. Il. 4.242 **b** (ante ἰῶν, οἱ μὲν om. **P**). *Apparatus fontium*: ἢ ὑπὸ βελῶν φονευθησόμενοι cfr. Eust. *in Il.* (= κυρίως δὲ οἱ περὶ βέλη μεμορημένοι).

[30] *Apparatus fontium*: πρὸς διαστολὴν – παλαιοῖς cfr. Eust. *in. Od.* 1760.23–6 = 2.72.7–10 ed. Stallbaum; λέγεται – ἐπ' αὐτήν Eust. *in Od.* 1760.26–8 = 2.72.10–12 ed. Stallbaum (ἀκούσαντα: ἀκούοντα **Eustath.** || ante καὶ πῶς, ὅτι om. **P**).

Corinth, when a *hetaira* was praised as hard-working, a man who heard it said: 'and how could she not be hard-working, she who in one single day took down two *histoî*?' The phrase seems to indicate two little 'woven tapestries'; however, its meaning was different, namely that the *hetaira* swiftly deprived of their riches two seamen who visited her.

The original context of the verse brings us to Odysseus' first speech to the swineherd Eumaeus, when the hero tells of how he managed to escape from a storm by clinging to the broken mast of the ship, according to Zeus' will. Even if Arsenios does not give us any clue about his paroemiographic interpretation, the 'firm mast of the dark-prowed ship' could have been used as a true symbol of salvation, when following a direct metaphorical transfer. But this does not seem to be the only possibility here, as there is a different reading which is also acceptable and, indeed, more appropriate. For Eustathios, in fact, the multiple interpretations possible for ἱστός (which broadly refers to anything set upright, including 'mast', 'beam [of a loom]' and 'erect male member'), inspire him to mention a χρεία, a succinct statement illustrated by an anecdote, which here pivots on the traditional sexual ambiguity of maritime vocabulary.[31] This anecdote concerns a prostitute from the city of Corinth – a centre which, not coincidentally, had been known for its brothels since antiquity – who was proud of being hard-working. When hearing it, a prankster insisted on the correctness of such a statement, considering that she was able to put her hand on and then ruin two 'masts' in a single day: not referring to completing two woven textiles – as might have been expected – but to tiring two seamen and making them fritter their money away.[32]

Eustathios' Reception in Renaissance Paroemiographers

The influence of Eustathios' thoughts and practice on the activity of paroemiographers during the Renaissance was significant. This is not only related to the physical transmission of materials gathered and commented on by him in the *Parekbolai*, although this was, indeed, fundamental. Eustathios' legacy consistently inspired the theoretical elaborations and

---

[31] Also of agricultural terminology; for the sexual metaphor, see also Young (1964: in particular 15) and Borthwick (1981). Χρεῖαι would be included in the section ὑποθῆκαι / ἱστορίαι, the fourth category identified by Arsenios in the division of his *Ἰωνιά*.

[32] See also Erasmus' *adagium* 301: *Non est cuiuslibet Corinthum appellere* / Οὐ παντὸς ἀνδρὸς ἐς Κόρινθον ἔσθ' ὁ πλοῦς. A similar anecdote is found in Strabo 8.6.20. Eustathios' final explanation could also have a pure sexual interpretation: the *hetaira* had sexual intercourse with two seamen so energetically that she rendered them completely incapable of continuing.

practical strategies of his more or less self-aware heirs. Research in this direction has been developing only in recent years, with new studies and translations of this quite complicated Byzantine work.³³ Various 'Eustathian features' emerge from the lines of the collections of Arsenios and Erasmus: I will focus here on the most important.

Arsenios used Eustathios as a springboard to integrate Homeric verses into a new section of proverbs dedicated to them, implicitly acknowledging Eustathios' role in the definition and development of Homeric maxims as well as apophthegms. It is not by chance that Arsenios selected particular entries from those in which, according to René Nünlist, Eustathios had provided Homeric verses with a universalistic explanation pivoting on ἠθοποιία and had even intervened in the original text itself.³⁴ By doing so, other than demonstrating that it was easy to paraphrase certain verses and insert them into other texts, Eustathios also suggested that each verse could be transformed into a generic, idiomatic expression which could be used in specific contexts with a new, precise meaning: he created what we can rightly consider a general proverb, or sometimes an apophthegm. In this respect, there are interesting occasions, unfortunately not included under the letter iota presented here, in which Eustathios reports Homeric 'apophthegms' that he has heard in the everyday dialogue of common people. Thus, Eustathios anticipated the importance of the vulgar tradition in paroemiology, which was not taken up again until Michael Apostolis, Arsenios' father.³⁵

The collection was, then, considered as a useful 'container of different ingredients'. As observed by Baukje van den Berg, the double image of the poet-cook/poem-banquet had a central role in the preface of the *Parekbolai on the Iliad* as well as throughout the commentaries themselves.³⁶ This

---

³³ The reception of Eustathios' *Parekbolai* has been discussed by Pontani (2017). Concerning more specifically the world of proverbs in the commentaries, see the still unpublished thesis of Andersen (2014, esp. 163–98).

³⁴ See Nünlist (2012, esp. 501–2) and his interesting hypothesis on the proverbs' vulgate tradition in Eustathios' work. See also Cullhed (2016: 17*–25*) in reaction to Nünlist. On the same topic, see also Koukoules (1955: 352–78), who pointed out proverbs common in everyday usage.

³⁵ The importance of these 'new' proverbs, in clear contrast to those derived from the classical tradition, has been pointed out in Lelli (2014) and Ciolfi (2017).

³⁶ This is the description in Eustathios' words (*in Il.* 3.36–8 = 1.5.2–5 ed. van der Valk): πρῶτον μὲν γάρ, καθάπερ τοῖς μαγειρεύουσι χάρις, οὐχ' ὅτι τὰ μὴ ὄντα δαιτρεύουσιν, ἀλλ' ὅτι τὰ ἐπιπόνως ἔχοντα τοῦ συναγαγεῖν αὐτοὶ ἀγείραντες εἰς ἓν παρέθεντο, οὕτω καὶ ἡμῖν ἔσται τι χάριτος, ὅτι πόνου δίχα οἱ περιτυχόντες ἔχουσι πολλαχόθεν ἐπισυναχθὲν τὸ ζητούμενον, 'for firstly, exactly as there is gratitude for cooks not because they prepare things that did not exist before, but because they have put together into one things that are toilsome to bring together, having gathered them together themselves, so too will there be some gratitude for us, because without toil the readers have at their disposal what they seek, gathered together from many sources.' For an extensive analysis of this image, see van den Berg (2017: 40–3), where the cited translation is found.

image allowed the author to underline his role in the arrangement of the work, as well as to show his readers one of the main features of his 'encyclopedic' collection: to be a rich, variegated and, above all, practical resource. Going well beyond the idea of self-indulgent erudition, Eustathios concretely shows how it is possible to take advantage of his text, a true reference book, and be abundantly fed by the delicious food offered both by Homer and – principally, perhaps in the author's mind – by his own intelligent re-elaboration.[37] Likewise, Erasmus, preferring instead the corresponding metaphor of a 'reserve supply', wrote in the preface of his *Collectanea*:[38]

> Quid enim aeque conducit ad orationem vel lepida quadam festivitate venustandam, vel eruditiis iocis exhilarandam, vel urbanitatis sale condiendam, vel translationum gemmulis quibusdam distinguendam, vel sententiarum luminibus illustrandam, vel allegoriarum et allusionum flosculis variegandam, vel antiquitatis illecebris aspergendam, quam huiusmodi paroemiarum divitem copiosamque suppellectilem et tanquam penum quendam extructum domique repositum habere?[39]

> What helps to embellish one's discourse with a certain enjoyable festivity, or to enliven it with learned witticisms, or to flavour it with the salt of refinement, or to adorn it with certain gems of metaphors, or to make it glow with the splendour of *sententiae*, or to create variety with little flowers of allegories and allusions, or to sprinkle it with seductive materials from antiquity, as much as having a rich and abundant repository and, so to speak, sort of storeroom of proverbs of this kind, built up and kept at home?

Moreover, the combination of usefulness with enjoyable relaxation plays an important role. In fact, this fusion already existed, originating in a famous and highly respected – almost proverbial – piece of advice given by the Roman poet Q. Horatius Flaccus to poets, *miscere utile dulci*, 'to mix the useful with the sweet'.[40] Eustathios, and later Arsenios and Erasmus, underlined these two fundamental components of their literary efforts.

On the one hand, we have the practical usefulness of the entries, to be put into practice when embellishing new compositions, explaining obscure passages or conveying complex ideas by simple figures or expressions where needed:

---

[37] See again Cullhed (2016: 2*–4*).
[38] This small book, ancestor of the more famous *Adagia*, was published in 1500 during a stay in Paris.
[39] The quotation is from the edition by Allen (1906: I 290–1, ll. 32–9).   [40] *Ars* 342.

Eustathios	Arsenios, *Preface of the* Ἰωνιά
1. Ἄλλα σποράδην ὁ ποιητὴς παιδεύει νόμῳ οἰκείῳ – *βιωφελὴς γὰρ πᾶσα ποίησις* (*in Od.* 1380.5 = 1.10.4–5 ed. Cullhed).	Παροιμία ἐστὶ λόγος ὠφέλιμος ἤτοι *βιωφελής*, ἐπικρύψει μετρίᾳ, πολὺ τὸ χρήσιμον ἔχων ἐν ἑαυτῷ.
2. Οὕτω παιδευτικὸς καὶ *βιωφελὴς* ὁ ποιητὴς καὶ ἐν μύθοις καὶ ἐν πλάσμασιν (*in Il.* 38.26–7 = 1.62.11–12).	
1. The poet teaches here and there other things in his own way: all poetry, in fact, is useful for life.	The proverb is a beneficial utterance – i.e. useful for life –, in a measured concealment, an utterance which has much usefulness in itself.
2. Thus the poet is pedagogic and useful for life, in both myths and fictions.	

On the other hand, Eustathios and Arsenios highlight the possibility of delight and relaxation, which one can have from enjoying and reading their works. If the latter says it clearly in his paratext, the former seems to conceal this idea behind a trope. Eustathios plays with the image of the Sirens, upon whom he had remarked in the preface of his *Parekbolai on the Iliad*, speaking of τῶν Ὁμήρου Σειρήνων. In fact, while commenting extensively on the allegory of the Sirens in the *Parekbolai on the Odyssey*, and especially dealing with the nature of their song, Eustathios is inclined to see in it 'stories, old tales, histories, compositions of myths, especially of those that can be elevated in a philosophical way',[41] that is to say, literature, broadly speaking:[42]

Eustathios	Arsenios[43]
Καὶ τὰ μὲν ἡσθεὶς ἐμφρόνως, τὰ δὲ καὶ τὸ χρήσιμον ἐρανισάμενος, ἐγκαταμίξει τὸ ἐκεῖθεν καλὸν καὶ οἰκείοις συγγράμμασι καὶ γενήσεται	Περιέχουσιν … ἱκανὰ … ἀνέσεως καὶ χαριεντισμάτων παρέξειν τὰς ἀφορμάς.

---

[41] In *in Od.* 1708.39–40 = 2.4.12–13 ed. Stallbaum: ἱστορίαι, παλαιοὶ λόγοι, συγγραφαὶ, συνθῆκαι μύθων τῶν τε ἄλλων καὶ ὅσοι φιλοσόφως ἀνάγονται.

[42] On the traditional figure of the Sirens representing the appeal of literature, see Hunter and Russell (2011: 79–80). On the image of the Sirens in Eustathios' preface, see van den Berg (2017: 32–5).

[43] The quote is from the preface to Arsenios' Ἀποφθέγματα φιλοσόφων καὶ στρατηγῶν ῥητόρων τε καὶ ποιητῶν (text and Italian translation in Ferreri et al. [2017: 270–1]).

θεσπεσία Σειρὴν οἷά τις καὶ αὐτός (*in Od.* 1708.41–2 = 2.4.14–15 ed. Stallbaum).

Having taken sensible pleasure on the one hand, and having collected what is useful on the other, he will mix what good he has taken from there [i.e. Homeric poetry] into his own compositions and will become himself – as it were – a divinely sweet Siren.

[Apophthegms] offer many opportunities for relaxation and for telling witticisms.

A close parallel between Eustathios and Erasmus, moreover, is that it was not necessary to read their 'encyclopedias' from the beginning to the end, which would have been a herculean task for any common reader, or to follow the fixed order of a given section:

Eustathios
Ἕκαστον τῶν χρησίμων καθ' αὑτὸ ἰδίᾳ κεῖται (*in Il.* 2.44 = 1.3.31 ed. van der Valk) ... ὁ διὰ τοῦ συγγράμματος τούτου ἐρχόμενος συχνὰ οἷον καταλύων ἀναπαύεται (*in Il.* 2.46 = 1.3.33 ed. van der Valk).

Each one of the useful entries stands on its own ... the person who goes through this book often takes rest as if lodging.[45]

Erasmus[44]
Mearum Chiliadum ea ratio est ut ubiubi quodvis finieris adagium, imaginari possis iam explicatum volumen.

The concept of my *Chiliades* is that, wherever you finish any *adagium*, you could believe the book already concluded.

Ultimately, an index of contents became a necessity. Conceived as a work in which every single entry was considered an independent part within a frame, as we have seen above, the full fruition and complete benefit of the *Parekbolai*, as well as the Ἰωνιά and the *Adagia*, could have been possible only with the creation of an index. Eustathios paved the way, a *unicum* in the entire corpus of Byzantine literature and erudition, by including a rudimentary index in the margins of the Florentine codices, Biblioteca Medicea Laurenziana, Plut. 59.2 and 59.3, essentially

---

[44] In Allen and Allen (1910: 466 n° 531 ll. 288–90).
[45] The translation of *in Il.* 1.3.33 is by van den Berg (2017: 39).

mentioning only the openings and possible keywords of the *lemmata*.⁴⁶ Furthermore, it was likely an advantage to exactly these sorts of reference books that, in a critical innovation, Renaissance printers began to add proper and exhaustive indices to their editions, advertising their presence in the frontispieces of the books published by their houses and presenting them as a kind of bonus feature. Of the authors analysed in this paper, only Erasmus' collection would be enriched by this important tool whose aborted development in the works of Eustathios is highlighted by René Nünlist.⁴⁷ In particular, this can be seen in the Venetian edition of the *Adagia* printed by Aldus Manutius, who proudly celebrated this new feature of his volumes at the end of the preface.

Conclusion

While using proverbs in order to convey his thoughts and stress his own reading of Homer, in his *Parekbolai*, Eustathios unequivocally celebrated the importance of proverbs in classical epics, considering the high number of γνώμας, αἶς καὶ αὐταῖς πολλαχοῦ ἡ ὁμηρικὴ σεμνύνεται ποίησις, '*sententiae*, by which Homeric poetry is exalted in many places'. Following the ancient tradition, he proceeded to point out every single verse of the *Iliad* and the *Odyssey* which, among other uses, could be read and adapted as an independent proverbial utterance. Although perhaps unconsciously, he also highlighted a new category of paroemiographic examples, which, on closer inspection and bearing in mind current understanding, can be seen to consist of a series of apophthegms: witty and model quotations from authoritative persons, which can be used in a specific context, where they gain a specific meaning in place of a universal truth.

From the point of view of paroemiology, his work represented a crucial moment in the creation and evolution of the *Homerici versus proverbiales* and was perceived as such by the Renaissance scholars who browsed his exegetical corpus. In fact, only because of the new needs of this innovative cultural movement could the greatest compilers of proverb collections, Arsenios in Greek and Erasmus of Rotterdam in Latin, experiment with the huge mass of materials gathered and wisely commented upon by Eustathios. Even if they did not acknowledge the major role of the *Parekbolai* in drafting their volumes, the influence of their author is evident and undeniable, shaping not only the structure of the Ἰωνιά and of the *Adagia*, but also influencing their mutual exchanges.

---

⁴⁶ See Browning (1992b: 142). ⁴⁷ See Nünlist (2012: 508).

Nevertheless, closer analysis reveals that the sixteenth-century compilers paid their dues to Eustathios: by adapting the ancient material to their contemporary context, they offered a new way in which his work could be honourably preserved, placed among the fundamental books kept in the libraries of the humanists and thus finally entrusted to the modern world.

REFERENCES

Allen, P. S. (ed.) (1906) *Opus epistolarum Desideri Erasmi Roterodami*, vol. 1: *1484–1514*. Oxford.
Allen, P. S. and H. M. Allen (eds.) (1910) *Opus epistolarum Des. Erasmi Roterodami*, vol. 2: *1514–1517*. Oxford.
Andersen, L. (2014) 'Unfolding Compressed Knowledge: Wisdom Expressions in the Homeric Commentaries by Eustathios of Thessalonike', unpublished PhD thesis, University of Southern Denmark.
van den Berg, B. (2017) 'The Wise Homer and His Erudite Commentator: Eustathios' Imagery in the Proem of the *Parekbolai* on the *Iliad*', BMGS 41.1: 30–44.
Boissonade, J. F. (ed.) (1851) *Tzetzae allegoriae Iliadis*. Paris.
Borthwick, E. K. (1981) 'Ἰστοτριβής: An Addendum', *AJP* 102: 1–2.
Browning, R. (1964) 'Byzantine Scholarship', *P&P* 28: 3–22.
  (1975) 'Homer in Byzantium', *Viator* 6: 15–33.
  (1992a) 'A Fourteenth-Century Prose Version of the *Odyssey*', *DOP* 46. *Homo Byzantinus: Papers in Honor of Alexander Kazhdan*, 27–36.
  (1992b) 'The Byzantines and Homer', in *Homer's Ancient Readers*, ed. R. Lamberton and J. Keaney, 135–48. Princeton.
Cavallo, G. (2000) 'Scritture informali, cambio grafico e pratiche librarie', in *I manoscritti greci tra riflessione e dibattito. Atti del v Colloquio internazionale di paleografia greca (Cremona, 4–10 ottobre 1998)*, ed. G. Prato, 219–38. Papyrologica Fiorentina 31. Florence.
Ciolfi, L. M. (2014) 'The Apostolis: A Family of Modern Paremiologists in the xvith Century', in *7th Interdisciplinary Colloquium on Proverbs: Proceedings*, ed. R. Soares and O. Lauhakangas, 174–84. Tavira.
  (2016) '"*Quia nihil aliud cupio quam prodesse vobis, studiosi*": il contributo di Aldo Manuzio alla paremiologia moderna', in *Aldo Manuzio: la costruzione del mito / Aldus Manutius: The Making of the Myth*, ed. M. Infelise, 142–59. Venice.
  (2017) 'Attraverso Venezia, da Oriente a Occidente: un codice di proverbi greci tra Michele Apostolis e Lauro Quirini', in *Venezia e l'Europa Orientale tra il tardo Medioevo e l'Età moderna*, ed. G. Arbore Popescu and C. Luca, 71–87. Collana saggistica. Crocetta del Montello.
  (2018) 'When the Proverb Collection Became an Encyclopaedia: Erasmus of Rotterdam and Arsenios Apostolis', in *Renaissance Encyclopaedism: Studies in Curiosity and Ambition*, ed. W. S. Blanchard and A. Severi, 371–413. Center for Reformation and Renaissance, Essays and Studies 41. Toronto.

Cullhed, E. (ed. and trans.) (2016) *Eustathios of Thessalonike, Commentary on the Odyssey*, vol. 1: *On Rhapsodies A–B*. Acta Universitatis Upsaliensis. Studia Byzantina Upsaliensia 17. Uppsala.
Dickey, E. (2007) *Ancient Greek Scholarship: A Guide to Finding, Reading, and Understanding Scholia, Commentaries, Lexica, and Grammatical Treatises, from Their Beginnings to the Byzantine Period*. Oxford–New York.
Di Lello-Finuoli, A. L. (1971) *Un esemplare autografo di Arsenio e il 'Florilegio' di Stobeo, con uno studio paleografico di Paul Canart*. Rome.
Erbse, H. (ed.) (1969) *Scholia Graeca in Homeri Iliadem (scholia vetera)*, vol. 1: *Praefationem et scholia ad libros A–D continens*. Berlin.
Ferreri, L., S. Delle Donne, A. Gaspari and C. Bianca (eds.) (2017) *Le prime edizioni greche a Roma (1510–1526)*. Répertoires et inventaires 2. Rome.
Fiedler, S. (2014) 'Proverbs and Foreign Language Teaching', in *Introduction to Paremiology: A Comprehensive Guide to Proverb Studies*, ed. H. Hrisztova-Gotthardt and M. A. Vargapp, 294–325. Warsaw–Berlin.
Gamillscheg, E., D. Harlfinger, H. Hunger and P. Eleuteri (eds.) (1981–97) *Repertorium der griechischen Kopisten 800–1600*. Österreichische Akademie der Wissenschaften. Veröffentlichungen der Kommission für Byzantinistik, III/1–3, A–C. Vienna. [= *RGK*]
Heinimann, F. and E. Kienzle (eds.) (1981) *Desiderii Erasmi Roterodami adagiorum chilias tertia. Pars altera*. Amsterdam–Oxford.
Henry, R. (ed.) (1960) *Photius, Bibliothèque*, vol. 2. Paris.
Hunter, R. L. and D. A. Russell (eds.) (2011) *How to Study Poetry: De audiendis poetis*. Cambridge Greek and Latin Classics. Cambridge.
Kambylis, A. (ed.) (1991) *Eustathios von Thessalonike, Prooimion zum Pindarkommentar: Einleitung, kritischer Text, Indices*. Veroffentlichung der Joachim Jungius-Gesellschaft der Wissenschaften 65. Göttingen.
Kaster, R. (ed.) (2011) *Macrobii Ambrosii Theodosii Saturnalia*. Oxford.
Koukoules, P. (1955) Βυζαντινῶν βίος καί πολιτισμός, vol. 6. Athens.
Kolovou, G. E. (2018) 'Homère chez Eustathe de Thessalonique: la traduction des *Proèmes* sur l'*Iliade* et l'*Odyssée*', *CCO* 15: 71–118.
Legrand, E. (1885) *Bibliographie hellénique ou description raisonnée des ouvrages publiés en grec par des grecs au XVe et XVIe siècles*, vol. 1. Paris.
Lelli, E. (2014) 'The Apostolis: A Family of Modern Paremiologists in the Renaissance Europe', in *7th Interdisciplinary Colloquium on Proverbs: Proceedings*, ed. R. Soares and O. Lauhakangas, 185–92. Tavira.
von Leutsch, E. L. (ed.) (1851) *Corpus Paroemiographorum Graecorum*, II. Göttingen. [= *CPG*]
  (1856) 'Commentationis de Violarii ad Arsenio compositi codice archetypo', I, in *Index scholarum publice et privatim in Academia Georgia Augusta per semestre aestivum*. Göttingen.
  (1857) 'Commentationis de Violarii ad Arsenio compositi codice archetypo', II, in *Index scholarum publice et privatim in Academia Georgia Augusta per semestre hibernum*. Göttingen.

(1859) 'Commentationis de Violarii ad Arsenio compositi codice archetypo', III, in *Academiae Georgiae Augustae prorector Georgius Waitz D. cum senatu successorem in summo magistratu academico Isaacum Aug. Dorner D. civibus suis honoris et officii causa commendat.* Göttingen.

(1862) 'Commentationis de Violarii ad Arsenio compositi codice archetypo', IV, in *Academiae Georgiae Augustae prorector Hermannus Sauppe D. cum senatu successorem in summo magistratu academico Aemilium Herrmannum D. civibus honoris et officii causa commendat.* Göttingen.

Manousakas, M. (1958) Ἀρσενίου Μονεμβασίας τοῦ Ἀποστόλη Ἐπιστολαὶ Ἀνέκδοτοι (1521–1534). Πρὸς Κάρολον τὸν Ε', Κλήμεντα τὸν Ζ', τὸν Ἔρασμον, τοὺς Καρδιναλίους Niccolo Ridolfi καὶ Egidio Canisio, τὸν Ἰανὸν Λάσκαριν καὶ τὸν Ἰουστίνον Δεκάδυον', *Ἐπετηρὶς τοῦ Μεσαιωνικοῦ Ἀρχείου τῆς Ἀκαδημίας Ἀθηνῶν* 8–9: 5–56.

Nünlist, R. (2012) 'Homer as a Blueprint for Speechwriters: Eustathios' Commentaries and Rhetoric', *GRBS* 52: 493–509.

Piasentin, M. and F. Pontani (eds.) (2018) *Cristoforo Kondoleon, Scritti omerici*. Orientalia Lovaniensia Analecta 271 and Bibliothèque de Byzantion 17. Leuven–Paris–Bristol.

Pontani, F. (2005) *Sguardi su Ulisse: la tradizione esegetica greca all'Odissea*. Sussidi eruditi 63. Rome.

(2017) '"Captain of Homer's Guard": The Reception of Eustathius in Modern Europe', in *Reading Eustathios of Thessalonike*, ed. F. Pontani, V. Katsaros and V. Sarris, 199–226. Trends in Classics Supplementary Volume 46. Berlin–Boston.

Schembra, R. (2006) *La prima redazione dei centoni omerici: traduzione e commento*. Hellenica 22. Alessandria.

Speranzi, D. (2013) *Marco Musuro: libri e scrittura*. Bollettino dei classici, supplemento 27. Rome.

Stallbaum, J. G. (ed.) (1825–6) *Eustathii archiepiscopi Thessalonicensis commentarii ad Homeri Odysseam ad fidem exempli Romani editi*, 2 vols. Leipzig.

Tosi, R. (2017) 'Proverbs in Eustathios: Some Examples', in *Reading Eustathios of Thessalonike*, ed. F. Pontani, V. Katsaros and V. Sarris, 229–41. Trends in Classics Supplementary Volume 46. Berlin–Boston.

van der Valk, M. (ed.) (1971–87) *Eustathii archiepiscopi Thessalonicensis commentarii ad Homeri Iliadem pertinentes ad fidem codicis Laurentiani editi*, 4 vols. Leiden.

Villa, E. (2021) 'Studi sulla Ionia di Michael Apostoles: tradizione manoscritta e fasi redazionali', *RHT* 16: 115–44.

Young, D. C. C. (1964) 'Gentler Medicines in the *Agamemnon*', *CQ* 14: 1–23.

Index

Achilles, 184, 202
administration, 204, 209
admonitory poetry, 52–3
Aegeus, 218, 231
Aelian, 12
Aeneas, 223, 225–6, 231
Aeschines, 131
Aeschylus, 6, 42–3, 135, 138
  Agamemnon, 215
  Persians, 15, 42
  Prometheus Bound, 215
Aesop, 9, 256–8
Agamemnon, 173, 183, 185–6
Agathias Scholastikos, 253
Agave, 222, 227–8, 230–1
Akropolites, Constantine, 14, 340
Akropolites, George, 296, 340, 347
Albert the Great, 19
Alexander of Aphrodisias, 78
Alexiad-Komneniad Muses, 52
Alexios I Komnenos, 46, 49–50, 52, 186
allegory, 9–10, 140
anabasis, 250
Andronikos Doukas, 71
Andronikos II Palaiologos, 13, 20, 197
Anna Komnene, 7, 17–19, 48–9, 53, 73, 78, 80, 85–9, 232
  Alexiad, 5, 186
Aphrodite, 113, 176, 179, 181, 221, 241, 249
  and Ares, 246–7, 251
Aphthonios, 14, 101, 107–8, 261
  Progymnasmata, 365
Apollonius Dyscolus, 309
  On Syntax, 305
Apollonius of Rhodes, 12
apophthegms, 366, 371, 375
Apostolis, Arsenios
  Ἰωνιά, 362–76
Apostolis, Michael, 371
Arabic, 111–14, 123, 131
Aratus, 12, 196, 204

Ares
  and Aphrodite, 241, 246–7, 251
Arethas, 343
Aristenos, Alexios, 50
Aristides, Aelius, 13, 339–56
Aristophanes, 6–8, 42, 46, 100–23, 131, 135, 138, 169, 200
  Frogs, 101, 107
Aristotle, 2, 9, 13, 16–22, 24, 48–9, 61–89
  Analytics, 296
  De interpretatione, 16, 67, 73, 81, 296
  Generation of Animals, 18, 79
  History of Animals, 79
  Metaphysics, 18, 20, 69
  Meteorologica, 20
  Movement of Animals, 18, 65
  Nicomachean Ethics, 18, 20, 64, 73–6, 79, 87–9
  On Divination in Sleep, 79
  On Dreams, 79
  On Generation and Corruption, 20
  On Memory and Recollection, 79
  On Sophistical Refutations, 154
  On the Heavens, 20
  On the Soul, 20, 77–8
  Organon, 20
  Parts of Animals, 18, 20
  Parva naturalia, 18, 65, 70, 78–9
  Physics, 20
  Poetics, 172, 175
  Politics, 18
  Posterior Analytics, 17, 48, 70, 73, 80
  Prior Analytics, 17, 82, 279
  Progression of Animals, 18
  Rhetoric, 69
  Sophistical Refutations, 18
  Topics, 16
  zoological works, 20
Armenians, 51, 203
Artemis, 222, 230–1
asteiotes, 149

astrology, 24
astronomy, 24, 71, 196, 203
Athena, 173, 176, 178–9, 181, 224–5, 249
Atticizing Greek, 3, 15, 100, 131, 138, 255, 258, 306, 308, 329, 331–2
Atticus, 76
audience, 2, 122, 139, 141, 143, 201–4
Ausonius, 229, 273–4
authorship, 62, 89, 123, 138
autograph, 254, 258, 262, 339–56
Avicenna, 19

Baldwin III of Jerusalem, 119
Balianites, Leon, 46
Balsamon, Theodore, 50
Basil of Caesarea
    Ethics, 341
Basilakes, Nikephoros, 14, 150, 155, 262
Batrachomyomachia, 257
Bellerophon, 114, 118, 123
Bertha von Sulzbach. *See* Irene, Empress
biblical exegesis, 47, 214–35
    catenae, 46
    didaskaliai, 46–7
biblical texts, 5, 47
bios, 74–5, 82–9
    political, 84–6
Blemmydes, Nikephoros, 66
Boethius, 240, 279
botany, 22
brevity, 80, 130, 143, 197
Bryennios, Nikephoros, 17, 48–9
Bücherverluste, 63–7
Bulgaria, 289–90

Cadmus, 227–8, 230–1
cartography, 196–8
cento, 214, 229, 231, 233, 235
Choerilus of Samos, 117
Choniates, Niketas, 120
    Dogmatic Armour, 51–2
    History, 119, 169, 256
Chora monastery, 21, 306
Chortasmenos, John, 14
Choumnos, Nikephoros, 13, 340
Christ, 75, 216–24, 226–8, 230–1
Christopher of Mytilene, 257
Christos Paschon, 15, 214–35
Circe, 160–5, 293
clarity, 143
Cleomedes, 71, 196
Cleopatra, 111–13
comedy, 6–8, 11, 170–89
competition, 3, 45–6, 89, 138–9, 149
Constantine X Doukas, 71

Constantinople, 17, 19, 21, 51, 54, 62, 65–6, 100–1, 111, 121, 123, 131, 143, 188, 196, 201, 214, 218, 233, 278, 284, 300, 306, 340, 344
consul of philosophers. *See hypatos ton philosophon*
Creon, 218–19, 231
Crucifixion, 216, 223, 227
Cyclops, 151–8

David, 114–15
Demosthenes, 13, 131, 341
Deposition, 216, 230
Diakonos Galenos, John, 10
dictionary, 44
Dictys Cretensis, 134
didactic context, 2, 9, 12–16, 19–22, 25, 41–4, 62–3, 70, 72, 102, 139–41, 175–6, 235, 261–5, 273–300
didaskalos of the Gospels, 47
dignity, 176–81
Dio Chrysostom, 13
Diomedes, 174, 176, 187, 225–6, 231
Dionysius Periegetes, 12, 195–209
Dionysius the Areopagite, 65
Dionysius Thrax, 14, 160, 305
Dionysus, 227–8, 230–1
Diophantos, 24
Disypatos, Nicholas, 81–2
Dolon, 225, 231
Dosiadas, 274, 282
Doukas, John, 201–4, 209

education, 100, 103, 142, 148–65, 195–209, 261–3, 273–300, 304–32, 340–1, 345–7, *See also* didactic context
ekphrasis, 261
Electra, 311–12, 330
eloquence. *See* rhetoric
emotion, 218, 221, 230–1, 234
encyclopedia, 372, 374
Entombment, 216, 219, 222, 227
epi ton deeseon, 202
epideixis, 141, 143
epimerisms, 7
epistolography, 254
Erasmus of Rotterdam
    Adagia, 362, 364–7, 370–6
eroticism, 241–8, 257–8
etymology, 285–8
Euclid, 24
Euripides, 6, 15, 103–4, 155, 196, 214–35, 259
    Bacchae, 215, 224, 227–8, 230–2, 234
    Hecuba, 215
    Hippolytus, 215, 221–3, 230–1

Medea, 215, 217–20, 230–1
Orestes, 215
Rhesus, 215, 223–7, 230, 232, 234
Troades, 215
Eusebius of Caesarea, 69
Eustathios of Thessalonike, 7–8, 10, 12, 46, 48, 50, 142, 306
  Commentaries/Parekbolai on Homer, 54, 149–50, 170–89, 199–200, 277, 331, 360–76
  Commentary/Parekbolai on Dionysius Periegetes, 195–209
  Commentary/Parekbolai on the Iliad, 5, 46, 116–17, 148, 176–81
  Commentary/Parekbolai on the Odyssey, 5, 148–65, 181
  Exegesis of the Iambic Pentecostal Canon by John of Damascus, 53–4, 200
  Inquiry into Monastic Life, 121, 180
  oration in praise of Michael III *ho tou Anchialou*, 47–8
  Preface to the Commentary on Pindar, 8, 200
Eustratios of Nicaea, 18–19, 49, 51, 62, 64, 75–8, 81–2, 86, 88–9
  Commentary on Aristotle's Nicomachean Ethics, 64, 73–5
  Commentary on Aristotle's Posterior Analytics, 49, 70, 73
Excerpta Parisina, 52
experimentation, 42, 44, 46–7, 50, 54, 214

fallacies, linguistic, 154–5, 157–9
flyting, 181–5, 189

Gabalas, Manuel, 9
  Introduction to Homer's Odyssey, 331
Gabriel, 102
Gabriel the Monk, 259, 310
Galen, 68, 70, 78, 112
Ganymede, 245, 247–8
genealogical embeddedness of commentary, 21–2, 25
genealogy, 131, 133, 137–8, 140, 143
geography, 22, 117, 195–209, 280–94
Geometres, John, 14, 253
George Choiroboskos, 306
George of Cyprus, 14, 262, 296, 340–1, 343, 346
Glykas, Michael, 112
Glykys, John, 309
gospels, 234
grammar, 2, 6, 11–14, 53, 79, 161, 163–4, 276, 279, 304–32
  syntax, 307–9, 331

Greek Anthology, 12, 169, 246, 254–5, 257–8, 261
Gregoras, Nikephoros, 15, 21, 196, 259, 262, 306, 340
Gregory of Nazianzos, 73, 80, 214, 233, 235
Gregory of Nyssa
  On the Soul and the Resurrection, 259
Gregory Pardos, 53, 172, 306, 309
  Commentary on Pseudo-Hermogenes' On the Method of Skilfulness, 14, 170
  Commentary on the Iambic Pentecostal Canon by John of Damascus, 53–4

Hadrian, 195, 274
Hebrew, 111–14, 123, 131
Hector, 174, 180, 223–6, 230, 232
Hellenism, 110, 119, 121, 123
Hephaestion of Alexandria, 8
Hephaestus, 178
Hera, 176, 178, 181
Heracles, 11
Heraclitus, 172
heresy, 50–2
hermeneutics, 62, 75–6
Hermes, 288
Hermogenes, 11, 14, 101, 107–8, 171
  On Types of Style, 184
Herodian
  Katholike Prosodia, 305
Herodotus, 116
Heroogony, 133
Hesiod, 11, 103, 130, 138, 196
  Catalogue of Women, 132–4
  Shield of Heracles, 12, 289
  Theogony, 130–4
  Works and Days, 12, 259
high-register Greek. *See* Atticizing Greek
Hippolytus, 221–3, 230–1
Holobolos, Manuel, 12, 273, 278–300, 340, 343
Homer, 2, 5–6, 9–10, 24, 79, 111, 138, 149–50, 170–89, 195, 247, 261, 263, 360–76
  Iliad, 3, 43, 45–6, 114–20, 133–5, 171–2, 175–86
  Margites, 172
  Odyssey, 3, 71, 114–20, 148–65, 171, 185, 249–50, 263
homoeroticism, 241–8, 257–8, 262, 264
humour, 102–4, 120, 156–7, 170–89, 240–65
hymnography, 53–4, 102, 233
hypatos ton philosophon, 16–17, 50, 65–6, 72, 289, 300
hypertextuality, 241–3, 247, 252, 256, 261–2, 264–5

insults. *See* flyting
Irene Doukaina, 49
Irene, Empress, 9, 119, 138
Irene, *sebastokratorissa*, 11, 44, 130, 138–41, 143
irony, 182, 185
Isaac Komnenos Porphyrogennetos, 5, 46, 50
Italos, John, 16, 19, 49, 64–6, 68–70, 89

James of Kokkinobaphos, 235
Jason, 218–20, 230
Jerusalem, 114–15, 117–20
jesting. *See* humour
Jewish culture, 110–23
Jews, 110–23, 224
John Charax, 306
John II Komnenos, 44, 46, 52–3, 119
John of Damascus, 53
John the Theologian, 216, 218–19, 224–5, 232
Joseph of Arimathea, 216, 219, 222–3, 227–8, 232
Josephus, 13, 117–18
  Jewish Antiquities, 118, 120
  Jewish War, 120
Judas, 218, 220–3

kairos, 311–13, 330
Kallimachos and Chrysorrhoe, 256
Kallistos Xanthopoulos, Nikephoros, 14
Kallistos, Andronikos, 12
Kamateros family, 201–4
Kamateros, Andronikos, 161, 201
  Sacred Armoury, 51, 203
Kamateros, John
  Introduction to Astronomy, 203
Kantakouzenos, John, 340
Kastamonites, John, 47
katabasis, 83, 250
Kataskepenos, Nicholas
  Life of Cyril Phileotes, 52, 235
kerdos, 312–13, 330
kertomia, 171, 181–5
Koine, 140, 198, 305, 330
Kosmas of Jerusalem, 53
Kotertzes, Constantine, 9, 108
Kyros, 253

Lakapenos, George, 7
lamentation, 216, 219, 222, 224, 227, 230, 234
late antique commentaries, 63, 71, 73–6, 78, 88
Late Antiquity, 61–2, 78, 260
Latins, 51, 65–6, 203, 278
laughter, 171–8, 188
Leo X, Pope, 362
lexica, 331
  Palaiologan, 307

lexis, 73, 76–7
Libanios, 7, 14
Libistros and Rhodamne, 256
logic, 19, 63, 69, 279
Longinus, 172
love, 241–8, 257–8
Lucian, 15, 233, 241, 250, 253, 255
  Icaromenippus, 245
  Lover of Lies, 249, 251–2
  Menippus, 83
  Philosophies for Sale, 15
  Symposium, 242–4, 246–9
Lycophron, 11, 46, 101, 137, 196, 274
Lysias, 131

Macrobius
  Saturnalia, 360, 365
Magentinos, Leo, 81
magic, 241, 246, 249–53, 255–8
Magistros, Thomas, 6, 310, 329
  Lexicon, 307
maistor ton rhetoron, 48, 199, 201
Manasses, Constantine, 139, 215
  Aristandros and Kallithea, 258
  astrological poem, 131
  Synopsis Chronike, 11, 131
Manuel I Komnenos, 44, 50–1, 119, 135, 141, 201, 203, 209
Manuel II Palaiologos, 344
manuscript publication, 102, 104–9, 122
manuscripts, 41, 63–7, 73, 80, 101, 142, 215, 277–8, 309–11, 341–2
  Alexandria, Patriarchal Library 62, 54
  Berlin, Staatsbibliothek zu Berlin, Hamilton 555, 260
  Biblioteca Nacional de España, 4617, 310
  Bremen, Staats- und Universitäts, b. 0023, 310
  Edinburgh, National Library of Scotland, Adv. 18.7.15, 196
  Florence, Biblioteca Medicea Laurenziana
    Asburnham 1174, 281
    Conventi Soppressi 139, 45
    Plut. 4.26, 363
    Plut. 31.3, 42, 104
    Plut. 32.16, 262, 278
    Plut. 59.2, 374
    Plut. 59.3, 374
    Plut. 60.3, 339, 343
    Plut. 60.8, 343
    Plut. 86.3, 42
  Heidelberg, Universitätsbibliothek, Pal. gr. 252, 107
  Leiden, Universiteitsbibliotheek, Vossianus gr. Q 1, 101, 107–9, 161

London, British Library
  Add. 19391, 196
  Harley 5542, 364
Madrid, Real Biblioteca de San Lorenzo de El
  Escorial, Y-II-10, 47
Milan, Biblioteca Ambrosiana
  C 222 inf., 104, 108, 196, 203, 209
  G 62 sup., 81–2
  gr. B 75 sup., 281
  gr. F 101 supra, 43
  N 166 sup, 310
Moscow, Gosudarstvennyj Istoričeskij Musej
  Mus. sobr. 3649, 342
  Sinod. gr. 10, 363
  Sinod. gr. 501 (Vlad. 480), 279
Mount Athos, Mone Batopediou, 655, 196
Munich, Bayerische Staatsbibliothek, gr. 430, 341
Naples, Biblioteca Nazionale 'Vittorio
  Emanuele III', II.F.9, 257, 259–60, 310
New Haven, Yale University Library, Beinecke 234, 81
Oxford, Bodleian Library
  Auctarium T.2.7, 45
  Baroccianus 131, 47
  Canon. gr. 30, 364
Paris, Bibliothèque Mazarine, Ms. 4461, 363
Paris, Bibliothèque nationale de France
  Coisl. 128, 341
  Coisl. 228, 197
  gr. 400, 44
  gr. 1853, 69
  gr. 1917, 80–1
  gr. 2696, 367
  gr. 2698, 367
  gr. 2705, 132
  gr. 2732, 208
  gr. 2735, 196
  gr. 2766, 367
  gr. 2771, 196
  gr. 2781, 282
  gr. 2832, 281, 299
  gr. 2852, 208
  gr. 2855, 208
  gr. 2884, 310
  gr. 2951, 339, 343
  gr. 2953, 343
  gr. 2998, 343
  gr. 3058, 362, 366
  gr. 3059, 363
  suppl. gr. 384, 275
  suppl. gr. 388, 195–6
  suppl. gr. 443A, 196
  suppl. gr. 655, 104
Ravenna, Biblioteca Classense 183, 259–60
Rome, Biblioteca Angelica, gr. 27, 363
Rome, Biblioteca Casanatense, 356, 208
  gr. 306, 132
Rome, Biblioteca Vallicelliana, ms. F 016, 132
Saint Petersburg, Rossijskaja Nacional'naja
  Biblioteka, Ф. № 536, 196
Salamanca, Biblioteca Universitaria, Ms. 31, 104
Uppsala, University Library, gr. 21, 281
Vatican City, Biblioteca Apostolica Vaticana
  Barb. gr. 30, 130, 132
  gr. 42, 282
  gr. 47, 310
  gr. 117, 198
  gr. 121, 198
  gr. 191, 196
  gr. 260, 79
  gr. 269, 64
  gr. 666, 50
  gr. 895, 142
  gr. 896, 142
  gr. 915, 282
  gr. 922, 208
  gr. 950, 134
  gr. 999, 198
  gr. 1087, 196
  gr. 1141, 279
  gr. 1298, 343–4
  gr. 1321, 364, 367
  gr. 1345, 104
  gr. 1396, 108
  gr. 1721, 259–60
  gr. 1825, 282
  gr. 1899, 339–56
  gr. 1910, 208
  gr. 2199, 65
  Rossianus 961, 367
  Urb. gr. 35, 81
Venice, Biblioteca Nazionale Marciana
  gr. 454, 45
  gr. 470, 310
  gr. 471, 196
  gr. 481, 254, 258, 263
  gr. 524, 256
  gr. Z 258, 78
Vienna, Österreichische Nationalbibliothek
  phil. gr. 118, 132
  phil. gr. 161, 310
  phil. gr. 163, 310
  phil. gr. 209, 310
  phil. gr. 300, 101
  phil. gr. 48, 259
  theol. gr. 134, 66
Manutius, Aldus, 365, 375
Marcus Aurelius, 12

martyrs, 75
Mary Magdalen, 216–17, 219–20, 222, 225–6, 231
mathematics, 19, 22, 24, 341
Matthew of Ephesus, 9
maxims, 8, 10, 15, 137, 254, 261, 360, 366, 371
Mazaris' Journey to Hades, 250
Medea, 217–20, 230, 232
medicine, 22, 196
meletai, 262
Menelaus, 183
Metochites, Theodore, 13–14, 19–22, 306
  Sententious Notes, 13
metre, 7–9, 260, 280, 286, 290
Michael III *ho tou Anchialou*, 47, 50
Michael of Ephesus, 18–19, 21, 49, 62, 64–5, 77–82, 86, 88–9
  Commentary on Aristotle's Generation of Animals, 79
  Commentary on Aristotle's Nicomachean Ethics, 79
  Commentary on Aristotle's On Divination in Sleep, 79
  Commentary on Aristotle's Parva naturalia, 70, 78
  scholia on Aristotle's *De interpretatione*, 80–1
Michael Synkellos, 309
Michael VII Doukas, 276
Michael VIII Palaiologos, 279, 340, 343
mimesis, 230, 234–5
modernism. *See* modernity
modernity, 43–4, 47–8, 50, 54
modesty *topos*, 70
monks, 75, 85, 88
Monotropos, Philip
  Dialexis, 52
Moschopoulos, Manuel, 6, 9, 12–13, 259–60, 304–32
  Collection of Attic Words, 307, 331
  Erotemata, 14, 307
  Schedographia, 7, 307
  Technologia, 331
motherhood, 232
Mouzalon, George, 340
multilingualism, 110–14, 123, 131
Muse, 223–5, 227, 230–1, 281
Muslims, 74
mythography, 293–5, 300
mythology, 287, 292–5, 300

Neoplatonism, 61, 63, 76–8, 86
Nestor, 148, 173, 187
New Testament, 46–7
Nicander, 195

Nicholas of Methone, 22, 49
Nicomachus of Gerasa, 24
  Introduction to Arithmetic, 81–2
Niketas of Herakleia, 10, 46–7
Niketas of Nicomedia, 80
Nonnos, 253, 261
  Dionysiaka, 248, 262, 293–4
  Paraphrase of the Gospel of John, 262–3
nous, 76–7
novels, 17, 48–9, 79–80, 169, 253, 258

Odysseus, 114, 148–65, 173–5, 178–9, 181–2, 185, 187, 223, 225–6, 231, 250, 293, 370
Ohrid, 289–90, 300
Oppian, 103–4, 196, 200
  Halieutica, 12
orality, 62, 66
Orestes, 311–13, 330, 332
orthodoxy, 50–2, 72
otherworlds, 241, 248–51

Pachymeres, George, 14, 19–20, 262, 340
  Philosophia, 19–20
paideia, 3–4, 72, 149, 155, 159–65, 340
painting, 229–31, 234
Palaiologina, Irene-Eulogia, 340
Pan, 188, 275, 280–2, 285–8, 291, 293–5
paraphrase, 9, 19–22, 43, 45, 67, 77, 80, 100, 230, 308
  of Dionyius Periegetes, 198–9
Paris, 178, 180, 185, 224, 226
parody, 241–2, 251, 264–5
paroemiographic collections, 360–76
parrhesia, 180–1
patriarch, 47–8
Patriarchal school, 19
patristic texts, 5, 50
patronage, 17, 21, 49, 62, 88–9, 101, 108, 130, 138–41
pattern-poem, 273–300
Pediasimos, John, 12, 16, 196, 273, 278, 288–300
  Commentary on Aristotle's Analytics, 296
  Commentary on Aristotle's De interpretatione, 296
  On the Labours of Heracles, 11, 289
Pentheus, 222, 227–8, 230–1
performance, 100–4, 120–1, 123, 214, 233
Peter Grossolanus of Milan, 66
Phaedra, 221–3, 230–1
Pherecydes, 135
Philo, 13, 121
Philoponos, John, 73, 296

philosophy, 2, 5, 15–22, 47–50, 61–89, 279, 306
Philostratus, 7, 12, 135
Philoxenus of Cythera, 103
Photios
  Bibliotheca, 120, 361
physics, 63, 72
Pilate, 220, 226, 235
Pindar, 8–9, 135, 138, 196, 200
  Olympian Odes, 259
Planoudes, Maximos, 6–7, 12, 196–8, 240–65, 278, 304, 306, 309–10, 329, 341
  Comparison of Winter and Spring, 259, 262
  Dialogue on the Construction of Verbs, 253
  Idyll, 15, 240–65
  Planoudean Anthology, 254, 257–8
  Scholastic Anthology, 12–13
  Synagoge, 198
  translations of Latin literature, 240, 253–4, 258
Plato, 2, 19, 22, 61, 73, 131
  and Aristotle, 75–6
  Phaedo, 75
  Republic, 75
  Theaetetus, 75
Plutarch, 13, 112–13
  Life of Anthony, 112
poetry, 279
  admonitory, 52–3
  ancient, 4–12, 130, 132, 135, 138, 175
  Byzantine, 214–35, 240–65
  didactic, 10–11, 130–43, 195–209
  polemics, 3, 13–14, 45–6, 100, 103, 138–9, 161, 163, 169
political philosopher, 83–6
political verse, 43–4, 46, 52, 101–2, 130, 140
politikoi stichoi. *See* political verse
Polyphemus, 151–8, 165
polyphony, 230–1, 234
Porphyry, 11
Priam, 180–1
Prodromos, Manganeios, 139
Prodromos, Theodore, 15, 42, 44–5, 53–4, 142, 150, 169, 215, 306
  Epithalamium for the Sons of the Most Blessed Caesar, 87–9
  Katomyomachia, 15, 169, 232–3, 235, 252, 256
  poetic diptychs, 44
  Rhodanthe and Dosikles, 17, 48–9
  Sale of Poetical and Political Lives, 15
  schede, 261–2
progymnasmata, 14–15, 233, 261–2
Proklos, 76
  Elements of Theology, 49, 76
  Prolegomena to Hesiod's Works and Days, 133

prose
  ancient, 12–14
prosification, 206–7
proverbs, 10, 15, 360–76
Psalms, 46–7
Psellos, Michael, 10, 16, 19, 64–6, 69, 78, 80, 83–6, 88–9, 150, 154, 169, 276–7
  Chronographia, 84, 159
  Paraphrase of Aristotle's De interpretatione, 67, 73
  Synkrisis of Euripides and George of Pisidia, 232
Pseudo-Apollodorus, 135
  Bibliotheca, 134, 289, 293
Pseudo-Aristotle
  De coloribus, 18
Pseudo-Dionysius the Areopagite, 16
Pseudo-Hermogenes, 172
  On the Method of Skilfulness, 170
  Progymnasmata, 261
Ptochoprodromika, 44, 169
Ptolemy, 24, 199, 208
  Geography, 197–8

Raoul Doukas Komnenos, John, 340, 342
Raoulaina, Theodora, 13, 339–56
  Life of Saints Theophanes and Theodoros the Graptoi, 341
readership. *See* audience
redactions, 104–9
Renaissance, 360–76
Resurrection, 216–17, 219, 222, 225, 228
Rhesus, 223–6, 231
rhetor ton rhetoron, 284, 299
rhetoric, 3, 14–15, 47, 84, 86, 89, 148–9, 152–7, 171–2, 175–81, 185–8, 201, 233, 261–2, 279
  good taste, 149, 152, 155–7, 165
  ridicule, 170–89

sarcasm, 156, 182, 264
Sarpedon, 179
satire, 169–70, 189, 251, 255, 257–8, 262, 264
schedography, 7, 12, 44, 47, 148–65, 261–2, 307
Scholarios, George, 21
scholia, 16, 24, 41–2, 45, 65, 67, 78, 80–1, 100–23, 240, 241, 254, 264, 339–56
  ancient, 71, 115–16, 163, 174–5, 198–9, 278, 280, 284–9, 292–3, 295–6, 342, 347, 368
  Palaiologan, 6–7, 12, 259, 304–32
  Renaissance, 363
school, 44, 47, 61–3, 79, 102, 142, 161, 195–6, 214, 233, 235, 257, 259–63, 273–300, 304–6, 329, *See also* didactic context

science, 21–4, 81–2, 196, 279, 306
scriptorium, 341
Second Sophistic, 86, 171
self-fashioning, 21, 25, 62, 82–9
self-legitimation, 71
Seljuq Turks, 53
Simmias of Rhodes, 274
Simplikios, 73–7, 88
Skylitzes, George, 51, 103
Skylitzes, Stephanos, 69
Socrates, 74–5
Solomon, 114–15
Solymi, 114–20, 123
sophistry, 154–9
Sophocles, 6, 155, 196
    Antigone, 310
    Electra, 304–32
    triad, 259, 310
Sophonias, 77
Sophronios of Jerusalem, 306
Spaneas, 52
Spheneas, Manuel, 42
staseis, 101
Stephanus of Byzantium, 197, 199
Stilbes, Constantine, 47
Stobaios
    Anthology, 361, 363
Stoudios Monastery, 66
Strabo, 197–9, 204
Symeon the New Theologian, 254
Synesios, 13, 22
synkrisis, 262

technopaegnia, 273–300
Teiresias, 227, 231
textbooks, 305–7
textual criticism, 7
textual transmission, 195–7, 207–8, 281–4, 309–11
theatron, 67, 141, 143, 150, 214, 218, 233, 235, 263
Themistius, 159
Theocritus, 15, 135, 241–3, 249, 253–4, 258–61
    Syrinx, 11, 273–300
Theodore II Laskaris, 340
Theodore of Smyrna, 16, 89
    Epitome, 66, 71–3
Theodoret of Cyrrhus, 75
Theodosius
    Canons, 305
theology, 19, 47, 49–51, 53, 61, 66, 80, 306

Theophylact of Ohrid, 46–7
    Commentary to the Four Gospels, 341
theoria, 73
Theotokos, 215–17, 221–8, 230–1, 235, 254
Thersites, 173–6, 181, 186
Theseus, 221–2, 230–1
Thessalonike, 17, 299, 306
Thucydides, 107
Timarion, 83–5, 89, 169, 250
Tornikes, George, 49, 80, 85–6, 89
tragedy, 6–7, 11, 15, 42, 172, 175, 214–35, 304–32
translations, 24, 196, 240, 258, 279, 365–6
Trebizond, 306
Triklinios, Demetrios, 6–8, 282, 310, 329
    circle of, 299
Trojan War, 11, 131, 133, 173, 224
Tzetzes, Isaac, 8, 137
Tzetzes, John, 7, 11–12, 14, 45–6, 169, 180, 215, 306
    Allegories of the Iliad, 9, 54, 118–19, 135, 138
    Allegories of the Odyssey, 9, 114–15, 119–20
    Carmina Iliaca, 11, 45, 135
    chronicle, 54
    Commentaries on Aristophanes, 8, 46, 100–23, 169
    Commentary on Aphthonios, 107–8
    Commentary on Hermogenes, 101, 107–8
    Exegesis of the Iliad, 5–6, 10, 45, 135
    Histories, 46, 51, 101–3, 108, 111–13, 115–16, 119–21, 123, 149–50, 160–5, 186, 264
    Letter to Lachanas, 102
    On Metres, 9
    Scholia on Lycophron, 11, 46, 101, 137, 277, 293
    Theogony, 11, 111, 130–43

Union of the Churches, 279–80, 340, 343

Venice, 364, 366
vernacular, 44–5, 52, 131, 141, 305, 308
Virgin. *See* Theotokos

Xenophon, 13

Zenobius, 112–13
Zeus, 176, 179, 245–50, 276, 370
Zigabenos, Euthymios
    Armour of Dogma, 50–2
Zonaras, Christopher, 2–3
Zonaras, John, 50, 53–4, 120

For EU product safety concerns, contact us at Calle de José Abascal, 56–1°, 28003 Madrid, Spain or eugpsr@cambridge.org.

www.ingramcontent.com/pod-product-compliance
Lightning Source LLC
LaVergne TN
LVHW011756060526
838200LV00053B/3610